11/08

Also by Laura Claridge

NORMAN ROCKWELL:
A LIFE

TAMARA DE LEMPICKA:
A LIFE OF DECO AND DECADENCE

ROMANTIC POTENCY:
THE PARADOX OF DESIRE

OUT OF BOUNDS:
MALE WRITERS AND GENDER(ED)
CRITICISM *(Coeditor)*

Emily Post

Emily Post

. . .

DAUGHTER OF THE GILDED AGE, MISTRESS OF AMERICAN MANNERS

LAURA CLARIDGE

RANDOM HOUSE

NEW YORK

Copyright © 2008 by Laura Claridge

All rights reserved.

Published in the United States by Random House,
an imprint of The Random House Publishing Group,
a division of Random House, Inc., New York.

RANDOM HOUSE and colophon are registered
trademarks of Random House, Inc.

Grateful acknowledgment is made to W. W. Norton & Company,
Inc., for permission to reprint lines from "In View of the Fact,"
from *Bosh and Flapdoodle* by A. R. Ammons. Copyright 2005
by John R. Ammons. Used by permission of
W. W. Norton & Company, Inc.

ISBN 978-0-375-50921-6

Printed in the United States of America on acid-free paper

www.atrandom.com

2 4 6 8 9 7 5 3 1

FIRST EDITION

Book design by Barbara M. Bachman

*The portrait of Bruce Price as an architect's apprentice is courtesy of the
American Institute of Architects, Baltimore Chapter (AIABaltimore).
The photographs of the Tuxedo Park tennis court and train station are courtesy
of the Tuxedo Park Library. All other illustrations are courtesy of the
Emily Post Institute, Burlington, Vermont.*

To Devon and Ian:
Indelicate as always, I wallow in your love.

To Dennis:
until we die, we will remember every
single thing, recall every word, love every

loss: then we will, as we must, leave it to
others to love, love that can grow brighter

and deeper till the very end, gaining
    strength
and getting more precious all the way.

—A. R. AMMONS, "IN VIEW OF THE FACT"

These States are the amplest poem,
Here is not merely a nation but a teeming Nation of nations.

—WALT WHITMAN, "CHANTS DEMOCRATIC AND

NATIVE AMERICAN, NO. I," *LEAVES OF GRASS*, 1860

Intellectually I know that America is no better than any other country; emotionally I know she is better than every country.

—SINCLAIR LEWIS, 1935

Damn it, I happen to love this country.

—J. ROBERT OPPENHEIMER, EARLY 1950S

MILY POST ENTERED THE WORLD ONLY SEVEN YEARS AFTER AMERica's Civil War ended. Though most of her family sided with the Union, a few renegade relatives fought with the South, the staunch loyalists who survived spinning heroic stories of General Lee and his horse Traveller throughout their lives. At the time of Emily's birth in Baltimore, women were being jailed for promoting birth control for married couples; when she died in New York City, women and men, married or not, were campaigning for legalized abortion. A few years before her funeral, befuddled but fascinated, even now, by the latest technology that celebrated the ingenuity of the age, she would watch, on television, the launch of *Sputnik*.

She witnessed Reconstruction and Jim Crow, as well as the emergence of Martin Luther King. Her youth was shaped by the high Victorian era, cosseted by the Gilded Age, and then tossed about in the restless years culminating in World War I. Through the Roaring Twenties, the Great Depression, World War II and its domestic aftermath (all revolutions of a sort), Emily Post's *Etiquette: In Society, in Business, in Politics and at Home*—magisterial, impatient, collegial, and neighborly—would outlast the ages it reflected and corrected.

When it debuted in 1922, *Etiquette* represented a fifty-year-old woman at her wisest and a country at its wildest. The preternaturally confident author had her feet firmly planted in the Jazz Age, taking its thoughtful measure in her meticulous way. What Emily initially called her "little blue book" debuted in a Manhattan society intrigued by the Algonquin's Round Table, where Harold Ross, editor of a new, quickly influential weekly, the *New Yorker,* held court with a whiskey in hand. Even as sales skyrocketed for

Emily Post's guide to the good but proper life, the same decade would also nurture Dorothy Parker and Ernest Hemingway, Claudette Colbert and Clara Bow, George Gershwin and Louis Armstrong. *Etiquette* assumed its position within the heady cultural milieu of the 1920s, shaped by the era of its birth even while modifying it.

At its broadest, etiquette—the measure of how we treat one another—reaches across class, race, gender, and culture. For many women, particularly (and through their transmission to their sons and husbands), *Etiquette* long fashioned our country's idea and ideal of what it was to pursue a gracious—possibly even a moral—life. Attention to behavior, after all, preoccupied the founders of our nation. Sixteen-year-old George Washington had written his pamphlet *Rules of Civility & Decent Behaviour in Company and Conversation: A Book of Etiquette* believing that everything he already knew about getting on in life was worth sharing with others.

Though never a head of state, Emily Post didn't lack for recognition. In 1976 and again in 1990, *Life* magazine would laud her as one of the most important Americans of the twentieth century. *Etiquette,* by the 1930s having sold over a million copies, would continue to be touted in the most unlikely moments and places. The list of extravagant citations the book has received in the past few years alone includes admirers as disparate as P. J. O'Rourke, reminiscing about learning how to fit into society through Emily's book; Joan Didion, using *Etiquette* to confront her grief over her spouse's death; and Tim Page, a *Washington Post* music critic, discovering that *Etiquette* could help him cope with Asperger's syndrome.

In 1934, more than a decade after *Etiquette*'s publication, Ruth Benedict, on the first page of her groundbreaking work *Patterns of Culture,* would state that "anthropology is the study of human beings as creatures of society." Lacking the intellectual tools to articulate her own cultural philosophy, Emily Post nonetheless worked instinctively from a similar model. While Benedict was exploring customs far from her native shores, Emily was a domestic anthropologist, plumbing the homegrown soil for its indigenous fertility. She assumed early on that change was endemic to humanity, and that the human task was to adapt to it, preserving the best of what came before and integrating what superseded the past.

Emily Post's life and work would have been inconceivable without the story of Ellis Island, and the millions of immigrants who sought to become what they considered real Americans during Emily's lifetime. Between her engagement party in 1891 and the twelfth reprinting of *Etiquette* in 1924,

Ellis Island was terra firma for more than 22 million immigrants. As a little girl, she was granted a singular privilege: while a family friend constructed its base, the Statue of Liberty functioned as her personal dollhouse, allowing the child to play inside its hollow core for weeks. When the statue was completely finished, her beloved father shared the dais with a select group, helping to dedicate Miss Liberty to the American people, especially to those future citizens streaming through the immigration corrals. Such mythical moments braid competing truths about Emily Post and the country she increasingly grew to understand and to appreciate on its own messy terms. Hers was a staggeringly ambitious hodgepodge of a nation that offered liberty and justice to all—but a justice whose blindness, for all its noble intentions, required continual redress.

How could the promise that etiquette bestows be maintained throughout the twentieth century? How, in the face of massive human and natural evils, could Americans believe that considerate social intercourse remained a significant issue? That politesse mattered? If misleadingly superficial at first glance, however, the lady's solution holds up after all. Emily Post was not alone in maintaining that the art of treating people well is the other side to the act of waging war.

PART ONE

. . .

She must not swing her arms as though
they were dangling ropes; she must not
switch herself this way and that;
she must not shout; and she must not,
while wearing her bridal veil,
smoke a cigarette.

—ETIQUETTE, PAGE 373

CHAPTER 1

✳

*I*T HAPPENED LIKE THIS—IN MANY RESPECTS AN OLD TALE, WITH nothing original to recommend it. A society man was caught cheating on his wife, and now, his blackmailers agreed, he would have to pay.

Emily Price Post, the adulterer's wife, was furious. Shocking even herself, for the briefest of moments the usually even-tempered young matron yearned for revenge. Against her spouse, his lover, the blackmailers, and society: anyone who had contributed to this pain. Still in love with her husband, the thirty-two-year-old woman had long ago given up hope that he felt the same about her. She had made peace with her private anguish. What she had not anticipated was public humiliation.

During the hottest days that summer of 1905, the aftermath of Edwin Post's betrayal played out daily on the front pages of New York City's newspapers. Such flamboyant publicity bolstered Edwin's damaged self-image even as it shriveled his wife's. Now Emily wore, to those few who knew her well, an aura of sadness only emphasized by her husband's exuberance.

Edwin's friends had warned him to be discreet, but he had ignored them, sure, as usual, that he knew best. By late April 1905 the cocky thirty-five-year-old stockbroker had become careless about how he conducted his affairs with chorus girls and fledgling actresses. So in the middle of June, when one of them whined, mistaking his attentions for relationship collateral, he made a fatal misstep. He reacted callously, warning her to vacate the Connecticut cottage he kept for such intrigues: she bored him.

Within days of toasting his new freedom from the starlet he had suddenly found cloying, Edwin received a call from a representative of Colonel

William D'Alton Mann, publisher of the articulate gossip sheet *Town Topics*. Mann, already embarked on this summer's vacation abroad, had left his business in the hands of Charles H. Ahle, his second-in-command. The officious Ahle suggested that he and Edwin Post meet—soon. On June 25 Ahle visited Post, who was unceremoniously instructed to ante up the cash or be exposed to scandal: *Town Topics* was about to go public with some juicy news of certain interest to Edwin. Luckily, Colonel Mann had left instructions to suppress this gossip if Post subscribed to a vanity book to be printed sometime in the distant future. Five hundred dollars would neatly cover the costs for Post's copy. He should be grateful, Ahle added unctuously; some other men—more important than Post—had been taxed a far greater amount for the same "project."

Thus it was that Edwin Post joined the Gilded Age prey, a group of select men (and several women) stalked by the redoubtable publisher. Colonel Mann abhorred what he considered the duplicity of society. He took immense satisfaction in supplementing his own income at the expense of a careless millionaire's misalliance. The jovial Civil War hero, a suave, condescending, robust Santa Claus, mixed in his complicated person two sometimes contrary impulses. He was a true believer—no sloppy grammar or careless vernacular would be published under his masthead. But he was also a cynical extortionist, impatient with public figures so inane that they discarded their private lives for a night of pleasure.

This hypocritical reformer had become an object of dread among the city's most prominent citizens: J. P. Morgan, Andrew Carnegie, William K. Vanderbilt, and William C. Whitney. His method was simple: hire aggrieved servants, disgruntled friends, or a furious spouse to spy on suspects. Then bully those miscreants into paying for a "subscription" to a mostly phantom, wildly expensive illustrated book about leaders of society. Various prices were assessed for each victim, with an eye to what the sinner could afford. What could be easier than such a scam, in the shadow of the Victorian mores that still darkened the resplendent Gilded Age? Money and fevered morality, a glorious mix for a con artist with ethics like Mann's.

Pleading a shortage of money, Edwin bought some time to consider his options. Two days later, Ahle came looking for him again. The wayward husband bargained with Mann's representative. "Give me a little more time and I'll get you the money," he pleaded, adding, "please don't publish the article on Friday"—the usual pattern for expensive gossip sponsored by *Town Topics*.

Here the truth becomes a matter of conjecture. The official line, constructed by Emily years later, maintained that the victim was unable to produce the $500 "fee" for the vanity book (worth about $5,000 in today's currency)—his extensive costs of paying for a mistress aside. Before divulging the news to his wife, Edwin had first sought advice from the couple's mutual ally, prominent society lawyer Phoenix Ingraham (whom Edwin knew to be smitten with Emily). Predictably, their friend had insisted that she be brought into the discussion, whereupon Emily immediately agreed to help bring down this corrupt operation that had netted so many of their friends. There was no question: the Posts should not pay off the bribe. The prospect of a public spectacle, with her husband its sacrificial lamb and she herself the object of prurient gossip, supposedly failed to discourage the always decorous Emily Price Post.

Throughout the years, Emily would contend that the couple's private discussions had centered upon Edwin's lack of money as well as their mutual determination to end the insidious blackmail of their friends. But such a grand explanation allowed Emily to displace her husband's painful, real weakness: his inability or, even worse, his unwillingness to protect his wife from scandal.

THE WEEK FOLLOWING July 11, 1905, both the *New York Times* and the *New York Tribune* sustained a running commentary on the sting. "Stockbroker's Way of Dealing with Bribe Offer" trumpeted the *Tribune's* front page. Edwin Post, the article continued, was a partner in a brokerage firm and lived—in the summers—with his wife and children in Tuxedo Park. A terse sentence followed: "[Post's] action in the case was taken on the advice of Mrs. Post." The *Baltimore Sun,* Emily's hometown paper, ran a short front-page article on the affair, failing to mention that the betrayed wife was the daughter of their famous homegrown architect, whom, till then, the city had proudly claimed as its own any chance it got. However briefly, Edwin Post was finally at the center of Emily's life.

She never forgave him.

⊱⊰

HE KNEW HE'D STRUCK GOLD WHEN SHE TRIED SO HARD TO impress him, stifling her girlish giggles and self-consciously checking her slight slouch. A fetching enough sixteen-year-old from the Pennsylvania countryside, she had been turned out by Baltimore's best finishing school, polished with the high patina of shiny anthracite coal. Josephine Lee won Bruce Price's loyalty, if never quite his heart, within minutes of their meeting at a debutante ball in the winter season of 1869.

Young Bruce, an aspiring architect, was undeniably looking to marry money, and Josephine's father, Washington Lee, possessed a postwar fortune in want of spending. The Lees were no anomaly: one of Lee's railroad compeers demonstrated his recent profits, in 1865, by throwing what was the most lavish party in memory. The menus were lettered in gold, the dining room "smothered in rarest flowers." Each of the host's guests was presented with a silk cushion embroidered with his name. The wines cost $25 a bottle, the prestigious singers were paid $1,000 for two songs, and the final bill for the extravaganza totaled $20,000 (almost $3 million today), to bravos all around.

Emily Bruce Price, Washington Lee's granddaughter, would be a daddy's girl throughout her long life. She unabashedly bragged about her devotion: to Emily, Bruce Price was a giant among men. At six feet, two inches, the architect whose charms were legendary came of age at the end of the Civil War, but he would have stood out in any era. Handsome, naturally convivial, confident, generous: it is easy to understand his daughter's lifelong infatuation. Her adoration, in the end, merely echoed that of Bruce Price's many friends and relatives, who, after being with him for five minutes, seemed convinced they'd made contact with something significant. His niece, a countess by marriage, still recalled, almost fifty years after his death, Bruce Price's "outstanding personal beauty and personal charm" and his "unpretentious confidence in himself." "Everyone" revered him, she said. Emily worshipped him.

Born in Cumberland, Maryland, at the end of 1845, Bruce Price had arrived a week and a half too early to be the Christmas baby his parents had anticipated. What would become his trademark of nearly obsessive punctuality stamped his earliest days. The boy, one of an eventual seven brothers and sisters, spent most of his childhood in Baltimore. Hugging the Chesapeake Bay, the nation's third-largest city enjoyed a seventy-mile buffer from the Atlantic, a distinction only one other major American port, Philadelphia, could claim. The location was ripe for a transportation liaison, which the railroad barons of the nineteenth century would pursue with relish, even when slaves were needed to turn dreams into reality.

William Price, Bruce's father—"eccentric," sniped some who didn't understand him—was an important lawyer in Baltimore during the turbulent 1860s. A restless man, Price graduated from college eager to leave the outskirts of Washington County in favor of the more prosperous legal garrets of Cumberland. There he met and quickly wed Marion Bruce, a Scottish lass who could minister to his practical side. Their obligatory Episcopal ceremony reflected no particular religious convictions on the part of either bride or groom.

Marion herself boasted a family renowned for its small-town achievements: she was the granddaughter of the first president of Cumberland's First National Bank and the niece of Allegheny County's first circuit court judge. She was even prouder to inform her already convinced suitor that her father, a Scotsman who had settled in the region twenty or thirty years earlier, was a first cousin to Francis Scott Key.

The agility of a Renaissance lawyer like Price (who would write a novel and build his own house) was in short supply at the time. Still in his twenties and fresh from school, he was elected a member of the Maryland State Senate in 1825. William Price enjoyed debating hard questions. Perhaps inevitably, many considered the complex man a contrarian. His moral allegiance was to the North, but his heart never deserted Dixie.

The lawyer came honestly by his often eccentric ways of doing things. After William's father died, you could practically hear the townspeople gasp at the idiosyncratic terms of Josiah Price's will. Josiah left behind a creative document; everyone agreed on that. He had bequeathed his four sons a choice: to attend college or to own real estate. Either/or. William, along with his older brother, chose an education. William's granddaughter Emily, who loved recounting the story, would always emphasize the proper decision her shrewd grandfather made: through his canny judgment, he got it all. The two brothers who chose property died early, their misfortune ensuring that William Price and his favorite brother, Benjamin, acquired both the land and the academic degrees.

Without a doubt, wealth and education proved a vigorous coupling. In the 1830s, William parlayed his inheritance into a law firm in nearby Hagerstown, Maryland. In spite of Price's somewhat confusing persona as an erratic gentleman farmer, the man's intellectual dexterity as he nurtured social connections led him quickly to become one of the lawyers sought out by the local powers. He knew about the art of doing people favors—sometimes just from kindness, but often out of expedience.

This was the lay of the land that would shape Emily Price's father, William's talented son Bruce. This was a family that believed in passing down its wisdom along with its genes. In the middle of the nineteenth century, when Bruce was two or three years old, William moved his family from Hagerstown to Baltimore. They lived at 27 Washington Street, across from a severe, newly constructed Greek Revival library. Inspired by the chance to enhance the aesthetic harmony in his still raw neighborhood, William Price, though untrained in the arts, designed his family's house to harmonize with the library. The self-taught architect created a one-story Greek Revival building whose enormous wide hallway ran through the entire house to the rear garden door. It takes no great leap of imagination to connect William's mildly chaotic vision with the bold design that informed Bruce Price's Gilded Age aesthetic. Or the panoramic view of the machinery driving her own age that would inspire his daughter.

AS THE LAST FEW YEARS of the 1850s teetered to a nervous conclusion, the prospect of war took up a permanent residence among William's legal cronies. The signs around him were hardly subtle: he could sense tectonic plates shifting beneath his family's feet, and he wanted to be ready.

The 1860s opened upon the heels of an unusually cold December, the thermometers shivering at zero. Nothing so frivolous as weather ruled the household of William Price, however, as agonized loyalties played out in his family, reflecting the schism at the heart of the city itself. Seaport or not, Baltimore was a southern town with a northern manifesto, its leaders primarily Union men. In more ways than one, Maryland lay on the fault line, geographically in the middle of the nation's coast.

Openly pro-Union, Maryland's official position was not without risk: in reality, Maryland was a border state. Though the state contributed men and matériel to the Union's efforts, the Baltimore southern sensibility was no small thing. Many secessionists pushing to legitimize the Confederacy resented the local abolitionists. In a telling paradox of the whole sorry debacle, the 7th Regiment United States Colored Troops and the 9th Regiment U.S. Colored Troops were heavily represented by Baltimoreans, in spite of the city's collusions with slave-owning states. But on April 19, 1861, as northern troops passed through the city on their way south to defend Washington, D.C., the first blood of the Civil War was officially shed. The Baltimore Riots claimed the lives of four soldiers in the 6th Massachusetts Infantry. Several civilians were killed, and many more were injured.

Thomas, William's and Marion's firstborn, was barely mentioned in family chronicles. But Bruce's adored older brother Benjamin joined the Yankee forces, while Adrian, four years younger, sided with the Rebels. It was a scene invading every neighborhood. Tangled loyalties rebounded in the anguish echoed across the city. Perhaps such misery motivated William to take the route open to upper-class men of his times: he paid authorities to ensure that young Bruce would not be drafted to fight, regardless of the nation's needs.

The Baltimore schism was in many regards a kinship dispute that would run its course. But the repercussions of the deepest confusions about race, class, and nationality that the feud reproduced would resurface repeatedly. On June 10, 2006, the Ku Klux Klan rallied at the Antietam battlefield, where some believe William Price's rebellious third son, Adrian, lost his life on the bloodiest day of the war.

BALTIMORE—"CHARM CITY" was its later nickname—was not a place where people with options chose to live out the nation's crisis. William Price decided that the early 1860s would be a good time to send his family to the country to stay with other relatives who shared their pro-Union sentiments. Price himself stayed in the city. Long respected for his prudence, he was soon appointed by President Lincoln as U.S. district attorney for Maryland.

Emily's grandfather dealt directly and effectively with the president throughout the war. Buttressed by his reputation as a sentinel of sanity, he could count on receiving an almost immediate response from an otherwise overwhelmed leader. If William Price was a prisoner's supplicant, Lincoln granted the pardon. And when William Price implied that he'd uncovered incendiary information, the president took notice. On October 22, 1864, Price telegraphed Lincoln: "Information has this moment come into my possession which I think ought to be communicated at once to the Govt. I will leave Baltimore in the three thirty (3 30) pm train for Washington & be accompanied by three (3) persons. Can we have an interview with the Prest [*sic*] in the evening & what hour." The president responded at once: "Yours received. Will see you any time when you present yourself. A. Lincoln."

In 1868, when William Price died, Baltimore's courts were officially adjourned so that legislators could attend his funeral. The lawyer bequeathed no sumptuous assets to his family, though his wife and two children at home could live comfortably on their inheritance. Still, the lack of wealth enabled Bruce Price to create a mythology that excused him from the classroom, which he had never enjoyed anyway. Newly matriculated at what is now Princeton, he dutifully dropped out during his first year to help support the family his father had forgotten to indemnify with a fortune.

From now on, Bruce's education would come from on-the-job training. He took a low-paying position as an apprentice with Niernsee and Neilson, one of Baltimore's most prestigious building firms, and, to better train his eye, he apportioned his inheritance so that he could undertake a yearlong tour of European capitals. Even when lack of money made it difficult, he kept to the standards of his class. Bruce Price would bequeath this talent to his daughter, Emily Post, a southern girl manqué, trailing wherever she walked the potent scent of lush magnolias tastefully tamped down by a life under tight control.

RIGHT UNTIL WILLIAM PRICE DIED, IN 1868, HE WAS STILL more interested in politics than fortunes. In contrast, Josephine Lee's father, Emily's maternal grandfather, was a cheerful coal baron gleefully taking the measure of the monied men of his wild new age. All that earlier laying of railroad tracks—thirty thousand miles already in place by 1860— had been stymied by the four-year break, and now it resumed with a vengeance. Men who had not inherited great wealth were nonetheless developing their own massive fortunes. Only four years after the war's end, the economy and mores that had shaped the men of William Price's generation already felt outdated and irrelevant. Life hereafter was to center on banking, commerce, transportation, coal, and steel—like the railroad, enterprises interrupted by the war and now in full gear, making up for lost time. Baltimore, the city to which both of Emily Post's grandfathers had returned, would become a new crossroads for this apparently endless proliferation of trains, charged with rushing crops and commodities to market. It was a new day and a new world, where speed ruled as much as anyone or anything.

Josephine Lee would always be envied—and, some say, her favor curried—for her rich family, wealthy from the staggering number of coalfields they owned. Like any commodity, anthracite had its ups and downs, but everyone knew that the Lees had invested well. Beyond the mines, Josephine's father had capitalized on the railroad investors eager to buy up the deposits and work the land themselves. A year before the war started, Washington Lee showed assets of $50,000, versus William Price's

$10,000. And it wasn't as if Lee were unlettered: after earning his law degree from Dickinson College in nearby Carlisle, Pennsylvania, he was elected district attorney of Luzerne County.

Pictures of Emily Post's mother suggest a pleasingly plump, good-natured woman, possessed of a certain bland sturdiness. Not quite pretty, even at sixteen Josephine carried herself with the self-possession of privilege. She had attended one of Baltimore's uninspiring girls' schools, which functioned primarily to supply the female quotas for the next town ball or dance at Johns Hopkins. Academics formed little of her education; school was a waiting station for upper-class young ladies tutored to catch the right train. In their photographs, in contrast to Bruce Price's air of dreamy distraction, Josephine's canny attention to the moment inhabits her every likeness.

When Josephine Lee debuted in Baltimore, 180 miles from her family's gritty Pennsylvania ore, she found Bruce Price at her side within minutes. The marriage of the Lee and Price families would be an equitable swap, great lineage for great wealth. Josephine's parents, eminently practical people, saw no advantage to a long engagement. The marriage would take place four months after they met, on April 10, 1870. From the outside, it looked as if the match granted the advantage to the struggling architect, a suggestion his daughter, Emily, would forever dispute.

In fact, Josephine staked her own proud ancestral claims through two shrewd, hardworking pilgrims, Priscilla and John Alden, who had disembarked from the *Mayflower* in 1620. Half a century later, having learned how to survive in their new country, the Aldens' descendants acted on a rumor they'd heard about coal blanketing faraway fields. Gathering up their sparse provisions, they migrated a few hundred miles west, where they picked quality ore by hand.

Great-grandchildren of the *Mayflower* Aldens built their own forge on Nanticoke Creek in 1778, a simple unit consisting of just one hammer and one fire. Even moving that weighty mallet had been an arduous ordeal: the miners brought it from Philadelphia to Harrisburg in a wagon, then on to Nanticoke in a Durham boat, a sixty-foot-long flatbed, the style made famous after Washington's troops used one to cross the Delaware River on Christmas Eve two years earlier. At least such effort proved worthwhile: not until Emily's great-grandfather spent a few years in the 1820s cursing his way around its peculiarities was the fifty-year-old tool retired.

A few generations later, in expansive gestures that would prove extremely beneficial to his future son-in-law, the canny and kind Washington Lee remembered to endow the township with the rewards of their quality coal, even as he prepared to live out the rest of his own life in larger cities. He donated an entire lot of prime real estate on Hanover Street for a church building, helping to lay the cornerstone himself in 1869. By the time St. Clement's was consecrated, in June two years later, Bruce Price and Josephine Lee would already be married.

IT IS HARD NOWADAYS to envision the mix of frothiness and gloom of the decade after the Civil War, the years when Emily Post's parents became adults. The exuberant North celebrated success even as the vanquished South mourned the loss of its empire. During the 1865 fall and winter seasons alone, Yankee socialites attended six hundred balls and spent $7 million in the process. The costumes averaged $1,000 each, excluding the jewelry. Fancy dress balls had defined New York City from the 1820s at least, and their stark absence during the Civil War created a rebound.

Precisely because they had forfeited so much, upper-class Baltimore citizens also felt the mandate to celebrate hard. Internecine warfare had cost their divided city heavily, and now the defeated compensated for their losses accordingly. Following the war, there was an overspill of everything that figured in southern society, from terrapin suppers to invaluable gossip. Properly credentialed couturiers would enter the ladies' boudoirs and chatter nonstop while they draped their customers' dresses and designed their hats. It was important to be happy again.

ON OCTOBER 8, 1871, the year after Emily Post's parents married, Chicago ignited. The great fire burned down a city but gave birth to an architectural race that would shape Bruce Price's career. First, however, the novice needed to position himself, and that meant forming connections. He would reap the rewards of Chicago's tragedy in due time, but for now, the nearly twenty-five-year-old Bruce gratefully entered a new familial world, one gloriously covered with soot.

The couple—accompanied by Josephine's parents and much younger brother—would make the Grand Tour for their honeymoon, traveling first-class on a Cunard cruise underwritten by the Lees. They were headed for the Continent, their trip a staple of the newly rich. Bruce, his extravagance justified by professional needs, had just returned the year before from his first exploration abroad. Though he was eager to study sites he'd not had time to visit on his previous trip, he was determined to be politic and manage his time carefully. He intended to show proper appreciation for the luxuries Washington Lee had funded. Crossing the ocean was a major event in itself, and grandly furnished suites sheathed in Victorian flocked wallpaper, as well as an excess of champagne and every culinary delicacy imaginable, made a few weeks of paying up, in essence, quite agreeable.

A delicate tension nonetheless surfaced. The well-meaning young husband quickly discovered himself unable to spend more than a few hours in the company of his hardy, stouthearted, and eventually stout-figured wife. The enclosed transatlantic voyage made him suddenly mad to explore a newly discovered gold mine in South Africa. As soon as the extended family docked, Bruce took off to make his fortune, abandoning the rest of the family in Paris for over ten months. His daughter, Emily, would gleefully repeat a version of this story to journalists, year after year, the variations depending upon her purpose.

The only problem with this postscript to the Price honeymoon was that it was largely Emily's fabrication. Accused, she would have defended herself, her method of viewing reality endemic to her generation; all she did was decorate the truth. Certainly, her version is more provocative than the unembroidered account, especially the way she told it. Nonetheless, the fact of her parents' honeymoon is that Washington Lee, Josephine's father—not Bruce Price, Emily's hero—intrepidly trekked off to Africa to find his (next) fortune. Bruce Price was left behind to babysit his new family.

A fresh but knowing bridegroom parking his wife on the Continent while he takes off for the wilderness is undoubtedly more exotic than the tale of a rich middle-aged man speculating with a new investment. As if the young bridegroom was above social custom, he was allowed, in Emily's narrative, to forge ahead, leaving his new family behind. What was so meaningful in this fairy-tale version to his daughter?

Washington Lee had sold the majority of his coal business by now, the transaction leaving the always restless man searching for a new project. For a decade, the dark continent had been beckoning him. And now he was even a bit ahead of the game: it would take until the late 1880s for Cecil Rhodes and his brother to gain near-total control over the Kimberley gold mines and the De Beers diamond fields. In 1870, Lee still had reason to try to stake his claim in South Africa. Gold, especially, beckoned him, along with many other eager speculators of the period.

The shiny rock sometimes seemed to dreamers like Lee to possess supernatural powers. A decade earlier, a hurricane overtaking a ship sailing from California to New York had definitively sunk a million dollars' worth of the precious commodity. A tidal wave of financial detritus from the disaster pounded the American economy without mercy, converting skeptics to the absolute power of gold. Later, when Jay Gould and Jim Fisk tried to corner the gold market, everything collapsed, ruining all but the canniest investors. But such wreckage served to romanticize the soft metal more than ever, and Washington Lee was nothing if not romantic.

Like most important fantasies, the family legend as Emily presented it—with Bruce, not her grandfather, at its heart—is richly overdetermined. Josephine is dumped unceremoniously—on her honeymoon—which is fine by the daughter, who preferred having her father to herself any chance she got and who, privately, always believed her mother unworthy of Bruce anyway. Unfettered by the conventions of matrimony, the bridegroom, refusing to be tied down, is allotted what in real life he had lost by his spousal bargain: freedom. It seems likely that in Emily's improvisation, she also played out her own yearning to be beholden to no one in an era that rarely allowed women such freedom. She made her father mythically act out the role she would have chosen herself, given the opportunity.

The surviving records suggest that the extended family stayed abroad for almost six months, several of which evoked panic in the confined architect. Bruce managed to take solitary "research trips" whenever the well-meaning banality of his teenage bride overwhelmed him. For all her immaturity, Josephine Lee would develop into a tonic for her quixotic husband. Already the hearty young woman was quite capable of constructing a family scene to her own specifications. "It's time to go home," she apparently told her groom. "I want to have a baby, and I don't want the child born here, where the doctors aren't entirely modern." So Bruce and Josephine, her mother and brother Henry in tow, returned to Baltimore and to Wilkes-Barre, both cities where the Lees owned family apartments. Eventually, Washington Lee would come back as well, determined to figure out an economical way to transport the gold home from Africa.

Lee knew his daughter was in good hands: Bruce was a worker too. Under the aegis of his own Baltimore firm, Baldwin and Price, the young architect quickly constructed four solid city houses at 12–16 East Chase Street, reserving his favorite, No. 14, for Josephine and himself. Upon Emily's birth—and surely as part of a deal Bruce cut with the doting grandparents—he moved the family back to Wilkes-Barre, where they would live for the next five years. City court records reveal that the young couple retained and even enlarged their Baltimore house, building sewer and drainage pipes as part of the expansion. Emily was always careful to refer to her father's professional grounding in Baltimore. After all, Bruce Price, architect, a descendant of the city's own Francis Scott Key, would belong to its history books as well.

SHE WOULD NEVER deny being larger than life. On October 27, 1872, one incontestable hard fact presented itself as metaphor and nature both, when Bruce Price and Josephine Lee, two giants in their different ways, produced a very large baby. Emily Bruce Price weighed in at over nine pounds, hardly the delicate creature more typical of her era.

Like clockwork, regimentation being important to young Josephine Lee Price, a son would follow the next year. According to burial records, William Lee Price was born on April 18, 1873, and died on December 6, 1875, within days of Bruce's birthday. This "fact" is impossible to reconcile with Emily's birth six months earlier. But the early death of little William in 1875, just before Christmas, mentioned only once in the lifelong flow of interviews conducted with Emily Post, became a kind of family secret, the creed of an age that expected personal problems to go unacknowledged.

Perhaps it was her desire to blot him from the family chronology that caused Emily to mesh her birthday confusedly with William's. Certainly it is odd, especially for as fastidious a record keeper as Emily Post, that the birth dates on the child's Wilkes-Barre gravestone and on Emily's own granite marker in Tuxedo Park overlap. Such lifelong "confusion" strikes a false note in a woman who recorded the yardage of every dress she sewed and the color of every bulb she planted.

CHAPTER 4

❖

THE YEAR EMILY POST WAS BORN, NEW YORK CITY, 190 MILES NORTH
of Baltimore and a few miles less to Washington Lee's coal fiefdom, braced
itself for a more complicated birth. Its gestation finally complete, Grand
Central Station tethered the old to the new surer than genealogy ever
could. Transportation reigned, and coal was king. The decade was switch-
ing gears, gentility displaced by a refusal to linger.

Emily entered a world barely stepping one foot ahead of financial disaster. The very tempo of her country's change, the relentlessness of its
progress, contributed to a near breakdown in its infrastructure. Not everyone, it is true, registered dismay during this first real test of postwar American monetary markets. Josephine, for instance, scarcely recovered from
Emily's birth, succumbed to the speculation spreading throughout the markets. She was good with money, and she made a tidy sum from her stock investments. Her enterprise did not lack for irony: more than any other
single event, the extreme overbuilding of the nation's railroad system—on
which Washington Lee had staked his fortune—had laid the groundwork
for the fiscal meltdown that year.

The fear in its wake shaped a depression that would hold the newly reunited nation in a nervous clutch for another six years. Along the way, institutions thought invulnerable were exposed as anything but. In 1873, on
an insufferably muggy September afternoon, the country's leading finan-
cier, the indomitable Jay Cooke, signaled to a nation that radical change
was indeed at hand. Cooke had played a significant role in the Civil War by
helping the Union raise over $3 billion in bond sales, portending the ways

modern governments would fund their wars in the subsequent century. More recently, he had sent General George Custer to clear out the Sioux Indians blocking progress on the Northern Pacific Railroad he had underwritten.

Now, to the shock of just about everyone, Jay Cooke & Co., the nation's premier investment bank, failed, finally and completely outmaneuvered by its only rival, J. Pierpont Morgan and his cohorts. Possibly Cooke took some perverse solace in the signs of his greatness: his fall on September 18 set off a national drama. The New York Stock Exchange closed for ten days; credit evaporated and companies folded.

With the failure of the banks, thousands of workers were suddenly without income. Such dramatic shifts in fortunes engineered momentous social change. To people of Emily's class, a new sophistication about the instability of the money markets fueled their concerns. (What would the market do? J. P. Morgan was often asked. "It will fluctuate," he inevitably answered.) All of which suited Washington Lee just fine. Developing strategies for playing the market with all that coal money proved a robust enterprise. Lee and his family would ride out the depression in style, in spite of an unexpected loss here and there.

Emily's grandfather had enjoyed the frenetic growth of the railroads unfettered by government regulation. Now he had his ear to the ground again, this time listening to rumbles of pending bank failures. In spite of her own preoccupation with her babies in the early 1870s, Josephine found herself engrossed in the household excitement anytime her father started talking about the current market realities. Father and daughter enjoyed dreaming together out loud. But while humble, unassuming coal was stoking Washington Lee's lifeline, his imagination kept returning to those gold mines in Africa.

Josephine didn't talk finance exclusively; she was equally interested, unlike her father, in the lives of people who inhabited the fabulous world of men like Jay Gould. She enjoyed regularly gossiping with her rich but down-to-earth relatives about the extravagant lives detailed in the local papers and tabloids. Still redefining itself as a country, the restored Union was being forced to confront class structure even as its national ethos preferred denying such undemocratic barriers. The newspapers described society's movement, in ever greater detail, as the gap between the haves and have-nots grew even larger. Of all the names bandied about, Caroline Schermerhorn Astor's was the bluest. She, more than anyone, inspired the postwar frenzy of lavish displays of wealth to prove one's worth. And yet, in one of the paradoxes endemic to the Gilded Age, between the Reconstruction of the 1860s and the early twentieth century, society depended upon ancestry, not the incidental (and implicitly vulgar) acquisition of a fortune, to rank its citizenry.

Shortly before the depression of 1873, Ward McAllister, a formidable social climber from Savannah, even founded an exclusive New York City institution called the Patriarchs. McAllister showed Mrs. Astor, whose toady he became, how to create a truly exclusive social circle: he devised a group of twenty-five men (enlarged to fifty the following decade) whom he alone deemed the choicest of the social crop, a set meant to represent bloodlines rather than mere fortunes. Fifteen years later, he would create his mythical list of the Four Hundred, said to enumerate all those worthy of gracing Mrs. Astor's ballroom. McAllister finally produced a catalog of the Four Hundred (really only 273 names) during his last gasp in the 1890s, the list existing only in his imagination until then. Such pompous self-aggrandizement was frequently mocked in the press: Charles Dana Gibson cleverly caricatured society's self-appointed leader on a hobbyhorse—referencing a common game played at the society dances—or as a goose girl (a figure in another such amusement) herding a flock of the elite Four Hundred.

Throughout Emily's youth, Mrs. William B. Astor—*the* Mrs. Astor, Caroline Schermerhorn—with Ward McAllister at her side, would help maintain Society's purity, whether in New York or Newport. Because of the circle her family inhabited, Emily had many opportunities to observe such members of Society. Without realizing the significance of her disdain at the time, the young girl disliked such posturing, her contempt later underwriting her personal code of ethics. She was, of course, influenced by her parents: though accepted into the ballrooms, they remained sufficient outsiders to levy judgment upon the society they had joined, and by training and heritage, they were too sensible to swallow it whole. Real quality, they taught their daughter, had nothing to do with money or birth.

SPENDING THE FIRST few years of her childhood in the bosom of an adoring extended family, benevolent lords of their local fiefdoms, Emily Price escaped the depression entirely. One memorable Christmas in Wilkes-Barre, her grandfather even presented her with a fine miniature china tea set. Outraged at not receiving a more exciting gift, the four-year-old demanded her young uncle Charlie's elaborate toy train instead, only to be

gently rebuked for overreaching: when she was older she could play with
the train. Soothingly told to go pretend to have tea in the garden, little
Emily marched outside, railing against her lack of power. There, she sys-
tematically smashed each expensive cup and saucer against the rocks, scat-
tering shards of china throughout the pool. The girl didn't want to play tea
party; she wanted to work an engine like Uncle Charlie.

Such petulance surfaced whenever Emily felt herself treated dismis-
sively, as if she wasn't mature enough to have what others, older and wiser,
possessed. One summer in Bar Harbor, Maine, for instance, where the
young girl and her mother vacationed while Bruce worked at enlarging several local estates for the Gilded Age set, Emily again displayed the entitle-
ment of a bright only child. The five-year-old was given a charge account
by her parents so that she could learn to manage money. Instead, she immediately ran up a bill for $5 at the local candy shop, feeding her sweet tooth.
To her surprise, her father refused to pay the bill: it was hers, he explained,
not his. To show her the size of her debt, Bruce filled up a box with five
hundred beans, which stood in for pennies. She had to use her weekly allowance until the beans were gone.

Throughout her life, Emily would remember this kind of firm, instructional discipline with almost as much pleasure as the lessons in design she
received from her loving but often preoccupied father. Either way, Bruce
Price was worth listening to. Whether truly attracted to his field or as an attempt to gain his attention, Emily began to show an early interest in what
Bruce worked on in his home office. The delighted father set the little girl
up on his oversized drafting table, allowing her to "work" alongside him
while he revised his blueprints, supplying her with a T square, paper, and
proper pencils. Soon the child was tagging along when he visited (startled)
clients.

Such concentrated moments compensated, in part, for the lack of attention her father typically gave her. Emily saw very little of the architect,
his frequent absences as he worked overtime at his business encouraging
her to idolize him. Josephine's father had delivered on his promise of an office in Wilkes-Barre for a wedding present. Profiting from his father-in-
law's gentle but direct suggestions to town councilmen, Bruce was able to
design local churches and homes that were unusually choice architectural
commissions for his age. He labored especially hard for the first five years
of Emily's life, capitalizing on the commissions both his father-in-law and
his own former colleagues in Baltimore steered his way.

Bruce's buildings were more or less subsidized into realities on the power of Washington Lee's name, both in Wilkes-Barre and Baltimore, one successful project begetting the next. During the professionally crucial years following Emily's birth, important firms in New York made note of Bruce Price, whose achievements were already on prominent display. Very few architects see the majority of their designs actually executed. Bruce Price's prolific blueprints, in contrast, would average a 90 percent rate of execution throughout his career.

Connections would only become more important as his business grew. Around the time of Emily's birth, the architect cemented a friendship with a longtime Baltimore resident that would prove seminal to his future. Bruce met Frank Hopkinson Smith when the two worked together on a project. An informally trained architect, artist, writer, and socialite, "Hop" Smith, probably after Bruce the most influential man in Emily's life, was a talented engineer and artist, as well as a riveting storyteller. His compelling, friendly masculinity supported a geniality Bruce Price admired. Born in Virginia a decade earlier than his friend, Hop had grown up in Maryland and considered it his home. He took pride in being the great-grandson of Francis Hopkinson, one of the signers of the Declaration of Independence.

Hop Smith informally sponsored his friend in the assorted circles he himself inhabited, social and professional. Years earlier, he had relocated to Manhattan, traveling back to Baltimore frequently. After hearing from Hop one more time about the opportunities he was missing in New York City, Bruce seriously began to consider moving. The business trips he had been taking to New York had already made him restless for more. He marveled at the changes sweeping their way across town with an awesome invincibility. Urban life was sprawling in all directions, even appropriating Fifth Avenue itself, New York's definitive promenade. The city, groaning under the unprecedented heft of new construction, seemed to flex its muscles more powerfully than ever. The recent opening of Central Park encouraged the building of new uptown residences. Such fashionable relocations were finally convincing out-of-town visitors like Josephine that settling below Wall Street was no longer the only viable—or even the best—sign of gentility.

Enhancing her own prestige was not Josephine's driving force: like her father, she usually gravitated to change and excitement for their own sakes. Her privilege blinded her to the ways her upper-class status offset the handicap of having been born a girl. Josie saw little to recommend equality with men. She shrugged off women who acted, she scoffed, as if they were ashamed of being female. Her sexual politics typified those of the readers of Baltimore's popular anti-suffrage magazine of the age, *True Woman*. Why would anyone willingly take on male responsibilities?

And yet for all her commitment to the traditionally feminine, Emily's mother was a strong woman. Now, invigorated by what she glimpsed when she accompanied Bruce to "the city," as the Baltimorean referred to Manhattan, she finally suggested that her extended family might move there. Her parents' rapid acquiescence—five-year-old Emily's energetic grandparents were ready for a change—spurred the young couple on. Eager for another adventure, Washington and Emily Lee financed the Prices' change of residence along with their own, enthusiastically endorsing their son-in-law's choice of a neighborhood. The Lees were already sold on the city, their granddaughter later recalling reasons for their immediate allegiance: "New York was built, is building, will ever be building in huge blocks of steel and stone, and the ambitions of every city and country in the world will keep pouring into it . . . and shoving it up higher and higher into towering cubes." The Lees and the Prices were quickly enveloped into its urban fold.

MILY POST WOULD ALWAYS BEAR THE IMPRINT OF A KNOWING southern girl, her antebellum roots as entrenched as her northeastern attitudes. Her convivial, artful restraint, her disdain for vulgar displays of wealth or beauty or personal information, stemmed partially and potently from her ties to a mixed heritage. If nothing else, an overspill of Baltimore relatives would keep her going back home for a good fifty years of debutante balls and weddings and christenings.

Her childhood house in Manhattan was one of several four-story red-brick houses lining Tenth Street between Fifth and Sixth avenues. By the time the Prices arrived in New York, society might have been moving uptown, but the less secure denizens still leaned toward real estate they knew was correct. And Emily's New York home was connected to her birthplace, after all: Bruce selected the building because its windowsills reminded him of Baltimore houses he had loved. Even today, *New York Times* architecture critic Christopher Gray lauds the 12 West Tenth Street town house's "fabulous door escutcheon . . . [which] looks like a spider web woven by a Gibson Girl, a terrific sinuous work. . . . Clearly custom hammered."

The two apartments, one above the other, ensured that the Prices and Lees saw much of each other. Yet it is easy to forget the Lees' proximity to their grandchild, Mrs. Emily Lee's namesake. In fact, without studying a few scarce family photographs, it would be possible to read everything Emily Post wrote, including the thousands of interviews she would grant through the years, without coming upon a single reference to Josephine's spunky if inelegant parents. It was Bruce and his family, not Josephine and hers, that Emily would venerate throughout her life.

Everything her father did was larger than life in his daughter's eyes. Soon after arriving in Manhattan in the late 1870s, for instance, Bruce had dared to renovate their Tenth Street building, though the Lees thought it fine as it was. Even as the local residents tensed over historical errors he might commit, the confident architect dismayed them further when he explained that he would rent out his in-laws' apartment when they weren't in residence.

The more subtle issue of Bruce's boldness dealt with class and custom, as well as the architect's imperviousness to outdated modes of conduct: Could a gentleman turn his house into a home for himself while leasing part of it for profit—and remain a gentleman? Emily's proud father answered yes: a person of quality was no less pure for earning a living.

WITHOUT SHORTCHANGING his formidable talent, and without taking anything away from what were apparently Bruce Price's almost unworldly magnetism and his preternatural good looks, we can admit the significant role luck played in his life. He came to New York hungry and wise, knowing that such an appetite was exactly what got things done. Manhattan could not afford to relax in the knowledge that it had the urban edge: significant rivals challenged the city's supremacy, especially in the form of the great midwestern capital eight hundred miles to the west. The year before Emily was born, after the roaring, uncontrollable fire gutted Chicago, the city had been forced to rebuild. Destruction spawned the forward-looking Chicago aesthetic. When Bruce moved to New York, the competition between Chicago and New York had evolved into a heated contest, one that shaped the work of any major architect of the period.

To New Yorkers' utter mortification—though the city's architects refused to admit being bested—the Chicago style aimed at the very heart of the skyscraper: its urban steel-frame construction made the sky the limit. As a result of putting function first, Chicago's designers had also, fortuitously, created a cleaner look than the present tired Victorian style of Manhattan. Gone was mere decoration with no purpose, an ethos that suddenly seemed dated and decadent. In its place, the Chicago style prophesied the future, an age of commerce and creativity. With innovations by prominent Chicago architects like Louis H. Sullivan and John W. Root, it sometimes looked as though the Midwest was pulling ahead of its eastern rival. Such urban competition energized Bruce Price's work, which seemed to grow in sophistication from the moment he relocated from Baltimore to Manhattan.

EMILY'S PARENTS QUICKLY shone in New York, reflecting the patina of the upper-middle class, befriended by social types who approved the blend of Lee millions and Price bloodlines. Josephine was in charge of the home, particularly of arranging for Emily's care. In an age when large families were still the norm, the couple was occasionally complimented for rearing their only child progressively, the girl sometimes accompanying them to social events instead of staying home with her nanny. Often her presence simply testified to Emily's success in wheedling her father into taking her along, if only to escape the dreaded German nanny who seemed a jailer to the independent youngster.

"Emilie, put your shoes straight. . . . Emilie, fold your hands. . . . Emilie, do this. . . . Emilie, do not do that"—Emily felt herself admonished throughout the day, and she didn't fail to report what she considered the most outlandish criticism to Bruce the minute she spotted him walking down Tenth Street after work. She knew he'd sympathize with her, especially since he was a Francophile and the nanny openly disdained the French. Shrewdly, the girl made sure she reported every critique the woman uttered. Josephine had employed the strict German governess in part because she herself had grown up in Wilkes-Barre under similar supervision and believed it the firm hand her willful daughter needed. Too, she did not trust French women around her husband. He was too charming, and they too artful. The fräulein, whose hands were so icy that Emily avoided her touch, aroused no such fears in Josephine.

"Bruce Price, playboy" seems an unlikely pairing, whatever a governess's charms. Even if so inclined, the architect didn't have time to misbehave. Soon after the family settled into their apartment, Bruce was commissioned to design an upper-class, income-producing, six-floor walk-up rental apartment building, still a rarity at a time when most city residences were owned. With one apartment per floor, rentals went for $1,400 per year in 1878, the equivalent today of $2,600 per month.

Bruce's eagerness to participate in urban transformation reflected the momentum of the day, with the citizenry no longer awed by the increased speed of change. Innovations that soon became mundane—stores with electric lights—were modifying the culture's habits, the new beats absorbed so quickly that they often went unnoted. And once women could shop after the sun set early on winter afternoons—such a trivial change to the men on Wall Street it was hardly worth mentioning—new social routines evolved, from later mealtimes to faster changes in fashions. Even the city government emitted a sense of cautious renewal, marked by a milestone that year when imprisoned Boss Tweed died, no longer able to bribe the Irish workers with citizenship papers in exchange for a vote for Boss.

Disgusted by the city government at Tammany Hall, still ruled by corrupt leaders who continued to illegally recruit immigrants' support, Bruce brought home the occasional story about city politics to his daughter and wife. He admired the newcomers. What subsidized their passage, other than their own raw courage? He was pleased that the engineering principles about to bear fruit—indoor plumbing, the Otis elevator, and steel structures—would free him and his colleagues to accommodate the masses, sheltering the citizens at the bottom of the ladder in addition to those living in luxury. He was right: ten years before the century ended, elevated trains, called "els," would traverse the length of Manhattan and continue on through the Bronx, Brooklyn, and Queens, moving several hundred thousand passengers each day, offering fares affordable even to the lower class, and transforming the landscape.

But of course his little girl was more interested in goings-on that affected her directly. Two weeks after Boss Tweed's death, Emily Post would make her first public performance, her society debut, twirling her way across the stage. That was all she could think about these days.

Her parents had allowed the six-year-old to accept a bit part in a tableau of The Sleeping Beauty. A charity function at New York's Academy of Music, the event overflowed with patrons, the theater's limited boxes apportioned according to the buyer's prestige. Emily's parents were on the committee of the Mount Vernon Endowment Fund, whose volunteers' months of preparation were now rewarded by a sold-out house. The audience, decked out in their finest evening dress, created their own bejeweled spectacle, the bijoux casting more illumination than the chandeliers. Local swells drew enough mutually admiring stares that the actors were nearly upstaged. So elite that the founders refused to let in the newly rich, self-made businessmen and their families, the academy members outdid even their usual luxuriant selves this time. (J. P. Morgan and other rising nouveaux riches would found the Metropolitan Opera a few years later in order to have a place where they could attend musical events.)

The Sleeping Beauty, which began at an unusually reasonable eight P.M. as opposed to New York's typical curtain time of nine or later, was a fairy tale in four acts with a climactic final scene, the five "gorgeous" choreographed pictures changing at intervals. Characteristic of late-nineteenth-century upper-class entertainments, the carefully held (and heavily rehearsed) poses commanded high admission prices and fulsome praise. The thespians onstage this night included so many prominent socialites that it's unclear who was left to appreciate them. Those applauding, however, were equally illustrious: the *New York Times* devoted nearly a full page to the event, since even listing the "remarkable" audience members proved daunting.

Leading the dance, front and center stage, were Bruce and Josephine Price. Josie shimmered in a long, pale pink brocade dress, while Bruce shone in evening clothes embroidered in rich gold and white. Other well-known local men, acquaintances of the couple, had to content themselves with playing beefeaters and court guards and spear-carriers. Satin and silver curls, antique armor and purple velvet: the scene was a welter of precious-metal threads. The lavish sequins dazzled the spectators as the elaborate new onstage lights caused Titania's costume to sparkle like a star. Among the bevy of young girls serving as stage fillers stood a proudly erect Emily Price, the girl who would say to the end of her life that she had always wanted to become an actress.

EMILY GREW UP respecting wealth, aware, through the example of her family and friends, of the great good it could serve as well as the comfort it bestowed. By the time that she was seven years old, the girl had heard how Catharine Lorillard Wolfe, a distant cousin through her father's mother, Marion Bruce, was playing a significant role in urban development. Her funding of the East Side Lodging House for newsboys and bootblacks was no small feat in an age when social services barely existed. According to her approving parents, Emily's large legacy from Catharine was reduced when the woman donated staggering sums to build an orphanage for boys, designating that no child could be turned away: if a boy couldn't pay the nightly fee of six cents, the debt was to be charged to his account, to be paid off when he was able.

The *New York Times* had written often about Catharine Lorillard Wolfe's projects to help the poor, and now the paper chronicled the covey of homeless children who carried their "effects" from their old, decrepit domicile to the new lodging house. At six-thirty in the evening, after the boys got off work, all but one were able to transport their entire possessions under their right arm. They were used to such paucity; what they had never experienced was the privacy the new residence gave them. The 175 beds in this upper-echelon orphanage were separated from one another with cloth partitions. As if that wasn't wonder enough, on their first night home the inhabitants were treated to a dinner of ham sandwiches, coffee, and ice cream, the dessert a special treat from their patron saint.

Wealth and doing good: both were staples of Emily's early life. Bruce's daily routine of handing out money to beggars as he walked to his office secretly made Josie proud. She bragged about her husband being such an easy touch even while she pretended to despair. Accommodation, of husband with wife, of compassion compounded on sound investments: this was the art of the well-oiled and morally ordered existence. This was the model of proper behavior shaping their watchful child.

Decisions about spending money were, for Emily, a natural part of life. It would have been hard for her parents to keep the subject from her, even if they'd wanted to. In 1879, the new year once again swept in on the frenzy of Wall Street. The price of a seat on the New York Stock Exchange was rising steadily (it would go from $10,000 to $20,000 during the next twelve months), an adjustment that didn't escape Emily's cagey entrepreneurial grandfather. Washington Lee had at least partially realized his quixotic dreams by establishing a precious-metals firm, and at the springtime meeting of the Columbia Consolidated Gold and Silver Mining Company's stockholders, he projected his optimistic earnings for the coming year. Success seemed to come with the prime real estate his office occupied at 33 Wall Street. As with the Internet companies of the 1990s, however, Lee's speculation quickly proved a brilliant blaze that would sputter to a wan conclusion.

Luckily, although Washington Lee preferred the glitter of fine metals, he recognized compelling reasons to bet most of his money on the railroads: the decade of Emily's birth had brought about a revolution in shipping methods. It wasn't a glamorous subject—and certainly lacked the luster of gold—but now crops could be shipped by rail. He would retain his interest in coal, Emily's grandfather decided. In the past, getting food to market had sometimes cost more than the goods themselves. This new speed, this new ubiquity of the humble, sturdy rails, changed everything: it changed the way Americans would eat.

CHAPTER 6

⊹

*I*N 1880, WHILE THE OTHERWISE STOLID JOSEPHINE MERRILY PLAYED the market, closely following her father's astute prognostications, the more ethereal Bruce Price pursued a different kind of speculation altogether. He had proven himself this past year by building several additional luxury residences in Bar Harbor. Now he qualified to compete with the more experienced professionals, the cadre of top-rung New York architects bidding against one another for choice projects. That January, however, he suffered his first defeat, though his inclusion in the contest was honor enough. The Long Island Historical Society had solicited drawings from five architects for its new home in Brooklyn. Bruce lost the contest to George Post, but in the process he and the older man quickly became friends. Post, among the era's most prominent architects, was leading the way with his technologically sophisticated designs, including New York's first metal-framed structure, the four-story Produce Exchange at 2 Broadway.

Throughout 1880, the almost militant excitement of the city's architects reverberated through long-running friendly arguments, their shared long-term vision underwriting their critical inventories of one another's projects. Exhilarated, Bruce spent long days at his office. Sometimes, when he found himself still working hours after dinner, he would simply spend the night at one of his men's clubs a mere block or so from his home, refining his designs until two or three A.M. Josie was as happy for her husband to sleep at the club, instead of waking her up with his restless movements.

Just as the architect had been searching for another—grander—project, he'd heard from Hop Smith about a perfect, plausible opportunity to make real money: Bruce could invest his time and reputation, Washington Lee his cash. Together, they would all become rich off Long Beach, New York, a town on a barrier island off the South Shore of Long Island. Hop Smith, the graceful amateur economist whose enthusiastic calculations and excellent track record could suspend anyone's disbelief, practically guaranteed the outcome.

A BORN WINNER, Francis Hopkinson Smith sometimes literally turned what he touched into gold. Bruce Price had always, good-naturedly, laughed about Smith's positioning himself as an outsider to society. New York artists of a certain ilk were encouraged to hang out at the swank Century Club, even if they weren't members, since their presence lent a raffish air to the otherwise august men's facility. In reality, the "bohemians" who were allowed into the establishment inevitably came from wealth and well-connected families, and Hop was a prime example: he had memberships himself in all the major clubs.

But none of that mattered to Emily Price, who doted on Uncle Frank, as she called him. He always managed to make his enviable adventures even more exciting in the telling. Years later, her favorite memories would include sitting on his lap as a child, awed by his tall tales—usually, if improbably, true. Once, when he dreamily described the barge trip taken up the Hudson by "the Club," his group of artist friends, Emily gaped, causing him to joke about her swallowing a fly. The born raconteur allowed her to feel part of the ride, traveling the Erie Canal from Troy into Lake Champlain. Next to her father, the girl admired Uncle Frank more than anyone else in her life.

Hop had developed an engineering firm that would stay in business for the next three decades, and he and Bruce often sent each other business throughout their careers. This current chance for everyone involved to reap rewards for a development project in Long Beach was just another example of the uncanny acumen Hop showed in combining commercial with artistic investments. The recently formed Tile Club was yet another example.

A group of illustrious men (twelve, with a few members wandering in and out over the decade) met periodically, ostensibly to promote the Arts and Crafts movement, then catching on in the States. Inspired by British artist and activist William Morris's decorative genius, the movement had reached America on the back of the new post–Civil War fortunes. The 1876 Centennial Exhibition in Philadelphia, with its almost neurotic emphasis on England, the mother country, had paved the way. New York's Hudson River school had had its time in the sun, and the Tile Club was determined to help art reinvent everything from painting to textiles.

More than most such organizations, the Tile Club ingeniously blended pleasure with business—and not only the business of making art. Painter William Laffan, a writer for the *New York Sun* as well as a passenger agent for the Long Island Rail Road, served as the unofficial leader of the club. Counted variously as members during the club's ten-year duration were Beaux Arts sculptor Augustus Saint-Gaudens; painter Winslow Homer; teacher, proponent of impressionism, and artist William Merritt Chase; and architect Stanford White, who eventually decorated the room on East Tenth Street where the club met. Even Mark Twain was briefly involved in what quickly became more of a social than a professional club. John Singer Sargent requested permission to join before he'd even consider moving to New York.

The Tilers actually stuck to their professional agenda for about one year, from around 1877 into 1878, but the club quickly devolved into a social organization, professionally affiliated in name only. Over the next ten years, a member would occasionally publish an article in *Scribner's* or *Harper's Weekly,* keeping interest in the Tilers' future alive by teasing the audience about what actually went on at their mysterious meetings. The Club functioned like a grown-up boys' fraternity.

Art had always been secondary to the agenda of the Tile Club, whatever its official mandate. And if camaraderie came first, doing business followed right behind. It was this primary business agenda that interested Hop's friends Bruce Price and Washington Lee. Club president Laffan had invested early in the Long Beach Development project, and he made it clear to Hop that the Tile Club would help commercialize Long Beach, making it, as well as the rest of Long Island, famous through the Tilers' travel, painting, and antics.

In keeping with its primary schema, one of the earliest products of the Tile Club was a commercial brochure for the Long Island Rail Road, the LIRR, called *The New Long Island: A Handbook of Summer Travel.* Using the Tilers' own visual record of their summer hike, the promotional package made for a slick product. During a couple of leisurely paced weeks, the Tilers had hiked the hundred miles from Long Beach to Montauk, at the tip of Long Island itself, racking up adventures to share with those less adventuresome and fortunate. Future residents would have it easier: the brochure promised a year's worth of free railroad passes for newcomers who bought real estate on Long Beach.

ALWAYS CONFIDENT THAT he would come out on top, Washington Lee viewed the business proposition, brokered by Hop Smith (who rarely bet wrong), as a savory opportunity. During the early decades of their rapid development, most railroads were tiny, owned by private stockholders who basically controlled the routes. Washington Lee was a railroad man, his specialty coal, along with equity in the occasional railroad company itself. Of course, he knew how to negotiate contracts with the Long Island Rail Road to transport thousands of customers to the beach development. And this investment would grant his son-in-law the chance to build a major project. The enterprise, inbred with shared artistic and financial interests, fit Lee's ambitions and generous personality. Everybody would win.

In spite of his complete lack of experience in designing large spaces that combined commercial and residential uses, Bruce Price was awarded the commission for the mammoth Long Beach resort hotel. Whether the timing was good for such an investment is a question that might have stopped many other men. The early 1880s were an unstable period for the nation's finances. Washington Lee believed, however, that this was the perfect moment to invest heavily in an ambitious scheme for the leisured classes. He figured that most financiers were erring on the side of caution.

And so he did invest, again and again, desperately trying to save an enterprise that proved a financial disaster almost from its beginning, an endless money pit that severely rearranged the aging man's finances. As a result, the legacy he bequeathed his family would be a small portion of what it was before the Long Beach behemoth took shape, a fraction of the fortune Bruce Price had anticipated when he'd married the coal lord's daughter.

The gigantic hotel complex, which the *Times* anointed as "the new watering place," officially opened on July 13, 1880. *Harper's Weekly* printed a full-page engraving, revealing the Long Beach Hotel as impressively large but fairly mundane in its design, its Queen Anne pretensions and seaside resort simplicity an ill mix. More important than the general, if tepid, praise Bruce's building received were the management problems that riddled the colossus from the beginning. On April 5, 1881, a new board of directors elected by stockholders of the Long Beach Company chose Lee and Frank Hopkinson Smith to oversee company operations.

That summer, the stockholders bet that the financial flux caused by the July 2 assassination attempt on President Garfield had upset the market only temporarily. But during the ten agonizing weeks it took for the president to die, the financial morass entangling the Long Beach Company kept getting worse. On August 9, A. T. Stewart and Company, the Saks Fifth Avenue of its day, filed suit to reclaim its furnishings, bought on credit. Seemingly undaunted in the face of the continuing foreclosures, the company finagled, within days of the department store's suit, yet another mortgage for $250,000. On September 21, 1881, when Chester Arthur took the helm as the country's twenty-first president, Americans became confident of the market again, and investors in the hotel became optimistic. Over the next few years the association publicized celebrity visits, including two trips Oscar Wilde made to the Long Beach Hotel in 1882.

That same year the hotel site was awarded a long-promised railroad stop. Now, surely, the crowds would come rolling in. Society might be agog over J. P. Morgan's purchase of a 185-foot steamer, the *Corsair,* the largest yacht in the nation. But even he depended on the trains over the long haul—everyone knew that.

HER SPOUSE'S AMBITION and the life he labored to provide for their family made sense to Josephine Price. She believed Bruce was correct to emphasize his career at the expense of conjugal socializing. The intrepid young matron simply recruited her women friends, including her mother, to accompany her to the theater and the opera. She appreciated her good life: some New Yorkers claimed that "tip-top" living in Manhattan was as fine as that of St. Petersburg and Paris. She also discovered that her New York friends were sometimes demanding in a way that Josie herself was not. They maintained, for instance, that there was no drinkable champagne under $3.00—whereas Josie herself would never pay so much. Her happiness was more likely to come from the tasty $1.50 dinner served on the train to Baltimore. Still, such frugality was her choice; the Price income had progressed nicely.

Nor was there any need to pity Bruce Price for his workload. Missing the theater (or the chance to spend more time with his child) didn't bother him much; Emily would later explain proudly that he was a man's man. His social inclinations lay more in debating his colleagues over the staying power of the new impressionist painters or in rehashing, endlessly, the future of tall buildings: How high would they really go? But he couldn't afford to overindulge in such fraternity, unless the friendship was linked to a job. He worked hard and fast, whether building a church or designing rural getaways for millionaires.

Only an hour or so from the city, the mansions dotting the Hudson Valley's gentle wilderness stretched from Bear Mountain to Rhinebeck, allowing people like Pierpont Morgan to escape into nature and, unlike the architect, enjoy a more leisurely pace. Between his country and in-town residences, Bruce had built eleven significant structures over the past year. When a census showed that New York City had almost doubled in population since the eve of the Civil War twenty years earlier, he joked that he had probably housed half of that number. By the end of 1880, Bruce Price was satisfied but worn out, in need of a vacation himself.

Like the flexible spouse she was, Josephine picked up the social slack created by her husband's relentless work schedule. In January 1881, in spite of frigid weather, she took eight-and-a-half-year-old Emily to Baltimore for a relative's wedding. Cornelia Barroll, Josie's niece, was uniting what the New York Times pronounced were two "well known families of Boston and Baltimore." Though a "blinding snow storm" raged outside, most of the fifteen hundred invitees still managed to attend a "social event . . . of much moment." Emily and her mother must have beamed with pride, sitting in the front pew of Baltimore's Christ Church, Bruce Price's presence embedded in the sanctuary walls. Against the bets that several cynical local residents had placed, he had somehow managed to finish the Chase Street building by the beginning of 1881, in time for his in-laws' ceremony.

BRUCE PRICE'S ROLE in the Long Beach project served him well. Immediately he moved on, engaged in his peripatetic life, with its gratifying mixture of work and pleasure. Josephine and their daughter traveled abroad late in the winter of 1881 before hunkering down back in New York City so that Emily could finish the year's classes at Miss Graham's School for girls, which the nine-year-old now attended. Finally, generously interpreting the school's spring break, the family of three traveled to Bar Harbor once again for Bruce to build a new house and for his wife and child to play.

Though Josephine and Emily enjoyed a vacation while in Maine, Bruce rarely paused from his work. Still, with his wife's full support, he managed to return to the city for important social events. Late in March, for instance, when the Titan Club honored Mother Earth, Bruce joined the select set of men gathered at Delmonico's, at Fifth Avenue and Twenty-sixth

Street, since 1825 the favorite restaurant of Manhattan's social set, to salute the vernal equinox. This was the kind of revelry the architect always seemed to find time for, an otherwise little-seen frivolous side that his daughter adored.

The Titan Club frolic was well matched to Bruce's current project, a theater at Broadway and Twenty-eighth Street that he'd been constructing throughout the previous year. A well-known capitalist had convinced a company to invest in a new stage for vaudeville and light musical entertainment. Acclaimed by the *New York Times* as one of the city's best recent buildings, Bruce's French Renaissance–style theater was praised widely for its exceptional design. Even the stylish boxes—"like the circle boxes at the new Metropolitan Opera house"—were lauded for deviating from the traditional model in order to obtain better sight lines.

The architect's daughter was, at ten years old, the perfect age to decide that the theater house her papa was constructing in 1882 was more magic of the type he always seemed to create. Bruce took Emily with him while he worked on the building and later, on special occasions, to an actual performance on the stage he had designed. The young girl watched the stage intently, its glamorous, slightly suspect ladies in luxurious costumes always meeting with tumultuous applause. By now, it was clear to the child that her father, not her mother, was the star in their family. This winter he also found time to help her build an intricate dollhouse, bringing home wood that he ordered cut and smoothed to the dimensions his daughter judged correct. Though he insisted on erecting the staircases himself, he encouraged Emily to create everything else. She took her assignment to heart, not allowing an inch of space to be overlooked. "Walls, ceilings and furniture and ornaments—complete!" she would recall with gusto decades later.

WHILE HIS SON-IN-LAW was marching ahead with his life and his career, Washington Lee was still agonizing over the finances of the Long Beach enterprise. Undeniably, he had been a holy fool with his fortune. By 1883, regardless of the refinancing, the various receiverships, and the repeatedly extended credit, the company officers had to concede they couldn't make a go of it. The sixty-two-year-old Lee died in the spring of 1883, altering his family's plans for the Monday circled in red months earlier on the city's best calendars: March 26, the day of the decade's most eagerly awaited social event, Mrs. Vanderbilt's ball. Lee's own pleasures had lain elsewhere, of course; he'd been more excited about the new Brooklyn Bridge, officially

opened by President Cleveland just a few days earlier. But Josephine's father had been devastated by the disastrous miscalculation he'd made with
the hotel. When he died, the Long Beach investment company was just
marking time until its own inevitably ignominious end.

His will—"I Washington Lee, formerly of Wilkes-Barre, Pennsylvania,
now of the City of New York"—was probated on May 31, 1883, by New
York State. Clearly he had underwritten Bruce Price's career, and yet Lee
appears to have been as admirably even-mannered as his granddaughter
herself would turn out to be. He left his estate to be equally divided among
all five of his children, after his wife's interests had been settled. But, he
noted genially: in light of the various amounts of money he'd given to one
child or another through the years (he tactfully refrained from naming
names), he did expect their inheritances to be reduced by any unpaid loans.
His wife could mete out the final rewards.

The man was generous by nature, even in death. He may have suffered
the mortification of his last investment, but his fine character lasted to his
final hour. Like Peter Cooper, who also died that year, having done more to
endow New York City than any other single citizen, Washington Lee performed charitably too, albeit on a different scale. Both left New York better off than they'd found it, the self-taught Cooper as a poverty-stricken
child and Washington Lee as a mature, cheerful adventurer who didn't
mind getting his hands dirty, smiling all the way.

Right up until her father died, Josephine and her friends had rattled on
about the same subject for weeks, Josie admitting to her family that even
she was finally bored by the gossip. Spilling over into the homes of the day's
most sensible women, the topic of the Vanderbilt ball, scheduled for March
26, 1883, had usurped center stage in society columns and at neighborhood
soirees throughout the winter. Years later Emily recounted having heard
the ladies buzz with the latest news on the great event. Gradually the girl
had come to realize that her mother's friends enjoyed the prelude as much
as the occasion itself. Monsieur Worth's latest designs from Paris were at
least as important as the guest list.

The ten-year-old, though interested in fashion at an early age, nonetheless grew impatient with the babble's monotonous rhythms. There was no
way, however, to avoid the excited chatter of her class as the stakes escalated
during the year's great melodrama. Its juicy details were rehearsed daily for
weeks, the gossip centered upon Alva Vanderbilt's audacious bid to unseat
Caroline Schermerhorn Astor as the potentate of social clout in New York.

Mrs. Astor was Old Blood royalty at its most incontestable moment. It was no secret that the Astors looked down on the Vanderbilts, whose riches came from mere trade, and who were now elbowing their way into society with their millions. The Astors had dirtied their hands the right way, trading pelts and selling pianos so long ago that no one remembered their past as merchants. Time—which in the new country moved fast—had made of them gentlefolk. And this new elite had no intention of letting the rabble join their group.

⛭

FROM THE SIZE OF HER NEW BALLROOM—SAID TO HOLD ONE THOUSAND guests—to the party favors Alva would furnish—Tiffany bracelets and silver lockets transported on a giant gondola rolled into the room—this dance was in no way an exercise in good taste. The housewarming for the Vanderbilts' opulent new limestone mansion at what was then 660 Fifth Avenue took the form of a March costume ball that would eclipse the most fabulous events of seasons to come. More important, the blatant confrontation between old and new would ante up the social stakes. This was no gracious dance in the southern style, in spite of Alva Vanderbilt's Alabama roots; it was an aggressive tango telling "Old Society" New York that the game was over. Now the arrivistes not only belonged in Manhattan, they owned a large part of it.

When she was informed of the upcoming Vanderbilt ball (so the myth's most popular version goes), the redoubtable Caroline Schermerhorn Astor had immediately doubled up on dance lessons for her marriageable daughter, Carrie. Even the jaded Mrs. Astor couldn't help getting excited about the Vanderbilt gala: its magnitude promised to be beyond anything even she had sponsored. Perhaps her excitement caused her to be careless. Or, more likely, it never occurred to Mrs. Astor that she would be excluded from the guest list. Whatever the reason, she failed to notice that the Vanderbilts had not invited her family to their ball.

Then she began to hear alarming rumors: Mrs. Vanderbilt was not expecting the Astors' daughter or her parents to attend. Prodded by her worried daughter, Mrs. Astor sent out a polite if typically haughty query about the missing invitation, mere days before the dance. She was immediately and "reluctantly" informed that the presumably misplaced invitation to the ball was in fact not lost at all: Mrs. Vanderbilt was not so uncouth as to invite someone who had not yet called on her. Mrs. Astor had never dropped her "pasteboard" (or calling card) at 660 Fifth Avenue, so of course Mrs. Vanderbilt couldn't expect her to attend the party.

The story, retold with relish in certain quarters even today, surely embellishes the inward turmoil purported to have kept Mrs. Astor tossing in her bed over the next few nights. Smoldering, purple with rage for several days, the defeated queen of society at last angrily acquiesced. Neighbors peeking through their curtains saw a footman in the blue livery of the House of Astor deliver Caroline's calling card—"Mrs. Astor" was engraved on it even more simply than were most socialites' names—to the maroon-liveried footman guarding the Vanderbilt gates. The victor purportedly bestowed a wicked smile of thanks upon her servant. That afternoon, the outmaneuvered Mrs. Astor received her invitation to the ball.

Alva Vanderbilt was only thirty-one years old when she took on Old New York, her battle signifying a larger shift in the city's power structures than partygoers realized. If the Vanderbilts lacked blue blood coursing through their veins, they could never, by any means, be considered bloodless. Raw power, not genes, was what counted. Alva had come to town, and the déclassé Vanderbilts planned to stay. Alva won everything she competed for, elbowing aside the Old Guard, breaking the stranglehold of two generations' refusal to let her husband's family into high society.

She helped maneuver her husband, William Kissam Vanderbilt, the Commodore's grandson, into the right clubs—the Metropolitan, the Knickerbocker, Union, Racquet and Tennis, Turf and Field, and the New York Yacht Club—the club culture allowing him to avoid what had quickly become his miserable home life almost entirely. Hardly missing a beat, Alva would divorce William a few years later and marry one of the Belmonts, soon following that marriage with a prominent role in the women's suffrage movement. She was a politic and political woman, such qualities setting her apart from her contemporaries, who tended to be one but not the other. The indomitable Alva was even willing to make her personal peace with Ulysses Grant, who could, after all, further her goals, though General Grant's victory had ruined Alva's father back home in Alabama. Alva Vanderbilt was the iron magnolia come to take her revenge on the Yankees.

So on the night of Washington Lee's death, the Vanderbilts were finally seated among the elect. On that fabulous March evening, they spent their way into society, becoming an "old family" overnight and making no secret of how they were doing it. They made Old New York swallow the ignominy of it all. The following spring, Mrs. Astor's colors would be seen fluttering outside the Vanderbilt mansion; the footman was delivering an invitation to Mrs. Astor's annual Four Hundred ball. Years later, as Mrs. O.H.P. Belmont, Alva would seek to protect Newport from the arrivistes, but for now, she was carrying the torch for the newly arrived. However implausibly, Mrs. Astor herself would become one of Alva's closest friends and most ardent champions in the age to come.

To most Americans, such a world might as well have been on a different planet. The housewarming at the Vanderbilts' cost a quarter of a million dollars at a time when $25 a week enabled the men who constructed the extravaganza's indoor arboretums to support their families comfortably. Such opulence also engineered trickle-down benefits less direct than paychecks for workers: it provided endless fodder for every type of tabloid.

HAVING BURIED WASHINGTON LEE instead of attending the Vanderbilt party, the Price family wanted a change of scenery. They decided to vacation at Newport for a full four months this year, since Bruce needed to be on a local construction site anyway. Emily's parents had come to realize that in many ways Newport was the most southern of the summer retreats, if only because rich old-timers had used it for generations to escape from the Carolina and Georgia coasts during the unremitting summer humidity.

The mecca for the well-off seemed even more packed than usual this season, the sheer number of socialites attracting press attention. Just a week into the summer season, the beach and cliff thronged "with excursionists," the *Times'* society pages declared, excitedly enumerating the upper-class vacationers. Who was visiting whom seemed the major preoccupation of the day. Henry Clews, Chauncey Depew, Edward Bulwer-Lytton of England, and Emily's own little family of three were listed as the early arrivals. The *Times* noted that the Prices were frequent guests at Miss Catharine Lorillard Wolfe's "palatial villa," so large that even the neighbors refused to call it a "cottage." Miss Wolfe had barely finished her new house in time for the season, and now she intended to share it with the Whartons of Philadelphia, the Goelets, the Van Alens, and the Jays, while they were busy laying the grounds for their own bungalows by the sea.

Newport hummed, though the gravity of losing her father must have slowed down even the indomitable Josephine for a few months. But the truth remains that Emily's mother was never one to show much emotion. Much like her daughter after her, she tended to her psychic pain by staying busy, digesting the psychological detritus piece by piece, everything in its own time. Josie valued things that affected life directly.

Josephine also believed in taking the measure of the signs around you. Back in Manhattan, that had included watching the majestic ten-story Dakota apartment building, far uptown on the Upper West Side, take its final shape. Solitary against the sky, the building, three years in the making, was almost completed. As what were basically permanent hotel suites begun substituting for conventional private residences, the urban sensibility seemed to shift, the cityscape ceding space to ever more restaurants and apartment buildings. Commissions burgeoned for the city's top architects, among them Bruce Price.

More work for her father meant less time for his daughter; Emily knew this. At least she had an increasingly full agenda herself these days. That autumn Emily turned eleven, an age that advanced her to the next, more serious echelon of studies at Miss Graham's School for girls. Convenient to her home—though during Emily's tenure it would move from West Twelfth Street to 63 Fifth Avenue, at East Thirteenth Street—Miss Graham's proximity proved opportune when Emily needed extra coaching to speak the perfect French now expected of her.

Her later disparagement of the school was almost certainly aimed at defending her halfhearted studies during girlhood: "For six years I attended a school in New York—the Misses Graham's Seminary for Young Ladies— don't you love it? But that didn't help much. I got my real education from listening to my father." When she was much older, and more confident about her native intelligence, she would admit that she "didn't like school much" and tried to avoid classrooms whenever possible. "I was absolutely the world's worst student," she would claim.

By the time Emily was enrolled, northeastern society knew what they were paying for when they sent their daughters to Miss Graham's: connections, after all, not test scores, guaranteed the best placements in life. And in reality, in spite of Miss Graham's willingness to let the girls' academics slide in favor of social events, Emily's school had a formidable history of hiring august teachers, including, while she attended, the founder of the *New York Times,* Henry Jarvis Raymond. Mentored by Horace Greeley, the well-respected founder and editor of the *New York Tribune,* Raymond was a promoter of disinterested, honest journalism at a time when tabloid news prevailed. Nor is it likely that the illustrious Morgans, the Rutherfords, or the Trowbridges, whose daughters also attended Miss Graham's, would be completely lax about their daughters' schooling. Jennie Jerome, the mother of Winston Churchill, did not appear ill-served.

THE SCHOOLGIRL EMILY had increasingly come to love Uncle Frank; for a change, Bruce Price wasn't the only man figuring prominently in the child's life. On August 18, 1883, Hop won the government contract to build the Statue of Liberty's base. Miss Liberty was a gift from the French government meant to stick in the British craw upon America's centennial. Her arm and torch had been displayed in Madison Square Park, at Twenty-fourth Street, since 1876, the next seven years spent in a national campaign to finance the statue's foundations. Now, the construction funded at last, Uncle Frank was the man of the hour. Almost daily, it seemed, Hop Smith's name appeared conspicuously in the city newspapers, as if he were as important as Liberty herself, whose concrete support would cost the government $8.94 per cubic yard. The end of the nineteenth century was an era of numbers, an age devoted to codifying and classifying; calculations were next to godliness. Expenses were meticulously detailed for the public: Frank Smith's base required $51,000 to $52,000. To be made of concrete composed of sand, cement, and broken stones, it would measure 93 feet square at the bottom and 70 at the top and stand 48 feet, 8 inches high. The pedestal, rising to an altitude of 112 feet, would require a platform 67 feet square at the base and 40 at the top. Reciting the numbers reinforced the statue's significance: Who would have thought so many layers compiled the Statue of Liberty's foundation?

From the beginning, Hop installed Emily Price at his side. She joined him in his small tugboat as he inspected Miss Liberty's support material. Sharing with her his sketches, as if Emily's intelligence justified adult respect, Hop Smith served as mentor at a key moment in the life of the girl who was "almost twelve" (as she constantly reminded her mother). This was the type of extracurricular education of which Miss Graham wholeheartedly approved. As Hop and Emily toured his work in progress several times a week, the girl strutted proudly. While the statue's foundation took form, Emily was allowed to explore the cavernous "secret" rooms in the monument's hollow interior. The experience turned out to be an idée fixe in the making. She pretended she was a princess, this strange edifice her castle. A not entirely singular fantasy for young girls, it nonetheless took hold of her imagination with a ferocity her other memories rarely exhibited.

Contributing to the literal foundation of what was to be her country's welcome to strangers eager to be Americans affected Emily deeply. That she worshipped Frank Hopkinson Smith second only to Bruce Price made for a potent combination: Liberty and a second father she adored. In her later spill of vivid memories of Smith, she never mentioned his children or his wife. If readers of Emily Post's life relied on her anecdotes alone, they would assume Uncle Frank was a lifelong bachelor—devoted to his ersatz daughter in lieu of his own family. Yet his long-term marriage and lifelong doting on his children were singled out in all the elegies to him years later.

Bruce proudly observed Emily's interest in understanding Miss Liberty from an architectural perspective. Spurred on to allow his precocious daughter to accompany him to otherwise all-male construction sites, he felt responsible for Hop's obvious success with Emily. Given this most recent evidence of her talent, Bruce was willing to forfeit the masculine solidarity he was accustomed to, in order to educate the girl. Throughout her adulthood, in an odd absence of larger cultural reflection, Emily would wistfully recall Bruce's sadness that her gender denied her the chance to become an architect herself. She so clearly had a talent for this kind of work; what a pity she'd been born a girl, he said more than once. Had she been a boy, she could have become his partner and eventual successor. Without ever pondering the motivation for choices she made as an adult, Emily would set out to prove to herself, most of all, that she was a worthy heir to Bruce Price.

In fact, by the time Emily thought seriously about a career, there were already women architects, however small their number. In 1886, Louise Bethune, who some said was the first professional female architect anywhere, had become a member of the prestigious AIA, the American Institute of Architects. Several journalists suggested that Bethune's birthplace, a small town in the center of New York State, had spurred her to achieve: she grew up next door to Seneca Falls, where Elizabeth Cady Stanton and Lucretia Mott had conducted the first Women's Rights Convention in 1848. In October 1881, when Bethune opened an architectural office in Buffalo, she ensured that the occasion coincided with the presence of the state's Women's Congress in town. Nor were women limited to artistic fields: in 1884, Belva Ann Lockwood, a well-known suffragist and lawyer from Washington, D.C., forty miles south of Emily's Baltimore home, ran for president of the United States—and she did so again in 1888. She received an astounding four thousand votes (from men, who alone could vote).

But if enlightened attitudes toward gender were slowly working their way into the American psyche, atonement for slavery and subjugation of black people seemed headed in the opposite direction. The same year that news about the Vanderbilt class warfare temporarily outstripped interest in maneuvering Miss Liberty to harbor, the Ku Klux Klan, nearly twenty years after its founding, was accelerating its efforts to cleanse America. Such extremism Emily would have abhorred and, offered the chance, tried to squelch. But ugly radical factions weren't what shaped her careless consideration of racial minorities; that culprit, a failure of intellectual sophistication, was more subtle. Throughout the decades, she would enfold her ambivalence about upper-class superiority into her belief in giving everyone a fair shake. People of color had to play by the same rules as everybody else: in America, men and women, girls and boys all had an equal opportunity to learn how to behave. As the idea of inherited class eroded throughout the twentieth century, Emily would breathe a sigh of relief. Now there was no contesting the idea that quality could be had by anyone who wanted it badly enough.

In light of her birth, Emily Price should have grown up in an era where the prejudices of her parents would soon become a thing of the past. After all, the Civil Rights Act of 1875 had been written three years after she was born. It outlawed racial discrimination in public accommodations, a major step in promoting equal coexistence. But instead of life steadily improving for former slaves and other black citizens, in 1883 a conservative Supreme Court took the extraordinary step of rescinding the landmark legislation. The "separate but equal" coexistence established by *Plessy v. Ferguson* in 1896 would remain the law of the land until the 1960s.

꙳

By late 1884, when New York's autumnal balls began, Bruce had served his family commendably, if sometimes functioning like a finely tuned machine. He had dutifully joined all the right clubs, from the Century to the Salamander and, most important, the Union, which dated from 1836 and had a yearly waiting list of five hundred applicants. Bruce Price, a real club man, society murmured approvingly.

Cleveland Amory has explained the appeal of club life to the upper-class man of this era: "Here he had the best of his well-bred friends, the most comfortable of his well-stuffed chairs, the best of food, drink and cigars from his well-stocked lagers and cellars, the least irritating of reading material from a well-censored library, and the best of games from well-mannered losers. Here he could do what he pleased when he pleased where he pleased and with whom he pleased; here, and only here, did he find sanctuary and his four freedoms: freedom of speech against democracy, freedom of worship of aristocracy, freedom from want from tipping, and, above all, freedom from fear of women." It was to the gentlemen's club, Amory pointed out, that lady friends not part of the intimate family circle wrote, the letters discreetly delivered by the club servants, facedown, on silver trays.

The only membership Bruce Price refused was the prestigious Union League. A product of the Civil War, the club had supported the North. The Union League had spearheaded the building of the Metropolitan Museum a few years after the war ended and had helped found the Red Cross. Now its members were working on the Statue of Liberty project. But the past still stung people like Bruce Price. Emily later explained that her father had refused the club's invitation because of the organization's occasional disrespect toward the South.

Though Bruce's prejudices were passionate, they were few. Always convivial, he became more gregarious with age. In the past he had needed much solitude, in spite of his easy nature. By 1884 he was thirty-eight years old, and operating with consummate social skill. He had realized that he thrived on the routine and comfort of club life and male social events, enjoying both rhythms more than the feminine home life he shared with Josephine and Emily. The era's frantic attention to speed suited his perfectionist tendencies well, but he had learned that he also needed a way to relax.

That autumn, everybody was actually keeping the same time, a very promising scientific advance, in the architect's opinion. Time zones hadn't existed previously; each town and city along a rail line had created its own slightly different noontime. Now there would be uniform schedules for the entire United States: Pacific, Mountain, Central, and Eastern. With the world split into twenty-four zones, routines such as determining railroad timetables acquired a new precision that would promote efficiency.

Still, most people, unlike Bruce Price and his friends, would know only one time zone all their lives. And New Yorkers, whether transplanted or longtime residents, could be forgiven for thinking their city at the heart of the world. New York was for everyone, and everybody came. That year the world's first roller coaster debuted in Coney Island, creating almost as much excitement in 1884 as the Ferris wheel would at the Chicago world's fair the following decade. Innovative entertainment unfolding in Times Square allowed New York ladies to participate in nightlife without losing respect—as long as respectable men accompanied them. Dance halls, theaters, and restaurants reached out to female customers, their presence driving prostitution and pornography to the tenement districts at the city's southern and western borders. Women of every class were seeing more of life than they had for most of the previous century.

THERE WERE THOSE in this exuberant age who pushed geographical limits even farther than crossing the newly regulated time zones. On November 22, 1884, while Josephine and her twelve-year-old daughter embarked on a monthlong holiday in Baltimore, Bruce attended a widely publicized dinner at Delmonico's, in midtown. Where else would the city's finest choose to fête a romantic explorer, a true hero of the age? Tonight's guest of honor was so important that the restaurant was closed to ordinary business.

Lieutenant Adolphus W. Greely was an Arctic explorer who had survived more than two years at the North Pole without supplies, from late 1881 until early 1884. Only a few years before, an expedition financed by the expatriate and social pariah James Gordon Bennett Jr. had been crushed, along with its brave leader, whom Bennett had financially supported, by the polar ice on its voyage to the North Pole, sinking all on board. Even the notorious Bennett, who had publicly urinated in the fireplace of his soon-to-be ex-fiancée's friends, flinched when told of the crew's fate. Greely, in contrast, had survived this latest polar disaster, leading the remnants of his group to safety. Now, as he was celebrated by high-ranking army and navy officials, Bruce Price, architect, sat among them.

Having grown a bit plumper on the requisite duck, oysters, tenderloin, and turtle that Delmonico's routinely served these days, the architect mixed easily with the illustrious explorers and military heroes. His connection, yet again, was the omnipresent Frank Hopkinson Smith. An unusually convivial event, the gathering encouraged the jolly company to vie with one another to show their appreciation of the honoree's pluck. But only after they had downed their coffee and lit their cigars, settling back to hear what they knew would be a once-in-a-lifetime story, did the real show begin.

It was the kind of compelling adventure Bruce Price relished and, still awed, shared weeks later with his wide-eyed daughter. He admired men indifferent to danger, knowing himself to be cautious by nature, though immoderate in desire. One reason he and his father-in-law had gotten along so well was his genuine admiration for Washington Lee's never-say-die spirit.

Now here he was, listening to Lieutenant Greely detail his near-death exploits in the Arctic sea. Nonstop press coverage guaranteed that his story was a repeat by now, but the men were still awestruck as Greely vividly detailed the ordeal: disaster had struck when the supply relief ship failed to show up. The result was horrific, only six numb men surviving out of the original twenty-five.

What heroes they were, larger than life, if they could face down such disaster and beat it. Yet Greely had survived in large part because his wife had galvanized an exhausted rescue team into giving it one more try—and that time they had finally found her husband. The spellbound listeners stood up to toast the woman behind the man, and after the convivial cheers quieted, the group smoked a few more cigars, drank some additional sherry, and then headed off for their favorite club to share some substantive nuggets with less fortunate friends.

The trip, and the audience's fascination with it, typified the period's sense of boundless horizons, suddenly within grasp. Toward the end of the nineteenth century, many Americans and Europeans romanticized distant and unexplored lands; the more exotic a place seemed, the more compelling the challenge. Africa, with its still virginal commercial markets, and the Arctic, ready-made for the true explorer, had particularly captured the popular imagination.

Bruce Price's professional skills, oiled by his social affability, assured him a nearly limitless run of invitations to such gatherings. On the increasingly infrequent occasions when he was home for dinner at 12 West Tenth Street, he jovially passed on detailed accounts of his office life as well as of the social events he attended. The glamour of her father's schedule reinforced Emily's sense that Bruce's activities and his personality were infinitely more interesting than her mother's. Though Bruce was always courteous and respectful to Josephine, he exhibited a restrained but obvious impatience with her heedless return to practical issues. Luckily, by the middle of the following year, while Emily attended what she viewed as increasingly tedious classes at Miss Graham's, her parents became aware that they were about to hit pay dirt, and the realization pleased them equally. Josephine's boosterism and Bruce's guileless but gutsy work ethic, undergirded by real talent, had irrigated the seeds of a project that set up their daughter better than any social opportunity they could have imagined.

DURING THE SUMMER OF 1885, Bruce Price finished a four-story addition to property Washington Lee had bequeathed to Josephine. Now he was eager to return to some business that would immediately make, not cost, money. But first he had to attend to lingering matters out on Long Beach.

The board of directors planted days of carefully calculated publicity in the *Times,* a final desperate payoff aimed at saving the limping, ill-fated investment. Six inches of well-positioned gossip listed the illustrious guests who appeared on a very hot summer weekend, along with the largest crowd since the beleaguered resort had opened five years earlier. Among the list of celebrity "late arrivals" was the architect himself, Bruce Price. The usual list of Van Burens and Baldwins and Turnures (whose family Bruce's niece would marry into) contained no mention of wives or children, suggesting that the men were dutifully showing up in spite of the heat to represent their stake in the company.

Nothing went right, the ragged celebration instead typifying five years of foredoomed efforts. The local stores ran out of bathing suits and clean towels by midafternoon on the record-breaking weekend. Hundreds of women and children couldn't get seats on the train. To make things worse for the would-be tourists who were able to board, the hot, muggy ride took twice as long as normal. Even the initially cheerful *Times* reporter seemed to have been wilted by the truth: the facilities were just not prepared for such numbers, he concluded. The owners weren't used to success.

The Long Beach Hotel housed over fifteen hundred "heated mortals" that Sunday night alone. The incredulous restaurant owners and hoteliers exulted. They had "reason to rejoice," having seen no such crowds the five years prior. But even such spurts of success couldn't rescue the failing enterprise. By the time the hotel's mortgage was foreclosed in 1885, the property loans amounted to $1.5 million, approximately $15 million now.

Today, city histories chronicle this project as a major investment of its time. Glossy accounts plug the history of the hotel as if it were a success story, barely mentioning its disastrous first five years. The Tile Club is largely forgotten, and the Long Island Rail Road once again trundles along to the beach. But Bruce Price came out ahead. Guarding against loss, he had been building the nearby Coney Island Inn back in the summer of 1880, even as he finished the mammoth Long Beach Hotel. Everything was completed in sixty days, speed central to his aesthetic as much as it ruled the railroads and the age they traversed. His reputation traveled almost as quickly.

So when Pierre Lorillard, the nephew of Bruce's distant cousin Catharine Lorillard Wolfe, asked Bruce to help investigate some prime hilly country land—or very rough, rocky terrain, depending upon who was talking—he was more than ready. Lorillard was a man worth heeding: his family had practically cornered the tobacco industry, moving on to finance the famous Rancocas Stable in New Jersey. Through his contacts, Bruce had recently designed a parlor car for the Pennsylvania Railroad. Now, in the fall of 1885, they would begin a new project that would change his daughter's future.

❋

CHAPTER 9

*E*MILY POST WOULD RECOUNT THE FOUNDING MOMENT OF TUXEDO
Park hundreds of times during her life: on a gray mid-September day in
1885, Bruce Price and Pierre Lorillard jumped off a train bound for Buffalo,
refusing to let the lack of an official stop thwart them. Hopping onto a
farmer's wagon, they explored Lorillard's ancestral Orange County acreage
in a pouring rainstorm. By the day's end, Bruce Price was convinced that he
could make Lorillard's dream a reality. With engineer E. W. Bowditch, the
architect would build a self-contained community, with roads, sewer, water,
nineteen mansions (or "cottages," in the reverse snobbery of the wealthy's
nomenclature), a police station, a clubhouse, and a village, sited around
three lakes at the base of New York's rocky Ramapo Mountains. If they
could quickly import eighteen hundred workmen from Italy, Lorillard
would see his latest whimsy in place in nine months flat.

Built on a six-thousand-acre game park shaped by the Ramapo hills, at
the foot of the Catskill Mountains, Tuxedo Park would quickly become a
playground for Lorillard's wealthy friends and cohorts—the community inspired by the millionaire's mistress. Early that year, Cora Brown Potter, a
southern belle who thought she'd married money, had discovered that her
husband didn't have much of a fortune left—and he wasn't very smart to
boot. Through the social circles the Lorillards and the Potters shared, the
exotic redheaded beauty became, in short order, Lorillard's lover, even as
she pursued her impressive talent for the stage. Several months before
Bruce and Lorillard's rainy walk about his land, Cora had given her restless
philanderer an idea of what to do with the vast, useless (so he complained)

tract of land he owned around Tuxedo Lake: Why not create a truly exclusive social club, one that played to its strength as an enclave against urban life? she suggested. Close to the city, yet only an hour from the heart of the Catskills, Tuxedo Park, with its lakes, crags, and hills, would be a perfect retreat where the affluent could pretend to relax.

Lorillard thought this a brilliant idea and immediately asked her to follow through. Cora arranged a meeting for 150 male friends and associates, where Lorillard discussed his—or Cora's—vision. As a reward, Tuxedo Park's founder gave her a desirable plot of land to build on. Her husband, deciding he should at least appear as if he weren't being cuckolded, insisted that the property be put in his name. A few years later, after Cora left him to become a professional actress, her husband and baby would inherit the Tuxedo Park house.

Not one of the carefully detailed histories of Tuxedo Park includes the part Cora Potter played in its genesis. Instead, the official version claims that Lorillard and his son Pierre Lorillard V precipitously decided that it was wasteful to let their country acreage lie fallow, especially since Pierre père believed the land could be converted to first-rate hunting grounds. To gauge the interest in turning their forests into a private resort, the Lorillards decided to hold a dinner in the city for like-minded friends who would appreciate the proposition: a location convenient to the city but cozily estranged from its inhospitable rhythms.

Reprinted in town documents, in city memoirs, and in myriad stories about Emily Post's life—repeated by Emily herself until she probably believed it—this account omits a central figure, the true force behind Tuxedo Park's existence. Cora Potter was blotted from the community's history.

THOUGH RARELY, ON A VERY CLEAR DAY from a certain lookout point in the Ramapo Mountains, the Empire State Building, built in the twilight years of Tuxedo Park's golden age, magically emerges from the squadrons of trees. The skyscraper's prominence among the stark pines captures the way Tuxedo Park integrated, even before the advent of the tall buildings, city and country. By car or train today about forty-five minutes from Manhattan, the community was meant as a rebuke to the Newport mansions that increasingly catered to the nouveaux riches. No urban realities would intrude on Pierre Lorillard's park, which instead showcased the designs of the environment itself. The local land, 90 percent woods and mountains, inspired Lorillard to cultivate a return to nature, even as he accommodated society's best, offering cottages for purchase or seasonal rental. In the 1950s, Emily Post would explain to a Yale doctoral student writing his dissertation on Bruce Price that, in truth, her father had had to work hard to convince Lorillard to stain the shingle cottages nature's humble hues: gray and dull brown and rust red.

Italian and Slovak immigrants built Tuxedo Park, most of them brought over by Lorillard or hired on the New York City docks to make his dream become a reality fast. He named the roads of the workers' temporary cabins (in the slang of the period called "shanties") Fifth Avenue, Broadway, and Wall Street; the workers' mess hall was "Delmonico's." Given her later insistent regard for others' feelings, especially for those in one's employ, Emily was probably sensitive to Lorillard's careless disrespect for his employees, even as she considered him family and tried to overlook what her mother called his peccadilloes. Children of the southern aristocracy, like Bruce Price, were taught not to take advantage of those in an inferior position; they spoke kindly to their slaves and, later, gently to their servants. As Emily herself would insist years afterward: a lady's "manner to a duke who happens to be staying in the house is not a bit more courteous than her manner to the kitchen-maid."

However he treated them, Lorillard got what he wanted out of his employees. His demands motivated the workers to do the impossible during what was the particularly harsh winter of 1885–86. Even in the relentless snowstorms, the men proved indomitable. By the time it opened, in addition to the thirteen cottages and massive clubhouse, the park would boast the first telephone, water, and sewage-treatment systems outside a major city.

The gargantuan project was a prize for any architect to have won, whatever his age. But Bruce Price hadn't just stumbled on it, no matter what a few jealous competitors would mutter. During the critical months leading up to the project's final planning, which included delicate contract negotiations with Lorillard, Bruce had already spent a great deal of calculated time socializing with Lorillard, best known as an aging playboy whose horses kept winning, as well as, according to a friend of Emily's, "the biggest bore anyone had ever met." The architect had also increased the time he spent socializing with Lorillard's two sons, both well-known philanderers frequently mentioned in the notorious weekly *Town Topics*. Gossip claimed that Bruce won the Tuxedo Park commission instead of Peabody and Stern (who had been led to expect it) solely because he made sure to play with the boys who made the decision. Instead, though he certainly appreciated the need to mix with those he wanted to work for, Bruce was able to balance his friendships with such men, their misbehavior too obvious for his taste, with his own decorous personal behavior.

IF THE SECOND HALF of 1885 (practically every day spent in the Ramapo hills) sped by in a blur for Bruce Price, the season proved, mercifully, fast moving for his daughter as well, even though she saw far too little of her father to be happy. While Bruce worked madly, pitching in with his own hands during an icy winter to get Tuxedo Park ready for its June opening, Josephine and Emily traveled back and forth to family soirees in the South. Even a good five years before her official New York debut, thirteen-year-old Emily attended countless family-sponsored teas in Baltimore—still the preferred way among Old Wealth to come out in the South, where anything grander was considered trying too hard, and prolonged dancing with young men during a debutante's first year out would be an embarrassing mistake.

Being able to pour properly—pristine white linen threatening to draw attention to any slipups made by the tense novice—was a rite of passage in Baltimore. Often Emily's favorite cousin, Sarah Price, would preside as junior hostess. The beautiful Sadie would end up marrying one of the Pell heirs to the sprawling lands ten miles from the Upper East Side of Manhattan, bought from the Siwanoy Indians in the mid-1600s. Emily, close in age to Sadie, showed off for her southern family, mastering the technique of the tea so that she could move deftly from one home to another, taking in four or more invitations during a single bloated afternoon in the Baltimore of her late childhood.

At Sadie's home, the older cousins chattered nonstop about what balls they planned to attend this season. The girls buzzed with the news about one innovation that actually seemed to consider them first, ranking their needs ahead of the adults' for a change. This year's sponsors were experimenting with a new scheme: they were going to start the dances earlier, the hour unfashionable but easier on the participants. When the idea expanded to the North, a scandalized few complained that a ball was supposed to be held late, but the New York Times squelched them, its reporters documenting the Baltimore experience with obvious relief. The proposed schedule would make the event far easier on both the press and the debutantes. The Baltimore matrons proudly saluted their local newfangled commitment to having their young men and women "safely tucked in their little beds" by one A.M. But when plaintive New York reporters, exhausted by their typically late hours, pleaded with local society to follow the southern trend, Manhattan's finest answered with a definitive no; it was not fashionable.

This seemingly trivial issue rehearsed the fault lines still dividing Emily Price's generation. The cotillions in New York invoked a mythical aristocratic past as the template for the present gilded reality. In Baltimore, twenty years after the Civil War defeat, people esteemed those among them who had been "well born before all had been lost." Here there was nothing to prove with overdone balls and obscenely late hours. Southern women, after all, still exchanged anecdotes about whose grandmother had summoned up the grace to feed the Northern occupiers.

Most of the women had nastily swept up their skirts when a Yankee soldier even nodded to them in their streets, or so the oft-repeated story went. But once in a while, a lady of real quality would come along—inevitably the speaker's ancestor—good and gracious in the face of devastating defeat, and able to stare, without flinching, into those Yankee blue eyes. Such a lady would give the enemy water and a place to sleep. Combining righteousness with grace under pressure: this was the model held up for the well-raised southern girl, even into the 1880s.

In part, the deliberate, carefully plotted gentility of the southern aristocracy—including the less outré, more refined party hours—was itself meant to rebuke the North: for its crass worship of money, and for failing to notice how naturally good people were supposed to act, even in defeat. Robert E. Lee had always behaved with genteel nobility: he was a gentleman, though bearing arms. It was his nemesis, General Sherman, who had burned his way through Georgia, in a story retold as if it had happened yesterday. The once luscious South, now desiccated, teased out ways to recall its lost culture, relying on its enchanting young women to perpetuate its traditions: "those good old days when women were safely on pedestals and lineage mattered most of all."

Back home, Emily found herself increasingly bored by spending her evenings with the servants as she made up homework accumulated during her frequent absences. She wasn't interested in mastering the latest French vocabulary or, worst of all, spending more time with her mother and her friends on the nights they stayed in to play cards. For weeks the girl couldn't help hearing all about the recent venue change for one of the year's important balls. The Metropolitan Opera House, not the redoubtable Delmonico's, had hosted the event. Outsiders might have missed the significance, but upper-class New Yorkers were agog. New money, flagrantly, had endowed the Met, creating the institution for those whose cash smelled too recent to gain access to society's top echelons.

🔆

CHAPTER 10

E MILY PRICE, WHOSE FOURTEENTH BIRTHDAY WOULD BE CELE-
brated at the estate's first autumn ball, worshipped Tuxedo Park. Bruce
built four "cottages" for his little family of three, so that the Prices could
stay in one and rent out the others. A domestic setting amid a coterie of
friends connected by wealth and family, a carefully manicured wilderness
her playground: for a precocious only child, Tuxedo Park was heaven, created by her estimable father himself.

In spite of the deliberately understated drama of this country community, Tuxedo Park was not lacking in luxury. Its provenance, was, however,
more tastefully disguised than that of the older, sometimes garish retreats.
While Bruce was building, Lorillard had stayed busy breeding foxes for fall
hunting and stocking the lakes with bass and pickerel for summer fishing.
The point of Tuxedo Park, as far as its founder was concerned, was to experience nature at its finest. Because whatever else you could say about Newport and Bar Harbor and even Lenox, nobody at either resort was ever off
duty. Only at Tuxedo Park was acting natural a virtue. Even the gestation of
the entire project was organic: from September 18, 1885, when Bruce Price
and Pierre Lorillard had braved the mud and rain of the embryonic park, to
its official opening on June 16 the following year, nine months had passed.
History books record the speed with which Bruce built Tuxedo Park, a near
miracle in engineering and construction. His pace is still legendary among
architects.

The turnout for the unofficial preview stunned even its organizers. On
Memorial Day, May 30, 1886, three special trains, loaded with seven hun-

dred guests, arrived from New York City. Green-and-gold buses and wagons, branding the scene with the club's colors, lined up at the station to transport the visitors to the park. For latecomers, there were the Tuxedo taxicabs—single-horse covered carts, locally called "jiggers"—to pick up the slack.

Striking an exotic, Vanderbilt-like tone out of tune with his determined paean to nature, Lorillard had commissioned specially constructed flatboats to ferry the guests across the park's lake. The two barges were crewed by men in white yachting uniforms. Throughout the day, costumed local woodsmen hired by Lorillard to meander the park roads would suddenly appear whenever a carriage drove past. Tasked with looking natural, the novice actors looked sheepish instead, their black-feathered green Tyrolean hats bobbing along the pathways, their feet occasionally mired in mud.

The land parcels sold quickly: within a matter of months, Lorillard's friends from New York's and New England's finest families snapped them up. At the beginning, most owners, including the Prices themselves, used the homes for a few weeks only. Within a few years, the Astors, Pells, Baldwins, Bowdoins, Bryces, Goelets, Kips, Leroys, Mills, Rices, and Schermerhorns—the roll call expanded until it included almost every grand name of the late nineteenth century—were spending much of the late summer and early fall in Tuxedo, preferring it to Lenox, Massachusetts, the seat of the Berkshires, and, eventually, even to Bar Harbor and Newport. Gradually, in part due to its proximity to Manhattan, Tuxedo Park became a year-round address for many of the Price family friends.

Tuxedo Park would be Bruce Price's greatest legacy. The park's design depended upon each site and its house working as one, an aesthetic, according to later architects, that encouraged Frank Lloyd Wright's "interpenetration of interior and exterior space." Experts in American architecture believe Tuxedo Park set the stage for what a student of Yale's Vincent Scully would call "the most interesting domestic architecture of the first half of the twentieth century." Scully himself, a prominent historian of American architecture, claimed that Wright's prairie homes were strongly influenced by Bruce's cottages, proving of "profound importance for the later development of creative American domestic building."

The New York Times critic Christopher Gray also admires the complex. "The distinction of Tuxedo Park," he says, "lies not in the individual architecture but in the planning and conception of the whole: to create a private enclave with appropriate architecture, with nothing showy or fancy. Bruce

Price when he was designing there in the eighties was competing against the big showy Fifth Avenue–type palaces, Astors on Fifth Avenue, and also in the Jersey shore and other resorts, and even in, to some extent, the Berkshires. Though those tend to be toned down, many of them are really quite aggressive. But the early Tuxedo Park houses are all very simple and unassuming and appropriate and nothing extra to them."

AS TUXEDO PARK'S demands lessened, Bruce Price's workload in the city accelerated. Adding draftsmen to his practice and expanding his office space, Bruce had entered a new level of achievement. He joined critic Russell Sturgis, with whom he would write several books, to reconstitute the neglected Architectural League (originally formed in 1881). Primarily through the efforts of the two men, the league became an influential arbiter of architectural taste in New York and nationwide. Bruce helped inaugurate a program of exhibitions, lectures, dinners, and annual juried shows of the nation's best buildings, a tradition that continues today. Motivated by Frank Smith's success with the Tile Club, Bruce supported artistic collaboration across the disciplines. He welcomed prospective members' divergent interests, their various roles as muralists, sculptors, painters, and landscape architects.

Bruce had been honoring nonstop commitments all year. Following the Tuxedo Park inaugural ball, the unveiling of Bartholdi's Statue of Liberty on Bedloe's (now Liberty) Island finally took place on October 28, 1886. Bruce Price belonged to the volunteer staff arranging the event. Taking the steamer *Florence* from Manhattan, he and several others arrived at the site at seven A.M. in order to ready everything on the dais for the afternoon ceremony. Around two P.M., boats started depositing guests on the island, including Josephine and Emily. One of the wives of the male welcoming committee actually climbed the 354 steps to reach the torch, surprising reporters most by her gender.

Everything from yachts to rowboats filled the bay, their vivid banners festooning the little island. French and American flags obscured the dais. Finally the *Tennessee* boomed, the gunship causing the water to shimmer from its vibrations. A smiling President Cleveland took the speaker's stand, where he stood for a solid half an hour, acknowledging the nonstop cheers. The French speeches that followed sounded a common theme: France, not England, had spawned America. America and France would continue to fight injustice together.

Recreational asides such as the Statue of Liberty pleased Bruce's wife and daughter, especially because Uncle Frank was involved, but it was the commissions inundating the architect's desk that changed their lives. Tuxedo Park had proven the Price family's ticket to success. Bruce had not yet put the finishing touches on the park when he accepted a project from Mrs. Alfred Lebbeus Loomis, whose physicist grandson, Alfred Lee Loomis, would, much later, use the park to convene cerebral firepower to construct the atomic bomb. But for now, Bruce was busy building a simple—in his manner of speaking—house for Mrs. Loomis in Ringwood, New Jersey.

DURING THE EARLY MONTHS of 1887, Emily, spurred on by stories of her cousins' scholastic success, meant to study harder than usual at Miss Graham's. Instead, she interspersed periods of concentrated lessons with the ramped-up socializing Bruce's commissions ensured, especially his recent magnificent creation in the Ramapo hills. While she waited, the fourteen-year-old was observing the life she would inherit. This summer would prove a whirl of dinner parties at Tuxedo Park that her father actually attended as well; this—all of this—was, after all, his creation. But it was the upcoming October gala at the park that guests always ended up talking about excitedly. In one short year, the fall dance at Tuxedo had become the hottest ticket in town.

A leading member of what would become Café Society in the 1920s, Elsie de Wolfe (a friend of Cora's from the instant they met in England), recalled the tensions throughout the social world of New York City during the weeks leading up to the park's autumn dance of 1887: "Women pulled every string they could master in order to be included. Failing, they wept bitterly. Men almost broke their necks in an attempt to get an entering wedge into what was tantamount to a closed circle."

It would prove providential to Emily's future that Cora Potter finagled one of the coveted invitations for Elsie to attend that year's dance, in spite of—or perhaps because of—the trouble it led to. Later, park residents insisted, the financially impoverished and, worse, short-term professional actress (sharing Cora's passion for the limelight) would never have been allowed in. Cora herself would recall that "the exclusive invitation and membership lists included the highly select only, and they had to pass the cold and exacting eye of Pierre Lorillard, who was a dictator in his own right."

Throughout that winter season and early into 1888, Cora Potter encouraged Elsie to ply her well-known thespian talents on Tuxedo's elaborate stage. Without scruples, Cora was training her handpicked replacement for Pierre Lorillard's lover. She assured Lorillard that Elsie would serve him well in every regard. Certainly the great age difference between Elsie and Pierre Lorillard wasn't a major impediment to friendship or to accepting help from a wealthy patron: Frances Folsom, a twenty-one-year-old, had wed President Grover Cleveland two years earlier, and he was nearly three decades her senior. If she could be first lady without Colonel Mann detailing their courtship in Town Topics, why couldn't the married Pierre Lorillard, without exciting spurious comment, befriend with his largesse an innocent young woman?

Inevitably, when the friendship did indeed become fodder for Town Topics, Lorillard was apoplectic. The newspaper published details the millionaire thought he had cleverly obscured. Maybe he had: more than one historian believes Elsie fed the gossip to Town Topics herself.

Stories spread through the park, irritating Josephine and infuriating her husband. The truth was not at issue: this publicity was an invasion of Lorillard's privacy. Whether the Prices believed the official story Lorillard promoted—that he was merely underwriting what he saw as a promising acting career—was not their point; that anyone dared suggest otherwise should offend them all. Secretly, Josephine must have reveled in the juicy innuendos about Elsie de Wolfe that circulated that November and ran in Town Topics through the end of January. She couldn't have felt entirely easy about her husband's association with the notorious philanderer Pierre Lorillard, but after considering the futility of complaining and the prospect of appearing a shrew, she chose to ignore it.

The fifteen-year-old Emily Price would suffer grievously, in her eyes, from the repercussions of the de Wolfe–Lorillard relationship. The Tuxedo Stage, part of the Grand Ballroom that Bruce had built for the compound, served as a venue for amateurs and, occasionally though unofficially, as a first stop that talents headed for Manhattan used to warm up. For several years, Emily had found ways to increase her appearances, whether participating in local benefits or in plays written and staged by Tuxedo Park residents. Predictably, the child nurtured by her father's always dramatic company proved a natural. Before long, there was little she enjoyed as much as basking in the limelight, mugging for laughs while exaggerating her vowels, and, most of all, being the center of attention. Later she would recall this period when she "loved to act." Secretly, she sometimes even considered becoming an actress. She craved the power she felt when an audience responded.

But the spotlight would soon be denied to the adolescent. The hoopla involving Lorillard's two actress-mistresses, who had both appeared on her father's Tuxedo Stage, caused the pompous millionaire to declare the proscenium off-limits to Emily Price. The girl was so talented that corrupt women like Cora Potter and her friends might seduce her into following their lead onto the professional stage. Look and learn, Pierre Lorillard instructed; this drama being played out at Tuxedo Park should be a cautionary tale for the Price family. Bruce felt the concern overstated, but Josephine had already become uncomfortable with the attention Emily was getting, as well as the slight hauteur it had encouraged. She welcomed the chance to command Emily to pursue a different hobby. Over the years, Emily would spin the story one way and then the other, allocating blame for her failure to become a famous actress first to Lorillard, then to her mother. If only her father had spoken up, she would imply: then she could have constructed a career for herself on the stage.

CHAPTER 11

⸙

At the end of the century, it was hard to access winter sports easily from the city—with the exception of the particularly urban pastime of ice-skating in Central Park. Achieving near-immediate eminence as the place for those of Emily's age to spend the snowbound weekends, Tuxedo Park quickly gained status among the children of the rich. Iceboats—basically boards set on runners—had become wildly popular, and cross-country skiing seemed to have been created for the local terrain. Every year Pierre Lorillard came up with a new idea: the toboggan run was quickly illuminated for nighttime events. Even winter hunting had a small cache of older devotees.

Sledding the clubhouse's indoor stairs was a special treat for the younger set. The girls in their voluptuous party dresses, Miss Price among them, slid down the staircase on tin trays, caught in a pillow at the bottom by their beaux. The game came to an abrupt end, however, when one of the Lotharios got sloppy with his remarks, questioning a friend stationed nearby a bit too loudly if he too had seen that last lass's "lovely laces" when her dress flew up. All participants were commanded to stop the activity immediately, the miscreant sent packing, and the game declared over forever at Tuxedo Park.

If anything saved the minor intrigues at Tuxedo Park from becoming Colonel Mann's topic of 1888, it was nature. On March 11 the Great White Hurricane, deflecting attention from society's dramas entirely, paralyzed the East Coast. The most famous snowstorm in America halted life on the Atlantic seaboard for one week, reminding the increasingly confident easterners that nature held the trump card. The Great Blizzard of '88 caused temperatures in New York City to fall as much as sixty degrees in one day. Winds whipped twenty-one inches of snow into twenty-foot drifts, costing four hundred lives. The *Times* published a daily death count.

When Emily was asked later about the blizzard's effect on New York, her reference was Tuxedo Park, where the storm killed off the quail Pierre Lorillard had so proudly supplied. That's about as far as the Price family's direct connection with the disaster extended. Not many in Emily Price's circle were interested in how the less fortunate lived. Even the concerned few considered it unseemly to introduce such an inflammatory topic into their social conversations.

Her own family was not entirely impervious to the lower class's needs: they wouldn't think of allowing their servants to live in penury, and they believed in being sensitive and respectful to their hired help, ensuring that they had proper and attractive, if modest, living quarters. Though Josephine meant well by others, it was Bruce who conscientiously translated good intentions toward the less fortunate into measurable results. Emily's own amateur house designs invariably included large and cheerful servants' quarters, including the unusual addition of a separate dining room. She worried about ensuring enough space for the servants of a household, explaining how important their well-being was to everyone else's. Predictably, she would rarely experience the "servant problem" that plagued so many upper-class households through the decades she was alive. Her staff tended to be loyal and long-employed.

During her childhood, the national census still listed the servants as part of the family they lived with, the practice suggesting the days when slaves or indentured laborers were considered part of a family's property. Emily's family believed that respect was due to those who performed well, whatever their job. In fact, if people were willing to work hard enough, they could do anything.

This was the era of social Darwinism. Well suited to the American belief in individualism, and tailor-made to the business interests of the age, Herbert Spencer's deeply flawed system surely influenced, if only indirectly, the assumptions shaping Emily as she grew up. As an adult, she would assume that people wishing to become successful members of society could do so as long as they possessed resolve. Those disabled by poverty or prejudice or physical misfortune failed to enter the scope of the young Emily's thought. After all, America was a nation built on the idea of freedom for all, the individual's rights central to its creed. Such convictions were fundamental to the Price family's ethics, and as long as Bruce and Josephine treated others well, they were not interested in further philosophical discussion. Their standards for doing unto others, however, were higher than was typical for their class, grounded in a generosity that refused to consider class or personal expedience the equal of unmotivated kindness.

By 1888, Bruce's life had acquired a distinctly New York City rhythm, and in spite of his continued habit of emptying his pockets for the poor every day, its tempo didn't encourage much worrying about the unfortunate. The networking, as it would later be called, the socializing, the getting close to people in the know, the solidifying of personal bonds: the Price family did everything right to further their patriarch's career. Bruce opened a new office at Seventh Avenue and Twenty-third Street, within easy walking distance of the mammoth construction under way at Madison Square Garden, Stanford White's current project.

Not only professional kinships succored the Price menagerie during this period. That year, the family's nurturing of their distant relatives came to fruition. According to the *New York Times,* Emily Price had been made an heiress by Catharine Lorillard Wolfe, she of the East Side Lodging House for orphaned boys, where she'd delivered ice-cream cones along with a bed to sleep in. How much of a fortune the elderly philanthropist left Emily Price is unclear. Wolfe's estate itself was worth between $8 and $10 million, but upon her death the previous year she had left a sizable amount to a great many people. Her bequest to Emily, however, was publicly deemed a large fortune.

ANOTHER VICTIM OF the March blizzard had been the Canadian Pacific Railway. Needing to recoup the season's losses, its officials distributed free passes to artists in exchange for promotional pictures of scenery visible from their trains. Through Lorillard's strong connections in Canada, Bruce got in on the offer early, parlaying the acquaintances he made through the project into serious architecture commissions. He ended up designing several buildings for the CPR, initiating the château style with his design for the Banff Springs Hotel.

It was the right time to go north. Self-consciously, the Canadian millionaires provided American architects an overflow of commissions as the new nation strove to separate its aesthetic from those of the United States and, more important, Great Britain. Now, at the end of the nineteenth century, architects Bruce Price and McKim, Mead and White heavily embossed the Canadian cities with their signatures. Bruce spent much of 1888 working on Windsor Station in Montreal, which would open the following year. Even as he was in the middle of the Tuxedo Park project, he had managed to start on what would be the main Canadian Pacific station, its profile still dominating the Montreal skyline today. The railroad terminal, with its massive stonework and rounded arches, was characteristic of the Romanesque revival popular during this period. At Tuxedo Park, the talk was often about Bruce Price—Bruce's brilliance, Bruce's popularity.

More than anything, Emily wanted to accompany her father on his ventures north; she was sure Miss Graham wouldn't object to additional on-site education. Instead, she felt herself oppressed by what now seemed like Josephine's almost constant presence at her side. Josie was spending all her energies plotting her only child's upcoming debut, and she thought her daughter well advised to take more interest in it herself. Should she return to Baltimore for the official first presentation or hold it in Tuxedo, perhaps at the autumn ball? Emily found herself wishing for longer school days and extra assignments to take her out of her mother's clutch.

These years that rendered Emily Post an adult were named by Mark Twain the Gilded Age. Historians argue for other labels, often revelatory in their contradictions: "*The Age of Innocence, The Age of Excess, The Age of Reform, The Age of Energy, The Age of Enterprise, The Mauve Decade, The Brown Decades, The Populist Moment, The Confident Years, The American Renaissance.*" As historian Jean Strouse concludes, the "final third of the nineteenth century has generated more divergent interpretations than any other period in American history." Broadly defined as running from the end of the Civil War to Queen Victoria's death, the period by whatever name paraded a wild mélange of newly minted American millionaires and their extraordinarily fortunate wives. The attention accorded by both the conventional and the popular press to such figures, especially the women, reflected the historical anomaly of such great wealth possessed by (relative to the past) so many. Newly liberated from the exhausting routines of the olden days, moneyed wives had to redefine themselves.

So it is no surprise that in such a vortex of change, while some women spent their energies practicing the latest dance with their daughters, early feminists met in Washington, D.C., to discuss women's rights. Their 1888 meeting was a sometimes exhausting rehash of what the Women's Rights Convention had tried to accomplish back in the autumn of 1853. Then a still young and optimistic Susan B. Anthony and Elizabeth Cady Stanton had led the national delegates, demanding not just voting rights but complete equality with men. Fifteen years later, in 1868, the women's writers group Sorosis was allowed to meet at Delmonico's, seeding the movement for women's clubs.

Josephine and her friends talked about the shocking independence of some of the erstwhile socialites from their own circle, including J. Pierpont Morgan's daughter Anne, whose radical tendencies already worried her more conservative father and irritated her older sister, Juliet. The brashness of Elsie de Wolfe and Cora Potter too, as they defiantly took to the New York stage, would track a seismic change in women's opportunities. Increasingly, if slowly, Emily would come to understand the politics of women's freedom. Certainly any courage she might have summoned to develop her talents would have been quashed by the monthly ridicule the press heaped on the Sorosis Club meetings, as columnists scoffed at the women's quest for civic clout and cartoonists mocked their appearance.

For now, Emily agreed with Juliet Morgan: she didn't support such bizarre behaviors on the part of their sex. She assumed that money and marriage—to someone, she hoped, like her father—would set her free. They would grant her independence, allowing her to become an adult at last. That was the reality she was focused on now, with no time to waste on silly fantasies of joining a man's world. Emily and her friends, including Juliet Morgan, struggled at least twice a week to master the complete set of complicated dance steps of the German. She hardly had a chance to miss her father, who was spending much of 1888 in Montreal. In contrast to the routines of her past, she visited him only once or twice, too intent now on preparing at Miss Graham's for her debut.

How to enter the young Emily Post's mind, in the context of her culture and the expectations of her parents? It is hard not to expect more of her, given her opportunities, good mind, and evident curiosity about her father's career. She could have pursued opportunities that her talents clearly suggested she could master. There were already singular women entering professions long assumed to be male: medicine, ministry, and the law. Colleges such as Vassar, founded in 1861, Wellesley (1870), and Smith (the following year, the year before Emily was born), had forced even rich socialites who spent their time directing their servants and plotting their social lives to confront, however privately, other options.

But though the leaders of the women's movement throughout history often emerged from privileged families, most upper-class women saw no purpose in upending their comfortable lives. The majority regarded the nascent women's movement with well-bred distaste. At this point in her life, Emily was ambivalent about women's place in society. She would come to an awareness of their second-class status only as the twentieth century disentangled itself from the late Victorian age.

You are a young girl on the evening of your coming-out ball. You are excited, of course you are! It is your evening, and you are a sort of little princess! There is music, and there are lights, and there are flowers everywhere—a great ballroom massed with them, tables heaped with bouquets—all for you! You have on an especially beautiful dress—one that was selected from among many others, just because it seemed to you the prettiest. Even your mother and married sister who, "en grande tenue," have always seemed to you dazzling figures, have for the moment become, for all their brocades and jewels, merely background; and you alone are the center of the picture. Up the wide staircase come throngs of fashionables—who mean "the world." They are coming on purpose to bow to you! You can't help feeling that the glittering dresses, the tiaras, the ropes of pearls and chains of diamonds of the "dowagers," the stiff white shirt-fronts and boutonnières and perfectly fitting coats of the older gentlemen, as well as the best clothes of all the younger people, were all put on for you.

—*ETIQUETTE, page 276*

SHE LIVED IN THE EMOTIONAL THICK OF FAMILY ADORATION: HER father approved and loved her, her mother assessed as first-rate her chances for a good marriage—even the Pierre Lorillards had anointed her their favorite. An only child with Tuxedo Park for her late-adolescence drawing room, Emily had used her father's creation as the ultimate finishing school, surpassing anything Miss Graham's could offer. The darling of the park's residents, she spent her winters skating on the frozen lake, appearing, though less frequently, on the impressive amateur stage Bruce had built, attending the autumn ball and practicing her dance steps with affectionate family friends, older gentlemen rather than the young bucks with whom she shared hot chocolate at the clubhouse.

Now she was ready to conquer the field of female competition. She was going up against the best, vying to gain the most attention, the choicest gossip, the champion husband. Just when her excitement at being Tuxedo Park's resident princess was wearing thin, Emily turned to a year of designing her own evening dresses, perfecting her dancing, experimenting with hairstyles, and exercising regularly to strengthen her stamina. Her days were suddenly busy with purpose.

EUROPEANS COULD BE excused for their confusion as they witnessed upper-crust Americans modeling their habits upon those of the defeated mother country. After the Revolutionary War, republican social leaders, most surprisingly among them Abigail Adams, had almost immediately replicated the same customs the new country supposedly disdained—habits that smacked of privilege and class. When presented at the court of St. James's in 1785, Abigail had written home with disgust about the whole sorry spectacle her new country had, thankfully, transcended. Yet on New Year's Day sixteen years later, she'd appeared at the first formal White House reception as an English clone, imitating the very stiffness she had earlier excoriated, even bowing instead of shaking hands the American way. Her husband had emitted equally confusing signals: for their magisterial party, John Adams wore velvet knee britches and powdered hair, fashions more redolent of London than Philadelphia or Washington.

The English court, the motherland, had unintentionally controlled the way the new country's social set measured worth. Impoverished nobility seemed a fair exchange to a rich American girl: money for a title. The post–Civil War wealth of railroads and finance funded most of the debutantes in Emily's day seeking to be presented at the court of St. James's. Their oft-innocent eagerness inspired old-schoolers like Henry James to tsk-tsk at their sometimes embarrassing ignorance abroad. Old-line Knickerbocker Edith Wharton practically sneered at the daring parvenus, so gauche, so obvious in their quest for a title.

But the newly wealthy were getting as good as they gave. They were investing in Old World class, with continuity and the implied link to important histories. After all, the "venerable" British custom of a young woman's debut even included that most American of icons, Pocahontas. In 1616, this daughter of an Indian chieftain "came out" at the court of James I. Within a few generations of such efforts, if all went as planned, even a Native American's granddaughters could be promoted to Old World status, the color of their skin long merged with the fairness of the Old World Dutch.

In Emily's day, coming out was the linchpin for an upper-class girl's entire future. The debut as we know it dates from 1870, when Delmonico's sponsored the first debutante ball held outside the home. By the time Emily was ready to take center stage at the end of 1889, young women took their coming out as seriously as today's students take their admission to college. Very few refused the unveiling. (Though the young Edith Wharton balked at the idea, in the end she simply sulked her way through the evening.) Nor did many object to being put on the market: it was, after all, no small matter to run households for men with great fortunes in those days, before the invention of conveniences our own age takes for granted.

Thanksgiving traditionally marked the advent of the New York dance season, which ran from late November through February or March. Most of the magisterial "Assembly balls" were subscription only, with groups of similar-minded people selling tickets that would in turn repay the costs they had underwritten. The fanciest dances required no subsidy, and they were inevitably overseen by Ward McAllister, who sought to import pre–Civil War correctness and southern class into the uncivilized North. Mistakes cost friendships: if demand for one's Madeira exceeded the host's supply, the household's reputation was ruined over the next morning's breakfast gossip. By the time that Emily debuted, during the holiday season of December 1889, McAllister controlled who was in and who was out, far more effectively than any high school clique has ever managed to do.

Partly because he himself enjoyed dancing—and, for an ungainly, pudgy short man, performed the routines fairly well—McAllister incorporated ever more elaborate steps into the choreography he usually supervised. After all, the mother of Caroline Astor had imported the complicated dance ritual called the cotillion to the States before the Civil War. The ever-changing taxonomies of the day thwart even experts on dance history. One could either "attend a cotillion" or "dance a cotillion," depending upon the favored vocabulary of the season. Other times the same dance was termed simply a German or, sometimes, a quadrille.

Whatever the nomenclature, the result was a four- to six-hour-long, heavily plotted production wherein only dancers who had seriously practiced the steps could hope to take part. The successful execution of the dances themselves, let alone the exhibition of any real skill, was impossible without long lessons. Dances at the society balls were no small matter, the stakes for the participants high. The ability to dance well was such a serious concern that almost three decades later, Emily Post would kindly but firmly advise any young woman with two left feet to stay at home and limit her socializing to afternoon teas. That way, she would avoid being the rejected wallflower at the dance. In Emily's youth, the cotillions were always led by an important male society figure, recycled throughout the season.

The format for the intricate evening dances was boringly consistent, at ball after ball. Several of the events called for special costumes, which needed to be meticulously planned in advance. After the guests arrived, a grand march officially opened the ball, with couples circling the ballroom in a slow procession. The guests then danced for a few hours, all ages joining in the day's popular steps: the quadrille, the lancers, the waltz, and the schottische. The gentleman held the lady at a respectable distance, and older guests and the official chaperones spent the evening talking and waiting for dinner to be served.

The dancing paused while guests sat down to the evening repast. They expected to encounter an appropriately light meal, if they were lucky, or, if they were not, a menu of terrapin (hard-shelled freshwater turtles) and canvasback duck, in danger of being overhunted. In his earlier days of planning society's galas, Ward McAllister had included a boiled sheep's head with hollandaise sauce, but it failed to elicit the response he desired and so the menu reverted to type.

Debutantes were taught to eat lightly on dance days, if they planned to show off their trim waistlines. After everyone finished dining, the men downed their cordials and smoked their cigars while the ladies attended to their toilette. Then the heat cranked up. The cotillion began in earnest, several hours of choreographed dances cantilevering seamlessly one upon the other.

The German, at least in one of its many semantic variations, was really four or five separate dances consisting of highly regulated formal steps, closer to what we today call a square dance than anything else. The figures of the German could include any number of combinations, depending upon the calls: the Fan, the Ladies Mocked, Blindman's Buff, the Cards, the

Ropes, the popular Mother Goose (where a prominent society matron would usually appear dressed as the Mother, with a live goose under her arm), the Dresden (with the dancers acting out pieces of china place settings), the Mirror (which the men hated because they were presented, one by one, to a prospective partner until she chose her favorite), and the Hobbyhorse, which one cynic has wryly called the most suggestive, with "whips and all." At Alva Vanderbilt's famous party in 1883, two of the ladies, wearing gold-spurred, shiny black boots, had even fallen off the overly rambunctious men they were riding.

To New York's unmarried girl in white, trying not to fidget with her abnormally long gloves as she waited her turn for a spotlighted waltz on the floor, there was one aim of this whole encounter, which everyone understood. Tonight these girls were going on the market. They needed to be among the ones chosen for marriage, usually quickly arranged within a year or so of their debut. Otherwise, they risked being passed over, left behind as part of the also-ran group. The pressure was intense, the occasion fraught. Unless you knew that you'd be the star.

BY THE BEGINNING of 1889, the year that would end with her debut, Emily had already spent several winter seasons in New York society. She felt constrained by her repetitive city routine, for the most part just more of the same classes at Miss Graham's—plus the inevitable practice in deportment.

In January, the endless sessions of dance lessons had turned serious. Emily's nervous friends filled up their weeks with different classes or actual dances nightly: Ward McAllister's Family Circle Dancing Class, the Assemblies, the Patriarchs, the Tuesday Night Dancing Class, the Wednesday Class, the Thursday, and so on. Although one could not predict the steps a dance master would call for his German, there were certain expected standards. Those routines currently in favor clearly deserved extra practice. All in all, a limited number of "sets" existed, though at times it seemed a terrifyingly large list of choices. Practicing her steps between lessons was the most important homework assignment a young woman of the Gilded Age would ever complete.

Whether attending parties for her own crowd or for the older girls in the classes ahead of her, Emily would be accused by jealous young women of deliberately making a spectacle of herself. It was true that her imposing height of five feet nine, the gift of her tall father, gave her the edge in terms of immediate attention. She usually arrived late in the evening, around eleven o'clock, for a dinner served at midnight. But Emily really did tire easily. In the pictures of her from that time, doctors note her protruding eyes, possible evidence of a thyroid problem; the condition would affect her energy and her weight, another problem she began having within a few years of her debut. She found the social schedule she was required to keep burdensome, and she felt forced to attend only the most important dances. Even so, her days now passed in a flurry of activity.

Elsie de Wolfe remembered vividly, even after all the histrionics her life had undergone, her own debut almost ten years earlier than Emily's: "My days were a whirl from shop to shop as I said good-by forever to plaids . . . and gathered brogans. There were silk stockings for eveningwear, and fine lisle for everyday. There was handkerchief-linen underwear and a real corset of white brocade, and Swiss embroidery corset-covers and voluminous petticoats starched until they could stand alone, and dresses of silk and satin and *mousseline de soie* and soft cashmere, tucked and ruffled and shirred in the elegant confusion of the styles of that day. There were hats, too, for every hour, and high-heeled shoes of kid and satin, and boxes of kid gloves of different lengths."

Emily and her friends, finally graduated from the years of monotonous dance lessons, now faced months of tedious dress fittings, the seriousness of the couturiers reinforcing the purposefulness of their mothers. When their season arrived, the girls needed to have everything in order. Josephine, always frugal, discovered the best immigrant seamstresses available in New York to sew her daughter's wardrobe; let the Astors order from Monsieur Worth if that's how they wanted to spend their money. And money was at the heart of the fanciest balls: the favors at the grandest cotillions came from Tiffany's or shops on the rue de la Paix, grandly delivered to the twelve hundred guests gathered at Delmonico's lavishly catered dinners.

On a clear December night in 1889, seventeen-year-old Emily Price was indisputably the belle of the ball, or at least one of the brightest blooms in a garden of rarefied flowers. As the *Times* noted, this dance brought together an unusually large number of distinguished society people in order to introduce several "fair" debutantes to their own. Tonight was the first exhibit of the season's cotillion, the novelty of a new group always exciting. If she couldn't be on a stage, this was an ideal venue for Emily Price.

At the beginning, Emily was put off her game by the late hour. Months earlier in Baltimore, she had been presented at a correct afternoon tea, where she wore a gown of white silk mull and lace and carried—with help—

almost fifty bouquets sent to her by admiring friends. Up North, however, they did things differently. The opera had kept most of the socialites otherwise engaged until eleven-thirty, a late starting time even for the notorious New York dances, and an hour when Emily preferred to be in bed. But the very point of Gilded Age revelry, after all, was to dispel the notion that people worked for a living, meaning that the hours had gotten longer, not shorter, over the past few years.

Immediately acclaimed as one of the most beautiful debutantes ever, Emily was one of only two (or ten, depending upon whose account we believe) debutantes that season and the next who knew how to cross a ballroom. She had enjoyed participating in the design of her gowns, and now her stark white mousseline de soie with off-white embossed embroidery looked angelic and glamorous at the same time. Emily's bodice was pulled even tighter than usual, her skirt a bit fuller, even diaphanous. Her delicate pale skin was heightened in color by the pink wax crayon she had used on her cheeks and mouth. Her dark hair was curled softly—not unnaturally, and not tortured into bangs and a tight chignon like the style chosen by some other debutantes that season. In the code for flowers that the late nineteenth century still used, the red roses twined through trellises throughout the ballroom symbolized a girl's coming adult sexuality, and Emily Price certainly looked ripe to be plucked.

She glowed. Nervous, but in a good way—challenged to live up to her own and to her parents' high expectations—Emily entered Delmonico's through the usual portal on Twenty-sixth Street, where she was redirected to the Fifth Avenue side of the building. Here she would enter a salon, where East Indian and Portuguese silken embroideries draped the walls and electric lights illuminated the marble. Moorish-style flowers by the society florist Klunder set the stage for the Hungarian band playing at full blast in the outer rooms. The fashionable Lander's Orchestra performed in the ballroom until supper was announced.

After dinner, Emily took center stage. In her excitement, the easily fatigued young woman summoned new reservoirs of energy, and she danced the cotillion almost continuously for three hours. No record exists of the exact sequence of steps employed during the early morning hours, but a typical agenda would have contained a set with a grand march, waltz, schottische, lancers, and polka. At least three sets—the limit was eight—were danced, the order of each dependent upon what was called. The dancers had to concentrate hard, especially when the dance master announced sudden variations within a routine. The few who executed the wrong steps looked especially foolish, causing others to trip. Man or woman, if you had failed to do your homework, you'd be completely humiliated and the object of communal pity and disdain.

By the time her official debut at Delmonico's was over, Emily was exhausted. As she would explain later, she'd nonetheless never faltered. Gracefully, triumphantly, she gathered so many lavish bouquets pressed on her by admiring young bucks that even her best friends expressed envy. (The smarter men, by sending extravagant flowers to Emily's home that afternoon, had obligated the debutante to invite them to tea.) The other girls were awed that she won so many of the prizes for best dancer, everything from a decorated hand mirror to a small mirrored jewelry box. After each routine, she needed help carrying her haul to the table.

Emily would find an excuse to recount the story of her debut throughout her adult life, noting that "the girl who is beautiful and dances well is ... the ideal ballroom belle." More importantly, "a young girl's success" was ruthlessly measured by her "ballroom popularity." Reality was best whatever the handicap: for "those not so blessed—some of the greatest belles ever known have been as stupid as sheep"—a cheerful disposition and lack of self-consciousness would compensate for much.

But in 1889, the young, triumphant Emily Price had no deficits. Nor any rivals. With her ramrod posture and delicate yet strong face, she commanded the stage, appearing almost otherworldly. Even her heavily lidded eyes added to her appeal, provocative when she was merely trying to strike a serious pose. The eligible swains vigorously pursued the young woman, permitting her (admittedly big) feet to rest only when she was too tired to dance any longer. Burdened by all her prizes and the flowers she had cleverly woven together into a kind of elaborate combination shield and muff, Emily required four men just to carry out the bouquets lavished upon her. Her carriage looked like a florist's shop.

CHAPTER 13

❊

THROUGHOUT HER LIFE EMILY REPEATED THE FABLE ABOUT HOW she and Edwin Post fell in love the night of her debut. She noticed him noticing her while she waltzed by with Phoenix Ingraham—though in fact Phoenix was four years younger and probably not present. Edwin and she danced a polka, equally smitten with each other's savoir faire and good looks, a Gibson girl twirled and thrilled by a Gatsby ahead of his time. The slender, boyishly handsome Edwin himself remembered it a bit less romantically: he realized very quickly that Miss Price would fit well into his life's plan, in spite of his being several inches shorter than the young lady in question.

Edwin Post loved theatrical women, and Emily's increasingly sure wit, her confidence fueled by the broad approval her dance skills were earning her, made her all the more attractive to the young man. She had developed a talent for mimicry that guaranteed she was popular at dinner parties, and she relished the sway she held over her postprandial audiences with the monologues she supposedly made up on the spot (though it is likelier that the perfectionist practiced ahead of time). Before long, Emily knew she was performing only for Edwin.

The young man must have been magnetic, because the belle of the ball quickly accepted him as her escort to all the major dances that season. In short order, everyone understood that she and Edwin were serious about each other. Still, Emily believed in having fun before settling down to the sort of family responsibilities her mother modeled. However brief, this was a heady period in her life. She meant to exploit being a debutante, if for no other reason than to recoup the effort it had taken to become one. And yet, the year following Emily's debut saw little press coverage of the well-regarded debutante. Newspapers recorded few appearances at social events or urban soirees. Emily loved ice-skating, making obvious her absence in the day's ubiquitous photographs of young society men and women skating in Central Park. Framed by the distant Dakota, the solitary tall building still far from the center of things in 1890, the shots were printed in the *New York Times* with almost weekly regularity that winter.

The early months of 1890 passed with no notices of Emily attending parties, social events, or family activities with her mother. Even the spring tea that her beloved cousin Sadie Price gave at her magnolia-laden Linden Avenue house in Baltimore didn't list Emily as a guest. Emily's appearances in Bar Harbor, where Bruce was building new "cottages" that summer, were noted in the society pages. Emily seems to have gone through some little-discussed malaise during this period. Perhaps she paused long enough after her debut to ask if there might be more to life than dancing. Her odd sense of discontent, her feeling that she should do more than suckle society, might have been the cause of Emily Price deciding to work for her father.

She spent much of that year, just as she had done as a little girl, accompanying Bruce to his job sites, from New Jersey to Canada. Having mastered the principles he preached, she would eagerly reiterate them in fairly technical language in her 1930 book *The Personality of a House*. Perhaps the training at her father's hands was simply parental compensation for thwarting her earlier dreams of a stage career, but the timing was in many ways perfect. This was the age of the architect, of men pushing the sky-scraper higher, shaping a radically new urban aesthetic from scratch.

Why Emily pursued her aspirations or training no further is unclear, but at the least, Josephine must have insisted that no real lady would choose to work for a living. Or maybe Emily lacked the talent: *Personality of a House*, though an impressive compendium, doesn't show the sophisticated aesthetic necessary to great architecture. She frequently refers to her memory of building her dollhouse with her father and making miniature cardboard replicas of Georgian furniture, which she would arrange and rearrange on paper diagrams of each room.

At least she was not forced to be part of the social mania surrounding her friends' newest passion, the yacht culture, an elite society Emily distinctly disliked. She had ample opportunity to participate, but she declined repeatedly. Just like Mrs. Astor, who refused to accompany her husband on his luxurious *Nourmahal* for even one inaugural trip (but who didn't demur at crossing the Atlantic in midwinter), Emily, when given the choice, maintained that she was not a sailor. Many of her friends at Tuxedo, including Juliet Morgan, delighted in spending time on the water, as their parents made yachting the center of their own recreation. In May 1890, J. Pierpont Morgan ordered a new boat to replace the *Corsair* he had bought in 1882, when there had been twenty-nine boats in the New York Yacht Club fleet. Now, in 1890, there were seventy-one. Yachting was "the Gilded Age's premier form of sport," and Emily was about to become enmeshed in its wash whether she liked the water or not.

Price family photographs from the winter of 1890—91 show a rustic post-Christmas vacation in the Berkshires; following a typical protocol of the times, the Prices had invited the debutante's favorite beau to accompany them. The holiday snapshots show "Papa" playing with Jack, the Price family dog. But the photograph that gives pause shows Josephine dreamily— even adoringly—gazing at the handsome young family visitor, Edwin Post. He was on break from his Columbia studies.

By the beginning of the New Year, whatever had kept her press coverage minimal during 1890 was no longer an issue. Emily attended the Ihpetonga ("High Place of Trees") Ball at the Brooklyn Academy of Music on January 21, 1891, having planned her outfit with her usual precision: her best friends, including Juliet Morgan, would be there. Ten days later, as if another coming out were being announced, the phrase "A Woman of Distinction" headed a syndicated society notice. Probably paid for by her parents, the piece about the "handsome and statuesque" Miss Bruce Price is most noticeable for the way Emily is identified, in addition to her name, as *the distinguished architect* (emphasis mine). Perhaps the phrase is just a bizarre misprint, the writer having confused Emily with her father, though her parents aren't even mentioned.

The newspaper announcement marking Emily's January 1891 reemergence onto the social scene pronounces her the belle of Tuxedo, Newport, and Manhattan. Detailing her soft eyes, "lustrous brown hair," and tall and "stately" physique, the description commends her cleverness and accomplishments as well as her beauty. "Quite a star on the amateur stage . . . perhaps the best banjoist in fashionable society," the newspaper recounted.

In the 1890s, banjo playing was a chic sign of the fast-moving times, and to be among its premier players was impressive. No longer only the stuff of minstrel shows, the instrument was now the new trend in Ivy League colleges. Their banjo orchestras were inspired by the fashion of the last thirty years, during which increasing numbers of society women had begun playing the classic banjo in the European picking style. Henry Dobson, a famous banjoist in New York, had created frets to help players improve their accuracy, an innovation that appealed to the ladies even as it distressed the old-timers.

In one of the quirks of American history, many historians have concluded that the banjo, developed in Africa and introduced to America by slaves, proved restricting for blacks and liberating for women. Socialites meant to legitimize the instrument's stature, hoping to elevate it, aided by the new silk or gut strings, to the status of a violin—an unlikely goal, for a number of reasons. Nonetheless, banjo bands proliferated. New York aficionados bought Buckbee banjos locally, though the most ambitious musicians imported banjos from one of ten specialty shops in Boston.

Emily plied her banjo like a flirtatious peacock fanning its tail. Used to getting what she wanted one way or another, she had been appearing lately as a musical performer, often enough to unnerve Josephine, Pierre Lorillard's warning ringing in her ears. On the last day of January, the syndicated newspaper column announced, in effect, that Emily Price was seriously on the market again, her informal apprenticeship with her father over. Her assets were coolly cited, among them her recent bequest: "She was a legatee under the will of Miss Catharine Wolfe and she will have a very large fortune besides." If the willowy socialite had her heart set on a perchance reluctant beau, this article was the perfect hook.

Something clicked. By April 12, 1891, Emily Price was officially engaged to Edwin Main Post. But six months later, in October, Emily found herself temporarily on hold, her parents submitting a formal announcement to the *New York Times* that the wedding had been postponed due to the prospective bride's "illness." Edwin, a favorite of the ladies, seemed little affected. A month later he penned an off-color poem, a "softly murmured song of the Babylon maiden," in the log of his family's hunting boat, the *Macy*:

He rumpled me so!
'Twas only a miracle,
Mamma doesn't know
He rumpled me so.

Shall I tell her? Hell no
He was really "not in it"
He rumbled me so!

'Twas only a minute.

He rumbled me so!

Edwin and Emily wouldn't marry until midyear 1892. The reason for the wedding's postponement—surely a remarkable event for the circumspect Prices to announce publicly—remains unclear. But it is unlikely that "illness," the polite euphemism of the day, was the cause. Edwin's father, H.A.V.—Henry Albertson Van Zo Post—was rapidly losing control of his financial ventures. Post's record of financial distress had begun the year Emily was born, when H.A.V.'s brother Edwin A. Post had sued him to recover funds that he and Mrs. Post no longer possessed: H.A.V. had just declared bankruptcy. More recently, Tuxedo Park home owners were divided over whose side they took when the same ornery family member, Edwin Post, on the A list of the social circuit in spite of his infamous truculence, very publicly argued that a survey map proved that certain cemetery grounds in Long Island's chic Southampton resort belonged to him alone—meaning that he had every right to raise his hogs and chickens on what most residents considered sacred land. Marrying their daughter into a family commanding such headlines as "The Desecration of a Graveyard in Southampton" was neither Josephine nor Bruce's idea of making a good match.

Most important, from their first meeting, Bruce had not felt completely comfortable with the young Edwin Post. The future bridegroom's volatile line of work—he was buying up office property seized during bankruptcies and then profiting from their resale—didn't sit right with Bruce; nor did it suggest the kind of financial stability he wanted for Emily. A photograph taken around this time shows the tremendously successful architect seated at his desk amid a tumble of plans. Handsome, successful, commanding, at the top of his game, admired and worshipped by his daughter, he must have been a difficult act for Edwin Post to follow.

EMILY SPENT MOST of the following winter in Manhattan. But by early February 1892, her family had apparently capitulated to someone's entreaties. She accompanied the Posts to a fancy party in Washington, a cotillion given by family friends Mr. and Mrs. John McLean (he owned the *Washington Post*). The ball honored a visiting young descendant of Napoleon Bonaparte.

Emily surely gloried in this southern departure from the numbingly familiar routine of the New York ballroom. Even the jaded social editor at the *Times* perked up a bit at the party's variation in theme: the favors, at least, were "unique," lending a slightly exotic air to the nation's usually staid capital. Proud attendants squired a wooden horse ringed with flowers around the room. Ladies were instructed to take one of the rosette garlands and adorn themselves wherever they chose. Gentlemen received violet rosettes and ribbons, including Bonaparte emblems in gilded orange, bees on tinsel cord, and purple streamers embossed with the requisite eagle.

Guests gathered from up and down the eastern seaboard. New York, Philadelphia, Baltimore, and Charleston were especially well represented. The event was a top-tier social affair, and the Post family's inclusion relieved Josephine and Bruce's concern over the stability of Edwin's family. The month after the Bonaparte fête, Emily and her mother were off to Tuxedo, where Josephine worked feverishly on the arrangements for the June wedding. The meticulous journals Emily kept of the dresses she ordered from Paris houses, many of which she herself designed from scratch, are the first known instance of her near compulsion to record the minutiae of her everyday life. She began keeping a detailed expense account of her clothes, though there was certainly no financial reason to do so; her parents were paying. She recorded the ribbons and trims she bought at Stern's or Altman's, noting when and where she wore an outfit and, interestingly, whether its effect was what she had hoped for. "Not a success. Can't tell why," said one entry. She was jubilant when she scored an exceptionally economical success: after one such triumphant evening, she noted, "And all it cost was $11.79."

Edwin and Emily spent little time getting to know each other. Several years into their marriage, Emily would clumsily fictionalize their relationship: "Do you realize . . . that I was only seventeen when I tucked up my hair, let down my dresses, and, imagining myself the Princess in a fairy tale, was married?" she has her heroine say. Even later, she would criticize the old ways, the complete strangers that young couples were to each other at the beginning of their marriage: "A young man was said to be 'devoted' to this young girl or that, but as a matter of fact each was acting a role, he of an admirer and she of a siren." At the turn of the twentieth century, "each was actually an utter stranger to the other," she recalled.

Dating, as we know it, was not acceptable among the upper classes in the early 1890s. In contrast, the working class had already integrated the term into its slang, and even the *Ladies' Home Journal* occasionally employed it during the new decade. The mixed messages of the gay nineties ensured that women of all social strata became adults informed by wildly contradictory values. One ideal was the upper-class Gibson girl, whose model, Irene Langhorne Gibson, was a friend of Emily's from down South. Oddly, though the Gibson girl's creator was Irene's husband, her profile embodied the new ideal of greater independence for unmarried females.

As the wedding neared, Edwin and Emily spent even less time together. In mid-April, during Easter weekend, he went out for a shoot on the *Macy*, along with several friends and male family members. At three-thirty P.M. on Friday afternoon, the hunters caught a train out of Babylon, Long Island's resort town on the Great South Bay where the Post family had long spent their summers, the bay itself a forty-five-mile arm of the Atlantic Ocean between the southern shore of Long Island and the barrier islands offshore. They arrived a mere ten minutes later at the boat, anchored just off the dock, located about halfway out on Long Island's South Shore. The men ritualistically removed what they called their store clothes and donned their shooting apparel before pulling up anchor and hoisting the sail. The *Macy*'s captain cooked a celebratory dinner in honor of the holiday: leg of lamb, potatoes, green beans, and cranberry dressing, the meal topped off with a rich vanilla pudding. As everyone settled back with a fine cigar or two, set on playing cards before they retired early, Edwin took the wheel so that the cabin crew could eat.

At four A.M. each of the next two days, the hunters ate a hearty breakfast; their shooting was abbreviated on Sunday so that they could return to town. Edwin commented in the log before he left that he was "broken hearted at having to leave hunting. Adios!" Until a week before the wedding, the prospective groom spent most of his nonworking hours on board, sometimes helping the cook fix the very early breakfast in order to bag more ducks, racheting up the day's tally toward the grand total killed that season.

Perhaps his fiancée had already admitted that she had no interest in sailing. If so, it would have been another point in her favor, Edwin might have thought: he valued his time alone with his friends, and would have been relieved that Emily was not one to seek pleasure through the pastimes her husband held in such esteem. Instead, she preferred what to him were boring cultural events. On April 23 she participated in a celebration of Shakespeare's birthday in another Manhattan socialite's home. One woman read an essay she'd written about Ophelia, others recited poetry, and Emily played the banjo—all in all, a feminine soiree typical of the times. A week later, she attended a luncheon given by a widowed family friend, Mrs. Algernon Sullivan, in honor of her niece. Mr. Sullivan, a prominent lawyer, had founded the New York Southern Society. Emily was expected to be Bruce's link to the Price family's southern roots whenever the occasion arose, an assignment that relieved her of the more tedious wedding details, which were happily assumed by her mother.

For the popular, busy nineteen-year-old, the months leading up to her marriage became a time of uncharacteristic introspection. Until now, she later realized, "she had always . . . taken herself and her world for granted." Her life was so carefully and thoroughly arranged by others that "there had been little time and no encouragement" to think "about herself." Instead, she had learned from watching her mother that "if you broke the rhythm [of life,] failed to do what the others expected of you and at the moment they expected it, you failed them. And yourself."

Realizing that he was about to lose his only child to irrevocable adulthood, her father had decided to have Emily's portrait painted, choosing someone from the Prices' own social and professional circle. Through Hop Smith, Bruce had become acquainted with the painter Rosina Emmet Sherwood, the daughter-in-law of etiquette writer Mary Sherwood, the matriarch of the well-known New York Sherwood family. Bruce and Josephine already knew Mary slightly. She had written a detailed social guide called *Manners and Social Usages* that had been invaluable to the family through Emily's debut, and now would serve as her wedding's bible.

No amateur, Rosina Sherwood had studied with William Merritt Chase in New York and at the Académie Julian in Paris. Her reputation was soaring, in spite of her "soft" subjects of mothers and children. Rosina, or "Posie," as her friends and family called her, painted alongside Hop Smith at Chase's building on Tenth Street near Sixth Avenue, not far from Emily's home. The atelier was a kind of commune, occupied by a close-knit group of student artists as well as long-established professionals. Chase was also expanding on what Hop had tried a decade earlier: along with such students as Rosina Sherwood and her sister Lydia Emmet, the professor would put the east end of Long Island on the map by choosing a location on its south fork, Shinnecock, as the site of his plein air movement, his protégés painting beside him in the healthy sea breezes off the Atlantic Ocean.

Cousins of Henry James's, the Emmet sisters—Rosina Emmet Sherwood, Lydia Field Emmet, and Jane Emmet de Glehn—were the Brontës of their day, though far more privileged. The three young women possessed prodigious talent, which they'd been encouraged to develop. Rosina was married and helping support her family with her portraiture. Eventually consisting of five children, the Sherwood clan would include the Pulitzer Prize–winning author Robert Sherwood. Rosina was the first professional woman Emily had known, a woman who combined marriage, motherhood, and a career, living in three worlds simultaneously and finding her life quite manageable for all that. Here was someone from a good family who seemed to have everything a woman might want, in late-nineteenth-century terms: a good husband, contented children, a productive and lucrative career, her family honor and genealogy undisturbed, if not enhanced, by her work.

Years later, while Emily Post was writing *Etiquette,* Rosina Sherwood's son Robert and his writer friends, including Alexander Woollcott and Dorothy Parker, were routinely meeting at New York's Algonquin Hotel. According to one close observer, the "Vicious Circle," as they mockingly called themselves, "received women on a more truly equal footing than any other group in the Nineteen-Twenties." Rosina Sherwood would raise a son who had been shaped by his mother's nascent feminism, the seeds of which were at least planted in Emily Post as well.

As she painted, her subject a captive audience, Rosina Sherwood suggested to Emily that she might do well to reflect upon her own life. Was a nonstop whirl of parties and vacuous entertainment really the best use of her obvious intelligence? "You are in a dream world now. But some day you are going to wake up," she said. Her advice unsettled her subject, and the resultant portrait—a tense, unrealized young woman—made Emily's father uncomfortable enough to complain.

Because Bruce was unsure that the painting was perfect, he sent several of his office staff to assess its likeness before he agreed to accept the finished product. When one of them voiced criticism, he then promptly dispatched important artist friends to view the painting. It was admired by all.

Upon their judgment, he relented, writing to Rosina of his deep emotions concerning his daughter.

"I hasten to say all this from a sense of perfect happiness in the possession of a treasure that in my heart has always given me pleasure," he wrote, "so that all that I said about the background was only the worrying of a soul distressed over very poor criticism. Of course I am impressionable and anything said about or against an idol of mine upsets me." After explaining how he had subjected the portrait to impartial review, he concluded, "I think it was mean in me to say what I did. I congratulate you first on your work, second on your proper sense of it. With sincere regards, very faithfully yours, Bruce Price."

More than Bruce Price could ever know, Rosina Sherwood's gentle query to the society girl as she posed for that portrait remained, decades later, a pivotal moment in Emily's memories. The timely discussion between the "woman artist" and the society girl tucked into the back of Emily's mind the realization that she had choices. On the eve of becoming an adult, of being under her parents' thumb no longer, Emily was asked what she wanted to be when she grew up. As if being a wife wasn't a complete identity.

Several decades later, Virginia Woolf would recall the stifling expectations that, upon their marriages, women of Emily's social class inherited. In 1931, Woolf spoke to the London National Society for Women's Service, where she discussed how her generation of women had been forced, finally, to kill off the infamous "Angel in the House," from a maudlin Victorian poem describing the ideal, long-suffering wife and mother. Much of the struggle Woolf described was awaiting Emily, though she had only a glimmer, through Rosina Sherwood, of its grip. "You who come of a much younger and happier generation may not have heard of her—you may not know what I mean by the Angel in the House," said Woolf. ". . . She was intensely sympathetic. She was immensely charming. She was utterly unselfish. She excelled in the difficult arts of family life. She sacrificed herself daily. . . . Above all—I need not say it—she was pure. . . . In those days—the last of Queen Victoria—every house had its Angel. And when I came to write I encountered her with the very first words. The shadow of her wings fell on my page; I heard the rustling of her skirts in the room."

Because she had been left an inheritance, Woolf explained, she could afford to be brave and not "depend solely on charm for my living. I turned upon her and caught her by the throat. I did my best to kill her. . . . Had I not killed her she would have killed me. For, as I found . . . you cannot review even a novel without having a mind of your own, without expressing what you think to be the truth about human relations, morality, sex. And all these questions, according to the Angel of the House, cannot be dealt with freely and openly by women."

To a large extent, Emily Price's class and Josephine's provincial beliefs about women had inured the girl to the increasing eruptions of sexual politics. Amid seismic changes for women, Emily's marriage was contracted on conventional grounds. She expected—and for the most part, assumed she wanted—the same life, more or less, that her mother had sought with Bruce. In a way, Emily got trapped on a cusp of social history: she married Edwin in 1892, just as her eyes were starting to open. Though she would never use such aggressive language, she would nonetheless come to share Woolf's conclusion: "Killing the Angel in the House was part of the occupation of a woman writer."

THE POST FAMILY coffers may have been depleted, but Edwin Main Post came from the bluest of blood, its worth on the stock market notwithstanding. The Posts were an old Dutch family with an impeccable pedigree. They had enough money to get by, even if they relied on the inheritance of their matriarch, Caroline McLean. Edwin's father, H.A.V. Post, had been born in New York City ten years before Bruce Price. After being wounded at Antietam, Henry moved to Cincinnati as a partner in the business of the day: manufacturing railroad supplies. In 1870 he returned to New York City and established businesses in Manhattan, eventually becoming a railroad banker. He even formed a steel firm. Yankee through and through, the good colonel and Baltimore's Bruce Price were unlikely to have had much in common, though if they had met under circumstances in which Bruce was less invested emotionally, a friendship might have ensued. H.A.V. Post, after all, sought fraternity even more fervently than Bruce Price did. He gathered his male friends onto the *Macy* every weekend he could escape his overbearing wife. He cherished his small yacht and would keep it no matter how his finances decayed. Ten years after Emily wed his son, H.A.V.'s little crew would honor the hearty gambler's even temper:

To our gallant Colonel Henry Post
We offer up this simple toast:

"May all his days be full of joy,
May drinking cocktails never lag,
May power reign and fishing please,
And may he always have a breeze."

H.A.V.'s marriage to the wealthy, stern Caroline Burnet McLean produced seven children. Edwin was born in the middle of the brood, in
Cincinnati on January 6, 1870, just before the family moved from Caroline's home to reclaim H.A.V.'s roots in the city. The daughter of General
Nathaniel McLean, Caroline was even more proud of her paternal grandfather, Justice John McLean of the United States Supreme Court. He was
one of the two judges who dissented from the high court's decision in the
Dred Scott case, believing that slavery defied and defiled the American
Constitution. Most of all—predictably, given her personality—Caroline
was impressed that she was a direct descendant of Oliver Cromwell.

It was undeniable that Edwin brought interesting family members to
Emily's table, as if making up for the only child's own dearth of local relatives. Edwin's older brother, the charming A.V.Z. Post, would be Edwin's
best man. One of society's finest and most popular cotillion leaders, Van Zo,
as he was also called, was a man who did things his own way: in 1900 he was,
by profession, a civil engineer, living with his parents at 140 West Seventy-
seventh Street in Manhattan, along with his sister Nathalie. Apparently too
busy to think about a wife until he was much older, he was an eclectic, wildly
talented man. His novel of 1913, *Diana Ardway,* would prove so popular that it
was made into a movie, his fencing talents prodigious enough to land him on
the U.S. Olympic team. At sixty-five years old, he married for the first time;
Nathalie Post was the only sibling who would remain single throughout her
life, while the others made illustrious matches and, in some cases, successful
careers.

Emily thrived under her brother-in-law's attention; the charmer made
everyone feel special, and now that she was part of his family, Van Zo's efforts doubled. "Angel sister!" an undated note he sent to Emily begins. His
most recent play, in Provincetown, has closed after two performances.
"With such a record no N.Y. theatre would let us in, so I just pocketed a ten
thousand loss and am sailing for Paris . . . by Deutschland. Thanks for your
good cheer and good advice, which I repent me of not following!!! Do hope
to show you my studio, 65 Boulevard Arago soon?" He signed the letter
"Affectionately."

There was also cousin Regis Post, who would become even closer to Edwin when, a few years after the Price/Post wedding, he married one of Edwin's sisters, Caroline. The Post-to-Post merger would last for twenty-seven years (though they were officially separated for nine of them). Finally Caroline filed for divorce, citing as the cause Regis's "misconduct with servants" in Manhattan, Puerto Rico, and the Post family home at Bayport, Long Island. Closer to Edwin than to any of his other relatives, Regis would become the governor of Puerto Rico while still a young man, enjoying his job immensely until 1919, when his marriage and good fortune had both clearly dissolved.

There were certainly enough Post cousins traveling the social circuit, frequenting Tuxedo Park as well as the other fashionable watering spots, for Bruce and Josephine to see up close that most of the family seemed respectable and well behaved. Even Uncle Edward A. Post, living on an "inherited income" as he raged against those claiming his pig farm for their graveyard, divided his time almost equally among the best watering holes in the country.

But it was the estimable George Browne Post, H.A.V.'s cousin, who was the crown jewel of the Post family. About ten years older than Bruce, he had attended the University of the City of New York (later renamed New York University), then studied architecture under the famous Richard Morris Hunt—favored among the high-society set—who designed his friend Cornelius Vanderbilt II's the Breakers. Just as he was making a name for himself, Post had been forced to switch gears and learn to fight, joining the Union Army at the outbreak of hostilities, promoted from captain to colonel in 1867. Three years later, as Bruce Price cast his lot with Josephine Lee down South, George Post reentered the civilian workforce in New York City.

In quick time, Edwin's relative had become one of the world's premier architects, one they all heard about in Baltimore. He was an engineer before he was an architect, almost a requirement in the early days of skyscrapers. His Equitable Life Assurance Society building would be the first office building to use elevators; his World Building and St. Paul's were both the tallest structures in New York at the time of their construction. His New York Stock Exchange still stands, its inventive use of steel supports reminders of how Post earned his fame. He would win commissions for the *Times,* the *Post,* New York Hospital, the Williamsburg Bank, the campus of the City University of New York, and major Gilded Age houses. His Western Union Building, the first office structure to rise to ten floors, was a prototype of buildings to come, twenty-five years before the great age of the skyscraper. By 1890, his World (or Pulitzer) Building, with twice that number of floors, would be the city's tallest structure, launching, some would claim, New York City's skyscraper age. The building would be demolished some fifty years later to expand the automobile entrance to the Brooklyn Bridge.

The bride must have believed herself bestowing a daughterly blessing upon Bruce Price. She would show her father that she was marrying well after all, in spite of his reservations about Edwin's financial reliability—and something else, though he admitted he couldn't say quite what. Her father was just nervous at the thought of losing her, Josie had reassured their daughter. Now Emily would set his mind at ease, linking him to George Post, who would soon be her family too. Maybe she couldn't be an architect herself, and perhaps Bruce would always rue the son he had lost. But Emily could present her papa with a therapeutic consolation prize. The attendance of the near celebrity at the Tuxedo Park wedding was the finest gift Edwin gave his bride, and the greatest solace she could offer to her bereft father. George Post's frequent presence on the *Macy* even redeemed her too frequent weekends spent at home alone.

AN INTELLIGENTLY CONTRACTED marriage in the Gilded Age could address two separate but equally compelling needs. A smart union would benefit everyone, accommodating both income and bloodlines, in this instance, the Prices' financial endowment (through Josephine's legacy), and the Posts' breeding. One enabled the future; one traded on the past. A perfect mix.

Edwin's family tree was deeply rooted and abundantly limbed. Emily later implied that it sometimes felt as if the generations of Posts were endless. Edwin Post's family had a summer home on Long Island's South Shore, where the various branches had been living for nine generations, intermarrying with all the other English families of the mid-seventeenth-century migration. The funds, versus the bloodlines, are less clear, at least in regard to the resources of Edwin's parents. Mrs. Post's money was clearly the major support. She let nothing stand in the way of her needs or her children's, whether she wanted to rent the finest cottage in Newport for the season or to take her two eligible daughters abroad after their debuts, presumably to expand their wardrobes or enlarge their prospects of snagging a title.

Henry Albertson Van Zo Post contributed his old Dutch name and his family lineage to the marriage—along with his good looks and great charm. Soon after Edwin and Emily's wedding, he declared bankruptcy. Nonetheless, the irrepressible H.A.V. kept buying and selling railroad companies, subsidized by his wife's money, until he died. Bruce Price's intuition had been right: this family was unstable.

CHAPTER 14

⚜

EDWIN POST DIDN'T EXPECT HIS PARENTS AND EMILY'S TO BECOME best friends. But even his worst fears hadn't predicted this disaster. In the spring of 1892, only months before the wedding, the Posts attended an exclusive engagement party given by Bruce and Josephine. The dining room at 12 West Tenth Street was perfectly configured for intimate groups of twelve. Among the guests saluting the young couple that evening were Pierre and Mrs. Lorillard, and Hop Smith and his wife—a lively, successful, culturally interesting group of people. The conversation seemed to flow smoothly at first, and the two young guests of honor began to relax. With that, the scene turned into a nightmare. Emily's prospective mother-in-law and her father had taken an instant, visceral dislike to each other.

The evening had actually gone wrong from the beginning, but Emily and Edwin were too nervous—or too young—to notice. Bruce had escorted a stiff Caroline Post to the dining room. He graciously paused to point out, proudly, the life-sized nude statue in the hallway. Emily had given him a reproduction of the *Apollo Belvedere,* he laughed, because "the sculpture reminds her of me." The pious woman blushed furiously.

More restrained attempts at social levity also fell flat. Frank Smith charmingly rehashed the stories of little Emily accompanying him to the Statue of Liberty construction site and begging to live inside the hollow statue, like the proverbial princess in a tower. Edwin's father, H.A.V., then gallantly toasted such royal femininity, and others urged more fine wine upon the party, hoping to loosen things up. But the fervently devout Mrs. Post refused the alcohol and abstemiously drank a half glass of water instead. Apparently the water renewed her, because she suddenly turned to the architect and asked what he thought about the wonderful recent crusade to clean up the Tenderloin, the seedy red-light district in western midtown Manhattan. The newspapers, she gushed, said her Long Island neighbor Dr. Charles Parkhurst was set upon reforming the city government.

Without a doubt, H.A.V. Post, whose charm was only slightly less than Bruce Price's, had ended up with a formidable spouse. The Prices were working hard to get along with the difficult woman. But any gain was now canceled by her vacuous polemics in the name of virtue. Bruce Price followed libertarian principles, though the philosophy would give rise to a political party only after his death. The architect tended toward the socially liberal and financially conservative. He believed that the less government interfered in citizens' business, both private and professional, the better.

The tension at the dinner table became palpable. To his credit, Emily's father tried to express his disdain for Mrs. Post's beloved celebrity minister gently, but the devoted woman persisted in her avid support. To her, one's position for or against Reverend Parkhurst's crusade to clean up city hall said it all.

As Bruce was wont to do when goaded by self-righteousness, he finally exploded—albeit carefully. "It is not men like me who support the vice in this or any other city," he retorted through clenched teeth, adding that Dr. Parkhurst's methods did more harm than good.

How so? the good woman huffed, incredulous. By encouraging some people to feel better than others, holier than their neighbors, Bruce was said to have replied, adding, "I consider [Dr. Parkhurst] a blue-nosed busybody, and if he ever came anywhere near me I'd feel tempted to kick him downstairs."

With that, Josephine firmly intervened, practically demanding her husband's opinion of the Metropolitan Opera's new box seats.

The Prices' other guests were not the sort to applaud the strong-handed tactics of a Charles Parkhurst either. A few months earlier, on a freezing winter morning in mid-February, the usually genial fifty-year-old minister had preached a fiery sermon in New York's Madison Square Presbyterian Church, a blistering indictment of the city government. Asserting that Tammany Hall was run by a "a lying, perjured, rum-soaked, and libidinous lot," he meant to derail its hellish evils. The parishioners were agog. Parkhurst, his imposing dark hair streaked with silver, was a society minister. He had recently served with J. Pierpont Morgan and Mortimer Schiff on committees fighting the hunger of Russian Jewry. His liberal Presbyterian parish was filled with upper-class citizens, including such aesthetes as Louis Comfort Tiffany. And he wanted these people to understand: their city had rotted at its core, and he planned to operate on the disease here and now.

And that was the problem. Russia was one thing, Manhattan quite another. As city historian Lloyd Morris maintains, New Yorkers, for the most part, knew their city was "open," and they liked it that way. "Cosmopolitan and pleasure-loving . . . many of them had no objection to leading a free-and-easy life in a free-and-easy town." Bruce Price was typical of those upper-class citizens disgusted by the minister's intrusion into what they considered private matters between consenting adults, whatever the subject. For the first time in the memory of the "average New Yorker," no saloon in the Bowery, the outré area of lower Manhattan notorious for its sexual exoticism, was open after midnight, the old, neglected city law suddenly enforced because of the reverend's exhortations. Under Parkhurst's sway, for instance, the largely ignored strictures against bars doing business on the Sunday Sabbath were now enforced, if haphazardly. Not content with curbing alcohol consumption, Parkhurst had tried to close down the high-class brothels, institutions that Bruce's social crowd assumed benefited everyone. Before long it seemed that the minister could locate sin on every city corner.

The narrowness of Parkhurst's vision offended Bruce Price, who would bequeath to his daughter his belief in a civic morality that didn't infringe on others' personal freedoms. The days when Parkhurst might have been seen as a liberator of oppressed women were still in the future; at this point, all he was doing was depriving certain deserving women of an income and their customers of pleasure, from the point of view of Bruce's crowd. The 1880s and 1890s were, after all, the "golden age of free thought," and the city's elite did not welcome the kind of religious interference in civic affairs Parkhurst urged. What may not have been clear even to the Price family was the part that the South, the Old South of Bruce Price's childhood, played in their values. Drinking, for instance (which Parkhurst distrusted), and, more importantly, the freedom to drink as one pleased (as long as one remained a gentleman) were considered God-given liberties. To the point of disaster, southerners believed themselves entitled to such escape from reality, and had done so even before the Civil War.

A few months after the disastrous engagement dinner, as if Caroline Post hadn't understood the depth of Bruce Price's convictions, she aggravated the wound that was just starting to heal. Once again she threatened the nuptials with her passion for Reverend Parkhurst, this time while Josephine was addressing the invitations.

As soon as Josie received Mrs. Post's list, headed by the name Reverend Charles Parkhurst, she knew that this was another crisis threatening the wedding. Even the usually implacable Josephine was disgusted at Edwin's mother, expressing to Emily her dismay before she told Bruce. "How can she?" she complained. "I don't know what to do. You know how your father feels about that atrocious man. And Mrs. Post must know after what he said that night at dinner. He certainly made himself clear."

When Bruce got home and heard the news about Mrs. Post's defiant gesture to include Dr. Parkhurst, he erupted. If that "damned bluenose" crossed his threshold, he'd shoot him, and then there would be a scandal, not a wedding. He finally played the age-old trump card: "I'm paying the bills" for the wedding, he reminded the Price women. No invitation was to go to the self-appointed potentate. Moral posturing was forbidden in this family circle.

Apparently Mrs. Post conceded defeat, since the wedding went forward. Presents started stacking up, and Emily's deft cataloging of wedding gifts in *Etiquette* years later hints at the haul she must have taken in. Fine pieces of silver should not be displayed next to poor imitations, she would explain, for fear of embarrassing someone. Colors should be arranged appealingly, imitation lace separated from the real, and duplicates thoughtfully spread out among the presents: "Eighteen pairs of pepper pots or fourteen sauceboats in a row might as well be labeled: 'Look at this stupidity! What can she do with all of us?' They are sure to make the givers feel at least a little chagrined at their choice." Protecting well-meaning individuals from shame was more important than acknowledging their shortsighted judgment.

Many years later, a middle-aged Emily Post would lament the ill-focused energies of the betrothed in her day. Instead of concentrating on the important stuff of intimacy, her generation had sought to avoid it, focusing on the gravy boats instead. "In nothing does the present time more greatly differ from the close of the last century, than in the unreserved frankness of young women and men towards each other. Those who speak of the domination of sex in this day are either too young to remember, or else have not stopped to consider, that mystery played a far greater and more dangerous role when sex, like a woman's ankle, was carefully hidden from view, and therefore far more alluring than to-day when both are commonplace matters."

ON JUNE 1, 1892, Emily Bruce Price married Edwin Main Post. An Episcopalian church in Tuxedo, St. Mary's, had been finished in 1888, but Emily got married at home. The wedding was held on the edge of Tuxedo Lake, at the family's Rocklawn residence, Bruce's favorite of the four Price family "cottages" he had built. (He gave his next favorite to Emily and Edwin as a wedding gift.) Bishop Whipple of Minnesota officiated, a concession to Mrs. Post: he was at least a member of her family, his son having married Mrs. Post's sister. By this point, Bruce Price must have been mollified by new family connections as well: the *New York Times* noted that George Post was among the highly select guests.

Emily had designed her wedding dress herself. She'd sent her sketches to Worth in Paris, who'd sewed everything on site, including the four bridesmaids' gowns. She kept her drawings for years in one of the calfbound ledgers she used to enter personal accounts. Explaining whenever asked that she didn't keep a diary—she wasn't the introspective sort—she failed to add that she nonetheless recorded her days in fastidious detail.

The bride had probably argued for a practical, local seamstress, but Josephine preferred the security of fine French fashion. Sending away to Paris turned out to be a mistake, however, for all the beauty it guaranteed. Promised the garments weeks earlier, Emily and Josephine received the package only two days prior to the big date.

Sixty-eight degrees at eight A.M., near ninety degrees by the afternoon: the weather for the wedding guaranteed a soggy affair that first day of June, in spite of the lack of rain. Tuxedo Park was hardly cooler than Manhattan. The *New York Times* urged city workers and those within a hundred miles to use umbrellas for the unremitting sun. Even if Emily had been willing to switch to the gauze undergarments the newspaper recommended for women that day (and she wasn't), the relief under her layers of silk and satin would have been minimal. Layers of material swathed the nineteen-year-old bride, the white mousseline de soie "and real old lace" surely ruined by her perspiration. Her high-necked corsage was trimmed with orange blossoms and a veil of *point d'Alençon*. Pale green mull (a fine muslin) draped the bridesmaids' dance-length silk dresses. Straw-colored corsages with delicate hints of pink cast the entire scene as a Watteau, down to the triple-plumed leghorn hats. Edwin's little brother Henry was the page, with his other brother, A.V.Z. Post, cousin Regis Post, and longtime friend Lyman Colt as attendants. When Regis married his cousin Caroline Post a few years later, he would placate Edwin's mother, ensuring that Dr. Charles Parkhurst sanctified at least one Post union.

Even more than with most weddings, it had been tense up to the last minute. The list of upcoming "country" nuptials that the *Times* published a week before Emily's listed her bridesmaids as "four Baltimore belles," friends and relatives from Emily's past. But the wedding announcement a week later indicated a few quick and pointed substitutions. Bruce and Josephine's Baltimore nieces, Sadie Price and Josephine "Georgie" Barrow, were still half of the equation. But two of Edwin's sisters, Beatrice and the dour Nathalie Post, now served as peace offerings to Edwin's mother, substituting for the two friends Emily had originally chosen.

We can only imagine the bride's irritation at the scene: perspiring profusely under the heavy fabric, irritated at her mother's belief in superstition. The marriage could have taken place in early May, a predictably cool time. Decades later, recalling her unnecessary suffering vividly, she would advise modern brides that "the superstition that Friday and the month of May are unlucky, is too stupid to discuss."

But by June 5, 1892, a few days after the Price-Post nuptials in the country, no evidence remained of the rough patches. The *New York Times* descanted on the three most "important weddings in the country" that had occurred that weekend. From Hempstead, Long Island, to Tuxedo Park, socialites vied for first place. Some of the papers used nomenclature from Edith Wharton, speaking reverentially of the "country seat" of the bride's parents. "Miss Bruce Price was the prettiest bride of the day," the *New York Times* boldly pronounced.

There was at least one wedding guest who would be convinced the rest of his life that no finer bride existed anywhere. If, as Emily later suggested, Bruce Price looked to others as if he had buried, not married off, his daughter, his sadness at losing his only child was matched by his pride in her exceptional character and her physical beauty.

PART TWO

. . .

My Dear Mrs. Upstart:

Thank you for the very handsome
candlesticks you sent us.
They were a great surprise, but it was more
than kind of you to think of us.

—*ETIQUETTE*, PAGE 466

CHAPTER 15

※

EMILY HAD PLANNED TO IMPRESS HER TWENTY-ONE-YEAR-OLD spouse by re-creating Josephine and Bruce's postnuptial trip to the Continent. The summer the Posts married, however, an epidemic of Asian cholera swept across Europe. Only because of stringent restrictions meant to dissuade even the most determined from traveling abroad did the scourge of 1892 largely bypass the United States. The couple reluctantly canceled their honeymoon voyage, whereupon they decided, with Emily's prodding, to visit Savannah, Charleston, and, of course, Baltimore, instead.

Proud of Edwin's charm and good looks, Emily delighted in showing off her handsome husband. For his part, though mildly curious about the life that moved his usually practical bride to wax nostalgic, Edwin was more eager to trap the tasty sea turtles studding the Chesapeake than to pass the time with his bride's southern relatives. Though everyone got along— Emily's relatives embodied the gracious Old South in so many ways—Edwin found the men strangely reminiscent of Bruce Price, who intimidated him, while the women, with their learned cordiality, somehow made him feel he was in danger of looking like an untutored Yankee rube.

Six weeks after their wedding, in midsummer, the couple returned to New York City to a rented apartment on Tenth Street between Fifth and Sixth avenues, the same block as Emily's parents. In early autumn, just after the bride finally finished hiring her house staff, she realized that she was pregnant. Now, along with mastering the routines of a flawless wife suitable for a man like her husband—so obviously making headway in the business world—Emily would have to marshal the resources to become a mother as well. In her ledgers, she painstakingly documented the world of a wealthy young matron, a job involving everything from planning the day's menus to scheduling the servants' days off. Though the upper-class women of the Gilded Age no longer needed to contribute to the household's physical labor, as in the past, they had found another way to imbue their privileged lives with meaning: by directing the labor of others.

Unfortunately, though their husbands depended upon such wifely resolve to manage their domestic lives, some of them, including Edwin Post, assumed their spouses could mature into their connubial roles while remaining the girls they had married. Emily had appealed to Edwin in part through her abilities on the amateur stage, her dramatic side promising hidden treats: actresses were sexual creatures—every man knew that. He had delighted in the sparkling, vivacious performances his bride had delivered ever since he'd met her that enchanted December night when she had occupied the center of attention. Clearly Emily Price had loved to show off, a trait Edwin appreciated. Now, as he uneasily observed several new mothers among their social circle, he began to worry that his wife would become tedious as her pregnancy progressed, boring instead of amusing him.

In fact, Edwin and Emily had little in common from the start, a lack of connection that had become painfully evident to Emily as early as their honeymoon, after she had struggled to find topics of conversation on long train trips that seemed never to end. The relief she felt when surrounded by her always chattering Baltimore cousins was short-lived when she noticed their carefully arranged facial expressions, revealing more clearly than words their suspicion of this young man so different from Bruce Price.

But now, back in Manhattan, Emily was determined to provide a satisfying home life for Edwin and their child, just like the one Josie had overseen as her daughter grew up. After consulting her mother, Emily established a routine whose morning ritual remained essentially the same throughout her life. She would be served toast and coffee in bed while she carefully reviewed her day's list of chores and prepared written assignments for her servants. Then she dressed for the requisite afternoon socializing, summoning John, her personal equerry. Until her pregnancy showed, she often went shopping, usually at Altman's or, less frequently, at Lord & Taylor's. After lunching at Delmonico's, she paid her social "at home" visits, directing John to deposit her card on the silver trays placed in the hallway entrances of those acquaintances whose "visiting day" it was, the network of socialites an important part of upper-class life. Visitors who were actual friends or who had been specially invited would be escorted into the study or parlor for tea.

When Emily called upon ladies whose company she enjoyed (their houses dotting Gramercy Park and even the newer enclave of Murray Hill), she usually stopped for the traditional twenty-minute face-to-face. Even these women were not among her closest friends—such formal calling hours were not required for them—and so she and her hostess stuck to a fairly routine list of subjects: the weather, current fashions, new menu items at Delmonico's, recent (noncontroversial) national or world news. By late afternoon Emily was back home, where she spent the remaining hours before dinner (hosted by the Posts half the week, the other times by their friends) reviewing her wardrobe for the next day, her final task being to ensure that her jewels were in ballroom condition. If the Gilded Age men were pushing themselves ever faster to make more money, their wives were expected to find conspicuous ways to spend it. Emily would later lament, "Men had not enough time and women had too much, so that they had to keep busily trying to find means, the former to save and the latter to squander it."

For a while, she found her new role as mistress of her own domain satisfying. This is what she had been trained to do all her life, and now she intended to show how well she could do it. Especially proud that her invitations were sought by the A list among the city's elite, she noticed that dinners at the Post home were seldom refused in favor of a competing offer. Emily knew that Edwin was eager to seem a social lion, and to her great satisfaction, their joint commitment to his success allowed the newlyweds to function as a team.

Emily's most important contribution to the couple's elaborate dinner parties was to purchase the finest specialties of the period, above all, duck and terrapin, the kind her husband had hunted on the couple's honeymoon. Terrapin, the ubiquitous society meal of the Gilded Age, had become a symbol of haute cuisine several years earlier when Delmonico's had first dared to serve the exotic reptile, the third-most-expensive item on the menu at $2.50 per meal ($55 in today's terms). Emily didn't understand the fuss; she had grown up eating this variety of freshwater turtle, popular in the South long before it appeared on northern tables. Upton Sinclair, approximately Emily's age, remembered how the Baltimore community accepted his grandfather, an unfashionable Methodist, only because of his infamous terrapin suppers. Terrapin soup, terrapin steaks, and terrapin ap-

petizers: you were in trouble if you couldn't stomach its taste, privately held
to emulate stringy beef—once you removed the sherry it swam in.

Luckily for Edwin, duck, the other requisite of the well-set table during
the 1890s, was a meat he knew well. Only half joking, he measured his
manhood by how many ducks—and what kind—he bagged during shooting
season every weekend that he spent on the Post family boat. Knowing that
most of the imported terrapin Emily and her parents served actually arrived packed in ice from Maryland motivated him to conscript the duck, at
least, into Yankee territory. The fowl, however, proved yet another southern specialty after all, a further reminder of fine cuisine below the Mason-
Dixon Line. As Emily gently explained, highborn southerners were
expected early in life to carve a canvasback with finesse, an art "once considered necessary to every gentleman."

Emily herself liked simple foods, but she knew she would have to put
aside her preferences in order to serve what Edwin, as well as their guests,
expected. Luckily, a copy of the cookbook written in 1889 by Delmonico's
chef, Alessandro Filippini, was among the gifts she had received following
her debut. *The Table* detailed the dishes the restaurant had been serving to
society for years. Now Filippini's meals could be replicated by society's
cooks, at home. In spite of her preference for plain fare, Emily would depend for decades upon Filippini's elaborate menus for entertaining, her
copy growing tattered over the years. His seven-course Thanksgiving feast,
with minor variations, served as the model for the countless winter dinners
she hosted, including her first Christmas as a wife in 1892. Flinching just a
little from the gruesome routine she was outlining for the cook, she read
aloud:

Take live terrapin, and blanch them in boiling water for two minutes. Remove the skin from the feet, and put them back to cook with
some salt in the saucepan until they feel soft to the touch; then put
them aside to cool. Remove the carcass, cut it in medium-sized
pieces, removing the entrails, being careful not to break the gall-
bag. . . . Cook for five minutes, and put it away in the icebox for further use. Put in a saucepan one pint of Espagnole sauce and half a
pint of consommé. . . . Boil for twenty minutes, being careful to remove the fat, if any; add half a pint of terrapin and boil for ten minutes longer. Then serve with six slices of lemon, always removing the
bouquet.

Edwin made his own contribution to the holiday meals. Over the past few years, he had become a true connoisseur of wines, and now he seized any opportunity to impress Emily's parents with his knowledge. His elaborate collection earned him respect not only from Bruce and Josephine but from their friends as well. Regrettably, Emily herself was never interested in alcohol—except for championing the nation's right to drink it in the face of Prohibition. In later years, she wrote briefly in *Etiquette* about the best temperature (warm, she said) for serving wines, provoking an otherwise sympathetic reader to lament, "She must have wasted a lot of time in France if this passage is the sum of her lore about wine." It was.

✣

FOR SEVERAL MONTHS INTO HER PREGNANCY, EMILY CONTINUED patronizing Delmonico's, the stalwart haven for her friends as well as the site for formal occasions—or for relaxed meals where children learned good table manners. Its safe, friendly atmosphere liberated women from the chaperones that proper society had required just ten years earlier. On Saturdays, when the crowd of businessmen weren't eating their lunches there, Emily's feminine clique could gather for the Gilded Age version of brunch. Omnipresent newspaper reporters decoded the diners' status by what they ordered: Emily's caste predictably requested oysters, scrambled eggs with truffles, filet mignon with béarnaise sauce, and toasted muffins. The respectable middle class preferred roast beef, mashed potatoes, and ice cream. Pretty, reputable unmarried women ordered quail on toast and a small bottle of champagne, their much-touted independence belittled by the married crowd whenever a nearby gentleman picked up their tab.

The restaurant's customers rarely graced the popular, crowded oyster palaces suddenly sprawling across the city: Delmonico's guaranteed a fresh supply of the best of the popular mollusks—no small matter when the Western world's second-largest city (only London was more heavily populated) was consuming a million oysters each day. The nationally famous gourmet Samuel Ward, Edwin's favorite tutor in things culinary, was rumored to have depleted the restaurant's entire supply himself one afternoon.

With one sip, Sam Ward could identify both a wine's provenance and its vintage, and his dinners were among the most celebrated in Washington and New York. He would eventually serve as the prototype for Edith

Wharton's Lovell Mingotts, who, in *The Age of Innocence,* presides over an extravagant dinner, his concentration on the most minute details of the menu meant to indict an overly fastidious set of people whom Wharton thought polluted society. For now, Edwin's wife held her counsel, not telling her husband that she failed to share his enthusiasm for fine food, and that she thought people like Sam Ward, regardless of their pedigree (he was the elder brother of Julia Ward Howe), vulgar.

To people like Emily's conservative mother, it seemed that vulgar excess was the favorite currency of the day. On March 13, 1893, William Waldorf Astor's opulent thirteen-floor Waldorf Hotel on Fifth Avenue, at the site of today's Empire State Building, opened its doors to the exceptionally well-heeled. Four years later William's jealous cousin John Jacob Astor IV responded to the challenge by building his own hotel, the Astoria, its additional four stories ensuring that, temporarily, it dominated the family power struggle. But in spite of the new competition from the hotels' restaurants, Delmonico's remained New York's premier place to eat, in large part due to the decades of loyalty it had bred among Emily's crowd. If a sense of foreign luxury was what you sought, you ate at the new fancy restaurants, where you were coddled if you were part of the privileged class and snubbed if you weren't. If elegance that didn't have to shout was more your style, you chose Delmonico's.

EMILY WAS TOO FAR along in her pregnancy to attend the marriage ceremony of Sadie Price, her absence making the wedding wardrobe she passed down to her favorite cousin all the more poignant for both her and the bride. That spring, in "the most fashionable wedding" held in Baltimore "in recent years," Sadie pledged her troth to the handsome, notorious playboy Archibald Pell. Accompanied by her father, lawyer Benjamin Price, she met her bridesmaids at the door of the Grace Protestant Episcopal church at twelve-thirty on the dot. Of course—this was Baltimore—the young ladies carried gardenias, the dense perfume of the lustrous white petals headily spiraling through the church air. To Emily's great joy, Archie Pell's business interests dictated that her cousin would be moving to Manhattan.

Though the Posts themselves would be relocating soon as well, they would still be able to get easily from their new neighborhood to Sadie's home. To their families' initial shock, Emily and Edwin had decided to move to Dongan Hills, an attractive but simple suburb on Staten Island. By this point, Emily had come to realize that as much as she worshipped

Tuxedo Park, its ceremony demanded more than she was up to these days. Wryly, years later, she would recall, "Tuxedo was the most formal place in the world. Nobody ever waved or hello-ed or hi-ed at Tuxedo. You bowed when you shook hands.... [F]irst names were considered very bad form. You might be Johnny in private, but you were Mr. Jones in public. There were only five men in Tuxedo who called me Emily, and then never in formal Society."

On Staten Island in 1893, the pace was slower and more relaxed, the expectations not so overwhelming, the afternoon at-homes far fewer—a perfect rhythm for a woman with child. In addition, Emily expressed to a few close friends her desire to escape the elaborate entertaining that held New York and Tuxedo Park social life in its thrall. That was exhausting for her to contemplate now; she was ambivalent, as well, about sharing her changing shape (however elaborately disguised) and dramatic new status as an expectant mother with the people who had nurtured her as their local princess. She always disliked being seen at less than her best.

Horse-drawn vans and local ferries transported the Posts' furniture from their Manhattan apartment to their undistinguished but still attractively homey neighborhood. Emily proudly considered herself frugal in light of what she deemed her modest five-bedroom rental, where, in addition to her little family, three house servants would live. An attached stable boarded the Posts' three horses, and the rooms above the stalls housed a groom and coachman who would double as an odd-job man. On most days, a gardener joined the staff as well.

Contrary to her later recollection that she knew no one when she moved to Staten Island, census records show that several of Emily's Baltimore relatives had moved to the island over the last few decades. Furthermore, Benjamin Price's wife visited the island frequently, bringing Sadie's sister Marie with her. Finally, Marion Price, one of Bruce's favorite siblings, had offspring living in New Brighton, Staten Island, a few miles from Dongan Hills. Such family members, Emily included, routinely appeared in coverage of the island's social events during the years that she and Edwin lived on the island. Given her love of the Baltimore clan, the Dongan Hills residence must have offered security, tranquillity, and companionship to an anxious young bride in need of all three.

UNDENIABLY, STATEN ISLAND played an insignificant part in New York City's sophisticated urban rhythms. When Emily first told Josephine about the move, her mother was bewildered. Everything her daughter needed was close at hand: Tuxedo Park even had its own resident doctor now, a recent Columbia graduate. The community paid Dr. Edward Rushmore the equivalent of $35,000 a year in today's currency, compensating for the modest salary by providing him with free lodging over the town drugstore. With the park's small two-horse wagons on perpetual duty, all Emily would have to do was pick up the phone for immediate service: Tuxedo, Pierre Lorillard was quick to boast, already had a universal telephone service, unusual for such a small organization.

Responding to Josephine's near panic, Emily explained that she'd already employed an obstetrician. Dr. Kinnaird had lectured on childbirth at New York Hospital, but when Emily told her mother that the new specialty was very scientific, Mrs. Price retorted that it sounded like another fad to her; midwives, after all, had been around for centuries. Who needed an "obstetrician"? she sniffed. What finally convinced Josephine was Emily's promise to install a telephone in her new house so that she could call her Manhattan doctor as soon as she went into labor. Dr. Kinnaird would immediately take his one-horse brougham to the South Ferry, where he would catch a boat—they ran regularly—to Staten Island. There Edwin would meet him for a quick two-mile trip to reach the mother-to-be.

But Emily really won the argument when she pointed out the ease with which Edwin could get from Dongan Hills to Wall Street. After that, Josephine put up no resistance. She enjoyed her son-in-law's company immensely, his interests far closer to her own than her daughter's had ever been. He was eager to join the successful young bucks increasingly in the public eye, such impatience much to his mother-in-law's approval. Edwin and Emily had married when society was undergoing a transition from promoting rich, idle men-about-town to a model where even the wealthiest sought self-worth from their jobs. Josie's easy alliance with Edwin, all the more obvious compared to his stiff relationship with Bruce, only inured the young wife further against her husband's charms. Josephine was not the parent Emily admired.

Not only Josie but Edwin himself had needed to be convinced of his wife's plan. He believed in the power of the right address, and his family had a long-established social history on Long Island, not Staten Island, where he'd never even had reason to visit. The Posts had been living on the South Shore for nine generations. Emily reminded him, however, that a decade before the Civil War, southerners (including the Price family) had started building what were often grand houses overlooking the Narrows, in order to escape the summer heat at home. More recently, Commodore Vanderbilt had furthered his fortune by ferrying passengers from White-hall Street, at the southern tip of Manhattan, to Richmond, the Staten Is-land loading site. The Vanderbilt ferries ran at frequent intervals around the clock, making the trip pleasant and efficient. It took only an hour for commuters like Edwin to get to Wall Street each morning.

In truth, for Edwin, anything would be better than spending the sum-mer at Tuxedo Park. He found its mise-en-scène absurd: the gamekeepers; grown men as property guards, walking around in Tyrolean costumes; the artificially stocked lake. It was all humiliating to a real sportsman like him-self. And Emily was right: this new residence made for a better commute as well.

In no time at all, Edwin began to consider keeping a boat moored nearby, though—or maybe because—he knew his wife would dislike the idea. Once he had gotten over his initial disappointment at Emily's disre-gard for the water, he had realized it might work to his advantage. Early on, he'd stopped trying to entice her to join him at sea, realizing that now he could always escape home life when it threatened to suffocate him

Even if he knew what he himself wanted, Edwin had little idea what made up his twenty-year-old wife. His feelings for her were based mostly on pride of possession; he had no interest in the actual contents of the ele-gant package. Replicating his father's failure to confront his unhappiness in the face of Caroline McLean Post's controlling behavior, he unwittingly set up his own marriage on a fault line. He neglected to notice that his wife and their relationship would benefit from a very different dynamic. Like his mother, Emily was strong and commanding. But unlike Caroline, she was funny and open to change. In the nostalgic haze cast by the passage of time, it is tempting to believe that the Edwin who loved Emily's type and the debutante who never got over her feelings for her handsome prince should have made a go of it.

By the time Emily wed, the women's suffrage movement and other feminist causes had begun exerting a national influence. Today, the solu-tions promoted by those early leaders seem as oppressive as they were lib-erating. A league of thousands of professional women, called the "new abolitionists," had sought to ban both abortion and contraception begin-ning in about 1860, because the members believed that the need for birth control stemmed from men's selfish impulses. These women, the well-regarded temperance leader and reformer Frances Willard among them, associated unwanted pregnancies with men who lacked a proper regard for women. If society would apply a uniform standard of acceptable sexual behavior, so that men and women "respected" each other equally, unwanted babies would not be born. Nor, of course, would married couples have much sex.

Around the time the Posts married, society marriages had privately begun to implode. Soon they would be blowing up publicly as well. Occurring on the heels of the Newport divorces of Mrs. Jennie Fosdick and Mrs. Henry Turnbull, the collapse of the marriage of Commodore Vanderbilt's grandson consumed the gossip sheets of 1887. The separations were often inspired by the women's unhappiness at what their unions had—or hadn't—wrought, the expectations not even voiced, let alone met. Most people believed that the rash of uncoupling was just a bizarre cultural glitch and that the world would soon right itself. Little did they understand that this was only the beginning.

CHAPTER 17

THE SUMMER OF 1893 WOULD PROVE A LESS THAN IDEAL TIME FOR Emily to have her first baby. Edwin was preoccupied all the preceding winter with playing the market, certain it was about to collapse, with spoils going to those clever enough to bet on the right side. His confidence incited him to gamble more than Emily liked, especially given his father's predilection for unwise speculation. But her husband, believing that any money he lost would be more than compensated for by his next win, loved the rush that followed a wager on the right stock. He saw himself as a wise cosmopolitan, though his spouse feared he wasn't self-aware and that his confidence was ill-placed.

While Edwin was consumed with building a profile in the business world, his wife's world was steadily shrinking—by her own choice. Emily was turning inward. To her alarm, in the middle of her pregnancy she had begun to sense an estrangement from her husband, though he seemed oblivious to any marital discontent. Maybe it was something wrong with her, she worried. But what if Edwin became even more of a stranger as the years progressed? Her parents seemed to have created a companionate partnership, while Emily, increasingly, felt unable to reach her husband. Guiltily perceiving that she actually preferred a certain distance, she became anxious that her child might suffer from her need for solitude and interior space; maybe she would prove to be a bad mother.

Edwin had no such concerns about his impending fatherhood. He was flying high—higher week by week. His acumen paid off, his native shrewdness and expensive education together justifying Josephine's confidence. Two months after Grover Cleveland took office, delivering the inaugural address in March, yet another stock market swing touched off one of the worst depressions in United States history. Banks failed, factories closed. Prices for farm crops, already low, went lower. Thousands lost their jobs. Layoffs, strikes: while the country's finances, not to mention its collective morale, continued to fall, Edwin Post's income, along with his high spirits, rose daily. He had bet just right.

During the subsequent crash and depression, railroad companies defaulted at such a rate that the 1890s would see one-quarter of the nation's railroads go bankrupt—more than at any other time in American history. In its impact on the entire country, the depression that spanned the nineties was on a par with the Great Depression of the 1930s. Yet in spite of such hard times—or because of them—an astonishing one-third of the nation's population would attend the Chicago world's fair that summer and fall. Even for a depressed economy, the fair's prices were affordable. General admission was 50¢, the rough equivalent of $5 today. The White City recorded 27.5 million visits in a country whose population numbered 65 million.

The exposition was the center of conversation whenever Edwin's extended family gathered that year. At least Emily, heavy with child, could talk architecture with her relatives: George Post was the man of the hour. The hallmark of the exhibition, the one that would go down in the history books, was the Manufacturers and Liberal Arts Building, which Post had engineered. By the end of 1893, anyone in Chicago or New York who followed the news had learned his name. Staged partly in response to Paris's erection of the Eiffel Tower in 1889, the fair was represented by America's best, with George Post leading the list.

Some historians consider the Chicago world's fair of 1893 an epochal event that portended events of the next several decades. Its legacies remain astonishing in both number and breadth: the first elevated electric railway, a movable sidewalk, and a kinetograph (Thomas Edison's test run for what would be the movie projector), to name just a few. And the more ordinary innovations were no less influential: Cracker Jack, Aunt Jemima syrup (its racist trademark unnoticed), Cream of Wheat, shredded wheat, Wrigley's Juicy Fruit gum, soda pop. The hamburger made its national appearance at the fair. Scott Joplin, a child prodigy born to former slaves, gave a show that let everyone know they'd be hearing from him for a long time to come.

Not a few New Yorkers had doubted that Chicago could pull off such an exhibition. Nonetheless, most easterners remembered their manners and expressed their reservations behind their hands. Sure, there was the occasional competitive tabloid jab at the country's premier slaughterhouse, but there were limits, and everyone seemed to know what they were.

Except for the tutor to high society himself, Ward McAllister.

To New Yorkers' chagrin, the affected, overbearing McAllister suddenly took it upon himself to pontificate on class—to tell the citizens of Chicago how to get it, how to show it, how to keep it. In an article for the *New York World,* McAllister even advised the natives on how to behave like New Yorkers. To begin with, suggested the self-appointed Yankee representative with the startling Savannah accent, Chicago hostesses should import French chefs so that eastern visitors could avoid the midwestern mutton he had been told was indigenous to their smelly city.

Emily would later use Ward McAllister, an omnipresent figure in her youth and young adulthood, as the model of a social misfit: "He works himself up into a perfect ecstasy over his own wit, holds his sides over the point of his own stories, and lets the tears run down his cheeks over his own pathos. When he meets with great genius he says he must bow to the dust, so he probably kisses his own shoes before he puts them on his sacred feet. He is clever, but his wit is directed towards the unnatural and distorted, and no subject is too bizarre for his pen. He thinks he is a student of nature, yet he worships only its freaks—himself."

She despised McAllister's kind of posturing throughout her life, sharing with her father the disdain for puffed-up self-regard that Bruce had expressed toward Reverend Parkhurst. McAllister's promise to teach his readers how to "arrive" smacked of the very parvenu behavior he warned people "of quality" to eschew. Emily's privileged background would at times blind her to her own prejudices, but her childhood training had successfully taught her to shun the pretentious. She sided completely with the irritated but good-natured Chicago journalists who put McAllister in his place by flourishing fulsome apologies in their newspapers for being obviously unworthy of his notice. They hoped, in fact, that their would-be tutor felt no need to ever step foot in their city.

ON JUNE 2, 1893, a day after Edwin and Emily Post's first wedding anniversary, Edwin Main Post Jr. was born. Although unusually large for the times, at nine pounds, four ounces, he was about the same size Emily had been as an infant. For weeks preceding his son's arrival, Edwin had talked excitedly about the way the silver market was quaking beneath their feet, and Emily had tried to look interested. Five days after the baby's birth, while the new mother was still resting in bed, the value of American silver fell dramatically, setting the stage for national disaster. Edwin, triumphant, didn't see it that way, assuring his wife that he had wagered well on their behalf.

The failure of the railroads earlier that year had helped precipitate one of the worst panics the country had known, resulting in nonstop runs on banks in Chicago and New York. But though the subsequent silver panic of '93 would ruin many investors, it would reward Edwin Post with his first million. Shrewdly, patiently, he extracted a killing from the calamity when it finally occurred. Not only he but, with his advice, Josephine had bought President Cleveland's new government bonds just before the market crashed. Bruce's predilection for letting his wife deal with the family income paid off handsomely, as Josie and Edwin both sold their bonds with an eighteen-point increase a few months later. With his profits, Edwin was headed for a Stock Exchange seat and the purchase of the dream yacht he talked about incessantly.

By September, Josie, always up for adventure, felt secure enough about Emily's postpartum expertise that she and Bruce headed west for the Chicago exhibition. Though they had lived in Staten Island for several months before the baby's birth that summer, Emily had still not changed her social register address from the Manhattan apartment. The register requested an update that October, a query that Edwin, not the harried new mother, finally answered six months later. His renewal indicated the Posts' "summer address" only as New Brighton, Staten Island, though they intended to stay throughout the winter of 1893–94. Edwin had invested his silver profits for social good: this year, in contrast to last year, when he'd answered "0," he listed two fairly prestigious men's club memberships, the Union and the downtown St. Anthony. Edwin Post was on the move.

That October 13, the young stockbroker, trying hard to impress his imposing father-in-law, took Bruce Price to a yacht race. Along with nearly four hundred other members and guests of the New York Yacht Club, among them wives who, unlike Emily, enjoyed sailing with their husbands, the two men boarded the steamer *St. John,* following just behind the yachts that were racing. The roll of the boat from side to side caused several men to lose their lunches, the turmoil almost seeming to reflect the tense relationship between Emily's two leading men.

The Prices and the Posts saw relatively little of one another anyway; both couples were always busy. As the season progressed, the first early snowfall made Emily nostalgic, briefly, for the times she had participated in the occasional winter sport, especially the iceboating so popular at Tuxedo Park. This year, however, she wouldn't have many hours to indulge in an activity best shared by lovers anyway, the glow of Tuxedo Park's new electric lights transforming the ordinary into the fantastic. She was too busy supervising her servants and tending to her infant. Decades later, she would emphasize that the regularity of a baby's routine leads to a healthier, "more tranquil," and better-adjusted individual. Everything from daily baths to exercise to bedtimes and meals to playing with family members and pets served children best by being predictable. No, she would not be iceboating anytime soon.

When her son was six months old, she put him (and herself) to the test. On December 10, 1893, Edwin Main Post Jr. (known from his youngest days as Ned, in order to distinguish him from his father) was baptized at St. Mary's Episcopal Church in Tuxedo Park. He performed beautifully. Because Bruce Price and Caroline McLean Post were still at odds over their disagreement about Dr. Parkhurst, Emily arranged the ceremony, with her parents' complete agreement, to coincide with her parents' unfortunate prior commitment. They needed to attend the official opening in Old Quebec of the Château Frontenac, Bruce's most recent building. Of course everyone knew that the baptism date could have been changed, but they pretended otherwise. After all, to save people's feelings, granting "loose rein" to the imagination was sometimes called for. "*Toujours la politesse, jamais la vérité*" (always courtesy, never the bare truth) was the motto Emily endorsed. As she later explained, it was incumbent upon decent people everywhere to avoid hurting others' feelings.

In any case, Bruce Price was always happy whenever his work took him back to Canada. Especially now that he had finished the Château Frontenac, high on a bluff overlooking the appropriately grandiose St. Lawrence River, he was treated as one of the country's own. Even three years earlier, when he'd toured the dominion with the Duke of Connaught (Queen Victoria's son, later governor-general of Canada), he had been mistaken for the duke himself when they exited the train side by side. The cheering crowds believed him princely looking, Emily later explained. Bruce had apologized to His Royal Highness for the confusion, only to be told "Never mind, Bruce. It isn't your fault that God made you in the perfect image of a duke." It was a story recounted by the daughter of the "duke" throughout her life.

EMILY STILL HAD PLENTY to distract her, her parents' expedient absence only one puzzle piece among many that needed to be set in place. The evening before the christening, the uncharacteristically nervous wife gave a lavish dinner at Tuxedo Park for family and friends, including Edwin's cousins Regis Post and Esther Voss and his best friend, Lyman Colt, all godparents to Ned. Delmonico's cookbook once again provided the menu, with a few southern flourishes. Among Emily's choices were doxie Rockaway oysters, consommé imperial, braised sweetbreads, sauce duxelles, spinach, roast canvasback duck with hominy, and apple fritters. The weekend was a success, just as Josie, before leaving town, had assured her daughter it would be. In her ledger, Emily entered, "Things about the Baby: Ned was christened Sun . . . at 11:20 A.M. . . . He was as good as gold until the water was put on him and then he howled. He threw Regis's matchbox around all during prayer."

Successfully handling such potential minefields as her baby's baptism, Emily grew in confidence. In her accounts book—which she repeatedly explained was not a diary but a practical record—she nonetheless began to record her thoughts, analyzing what made her especially happy. Thriving on the approval sure to follow her finely tuned dinner parties, she realized that she gained great fulfillment by supporting her husband's efforts to shine. Increasingly reflective, she noted what she had discovered about her own needs and desires: "I don't want men to be in love with me, but to enjoy me, admire me, love me a little. But not make demands. I don't want to be emotionally stirred up. I want to be left to myself. Perhaps that's why I wanted to be an actress. An actress has, or she should have, the footlights between her and her audience. I think I don't want anyone to come too close."

It seems likely that such reflections were defensive, the disillusioned young wife hiding from herself the depth of her marital disappointment. From observing Bruce and Josie, she had assumed that she and Edwin would naturally accompany each other to most social events, or that she at least would receive Edwin's sincere gratitude for enabling him to succeed in society while she stayed home. In part, she had simply failed to consider that by the time she observed her parents she herself was no longer a baby in need of constant care. The other conflict drew upon Emily's nature, private in spite of her extroverted personality. Recently, as the December balls and the season's society pages had focused on the season's new debutantes, she'd realized with a start, as she'd listened to Edwin brag about how his gallant older brother, A.V.Z. Post, led Mrs. Twombly's dance for the "younger set," that she was oddly content with her solitude.

The energies she had once used dancing until the early morning hours she redirected to the demanding routines of a new mother and an exemplary wife. Determined to be a perfect spouse for a successful man to come home to, she was more likely these days to be overseeing the apple fritters Edwin relished than learning a new dance step. She never liked to do less than her best. That Edwin had been attracted to her precisely because of her dramatic sensibility escaped her notice. Determined to please, Emily gave up the very part of herself that had seduced the man she'd married.

WHILE EMILY WAS immersed in the quotidian, her father was at the peak of his professional and social power. Bruce Price would return from Montreal that December to work on what would be the highest structure in his own country, the American Surety Building. Located in lower Manhattan, at the southeast corner of Pine and Broadway, the skyscraper was the prize won in a fierce competition. The contestants had been told that the first priority was to plan "the greatest possible amount of renting area . . . on each floor, and then to give an outward form in keeping with the importance and height of the structure." In order for the $1.25 million construction to be economically feasible, it needed to be at least fifteen stories high.

Bruce had been honored, even surprised, to be invited to compete against the city's nine most important architects, including McKim, Mead and White, Carrère and Hastings, and N. LeBrun and Sons. Of course, as always, George Post had been asked to submit designs as well. If going up against Edwin's older, illustrious cousin bothered Bruce—he had lost to him many times in the past—he knew that such feelings were self-indulgent. George Post was considered a giant among the New York group, and a worthy man to lose to.

But Bruce Price had won instead. His design was the simplest and most severe of all the proposals, exceptional for its flat roof. Though no one in the Price family recalled the circumstances of the commission, years later, the architect Warren Briggs, Bruce's friend, cheerfully filled in the details. As he recounted how Bruce had been selected to design the skyscraper, he clearly meant to flatter Emily's father, but the story demotes him professionally instead. The competition narrowed to two renderings, with the committee certain that they recognized the architects behind their preference. They agreed to act surprised when McKim, Mead and White was pronounced the winner, the design's mannerisms speaking distinctly of its firm's provenance. In private, the committee was pleased they had chosen a firm that would pose no risk, given the size of this project. The men "were more than astonished, upon opening the sealed envelopes containing the authors' names" to find that the award was going to Bruce Price. "So a new architectural star of the first magnitude was born. My friend had reached his goal, his perseverance was finally rewarded," Briggs remembered happily.

It was particularly sweet justice at that. Four years earlier, Bruce had created a building proposal for the New York Sun newspaper, the city's largest daily, a thirty-one-story version of the campanile in Venice's St. Mark's Square, complete with a three-story triumphal arch. Though the building was never constructed, it would remain a point of reference for architects for the next fifty years. More important to Emily's father, it was a design to revisit in 1894, when he transformed the much lauded but unexecuted Sun building plans into his even stronger vision for the American Surety skyscraper, recycling those blueprints into a little bit of Italy down near Wall Street.

Hundreds of spectators, enabled by new mass transportation, gathered daily to watch Bruce's building in progress. Modernity had staked its ground: the els ran the length of Manhattan and through the Bronx, Brooklyn, and Queens, each day moving several hundred thousand passengers for modest fares. Getting into and out of Manhattan no longer required elaborate planning. Now the yard of Trinity Church, across the street from Bruce's building, filled each morning with anxious onlookers who believed the odds were against the behemoth standing once it conquered twenty stories. But it did. The original steel-frame superstructure sheathed with Maine granite (altered through the years) measured 312 feet high, its bulk resting on concrete and brick caissons sunk 72 feet in order to rest on bedrock.

The American Surety Building at 100 Broadway, still in the heart of the city's Financial District today, quickly became a popular and fully tenanted success. For one year, it would be the tallest building in the world. Bruce Price's skyscraper, dug deep into the ground the same year his daughter's marriage was getting off to an earnest, well-intentioned start, would, according to the New York Times architecture critic, "set a new standard of clarity of composition, lavishness of classic detail, and careful refinement."

Bruce was the right man for the right job at the right time, and his daughter beamed with pride at the plaudits he earned. As soon as she was able, she spent hours at the construction site, watching the skyscraper take its final shape—just as she had tagged along with Bruce as a girl. Years afterward, Emily Post would acknowledge the role successful adults play in a child's development: "That children, whether small or grown, admire [their parents'] actual achievement, is not even to be questioned," she asserted, still in awe of her gifted father decades later.

⁂

CHAPTER 18

E DWIN WAS SPENDING MORE TIME THAN USUAL WITH HIS OWN FA-
ther these days, probably to escape the demanding newborn at home.
When the weather was even marginally warm, the *Macy* log records an average of two or three days a week that would find him on the water with
family or friends. By March 1894, he was shooting so well that an early
spring weekend caused him to crow: "Red letter day," followed by "another
clear delightful day," enabling him to take home a "bag of 69 birds for the
two days." Growing giddy from his success, Edwin quoted Coleridge in the
ship's log: "a painted ship upon a painted ocean," he wrote, assuming that
anyone reading the entry would understand the allusion to "The Rime of
the Ancient Mariner."

He loved the *Macy*. But this was his father's boat, not his. And it was not
a boat built for speed. Everyone around him seemed to be moving up, as if
the Dutch word *yacht* itself conferred instant class as well as the implication
of astonishing new fortunes. By 1890 yachting was the Gilded Age's premier activity for the rich, and the owner of a yacht was assumed to possess
"really big money." Edwin's crowd might be nervously finessing the current
economic climate, but most of them had no trouble building on their net
worth.

If yachting was society's most expensive sport—and Edwin's passion—
it was among Emily's least favorite activities. The annual cruise of the entire New York Yacht Club to Newport each August was the year's highlight
for the rich. Members jostled for the fleet's best positions, and Edwin was
calculating stock market earnings that would enable him to join them. His

aspirations cast a cloud on Emily's vision for leisurely family summers. She found the yacht culture ostentatious, if only because it seemed built upon greed and competition—unlike, for instance, that of the Knickerbocker Club and its kin. Emily assumed that underneath his bluster, her blue-blooded husband sympathized with her view and that at some level, his boyish enthusiasm aside, he agreed with her assessment. Such confidence was dangerously ill-placed.

That spring, at least, her determination to take a positive view of her life seemed justified when Pierpont Morgan gave his daughter Juliet a cottage at Tuxedo as a wedding present. The two longtime friends would share motherhood and marriage—however poorly the latter served them both—through the years. Juliet had requested that the bishop who presided at Emily's wedding, a relative of the Hamiltons as well as the Posts, return from Minnesota to preside at her own nuptials. Unfortunately, Reverend Whipple seems to have functioned as a bad-luck talisman. Juliet Morgan Hamilton would divorce, though her husband would hold on strategically until his illustrious father-in-law was long dead and the estate settled, with William Hamilton himself as one of the will's executors.

But for now, as radiant a bride as Emily had been, an equally exquisite Juliet Morgan walked down the long aisle of Manhattan's Protestant Episcopal Church, overcrowded with three thousand guests from Boston, Philadelphia, Washington, Baltimore, and London. Her white satin dress was trimmed with point lace ruffles on the bodice and skirt, and a crown of diamonds fastened her lace veil, which hung delicately over her train. Elaborate masses of lilies and Jacqueminot roses filled the vestibule, while rare tropical palms crisscrossed the chancel, white ribbons trailing the plants at the front of the church. Perfume had become the habit among well-bred women, but it was utterly superfluous in this setting: the luxuriant scent of hothouse flowers enveloped the guests and wedding party both.

SHORTLY AFTER THE MORGAN WEDDING, the *New York Times* ran a full-page article that touted Emily's more modest environs, noting, "Staten Island Has a 'Boom.'" The enthusiastic headlines continued, bubbling awkwardly: "Its many attractions coming to be appreciated. General Movement this spring towards the island—People Going where they can get more for their money than in this city—pretty homes at reasonable rents." Until now, only Staten Islanders had thought they inhabited New York's "most attractive suburb." But the depression of the past few years was affecting the stock markets as well as the ordinary citizen these days. Manhattanites realized they could get a larger house with more property for much less money if they lived on Staten Island, and they'd still be within minutes of Wall Street. Admitting he'd been dubious when told to explore the mass exodus to Staten Island, the *Times* reporter was so impressed by what he saw that he wondered why everyone wasn't relocating to this heretofore hidden paradise.

Emily had reason to be proud: her instincts had proved right, and she had picked a good home for her family. Her choice felt especially fortunate now, since she was pregnant again. She wasn't worried about her husband's occasional frivolity, just privately disappointed. If her father was the pillar of reliability, her husband, she'd already realized, might prove a bit less stable, less straightforward in his personal and work ethics—and less aware of the prize he had in Emily. She consoled herself by deciding that at the very least he was working hard. Edwin was a partner with his own father at H.A.V. Post's Railroad Equipment Company, itself an unstable business. Still, he was always frenetically brokering deals on the side.

His wife took care to work as hard as her husband did. But if Edwin noticed his wife's exhaustive and exhausting contributions to their lives, his appreciation goes unremarked; though he expected kudos at home for his financial acumen, his wife was just doing her job, the details of which she faithfully recorded in her daily log. For the next five years, Emily's ledger highlights her earnest, unceasing efforts to be the proper society wife Edwin expected—and that she had assumed she wanted to be as well. But for a woman accustomed to following the rhythms of an only child all her life, at times her schedule seems to have allowed her no breathing space.

Emily understood that a millionaire in the making needed a wife and a life that would elicit envy and curry favor with other magnates. She worked so hard to fill the role she had signed on for—polished wife and nurturing mother—that she became, in modern parlance, overextended. When she'd had only her husband to think about, it had been challenging enough. Now, parenthood and a pregnancy besides pushed her too hard and she found herself much more irritable than usual.

It's difficult to be sure how much energy, psychic or physical, Emily spent on mothering. Society mothers in the Gilded Age often hired wet nurses and spent little time with their children on a daily basis. In addition to their domestic duties, society women were obligated to drive up and down Fifth Avenue every day during the season, exquisitely bonneted and veiled, wrapped in fur whenever the temperature dropped. At the very least, a retinue of baby attendants allowed Emily more leisure time—however circumscribed by the chores of a lady—during her second pregnancy than most women enjoyed then or do now.

In any case, pregnancy allowed her to read without guilt, begging off daily visiting obligations and other social events whenever she felt like it. Ouida, the pen name for a society woman who turned out popular romances, was one of Emily's frivolous pleasures during her months of confinement, a time she was allowed and even expected to seek the lighthearted. But there were other novels dear to the expectant young mother as well. Her two favorite authors were Mrs. Humphry Ward and Frank Hopkinson Smith, her "Uncle Frank," whose latest book, *A Day at Laguerre's*, was receiving strong early reviews. A robust, warm story based on Hop's life and travels abroad, it clearly reflects its author's liberal good nature.

Emily's ledger sometimes deviated from reporting on her activities in favor of ruminating about child rearing. Treating the emotional highs and lows of her days as if making an inventory of kitchen supplies, she also considered mistakes that wounded her as well as her child: "I started to spank Ned. . . . The more I hurt him, the more determined he became not to obey. . . . I will never spank him again." She was worried about her mothering. The countless hours she spent daily on preparing her wardrobe, supervising the servants, and tending to whatever tasks the household presented left her unsure that she, not the nannies, knew best; perhaps they were the greater influence on her child's development.

THAT AUTUMN, EMILY again didn't attend the Tuxedo ball, her socializing temporarily diminished. Edwin, however, spent more time away from home than ever, energetically mixing with chaps who could forward his career. He found himself enjoying his forays into the men's clubs almost as much as his time on the bay. Almost, but not quite: very little could compete with the savory smells of the four A.M. breakfasts he anticipated throughout his workweek. As in the previous year, at least two weekends a month all season, according to the *Macy's* log, Edwin went out with family or friends on the Great South Bay. He was bagging so many ducks that it was impossible to give them all away.

While her husband hunted, Emily's father prepared to finish the American Surety skyscraper—making its creator a hero. Though still in progress, the nearly completed building—and Emily's father—were touted in the press almost daily, and Bruce's name was cited even more often than usual in the social pages. At times it seemed that any excuse to hail the architect would do. Two days before Christmas, he attended the annual Virginia eggnog party at Delmonico's, held for the "New-Yorkers, late of Dixie land," who were "known collectively as the Southern Society." Among the attendees—the Polks, Fishes, Olneys, Calhouns, Churches, and Potters, some of the finest old families from the South—Bruce Price's name figured prominently. Here was a man who could gracefully maneuver between past and present, such flexibility among the greatest gifts he would bequeath his daughter.

Named after Emily's father, Bruce Price Post was born on February 9, 1895. Emily and Edwin's second child entered a well-managed household, though it is unclear if it was ever a happy one. An evocative formal portrait of a slender and shapely young mother, due to her prolonged postpartum recovery thinner than she'd been before her pregnancy, shows her in a high-necked dark voile-and-satin gown, a white fringe of lace over the front, an angular navy blue hat pulled close on her head. A depressed, almost sad expression grazing her hooded eyes guaranteed that spectators in real life would keep their distance. In contrast, an insouciant Edwin was appreciating his legroom these days. A well-thumbed snapshot divulges a handsome young buck lying in a hammock on the Posts' Tuxedo Park porch, legs splayed open as he sleeps. His riding boots are still on, as if he can't totally relax in this rarefied environment.

CHAPTER 19

❧

AS THE CENTURY WOUND DOWN, THE PROMISE OF CHANGE IN-
evitably implied by a fin de siècle dovetailed neatly with late Gilded Age
ennui, a merger that would further loosen Victorian holds on the fairer sex.
The right to participate fully in the laws of the nation was important to
most upper-class women. "We have got the new woman in everything except the counting of her vote at the ballot box," Susan B. Anthony said in
1895. "And that's coming." Outspoken feminists were not the only ones
marching: society women were often at their sides or, if at home, sponsoring teas for suffrage.

A strong contingent, nonetheless, did not support the efforts to place
the softer sex in the public's eyes, including Juliet Morgan, who disapproved of her younger sister Anne's public works. Two contrasting visions
clashed as the decade waned. Josephine, for instance, fettered by insecurity
over her anthracite heritage, still felt the need to prove she was genteel. A
strong, independent woman in charge of the family's finances, she was
nonetheless contemptuous of forward ladies who took public credit for
their accomplishments. She agreed with the etiquette spokeswoman of her
generation, the Post family friend Mrs. John (Mary) Sherwood, who had
recently declared, "Society is going to the everlasting bow-wows." It was
bad enough that the bicycle was threatening the city's morals. Even worse
were the appalling, aggressive, noisy socialites such as Mrs. Belmont, Mrs.
Fish, and Mrs. Vanderbilt—the very kind of women who gave society a bad
name.

As Anne Morgan had proved, some society women were willing to be pioneers, in spite of the ridicule they had to suffer. More women of all ranks joined the feminist cause daily, even if they failed to name it thus. Increasingly liberal ideas toward gender coincided with reconceived notions of racial differences. On June 15, 1895, New York's governor signed civil rights legislation, the Maltby Act, into law. The next day, three "Negro gentlemen" set out to test their liberation by visiting three restaurants. They were refused seating each time. Finally, at Delmonico's—though with scenes of nervousness and disapproval—they were politely served, the momentous event documented by excited reporters. From comments Emily made ten years later, she would have disapproved of the discomfort the scene created, and would undoubtedly have glossed over the real issue of skin color.

COMFORTABLE WITH THE STATE of her family finances and proud of her quick adjustment to motherhood, Emily turned her attention to moving back home. Edwin's investments were paying off, and so the Post family left Staten Island for Manhattan, where, with help from Emily's in-laws, they bought a handsome row house at 217 West Seventy-ninth Street.

The Posts' financial assistance, predictably, came with obligations. In lieu of spending much time in Tuxedo or traveling abroad during the unseasonably hot weather, Emily had to consign most of her vacation to Babylon, an enclave of old families who, as she saw it, were obsessed with the water. But the children could go swimming there so easily, as well as accompany their father on the *Macy*, and Emily reluctantly admitted that the South Bay Post family residence made sense just now, especially since it allowed her children to escape the dangerous heat wave reaching almost to Tuxedo as it blanketed Manhattan. During the nine days that the temperature rose above ninety degrees, 420 people died in the city. Hundreds of dead horses were left to rot on the streets, dying faster than they could be collected. Because of the weather, the Posts stayed in Babylon until the end of the summer.

Finally, sequestered back at Tuxedo Park for the fall season, Emily felt her relief short-lived: Edwin was working even longer hours than he had last spring. To make matters worse, he explained that such exertion earned him the right to use his rare leisure hours taking the *Macy* out on the already chilly bay—this season without his children. According to one of his typically effusive log entries, when a man stepped aboard the *Macy*, "all his cares in the world vanished." Though Emily failed to acknowledge the *Macy* in her otherwise meticulous records, the rest of the Post family practically revered the fifty-foot-long sloop. Considered luxurious for its day, it was furnished with one coal stove in the galley, a second coal stove for winter, and a toilet (or head, according to the proper nomenclature of the sea). Emily could have been put to good use on the boat: if ever a sport called for her skill at inventory, this was it, at least the way the Post men treated their weekend voyages. Long lists of every species of duck they bagged fill the ship's log, complete with Edwin's talented, playful caricatures of all mates on board.

At least Emily was not expected to serve duck dinners all season. Her infrequent social appearances throughout the winter, coupled with vague references Ned later made, suggest that she probably had both a hysterectomy and a gallbladder removal before the year was over. The Roosevelt Hospital doctors were amazed at her eagerness to learn everything, from understanding medical procedures to the way prescriptions were compounded. Her boundless, intelligent curiosity earned their respect, and after her recovery she was invited into the operating theater to sit with the medical students. In gratitude for the first-rate care, the ex-patient subsequently established a weekly hospital visit, a routine lasting for several years: as a volunteer, she read mail to and wrote letters for patients, sometimes even directing her driver to deliver the correspondence to the invalids' friends and family.

By early March the following year, fully healed, the young matron found herself tending to corporeal matters again, this time as part of the tight inner social circle at Tuxedo Park. James Powell Kernochan, a constant presence at Tuxedo (he was married to Catharine Lorillard, Pierre's daughter), had been rushing down Fifth Avenue to the Waldorf for a meeting of what was still New York's most exclusive social organization, the Patriarchs. (Though steadily diminished in numbers over the years, the Patriarchs lumbered on, a vestige of the past.) Kernochan, crossing the street without looking, was knocked down and killed by a carriage driven by the banker George F. Baker's daughter, a friend of Emily's. Tuxedo was in an uproar: Baker and Kernochan were both among its premier residents. The tragedy hastened the Patriarchs' collapse, with only eleven of the fifty members attending the next month's meeting. Those present voted to disband the formerly august club.

After caring for her bereaved friends, Emily announced that she needed a vacation, a trip to Europe. She, Edwin, and their sons (toddler Bruce was already one and a half) took the *Teutonic* across the Atlantic. The boys' beloved French nanny, Melanie, carted the children to her family's farm in Normandy. Emily meant for this trip to revivify the romance of her husband's courtship; she wanted Edwin to see her again as the girl he had desired so badly the night of her debut. She was sure that if she worked hard enough, she could rekindle his interest. As they visited mutual friends and relatives in England, France, Germany, and the grand Austro-Hungarian Empire, she would further impress him by teaching him about great European art and architecture, repeating the lessons her tutor Bruce Price had taught her. She meant to win her husband's heart all over again or perhaps, she reluctantly allowed, even for the first time.

Inevitably, given the couple's radically different priorities, the trip was less than successful. When the Posts arrived at the fashionable Brown's Hotel in London, where the afternoon tea was said to be the best in England, Edwin immediately tackled the stack of invitations awaiting them, while Emily wrote long reflective letters to her cousin Sadie. She became preoccupied with the refined Englishwomen she saw everywhere, perhaps in part due to the appreciative gazes they received from Edwin. Though Americans could be quickly identified because they dressed "exquisitely," Emily admired the more subdued English style: "the born Englishwomen . . . wear evening dress with an air many Americans would do well to copy. They never seem to be afraid of it, if you know what I mean. And they don't seem to be blazoning it, either."

In Paris, Edwin repeatedly begged off Emily's intricately choreographed museum excursions. In addition to being deeply disappointed at her husband's lack of interest, she grew furious at her expatriate hostess's condescension. Esther Voss's superior attitude as she commanded Emily along with the castle's servants irritated the now experienced housewife. Unfortunately, the offender was Edwin's favorite cousin and Ned's godmother, a countess by marriage. The night the Posts arrived, Esther had presumed to instruct her cousin-in-law on appropriate dress for Maxim's. Compounding her humiliation, Edwin had been graceless enough to suggest that Emily listen and learn, his easy assumption of his cousin's superiority making Emily almost apoplectic. She prided herself on her unerring sense of style, a self-assessment echoed by others, and Edwin's lack of appreciation offended her more than his cousin's recently acquired hauteur.

But Emily knew how to give as well as she got, and now she seized the chance to employ her talent for impersonations. After all, she reasoned,

Edwin, who reveled in her theatrical nature, had urged her to exploit her gift of mimicry. Playing charades, Emily imitated Esther's cavalier treatment of the maids, her performance drawing applause from everyone except the countess, who turned bright red and left the room.

The escalating tension between the two women encouraged Edwin to turn his wife over to another royal relative, Viktor, or "Vico," the younger brother of Count Hans Voss, Esther's husband. While Edwin escaped to go hiking, Emily, Vico at her side, could tour the art galleries. After a few weeks of his wife's daily museum trips with the officious count, however, Edwin grew nervous; intuition told him something was amiss.

His instincts were correct. Vico picked flowers for Emily and insisted that they stop for long, extravagant midday meals. He took her to outdoor gardens filled with nude voluptuaries, one of which she mentioned, quite deliberately, to Edwin. Vico was flirting outrageously with someone he viewed as a typically neglected American wife. And Emily was luxuriating in the perfectly proper attention kept within the boundaries of decorum, its sexual tension genteelly implied.

Alarmed at what he sensed was Emily's potential love affair, Edwin missed his wife's plea for his attention: Didn't Vico have the worst possible taste in art? she asked, urging him to understand. Instead of listening, Edwin rushed out and bought Emily an oversized copy of a Jean-Léon Gérôme garden sculpture Vico had appreciated, to Emily's private dismay. Gérôme, a late-nineteenth-century artist who specialized in nudes, including slave women, was at best full of passion. To some, such as Emily's teacher Bruce Price, Gérôme's sculptures were ridiculous and overwrought. Edwin proudly presented the overlarge statue to Emily before they boarded the ship home.

She wanted to laugh. Looking at her still sophomoric and certainly untutored husband, Emily realized that he couldn't tell the difference between the original that Vico and she had examined and the replica—to him, they were equally expert. Edwin's look of pleasure, what she would later call a "little-boy look of satisfaction from having done the right thing," stopped her from lecturing him on quality. She could only hope, she would recall in later years, that the statue would break on the way back to the States, but it didn't. In fact, the safe passage managed by the suspiciously well-packed replica every time Emily moved suggests she associated her husband's purchase with a rare effort to win her heart.

But Edwin's attempt to impress Emily through his knowledge of the

arts was a bad idea that only emphasized his lack of awareness: Bruce Price
had the lock on that showground, and Edwin's obviously weak aesthetic
judgment further alienated Emily. Comparisons between classical statues
and one's lovers were popular these days, and frequently, at dinner parties
just before they'd left for France, Emily had recounted how she had happily
rearranged her father's hands in his lap throughout her adolescence. They
were, after all, the exact measurement of those of a famous marble statue
he had once shown her in a museum. One of the Tuxedo Park crowd
bragged that his own body dimensions matched exactly those of a certain
classic figure in the Louvre. Edwin, however, hadn't done the groundwork
to exploit this particular trend, and now he looked foolish in his wife's eyes.
When Bruce Price saw the imitation piece as it was being uncrated, he exclaimed, "My God! Where did that come from?" Or at least that's how
Emily remembered it.

Decidedly a stranger to the art world, Edwin was in his métier as soon
as the Posts returned home from their trip. The *Times* had decided to list his
beloved Great South Bay as one of the best of the New York resort areas,
and he felt the ranking as a personal victory. The community of Babylon
was pronounced "the Newport of Long Island," where one could now boat,
fish, or explore the village's charm, its streets completely illuminated by
electricity. One hour from Manhattan by express train, the community was
notable, the *Times* added, for two illustrious residents, H.A.V. Post and Dr.
Charles Parkhurst.

In spite of his mother's stifling presence, Edwin still much preferred the
authentic South Shore to what he considered the artificially natural environment of Tuxedo Park, a place he found increasingly silly. He'd realized,
after years of efforts on everyone's part, that Emily and Caroline Post
would never get along. Yet for several seasons more, however much his wife
disliked his mother and stern sister Nathalie, Edwin's family of four would
spend part of each summer at Babylon, Emily gamely hiking her long skirts
to her thighs in order to take the boys into the water. She and Mrs. Post du-
eled often over their equally strong beliefs about children, Mrs. Post demanding that her daughter-in-law choose between soft and strict. Instead,
Emily insisted both were appropriate approaches, correct at different
times. Such flexibility made Caroline Post think Emily little more than a
pushover, and she didn't try to hide her disgust.

Feeling alone in the marshy lands Edwin loved most, Emily couldn't
wait to get back to Tuxedo that fall. The Price Colliers had returned to the

park after a five-year self-imposed exile. Emily had found the couple interesting and lively the brief times they'd met years before, and now, in 1897, they would all be reunited at the park's annual autumn rituals. Katharine Delano Robbins, an attractive young widow and sister to F.D.R.'s mother, Sara ("Sally") Delano Roosevelt, had caused a scandal when she'd married the defrocked Unitarian minister Price Collier. A successful diplomat, intellectual historian, and, eventually, bestselling author, he would found the Tuxedo Park Library.

That fall, Katharine, who was to become one of Emily's lifelong friends, seemed to chatter nonstop about the grand house Bruce Price was about to build for her and her husband. Emily loved having someone appreciate both her father and Tuxedo Park almost as much as she did. And now she had this someone to talk to on a regular basis.

As Emily reinstated her annual fall and early winter rituals—dancing at Tuxedo's opening ball, playing in the season's snow with her children—Edwin worked, she sometimes worried, nonstop. Even without his participation, Emily was determined to create the childhood she thought their children deserved. In early December she helped craft a scene for her sons similar to the ones she had reveled in as a child. The boys, dressed as colorful blossoms, strolled through the benefit audience, selling the flower each represented. The fairyland stage reminded her of that magical moment when she was six, debuting on stage in *The Sleeping Beauty*, her parents leading the march. But nostalgia had little place in the Price household, as Josie inadvertently reminded her daughter.

This current event at the Astoria Ballroom raised money for St. Mary's Free Hospital for Children, a charity that Josephine pooh-poohed in favor of trusting to the healing powers her own body and soul possessed. Over the past few years, Josie had come to embrace the Christian Science philosophy of mind over matter. There was no need for hospitals, she believed. Irritated, Emily changed the subject.

⧉

BY AN ACT OF THE STATE LEGISLATURE, ON JANUARY 1, 1898, NEW York City instantly tripled its population. Now, in addition to Manhattan, it included Brooklyn (previously an independent city) and the boroughs of Queens, Staten Island, and the Bronx. That New Year's Day, the new New York encompassed more than 3.5 million people, in contrast to the 1.5 million populating the region when Emily was a baby. Clearly, this was a city marking progress, its horse-drawn carriages yielding to the streetcars that would dominate the city's public transportation till the end of World War II.

As if such expansion and modernization encouraged movement in the social sphere as well, the feminist Elizabeth Cady Stanton and her Revising Committee released *The Woman's Bible,* a reinterpretation of biblical scriptures that the women believed demeaning to their sex. The project managed to offend almost everyone, and the women were widely denounced as deranged. Though such conversation was completely outside of Emily's interests, she took note when the hoopla caused her mother, as intolerant as ever of feminists, to reiterate her belief: in order to change things, people had to emphasize their strengths. Especially for women, calling attention to what they lacked smacked of whining.

Emily, to her surprise, found herself missing Josie these days. Rather than tending to her daughter's toddlers, as Emily had envisioned, Josephine lived for weeks at a time in Canada, where Bruce was working for a large English syndicate, building hotels in Halifax, Montreal, Ottawa, Toronto, and Niagara Falls. The experience of designing the mammoth complex on Long Beach had paid off handsomely: Bruce Price was at the top of his game, while his daughter was just getting started on hers. Emily digested her disquieting realization: she suddenly needed her mother, not her father, to tell her what to do.

IT WAS PROBABLY BETTER that Josie was unable to watch her son-in-law operate just now. Edwin had gone into business with the disreputable cad E. R. Thomas, the louche head of the newly opened Thomas and Post banking offices at 71 Broadway. Hearing that Edwin had teamed up with Thomas could not have pleased Emily's parents. It was well known that Thomas had an indulgent millionaire father who lavishly endowed his son's pleasures, fast actresses and even faster cars. A notorious playboy, Thomas had quickly replaced his first wife, the Posts' friend Linda Lee, a southern belle like Emily, with a succession of minor stage stars.

Thomas's misdeeds took their toll on more than his marriages. During the years Edwin worked with him, his partner's infamous driving killed two people, including a child, in separate accidents. Finally, after being granted legal immunity on one flimsy excuse after another, Thomas would be forced to pause. One day, his 120 horsepower Hotchkiss Vanderbilt Cup racer couldn't stop in time for the carriage in his path. Horses went flying, the passengers lucky to get away with their lives even if the animals didn't. Impatient as ever during his interminable recuperation, Thomas left the New York hospital early and traveled south, where, he believed, the tonic of southern friends would help him heal faster. This was the man Edwin had decided to partner with in 1898.

Giddy with success and the promise of ever more money, Emily's husband had arrived. He now ate a hearty breakfast every morning at the new Luncheon Club at the Stock Exchange, its wood-paneled dining room on the seventh floor encasing the clubby timelessness modern men of the day sought to embody. Here, feasting on oysters before returning to their offices in the late afternoon, the weary but still excited members retired to discuss their latest transactions. This was the life Edwin had confidently expected, but even he was surprised at how quickly it had arrived. As if such triumph on the floor of the exchange wasn't enough to swell his ego, he also was ranked among America's ten best bridge players. During bridge games—yet another enthusiasm he did not share with his wife—Edwin's carefully honed talent for waiting out the other's bluff served him well, while Emily's impatience at lingering inevitably derailed her. Bridge, of all card games, she found particularly exasperating.

A bit startled herself at her zealous domesticity, Emily had discovered that her pleasures lay more at home. She genuinely enjoyed functioning as a prudent and frugal helpmate, though she wished her husband would notice her efforts. Bruce had always appreciated Josephine's thriftiness and eye for a bargain; without his wife's attention to the mundane, he could not have indulged so freely in the imaginative. Mindful of the grandiloquent effect her own husband preferred, Emily religiously recorded the dress she wore to each social event, to ensure that she wouldn't repeat her ensemble when revisiting the same crowd.

Perhaps such outlays of energy on behalf of her family did impress Edwin, but the *Macy*'s logbook that autumn suggests otherwise. While his wife sought little more than his appreciation for her hard work, Edwin was busy scribbling about his discontent at home: For five years he has been living as a married man, having "committed matrimony," and, he wrote, been "sentenced to life for it!" Jocular as always, he penned: "I confess my crime was great; but look at Don Alonzo [Edwin's brother A. V. Post, the bachelor who led all the cotillions], who didn't! He is simply a degenerate. Smokes, swears, drinks 'slow' gin and quick cocktails and has acquired many other habits which render life happy tho unmarried!"

Bright, talented, vivacious young members of society, Edwin and Emily Post lacked guidance in negotiating the cross-purposes of their marriage. Models allowing both husband and wife to express their skills were scarce. Even the exceptional few had to compromise their unions: five years later, Marie Curie was denied the opportunity to accept her half of the Nobel Prize, forced to sit in the audience as Pierre was given the award for both of them. A template for a marriage that comfortably and logically accommodated both wife and husband didn't yet exist.

At least such inadequacies were starting to gain attention. At the end of the summer of 1898, yet another article directed at Emily's social set and its unsatisfying marriages appeared in the *New York Times*. The essay, written by an Englishwoman, bluntly decried the state of married American women, whose lives everyone assumed to be "immeasurably superior" to those of their sisters elsewhere in the world. Englishwomen, especially, were envious of the freedoms granted young American debutantes—until they noticed the girl's odd transformation after her wedding. Subsequent to her earlier freedom, the American socialite had to be "content to sink gracefully into the background as soon as the wedding march is over," the writer noted, her life converted to a "path of duty." The young American wife found herself submerged into "an almost Turkish seclusion," she added. Discouraged from forming friendships with men or participating in sports, she was even denied true companionship with her own often absent husband.

It is tempting to think of wives like Emily sharing the article with their husbands, suggesting options to the lifeless path their marriages had followed. But at the turn of the twentieth century, even voicing the problem took courage. Emily and her friends were not the type to denigrate the institution they had inherited; nor were they willing to shirk what they assumed, unthinkingly, were their proper duties. A "Turkish seclusion" seemed, to most of the socialites, the price they were meant to pay for the financially lucrative life they had signed on for.

THAT AUTUMN, EDWIN, who seemed to find time for any activity that interested him, submitted an article to *Field and Stream*. In January 1899, the magazine published the essay, a reverie about hunting in the Great South Bay. Graceful and informative, it would be anthologized over one hundred years later in a book of sixteen classic hunting tales that included authors such as Theodore Roosevelt and Zane Grey.

"Brant Shooting on Great South Bay" commemorates the intimacy Edwin and H.A.V. Post shared on the water over the years. "Father named the boat *Macy* after an old friend," Edwin wrote, "and has had her continuously in commission since she was launched; ... her first captain is still in charge—a bit gray now." In loving detail, he rehearsed the routine of the hunting party as they lay flat in the boat, waiting to get off their first shot at the ducks. Edwin Post was a more than competent writer. His prose was smooth, while a knowing urbanity offset his temptation to be merely glib. Though in 1910 he would also publish a short story in *Smart Set* magazine, sharing space with major contemporary writers, Emily never encouraged his avocation.

By 1899, the separate directions the couple took daily, emotionally and otherwise, seemed set. On February 11, a blizzard paralyzed New York for most of the month, forcing snowbound market traders such as Edwin to sleep over at their downtown clubs. Emily's ledger noted such absences from home as if they were the norm, business matters their cause as often as foul weather. Her life was not matching the image she had envisioned. She had neither the companion nor the lover that she had assumed marriage would confer. Only the springtime photographs of a laughing young mother standing next to Minnie Gray, Emily's longtime friend from childhood revelries at the park, recapture the vibrant woman who had married Edwin a long seven years ago.

That summer Emily once again joined the legion of wives usually left behind while their husbands navigated the seas. A few days after the annual Fourth of July celebration at Tuxedo Park, Edwin escaped to sail his company's yacht, the *Constance,* to victory in a Long Island Sound regatta. The boat, though modest enough to be entered in the "small category," still triumphed as "best in class." For the entire season, the *Constance* kept winning its seemingly never-ending races, the nonstop success ensuring that Emily saw even less of her husband than usual.

Any blemish on Edwin's happiness that summer came from his father's business troubles, which Bruce Price had almost certainly predicted after quietly investigating his daughter's future family back in 1891. Widespread newspaper coverage announced that H.A.V. Post had filed for bankruptcy. As treasurer of the Railroad Equipment Company, he was sued by the government, his personal assets and those of the company attached. In July the court's conclusions were published: liabilities of $3.5 million and assets of $2.6 million. Fortunately, most of his private property was in his wife's name and therefore safe from seizure.

The senior Posts obviously had adequate financial resources, so Edwin wasted minimal time tending to his parents' futures. Instead, he excitedly parked his own family of four at the Babylon house for yet another summer, so that he could continue sailing the *Constance.* Emily dutifully spent an additional season with her mother-in-law, the women's shared events with the children marked tersely in her agenda by date only. A photograph captioned "Emily swimming" seems almost a duplicate of one from the year before, again revealing a harried and tense young mother, this time with water halfway to her thighs, one son in her arms and the other clinging to her. No one looks in high spirits, least of all the overheated matron. Clothed in long, cumbersome skirts that are hitched up around her knees as she wades through the West Islip bay, Emily seems grimly determined to be the daughter-in-law drawing her extended family together.

Back on her own turf by the autumn ball of 1899, she was relieved to have regained her sense of rhythm. This year the October dance at Tuxedo Park was more popular than ever. In contrast to the dull autumn parties mercilessly flagellated by the city's social pages, Tuxedo Park, the *Times* noted, had everyone "flocking" to its doors. And within a month, the Tuxedo horse season would open.

Given that he was a betting man, it was a blessing that Edwin was not at all interested in horses. He devoted his leisure time that autumn to racing around in his shiny new red Pierce-Arrow, whose horsepower he found infinitely more rewarding than what thoroughbreds could offer. To some extent, Edwin's success during these perilous financial days had even won over his father-in-law. The two men occupied box seats for the December opening of the Metropolitan Opera's new season, where hundreds of disappointed spectators could buy standing room only in the packed house. But though the nineteenth-century piece by Charles Gounod was magnificent, the scent of upper-class anxiety hung heavily in the air, threatening to tune out the talent on the stage. Operagoers were on edge with news that a market crash seemed imminent. "So close are the relations of finance to the world of society that even those who hold great fortunes felt and saw that a chill was in the air," the *New York Times* solemnly reported.

The following day, Emily went to the first Assembly dance of the season—without her husband. Among the Old Guard receiving guests for the Assembly, three were cited in the *New York Times,* their leader Mrs. John Jacob Astor. Only one of the "young matrons" was singled out, the "new patroness" Mrs. Edwin Post, the appellation lacking the éclat of "debutante," but it reassured Emily that she hadn't been forgotten.

A week later, both she and Edwin attended the fabulous George Gould party, where Bruce Price was the star. Everyone at the dance knew the architect was just a few months away from finishing the Goulds' Lakewood, New Jersey, estate, an extraordinarily sumptuous site even in a period of decadent overbuilding. George Gould, influenced by the royal French châteaux on the Loire, had commissioned Bruce to construct what some historians today still believe to be one of the country's most magnificent private residences. Georgian Court, with its forty-bedroom residence and a casino and a racetrack the size of today's Madison Square Garden, became notorious overnight when it was announced that the exercise square, or "palestra," alone cost $250,000 ($5 million in today's dollars).

But grandiosity on its own couldn't guarantee knowledge of how old society behaved, as Josephine had lectured her daughter, it sometimes seemed, from birth. After all, George was the son of the infamous Jay Gould, a scion of recently acquired wealth himself. Gould had had no time to learn the conventions of the rich, and so, though he'd passed down his money to his son, George found himself unsure of court rules. Frightened of their English servants when they arrived en masse at the new manse, George Gould's un-

tutored family had reportedly huddled on the second floor, completely ignorant about handling their staff. Shamed and intimidated, according to the
gossip Gould's niece shared with Emily, the family turned to Bruce Price,
who kindly instructed them in the ways of old money with the same expertise he had applied to designing their house.

Bruce's easy assumption of such authority would be reprised in his
daughter's willingness to tell the country how to behave. Aesthetic and ethical priorities his daughter would value emerged in Bruce's four-part interview about Georgian Court, written for the *Architectural Record* and later
republished in the *New York Times*. Bruce explained that practical sense had
dictated his design for the palatial Gould estate. Its appearance was not
nearly as important to him as its function: "The moment you enter the
house you have the whole thing before you. You not only know where you
are, but you see the entire house as soon as you have come into it. . . . Not
only is it a perfectly logical utilitarian plan, but also you are at home the
moment you are inside the door. There is no need to find your way
around." Just so, his daughter would tutor others that good manners were
always a practical matter of being at home in the world, of going through
life pleasing oneself as well as others. It was all a question of balance.

CHAPTER 21

✥

EMILY WAS LARGELY ABSENT FROM THE CITY'S SOCIAL PAGES IN
early 1900; she was busy moving her family yet again, this time to 18 West
Tenth Street, just three doors down from Josephine and Bruce's apartment and in the neighborhood the young Posts knew well from their early
temporary rental. The new location, along with its household staff of
seven servants—including a Japanese butler, a Danish maid, French and
Swedish nurses, and an Irish laundry maid—implied a substantial increase
in income.

On August 26, when the heat was so intense that even the golf links
were deserted, Emily and Edwin hosted a lunch at Tuxedo Park, one of only
two society meals described that week in the press. Emily looked especially
pretty these days, trim with a rosy complexion, a tireless hostess working
hard to be the perfect spouse to an increasingly successful stockbroker.
From her smooth-running household to her much admired dinner parties,
Emily was the model of an ideal wife for an ambitious businessman. But
photographs reflect a new flatness in the eyes of the twenty-seven-year-old
woman, as if her life didn't allow the light in.

Edwin, on the other hand, was in his element. He had become quite the
epicure, some ranking his wine cellar with Sam Ward's. His pride in the
cuisine his table boasted took a beating, however, when he returned from a
hunting trip to South Carolina, eager to stock the family larder with the
dozen modestly sized terrapins he had trapped. The reptiles, meant as a
fresh source of turtle meat for months to come, were scheduled to live in a
wooden pen Edwin had built in the Tuxedo Park basement. He had failed

to consider the viciousness of the little creatures, however; they inflicted bites with beaks somewhat similar to a bird's, the result so nasty that most of the servants refused to go into the dark cellar, where the terrapins had quickly escaped from their cages. A struggle between Edwin and his creatures lasted for weeks. When a reptile escaped into the heating ducts, its lingering demise emitted a stench through the house. On another occasion, an even larger specimen sank the hard, sharpened edge of its bill into Edwin's leg and refused to let go, unmoved by Edwin's blood dripping onto the floor. Emily finally made a deal: Catch them all and I'll order them cooked for a series of dinners over the next two weeks.

But she couldn't help teasing her husband. "As a gourmet you know that terrapin should be boiled alive," she playfully scolded. "Smashing them with an ax"—as Edwin had done—"destroys the fine flavor." The southerner Uncle Frank, she said, would disapprove. After the turtles were finally collected, she quickly turned her husband's melodrama into grist for amusing dinner conversation. Emily's sons had observed their mother's style, and they worried that if she kept telling the story it was bound to be passed around the park, trickling down to their schoolmates. Then the other children would taunt the Posts about their father being scared of "a little turtle."

The boys asked their mother not to ridicule Edwin, saying they would end up being embarrassed too. At this entreaty, Emily recovered the better part of decorum and consideration. Her children's intervention caused her to rethink the quick wit she sometimes deployed at others' expense, all in the name of innocent fun, she'd assured herself. As a result of such reflection, she resolved to avoid hurting others unless doing so averted a greater harm.

To compensate for her lack of marital camaraderie, Emily found herself depending on her women friends more than she had anticipated. Such companionship was far from reliable, however, as so many households reformed and relocated. Dear Minnie Gray, for instance, was finally getting married and would no longer be as accessible as she had been. Until recently, since the time they had traveled the same summer social circuit as girls, Emily and Minnie could depend on frequent visits both at the resorts and back in the city during the winters.

At the end of September, Emily and Edwin traveled to Bar Harbor to attend Minnie's wedding. As Emily saw it, her dear but undeniably homely friend had herself a catch. Her betrothed, handsome William Coster, had recently opened a stock brokerage office with his brother Charles, where, admittedly, they were still at the point where they needed more clients. Most of the wedding guests assumed that the plain bride was exchanging heritage and money for an attractive husband. Loyally, Emily maintained that any physical inequity was more than compensated for by Minnie's radiant charm.

One of the groom's attendants arranged a surprise, and when Maria Griswold Gray Coster and her groom processed out of the church on October 2, the Bar Harbor band serenaded them with ragtime tunes that, typical of Minnie's style, "soon destroyed every vestige of formality." The nuptial festivities captured the pleasing unconventionality of Minnie's new husband as well. William Coster had already gained an odd renown in Manhattan as a speed walker, traversing the sidewalks between the New York Athletic Club and the stock exchange in record time.

DURING THE PIVOTAL YEAR of 1900, Edwin struck it rich. He was making $100,000 a year, and the yacht of his dreams was within reach. His life had never been sweeter, and he felt invincible. In November he was one of three men elected to the New York Stock Exchange, his achievement noted in the *New York Times*. The New York stock market at the turn of the century was as heady as anything before or after, and Edwin drank it all in—the speed and volatility, the theatricality and flair. A few months later, Archibald Pell, Sadie Price's husband, would join him. This was truly a man's world, and Edwin exulted in it.

One of Emily's Tuxedo Park friends, Julie Olin Benkard, would later recall how tense marriage to a Wall Street stockbroker could be during this period: "Was it a Bull Market or a Bear Market? Were new customers coming in? Were old customers being wiped out? Were we in a position to have an extra maid, or maybe we shouldn't have any maid at all!" Sometimes there would be a stream of luxuries, other times husband and wife "would sit up all night for it was useless to even try to sleep." But Emily's husband knew no such limits. He wasn't the type to stay awake from nerves. And he was rarely home to bother anyone's sleep, even if he did.

Just as 1900 had turned into Edwin's best year yet, it was proving oddly discomfiting for his father-in-law. Bruce lost several important competitions. Even his submission for the courthouse in Wilkes-Barre, Josie's hometown, proved unsuccessful, though much of the community's architecture had been designed by Bruce and lavishly endowed by Josie's father.

Instead, the town awarded the contract to Carrère and Hastings, their plans contrasting dramatically with Bruce's top-heavy concentration on an enormous, dated cupola. Further dampening his spirits, Daniel Burnham from Chicago won a prestigious commission to create what would become known as the Flatiron Building, one of New York City's icons.

By late autumn Bruce appeared at loose ends. As if casting about for something to do, he bought Lady Stratmore, an expensive mare, in time for an elaborate horse show at Tuxedo Park. Anyone professionally and personally connected to Pierre Lorillard always felt pressured to share in his equine passions. The family's racing colors of cherry red and indigo black dominating the Saratoga racetrack, Lorillard poured as much money into his prize mounts as other men lavished on their yachts. In 1900, everyone marveled at a man who currently maintained eight stallions, eighty brood mares, forty-eight racehorses in training, and forty-five yearlings at his 1,244-acre Rancocas stud farm in New Jersey. Before he knew it, Bruce was forcing himself to memorize thoroughbred facts and figures that held little interest for him.

Spending her time supervising her young children's schedules, preparing her wardrobe and the guest dinners each week, overseeing her servants, and handling the family finances, as the year drew to a close Emily seems to have felt that she, like her father, had unfinished business, no matter how carefully she planned her days. Her efforts to give some shape to her life, and the increasingly detailed attempts in her ledger to itemize her family's pleasures, recall the words of the writer she admired the most: "If we'd stop trying to be happy we could have a pretty good time," Edith Wharton would grumble.

CHAPTER 22

❖

FINALLY, IN THE SPRING OF 1901, EDWIN MAIN POST WAS ELECTED TO membership in the New York Yacht Club. Now he could take his father out on a boat even better than the *Macy.*

The timing alone suggests that Edwin had made a killing in the market. These days, more businessmen were exiting than entering the yacht club. On May 9, 1901, the New York Stock Exchange turned into a chaotic scene of men climbing over each other to buy and sell stock in the Northern Pacific Railway, property Edwin had bet on months earlier. Pandemonium ruled for days. The public would bear the greatest loss, but, as one anonymous high-placed official pungently admitted, "While it was a hard trial, there was money in it for the rich."

Edwin had no one at home to celebrate with, even had he tried. For months Emily had been more subdued than usual, feeding off of her cousin Sadie's melancholy over her impending divorce from Archie Pell. However miserable the Pell marriage had proven, ending it officially was still a radical step. Sadie's decision—or Archie's in her name—further depleted the store of certainties Emily had assumed ruled her world.

But at least the support of those friends who knew Archie Pell to be a scoundrel emboldened Sadie Price Pell, and she was soon smitten by a much more solid man, everyone agreed. The Baltimore surgeon Percy Turnure had quietly declared his love during the past miserable year, while Archie Pell flaunted his mistresses. The unmarried couple (Sadie was formally separated) asked Emily to chaperone them on a trip around western Europe, a request she was happy to honor. But as much joy as she received from being with the love-struck duo, Emily's displeasure with her own marriage confronted her anew. However proper the behavior of the amorous pair, their obvious devotion caused Emily to realize more than ever what she lacked.

The trio separated at times. Sadie and her fiancé stayed with his professional associates, while Emily hired a driver to take her from Paris to Naples. She decided to travel to Capri to visit the always interesting Cerio family. Mrs. Cerio was the daughter of the Freddy Princes of Newport, Emily's friends from Tuxedo Park, where the Princes often spent their autumns. Her husband, Ignazio Cerio, a doctor, had already created a buzz with his local explorations; a few years later he would become a minor celebrity when he discovered the remains of prehistoric animals and stone weapons on the island. Today it is nearly impossible to travel to Capri without stumbling upon the name Cerio, attached to everything from hospitals to restaurants.

The Cerios warmly welcomed Emily to their villa at Anacapri, close to the ancient house of the notorious Dr. Alex Muenthe, a controversial island presence and the leader of a cult that practiced Satanism. Emily found Muenthe sinister, and she sensed that he didn't approve of her either. Their mutual dislike thickened the island air for several uncomfortable weeks. Muenthe preferred "neurotic ladies," and he found Emily "too forthright" and "too sure of herself." Without a doubt, in spite of the faddish interest in "metaphysics" in which Emily herself would indulge a few years later, she had no tendency toward the dark side.

Back at Tuxedo Park for the Fourth of July fireworks, she walked right into a more compelling melodrama than any scenario Dr. Muenthe could have conjured. In weather hotter than usual for the typically moderate Hudson Valley, Emily and her friends complained about the temperature nonstop even as they tried to negotiate the local and very palpable tensions between the park's founder and his wife. When Katharine Collier wrote to a friend that the heat was oppressive, it wasn't clear if she meant the eighty-six degrees or the local hostilities. Pierre Lorillard, Emily's ersatz godfather, was critically ill with Bright's disease (the term is loosely used to denote kidney deterioration). And his wife couldn't have cared less.

Throughout the summer of 1901, the *New York Times* kept a highly public death watch at Lorillard's Manhattan apartment, in the process daily confirming long-muttered gossip about the apparent schism within his marriage. This was high drama indeed, demoting the earlier rumors about

Cora Potter and Elsie de Wolfe to mere child's play. It had been public knowledge—among Tuxedo's crowd, at least—that the Lorillards had not lived together for two years, a circumstance the *Baltimore Sun* would unceremoniously confirm in print. The *Times*, with the wealthy Lorillards closer at hand, elected to report the facts more discreetly.

Lorillard, his passion for horses unabated as he aged, had been attending Ascot when he fell ill. One of his innumerable paramours from a "fine family," Mrs. Lillian Allien, accompanied him back on the *Deutschland* to New York, where Mrs. Allien's brother met them aboard ship and helped the sick man debark and enter the hospital. Almost in the same breath that the *Times* solicitously reported Lorillard's daily kidney deterioration, the reporter noted the conspicuous absence of the mortally ill man's spouse: "Members of the dying man's family have been almost constantly at the bedside, but so far as can be learned Mrs. Lorillard has not been to her husband's apartments." Lorillard was said to be alive at this point only through the heavy use of "stimulants" given him by the doctors, to ease the pain of his acute disease. Asked by reporters if there was any chance of his recovery, the doctor admitted that there was always a chance, "but in this case it is a very, very slim one."

Whatever emotions Emily's parents felt, they surely condemned the scandal surrounding the man's final days. Previously private information had once again turned into fodder for the public. Given the closeness between Bruce Price and his patron, it is impossible that Pierre Lorillard's extramarital liaisons had not, at the least, been implied if not discussed in the Price household. What Emily thought of the double standard—of Lorillard grandly commanding her as an adolescent to renounce the amateur stage (lest she be tainted like the bad women he was bedding)—is a matter of conjecture. Probably it was merely another of the contradictory messages of the age that she had absorbed unthinkingly. After all, Josephine, if only tacitly, had made her daughter realize that her beloved father had been forced to play with the big dogs at times, however distasteful their conduct, and that Edwin would have to do the same.

As rumors circulated, within a few weeks of Lorillard's death the truth emerged: he had made the mistake of falling in love with the undeniably married Lilly Barne Allien. For fifteen years, it seemed, he and Mrs. Allien had been conducting their affair, which included her managing his best thoroughbreds for over a decade. Even worse, Lorillard had bequeathed her a sizable portion of his fortune, including the racetracks and the horses for which he was now famous. He left a total of $4 million (approximately $40 million today), granting his estranged wife a yearly annuity of a mere $50,000.

As the *Times* unearthed the details of the founder's private life, the overflow of information must have caused Emily to reconsider some of the facile assumptions she'd inherited. She could not deny, however munificent he had been to her own family, that Pierre Lorillard had never really cared about anything but his own pleasure. Now his wife was unwilling to let him go to his grave without payback. Instead of acting the part of a long-suffering Victorian wife, Mrs. Lorillard, long a companion of Emily and her mother's, sought revenge, in public and on her own schedule, and she found many ways to show her marital disregard, throwing parties and wearing flamboyant new clothes.

The papers were agog over the court battle, which would drag on for years, while Mrs. Lorillard pointedly set about entertaining socially even before twenty-four hours of mourning had passed. Two of her daughters, Mrs. T. Suffern (Maud) Tailer and Mrs. William (Emily) Kent, took their father's side. They remained resolute throughout the winter, even missing Tuxedo's holiday ball. For months everyone watched the comic tragedy play out, as the *Times* noted that the young matrons remained in mourning, while "Mrs. Pierre Lorillard wore no mourning whatever." Mrs. Allien remarried a few years later, taking with her to the marriage a grand inheritance from her benefactor.

By the end of the perfervid summer of 1901, Emily began to think about a second respite abroad. Few wealthy New Yorkers had stayed in the city the past few months if they had any other options. The heavy air bearing down on the streets, shimmering with heat, once again proved fatal: a hot spell from June 28 to July 4 had killed more than seven hundred people and one thousand horses in the city alone, leaving carcasses piled high and smells that gagged its citizens.

At Tuxedo Park, such misery was largely bypassed; extremes of temperature had never been its problem. Still, most of Emily's friends were in Europe this summer; in July, Tuxedo was already hot, or at least muggy, no matter what Josie insisted. So in August, Emily debarked, the two children and Melanie, the children's sweet French nanny, in tow once more. After she again deposited the boys at Melanie's family farm in Normandy, Emily, newly on her own, set out to visit friends.

Near Paris, she stayed for several weeks at a distant relative's country estate, where a lavish weekend was planned for twelve guests. With amused irony, Emily reported it all to her father, writing lengthy letters home about the daily minutiae of the visitors' lives, including her own. The closet games of hide-and-seek lent themselves admirably to intrigue by bored spouses, she commented dryly, affecting for Bruce's sake a tolerant but disengaged authorial voice.

Emily especially enjoyed reporting on the silly maneuverings of any guest who put on airs. She particularly disliked the way "Mrs. B-F" (as she labeled her fellow houseguest) kept trying to pry information from Emily about "a number of people you and I know and some of whom we like very much." Since Emily despised scandalmongering, she deeply resented the ways the overbearing Mrs. B-F was trying "to ferret out things I might possibly know" regarding others' private lives. As if reminding her father how much she and he were alike, Emily emphasized that she was willing to offend the woman rather than answer her questions, leaving Mrs. B-F to flounce away indignantly. The stage was thereby set for Emily to extend herself on behalf of a well-meaning but unsophisticated Chicago ingénue whom Mrs. B-F treated poorly.

The young houseguest, Elaine, was the daughter of a millionaire butcher. She had recently married a "dapper little Baron" who seemed, Emily observed, to adore his wife. Several days into the house party, after repeated haughty treatment at the hands of several of the female guests, Elaine, the "Chicago whirlwind," knocked on Emily's bedroom door just as she was about to put out the light. Emily started to dismiss her, apologetically but somewhat coldly. To her great surprise, the girl's eyes teared up. "I was thoroughly ashamed of my rudeness and anxious to make amends," Emily wrote to Bruce. The girl had approached Emily in hopes that the older woman, whose taste she greatly admired and whose friendliness had encouraged her, would teach her society manners. She was a rube, Elaine admitted, and she didn't know what to do about it. Worst of all, she was picking up signals that her husband was becoming intrigued with a few of the more sophisticated lady guests.

Emily quickly leapt at the chance to help the deserving young wife while putting an arrogant older woman in her place. She agreed with Elaine, who carefully explained: "We may not be old nobility in Chicago, but where I come from, a woman loves her husband and sticks to him. Or she gets a divorce. But here . . . where do you draw the line between these women and the *demi-monde*?"

Setting to work immediately, even though it was bedtime, Emily experimented with Elaine's hair, then pulled "geegaws" off her extravagantly decorated evening dress, explaining that overloading made the girl look twenty years older and forty pounds heavier. Upon discovering that Emily designed her own clothes, Elaine was shocked, saying that she thought her new friend was rich. Laughing, Emily said that she liked creating the patterns she then sent to the couturiers; she'd be happy, she offered, to do the same for Elaine. It wasn't money that counted as much as taste.

The following evening, when the girl from Chicago made her entrance—at Emily's instruction, she was the last to arrive to dinner—everyone gasped. Elaine looked like a "Greek goddess," her new confidence as much as her appearance guaranteeing the return of her husband's attention.

Though she was apparently always sexually faithful to Edwin, Emily flirted her way across France during this particular trip, at times actually fantasizing her husband's demise. She was just starting out upon what she felt to be a new life, she would later remember. Perhaps sensing an incipient rebellion, Edwin decided to call her back home. In a bizarre conspiracy with his mother, he dictated an overseas cable that Caroline sent to Emily, stating that her husband was gravely ill. She must get home as soon as possible. Quickly gathering the children, Emily returned at once, only to find a beaming, sunburned husband greeting her at the Hoboken pier, eager to show her his new purchase: not the sloop or cutter he'd tried to convince himself to settle for but a 129-foot screw schooner, a popular hybrid boat rigged with fore-and-aft sails on two or more masts, its screw propeller classifying the vessel as a steam yacht. He had planned a surprise, he claimed, worth tricking her back to New York however he could. The family was going to enter the Newport race in just a few days with their very own boat, he announced. The *Taro* could easily accommodate a large crew along with the four Posts and their friends.

Emily was furious. In addition to his thoughtless deceit, buying a yacht was far too significant a decision for one spouse to make without discussing it first with the other. After his wife calmed down, Edwin persuaded her of the family fun the boat would provide, and she reluctantly agreed to participate in the upcoming gala in Newport that would await them at the end of the race.

In confirmation of her fears, however, lurching from side to side made her so seasick that she missed the onshore celebration when they arrived. Though the *Taro*'s crew of eight seamen, an engineer, two stewards, and a cook, ensured a well-run household at sea, she insisted that one of their servants take her home by car, leaving her sons delighted to have their father all to themselves.

What Edwin considered her recalcitrance further earned his disapproval, his sour reaction buttressed by earlier disappointing discoveries about his wife. The feminine looks he had initially regarded as enigmatic now seemed evasive or, worse, saturnine. Only during the summers at Newport or Bar Harbor, when women other than his wife entertained Edwin, could he fully indulge his love of the water alongside guests who shared his passion. He had been ambivalent about his desire for her company when he took to the seas, and now this maiden trip on his new yacht convinced him that he would do better without his wife on board.

That summer, Edwin nonetheless meant to show off his newest toy, to parlay its purchase into admiration from others, including his in-laws. A month after Pierre Lorillard's death, Bruce and Josephine took a weeklong yachting cruise "as guests of Mr. Edwin Main Post on L.I. Sound and at Newport." Emily, in contrast, almost immediately began defining herself as a "yacht-widow," comparing her life with that of women who were "golf-widows." She was hardly alone. Alva Vanderbilt didn't dislike the water nearly as much as she detested her husband, but the couple's tacit agreement that she hated the sea allowed William an assortment of onboard female entertainment while Alva was vouchsafed the occasional escape from a man she abhorred.

If not so public, the Posts' alienation had become obvious at least to their older son. Ned later recalled this period as the time he first realized, though only eight years old, that his parents led separate lives except for public entertaining. "Many husbands and wives did this, [my mother] knew," Emily's firstborn would reflect years later. But not many women were as sure of themselves as Emily Price Post, and this complete failure at domestic happiness shocked her.

THE 1901 FALL EXTRAVAGANZA planned for Tuxedo Park, dubbed "the best horse show Tuxedo has ever had," smelled of Mrs. Lorillard's revenge. Guests and residents returned to an autumn season at the park that promised to be better than ever—as if its founder's absence made no difference to anyone. The implication was clear: the lavishly and tastelessly detailed demise a few months earlier of Pierre Lorillard had barely caused a pause, instead inspiring residents to hold up their heads even higher. According to the press, Tuxedo, newly "full of life . . . is gayer this autumn than usual," with the current season certain to be well patronized, especially by the younger set.

The guest rooms were booked through the season, and park members with their own cottages were already in residence. Emily's crowd was once again front and center, with cousin Sadie close at hand. Alice Post, Emily's favorite of Edwin's stable of cousins, frequented the park that fall. The George St. Georges, for many years frequent visitors during the season, now had their own place, where their dinner parties inevitably included Mr. and Mrs. Edwin Main Post. The Price Colliers had arrived, their presence a particular pleasure to Emily. She and Katharine Collier would grow even more intimate in years to come as marriage linked Emily's progeny with those of the Colliers and St. Georges.

It's a good thing that Emily had the Tuxedo community to keep her distracted that fall. In November, the simmering household tensions she had intuited ever since early summer suddenly began to make sense. She had already read the details in the New York Times: a "large proportion of the stockholders of the General Carriage Company of New Jersey" had requested Edwin M. Post and several other partial owners to present a plan of reorganization. Still, Emily never pushed Edwin about what he called the minutiae of his various deals. At least now she could assign her husband's prolonged absences to the demands of working extra hours. Perhaps he really was busy trying to preserve their assets. Perhaps this latest failure placated rather than vexed her, allowing her to fantasize real, desperate late-night business meetings in place of the love nest that, even before Lorillard's death, she'd realized was the mainstay of many successful businessmen.

From her subsequent writing, it is clear that by this time Emily had privately acknowledged that she and her husband were disastrously ill-matched. They had no intimate or truly companionate life together. Still, she continued to hope. Instead, as even their young son realized, over the coming months they would set themselves free, with circumspection, to go their own ways. Emily would care for the children, and, as long as Edwin kept his family out of harm's way, her husband could discreetly take lovers. It never occurred to either of them that Emily might do the same.

CHAPTER 23

W HILE EDWIN ATTENDED POST-CHRISTMAS PARTIES IN MAN-
hattan, Emily and their children traveled to Baltimore to celebrate the New
Year. In mid-January 1902 she went to a Monday night German, the first
she'd attended in a long time. Other than one local Baltimore debutante,
only Emily was mentioned by name: among the assembly, the New York Times
noted, was "Mrs. Edwin Post of New York, formerly Miss Price of Baltimore, a prominent out-of-town guest. She . . . was magnificently gowned,
wearing an exquisite creation of pale pink satin and duchess lace, with diamond and pearl ornaments." Once again, at age twenty-nine, she was the
belle of the ball, a conquering heroine who had held captive not only New
York City but ports south as well.

Emily's respite from domestic worry was brief. When she returned
home, even she realized that her preternaturally agile husband couldn't
bargain his way out of the mess he'd made this time. Coasting on his past
success, Edwin had failed to factor in the radical expansion and contraction
of the market; he had made the fatal mistake of neophytes and believed
himself invulnerable to its flux. In spite of a few months of scurrying for
solutions—investing here, selling short there—he was forced out of the
fast-moving Thomas and Post company before the summer was over. On
August 10, 1902, the Times politely announced his resignation, ostensibly so
that Thomas could bring in a relative but clearly the result of some financial disaster instead. Mr. Post, who "retire[d] from the firm," was "well
known from the thirteen or more clubs he now belonged to," the Times
noted, adding, "The clubs do a very large Wall Street business, and a man

with influential club backing is a good plum." The newspaper seemed to be rooting for Edwin Post as he announced that he was moving to a new job: "Mr. Post enters another firm. He married the daughter of Bruce Price, the architect."

Not even Tuxedo Park offered much bucolic compensation during this tense period for Emily. Rather than fawning over the life of country squires, the New York Times recounted the scandalous, scabrous details of the troubled marriage between Pierre Lorillard's youngest child and her husband, a tabloid-worthy saga of desertion, parental kidnapping of their only child, and the loss of a magnificent diamond ring. The Times explained that "last winter at Tuxedo it was apparent that they intended to separate ... and there was a great deal of general gossip about the matter." It seemed as if the park was starting to lose its luster.

By September things had settled down in Tuxedo, and the newspapers resumed their usual accounts of popular dinners for the well-connected, which were frequently hosted by the Posts. Edwin went about, as Josephine stressed to her daughter was appropriate, making their living. Reorganizing his finances that fall, however, he depleted Emily's inheritance from Catharine Lorillard Wolfe to form Post & Co. The company agreement required Edwin, as majority holder, to contribute $200,000 of his own money (approximately $2 million in today's value), toward which his seat on the stock exchange would count for $75,000. Three other partners would supply the remaining $300,000 that the new company required.

EDWIN'S FINANCIAL REINCARNATION occurred just weeks before Sadie Price Pell's early autumn wedding, and Emily's husband was not on the list of attendees. Divorced from playboy Archie Pell only four months earlier, Sadie radiated happiness begrudged by no one in the Price family. Celebrated on October 8 at Manhattan's Church of the Ascension, at Fifth Avenue and Tenth Street, Sadie's ceremony, while modest, seemed bathed in the warmth of the crowd's satisfaction, her gray gown shining in what seemed a reflection of the bride's happiness.

Though the wedding was set in New York, the bride still managed to carry gardenias, just as she had in Baltimore. Percy R. Turnure stood tall and obviously smitten with his bride. A physician from one of the oldest families of the city, Turnure brought as varied a roster of talents to the Price family as the Post wedding had over a decade earlier. When Percy's father, Lawrence, had died a few years before, the New York Times had pronounced him among the best-known bankers of New York and the most "prominent representative of [an ancient] Huguenot family." Sadie's new uncle, Arthur Turnure, had helped found New York's Grolier Club in 1884, America's oldest and largest society for bibliophiles and lovers of the graphic arts. He had also speculated on the more frivolous side of life by funding the start-up of *Vogue* magazine.

In spite of marrying into a prominent New York family, Sadie had issued only a few verbal invitations to her "very small wedding," the *Times* noted. Mrs. Edwin Main Post was her attendant, and once again, her father, Bruce's brother Benjamin Price, gave his daughter away. The select guests included Phoenix Ingraham, who seemed these days to be present whenever and wherever Emily was. The suave lawyer was such a good family friend—though a few years younger than Emily, he had grown up knowing Josephine and Bruce as well—that he came to dinner at the Posts' even when Edwin was away. Phoenix was the type of man Bruce Price admired: the boy who had matured into an impressive young man was named after his paternal grandfather, the Honorable Daniel Phoenix Ingraham, a justice of the New York Supreme Court.

A modest party was held at Bruce and Josephine's apartment. Probably the couple would have sponsored Sadie's reception whenever it occurred, but there were compelling reasons for Bruce to celebrate his family these days. Emily's father was sick, for the first time in his life, and at moments he seemed seriously ill to his worried daughter, in spite of her mother's optimistic bulletins. Managing her husband's care, Josie had recently sanctioned far more than the Christian Science beliefs she ordinarily preferred to medicine, an overriding of her convictions that caused Emily to grow anxious. Then, when she heard that her father sometimes felt too weak to go to his office, she got scared. For Bruce Price, his job came before everything.

Bruce had begun to limit his creative work, even as his firm was burgeoning into one of the nation's most prestigious. Before long, a new routine had developed at his home, with Bruce's most recently appointed associate, the ten-years-younger John Russell Pope, stopping by the house daily on his way to the office. Having been employed briefly by McKim, Mead and White, Pope had joined Bruce's firm both because he knew the older architect personally and because Bruce had promised to promote him rapidly. Now, however, Bruce increasingly spent his days at home, where Pope paid him loving homage with his calls, ostensibly to talk shop but, as everyone knew, to bring a sense of normalcy and hope to the sick man's surroundings.

Taking the measure of her father's bad health, Emily came to a decision: she would stay in town to watch over him rather than spend the autumn at Tuxedo that year. She soon found that she enjoyed being included in the talks at Bruce's bedside, where she was treated as more than just a wife and a mother, even more than a daughter. Hop and Pope were there daily, their presence calming even as the men cheered up the invalid. During one such visit, as the guests engaged in idle talk, Josephine grumbled that Emily's letters to Bruce from Europe a year earlier were far more vivid than the boring epistolary novel she had recently wasted her money on. *The Visits of Elizabeth,* by Elinor Glyn, was a current bestseller, whatever Josie's disdain, and Emily was surprised to hear herself compared to a successful author. Secretly she had envied her husband's success in publishing the story about his father and the *Macy,* but she'd never considered herself talented enough to write for others.

She was startled, too, that her mother had not only saved her letters but so clearly valued them. Most of her life, Josephine had felt the need to constrain her daughter, arguing against what she considered the flights of fancy Bruce and Emily tended toward, in place of grounding themselves in reality. But now Josephine was flourishing Emily's letters in front of Uncle Frank, who, as the author of several commercial novels, was well connected to the publishing world. Hop immediately offered to share the carefully crafted letters with Richard Duffy, an editor of *Ainslee's Magazine.* Within weeks, Duffy had struck a deal with Emily to publish a fictionalized version of the letters in his magazine.

Emily was thrilled. She had been deeply disappointed when Lorillard convinced her parents to take her off the stage. Dutifully, as a young matron, she had stopped all acting and had given up playing the banjo. Now, overcome with disappointment that her marriage had failed to provide the partnership she had expected, she needed a purpose again. Her relationship with her father had provided a port of entry into a professional world of her own: this chance to write for the public was a gift to her and to her father, whom she would honor with her words. When she told him what she was doing, he encouraged her, saying that she could write "not only this book, but others, probably better."

"You and I are alike," he explained. "We are workers. We are only fully ourselves when we are working."

And so, as Emily's father deteriorated in front of her, she wrote her first book. Soon realizing that his illness was probably mortal, she was determined to finish it before he died; she would make him proud of his daughter. At the beginning of 1903, Bruce rallied to visit the George Gould mansion he had designed, asking Emily and Edwin to accompany him to the opening. But within days he collapsed, and his family convinced him to go to New York Hospital, where Emily arranged for him to be seen by a specialist. Following surgery in March, the doctors acknowledged that Bruce Price had stomach cancer, a malignancy that killed more Americans than any other at the beginning of the twentieth century, probably as a result of the popular cured and smoked meats, a favorite of Emily's father's.

Privately, the doctors told Bruce's family that there was little hope for his future. Everyone agreed to pretend otherwise, and when Bruce suggested that he recover in Paris, Emily immediately set sail. Determined to prepare the way for her father's recuperation, she procured spacious rooms at the Hôtel de la Trémoille for her parents' tenure abroad. But within a few days of his arrival with Josephine, after a hellish passage during which he was in constant pain, on May 29, 1903, Bruce Price died.

Emily helped her mother transport to New York the remains of the man they both cherished. The women sailed home from Le Havre on June 2, 1903. They returned on *La Savoie,* the ship only a few years old and capable of a sea crossing in a mere seven days, sufficiently fast to preserve a body if it was packed heavily in ice and watched closely for signs of thawing. Ever practical, Josie chose to have Bruce cremated instead, his ashes placed in a coffin for transporting back to New York. When Emily and Josephine arrived in Manhattan they were driven at once to the Lee family plot at Wilkes-Barre's Hollenback Cemetery, where services were held and Bruce Price buried.

Emily's father had impeccable timing, one of the many gifts he would cede to his daughter. He even died at the right moment. Bruce Price was one of the leading architects of the American Renaissance, an aesthetic born of the post–Civil War wealth and the rash of American artists who went abroad to study, returning determined to mesh the great European past with their country's brash new promise. Now the movement was dying, just behind the architect, his nation's culture seeking original new ways to celebrate modern life.

Bruce Price's contributions, like those of his father, would be lauded by his profession. The *New York Times* rehearsed his achievements as an architect and the "many monuments of his genius" that he bequeathed the country. The paper also honored his distinguished heritage, from the eminent lawyer William Price to his mother's family, the Bruces of Scotland. The obituary concluded with a list of all the clubs Bruce had belonged to, followed by a line that would have meant the most to both his daughter and to the man himself: "He was also President of the National Architectural Society."

The Architectural League of New York printed its own appreciation that week: "Resolved. That we deeply mourn the death of our former President, Bruce Price. We realize that not only as friends and associates have we sustained an irreparable loss, but that the profession of architecture has lost one of its most eminent members, one who was found ready at all times to advance its interests in the highest sense. He was sincere, earnest, and always willing to make personal sacrifices for the general good. Resolved. That we tender to his family our heartfelt sympathy and condolence."

Though Bruce's wife quickly and stoically resumed her social life, the architect's daughter did not rebound so easily. Bruce Price had always been the one to grant Emily her full worth, though Josie had generously fostered the relationship of her two intense family members, even at the expense of her own needs for intimacy. If the stalwart mother was unable now to provide a conduit for her daughter's grief, Emily got even less support from her increasingly estranged husband, who finally had Emily all to himself—if he wanted her. He didn't, and Emily mourned alone.

BRUCE LEFT LITTLE money for his family. His style of living, as well as that which he underwrote for his family, had absorbed most of what he'd earned. Emily's frugal mother, protecting her father's bequest, decided to move into a smaller—although perfectly appointed—house in Tuxedo Park, and the park's records and newspaper accounts confirm that she rented out property she had previously used for friends and family. But the encomia lavished on Bruce's head must have gratified his widow and daughter more than great monetary inheritance anyway: Josephine had traded her wealth decades ago for exactly what she got, the deal as close to perfect as any she had made during her subsequent dabbles in the stock market. Through the years she would sometimes feign dismay at her husband's generosity to everyone from apprentices to beggars, but in truth she basked in his generous spirit—the mark of a true gentleman, the girl from coal country often proudly noted to her daughter.

One of the last official notices involving Bruce Price would appear on June 13, 1903, just around the time his ashes had made it to the burial grounds in Wilkes-Barre. He was sued by James N. Stout for failure to complete a task (as he was dying) and for costs incurred during the delay. The judgment was for the plaintiff. It was the first and only time Bruce Price would not finish a project, let alone fail to pay a bill.

While her father's obituaries recalled the Civil War, Emily was steeped in a culture that witnessed an entirely different world. Helen Keller, blind and deaf since the age of two, would graduate from Radcliffe College—the same year that another woman was arrested for smoking on Fifth Avenue. The first New York subway opened to anyone who could pay a nickel, revolutionizing work and city neighborhoods. The New York Cancer Hospital (now Memorial Sloan-Kettering) was the first in the country to capitalize on what the Curies had discovered: only six years after the discovery of radium, the institution was using radiation to treat patients. The twentieth century marched on, and Emily Post would assume a place in its history books, her edifice more monumental than Bruce Price's own.

THE POST MARRIAGE WAS BEING PUSHED FAR BEYOND ANYTHING Emily's parents' relationship had endured. In light of the grief Emily suffered upon Bruce's death, Edwin's increasingly serious money problems at least proved a distraction for her. After opening Post & Co. in September 1902, Edwin overextended the company to include four branches, located by July 1903 in Baltimore, Washington, Philadelphia, and New York. Now, just a month later, a newspaper column announced that these offices were being "discontinued." In the process of expanding his stockbrokers' company, Edwin had run it into the ground, barely escaping legal charges and losing his entire investment besides. Apparently he had tried to sell his seat on the stock exchange without, in effect, actually giving it up. It also transpired that Edwin had invested in two trust companies in Baltimore, probably calling upon his wife's family's local stature. Both companies had failed, their liabilities estimated to hover at $10 million, a fortune even in turn-of-the-century dollars.

When the *New York Times* announced the "dissolution" of the one-year-old stock exchange firm, no one was surprised, least of all Edwin's wife. But the Posts weren't even allowed the chance to deal discreetly with their present disasters. On November 1 Edwin faced a judgment involving failed enterprises belonging to his old partner E. R. Thomas. Unlike the friendly publicity surrounding Edwin's "voluntary" departure from the firm, the current article didn't pretend that Edwin and Edward Thomas had parted amicably: there had been "differences of opinion regarding the handling of International Silver securities," the *Times* reported.

Emily's novels suggest that she was less concerned about money than by his boredom with her—and by his lack of integrity. Whether yachting or spending time with friends, relatives, or actresses, he preferred to be with anyone rather than his wife. Cavalierly, he sold his carefully stockpiled wines for $10,000, explaining to Emily that his wise collecting would help them through the bad times. She saw none of the money. Alone night after night in Tuxedo Park, except for Josephine at her side, she knew that her current residence made sense in light of her mother's desire for companionship, her husband's neglect, and her sons' pleasure in the on-site grammar school. At least she could devote her energies to the epistolary novel based on her European letters to her father.

In typical fashion, she was soon immersed in her assignment. To her surprise, she even grew to resent the time consumed by her society life in the city, though it took at most two hours to travel to Manhattan. Still, she did her wifely part. That fall, just after Edwin sold his yacht, the couple was one of thirty at a party Mrs. Astor gave for the Dowager Duchess of Roxburghe and her daughter. The illustrious gathering also included the Elbridge Gerrys, the Cornelius Vanderbilts, the John Drexels, and the Robert Goelets. Increasingly distressed at the careless disregard to which Edwin subjected her, both in public and private, Emily found herself concentrating on the next chapter she was planning to start, even as she danced with her undeniably handsome husband.

By the beginning of 1904, Emily and Edwin were long settled into that most typical of society marriages, one maintained for appearances and for the sake of their children. The spouses were estranged in heart if not in fact—a pattern inherited from their parents' generation. Emily's accommodation came at a high price, and she could not have been unaware of the cost. She'd observed friends who had to hold their heads up high in order to avoid seeing the pity or condescension in other women's eyes.

But she went about creating her own satisfying life within the outer shell of her marriage, if only because she, unlike her cousin Sadie, had children. In addition to the boys, she had her friends. She and Katharine Collier saw each other frequently, and her long friendship with Minnie Coster remained as energetic and forthright as it had been when they were children, though she had to go to France, where Minnie had moved, to enjoy it. At least she saw more of Juliet Morgan Hamilton now than before both of them were married.

Worried at times that Emily seemed too curious about pursuing outside interests, instead of being content with the society she moved in, her friends nervously warned her not to become too serious about her writing. Don't be silly, she retorted. Whatever do you mean?

The Flight of a Moth began its monthly serialization in *Ainslee's Magazine* in January 1904, less than a year after Bruce's death. The architect's encouragement, given to Emily as he lay dying, had inspired his daughter to believe that she might have a literary career, forever linking the idea of writing with the beloved figure of her father. She wrote nearly nonstop on *The Flight of a Moth,* even allowing for her surely exaggerated claim of working through thirty-eight drafts. The forum itself was auspicious: *Ainslee's* was a well-received if recent addition to the monthlies, publishing fiction whose authors' names were usually recognized. Though she had called on Uncle Frank's literary connections to ensure an initial reading, Emily knew her novelized correspondence to Bruce Price was published on its own merits.

She earned $3,000 (around $68,000 today) from serial and later hard-back sales, a very respectable showing for a first book. By the beginning of October, the serialization in *Ainslee's* was complete, and a display ad in the *New York Times* announced Appleton's fall publication of the novel. *The Flight of a Moth,* a correspondence between two friends, allows the heroine to narrate "an unusual and unheard of" tale "that will be the talk of the town." Grace, a beautiful, vivacious twenty-five-year-old widow with an "enthusiastic pleasure-loving temperament," has had "very little chance" to put pleasure first, never in her childhood and certainly not "at all in her married life." At seventeen, she had married an "egotistical, faultfinding man of the world," who recently—unexpectedly, dispatched by Grace with a sentence—had dropped dead.

Writing to her friend back home, Grace details her adventures abroad. Tempted by a Vronsky-like character right out of *Anna Karenina,* the heroine renounces her quest for experience and, after the kindhearted "Lord Bobby" squires her away from the tempting exotic men who woo her, chooses the pleasures of the hearth instead. The lord's patient attentions cause her to "open her eyes" to the virtues of matrimony. The young widow gushes that she had always assumed she would "hate marriage. [But] if I knew what it was to be 'in love' I wouldn't feel as I do, would I?" Bobby, she concludes, has taught her what life should be.

A novice writer, Emily is often obviously present in the text, using her own experiences too visibly as grist for her story. *The Flight of a Moth* records (at times literally) the increasing marital distance Emily was enduring just as she needed her husband more than ever. While she'd written her first drafts, her father had lain dying. It was not, she was telling Edwin through her text, fashionable European counts who should arouse his jealousy. They were good for flirtations. But for life, for love, she wanted a Lord Bobby, and she was throwing down her ladylike gauntlet as hard as she dared.

That October, the *New York Times* took its first notice of Emily Post not directly connected with her social world, in an article titled "Recent Fiction: Emily Post's Study of the Restless American Woman." The reviewer, admitting that there had been a run of the fictional-letters genre of late, noted that occasionally something rose to the top of the overstacked heap and declared Emily's version a contender. Her novel was "lively and thoughtful, more than the spate of similarly structured novels" by virtue of its "wit, grace, and liveliness of style" and, the journalist added, the author's firsthand knowledge of society.

Even as the reviews appeared for *The Flight of a Moth,* Emily was plotting her next novel, which she would title *Purple and Fine Linen.* The positive press and decent sales figures for *The Flight of a Moth* ensured her respected publisher's continued commitment to its author. As she added to the daily hours she spent writing, her friends began to worry aloud. "You will be careful, won't you? . . . It would be a great pity if you became Bohemian. It is not your style, my dear," Juliet Morgan Hamilton gently counseled. As Emily worked at becoming a writer, she made fewer appearances in the social pages. Her friends, of course, proved right: her writing cut into what had been called her free time. In November the *Times* further validated her plan for a career. "Magazines for 1905: Some of the Plans of the Important American Monthlies for the Coming Year" listed under *Ainslee's* "clever" fiction, including "novelettes" from, among others, Ralph H. Barbour, Elizabeth Duer, and Emily Post.

Emily's older son recalls a significant flirtation his mother engaged in at this time. A temporary lodger at Tuxedo Park (carefully coded in Ned's memoir as "Mr. G.") started spending afternoons at their house, especially when Edwin wasn't home. The mysterious Mr. G. used his knowledge of the period's so-called spiritualist writers, steeped in a false medievalism, to woo Emily. Mr. G. begged her to be his lady and to listen to him recite poetry daily—after he had read aloud yet another scene from *Joyzelle,* Maeterlinck's drama about love triumphant first produced in Paris and Brussels in 1903. *Joyzelle* relied on signs to represent ideas, though few of his audience were sure what their correspondence was. Emily encouraged Mr. G. to tutor her on the arcane; Maeterlinck, who would win the Nobel Prize in Literature a few years later, was the name on the literati's lips those days, and it felt good to be in the know.

She saw herself as an autodidact, the model of which she would create in *Purple and Fine Linen*. Mr. G.'s literary gruel, however, was too thin for Emily's taste. As she gradually gained confidence in her own powers of perception, she explained to her dismayed, ethereal tutor that she found bestselling F. Hopkinson Smith's writing far more credible than the "wispy Princesses and knights-at-arms alone and palely loitering." Such people did not exist, she insisted, and even fantasy had to be rooted in reality to keep her attention.

Emily wrote *Purple and Fine Linen* while her own marriage was in limbo. Her husband, flouting minimal protocol, hardly bothered to show up at Tuxedo Park anymore, much to the writer's embarrassment. Ned and Bruce observed their mother dressed beautifully for the evening, hopefully taking the carriage to the train station, then returning by herself, night after night, head still held high. "Jealousy is the suspicion of one's own inferiority," her narrator would claim in *Purple and Fine Linen*. Perhaps she planned to effect Edwin's spousal resurrection through her text. In part, she was writing to save her marriage. If she rewrote and revised often enough, she knew she could make it all come out right.

BUT IN EMILY'S real world, she didn't get to choose the ending. Her friends understood the type of marriage she had settled into, or settled for. Tuxedo Park held its first round of winter parties, and at one of the few Edwin bothered to attend, he talked to the *Times* social reporter about his business ventures. Cocky as ever, he explained that he was busy reorganizing a new firm, an "alliance with some large financial interests." In fact, nothing was in the works.

Whether from shame, or job pressures, or romantic liaisons elsewhere, Edwin increasingly missed important social functions where the husband was expected. He completely ignored the large weekend crowd of well-known society people who showed up for the season's inaugural weekend of Tuxedo's parties, luncheons, and dinners. The gala honoring England's Duke of Newcastle, which included the Grenville Kanes and the Cooper Hewitts, was "led off by Mrs. Edwin Post." Edwin was not present. But when a "special dinner" was given at the clubhouse, with a "bridge whist tournament" afterward, both Mr. and Mrs. Edwin M. Post participated, though Emily left early.

Cards were ideal for Edwin's personality; anything that required strategy excited him. Unlike his wife, who disliked lingering over a task, Edwin appreciated the art of waiting out one's opponent. After all, a hunter had to be patient. Edwin Post was a man of extremes: he could linger as long as a duck dared him, or he could enter a bid in a heartbeat and lose a million dollars almost as fast. His two published short pieces, his hunting chronicle in *Field and Stream* and his fiction a few years later in the prestigious *Smart Set,* showcase his intelligence and his fine sense of style, a benefit of his having had his already strong mind further educated at Columbia. But while he respected sophisticated, knowledgeable men, women confounded him. On the one hand, he appreciated those who could transcend the limits society had levied on them. Yet he also assumed that his wife would devote her energies to being his helpmate and the mother of his children, and that she would define herself completely in those terms.

Emily's husband was clearly dissatisfied with his marriage. The trail of elegant actresses he would pursue for years suggests that he really had valued the Emily Price he thought he was marrying, the theatrical woman of the amateur stage, the dauntless banjo player who commanded the limelight in her own right. Emily, neglecting her own sensibilities while trying to emulate Josephine's support of Bruce, had instead deeply disappointed her husband, who felt betrayed. Edwin had counted on having it all: the usefulness of a Josephine but the glamour of the stage that his bride had promised. He had played straight from the beginning, as he saw it, but his wife had shifted the ground under him. The reality was less dramatic: Emily had found such a complicated, contradictory role beyond even her prodigious abilities.

AT MIDNIGHT ON JANUARY 1, 1905, AN EPOCHAL DISPLAY OF fireworks illuminated midtown Manhattan's first skyscraper, the thirty-two- (or, depending upon the person counting, twenty-five-) story Times Tower at One Times Square. The year that Emily became a published author ended with the modern city emerging during that celebration at Times Square. At Seventh Avenue and Broadway, the building embodied the paradox of New York City: like the Price family, the tower looked forward and back at the same time, its awkward Beaux Arts façade defining its aesthetic as much as its steel-frame construction, electric lights, and fast elevators.

It would be another ten years before New York's grip on the nation's cities was secure. But even now, with horns blasting and ragtime blaring, crowds accustomed to commemorating the New Year at Trinity Church capitulated noisily to the celebration at Times Square. With the showy fireworks, New Yorkers' self-contained, cloistered little island magnanimously reached out to the entire world, a world well represented here, with subgroups ranging from the Dutch to the Irish to the French to the German; it seemed possible to find someone from every nation on earth in this city. Such an assortment of several thousand unrelated families couldn't possibly trace their roots to society's idealized, largely fantasized homogeneous beginnings. Instead, they braided together an innovative social order, spawned by a bigger and better New York that seemed to grow daily in impossible new directions.

The old order didn't stand a chance. Later in 1905, Alva Vanderbilt, her divorce final, would memorably declare herself an activist when she flouted marriage to William. "I was the first" she claimed, proud of "show[ing] . . . the way" to society women. Though Josephine scoffed at women campaigning for equal rights for her sex, she admired Alva's strength, even if she abhorred her bullying methods. Josie went her own way, quietly counseling her daughter to move with the times even as she held steady to the old. In their dissimilar conduct, both Josephine and Alva nonetheless bore the marks of strong self-determination.

Josie, after all, came from a family of forceful and eccentrically creative women. Her mother, for whom Emily was named, had resolved to flee the boredom she'd suffered since her husband, Washington Lee, had died. "She learned to ride a bicycle at 80," Emily would recount proudly. Then, when she was eighty-six, she bought a letter of credit and booked herself a ship berth. "Goodbye, I'm off to Europe," she wrote to her son.

Not everyone of Emily's class welcomed the new freedoms of the age. Much of the Old Guard seemed moody, even moribund. For many, the city's quilt of cultures evoked real anxiety. Wealthy newcomers encroached upon the old good neighborhoods, whose protective barriers were crumbling. Even society's well-established haunts were being forced to compete against newcomers. Replacing Delmonico's as the modish place to go, Sherry's Hotel paneled its ballroom doors with mirrors, flattering the dancers as well as such visiting celebrities as Sarah Bernhardt. The upper class looked to the perpetuation of their own bloodlines for security, in events such as the Hyde Park–Oyster Bay marriage merger of the Roosevelts, which reassuringly supported the nation's founding myths. Emily's Tuxedo Park friends the Price Colliers and Katharine's son Warren Delano Robbins proudly attended the house wedding of their nephew and cousin Franklin to their other cousin Eleanor.

Though he half listened to the detailed accounts of the dynastic merger that the Roosevelt nuptials promised, Edwin found the talk boring. He saw himself as a new son of an old family, eager, unlike society's dinosaurs, to seize the moment, to play one opportunity off another. Yet however modern he believed himself to be, it was on his wife's inheritance, first from Catharine Wolfe, and now with the nominal bequeathal from Bruce Price, that Edwin brokered yet another shaky deal and dallied with an ever more beautiful mistress.

And then he grew careless and ruined everything. In the spring of 1905, Edwin returned from a pleasure trip only to be confronted by a comely actress he had already forgotten. The young woman had been waiting patiently for him in their lovers' cottage, misunderstanding the finality of their last good-bye. Within days of being scorned, she had contacted the gossip broadside *Town Topics.*

EDWIN HAD INTENDED to spend much of that spring and summer out on the Great South Bay, putting in the obligatory family appearance now and then. On May 17, he had even asked Emily's good-natured mother—whom he continued to enjoy far more than her daughter—to join the couple at the wedding of a mutual acquaintance; the reception was sure to be full of alcohol and male bonding, since the couple's always amusing, buoyant friends Phoenix Ingraham and Fred Kernochan were attending as well. It was going to be a superior season, he could tell: hot and humid, just the way he liked it—and it was officially still spring.

When he was approached by one of Colonel William D'Alton Mann's employees that inglorious summer, Edwin already knew the extortion scheme the publisher boldly exacted, using the pages of his weekly tabloid, *Town Topics,* more widely read than any other paper in town. Only a few of the bravest, including Edwin's high-living ex-partner E. R. Thomas, had ever dared defy the colonel, who looked like Santa Claus but never failed to demand his pound of flesh. Edwin had envied Thomas, who didn't care if *Town Topics* talked about his love affairs or not. More recently he had experienced a guilty pleasure when word had circulated about the less than dignified resolution of Thomas's latest contretemps. Even as the blustering stockbroker had noisily flouted the colonel, his bride was quietly paying up to avoid suffering public humiliation. Colonel Mann got his claws into the Thomas bank account after all.

So on June 24, when Edwin Post was called and asked to meet with a representative of the "Society Editors' Association," a group vaguely associated with Colonel Mann and *Town Topics,* he knew what was coming next. Sure enough, the following day, he received a visit from a Charles H. Ahle, who promptly informed him to pay up or be the subject of a soon-to-be-published article about Edwin's adulterous habits. Ahle's bosses were willing to suppress this scurrilous gossip if the stockbroker contributed to a cause they designated—their (mythical) vanity project about the rich and famous.

If Edwin had really wanted to save his marriage, he could have easily borrowed the $500 (one of Mann's more modest levies). Emily need never have known about the affair; the colonel was a man of his word—you'd have to give him that. And appearances, Edwin knew, mattered greatly to his wife. Almost as if writing a warning to her husband, a year earlier she had assigned her heroine in *Flight of a Moth* these words: "The eleventh commandment, 'Thou shalt not be found out,' is despicable but nevertheless it is the one thing you cannot get away from." Or he might have come clean with Emily, his brave decision so impressing her, he could imagine, that in spite of her insistence on discretion she would be willing to give him a second chance. He would stop playing the field and they could bring down *Town Topics* together. Either way, the newspaper would be unable to stake any further claim to his marriage—as long as he gave up the extramarital liaisons.

These are things he could have done.

But before Edwin even told Emily, he had already decided: he would set up a sting, becoming a hero in the process. The decision made, he visited the assistant district attorney to put things in motion, and only then did he send word to his wife, "warning her that some attempt might be made to approach her with a view to blackmail." He would explain everything later, he said. In other words, Ned Post's subsequent version notwithstanding, Edwin had determined to go public by the time he confessed to his wife.

AT THREE-FIFTEEN P.M. on July 10, 1905, the Holland House, on Thirtieth Street and Fifth Avenue, a restaurant and bar "renown[ed] for its aristocratic tone," would cater to less than elegant purposes. Edwin would remember the thunderstorms and the mugginess of the air as he waited in the second-floor lavatory of the ten-story white stone building. From later exhaustive court testimony, we know he was rehearsing his part even as Ahle swaggered in. A policeman had been planted in the toilet stall, and Edwin sought to entrap Ahle into admitting that the "payment" he demanded was, in fact, a bribe. At first, the man failed to take the bait. Then, all at once, Colonel Mann's tired underling grew envious of this expensively dressed pretty boy strutting in the men's room. The minion bragged that such an insignificant stockbroker as Post, after all, was just a minnow in the sea of far larger fish his boss routinely snagged. At that, the policeman threw open the door. In what was surely one of the least attractive locations assigned to a high-society rendezvous, Edwin had caught his man.

The *Times* publicized the sting, and cheers greeted Edwin as he strolled onto the floor of the New York Stock Exchange. "Go for them, Post, my boy," one member shouted. "Don't let the blackmailing scamps get away. We are with you, for we've all been through that mill ourselves." The men rose as one, as Edwin received the standing ovation that Emily herself had long coveted. For one day, at least, Edwin Main Post was a hero, his sexual profligacy as much as his courage in bringing down Colonel Mann honored by implication. The almost cheerful defiance he would exhibit on the witness stand proved him in great form. In contrast, Emily was humiliated. Known among both her friends and jealous enemies as a proud woman, she had been felled in front of the entire world—and the particular world that mattered to her. The *New York Times* would replay the saga throughout the sizzling summer. The unbearable July heat was just beginning when the Posts were splashed across the front pages of all the city's newspapers.

CHAPTER 26

❖

*I*F EDWIN HAD BLITHELY TRICKED EMILY INTO ABBREVIATING HER trip abroad several years earlier, it was with real trepidation that he forced her to cut short her vacation this time. When the *Town Topics* imbroglio occurred, she was already at Camp Uncas, J. P. Morgan's resort in the Adirondacks, where the idea of "roughing it" was quite to her taste. Like most other guests, she had traveled to the "camp" in a private railroad car. Once there, she ate food prepared by French chefs, with rustic, handcrafted birch-bark butter plates one of the few concessions to the setting. Even Sigmund Freud, when vacationing at the site, was dumbstruck at the "incongruous luxury in the wilderness." The camp in the woods overwhelmed him: "Of everything I have experienced in America," he said, "this is probably the strangest."

Emily, however, had no time to form an opinion. She was at Camp Uncas for only a few days before her presence was urgently required back home.

As always, she came through. Edwin was right: he could count on her. This time, after what must have been a very delicate negotiation on the sinner's part, the couple agreed to work together to put blackmailers such as Colonel Mann in their place. Nothing, however, could alter the fact that Edwin had broken their unspoken connubial contract, forcing his wife's hand, while brilliantly appearing a man of principle in the process as he helped rout the scourge of high-society men. Given who she was, Emily had little choice but to support him publicly, and he knew that.

Her son's memoir emphasizes Emily's heroic agreement to a highly public fight—she was protecting the right of law-abiding men and women to make private choices that should remain just that—but in truth Emily Post had no say in the matter. At least her husband gave her the chance to play the brave, supportive, honorable wife. And perhaps Edwin knew he was doing them both a favor by furthering the demise of their marriage. Maybe, at some level, Emily even recognized his idiosyncratic sense of justice as well.

By July 22, a week after a collection of breathless articles began appearing daily in the *Times,* the newspaper had begun listing prominent citizens who had "subscribed" to Colonel Mann's various schemes in the past. Almost every major society figure had been bribed, from J. P. Morgan to the Vanderbilts, from Chauncey Depew to O.H.P Belmont. It seemed as if all society men cheated. Occasionally a woman's name jumped out at the reader, its inclusion implying that the wives were paying for their husbands' protection, much as Emily might have chosen to do, if only for her children's sake—if Edwin had allowed her such an option. Instead, following a few weeks of sympathetic newspaper publicity, Edwin took the witness stand and recounted the entire saga with relish.

Emily had accompanied him, and now she appeared in the overheated courtroom as a boldly dressed fashion plate, practically daring anyone to pity her. Her husband, after all, was the star, and his supporting actress knew how to play her role as well. As usual, Emily had designed her clothes and then sent sketches to her favorite local seamstress. A *New York Times* reporter described in detail her exquisite outfit: "The skirt cleared the floor about three inches, and was laid in groups of three-inch side plaits, two in each group, and each group of two plaits its own width from the adjacent group." Fulsome attention was lavished on the color of the stripes at the wrist bands, the precise shape of the sleeves, the stitching, the buttons, and the type of feathers in her hat—red quills. The *Times* reporter also recounted an appearance earlier in the trial: "She wore the other day a smart linen costume, a short skirt and Eton, topped by a scarlet hat." Like any savvy politician, Emily understood that red conveyed power and confidence. From now on, it would be her favorite color and would figure prominently in her self-presentation, from her shoes to her fingernail polish.

But during the summer of 1905, an occasional glimpse of the wounded wife's fragility peeked through, in spite of her flamboyant subterfuge. Most telling was a reporter's odd misjudgment of Emily as "small." Substantial midnight anguish must have diminished the usual grandeur of the five-foot-nine clear-eyed beauty from Baltimore. An uncharacteristic loss of appetite surely affected her weight: for once, the Gibson girl shape that her husband demanded was no longer a struggle to maintain.

DURING THIS PERIOD, advance publicity began appearing for fall publication of Emily's *Purple and Fine Linen,* set in New York and Newport. The novel must have titillated the Tuxedo Park crowd, quick to identify its point-for-point correspondence with the life they knew Emily lived, and in which, in some cases, they participated. To those envious of what seemed her easy success, *Purple and Fine Linen* was a delicious payback, with its virtual almanac of the author's marital depression. Nonetheless, the novel's blissful ending, which Emily had surely hoped would predict her own life story, now appeared a humiliating chimera, the desperate hope of a disappointed wife.

But Emily's new position as a writer whom critics took seriously proved a soothing unguent to her personal shame. The *New York Times* cited, in "Authors' Summer Locations and Plans," her forthcoming novel among its top selections. The very title of the article, with authors as its subject, signaled a shift in the way she was being perceived now: no personal references to parties, no catalogs of food or clothes were included. Instead, *Purple and Fine Linen* was described as literature.

Purple and Fine Linen was published in October 1905, to generally positive if condescending critical response, similar to that given *Flight of a Moth.* Reviewers explained that the novel dealt "with the world-old questions of love and marriage, riches and happiness, and all the other things that go to make life bearable or unbearable." Camilla James, the protagonist with no education outside of finishing schools, is a wildly successful debutante at Tuxedo Park—her cache of beaux' favors reminiscent of Emily's own—when she first lays eyes on Anthony "Tony" Stuart. She loves him at first sight, but he is obviously in thrall to the most theatrical, vivid, outspoken woman in the room, who is dramatically recounting the gossip about the sordid demise of a Pierre Lorillard figure. Soon, however, Tony is convinced by his father to pursue the lovely young girl instead, and he marries Camilla.

Disappointingly, though Tony appreciates that his bride is "madly and demonstratively fond" of him, he himself seeks neither companionship nor sympathy from a wife, even though she is a "dear kid." Camilla soon laments the hours her husband spends working or playing at the club: "If you love me . . . you ought to want to stay at home. Do you realize that you are never with me unless we go out?" Tony impatiently responds that between tending to their business interests and his father's as well—echoing the real-life havoc of H.A.V. Post's investments—he has no time for himself: "I work very hard all day and when I don't have to go out with you, I do want a change myself. I want to go to the club, not only for pleasure, but because there are also important business affairs which I can arrange there."

"All right," Camilla blurts out, "but you may be sorry some day if I become like all the other women, and don't care whether you go out or stay in." She worries privately that he values her only for her ability to shine at dinner parties. "I wonder if Tony thinks me an idiot?" she ponders. "Why does he take it for granted that I can't understand [his business interactions]?" Left on her own so often, Camilla begins to read serious literature and to associate with literary types at social events. "She liked the satisfaction of feeling the growth of her mind. And yet the more she read, the more unsettled she became. She was less and less like the people she knew; it was getting harder and harder to be interested in the same continuous chatter. . . . But after all, these were her friends and this was her life; and both were the best of their kind."

As for loving her husband? "She supposed . . . she was in love with him. It never occurred to her that she was not. She did not believe that there was such a thing as the love she read about in books. She saw none of it in real life. The married people that she knew all seemed to lead their own independent lives irrespective of each other." She concludes that "the trouble was that they did not seem to like the same things." Tony soon takes a voyage abroad, which Camilla declines, though she would certainly have gone if she "were not such a bad sailor."

Inevitably, the heroine finds thoughts of "another man crowding out those of her husband" and finally contemplates divorce. Running off with a would-be lover, she turns back just in time. Temptation resisted, Camilla tries to rechart her future as she "thought of her father and mother. . . . Her conscience knew exactly what road they would point. . . . But when her husband came into her bedroom, her first instinct was resentment." Realizing that a husband has "the right" to enter her boudoir, she finds herself even more resentful: "What and for what reason had he the right? . . . [H]e suddenly seemed a stranger and yet a fellow prisoner handcuffed to her. And she felt in the same moment that the shackles were stronger than she was able to break. She wanted to scream aloud."

Just as she decides to tell her husband she is leaving him, he assumes full responsibility for her unhappiness: "A woman never gets into your frame of mind except through great unhappiness. As for the blame, I take it upon myself. When a man neglects his wife, there are always plenty of other men willing to keep her from being lonely." The fairy-tale ending to *Purple and Fine Linen* grants the author what she sought in real life. Her husband has realized, at the last minute, what he has in his spouse. He is willing to fight for her. "Don't think for one minute," he tells Camilla after her confession of ardor for another, "that I intend to let you go without an effort on my part to keep you. . . . I love you! I love you! And I won't let you go!"

THE ENDING TO her own real-life fairy tale still in question, Emily was not in a celebratory mood that autumn, in spite of the professional success she had clearly achieved. In dramatic contrast to her past, she did little entertaining and made even fewer social appearances, seeming instead to marshal her resources to succor her sons and to think through how to handle her marriage. On November 15, 1905, when Emily attended a ball held on the famously fast three-year-old British ship the *Drake,* docked in Manhattan's harbor, Edwin did not accompany her. In 1917 the ship would be blown up by German U-boats, but for now, it was an ideal venue for a dance, if you had any interest in the water or in speed itself. Emily had neither, and Edwin had both.

HMS *Drake*'s setting was an irony that her husband could not have missed when he read the social pages and learned that his wife, who hated the sea, had taken sole possession of the party invitation. Emily, lurching and staggering through the evening, had her own way of paying her husband back.

More to her tastes, Emily was one of the 170 illustrious guests invited to Mark Twain's seventieth-birthday party. Staged at Delmonico's, the event began with a cocktail reception, followed by dinner in the Red Room, music issuing from the forty-piece orchestra on loan from the Metropolitan Opera. Five hours of speeches came after the meal, their length making it fortunate that the chef had opted for hearty food: "fillet of kingfish, saddle of lamb, Baltimore terrapin, quail, and redhead duck washed down with sauterne, champagne, and brandy."

The press, clearly surprised at the guest list, observed that "a particular feature of the dinner was the strength of the feminine contingent. There were fully as many women there as men, and they were not present as mere appendages of their husbands, but as individuals representing the art of imaginative writing no less than the men." Furthermore, these female achievers were relatively young: "The whole gathering did not seem to include half a dozen women with streaks of gray in their hair."

The published list of the guests carefully noted the few "wives of" by citing them as "Mrs." Until now, even Emily's novels had positioned "Mrs." in front of "Emily Price Post." In contrast, women writers at this event were granted a listing by name, marital status ignored. Except for six or seven illustrious socialites, all the invitees were "genuine creators of imaginative writings," vetted by the host of the evening, George Harvey, the editor of the *North American Review*. The sponsor, *Harper's Weekly*, published an end-of-the-year special edition for the event. The spill of photographs shows writers Willa Cather and Dorothy Canfield and, at Emily's table, May Sinclair.

Seeing herself endorsed as a professional restored some of the strength the summer had robbed from Emily. "Never before in the annals of this country had such a representative gathering of literary men and women been seen under one roof," the *Times* crowed. In light of her confounded expectations regarding the life she would lead, Twain's advice to his spellbound crowd must have resonated for Emily Price Post: "I will offer here, as a sound maxim, this: that we can't reach old age by another man's road."

Perhaps the event—or the single women in attendance—provided sustenance to Emily, convincing her she could save her marriage if she tried hard enough. Or perhaps it scared her. Whatever the reason, something motivated her and Edwin to reunite at Tuxedo Park for the December holidays. On the day after Christmas, they watched their sons cavort with friends on the frozen trout pond, flying down the iceboat run. Basically sail-powered sleds, iceboats encouraged the kind of camaraderie Emily enjoyed most, even though they required more physical exertion than she preferred these days. She recalled wistfully that she had somehow found the energy to maneuver both beaux and iceboats during that long-ago winter of 1891.

Now, as 1905 drew to an end, its finale stuffed with sumptuous holiday dinners, laughter, and libations, she was hopeful. Out on the lake, there was bravura skating, but Emily preferred watching the young lovers glide by arm in arm, her own arm linked, resolutely, through Edwin's. The couple attended the house parties at the cottages of the Pells and the Lorillard sons, as well as giving their own, just as in years past. Given her unwavering disapproval of divorce, Emily was undoubtedly bartering for her husband's affection. But their marriage was merely on hold. Whatever crusade Emily mounted to resurrect their severely bruised union—hoping to re-create the scene of conjugal reconciliation she had written for her last novel—failed to convince her real-life spouse.

CHAPTER 27

❖

*T*HE POSTS' DIVORCE, ANNOUNCED EARLY IN 1906 THOUGH NOT granted till the end of the year, was postponed upon Phoenix Ingraham's recommendation. Phoenix, though admitted to the bar only four years earlier, was well connected in legal and state circles through his illustrious father and grandfather. Now he was trying to protect his friends' privacy until the legal hurricane over the exposure of New York City's confidential divorce records had passed.

The federal government's investigation had been well intended. What should constitute a nationally uniform divorce law? As it stood, citizens could be legally divorced in one state, travel to another to be married to other people, and then honeymoon in a third state that not only failed to recognize their new marriage but considered them legally bound to their former spouses. Partly in response to what seemed a national epidemic of divorce, the government had concluded that a special summer census would, for the first time, assess official court records of failed marriages— including files previously sealed by law, destined to remain interred in the vaults, their truths about who did what to whom carefully concealed. Citizens who had testified under oath were horrified and outraged when unannounced staff from the U.S. Department of Commerce and Labor descended upon the New York City County Courthouse, seizing state-filed divorce documents.

Officials from Washington and the New York Supreme Court threatened one another in a tense standoff. Then, after watching federal workers delve into all documents pertaining to a divorce or separation less than twenty years old, the state defiantly intervened. Albany wouldn't permit this travesty of justice, New York lawmakers told their superiors. New Yorkers had taken the government at its word when they'd testified under oath. A state's rights action was filed, and furious federal officials were forced to substitute a census that allowed New Yorkers to keep their secrets.

And there seemed to be a burgeoning number of them. These days, the upper class seemed mad for divorce. It was as if the privileged generation following Josephine and Bruce had suddenly found their parents' model of marriage intolerable. But Emily Post would never waver throughout her life: divorce, when there were children involved, was to be avoided at all costs. Adults could contain their differences within a household for the sake of those they'd brought into the world. After all, she'd watched her mother and father and their good friends, such as the Lorillards, do exactly that, at least while their children were young.

UNLIKE MANY OF her era, Emily was ashamed that her marriage had failed. Luckily, that spring, further attention to her professional success soothed the sting of her looming divorce. The *Washington Post* explored the new claims of "women of wealth" who scorned idleness, preferring "to work, to do things, to accomplish." Near the end of the column, after discussing the "brush, pen and chisel" work of women ranging from Mrs. Harry Payne Whitney to Catherine Duer—and the obligatory Edith Wharton—the article's author enlisted a new figure, noting, "The signature 'Emily Post' is appearing with increasing frequency. This is the pen name of Mrs. Edwin Post, famed in society as Emily Price, daughter of the late Bruce Price, the architect. So far she has confined herself to fiction."

Such professional attention, along with the solace of time, encouraged Emily to focus on the present. Nonetheless, even though she no longer noticed conversations pausing when she walked by, reminders of the previous summer's scandal lingered everywhere. The annual Tuxedo horse show in June 1906 received a suspiciously large and sympathetic notice by Colonel Mann, just months before he managed to get himself acquitted of the convoluted charges finally filed against him by various society men. The illustrious and circumspect banker George F. Baker took over as the horse show's president, further motivating Mann to pander to the crowd he despised: Tuxedo Park had become "a colony more select if less wealthy than Newport . . . undoubtedly the most exclusive retreat on the American continent," he wrote in *Town Topics*. "Climbers have scaled the Newport cliffs only to find the hills of Tuxedo far more treacherous." Unlike Emily, Edwin was not ashamed of the public collapse of their marriage. In spite of his oft-expressed disdain for Tuxedo Park, he spent the rainy weekend of the horse show in residence. By now a first-rate tennis player, he wasn't about to miss the chance to compete in the June tournament. His estranged wife wasn't present.

Emily was working nonstop these days, finding in her writing a refuge from reality and from the rawness of her largely unexplored emotions. Sometimes, however, she was forced back to earth against her will. On October 25, 1906, on Nassau Street in lower Manhattan, mere blocks from her father's skyscraper, thirty-four-year-old Emily Price Post appeared at the Office of the Referee. Day after day, for two weeks, Emily was subjected to the details of her husband's forays with the actress Grace Fields, a witness in *Emily Post v. Edwin M. Post*.

In spite of his part in orchestrating the divorce for his friends, Phoenix Ingraham appeared now as Emily's advocate. Over the past year, the lawyer had gone through the necessary charade of hiring private detectives to "catch" Edwin going in and out of Grace's apartment. However cooperative with and sympathetic toward Edwin Phoenix had been, his subsequent, almost immediate courtship of Emily suggests that he was promoting his own interests as well.

Routine for its time, the hearing demanded that Emily swear under oath that she had not "forgiven" or "condoned" the relationship between Miss Fields and Mr. Post. Nor had she lived with Edwin since discovering his adultery. She had never visited the West Side Manhattan residence at 907 Seventh Avenue her husband shared with the actress. Edwin (with Emily's family money) had hired two servants to assist his paramour, who was, to make matters worse, a lovely, intelligent-looking young woman. Exhibit B consisted of photographs passed around the courtroom, including a handsome picture of Edwin and Grace, eerily similar in looks, both square-jawed with knowing but kind eyes. Grace's provocative face has nothing of the tawdry in it: she was classically beautiful. Her forthright gaze into the camera implies a certain feistiness, though her looks could have commanded the crowd's attention in the most genteel of Gilded Age ballrooms. Edwin had lost some hair this past year, but he only appeared more distinguished because of it. The five-foot-six bantamweight carried a mere 140 pounds on his slim frame. He and Grace seemed a good fit.

The hearing took two of the longest weeks in Emily's life, ending on November 6. Then, when it was all over, she was free to work. She could have a career; she would have to, she would claim, as a single woman supporting herself and her children in a manner to which they were accustomed. By the 1906 Christmas holidays, the Posts' divorce decree would be final. That December, almost twelve months following Emily and Edwin's last joint appearance, Edwin Main Post entered the New York Stock Exchange as a member for his final workday; henceforth, he would find odd jobs around Babylon to keep him afloat financially. On January 23, 1907, the front page of the *Times* updated society: "Divorce for Mrs. E. M. Post" explained that the divorce was a month old, its verdict sealed. Mrs. Post still owned the Tuxedo house, and it was "understood" that her attorneys had not asked for alimony. (Four years later, a small newspaper announcement of Edwin's remarriage rendered a different version: Edwin Post had been levied monthly alimony and child support of $200—the equivalent of $2,000 today—upon his divorce.)

Perhaps during the divorce proceedings Emily had nudged the *New York Times* writer to emphasize that she didn't ask for alimony. The newspaper's wording was just ambiguous enough to leave room for conjecture. But Edwin had no money left anyway, and it is unlikely that he made regular payments, whether assessed or not.

Every summer the well-tended children would take the train to their father's family home in Babylon. The two boys would come to love spending summers with their witty half brothers and their British stepmother, Eleanor. This time, he had found himself a real actress, not one who had taken to the amateur stage as if the limelight were her natural home, misleading Edwin Post about the obedient daughter he was about to marry instead.

For her part, Emily operated efficiently and quickly: she cut her ex-husband out of her life forever. He had become, in her household, a ghost. She would continue to set an extra place at the table for as long as she lived, though the identity of the absent guest remains unclear. According to family legend, she refused to see or speak to or hear about Edwin Post again. William Post, Emily's beloved grandson "Billy," remarks: "She never once mentioned Edwin in my hearing. Nor did she ever speak of remarrying. I have absolutely no idea whether my grandmother wanted to divorce Edwin or not. What I do know without a doubt is that she did not wish her personal problems to become public, ever."

—

NEITHER EMILY NOR EDWIN Post was a bad person in any conventional sense of the word. They had needs that a Gilded Age society marriage could not accommodate. Strong individuals, they fit better into the modern age on the horizon than into the Victorian era where they'd been young adults. Through no one's fault, they had fallen into a marriage conceived in the cracks of a decrepit model, one bequeathed them by their parents. Edwin replayed, in the way he treated Emily, his father's own family drama. And Emily, confused by her mother's adoration for Bruce alongside Josie's own diminished self-worth except as a helpmate, didn't know how to connect her marriage to the larger world she was yearning to join, or how to find a place in which to express her own prodigious talent.

Edwin liberated Emily Post. And perhaps she was so large of spirit, so honest with herself, that she realized her own complicity in the hollow formality her marriage had become. The divorce signaled, as much as personal freedom for both spouses, a new era of self-determination for unhappily married middle- and upper-class citizens. Like it or not, Emily Post was part of her age.

🕂

*E*MILY LISTENED WITH WONDER TO HER FRIENDS' DESCRIPTIONS of the brilliantly illuminated iron and wooden ball, a seven-hundred-pound colossus five feet wide. One hundred twenty-five-watt bulbs harbingered the future, as the unwieldy globe descended a flagpole at Times Square. It was the new way to mark the New Year, but Emily preferred to retreat to the past, where she could reclaim her sense of self. She sailed to Europe in January, the solace of travel abroad meant to clear her mind of the tragic farce she'd been part of at home. But innovations in communications meant that distance no longer protected the rich: she had barely debarked when she heard that a colleague of her father's, the architect Stanford White, had been killed in a lovers' triangle.

As frightening as it all sounded from afar, at least it stayed distant to her while she was in France, where she reveled in Paris's diverting squabbles instead. Increasingly important to Emily following her divorce, these annual respites would satisfy her need for reconnecting with the Old World, where she felt safe psychologically as well as physically. She soon developed a routine that varied little during the next ten years: after spending a week or two at Minnie Coster's apartment in Paris, she'd visit her friend Leila Emery, whose baby daughter Audrey would marry Grand Duke Dmitri—long after he had betrayed his Romanov family and helped to assassinate Rasputin. Emily went from friend to friend (or distant relative), spending several summers motoring through the Black Forest or the Dolomites and finishing the season in Normandy, where Uncle Frank often painted *en plein air.*

All these signs—the focused writing, the visits to friends she grew closer

to—indicate that Emily managed to digest much of the lumpy psychic matter of her dissolved marriage within months. The divorce had, after all,
been a long time in coming. Resilient by nature, she was becoming centered
again, maybe more content than she'd ever been, except as the darling of
Tuxedo Park. She returned to New York City in time to attend a benefit at
the Waldorf-Astoria for Rome's Keats-Shelley house, featuring Uncle
Frank at the dais with Mark Twain and five other luminaries at his side.
Mrs. Grover Cleveland was among the guests "prominent in society, literature, and art."

As gratifying as her writing was, what gave her at least as much pleasure
was her talent for interior design and construction, which was suddenly
valued in her father's world. Family friend John Russell Pope had begun
seeking her help in creating models of the houses he was building. Brilliant
designs on the outside, he'd realized, didn't ensure livable interiors. Might
Bruce Price's talented daughter, whose drawings he'd admired years before,
pursue ways to solve his problems? The resultant models Emily began constructing from waxed paper, paint, tape, and glue provided exactly what he
needed. Month by month, more architectural commissions poured in, and
Emily's employment gave her more joy than anything she'd ever done.

By the spring of 1907, Emily had found that life as an unmarried woman
suited her quite well. Her sons—Bruce, now twelve, and Ned, almost fourteen years old—were installed at the prestigious Connecticut boarding
school Pomfret, and she was free to arrange her schedule as she preferred.
Often she'd spend long weekends, extended sometimes even to a month, at
Connecticut's Ben Grosvenor Inn, visiting her sons nearby, always treating
them and their friends to ice cream. Vivacious and pretty, she made Ned
and Bruce proud, as the other boys clearly envied them for their fine
mother. "She was then just past thirty-five [actually, she was thirty-four]
and at the height of her beauty," Ned remembered. "Her freedom and the
sense that she was coming into powers whose full scope she did not yet
know exhilarated her to an even greater loveliness, gaiety, and charm. The
entire Sixth [his class] was in love with her." An overeager master, having
palavered her with compliments and plied her with Dante Gabriel Ros-
setti's lush poetry, "gorged" one early May afternoon on Emily's "beauty,
wit, and flattering attention to his somewhat jejune observations, and he
succumbed to her charms: he begged her to marry him." Gently, she said no,
sweetly asking him, "If I were to marry you, what would the boys call you?"

Occasionally Josephine accompanied her daughter to the inn, and Ned

Post remembers his grandmother's visits in a tone of affectionate conde-scension: "When she would come up to visit us at school, the boys never be-lieved she was our Granny. She looked younger than many of the mothers, though she was always impatient about spending time on the punctilio of her appearance. Emily had persuaded her to use an eyebrow pencil to rem-edy her lack of noticeable eyebrows. The improvement in her looks was great, when she remembered to pencil both brows. Often she would go down ready to go out, but with only one eyebrow. . . . Bruce and I were con-stantly on guard to see that this did not happen."

In spite of their pride and affection, Emily's sons occasionally wished their mother as well as Josie would stay home. As active adolescents, they didn't particularly want Emily's gaze fixed on them or her presence interfer-ing with their plans. Sometimes, too, her well-meaning attentions threat-ened to smother them. Her grandson would recall: "She could seem stifling at times, even though she was in general a formal-type woman, a product of her times, even with me, who was very close to her. But when she turned her gaze on you, that was that. It was like a spotlight, very intense. I'm sure my father and my uncle wanted to beg her to leave, but they would never hurt her. That was the problem: she always meant well and you couldn't just push her away."

DURING THAT YEAR Emily exhibited the classic signs of a newly divorced woman trying on various identities for size. She developed what would prove a passing interest in a field hitherto foreign to her, "metaphysics," as the pseu-doscience was grandly called. The vogue of the day, metaphysics functioned as an umbrella for various occult and spiritual systems, all heavily weighted with arcane symbols. When "Mr. G." had flirted with Emily through intima-tions of the otherworldly, she had dismissed him.

But that phase of her life had given her an idea for her next novel, the treacly *Woven in the Tapestry*. While working out her short-lived fascination with metaphysics through writing the book, Emily deepened her friendship with Tuxedo Park's Julie Olin Benkard. According to Julie's memoir, she and Emily progressed from mere acquaintances to fast friends the day they both called the clubhouse at the same time to request a "jigger," the "tiny rickety bus" that ferried Tuxedo Park residents around the complex and to the train station. Emily boarded a few stops after Julie. Aware of the younger woman's occult interests, she almost immediately began talking about "thinking out" the plot of *Woven in the Tapestry*. The two women saw each other frequently from then on, Julie especially pleased to have a friend at the dauntingly regular dinners at Tuxedo Park. She, like Edwin, found the social scape here in the Ramapo hills claustrophobic, the identical guests showing up night after night at dinners sponsored by a select group. "Emily Post, Newbold Edgar, the Pillots and Tiltons and the Freddy Piersons alternated locations, each evening one group hosting everyone else at his or her cottage," she would recall. Such a "glass house" didn't upset Emily, but she could nonetheless sympathize with Julie's wry lament. "There weren't any secrets in the Park. Still, it was fine if one simply sustained social expectations and didn't strain the atmosphere for others. Your private life was your own."

Though it would quickly become clear to Emily that Julie (who later converted to the Baha'i faith and endowed the organization handsomely upon her death) took inquiry into the mystical far more seriously than she did, the combination of Julie's flamboyant life but impeccable breeding implied a courage Emily respected.

When Emily and Julie became friends, they both already knew Lewis Chanler—Julie far more intimately than Emily. Chanler (later lieutenant governor of New York) had built a house at Tuxedo Park for his wife and children. There and in Rhinebeck, where Julie also had a house, Lewis Chanler and Mrs. Philip Benkard, née Julie Olin, had met and fallen dramatically, flamboyantly, and entirely indiscreetly in love. They would live in sin for seventeen years because Alice Chanler, unlike Philip Benkard, refused to give her spouse a divorce. That Emily felt comfortable now, as an adult on her own, drawing close to Julie and sharing her and Lewis's set of friends, speaks potently to the changing times, and to Emily's own sense of belonging to the "blemished" circle. Nearby Rokeby mansion, for instance, was no longer open to Emily because she was a divorcée and Margaret Ward Chanler emphatically did not receive divorced people; her ill-behaved brother Lewis was not, after all, divorced. He was just living in sin with a woman who was not his wife.

Julie and Emily quickly discovered that they were each a connoisseur of dressing well, their clothes a major pleasure to them both because of the self-expression they allowed. By this time, Emily had found a perfect seamstress in Manhattan, and she generously shared her with Julie. Bertha Leach was a "genius" with a needle, according to her grandniece, Evelyn Perrault. Married young, Bertha was early widowed and needed to earn a living. Though the divide between employer and employee was always present, Emily and Bertha developed a friendship that granted them both great satisfaction.

Bertha could provide only one of the outfits for the charity bazaar at Tuxedo that year, and her loyalty lay with Emily. The "Best Dressed Woman in the Park" contest nonetheless ended up pitting the two friends against each other for the winning entry. Julie would recall the event years later: A "tall dial recorded the way things stood. As the proceeding went on, the candidates having few votes were progressively eliminated and finally only two remained, Emily Post and myself," neck and neck. Emily just pulled it off, at the end. It was fun "because we were great friends," Julie remembered. Apparently, in spite of her determination to be seen as a professional woman, she allowed herself time off to be silly once in a while.

Emily and Julie probably were "only" friends, in spite of the paradoxical ease with which women of the period could have lesbian relationships. In light of the lingering Victorian assumptions about female sexual desire, females were granted extensive cover for same-sex relationships, and certainly Julie was quite willing to break rules and cross boundaries. But by the time she got divorced, Emily had accustomed herself to Victorian expectations of limited physical pleasure for wives. Even her grandson would decide that Emily "wasn't a sexual person. She wasn't gay but she wanted to live her own life. She liked what she had made of her own life; she was asexual but passionate about life." She had decided: no man—or woman— would ever hold her hostage again.

In her astute analysis of the late-Victorian mores that shaped major female writers of the early twentieth century—Virginia Woolf, Willa Cather, Gertrude Stein, and Edith Wharton—Claudia Roth Pierpont has remarked on the "astonishing" lack of "practicing heterosexuality," the extreme "aversion to the male." The "ambitious woman" making the "dangerous crossing from the nineteenth century into modernity" had no model that underwrote her role as a fully invested, highly successful professional woman with a man at her side. Wharton, whom Emily would closely observe in person and in her writing, was ruthless as she portrayed ways society deformed the fairer sex, including teaching her to waste even a formidable intellect in the pursuit of the trivial. At least Emily recognized the danger of entering too many "Best Dressed" contests, however much in jest.

EMILY POST WAS BECOMING a professional, and she reveled in her new identity. Her longtime friendship with Hop Smith was furthering connections worlds away from metaphysics, which was at most a passing fancy for the pragmatic daughter of Josephine. She was much more at home at Uncle Frank's Sunday night buffet suppers, where she mingled with important male figures in the art and literary worlds: the elderly poet Richard Watson Gilder (the editor of *Century* magazine until he died in 1909 and, equally impressive to Emily, one of the founders of the Society of American Architects); George Barr Baker (an editor who, through Uncle Hop, had become like family to Emily); Condé Nast (the publisher of *Vanity Fair,* who would convince Frank Crowninshield to become its editor in 1914); and Frank "Crownie" Crowninshield himself, he who was equally expert in the art and literary worlds. Decades later, Emily would let it drop, in an unguarded moment, that Crownie, between his convoluted romantic relationships, had been "a one-time suitor."

The divorcée's freedom to attend social dinners at friends' houses reflected the changes in society that had even upper-class women rethinking their assumptions about the old restrictions of gender. If Emily had needed a place to work away from home, for instance, the Colony Club, an organization her friends were forming—Mrs. J. Borden Harriman, Mrs. John Jacob Astor, Mrs. Walter Damrosch, Miss Elizabeth Marbury, Mrs. Payne Whitney, and the diligent, hardworking suffragette Miss Anne Morgan—ministered both to the professional working woman and the nonemployed socialite as well.

On March 12, 1907, the club had finally opened, complete with guest rooms for visitors from out of town. Local papers were confused at the egalitarianism of an upper-crust organization that charged $100 for annual dues (around $2,000 today) and an initiation fee of $150. "Women of the highest social standing in New York are numbered among the club's members, and with them are literary women, women of the stage, and business women. There is not one member of the type known in New York as 'the club woman,'" noted one newspaper. The Colony Club was a place where even eligible middle-class working women could belong. Almost as notable, most of the club's spaces had "no restrictions against smoking"—and it had a woman chef.

Emerging from a city and an era both in flux, the Colony Club was inevitably denounced as immoral, elitist, and damaging to women's health. It was unworthy of inhabiting a neighborhood of churches, clergymen complained. Would the women drink as well as smoke? The club would surely doom families, suddenly bereft of their guiding light, as women began aping their husbands and spending their evenings away from home. Civic opposition also arose: How could sensible women justify the luxury of such an innovation? The country was still struggling to help rebuild San Francisco in the wake of the earthquake, whose reverberations had followed by a year the Russo-Japanese War, pinching the American money supply. As if to emphasize the women's supposed oblivion, the day after the Colony Club opened, there was a sudden collapse on Wall Street. One commentator noted wryly that, all in all, the timing was not good for "conspicuous luxury."

Because of her friends' outrage at the opposition, Emily tried to care about the Colony Club debate. For the most part, however, she was single-minded and felt no desire for camaraderie these days. She sought the opposite: to be left alone, allowed to adhere to her now rigid daily writing routine. Initially, she woke at six-thirty, then ate toast and drank coffee in bed, served by her kitchen staff. After noticing how sleepy her servants were at that hour, she switched to a self-service routine, her tray set up the night before. She wrote in bed until noon, with a midmorning break to talk to her household help, and then she rose to visit friends or tend to business matters.

When she was not writing, she accepted commissions from Bruce's associates to construct models for their buildings. Her knowledge of furniture and fabrics was considered first-rate, well served by her keen sense of style and fashion. Often using paper cutouts for staircases, windows, and doorways, she didn't hesitate to suggest structural changes to her employers, most of which they accepted. From such work, she received tremendous pleasure as well as a generous supplemental income. According to her later, probably unreliable memory, for the first few years following the divorce, her writing and decorating together earned her an average income of $2,000 a year (or $40,000 today), none of which went toward housing: she owned the Tuxedo Park house given her upon her marriage by Bruce and Josephine, as well as the Manhattan residence bequeathed her by her grandparents. Hers was no hardscrabble life. She was suffering in genteel poverty, enjoying every minute of her current independence. Her new life included her cheerful mother occasionally underwriting her daughter's lifestyle with a surprise delivery of groceries or an unexpected dress and plumed hat she thought perfect for her daughter.

From an interview Emily would give decades later, she was also supplementing her income during this period with "anonymous confession writing" and with jokes she sold to magazines. Though no record of them remains, we do know the way she tested them. Before she sent an item to a publisher, she first read it aloud to her mother. If Josephine laughed, the joke was no good. If she didn't get it—or, just as bad, was "disapproving"—Emily knew "she had a winner. The system never failed."

Frequently letting her apartment and staying at Josephine's home on West Tenth Street, Emily carefully compressed her household expenses, even leasing her Tuxedo cottage for a few months in the spring or autumn, when rentals went for top dollar. Reduced appearances in public and her decision to rent out the city apartment she'd inherited from the Lees suggest that, however luxurious her reduced circumstances must have appeared to many, she was taking seriously the mandate to support herself and her sons. When gently reminded by her friends that of course she should remarry, she shocked them by suggesting that she actually preferred being single.

FINALLY, DURING THE SUMMER of 1908, *Woven in the Tapestry* was released. It was a very bad book and a brave one: Emily Price Post was willing to fail. An odd blend of the occult, the mysterious, and the philosophical, the novel, meant to be semihistorical, is a wobbly period piece that reflects Emily's era. The early part of the century thrived on fantasy, whether the Nordic myths of *Das Rheingold* co-opting the Metropolitan Opera those days or the general intellectual preoccupation with magic. Five years later, Emily's ex-brother-in-law A.V.Z. Post would write a bestselling novel, *Diana Ardway;* its Hudson Valley heroine's "strange insight for the occult" was inspired by the Rhinebeck crowd whose parties Emily attended. Around the valley, traveling in their cars or on the train into New York City, partygoers claimed to have witnessed table turning at the séances sweeping the elite parlors of the Rhinebeck mansions. The phenomenon, noted jaded observers, was amazingly similar to an epidemic several years earlier.

A small press, Moffat, Yard and Company, noted for its specialization in books on metaphysical subject matter, published *Woven in the Tapestry.* The novel had a second small printing soon after its modest publication, suggesting perhaps that at least some of the readers Emily had developed with her previous two books were willing to take a risk. They must have been bewildered, if not slack-jawed, as they read prose of outlandish artifice:

"Why do you look so searchingly? What do you seek, Artaras?"

"Only that which all men seek—which I am seeking ever! Taking all that I can make my own—whether it falls my way, or whether I must needs pursue."

The plot is entangled in windy language that no one, including the reviewers, seemed to understand. Emily intended the novel as an allegory of life versus art, but the plot is so underdeveloped and the language so overwrought that the reader remains unsure of the story's meaning. The *Times'* reviewer seems to have deliberately aped the novelist's opaque style: "There are times of fairy and dream, to every young soul, entering upon life, feeling rather than knowing the mysteries before him, seeing the task of living through some medium, that lends it hues of purple and gold, seeing it unreal, not as it will be, but akin to it, as the shadow in a lake is akin to the rocky height it reflects." By the end of the review, it still wasn't clear if the journalist admired or detested the novel.

Several weeks after *Woven in the Tapestry* was published, Emily was transported back to her less fantastic world with a wallop of a stomachache. She suffered through several days of severe abdominal pain—probably, according to later suggestions, endometriosis, a gynecological complication. Her mother urged her to rely upon the Christian Science doctrine of self-healing, which Josie herself still embraced wholeheartedly, in spite of its uselessness when her husband lay dying. But if Emily had ever been so inclined, Mark Twain's open contempt for the religion's founder, Mary Baker Eddy, expressed in his recent visit to Tuxedo Park, had won Emily's allegiance; he'd excoriated Eddy for what he considered her cruel concept of "healing."

Josephine's insistence that Emily could control her "indigestion" with mental nostrums backfired when, a few months later, Emily paid her mother back for her lack of sympathy. When Josie herself started crying from the throbbing of an abscessed tooth, Emily tartly reminded her of Christian Science doctrine: "You have no pain . . . that is just error. Error of mortal mind." The two women had never really understood each other, and now their alliance was based on little but familial love, which, luckily, they were finding was more than enough.

CHAPTER 29

🕸

EVER SINCE ALVA VANDERBILT'S VICTIMIZED DAUGHTER, CONSUELO, had wept openly as she walked down the aisle to wed her disagreeable but aristocratic groom, readers had gobbled up tales of American fortunes traded for Old World bloodlines. With some embarrassment at her own untoward curiosity, Emily herself, along with her cousin Sadie and her friend Minnie Coster, had lunched at Juliet Hamilton's house in order to compare notes about the lavish wedding, the high point of the autumn social season in 1895. One of Consuelo's bridesmaids, Edwin's cousin, armed with firsthand backstage chitchat, was clearly the star for the day, and the other women tried, without success, to look nonchalant as she launched into her stories.

Now, thirteen years later, Emily shrewdly realized that the time had come to capitalize on her familiarity with this highfalutin social world by writing a novel about exchanging European titles for American cash. She had been making good money writing articles on royal romances for *Everybody's Magazine*, even winning the lucrative $5,000 first prize in the monthly's short-story contest. Wisely, she spent much of 1908 expanding that story into *The Title Market,* which would prove her strongest novel yet. Some of its most memorable anecdotes were supplied by her friend Helen Gould, who happily repeated stories about the reconstruction her niece Anna had undergone at the hands of her husband, Count de Castellane: after the count had tactlessly revised his homely wife's wardrobe and restyled her hair, he'd proceeded to shave the trail of black hair that grew up her back. Certainly Emily didn't lack for material.

Intent on searching out the choicest of such stories, Emily had begun treating herself to short trips abroad in addition to her annual pilgrimages to visit her titled relatives and friends. Visiting the best addresses, she eagerly collected tales about royal marriages and their aftermath, a subject the upper class loved to chronicle. Even as the oldest European coffers were being emptied distressingly fast these days, Gilded Age fortunes with no titles to precede them were in great demand.

Whether it was Monte Carlo, the Swiss Alps, or the Portuguese coast, Emily's travels left her little time to feel sad. Even in Europe's choicest resorts, there were problems more pressing than hers. It was impossible, for instance, for guests to mistake the despondency in residence at Minnie Coster's French villa these days. Minnie's husband, the investor William Coster, was torn over whether to move the family back to New York while the New York Stock Exchange investigated his brother's suicide. Charles Coster, it seemed, might have killed himself after he was discovered to be embezzling investors' funds. The haze of uncertainty that hung over Minnie was one with which Emily could sympathize: she had experience now.

Such hard-won wisdom paid off handsomely, and Emily's confidence grew. That autumn, her self-assurance clearly impressed those around her. The *New York Times* commented that even her wardrobe seemed to be making a new statement these days. The photograph titled "Mrs. E. M. Post in Pink" captures a secure young matron aware of her good looks. Still fresh and vivacious, she emits a new seductive certainty. To the Tuxedo Park horse show, she wore a "walking skirt and coat of dull rose-colored cloth" in a "modish" short length. The suit's "plainness" subtly managed to emphasize the wearer's figure. As always, her subtly stylish hat harmonized with her ensemble. Given the article's topic—the dark and subdued colors predicted for this fall's fashions—Emily, brightly and boldly dressed, was asserting her individuality. Her patrician good looks almost daunting, she felt she was in control again, just as she'd been before she'd married Edwin.

THE FOLLOWING FEBRUARY, *Everybody's Magazine* began its monthly serialization of *The Title Market*, the installments appearing from February through September 1909. At the end of the novel's run, the *New York Times* helpfully recounted the plot, which trotted out the shopworn contest between American ingenuity (and innocence) and European sophistication (and decadence). What kind of life would a girl from Fifth Avenue discover if she married a duke or a prince from the old country? Was life in a drafty,

decrepit castle better or worse than living more modestly in familiar surroundings?

The novel is less tentative than her earlier work; her prose had gained
texture that it lacked before. In spite of its tired subject, *The Title Market* is a
credible romance in part because of the charming Old World stories her
friends and relatives shared with her. The novel's Italian husband, a charming, handsome gambler, was based on the spouse of a distant cousin of
Bruce's. Every time *The Title Market*'s Prince Sansevero needs more cash, he
convinces his American wife that this time his will be the winning bet: "Just
this once—you will help me, won't you?" The wife inevitably yields to his
charming, "boyish" entreaties, though in the ten years they've been married
his schemes have almost depleted her inheritance. Her "boy-like" husband
has also caused the woman to age prematurely: she has the worried "verti-
cal lines" of a woman of "thirty-five."

Emily's cousin Nina (the daughter of Josephine's first cousin) was the
model for the story's eponymous ingénue. Relying upon her own new
reality—paying the bills and keeping tabs on the family's expenses—Emily
portrayed a heroine learning to pinch pennies. In an exchange the author
could not have written five years earlier, Nina worries aloud about her
aunt's lack of heating oil: "I don't understand! You don't have to think of
such a thing as the expense of keeping warm, do you?" Nina asks, horrified.

"Indeed we do," the older expatriate (Prince Sansevero's wife) answers.
"Fuel is a very serious item."

The Title Market "is one of the most convincing stories of the season, and
one that a reader cares to remember," the *Tribune* pronounced. Nina comes
to prefer the forthrightness and sturdy good character of the American
man to the admittedly smoother manners of her European suitor. Emily
probably modeled Nina's choice, the gallant and trustworthy Jack, upon
George Barr Baker, the magazine editor who had given her her start when
he'd recommended publishing *The Flight of a Moth*. Her subsequent appointment of Baker, Uncle Frank's longtime friend, as guardian of her sons testified to the high regard he elicited in Emily.

She continued writing about marriage, a subject she felt she knew well.
In April, while *The Title Market* was still in magazine serialization, Emily
published a short article in *Life* magazine that must have startled even her
closest friends. "On the Care of Husbands" gently satirized the woman
who greeted her tired husband at the door with a list of complaints. Warning that such insensitivity was a sure way to lose a man, Emily implied by

her writing that she herself, a very publicly divorced woman, was an expert on preserving one's marriage; she, in other words, was the innocent party in her own household's demise.

That summer, partly to promote *The Title Market*'s forthcoming publication as a book, Emily wrote a long piece for the *New York Journal,* one of New York's popular dailies, on real-life marriages of the sort her novel depicted. " 'Outrageous to Wed Titles': Mrs. Post Blames Mothers," the headline trumpeted in bold letters, though the article itself proved less provocative. Emily's brisk tone betrayed her impatience with any but practical considerations. Should American girls marry titled foreigners? It all depended on the individual's circumstances: a girl should weigh the options against her sense of self. In what follows, however, Emily made it clear which side she was on:

> If she prefers a man who will smooth out the path of life; who will always be alert to please; to serve in the lesser things; who has finesse, manner, an amazing understanding of the art of making women comfortable, then I say an American girl might marry, and marry happily, a foreigner. [But] if she prefers the man with the stalwart, reliant, almost brutal force of love; with no frills; with no understanding of what might be termed the art of life—rather one who has a contempt for it—then she is happier as the wife of an American.

Even during the courtship, Emily pointed out, there were trade-offs no matter which model you chose. In America, for instance, men tended to ignore the older generation. In Europe, suitors virtually courted the parents of the girl they sought. A European sophisticate "devotes himself to the mother," she wrote, deferring to her power over his marital prospects.

Just as important were the dissimilar aftermaths of the weddings. American women, unlike their European counterparts, failed dismally as intellectual equals. Often they couldn't even talk about detailed household finances with their husbands, let alone discuss international politics. Those few American women who took the time to learn the nuances of export and import tariffs gained the potential to exert a strong impact on the economy. Indirect influence, in other words, the same method Josephine had deployed to handle Bruce Price and the family finances, was the key to a married woman's success.

For a while, in 1909, as her novel's installments were appearing monthly in *Everybody's Magazine,* Emily was satisfied. Indeed, it seemed that everyone— at least everyone she and her mother knew—was talking about *The Title Market.* Even Josephine, while warning her daughter of the dangers of pride, must have been gratified to see neighbors reading a chapter from her daughter's novel. Increased warmth between the two women following Emily's decision to share her mother's Manhattan apartment surfaced in their frequent mutual social appearances.

And to Josephine's great relief, Emily was beginning to understand how to market herself. Proud of her daughter's strength, she had accepted her headstrong child's success as a professional writer. At least Emily looked the way she should, a successful young woman back on the marriage market— while she wrote her books in the meantime. For now, Josephine enjoyed the chance to claim her own time with Emily, but she also believed her daughter far too young to become an old maid, even a formerly married one.

Emily was indeed thinking about men these days, though not for the reasons Josie anticipated. One day, striving to sound nonchalant, the writer confided to her mother that she thought she was ready for the next step: she needed an agent.

⚸

ON OCTOBER 17, 1909, THE INTREPID FIFTY-FIVE-YEAR-OLD JOSEPHINE, always ready for an adventure, accepted the offer of her friend Mrs. Charles Coulter to accompany her and her twelve-year-old son Charles on a beautiful, color-drenched Sunday drive in the Hudson Valley. Crisp and bracing, it was the perfect autumn day to take the car out, chauffeur John Scully had proclaimed. Mrs. Coulter stopped to pick up Mrs. Price at around three-thirty, and they drove to Arden, six miles away, where they leisurely toured the grounds of Tuxedo Park's late railroad tycoon Edward Henry Harriman. His assets (estimated variously at $100 million to $400 million) would surpass the $80 million worth of J. P. Morgan's estate when he died a few years later.

There was no reason for the women to feel worried about others observing their curiosity—who would even see them in the seemingly endless miles of forested roads? The grounds were said to be magnificent: several decades earlier, Harriman had bought 7,863 acres for $52,500, adding 20,000 acres over the next few years, all of which he connected with forty miles of bridle paths. Mrs. Price and Mrs. Coulter had already heard the rumors about Harriman's widow planning to donate the lands to the state, and they wanted to see the property up close while the estate was still off-limits to the general public.

As they drove with the breeze wafting over them in the open touring car, the gentle swoosh of late-afternoon air against their faces felt divine this time of year. The low rumble of the tires against the gravel, lulling them as they drove, probably quashed any desire to talk. Maybe the little group lingered too long, unable to tear themselves away from such perfect weather. Maybe, suddenly aware of the lengthening shadows, they urged the driver to go just a bit faster: they were returning home and it was time for the substantial tea that the women assumed would segue, as usual, into an early dinner.

Chauffeur Scully sped up a bit when he got onto the clear, level roadway cut through the estate. Nearly in front of the manager's house, the Coulter car came upon another tourist driving more slowly in the same direction. Scully maneuvered to pass the vehicle, but he misjudged the width of the road. His car's wheel caught in a rut, causing the vehicle to skid off the edge of the lane, toward a ditch three or four feet deep. The roadway crumbled beneath the heavy touring car, which then plunged into the ditch, over-turning against a tree straight ahead, the front of the auto "striking the trunk with considerable force," as the *New York Times* later reported.

Josephine Lee Price slammed headfirst into the oversized pine border-ing the road. Thrown from the car, she had her "skull . . . crushed," the newspaper related, the graphic description surely numbing Emily as she read it. The "machine" pinned Josie's body against the tree, the smashed car and the tree making a gruesome sandwich out of Josephine, who died while the driver of the other vehicle tried to pry her from the entrapment. Mrs. Coulter and her son were not seriously injured, though the broken, twisted arm the mother sustained as her son landed on top of her required that she be hospitalized. They and their bruised chauffeur would recover.

The woman who'd meshed the Civil War era with the brash Gilded Age was finally claimed by the very emblem of modernity, the automobile. Her blameless daughter yet again became the object of the public's prurient at-tention, as Josephine's violent death among society's lush private grounds naturally proved irresistible fodder for the city's papers.

EMILY, TELLING HER sons their grandmother was sick, arranged for them to take the train home from Pomfret. Instead, when the boys arrived in Tuxedo, she gently explained why she was taking them to buy new suits. Concentrating on her sons' sadness over Josie's death, Emily was relieved to have something to distract her from her own grief. Since her father's death, she had drawn increasingly close to her mother, in spite of what she consid-ered their radically different personalities. She had even come to appreciate how important Josie had been to Bruce's achievements, through her stolid financial wisdom and her no-nonsense determination to anchor the architect's fancies. Maybe, Emily had reflected, there was more of Josephine in her than she'd realized.

Josie was cremated, her funeral held on a late Tuesday morning at St. Mary's in Tuxedo Park. After the service, Emily and the boys took a train to Wilkes-Barre, where Josephine's ashes were buried alongside Bruce's. Following her mother's interment—which her sons, always more amused than moved by their grandmother, remembered primarily for their pleasure at seeing Great-Uncle Charlie again and for the chance to miss school—Emily returned to the solace she always sought in times of distress: she went to work. Her next novel, *The Eagle's Feather*, which Dodd, Mead hoped would ride the crest of her successful serialization of *The Title Market* the year before, was due to the publisher soon. Finally, she meant to honor her mother as well as her father through her success.

On November 5 the will was read. Lack of income would never again be a problem for Emily Post. Josephine had bequeathed her daughter and her grandsons all her carefully controlled assets. She also asked Emily, in the name of Bruce Price, to continue the monthly $75 allowances she had been making to two of her late husband's relatives, until they died. Josie made generous $10,000 gifts to various extended family members—to be bestowed, however, only upon the premature deaths of Emily and her sons. The exact amount left to her only primary heir, her daughter, went unspecified, but it included all of Josephine's real estate: four houses at Tuxedo Park and her apartment in New York City as well.

On the dedication page of the second printing of *The Title Market,* Emily would acknowledge her mother's untiring willingness to listen as her daughter tried out plot alternatives aloud: "As though you did not know each page, each paragraph, each word; as though for months and months the Sanseveros, Nina, John, and all the rest, had not been your daily companions—Madre Mia, this book is dedicated to you." Four months after the accident, Josie's mother, Emily Lee, died. For some years she had been living in the New Jersey home her husband had maintained for two of his unmarried sisters. Now Emily's mother and grandmother were both gone. Increasingly, Emily Post was on her own.

Taking solace in keeping busy, Emily appeared at the Tuxedo Park horse show the following month in a much-noted "hand painted chiffon gown with a cerise cloak" and a "small little black hat, much like a tricorne, with a great brush of stiff, rose-colored aigrettes pointing backward." Between her mother's bequest and her own income, she had enough money to splurge on a luxury or two. In later years, as if unable to justify continuing to work any other way, Emily would simply dismiss the inheritance and vaguely suggest that her mother had left her a "small fortune" which soon "vanished in bad investments." All evidence suggests otherwise.

Josephine would certainly have appreciated the kind of attention, all within the boundaries of good taste, her daughter was receiving these days. *Publishers Weekly* focused on Emily's charming home design instead of her books. A month later, a few days after Christmas, a short syndicated newspaper interview meant to promote *The Title Market* identified the author as "particularly well-suited" to discussing overseas romance. Was marrying a title a good thing or not? The novelist advised that as long as a wife created a fulfilling home for her family, domestic or foreign marriages contained equal opportunities for happiness. Women didn't fully appreciate the influence they exerted within their own households, private kingdoms that could inspire "state and country," wherever the wives lived.

Such domestic scenes were far removed from the concerns of most contemporary women: at times Emily's emphasis seemed anachronistic, harking back to her parents' era. Debates about social injustices rather than royal weddings held sway these days in the conversations of most educated women. The classes were mixing things up, and the newspapers were full of the urban potpourri that followed. Readers learned about the Colony Club speeches, where striking shirtwaist factory workers were the guests of honor. The incongruous images skillful writers conjured of such a social mix seemed far more relevant than the fairy-tale kingdom of overseas marriages. Right here, in New York City, sympathetic club ladies were passing the hat in the name of their less privileged sisters, in one meeting collecting $1,300 (worth $27,000 today) on the spot.

But women would prove a no more solid voting bloc than any other constituency, quickly separating into their own idiosyncratic concerns. Workers, for instance, broke ranks among themselves when some of their members dared accept support from high-profile society suffragists. Newspaper articles about rich, outspoken women like Alva or even the notoriously shy Anne Morgan parading against sex discrimination only irritated their less fortunate sisters. The image of J. P. Morgan's earnest but incalculably rich daughter—interested throughout her life in the welfare of women—setting up meetings to support factory workers incensed some observers. Class issues became more confusing than gender; what seemed like logical alliances didn't fit after all. Girl strikers might be recounting their woes to millionaires one day, while the next morning the same young women would denounce these wealthy socialites for wasting their time on the vote: What did such privileged ladies think they knew about politics anyway?

In some cases, their rage was well aimed. Emily avoided the maelstrom by claiming, when asked her opinion, that she hadn't studied the issues enough to justify taking a position. It was an ignorance she later rued, a lack of awareness that her uninformed mother had unwittingly fostered. Gradually, as she educated herself about the ways a society functioned, Emily would realize that class and gender were issues that never went away, regardless of the vocabulary they came clothed in.

CHAPTER 31

❊

ON JANUARY 1, 1910, ENRICO CARUSO SANG IN THE METROPOLITAN Opera's first live radio broadcast. Though the country was still a decade away from easy access to radios, this moment marked the real changing of the cultural guard, a democratizing of possibilities. Emily Post, never as strongly interested in music as in its spectacle, would nonetheless grow to value the radio for its unimaginable potential to connect her with her readers. She understood that the future was upon her and she had to find a new way in. That awareness is part of what funded her decision to hire an agent.

She was also motivated by her ex-husband's trespass onto her territory. Weeks earlier, Emily had heard about Edwin's own impressive achievement, writ large on her landscape. His glossy piece of fiction entitled "The Blue Handkerchief" had appeared in the relatively new journal the *Smart Set*. Until its demise in 1930, the magazine would present important new writers, introducing its readers to literary modernism as it published new authors from F. Scott Fitzgerald and Dorothy Parker to Eugene O'Neill. Though its circulation was small in 1910, the *Smart Set* already enjoyed a reputation for being intelligent but slick. When Edwin's story appeared that February, Emily must have been annoyed to see her ex-husband listed among a group that included George Jean Nathan, H. L. Mencken, and Louis Untermeyer. Even harder for her to swallow was the source of Edwin's good fortune. William D. Mann—Colonel Mann himself, the hated publisher of *Town Topics*—had founded the *Smart Set*, his name listed prominently on its cover for all to see.

"The Blue Handkerchief" is a fluff piece full of double entendre and smug club references. Based on actual anecdotes that Edwin's sophisticated, unmarried older brother had heard and shared with him, the story features a couple of society men who duel over the dishonor dealt to a third. Only at the end does the reason for the rapiers surface: Monsieur de Nancy, the man challenged to fight Raol, had implied that Raol's friend Armand fathered the child of the Comtesse de Crèvecoeur. Because the toddler possessed the eccentric carrot-red hair of Armand himself, Monsieur de Nancy had dared conjecture about the boy's patrimony. The story ends with everyone laughing, merrily reconciled.

Those socialites in their old circle who had preferred Edwin to Emily must have relished his current success. Surely the snider ones connived to ask Emily her professional opinion of his piece. She was too savvy not to deflect such arrows easily. But she was smart enough, and a good enough novelist, to realize that Edwin was a natural writer in a way that she could never be. Her ex-husband could produce on the spur of the moment highly crafted sentences that would have taken Emily several rewrites to create. Still, she also realized that he had never written anything over ten pages; even his prose might flag if he held himself to the grindstone, discipline he'd never be able to exert.

PAUL REYNOLDS, a "tall, spare, awkward, shy, and modest man," had done graduate work under William James at Harvard, earning an M.A. with honors in philosophy. The gawky, earnest gentleman scholar moved to New York City, where he meant to follow his dream to become the junior editor of a publishing house. Instead, he became the country's first literary agent, the luminaries his office represented ranging from Willa Cather to Sir Winston Churchill, Theodore Dreiser to Havelock Ellis, George Bernard Shaw to Norman Mailer. Reynolds was successful enough from the start to turn down Gertrude Stein because, he confessed, he couldn't understand her writing.

Reynolds's acceptance of Emily as a client suggests his confidence in her literary future. Luckily, Reynolds hated the phone. The resultant frequent— sometimes several times a day—exchange of letters between his New York City office and her Tuxedo Park home, the trains running reliably between Manhattan and the park every few hours, document her writing career in ways available nowhere else. Clearly building upon Emily's reputation as a society novelist, Reynolds immediately sought magazine commissions for his new writer. The *Cosmopolitan* contracted for a piece entitled "What

Makes a Young Girl Popular in Society?" for $250 ($5,000 today), and Emily spent February and March working on the article, her usual pace slackened due to a respiratory problem that wouldn't go away.

She had been disappointed in Dodd, Mead's efforts on behalf of *The Title Market,* its sales (ranging from 40,000 to 70,000 copies, depending on the telling) entirely respectable if not impressive, yet still far less than she'd anticipated. Now, holed up in Tuxedo Park during the late winter and early spring to write undisturbed, she told Reynolds, who was in England, that her new novel, *The Eagle's Feather,* was definitely "not finished" yet and needed heavy revision before it could be published.

In March Reynolds commented in an internal memo to his staff that Emily would be sending him a few trial essays from her proposed new series, "Letters of a Worldly Godmother." He hoped to get the collection published as Emily's first nonfiction book. The rough drafts proved strong, and the agent peppered Emily with enthusiastic suggestions. Why not discuss one particularly sticky topic: young women forced to marry for financial reasons? Or might she tease out the consequences of a girl entering society without a chaperone? Emily was amenable to all his suggestions, though she insisted on including one subject of her own: dance partners for young ladies. Without hosts' tactful preplanning, parties too often relegated the unpopular girls to the sidelines for the entire evening, and in the social world, this was a crime for everyone involved.

In April, the agency was disappointed when it received the month's figures for newspaper syndication rights to *The Title Market.* Breaking this news to Emily, Reynolds assured her that he'd come visit her in Tuxedo Park within the next week to think through new strategies. Instead of placating his author, however, his letter elicited a frantic telegram: "In midst of moving cannot think writing for two months postpone visit for present." Emily had made the mistake of assuming that her career would automatically accelerate, but instead she felt she was lurching forward at best, in spite of having an agent. Now she used her yearly transfer to a summer cottage and a trip to Europe as a smoke screen to buy herself time to think.

Reynolds responded promptly, gently explaining that even the "sure sale" of her essay "What Makes a Young Girl Popular in Society?" to *Cosmopolitan* had proved less than definite after all. There was good news, however: the popular *Delineator,* a monthly women's magazine, had requested a few more pieces of advice from Emily's "worldly godmother" persona. In spite of the jaunty air of her response, Emily was clearly disappointed: "Perhaps I had better go into house furnishing—I have to go into something to pay my bills since I find [even small] dolls' houses come high." She had decided to move into one of Bruce's smaller cottages, refurbishing it to her taste.

In fact she had no real financial problems, even with the perhaps surprising expenses young men of fashion, such as her two adolescent sons, could incur. Harvard, which Ned was eyeing, didn't come cheap, and Emily may have legitimately worried that her safety net from Josephine could easily collapse under too much pressure. But the real concern her household worries voiced was her deep disappointment that her career as a writer seemed to have gone off track.

She decided she would accept almost any editorial request but one: under no circumstances was anything she wrote to be submitted to the several magazines connected financially with Colonel Mann, the person she held responsible for her humiliation. As she reminded Reynolds, "Frank Crowninshield read 'Negative 7' when he was at Munsey's [a fiction magazine] and Munsey's wanted it. I was furious that Frank had let the Munsey readers read it as it was sent only to him personally as he and I had talked of the story at Monte Carlo and it was a purely personal thing. I do not want to sell anything to Munsey or Town Topics or the Smart Set or Pearson or Smiths or the Black Cat!!!!!! Please never to any of those!" Then she went on to explain what she really wanted—to appear in a more intellectual publication: "I'd burst with pride if I ever got between the Atlantic's covers."

In July she received a check for $300 from the Delineator for the advice piece intended for Cosmopolitan, "What Makes a Young Girl Popular in Society?," which would appear in November. Though Emily was eager to publish in journals that scholars bought, she understood that the Delineator reached a larger audience. Theodore Dreiser had edited it until that year, and the magazine published everyone from Jacob Riis to John Burroughs, Rudyard Kipling to A. Conan Doyle; at least it was not just another women's magazine. A full-page photograph accompanying Emily's rather slight article shows the writer at her best. Her hair is softly dressed around her face; she is serious, not sad; and she shows a touch of the demure even while commanding the space with an authoritative upright pose.

The article itself promoted a thesis Emily would revisit throughout her life: though beauty, grace, intelligence, and radiance make a young woman popular, the "greatest of these" is the last. Every woman alive could possess all four gifts—if she understood that some people have to work hard for what appears to be bestowed by luck. Girls with limited assets were the potential equals of those blessed by nature or by a rich papa. It was the illusion, not the reality, of being thus endowed that guaranteed a girl's success. "And even so," she noted, "the one great attribute" above all the rest was "the sense of enjoyment, the gift of happiness."

To support her opinion, Emily told a story based on her cousin's marriage to a wealthy Italian nobleman. "She [the American abroad] was not pretty and she had no money at all. The secret of her success was really one of good manners; manners that came from a happy and kindly attitude of mind that looked altruistically outward instead of egotistically inward; in other words, an appreciation of other people's feelings and an equal forgetfulness of her own." Most of all, Emily insisted, "people are drawn to others who seem happy." In articles like this one, Emily seems every bit the natural writer her ex-husband was. Her voice rings with conviction, her ease in the role of advice giver apparent in every bend of the sentence.

BY THE END of 1910, Emily Post seemed to be back on top. Impatient at the speed with which her agent got results, she bypassed him entirely and directly submitted two essays to the *Delineator,* and they were promptly accepted. The payment went by mistake to Paul Reynolds's office, and the agent scribbled plaintively: "As I have never seen the manuscripts you turned over to them, I do not know whether this is in accordance with the previous rate or not, and I am holding the check until I hear from you if this is as it should be. Will you let me have a line from you?"

A few days after Reynolds mailed his slightly querulous letter, the *Washington Post,* prompted by the upcoming publication of *The Eagle's Feather,* due out, finally, at the beginning of the year, published "Emily Post, Author," an interview that would have driven her mother to despair. Emily professed to have "given up society life almost completely that she may devote herself" to letters. "A woman of extraordinary talent," she had written "several excellent books," the interviewer explained. Though she lived amid the great temptation of Tuxedo Park, she yielded "few hours to frivolities. She has broken away from her old habits of ease and amusement, and devotes at least eight hours every day to literary work." The article's emphatic separation of her "wealth, social gifts, luxury, and friends among the members of the 400" from her present life suggested that Emily was redefining herself publicly.

Her schedule as a working woman was given in detail. She now wrote until "luncheon" time, and then spent the afternoon revising her work. Al Winslow, the official chronicler of Tuxedo Park, recalled in his memoir that while Emily was writing in her cottage, he and his brother would run over there in the midmorning, and "she'd share toast with us two kids, as we sat on the edge of her bed." Quietly, the boys watched her, awed by her concentration. She took her daily walk at five P.M., and, except when she dined out at friends' houses, she reserved her evenings for reading books to provide her better "style and stimulus." But in spite of her increasingly reclusive habits, Emily continued to seek new friends. "She is fond of bright, witty persons," Winslow pointed out, "and makes it a point to meet as many as possible" on the weekends. Finally, Emily threw down the gauntlet, challenging the social set who disapproved of her professional profile: "She . . . shuns mere society," Winslow said. Emily Post had joined the ranks of female professionals whom Josephine had scorned and taught her daughter to disdain.

CHAPTER 32

HE EAGLE'S FEATHER, EMILY'S MOST AMBITIOUS NOVEL, WAS PUBLISHED to tepid praise in January 1911. The story of an artist torn between his need to create and his love for a woman, the adroit melodrama features a European playwright unable to finish his masterpiece unless he destroys his real-life heroine first. Rather than allow brilliant, tortured writer Jan Piotrovski to divorce his long-estranged wife, his mistress, Vera, insists on living with the author in sin so that they will not betray the church. "For love of him she had given up her greatest possession, her honour, her reputation. Beautiful and pure as her own soul might still be, in the eyes of the world she was lost." In a predictable ending, the love affair fractures only to recommence at the hour of the heroine's death.

Such a romantic yet desperate ending reflects Emily's own confusion about norms that, in 1911, were supposedly now outdated in the Western world but, in fact, were often reconstituted in renovated garb. Society's expectations of and opportunities for women were bifurcated; Emily was not the only Gilded Age baby to find herself utterly confused. In her beloved France, for instance, Marie Curie appeared in the news again, not only for winning her second Nobel Prize but because Stockholm authorities had suggested, in light of the widow's married lover, that she send someone else to accept the award on her behalf. Rebelling at the spurious connection between her personal and professional lives, she attended the ceremony and then suffered a nervous breakdown.

Closer to home, aspiring lower-class working women made the front pages as well. On a late Saturday afternoon in March, shortly before closing time at Manhattan's ten-story Triangle Waist Company, just east of Washington Square, the factory workers, mostly immigrant girls between fourteen and twenty-five, were encased in a virulent fire speeding throughout the top floors. Witnesses would remember that spring day for the rest of their lives, the image of the young women workers desperately jumping from the ninth-floor windows. Piles of flattened corpses littered the sidewalks. Sharing the grisly details in photographs, the *Times* reported that most of the corpses were "headless and charred trunks . . . just a mass of ashes, with blood congealed on what had probably been the neck."

At the time of the city's inferno, Emily, as usual, was not engaged with topical issues such as the plight of factory workers. She was busy reading proofs for another article in the *Delineator,* this one titled "The Traveling Expenses of the Stork"; the piece allowed her to catalog household expenses, clearly an activity that gave her great satisfaction. She counseled an imaginary young couple living on "Jim S.'s" annual salary of $1,800 (or $35,000 today) to be prepared for the unexpected. The twosome managed very well, Mrs. S. sewing charming curtains and proudly making their house a home. But unexpected medical costs during her pregnancy had threatened to ruin them, and Mr. S. has had to take on an extra job in the evenings.

Everything continued to go badly for Emily's well-meaning but misguided fictional family, from Mrs. S.'s need for medical specialists to her potential inability to produce enough milk to feed her baby. Emily counseled them about their options: families with reduced incomes could petition the doctors and the hospital for lower rates, and hire an inexpensive wet nurse from a small town near their home.

Next, she tutored the future parents in ways to allocate the baby's resources from their modest annual income. The minimal cost for a layette was $100, but a truly adequate one would cost $300 (in today's terms, $5,500). Perhaps the mother-to-be could sew the layette? If not, she might obtain the bare essentials for a modest $50, as long as her friends and family supplemented her purchases with practical gifts.

Such articles proved Emily sensitive to the financial realities confronting middle-class women, and her tone is breezily respectful, suggesting that with gumption and hard work, anyone could create a rewarding life. In contrast, during this same period she wrote an article for *Century* magazine that positioned Tuxedo Park as if the retreat were locked in time, subject to none of the social explosions that had made it an endless source of gossip from its beginnings. "Because of a long felt ambition to appear in the *Century,* and because of some familiarity with the development of Tuxedo, I shall be glad to write the article for you—and at your price," she had grandly written the editor the summer before. She sought to layer the park's founding myth with her personal investment in the subject: Tuxedo was her father's development, and *Century* was the most respected monthly yet to publish her work.

In her eagerness to complete the *Century* commission, she sent the well-respected editor, R. U. Johnson, a rough draft, unaware that he was not accustomed to commenting helpfully on writers' unfinished manuscripts. He abruptly returned a detailed critique, advising her to "make [her] writing interesting." Embarrassed, she apologized, explaining several times that she was "the kind of writer who has to get things down 'anyway at all' and then write it all over again fast."

Until now, Emily had been coddled by editors willing to spend time sifting through her ideas and suggesting the best ways for her to develop a piece. The *Century* was different: Johnson wasn't about to do her work for her. Between Emily's nervousness and her desire to get on with her more relevant current work, the essay on Tuxedo Park would prove one of her least interesting pieces. But it turned out to be a valuable learning experience nevertheless. Tuxedo, Emily began to understand, had always been a mirage as well as a reality to her. It was time for her to let go, both of her actual life at Tuxedo Park and—this would be even harder—of the fantasy she had spun from its more banal truth.

Her past nonetheless still informed her present in very specific instances. That same year, Uncle Frank, who had inspired Emily to become a writer, saw his latest book, *Kennedy Square,* become a national sensation. For his heroine, Hop had surely drawn upon Emily as she had appeared at the time of her divorce. Kate—tall and stately and beautiful—takes no prisoners. When her betrothed drinks too much one night—and in public, at that—their engagement is called off, in spite of her love. Whether Kate will forgive or not is the crux of the tediously long novel, the climax occurring even as she serves the ubiquitous canvasback ducks for dinner. Kate is "as proud as Lucifer and dislikes nothing on earth so much as being made conspicuous" (except when she has prepared for the spotlight). Nor would she ever forgive "anybody who breaks his word." Like Emily, the only daughter, the narrator describes her as "the proudest and loveliest thing on earth."

"I won't hear a word about him," she says of her soon-to-be ex-fiancé. "He's broken his promise to me . . . and I will never trust him again. . . .

Some of my girl friends don't mind what the young men do, or how often they break their word to them . . . I do, and I won't have it." It was as good as a flashback, a replay of Emily Post talking to her husband five years earlier, if only in the version she told to others.

THE "PROUDEST THING on earth" was feeling tense that spring, as if her experience of being treated like a professional had chafed her sensibilities and roughed up the edges of her idealized image of a writer. She had expected to revel in this moment, and instead the tensions of getting her prose exactly right vitiated her pleasure. This wasn't like being a star at all.

Bruised, she took out her frustrations on her agent. Paul Reynolds had secured a commission for a summer article in the *Delineator,* but Emily clearly didn't have her heart in it. Another episode of "The Traveling Expenses of the Stork" admonishes the next generation for failing to see how easy and natural having and raising a baby used to be. But Emily's impatient tone bullies the reader, lacking the humor that usually leavened her reprimands.

However unrewarding the "Stork" piece proved to be, the article, part of the planned series of "Letters of a Worldly Godmother," confirmed the importance to Emily of being useful. In a moment of insight that surprised none of her friends, Emily Post suddenly realized that she liked giving advice. "Don't you think it is about time to do something about selling the Worldly God-mother letters . . . to a publisher for book form? I don't see why it is not of the same order as *Letters of a Self-made Merchant* [a current bestseller], etc. [The Godmother letters] are having a wonderful success in *Delineator* and it might be a profitable book. . . . Let me know in regard to this, will you?" she had prodded her agent.

She waited a few days and then telegraphed Reynolds that she would simply circulate the pieces on her own; he was to return them. "I am interested in doing my best for anything of yours," Reynolds replied, so busy these days that he had recently added Harold Ober to his firm, "but of course I want to help you in any way that I can and not hamper you, and I hope you will place 'The Letters of a Worldly Godmother' well and satisfactorily." He expressed interest in the novel she had mentioned writing, asking, "Do you expect to have it finished at any definite date?"

After two months had passed, he wrote her again: "I know five magazines that want serials. Have you ever started on the new novel, and could it be offered serially? Several of these magazines say that they would pay a large price if they could get the story they wanted." From his plaintive tone, we can guess that communications between them had been sparse. "Won't you let me have a line from you about this?" he pleaded.

Two weeks later Reynolds tried to woo Emily with the news that the editor George Barr Baker, at *Everybody's Magazine,* thought the proposed novel was the "kind of story that you could write and write very successfully." She failed to answer with her usual alacrity. Reynolds pushed harder: "You know that I am very interested in that story, and very keen on it, and I do not want to see it go up the board." Flattering her, he continued: "I know you could write it better than any woman in the United States that I know, and I want you to do it and I believe if you do it I can sell it for a large sum." Desperate, he concluded: "You can add just a line to this letter if you like and say 'I am hard at work.'"

But by now her *Century* piece was out, and she still wasn't a star. Nor was she hard at work. Instead, in early July, she finally confessed to Reynolds, "No use—the book has got to wait. I am really stagnated—although I did get a start—have my characters blocked." She had meant to visit Maine's coast for a while in hopes of rejuvenation—as she explained it, "just as a man decides to put his capital into a new venture." Nor had Reynolds' well-meaning use of George Barr Baker shored up her confidence. "Alas!" she responded. "I got, I fear, little incentive in hearing that your editor whom you wanted to interest was G.B.B. . . . It is scarcely an inspiring bit of news that your brother or your mother 'will take an interest'! Geo. Baker could not be nearer to me, or more wrapped up in my life were he my brother. He will be the boys' guardian should I die. And next to one other person, my aunt, he is the nearest family I have." What she most sought was affirmation from outside. "I wish you could procure me a job—even a little one— from Bok," she wrote, referring to Edward Bok, the editor of the *Ladies' Home Journal.*

Reynolds apologized at once; he hadn't known of Baker's close friendship with Emily. Now he entreated Baker to join him in urging Emily to visit a Hudson Valley spa in Kerhonkson, where an outdoor regimen would surely revive her flagging energies. While she was gone he could seek out Edward Bok's opinion about a few of her recent pieces, since she was so keen to publish in his magazine.

Several weeks later, Reynolds wrote to her about a subject she had obviously broached months earlier. Apparently, Emily had laid out for her agent her desire to become an advice columnist. After all, her roots allowed her an automatic advantage, as most European visitors found southern society to exhibit the most sophisticated manners in the country. Reynolds had followed through on her request, with disappointing news. "I talked to the *Ladies' Home Journal* about you," he explained. "They said that only [recently] they had got somebody new to run a department on proper social observances. I do not know if you would have liked running such a thing because there is such a lot of uninteresting work about it. Writing and deciding what kind of finger bowls people ought to have on their table when they give a luncheon, gets after a while, I think, to be a very tiresome pursuit."

This extraordinary letter buried deep in the archives of a literary agency lays to rest the myth of *Etiquette*'s genesis—most significantly, that of Emily's initial horror at the very thought of such an assignment. Paul Reynolds never urged her to pursue her interest in the subject; in fact, he tried to dissuade her, carefully implying that the subject was not worthy of her writerly ambitions. Consoling her and perhaps hoping to sweep the whole social advice idea under the rug until she forgot about it, he concluded, "I have never known how serious you were in this, but I thought I would go ahead and see what I could do anyway. *The Ladies' Home Journal* people were very interested in the idea, and I daresay it will bear fruit in some shape or other later on."

PART THREE

. . .

Before you can hope to become even a passable
guest, let alone a perfect one, you must learn as it were
not to notice if hot soup is poured down your back.
If you neither understand nor care for
dogs or children, and both insist on climbing
all over you, you must seemingly like it.

—*ETIQUETTE, PAGE 436*

✳

CHAPTER 33

MILY POST WAS EXHAUSTED, EMOTIONALLY AND PROFESSION-
ally. She had written and published five novels in six years, suffered the
deaths of both parents, and, most unsettling of all, ended her marriage.
Since the divorce, she had worked nonstop to create a new identity, but her
career was stalled now, just as she had learned to define herself through her
work. Never one to mope or stagnate with worry, she opted to direct her talents elsewhere, employing the architecture skills she had learned from her
father, while she allowed new literary ideas to incubate.

Whether she realized it or not, this path was the way to heal her psyche.
Almost one hundred years after the demise of Emily's marriage, *House and
Garden* editor Dominique Browning, when confronting personal chaos herself, would comment on the emotions played out in designing a place to
live: "I began to pay close attention to how people talk about making
homes, whether they are decorators, architects, clients, or people like me,
who have always done it—or not—themselves. I began to appreciate how
deeply charged a subject home is. . . . We invest our homes with such hope,
such dreams, such longing for love, security, a good life to boot. . . . [M]aking
a home is a materialistic endeavor. But it is often, maybe usually, undertaken with intense spiritual energy."

Encouraging others to see their homes as their cocoons further helped
Emily to recuperate from her losses. Instinctively, she felt the need to insu-
late herself from the sadness that she could not entirely shed. As she sought
to regain her balance, she helped others build their dreams. Buildings represented wholeness. Just as her father was eulogized as having "the will to

experiment with [the] traditional past and to create something new from its very root," so Emily hoped to do something similar.

She began working for architect John Russell Pope, with whom she felt deeply connected through the deathwatch he had kept with her and her mother at Bruce's bedside. Now, under Pope's guidance, she refined her amateur's techniques, discussing with builders and customers her ideas for interior construction and decoration. Developing her own design methods, Emily cut out paper windows and taped them to walls, in order to show customers the effect she sought. Commissions poured in through the grapevine of her social contacts.

Nonetheless, however determined she was to define herself as a working woman, Emily was inevitably reminded of the privileges of her class. On April 14, 1912, an iceberg bested the supposedly unsinkable *Titanic,* and only the first-class passengers' access to lifeboats saved Tuxedo Park's Spedden family. Picked up by the *Carpathia,* one of Emily's favorite ocean liners, the Speddens were welcomed on board by the Ogdens, fellow Tuxedo residents who succored their neighbors after a disaster they'd been told couldn't happen. Anne Morgan quickly joined the *Titanic* relief committee and greeted survivors as they debarked, her passion for helping others admired by Juliet even if she privately noted that her sister tended to overextend herself.

To the upper class, such catastrophes as a luxury liner that had been guaranteed to be unsinkable going down on its first voyage portended an unhinged society, its ruling classes as vulnerable as any others. Nothing seemed fixed; even society women were no longer dependable. Elsie de Wolfe, Mabel Dodge, and Mrs. O.H.P. Belmont were suffragists. Mrs. Belmont (formerly Alva Vanderbilt) was willing to let her society peers jeer at her as much as they liked, in order to advance equal rights for women. She led a heterodox parade of women in white: socialites, seamstresses, factory workers, housewives—class unified by gender—down Fifth Avenue. They marched from Fifty-ninth Street to Washington Square, drawing hoots and laughter all the way.

These "radicals" included women Emily knew. Inevitably, and in spite of her mother's early urging to mind her own business, she was increasingly aware of the effects of gender (and, later, class) on social and civic power. But she had to find a cause that made sense to her own proclivities. She chose one that allowed her to further the professional needs of writers— women as well as men. As a founder of the Authors League, Emily helped develop an association crucial to the life of city writers who lacked financial resources. Though not involved on a regular basis, she raised funds and lobbied New York legislators several times on behalf of the league's members. The agenda she helped draft covered everything from copyrights to fair contracts.

More flexible than most of her friends, she was finding the world taking shape around her more hospitable than the one she'd inherited. Even trivial changes often seemed ready-made for someone like her, someone tired of the overemphasis on fine food and elaborate, time-consuming preparations. Although she might not patronize the city's first Automat, the Horn & Hardart recently opened in Times Square (she still had her cook, after all), she approved the principle, as long as people sat down while they ate. Mayonnaise became a lifelong mainstay of her diet, once she tasted sandwiches from Hellmann's Delicatessen that year. One new practice did distress her greatly: social life for the upper classes had shifted rapidly from home to fine, expensive restaurants, but Emily believed such meals a waste of her precious work hours. Until her death, having to kill time while awaiting one's order—the diner at the leisure of the waiter, not, as at home, in charge of how the meal would proceed—and resisting the urge to beg for the check immediately tested her patience and courtesy to their limits.

IT WAS A NEW DAY, like it or not; everyone could sense it. If a couple of years ago the nation had learned, as a popular title put it, *How to Live on 24 Hours a Day,* 1913 would dazzle readers with *Psychology and Industrial Efficiency,* a variant of the now firmly launched self-help genre. Paradoxically, the very speed of progress seemed to be immortalized in stone, as the year's tallest structure, the Gothic Woolworth Building at Park Place and Broadway, began its long reign over Gotham's panorama. More than twice as high as Bruce Price's skyscraper, the 792-foot tower, vertiginously sheathed in neo-Gothic detail, seemed equally to evoke an ancient Christian ethos and the contemporary secular city. But women who wanted to gaze at its summit, whatever era it called to mind, still found themselves constrained to the ground: the average dress even now required at least $19^{1}/_{4}$ yards of fabric.

Yet this was also the year that a woman's voluminous skirts were allowed to compete for office space. Tuxedo Park's Mrs. William Laimbeer, who had rolled up her silk sleeves and taken on whatever work she could get to support her three children when she was widowed twelve years earlier, became an executive with the National City Bank of New York. She would supervise all business that dealt with women, instituting a new financial branch of the bank. Instead of garnering praise for its announcement, however, National City was chastised. It was about time, the local newspapers huffed, clearly aligning themselves with their increasingly enfranchised female audience. The *New York Times* criticized the bank for so belatedly recognizing "women as an economic factor."

MOST OF THE WOMEN in Emily's circle, when their spouses died, didn't have to go to work and chose not to. In late autumn, the writer found herself consoling her friend Katharine Collier upon the recent sudden death of her husband, Price, who, while with a shooting party at a royal Danish estate, had dropped dead. Mere months before, Katharine had proudly witnessed his prizewinning but controversial work *Germany and the Germans* climb to No. 2 on the bestseller list. Now he left behind a widow whose life meshed well with Emily's, from her background to her warm personality. Katharine Collier was loved for her generous spirit, and she was able to depend upon a physical energy that Emily lacked.

Other friends, not widowed, nonetheless faced upheaval. On December 22, 1913, the forty-six-year-old Minnie Coster, with her husband, William, and their three children, sailed home from Bologna, where they maintained a residence. It had been five years since banker Charles Coster, William's brother, had committed suicide after he'd been caught bilking his customers out of millions of dollars. In spite of the accusations against William, he was subsequently declared completely innocent in the affair; he and his sibling had conducted their business out of the same office but otherwise acted completely apart, the court ruled, much to Minnie's relief.

Such individual cases aside, by the end of the year the country's economic future rested on far sounder ground than ever before. J. P. Morgan's group of influential friends, dressed as duck hunters in order to throw nosy reporters off their track, had held a secret conference on Georgia's Jekyll Island, where they'd created a new recipe for the nation's long-term financial security. In spite of the tremendous importance of that backwater moment, the systematic reorganization of the nation's money management meant little to most Americans. Nearly everyone thought the innovative but boring Federal Reserve Act of late 1913 was worth no more than a minute's attention. To the men and women unfamiliar with the heady world of high finance, however, the new plan was an invisible sign of change.

Far more meaningful to most urban New Yorkers was the animation driving their city, whether New York's Armory Show, with its crazy modern art, or the world's first movie palace, Manhattan's Regent Theatre, or the sensational Ziegfeld Follies. But of all the new landmarks that defined the year, the official opening of the New York–to–San Francisco transcontinental highway would affect Emily's life more dramatically than anything indigenous to her city alone. In honor of the president who had unified the nation, the cross-country road would be called the Lincoln Highway.

THE BRIGHT, SOMETIMES BITTER SOCIETY MATRONS WHO HAD MADE their debuts a quarter of a century earlier registered the inexorable, enviable shift toward freedom evidenced in both popular and high culture. Edith Wharton spoke for many of them when she acidly observed, "What a woman was criticized for doing yesterday she is ridiculed for not doing today." By 1914, signs that the distaff sex was on the move seemed to radiate from all directions, women's burgeoning confidence reflected vividly in the period's literature. Charlotte Perkins Gilman's infamous novel *Herland*, published as a magazine serial, dared take as its subject a land where, after procreating, mothers lived among themselves. Banding together to raise their children without men, the fictional amazons solved the quest for feminine autonomy by uprooting privileged Victorian males and taking on their professions and positions themselves.

Emily was more sympathetic to Edith Wharton's asperity than in line with the agenda of radical feminist writers. That winter, during a fierce snowstorm on January 10, 1914, she mingled with the formidable Mrs. Wharton when the two women appeared at the Ball of Fine Arts. Sponsored by the Society of Beaux Arts Architects, the event featured Emily as the official representative of the invited prose writers while, in homage to her volume from five years earlier, *Artemis to Actaeon, and Other Verse*, Wharton led the poets. (Ethel Barrymore headed the list of actors, now more or less admitted into society.) The Beaux Arts Architects had been a second family to Bruce Price, and tonight it seemed to sanction his daughter's talent in his stead. Emily Post, her head held high, felt herself a winner among equals.

She was not the only one from her social set who had become a professional scribbler, as women writers were often still called. Throughout the year, Anne Morgan saw her essays published in *Woman's Home Companion*. Anne intended her articles to ease young lower-middle-class women into life beyond what they already knew. Forget about the Victorian mind-set, she urged: there was no need to hunt for a man to take care of you. Instead, go to work yourself—and early. Even if you married, you might find that you needed to bring home a paycheck.

Increasingly over the past few years, formerly domestic jobs had been driven out of the home and into the marketplace. There was, J. P. Morgan's earnest daughter believed, no turning back. So many of today's young women, like Anne herself, had "great men" for fathers, men whose "vision" and "Pioneer spirit" had more than once carried the day. Why, then, she asked, was it their daughters' duty to do nothing more than find a mate? Why not learn history and arithmetic? Why remain an ignorant and unformed child?

Emily Post wasn't a rebel like her friend Juliet's courageous, quietly feisty younger sister; nor was she an innovator, though she admired the many such women taking center stage these days. But she was headstrong and smart, and she knew that the life bequeathed her wasn't stimulating enough. She fully expected that once she had proven herself, her success would continue.

Instead, that spring, she became worried that her writing career had stalled for good. "The Chase of the Calico Girl," the story of yet another society girl, had been serialized for the past year in the *Woman's Magazine,* and at this point with her other novels, she had always secured book deals based on her installments. So far, there were no takers, and she was concerned that the story was dated. Reynolds demurred, insisting that her audience remained solid. "I am glad to have something of yours once more to sell, and I am interested in this story and expect to make a good arrangement for it," he wrote her encouragingly.

In part to avoid waiting around to hear updates from Reynolds, Emily devised a perfect distraction, one that combined her love for her sons with her passion for traveling. She had recently learned that Ned and Bruce would not be spending July in Babylon, as they usually did. Edwin and his wife, Nellie (Eleanor), planned to go abroad this summer due to Nellie's pregnancy and her wish to give birth in her native England. Emily knew that the boys loved both their father and their stepmother, and Emily had

supported such loyalty. Now she realized that her sons, even the sophisticated college student Ned, would be deeply disappointed to miss their annual outing on the Great South Bay, where, just like their father, they rose
every weekend morning at four to take the *Macy* onto the marshy water-
ways with their father in search of ever-dwindling numbers of canvasback
ducks.

Both to compensate for her sons' letdown and to clear her head so she
could write again, Emily suggested that she and her tall, strapping young
men spend the summer driving across Europe. They would stop along the
way to see friends such as Minnie Coster in England, back at her latest
leased country estate, and Uncle Frank in the quaint French farmhouse he
had rented near the coast. Ned and Bruce needed little persuading, especially because Emily agreed to stay in London for a few weeks to get their
car remade to Ned's specifications.

At the beginning of June, before the threesome left on their trip, Emily
again wrote to Paul Reynolds. Deeply discouraged by his failure to interest
publishers in her recent manuscripts, she sounded an unusual note of defeat and peevish ill humor in her correspondence: "What is the matter with
the 'Calico Girl'? . . . Why no news? I am sailing soon, now, and should like
it settled." Emily, instead of the usually astute Paul Reynolds, was the one
who recognized the waning of her readership. Or perhaps she had admitted to herself that "The Chase of the Calico Girl" was little more than *The
Title Market* and *The Flight of a Moth* combined and recycled. Reynolds replied
two days later: "I offered 'The Chase of the Calico Girl' to Little, Brown
and Company; then to Harper. Both of them have declined it. . . . I have
not offered it to Dodd because I thought you felt that they didn't do well
enough with *The Title Market*."

AT LEAST HER SONS' excitement took Emily's mind off her career for a
while. With his mother's permission, Ned had ordered a Mercedes for the
family. Now he would have it Americanized with parts from the States
added on by an English entrepreneur who specialized in "souping-up Mercedes and providing them with eye-popping aluminum touring bodies, external exhaust pipes . . . great disc wheels, and flaming scarlet upholstery."
Though no record of the Post amalgamation remains, a similar car commissioned from a London firm three years earlier had cost J. P. Morgan
$7,275 (the equivalent of $150,000 in the early twenty-first century)—this

at a time when Henry Ford had proudly announced that his workers would be paid $5 a day.

Emily, grumbling about the price tag for a car that one entered as if climbing into a bathtub, was further annoyed when her son showed her the bill for his "improvements." The Mercedes still had no doors, she pointed out, even after all the supposed upgrading. At least the car's ferry delivery onto the Continent proved relatively inexpensive. After warning her boys that if they kept spending at this rate they'd be forced to economize severely, Emily settled back for a summer of being chauffeured in luxury by her precious sons across the countries she had loved since she was a child.

Within days of their arrival in Paris, however, in contrast to the reassurances their friends in England had expressed, the threesome heard nonstop rumors of war. Still assuming the rumblings to be more gossip than reality, the Posts delayed making arrangements to return home, until they found themselves in danger of being stranded overseas. Just as chilling, when they made rest stops in France, they were unnerved by anti-German sentiment aimed at the suspicious foreigners driving a car whose Daimler-Mercedes engine had been built in Stuttgart. Nonetheless, in spite of the extraordinary and potentially dangerous political events surrounding them, Emily insisted that Ned and Bruce receive an encyclopedic tour of the Louvre, not just a pause at her favorite pieces. Determined to view each exhibit, she hardly noticed the excitement that had commandeered the entire first floor. A breathtaking museum heist was under way even as the single-minded mother coaxed her sons up the stairs.

Finally they began making their way back to the docks, though at times their eventual arrival seemed no sure thing. Because of their overwrought German car, the Post family needed to clarify their loyalties—fast. The tirelessly creative Bruce came to the rescue with "Henri," a stuffed animal he tied tightly to the car's hood. Beneath the little black-and-white dog he and Ned attached a sign that said, "I eat Germans." As the Posts slowly made their way back to the docks, they were greeted every few miles with cheers, all because of Henri.

But borders were closed, banks weren't open—and cars were impounded for the war effort once they reached the port. Even the charming talisman failed to protect Ned's pride and joy. Commanded by French officials to leave their expensive, shiny new automobile behind, he finally managed to convince a tired soldier, confused as the Mercedes was hoisted up into the air, that it would not be worth his effort to disconnect the cables already conveying the automobile onto the ocean liner. Emily, her sons, and their car quickly set sail for England, unscathed by an adventure they promptly turned into family lore.

Once they reached London, the Posts vacationed merrily until early September, when the boys returned to school and Emily went to stay for a month at the Turnures' Mount Kisco house, about an hour from Manhattan. Emily's cousin wasn't often in residence, due to Dr. Turnure's efforts to organize the first French mobile health unit near the Somme trenches, with Sadie herself preparing to work in a hospital in northwestern Burgundy. Emily listened to their plans with trepidation, realizing that her sons were now old enough to volunteer as well.

WHEN THEY GOT HOME, Ned immediately began writing an article about the overseas trip. Published in the *New York Times Magazine,* it was striking for its graceful prose. The following summer he would write a follow-up for the *New York Times,* the newspaper hawking a brochure about "Henri the War Dog" to raise money for the Allies. First her husband, then her son: Emily's secret conviction that a solid, traditional college education underwrote a writer's tweaking of syntax had only grown as she'd watched her firstborn effortlessly toss off his piece about their European adventure.

Compounding her wavering confidence, Harold Ober, Paul Reynolds's partner, soon conveyed the disappointing news that he had sent the already published story "The Calico Girl" to every plausible publication, and each had declined to option it as a novel. "Dear Mr. Reynolds—it is rather discouraging, isn't it! However, if it is no good—it is no good!" Emily tersely wrote to her agent, rather than responding to Ober directly.

Her subjects felt increasingly out of date, even to her. That spring, the country was largely preoccupied with the war overseas, not society. For a short but violent few months, the nation temporarily discharged its anxiety by returning to its past, reassessing the Civil War through the safety valve of fiction. On March 3, 1915, *The Birth of a Nation* mesmerized Manhattan when it made its New York debut at the Liberty Theater on Forty-second Street. Though the movie's violence felt radically at odds with the domestic plots Emily favored, she found herself deeply moved. The portrayal of old friendships sundered when sons joined opposing armies reminded her how her father's brothers had suffered just such anguish.

More insidiously, *The Birth of a Nation* paved the way for a renewal of racial violence barely suppressed since the Civil War, and it dangerously romanticized the Ku Klux Klan in the process. At least Emily's novels, however dated they seemed, were safely stationed in a rarefied past no one sought to resurrect. The War Between the States—between families—was something else, seeming to have been fought only yesterday to many of the movie's audience. Even the academic, usually liberal Woodrow Wilson honored the silent film, making it the first feature picture ever screened at the White House, with Thomas Dixon, upon whose book the movie was based, at the president's side. "The Calico Girl," not the Civil War, seemed from a bygone era.

It is unlikely that Emily Post's family and friends saw any connection between the racial stereotypes influencing even the most sensitive of their crowd and the ugly local warfare promoted by the stunning silent movie. Neither Emily nor her Uncle Frank believed in a class subjugated on account of race. But they failed to see that an exalted "Best Society" coexisting alongside ethnic segregation was as illogical as the chimera of exalted "pure" Dutch ancestry they had always found ridiculous. The racial condescension and ignorant assumptions of Hop's genial novels coexisted uneasily with his avuncular aura. Even his popular novel *Colonel Carter's Christmas,* for instance, read aloud in the presence of Mark Twain nine years earlier, referred to the benevolent protagonist's loyal prewar slave as a "worthy darky" with a "scrap of a pickaninny" son.

However the company she kept discouraged Emily from rethinking her views on racial relations, it's a good thing that she could depend on Uncle Frank and his circle for socializing just now. Her decorating projects were rewarding, but they didn't provide the same sense of accomplishment—or the large audience—that writing her books had. Stationed among other authors at Hop's Sunday night soirees, she could define herself as she wished—who would argue, whatever her subjects? Still, she could take only so much chatter, no matter how sophisticated; she had long preferred work to endless repartee. Using his mother's ennui as leverage, Ned began to badger her about taking a coast-to-coast trip in their own country: once again, he pointed out, he could be the chauffeur. They had the automobile, and it was a shame not to use it. A brilliant idea, Emily concluded, her sudden enthusiasm scuppering her listlessness.

Soon thereafter, at one of their habitual weekend dinners, she proposed to an editor friend of hers, the elegant Frank Crowninshield, that she spend the spring driving across the United States, penning an account as she traveled. Within weeks, Crownie called and suggested that she motor from New York to the sumptuous world's fairs at San Diego and San Francisco, describing the western extravaganzas for *Collier's,* owned by his friend Condé Nast. An omnibus magazine that competed with the *Saturday Evening Post* for readership, it featured such writers as Ernest Hemingway, Winston Churchill, and Willa Cather. What a perfect forum to advance her writing career—and with such a subject! Remember, the persuasive bon vivant reminded Emily, President McKinley, just a few minutes before he was assassinated at the Buffalo world's fair, had asserted that "Expositions are timekeepers of progress." Now the West was making its bid for fame, and Crownie encouraged his friend to explore her own country for a change. Emily Post, reporter, agreed to visit both exhibitions.

But in the middle of her cheerful flurry of preparations, Emily received the sad news that Uncle Frank had died, at the age of seventy-six. Obituaries, inevitably noting his modesty, emphasized his unusual prowess at multiple careers: engineer, artist, illustrator, and short-story writer. In spite of his considerable success with portraiture and illustration, Francis Hopkinson Smith had always insisted that he be termed an amateur. Similarly, his accomplishments as a writer, a talent exercised only after he turned fifty, were equally serendipitous. A natural after-dinner raconteur, he had been persuaded by friends to commit his stories to paper, whereupon he'd discovered that others enjoyed his deceptively light touch as well. Though he wrote and illustrated volumes of personal travel narratives, covering Cuba, Mexico, Venice, Constantinople, and Holland, his most widely bought novels and short tales dramatized life in the Old South, elegies for the distinguished family he had been born into.

More personal reminiscences also appeared in the New York city papers. "There never was a kinder nor cleaner gentleman, nor yet one capable of more withering indignation when indignation was deserved," a letter to the *New York Times* declared. "If ever there was a radiant center of cheerfulness and light, he was one." The wide-ranging praise suggested why Uncle Frank had been a family favorite, with a natural gregariousness that had reminded Bruce Price not to take himself too seriously.

🎋

O N SUNDAY, APRIL 25, 1915, THE YEAR VIRGINIA WOOLF PUBLISHED her first book, *The Voyage Out,* Ned, Emily, and her favorite cousin through marriage, Alice Beadleston Post, began their drive across the country. The writer traveled in her long, elegant Mercedes, with steel tires and a pull-up half top that look primitive today. The threesome was in frequent danger of getting stuck in the mud, the Lincoln Highway proving years behind schedule, its official dedication having been held months earlier.

Begun in 1912, the United States' first transcontinental highway, extending from New York to California, had been planned to officially open at the same time as the world's fairs in San Diego and San Francisco. With the help of Goodyear and the Packard Motor Car Company, Carl Fisher, the developer who had recently created Miami Beach by dredging a swamp, was building a highway worthy of a president's name. But in 1915 it couldn't be considered finished by anyone's standards.

In spite of warnings from car clubs and officials connected to the Lincoln Highway about its still primitive road conditions, Emily was determined to see America. Nor would we know from her subsequent chronicle of the voyage west that a year earlier she and her car had barely made it out of France. As if averting her eyes from the European battlefield, she held war stories at bay as she discovered her own nation. The forty-five-day trip during one of the wettest springs on record would prove seminal to the writer's psychological maturation, enhancing her ability to look beyond what she already knew.

Collier's suggestion that Emily keep a journal of the itinerants' most mundane experiences appealed to her compulsive nature from the start. She had already shown herself to be infatuated with accounting, recording everything from the number of yards needed to cover a couch to the cost of decorative lace by the foot. Now she put her fastidiousness to professional use, documenting the minutiae of the trip: gas, food, lodging, car repairs, and generous tips, all of which would cost $1,800 (in today's money, around $36,000). The magazine articles and the subsequent book, *By Motor to the Golden Gate,* captured Emily's deep satisfaction at understanding life around her through what would ordinarily be considered insignificant details.

As the intrepid threesome trekked the rough, sometimes impassable trail from New York to California, Emily's keen observations of social and cultural differences fairly shimmer with intelligence, her excitement inscribed within the precisely detailed ledger pages. Surprised at the towns' variety and the variable landscapes she encountered, Emily compared New York favorably with Europe. Leaving Albany, she noted, "the roads have been wonderful, wide and smooth as a billiard table all the way. There were stretches of long wide roads as in France—much better than any in France since the first year theirs were built. One thing we have already found out; we are seeing our own country for the first time!"

"We had expected the scenery to be uninteresting!" she continued exuberantly. Instead, "No one with a spark of sentiment for his own country could remain long indifferent." Alongside the "splendid-looking cows, horses, houses" she observed "in every barn, a Ford." Culinary specialties created outside of Manhattan and even beyond the reach of her beloved Hudson Valley amazed her: "Crepes Suzette, which were delicious" ended a lavish dinner that cost only "a dollar and thirty cents" per person. Her hotel was practically sumptuous, she declared, though a modest but clean inn was all that she had expected. Such plenty explicitly reminded her (uncharacteristically) of those less fortunate: "Going through these miles after miles of perfect vineyards and orchards, it seems impossible that in New York City are long bread lines, and that in other parts of our great country there is strife, hunger, poverty and waste."

When the travelers reached Chicago, they paused to wait out the record-breaking rains, which had turned the highway into furrows of mud. Emily couldn't help comparing Chicago high society, among whom was a good friend of hers, with society back East. Though she didn't name her prototypical Chicagoan, it was probably Elaine, the naïf Emily had taken under her wing at the weekend party near Paris years before. After Emily had taught her how to fit into the social gathering, helping her alter her dress and arrange her hair, a spontaneous friendship had grown between them, and now Emily apparently used the woman herself as an analogy for appreciating Chicago. "Once in a very great while," she wrote, "one meets a rare person whom one likes and trusts at first sight, and about whom one feels that to know him better would be to love him much. To me Chicago is like that."

Attending a dinner Elaine gave in her honor, Emily thoughtfully monitored which topics were most popular at the table. Unlike the witty, acerbic barbs of her youth, her observations showed insight and imagination, as well as a strong sense of fairness in the name of difference. "Boston society is distinguished and cultivated. Chicago society interesting and stimulating. At least that is what the people I have met in these two cities seem to me," she averred. Furthermore, she observed, "the Chicagoans love their city, not as though it were a city at all, but as though it were their actual flesh and blood." They despise the very mention of New York City, she said, just as a loving parent doesn't enjoy hearing about the Smiths' beautiful baby. Instead of finding such urban devotion ridiculous, she thought Chicagoans' "love of their city ... something wonderful, glorious, sublime.... I don't suppose a New Yorker ever wants to live anywhere else, but if sentence should be passed on me that I had to spend the rest of my life in Chicago I doubt it I would find the punishment severe."

After her little entourage passed through Chicago, however, Emily grew careless, offering less than enthusiastic descriptions of the diners and hotels she experienced farther along the road. *Collier's* midwestern readers sent irate mail to the magazine, responding negatively even to the writer's most determined praise. The "many pleasingly plump" husbands and wives at the Bakers' Convention in town made delicious bread, Emily offered; but the compliment felt compensatory. A local paper in Iowa City chastised her for speaking ill of the area's roads and disparaging its food. Citizens of Cedar Rapids were particularly pained by Emily's unflattering description: "The rooms we were in depressed us to the verge of melancholia. Dingy bottle-green paper, a bathroom in which the plumbing wouldn't work, a depressing view of a torn-up street."

She would apologize in the preface to *By Motor to the Golden Gate* the following year. At least she had reconfirmed for herself the power of the pen, the care necessary to avoid giving unintentional offense when writing nonfiction. Carefully choosing her words, she explained that travelers passing through an area for the first time naturally relied upon their initial impressions, noting, "An ugly, down-at-heels, uncomfortable hotel makes you think the same of the city." But she also acknowledged that the truth was not always as uncomplicated as it seemed at first thought. "I do realize . . . it is a very distorted judgment that appraises a town by a few rooms in an hotel," she admitted.

Any disappointment was more than compensated for by what lay ahead. By the time Emily reached Santa Fe, she was in awe of the wide spaces and vivid colors of country hitherto a secret to her. The experienced traveler confessed, "We, ourselves, to whom the antiquities and wonders of far countries are perfectly familiar, did not even know the wonders of our Southwest existed." Even as she extolled nature's beauty, Emily was learning to relax into the mundane pleasures of daily living far from the bustling East. Extremely hungry, having postponed their meal all day, she and her party eagerly anticipated their dinner at "Mrs. Seth Brown's," a restaurant they had seen advertised for its home cooking. Its specialty was southern fried chicken. "Couldn't we speed it up?" the ravenous woman urged her son.

The restaurant turned out to be a saloon, its food served "in the rear of a bar . . . smelling of fried fat and stale beer." Their fantasized dinner consisted of some "greasy fried fish, cold bluish potatoes, sliced raw onions, pickled gherkins, bread and coffee." Nevertheless, upon reflection, Emily appreciated the peculiar pleasure of the unexpected. "There is one consoling feature in such an incident," she wrote. "Although it is not especially enjoyable at the time, it is just such experiences and disappointments, of course, that make the high spots of a whole motor trip in looking back upon it. It is your troubles on the road, your bad meals in queer places, your unexpected stops at people's houses; in short, your misadventures that afterwards become your most treasured memories." Such a realization was not new to Emily; it captured her joy in integrating what was current or surprising with the nostalgia for time past, a recipe for the best that life could offer, as far as she was concerned.

TO EASTERNERS, IT SEEMED preposterous for one state to sponsor two world's fairs at the same time. But this was California, its residents insisting that their vast territory was really two different countries in one. The prevalent opinion held that San Francisco was the grande dame, with Los Angeles and its region "abjectly bourgeois, upstart crass." Somehow the spunky stepsister, San Diego, had won the bid to join in a two-for-one exhibition that year, with visitors allowed to buy a single ticket for admission to both fairs. Everyone understood that San Francisco, its accreditation ensured by committee, was the official world's fair.

When she finally crossed into California, Emily was initially put off by how "overdone" she found Pasadena and Los Angeles. San Diego, however, proved so satisfying it justified her entire trip. The city's central plaza reminded her of Venice, while the modestly sized fair itself was "a pure delight." She wrote so appreciatively of the event that the San Diego Historical Society's website uses her description today:

> The composite impression of [San Diego] is a garden of dense shiny green in great mass and profusion against low . . . buildings of gray white, no color except gray and green until you come into the central plaza filled with pigeons as in St. Mark's in Venice, and see a blaze of orange-and-blue striped awnings, stripes nearly a foot wide. . . . [The exhibition's] simplicity and faultless harmony of color brought out [the city's] values startlingly.

Omitted in all of Emily's discussions of the fair, including her three articles for *Collier's,* was the palpable tension surrounding the organization of the San Diego exhibition, a buzz that energized the fair and filled the city's newspapers but that Emily found indecorous to include. The board of directors had initially refused to allow women to be on the planning committees. Only when the San Diego County Women's Association threatened to plaster the fair's restrooms with posters denouncing the men had the board agreed to include women in all future decisions.

Yet for all her interest in San Diego, it was San Francisco's spectacle, with its proof of history's progress, that dazzled Emily. The Panama Pacific International Exposition, held from February 20 to December 4, 1915, had taken over three years to complete, and its success was a morale builder as well as an economic tonic for a city almost destroyed by the 1906 earthquake and fire.

She could hardly choose a favorite from the bounty displayed everywhere she turned, though the astonishing forty-three-story Tower of Jewels, covered with glass "gems," happily reminded her of her father's gift to his young bride so many years before. She still had the gilded box that Bruce had handcrafted himself in order to set off the exquisite stones he and his father-in-law bought Josephine on the Prices' honeymoon trip of 1870. This current Tower of Jewels used colored tin mirrors, "shimmering in the wind through the Golden Gate" and looking, Emily believed, "like a diamond and turquoise wedding cake."

With obvious excitement, she detailed the technological wonders of the fair, including the assembly-line production of Ford automobiles, an exhibit that left Ned agog as well. She was also fascinated by the 250-foot-long replica of the Panama Canal, which dramatized the ships passing through its locks. Some citizens felt that for a national feat of this scope, engineered by the United States Army, the nation's homage was "strangely scanty," with the canal's recent opening almost staged to appear as if dug primarily for the Golden State. Such antagonism didn't affect Emily at all. She was far more interested in the showy presentation than the politics behind it.

Even so, a theatrical presentation had to be grounded in reality in order to impress her these days. She barely noted the darling of the newspapers: a futuristic space-battle fantasy set in New York City in 2000, with Asians and Africans arriving in battleships and airplanes, eventually destroying the city under siege. She clearly preferred the nonglamorous Sperry Flour demonstration, "quite as ingenious and if anything more interesting," she believed, than everything else at the fair. The Sperry exhibit included specially built sample kitchens from all over the world, each one illustrating a foreign nation's use of flour in its diet. More than she herself was quite aware, Emily thrived on comparing cultures and the ways they differed from one another.

At the conclusion of her travel reports, Emily wrote a tribute to the country she felt she had just begun to know:

New York dominates the whole of the Western Hemisphere and weights securely the Eastern coast of the map, and because of all this weight and importance, New Yorkers fancy they are the Americans of America, but New York is not half as typically American as Chicago. . . . Chicago is American to her backbone—active, alive and inordinately desiring, ceaselessly aspiring. . . . I feel as if I had acquired from the great open West a more direct outlook, a simpler, less encumbered view of life. You can't come in contact with people anywhere, without unconsciously absorbing a few of their habits, a tinge of their point of view, and in even a short while you find you have sloughed off the skin of Eastern hidebound dependence upon ease and luxury, and that hitherto indispensable details dwindle—at least temporarily—to unimportance.

For a woman who always bet on the detail, who preferred to be in control of every aspect of her life, this was extraordinary homage to the unknown world outside her own. As she traveled West on her car trip to California, Emily Post became a watchful, even vigilant student of American culture. Europe had arrived ready-mixed, a formula for her to memorize as a child. America, it seemed, was a land of opportunity.

Back home, she believed her stalled career to be recharged. On September 18, 1915, *Collier's* trumpeted the second of her three-part travel series on its cover. Even as she was editing the essays that fall for publication as a book, Dodd, Mead wrote her that its editors would like to submit a select group from the company's catalog to "various moving picture concerns," and they wanted to include two of Emily's novels, *The Title Market* and *The Eagle's Feather.* She, however, would have to accept a commission of 50 percent on any deal their time-consuming efforts might achieve. She answered enthusiastically, appending to the bottom of their inquiry, "With pleasure! O.K., Emily Post."

CHAPTER 36

✠

NATHAN AND IDA HANDWERKER'S NEW CONEY ISLAND HOT DOG
stand excited average New Yorkers in the spring of 1916 almost as much as
the events overseas concerned them. The war in Europe was already looming over America, and many families had relatives trapped abroad. To aggra-
vate citizens' worries, in March President Wilson had amassed troops out
West, eventually sending ten thousand soldiers into Mexico to avenge the
raiding of a border town by Pancho Villa, a Mexican revolutionary terror-
izing parts of Texas, New Mexico, and Arizona.

Emily and her friends soon began raising funds for the European war
effort in earnest, collecting pledges, selling tickets to Allied bazaars, pushing one-dollar chances on a Niagara Falls honeymoon trip, and bartering
postcards of Henri the War Dog, Emily's talisman from the trip abroad in
1914. The volunteer headquarters at 120 Broadway announced that Mrs.
Emily Price Post was one of three women who had secured an unusually
"large sale of tickets." As part of the promotion, she had ridden in a motor-
cade of cars ferrying along Fifth Avenue women "prominent in society," including well-known actresses—a sure sign that the times had changed.

Shrewd as always when it came to business, Emily was aware that her
visibility helped promote her forthcoming book even as it genuinely contributed to the war cause. On June 11, 1916, when the *New York Times* Review
of Books section listed on its front page "Important Books for Summer
Holidays," Emily's *By Motor to the Golden Gate* led off its list of perfect leisure-
time reading. Though no critical opinion was rendered, the book's inclu-

sion signaled recognition and respect for its author that she found most gratifying.

But the hopes such publicity raised would soon be dashed. In other years, when global urgencies weren't so pressing, Dodd, Mead's *By Motor to the Golden Gate* might have sold well. Now, however, caught in the crucible of war fever, the book met with little interest. In the midst of anxieties about troops deploying overseas, a lady's (already serialized) account of life with her Mercedes during a costly cross-country vacation seemed frivolous and ill-timed. It also lacked the novelty such a narrative would have carried just a few years earlier, before several dozen men had individually motored coast-to-coast. Even worse for Emily's implied singularity, a twenty-two-year-old housewife and mother from Hackensack, New Jersey, had already chauffeured three women companions from her state to San Francisco five years prior to Emily's trip. Shrewdly, Alice Ramsey, driving a stolid Maxwell, one of the early successes of the car industry, had arranged for a *Boston Globe* reporter to drive ahead, so that he could record the women's journey for his newspaper.

In short, Emily's book failed to find an audience. Stories of the torrential spring rains that had dramatically turned the phantom Lincoln Highway into "mud wallowing agony" through much of the Midwest took a back seat to the torrents of gunfire that rained down on real muddy battlefields. Yet even today, Emily's detailed account provides a rich cultural foray into the prewar era. *By Motor to the Golden Gate* was reissued in 2004; it proved oddly fresh, still exuding the vibrant voice and vitality of its author.

IN THE TRADITION of other well-heeled young gentlemen of their day, Ned and Bruce Price were eager to help lead their country through the war, both joining elite corps almost a year before President Wilson enacted the draft. While they awaited training assignments, Ned with an ace flying unit, Bruce with a select National Guard regiment, they joined Emily in the Berkshires to escape the polio epidemic sweeping through New York City that summer. On July 9, 1916, after Bruce had left for the Massachusetts cavalry, Emily drove with her older son to Buffalo, where he was due for pilot training. Recently, Ned had been finding Emily's attention smothering, and now he was especially irritated when she found an excuse to follow him around like a mother hen, even in Buffalo. Eventually she compromised and took a hotel room in Albany for the six months he was in flight school. Consistently deferential and sweet toward his mother, Ned suffered silently for the most part rather than complain. He knew, he would later explain, that she was nervous about his safety, and lonely besides.

By October, with Ned fully credentialed, Emily moved on to Texas, where her younger son was stationed. Bruce, "galloping away on the border," was now guarding El Paso, according to his mother's latest interview. "He doesn't mention college in his letters, but talks of his horse, his pets, horn toads, a goat, an armadillo, a tarantula," she reported. Even though he assured Emily that he planned to return to Harvard that fall, she knew her son: he was Bruce Price's heir in every way.

The years traveling back and forth to Pomfret had helped reassure Emily that her mothering skills were still needed. But recently, both in upstate New York and during her quick trip out West to see Bruce, she had sensed her sons' frustration. As she entered middle age with no strong sense of where she was going, she realized it was time to find a purpose to her life other than depending on her children to need her. Still, letting go slowly, she circled around the issue of losing them.

When asked by a reporter from New York's *Morning Telegraph* how it felt to have both her sons in harm's way, especially now with her younger boy involved in the dispute with Mexico, Emily answered ambiguously, in part claiming responsibility for her children's lives. "The only 'consolation' I had all summer was the thought it would be my fault if the boys were killed," she said. "I brought them up to give what they could to life, and to get what they could from it. And the feeling I have for them isn't a bit short of worship. Whatever happens to Bruce, he lands on his toes, and he has dancing feet"—with this last phrase, she referred to the bond mother and son shared.

Emphasizing that she stayed in constant touch with her sons, Emily grew pensive, explaining that she had recently grown "close to real things." Currently she was exploring "things that mattered," no longer scared "to look into the texture of the spirit." The alert journalist cannily remarked that "there is a certain sadness in the author." Although she noticed that Emily was good at hiding any negative emotions, she herself dared not probe her subject further.

The interviewer quickly switched subjects: "But through it all you never neglect your dressmaker," she commented, a feint to which her grateful subject immediately yielded. Taking comfort in her familiar routines, Emily managed to emphasize the efficiency she valued, whatever the subject. In only a half hour, for instance, she had recently planned and ordered her entire upcoming winter wardrobe from her seamstress, Bertha. "That is something of a record for New York, isn't it?" she asked proudly.

MAYBE IT WAS her awareness that she could no longer protect her sons from danger that made Emily unusually irritable when she dealt with the Paul Reynolds agency these days. She hadn't been pleased with the publicity for *By Motor to the Golden Gate,* and her relationship with the agency had chilled as a result of the poor sales, the notes back and forth stiff and charmless. Even while sequestered at Buffalo's Hotel Statler during Ned's training, Emily had scribbled a churlish response to a mismailed letter about payment that she'd accidentally received: "What are you talking about? Wrong name and address somehow." Reynolds had hastily apologized for his new secretary, who hadn't recognized Emily's signature. The explanation hardly reassured her about her status within the agency. Now, at the end of the year, she wrote to Reynolds: "I'm up in the back roads of Connecticut working on the book. A novel of N. Y. Society!!! Hurray!"

Back in New York, as if to will herself into the right mind-set to write such fiction again, she participated in one of the many relief projects organized by Edith Wharton while she lived abroad. Emily gracefully spearheaded the fund drive to benefit Belgian children displaced by the war. In newspaper photographs, she looked serenely preoccupied, teaching the smiling children (clearly mesmerized by their patron), how to make sure their shoes fit properly. As if to match the identity Reynolds believed marketable, she was soon photographed for the *Times* as a beautiful society woman in fur neckpiece and muffler, outfitting four starstruck waifs. The boys' benevolent but clearly efficient patron busily selected boots to help the children brave the cold weather. She had a purpose again, no matter how temporary it proved.

CHAPTER 37

❊

ON JANUARY 31, 1917, GERMANY GAVE TWENTY-FOUR HOURS' NO-tice of its new commitment to "unrestricted warfare" in the seas; neutral or merchant vessels would no longer be allowed free passage. Though infuriated, members of the United States government resisted going to war until early March, when the public learned of the "Zimmerman note," which revealed a secret plan the German foreign minister had offered to Mexico's government. Berlin's official had made the ill-advised suggestion that the two countries join in declaring war on the United States, appropriating for Mexico a few of the western states in the process. On April 6, the nation's headlines were uniform: President Wilson had declared war against Germany. State laws soon forbid teaching the German language. In New York City, Columbia University's president fired faculty who had disparaged the American government. The purportedly liberal Wilson through the Espionage Act, amended the following year by the Sedition Act, even went further: he ensured that citizens could be jailed for criticizing the government, whether the accusation was true or false.

Now that the country was officially at war, Emily continued her limited charity work, though she didn't feel the need to step it up. Privately, she believed that contributing both of her sons to the military paid much of her own debt to her country. In March, she traveled to Albany on behalf of the Actors Fund, which her own Authors League sponsored. At the state capitol, Emily and her close friend, the editor George Barr Baker, along with the illustrator Charles Dana Gibson and the novelist Gertrude Atherton, successfully argued the case for increased funding for the arts.

By early spring, she was redirecting her energies to national causes. On May 9, the *New York Times* featured a photograph of J. P. Morgan Jr. buying a $10,000 Liberty Bond from his childhood friend Emily Post. Then, in June, after Congress had enacted the first national draft law since the Civil War, she pitched in at Tuxedo Park, where 254 men from the town and the park reported for military duty.

Not everyone from backgrounds similar to Emily's was cooperating with the government. Only a few months later, forty miles from her hometown of Baltimore, picketing by the National Woman's Party in Washington turned violent. Any criticism of the government was immediately suspect those days, and these protestors, who were marching for voting rights for women, were deemed probable Communist agitators or something similar. Suffragist Doris Stevens, a close associate of Alva Vanderbilt Belmont's (later her assistant) and a soon-to-be friend of Emily's, was arrested, stripped naked, and jailed at the Occoquan Workhouse. She was released, but a month later she was rearrested with dozens of other women, including a "frail seventy-three year old" who was "manhandled" and "knocked to the ground," in what became known as the "night of terror." A federal court subsequently ruled that every arrest had been illegal.

Emily didn't like to talk about such distressing matters, or even think about them much. She still maintained that flagrant displays of anger harmed rather than helped any cause, however just. There were less extreme ways to draw upon one's talents: look at how Juliet Morgan's brother had enlisted the Morgan bank to facilitate finances between the Allies and their American suppliers. And there was Juliet herself, donating her land near Tuxedo Park as a temporary experimental training camp for women agricultural workers.

But it was Juliet's sister Anne who took the Morgans' war efforts to the battlefield. Anne, who had worked indefatigably in New York for women's causes, now assembled an all-women staff overseas to provide everything from car repairs to medical care. She soon organized CARD, the American Committee for Devastated France, stationed in northern France. Juliet's little sister, the daughter of one of America's best-known Gilded Age tycoons, had become the model of a selfless international citizen.

Nor was she alone among the Tuxedo crowd of stellar patriots. On September 25, Ned Post executed a piece of notable legerdemain that made it clear that his summer automobile trip with his mother the year before had been a mere prelude to real adventure. Five months after enlisting as one of fifteen elite aviators chosen as "the nucleus of General Pershing's aerial corps," Lieutenant Post found himself in the midst of a fiery chaos. His plane broke into flames above the aviation school in Pau, France, where he was instructing others in how to fly. As flames rose on all sides, Ned landed the plane safely. Ever his mother's practical son, he even salvaged the instrument panel before lurching his way to freedom as his plane exploded.

His citation was the first award conferred upon an American pilot in World War I. General Pershing's chief of staff forwarded the letter of commendation: "His example . . . should serve as an example for all the aviators. . . . The Commander in Chief is particularly gratified in having an American officer so soon get honorable mention from our French allies and I am very glad to congratulate him." The *Times* piece, yet again, ended as if Ned's father didn't exist: "Lieutenant Post Jr. is a son of Mrs. Price Post of this city and Tuxedo Park."

In a subsequent feature that would appear in the paper's magazine, Ned was hailed as "immensely popular" in New York even before this feat. The lieutenant was said to possess "the natural equipment of calm, steady nerves, good judgment and a sportsman's keen love of the game." He even came accompanied by a famous mother, a writer "known for her beauty and well known socially in Tuxedo and New York" and the author of a "best seller besides, *The Title Market.*"

Over the next six months, Emily accelerated her war relief efforts. She joined the female contingent in Tuxedo Park that was rolling bandages for the Red Cross, which, nationwide, was spilling over with volunteers—more than would help during the following world war. Americans were cautiously optimistic. When, on November 11, 1918, Germany sued for peace, many even believed that the United States had proven itself the most powerful country on the globe. For a few magical weeks, life seemed mythical, good conquering evil once and for all.

THE FIRST WORLD WAR empowered Emily Post just as it did much of America's female population, granting it a belated respect. As she took the measure of those around her, Emily opened her eyes wider every day: women's talents had been shortchanged all these years. Belva Ann Lockwood, who had run for president of the United States when Emily was an adolescent, had recently died, and women still couldn't elect their leaders. Yet, from later comments she made to interviewers, Emily even now was not persuaded that the ballot box held the answer. Though she was not averse to the voting rallies that surrounded her, she believed her sex could best wield power indirectly, through managing the home.

She would be forced to reconsider. Over 100,000 women worked in munitions factories alone during the war, many discovering that they excelled in heavy industry. More than a few also found that they liked their independence. Liberated not only by modern housekeeping but by changing attitudes as well, women realized that they could perform paid jobs more than competently, working simultaneously inside and outside the family. Nonetheless, war was one thing, ordinary life another. After the smoke cleared, the men wanted their jobs back, even if the women meant to keep them.

Before the country could confront such new social issues, however, history paused, reconnoitering with the detritus of battle. In the worst influenza outbreak ever recorded, deaths worldwide ranged from 20 to 100 million, depending upon the scribe doing the frenzied reporting. The 1918–19 epidemic killed more people in one year than the Black Death of the Middle Ages did in an entire century, claiming greater numbers in six months than AIDS would record in twenty-four years. For all of its notoriety in America as a decidedly unwelcome immigrant, evidence suggests that the "Spanish flu" originated in Haskell County, Kansas, then traveled across the state to an army base. It accompanied the soldiers going overseas, afterward hitching a trip back to the United States with the troops returning home after the war.

In spite of its protection from the urban crowding feeding the virus, Tuxedo Park shared in the fatalities, underwritten, like New York City's 33,000 deaths, by the anomalous summer of 1918, when the region recorded a record high temperature of 104. Subsequently, just as the entire Hudson Valley rebounded from being held hostage to August's heat, the Midwest was hit with its coldest winter on record, making some mutter that God's wrath was upon the nation.

At Tuxedo Park, women not affected by the flu epidemic tended local patients, 400 of whom died. One apparent victim was Minnie Coster's husband, William; another was Juliet Hamilton's eleven-year-old daughter, Elizabeth. The new fear of the crowded germ-riddled city inflated prices for the seemingly safe property in the country, so Emily decided to sell the houses she'd inherited from her parents. After all, her writing was producing little income these days. She disposed of three of them quickly, retaining the smallest lot, with the beautiful little cottage Bruce had loved, for herself. When she finally sold it in 1927 to Katharine Delano Collier, the transaction would signal the end of Emily Post's legendary reign at Tuxedo Park.

CHAPTER 38

✠

EMILY POST WAS LUCKY, AND SHE KNEW IT: BOTH HER SONS HAD returned from the war intact. Now the three of them would step into the modern age together, traveling routes that would test the fortitude of this family beyond anything they could imagine.

Bruce Post was still trying to figure out what to do with his life. Though he had served honorably in stateside duty, patrolling the Mexican border for two years, he knew his tame service record didn't compare with Ned's dramatic exploits. After the war, when Emily took a new city apartment at 350 Park Avenue, she ensured that there were plenty of rooms: for both sons, three female servants (all Swedish), and even one of their daughters. But Bruce would elect to live with Katharine Collier for a brief period, possibly to get away from the hoopla surrounding his handsome, romantic war hero brother. He occupied the third floor of Collier's town house, his bedroom cheerily ordained "the Bruce Post room" thereafter. The Colliers, with their mixed family of two sons and two daughters, had become like close relatives to Emily's "baby," as she still fondly called the charming six-footer.

In contrast to his younger brother, Ned Post had been dating girls from an early age. He was perfectly positioned to take advantage of the independent youth culture that had developed upon the war's end; he had, after all, returned from overseas a hero. He happily moved into his mother's city apartment, quickly becoming a popular figure on the Manhattan party circuit—and, of course, at the resorts of the rich. Soon he was spending time with a childhood acquaintance from Tuxedo Park and Newport, Barbara Loew. The two had grown up together, and Barbara's mother, Florence Baker Loew—and even Barbara's grandparents, Mr. and Mrs. George F. Baker—were friends of Emily's, all from the same set. Beautiful, blond Barbara Loew enjoyed society more than did her august grandparents or even Ned, her pleasure apparent at her lavish formal debut during the summer season at Newport two years earlier.

The genial if reserved Baker family would have impressed anyone. Two years earlier, just after the reclusive patriarch helped finance wartime flying lessons on Long Island for Yale undergraduates (the fraternity later known as the Millionaires' Unit), the Forbes 400 list had ranked him fourth among the nation's wealthiest citizens. In 1931, the legend of George Baker's fortune would be immortalized when his *New York Times* obituary, listing his assets, pronounced him "one of the richest men in America"—and, equally daunting, the third-wealthiest man in New York City.

Emily was pleased when the engagement of two of Tuxedo's finest was announced on February 2, 1920: Barbara, the daughter of Mr. and Mrs. W. Goadby Loew, and Edwin Post Jr., the son of Mrs. Price Post and the grandson of the late Bruce Price. Though Ned was close to his father, he didn't even consider asking his mother to add Edwin's name to the announcement; he and Bruce had always played by Emily's rules, which included omitting their father's name from any occasion where hers was listed.

Even as such conventional manners reinforced the sort of strict behavior nurtured in the postbellum South, Emily observed other people she respected chipping away at it. In Harlem, a much-discussed uptown energy could be purchased temporarily by white people like Ned Post and his friends, eager to participate in the feverish new nightlife. But activity that integrated black and white citizens was generating unease as well as excitement among Emily's crowd, breeding deep-seated fears even among the most enlightened liberals. The respected novelist, critic, and photographer Carl Van Vechten, defiantly mixing the races at his dinner parties, nonetheless assumed that "Harlem's rhythm and heated sexuality" came from "primitive, primordial roots, no longer extant in whites."

Such so-called heated sexuality was increasingly considered a valuable commodity, wherever it appeared. At times, the 1920s seemed to be preoccupied, even obsessed, with sex. In the face of daunting publicity, while the war overseas was being fought, Margaret Sanger and her sister Ethel Byrne had opened the country's first birth control clinic in Brooklyn in 1916, outraging the authorities, who shut it down ten days later and imprisoned the women. Still, the Victorian Angel in the House was yielding to a new model who not only expected a public vote but demanded a type of personal fulfillment that her mother, taught to sublimate bodily pleasure, hardly knew existed. During the final years of the decade, even the *Ladies' Home Journal* fully supported sex education.

By 1920, the transition from the Victorian age was complete, the war's end a mere exclamation punctuating an era long outworn. Young adults started "to sample the merchandise before making their final selection," their casualness leading the journalist H. L. Mencken to declare confidently that "the veriest schoolgirl . . . knows as much [about birth control] as the midwife of 1885." Furthermore, the New Woman demanded satisfaction on all levels of life, just as men did. Let her mother extol the shiny synthetic fabrics and the sturdy Bakelite: such domesticities failed to interest her. She was too busy admiring the brevity of the skirt she bought at Gimbels.

Emily's firstborn would plunge with the complete confidence of his class and gender into that liberated new world. On May 6 at four P.M., Ned Post and the dazzling socialite Barbara Loew married at St. Thomas's, Manhattan's premier church. Described in detail by the *New York Times,* the wedding was represented by "the society life of New York, Tuxedo, Long Island and Newport." Hours before the event, guests lined the pavement outside the church, hoping to get good seats. Even so, many stood in the aisles. For the groom's mother, the bridesmaids, all of them children of her friends, connected Tuxedo Park to Manhattan in a blur of nostalgia. After the ceremony, the guests attended a wedding reception at 258 Madison Avenue, the home of the bride's parents, just a few doors down from where Barbara's mother, Florence, had grown up. Back in the Gilded Age, the Bakers had sponsored an even more lavish wedding for Florence: their house at 262 Madison had easily accommodated the afternoon's "light breakfast" for five hundred. Though the number of guests was almost the same, today's feast was relaxed by comparison, a product of the more casual decade.

CHAPTER 39

⊰✦⊱

THE WAR WAS OVER, NED WAS LAUNCHED, WORKING AS AN ENGINEER for the Mack Motor Truck Company, and Bruce was trying to find himself, while his mother nudged him gently as he explored his options—which did not, he reasserted, include returning to college. Life seemed to have settled back into its prewar routines, and Emily found herself once again attending dinner parties instead of allotting her time away from work to volunteer activities.

Though they could drink to the newlyweds in the privacy of a family setting, in 1920, she and her newly empowered female friends were still unable to raise a champagne toast at Delmonico's in honor of their hard-won status as fully enfranchised American citizens. Prohibition reigned, promoted in many cases by the very women who had lobbied hardest to get the vote. Emily didn't drink, but, ever her father's daughter, she was disgusted with the government's interference with what she believed were citizens' rights.

At one of the Saturday evening dinners for twelve where the guests routinely waxed indignant at the restrictive liquor laws, she was feeling particularly feisty, and she argued eloquently that all citizens should have the right to make their own decisions. Before long, the discussion turned to problems of civic versus personal domain, whereupon one of the erudite guests reminded the others that the French word for *ticket,* used to remind citizens to distinguish between private and public space, was actually the source of the English word *etiquette.*

With that, *Vanity Fair* editor Frank Crowninshield, lingering over dessert alongside Emily's longtime family friend and legal adviser Phoenix Ingraham, now happily married, launched into a lament for what passed as etiquette books those days: mostly pretentious babble, he huffed, that had no grounding in ethics. He himself had written the satirical *Manners for the Metropolis* over a decade ago, a book that skewered both the pretensions of the newly rich and the snobbery of old money. As if suddenly inspired, Crownie turned to Emily, his dinner partner, and urged, "Why don't you compose a book on how to behave?" Emily pooh-poohed the idea, embarrassed, in spite of the instructional articles she had penned for magazines over the past few years, that she was being asked to write a book about something as uninspired as manners.

Perhaps the story about Frank Crowninshield inspiring Emily Post to write *Etiquette* is true. A savvy interpreter of others' abilities, the editor surely recognized in his friend a hybrid perfect for the age, a woman proud of her past even as she sought to be part of the future. Crownie, ten years older than Emily, had deeply enjoyed getting to know her over the past twelve or thirteen years, first at Frank Hopkinson's Sunday soirees, then, since Hop's death, at more irregular but still frequent dinners that mutual friends gave. For her part, Emily had found Crownie smart, though a gentleman who wore his learning and his breeding lightly. Born in Paris to a well-connected but poor Boston Brahmin family who soon moved back to the United States, Frank had been tutored by his father, a mural painter, who'd passed on his knowledge and love of art to his son—just as Bruce Price had trained his daughter. A member of the exclusive Knickerbocker and Union clubs, Crowninshield, since he'd begun editing the year-old *Vanity Fair* in 1914, had already turned it into the premier omnibus periodical for men and women.

Weeks after the dinner party, Crowninshield called Emily again about writing an etiquette book, luring his friend with his erudite but breezy take on America's postwar needs: all those new war wives desperate to know how to write a thank-you note, all those immigrants who had made it to our country before the rules tightened, all those new-money people, ashamed to admit they had no idea how to behave in society. Over the past decade, the country had also witnessed unprecedented numbers of rural American women, the purveyors of the nation's manners, moving to cities. He smoothly explained that he had taken the liberty of setting up a meeting between her and Richard Duffy, the new editor at Funk and Wagnalls, who had been one of Emily's first supporters when he worked at *Ainslee's*. Crowninshield also disparaged the present competition published by Doubleday, knowing he was appealing to Emily's prodigious vanity.

The Doubleday book to which he referred was the two-volume *Book of Etiquette,* actually an old compendium newly spruced up by a nineteen-year-old copywriter, Lillian Eichler. The original version, written by Emily Holt, emphasized "elaborate rules and petty details," Crownie explained. Recently, the publisher had sought to increase sales by underwriting a publicity campaign of monthly cartoon advertisements depicting humiliating social blunders, especially those of young married couples and aspiring social classes. The offenders were shown ruining all future chances of success through their unwitting faux pas, born out of crass ignorance. Doubleday's ads "infuriated" Emily, who later remembered that they "made me so blind mad that I couldn't see straight." She had grown up believing it wrong to shame others, a belief that had only strengthened with age.

The myth of *Etiquette*'s origin is one of infinite delay, with Emily deciding only at the last minute to take on the project, almost (though she would never have said so) as a social obligation. Throughout the years, she would retell the genesis of *Etiquette* as if she had been horrified at the idea Crowninshield proposed, then appalled, even insulted, by this subject that he and Richard Duffy kept urging on her. Why would she be interested in telling people which fork to use? To write about such matters was beneath her. Just as bad, the subject was boring. Only when Crownie and Duffy convinced her that she would be serving the citizenry did she capitulate. With every recounting, *Etiquette*'s birth would grow more miraculous. The psychoanalyst Sue Erikson Bloland explains Emily's myth as typical of the famous: "They came to me and made me do it."

Emily's later description of her friends' begging her to write about manners is, of course, betrayed by the hard evidence of the letter she had written to Paul Reynolds nine years earlier. She had beseeched her agent to arrange for her to write a monthly magazine column on the subject of etiquette. Emily Post should have known better than to commit such supplication to the archives. Two years later she would pen these words, as if she had learned her lesson: "Remember that every word of writing is immutable evidence for or against you, and words which are thoughtlessly put on paper may exist a hundred years hence."

ETIQUETTE BOOKS, CALCULATED to placate the demons of insecurity, had been wildly popular in America from the country's inception. Citizens of the raw, new nation were ripe for instruction as they looked to their future, far from the motherland. New Yorkers especially proved a fruitful market for etiquette books; the mandarins of Boston or Philadelphia had names or property to confirm their worth, while New York was still up for grabs, a center for commerce and new money and for immigrants attracted by stories of both.

The city's mad mix of backgrounds had created less than uniform manners. Recently minted gentlemen had to learn to stop blowing their noses into their bare fingers and to avoid hitting the backs of ladies' dresses when spitting out their chewing tobacco. By the early nineteenth century, Manhattan bookshops and newsstands overflowed with books and articles on "good form" and "proper social usage." Such etiquette writers were talking to the new Americans, unaccustomed to being "in society."

These social novices, as they created a uniquely blended middle class, needed to learn what to wear, what food to serve, and which people to invite to their parties, or they might be blindsided by those just a rung down the ladder, always nipping at their heels. The country's exotic blend of backgrounds and world cultures demanded constantly updated instructions on conduct. Manuals seemed to appear nonstop, trumpeting opportunities for everyone. No matter where you came from, etiquette indicated where you could end up. As Arthur Schlesinger has maintained, the story of etiquette in America illustrates the opportunities engendered by the "leveling-up process of democracy" itself.

From 1870 to 1900, five or six books a year appeared on the broadly defined topic of manners. Then, for the first two decades of the twentieth century, the subject spilled over into the popular magazines littering American living rooms, driving the quest for the good life until the First World War, when there was a predictable lull in inquiries on local behavior. By the time that Emily Post was asked to write her book, the market was bulging again, full of volumes that, as far as she was concerned, were second-rate.

Her assessment was correct, according to most historians: "Few of the hundreds of etiquette books published in America since the time of Jackson left any more than a thumbprint on American behavior until Emily Post came along in 1922," according to the historian Esther Aresty. "Then, in the way that Victrola identified phonographs, Kodak cameras, Frigidaire refrigerators, and Kleenex cleansing tissues, 'Emily Post' became a synonym for etiquette. Purchasers of her book rarely ask for it by title, let alone its full title. . . . To ask for 'Emily Post' was sufficient."

H ER SONS TRIED TO DISCOURAGE HER FROM THE NEW PROJECT. The flamboyance of the early twenties, they believed, hardly appeared an ideal time for yet another book on manners, in spite of Frank Crownin- shield's enthusiasm. They themselves knew no one who would buy such a book. Emily appreciated their advice: the flappers and petting-party devo- tees eager to create their own rules seemed unlikely to engender a run on etiquette manuals. Ned and Bruce worked hard to persuade their mother that her timing was off, further arguing that for an already established au- thor to write an etiquette book was surely a step down from her previous work.

Their skepticism was well placed, for more than one reason. After all, Sigmund Freud and Havelock Ellis filled the popular press those days, boldly asserting the sexual nature of the female, who, it turned out, was relieved to shuck her Victorian constraints. Defiantly uninhibited, these liberated women sought new, not traditional, representations of what they were and wanted to be. As if unbinding their fetters, by 1920 women everywhere—from France to Brazil, Japan to the United States—were busy freeing themselves of any signs of repression or rules. Everything from dress lengths to hairstyles was abbreviated. Women, the primary consumers and purveyors of etiquette, were currently otherwise engaged. An age of gangsters and speakeasies and flat-chested women seemed entirely out of Emily Post's domain.

But Ned and Bruce's seemingly easygoing mother, more strategic than even they realized, was convinced that change was endemic to culture. As she had witnessed her sons and their cohorts readjusting to civilian life, she had accurately gauged a renewed opportunity. Not only were increasing numbers of immigrants hungry to learn how to become well-bred Americans; wartime brides and their husbands were confronting a home front whose landscape had shifted radically in the past four or five years. The war had sent two million soldiers back from Europe, many of whose tour of duty had opened their youthful eyes to freer sexual mores abroad. Even Prohibition, paradoxically, had furthered a cultural revolution, creating disgusted citizens whose defiance helped double the number of legal and illegal saloons in New York City, from fifteen thousand in 1917 to thirty-two thousand a few rebellious years later.

So Emily saw her opening, and, in the summer of 1920, with no travels to distract her and no book proposal languishing on a publisher's desk, she either asked Frank Crowninshield to broker a deal or she jumped at one he had already offered her: she would compose a book about how to behave. Seated on a high stool in front of her father's drafting table, she in effect wrote from and of her own life. Her reaching out for advice would prove one of the few avenues by which she socialized, otherwise cutting off society—of every ilk—more resolutely and severely than she'd ever done before. Humble enough to realize that she lacked expertise in this area or that, she occasionally embarrassed herself with her enthusiasm, so carried away that she grilled everyone around her to supplement her own knowledge. A substantial portion of *Etiquette* came from Emily's polling of friends, family, even customers waiting for taxis.

As the summer of 1920 ended, Emily focused exclusively on her new project. She was well aware that her former agent's business had expanded, his clients now brilliantly capturing the nation's anxiety. This was the age of the "Lost Generation" of writers, those such as Ernest Hemingway and F. Scott Fitzgerald who were convinced that the old values had rotted to their core. *This Side of Paradise* serenaded the Jazz Age inchoate, while *The Great Gatsby* would lament its decline. The Paul Reynolds agency had little use for Emily Post these days. It was not surprising that her sons were convinced she was out of touch.

NEVER A SLOUCH, she now worked nonstop, every day but Sunday. First she reviewed Mrs. John (Mary) Sherwood's etiquette book, which Josephine had reared her on. Next she made herself read the brand-new version of the out-of-date Emily Holt book. Reading others' compendiums of everything from table settings to funeral services, Emily quickly realized she needed a more elaborate filing system than she'd used for her novels or even for her road trip. To organize such an expansive project, she spent weeks devising categories for the subjects she would discuss. Next, she thumbtacked rows of cards across one entire wall of her home office, positioning new research under the appropriate heading: "Weddings," "Introductions," "Traveling," "Cards and Visits," "Correspondence," "The Debutante."

Organizing, cataloging, sequencing, designing, constructing, teaching: she was performing the tasks she excelled at, and she was satisfied. "When she had a job in hand she was like a bird dog on a scent," her son Ned remembered. Emily's panoramic vision of her subject contained advice that today would come from a marriage counselor, psychologist, doctor, or fashion consultant. Several of the resultant thirty-eight chapters, such as "Fundamentals of Good Behavior," consisted of a mere five pages; others, including "Balls and Dances" required twenty-six.

Throughout 1921, with Emily in semi-isolation, writing *Etiquette* in her resolute, relentless fashion, she experienced the culture's hybrid reality primarily through her sons' anecdotes. She heard that Edith Wharton's *The Age of Innocence* had won the Pulitzer Prize. The book's backward glance complemented Fitzgerald's lament: an era was almost over before it had had a chance to take root. How to move forward while saving the best of the past? As if determined to appear at least among the minor league of the day's novelists, Emily created vivid fictional characters in her own text to play out such scenes as happened in the seemingly ever-changing life of the day.

She did take a short break when William Goadby Post, her first (and only) grandchild, was born that year, on her favorite holiday (or so she told him), the Fourth of July. As if to ensure that Bruce didn't feel overshadowed by his older brother, Emily found extra opportunities when she could share time with him as well. A few months after Billy's birth, Emily and Bruce, who had developed performance skills much like his mother's, appeared in a privately made movie, a story about a moonshine still. *The Kick in It* was based on an actual incident described in city newspapers the preceding spring: a family living as if untouched by civilization had been discovered in the Ramapo Mountains, within a few miles of genteel Tuxedo Park.

Local residents, including Emily's friends Mrs. George St. George (Katharine Collier's daughter) and Mrs. Philip Rhinelander, a relative of

Edith Wharton's, worked hard on the private production, which Tuxedo Park was sponsoring as a benefit for its town hospital. Nonetheless, in light of the inelegant subject, Emily's sardonic, witty son couldn't stop himself from teasing his mother about having taken Lorillard's fairy-tale village so seriously throughout the years.

EMILY SIGNED HER CONTRACT with Funk and Wagnalls on January 27, 1922. The book, written in longhand, had taken a year and a half of almost nonstop work. Though her friends still complained that she was rarely available for lunches at the Colony Club, Emily no longer even tried to make excuses for putting her profession first. She had become convinced that there was not enough sustenance in her old way of life for her to ever return to it, or to the person she had assumed, as a young wife, she had to be.

Even the packaging of the royal blue *Etiquette* reassured while it motivated, striking a fine balance between contentment and desire. Illustrated with "private photographs and facsimiles of social forms," its 250,000 words required 627 pages. The unadorned title, *Etiquette,* and the name Emily Post stand alone on a dark blue case. Both are printed in a gold Art Deco font, the up-to-the-moment aesthetic cleverly offsetting the potential stuffiness of the subject. The book's long subtitle—*In Society, in Business, in Politics and at Home*—was wisely relegated to the pages inside.

Etiquette was published in July 1922. It cost a hefty $4 (approximately $44 today). According to an account Emily gave years later, rival publishers pronounced her book "too full of footmen" to be successful—a prediction quickly proven wrong when their stenographers rushed to buy the volume within weeks of its debut. During the subsequent four decades, Emily would revise *Etiquette*—its subtitle changed after this first edition to *The Blue Book of Social Usage*—ten times.

In his introduction, Richard Duffy, a scholar of Romance languages, would make serious claims for its importance: "As a social document, it is without precedent in American literature. In order that we may better realize the behavior and environment of well-bred people, the distinguished author has introduced actual persons and the places of her own world; and whether we can or cannot penetrate the incognito of the Worldlys, the Gildings, the Kindharts, the Oldnames, and the others, is of no importance. Fictionally, they are real enough for us to be interested and instructed in their way of living. That they happen to move in what is known as Society is incidental."

Etiquette became—and arguably still is—a ticket into the American establishment, even as that monolith changed shape at an ever-faster rate. Emily's subject took form in the crucible of race, class, and gender, the ghost in the machine of an ambitious, multifarious nation. As the University of Chicago's Professor James Cate has claimed, "With rigid standards in matters of principle, she showed a spirit of compromise in the unessential; the successive editions of her book reveal how aware she was of the changing scene in America and how she sought to accommodate herself to the changes. But perhaps the test of her significance is the degree to which she herself was responsible for these changes in the mores."

America had expanded, geographically and culturally, to accommodate newcomers and new economies. The United States, at least until World War I, and with the exception of the stunning, steady vitriol aimed at Asian immigrants since the early 1800s, had prided itself on accepting foreigners, the country's magnificent Statue of Liberty appropriately lodged, at the end of the century, at the mouth of the mighty Hudson River. There Emily had proudly watched her father standing on the dais during the statue's dedication. Though she never publicly articulated the symbolic connection between that moment and the role her book on etiquette played for the masses greeted by Liberty, at some point, surely, she realized it. With *Etiquette,* an amalgam of the experiences that had shaped her along with her epoch, she was in perfect step with both time and place.

⁎

*E*TIQUETTE WAS A HIT. IN MARCH 1923, EIGHT MONTHS AFTER ITS publication, Emily's "little blue book," as she self-deprecatingly referred to it at first, would finally top *Publishers Weekly* sales list for nonfiction, having occupied second to fifth place throughout the fall of 1922, and would stay in fourth place for much of the following year. Its author was in good company: Sinclair Lewis's *Babbitt* took the honors on the fiction list, and Edith Wharton's *The Age of Innocence* was still selling strongly two years after its publication. *Babbitt, The Age of Innocence,* and *Etiquette*: this triumvirate of the modern moment, nostalgia lacerated by a sharp-eyed honesty, made odd but perfect sense. Mrs. Wharton skewered society, while Lewis lacerated the joyless businessman. Emily Post would represent the truth of their fiction, her prose teaching the country that manners, in the end, mattered even more than money.

In the ages-old tradition of Horace, *Etiquette*'s dramatis personae entertained the audience through amusing, occasionally painful lessons, providing instruction that was both sweet and useful. The Toploftys, the Eminents, and the Richan Vulgars were composites of Emily's acquaintances. Though her book frequently invoked a mythical, sometimes contradictory "Best Society of Best People," Emily knew there was no hereditary ruling class in the United States: the leveling ideals of a democracy funded its very foundation. Her heroes and overwrought villains implicitly acknowledged the fiction at the base of Best Society: "Best Society is not a fellowship, nor does it seek to exclude those who are not of exalted birth, but it is an association of gentle-folk [in which] charm of manner . . . and instinctive consideration for the feelings of others, are the credentials by which society the world over recognizes its chosen members."

Whatever their expectations when they opened *Etiquette,* readers such as F. Scott Fitzgerald, Arthur Schlesinger, and Edmund Wilson quickly found themselves transported by the travails of Emily's vivid characters. According to Wilson, after finishing the book, Fitzgerald "became inspired with the idea of a play in which all the motivations should consist of trying to do the right thing." Mrs. Worldly, Mr. Bachelor, Mrs. Younger, Constance Style, Mrs. Bobo Gilding, Mr. and Mrs. Littlehouse, the Kindharts, the Titherington de Puysters: all starred in leading roles, with the Joneses, the Smiths, and the Browns contentedly confined to the chorus. Wilson would note that the names of Emily's actors sounded like stock figures from a fifteenth-century morality play, a drama that drew the reader into the text's mise-en-scène. Snobs such as the Gildings, for instance, revealed the small cruelties thoughtless people committed against those they considered their inferiors. In contrast, "real Best People," such as the Kindharts, converted a failed dinner party into a chance to encourage a pair of nervous newlyweds, reassuring the young wife that the disastrous meal she had just served was of no consequence.

Some of the characters resonated with New York readers more than others. "To you my friends whose identity in these pages is veiled in fictional disguise it is but fitting that I dedicate this book": this edgy, provocative dedication implied a tension about Emily's past that she kept close to the chest. Among Emily and her parents' crowd, the Prices, in fact, had not been the social equals of their peers. Bruce and Josephine could afford to criticize the gilded crowd privately, while making a strong show of personal and family pride, because they themselves never really fit in with the Yankee elite.

Though she would claim Francis Scott Key in her ancestry, Emily still couldn't match the Dutch ancestry that passed in New York society as the real thing. Her parents were not the integral part of Gilded Age society to which, for instance, George Post belonged. Post represented old money. Emily and her parents were belated, allowed in because they knew how to act and because they were genteel; they bore an air of "breeding." Lacking the requisite bloodlines, Bruce and Josephine had had to depend on their wits and their manners for their ticket into Best Society.

There must have been slights through the years. Bruce was a professional man, his Maryland family distinguished but still suspiciously southern, and certainly not rich. Josephine's moneyed parents commandeered the coalfields more often than the ballrooms. The Prices were in society primarily because Bruce had built Tuxedo Park, his friendship with Pierre Lorillard deepening in the process. If Emily was the park's princess, she was still just another ordinary upper-class girl when she moved to Manhattan. Many of those whose company she kept were aghast as they watched the "army of nouveaux riches advancing on Fifth Avenue from Pittsburgh, Chicago, and Detroit; and the march of the miners from Montana, California, and Nevada." At times, the Prices probably felt themselves uncomfortably close to such a crowd.

Maybe Emily Post had had enough. By creating emblematic characters easy recognizable by the Manhattan cognoscenti, she was putting into the text those who had undoubtedly snubbed her and her family along the way. From *Etiquette*'s 1922 edition to the final volume under her personal supervision, almost forty years later, she would maintain that no error of etiquette could ever match that of the cruel arbiters of society, those "real outcasts," who acted unkindly with "inexcusable" crudeness and attracted attention to someone's shortcoming whenever they had the chance. Now that she no longer had anything to prove, Emily was able to attend to the worth in the ordinary people of the working world, people who sincerely wanted to improve themselves, the type that had always impressed Bruce Price. She emphasized in each edition of *Etiquette* that knowledge was power. Knowing how to give a formal dinner party was one thing; actually spending the money to do so, if you didn't have it, was caving in to the wrong, not the "Best," people.

THE THEME OF APPEARANCE versus essence, the superficial versus the significant, recurs throughout *Etiquette*. A naturally beautiful bride turns instantly unattractive if she fails to treat guests courteously at her wedding, whereas a "plain girl" becomes stunning when she glows with joy: "No other quality of a bride's expression is so beautiful as radiance; that visible proof of perfect happiness which endears its possessor to all beholders and gives to the simplest little wedding complete beauty." And pity those unlucky brides marrying against their will (Consuelo Vanderbilt's fate was never far from Emily's mind): "The sight of a tragic-faced bride strikes chill to the heart."

Doggedly, Emily reinforced her central message every chance she had: the way people treated others was more important than an address or last name could ever be. With each subsequent version of *Etiquette,* she further defined "good breeding" or "class" as an external sign of people with good character. She had thought through this issue much earlier, when she confessed to her father that she had spoken roughly to a new acquaintance whom she deemed "common." After seeing how her abruptness hurt the young woman, she had made amends. Now Elaine and she were close friends.

Counseling generosity of spirit toward the underclass or the unsophisticated, she nonetheless wrapped such advice in the cloak of privilege. In 1922, she'd still failed to think through the class implications of her advice. As Emily insisted, anyone could be a "thoroughbred" in behavior or habits, but in fact few readers of *Etiquette* could afford to hire help, a problem she underestimated. One of her most earnest pronouncements throughout the years maintained that "all thoroughbred women, and men, are considerate of others less fortunately placed, especially of those in their employ." Most of her audience rarely had such a problem, though if they did, Emily had spoken clearly: the way to distinguish between a "woman of breeding and the woman merely of wealth" was to observe the way she spoke to her servants.

Treating respectfully those with less power or position than oneself remained central to the message of *Etiquette* and to Emily's own life. Almost fifty years after her death, the Post great-grandchildren would receive a letter from a woman in New Mexico, attesting to the difference such concern made in real lives: "My father grew up [outside Tuxedo Park] in the village, on Augusta Place, more commonly called 'the hill.' As a very young man, perhaps late teens, he acquired the temporary job of census-taker. Being from a family of English/Scots who had sometimes worked 'in service,' he proceeded to the Park [to take the census], and knocked on many back doors, to be correct for that time. At your great-grandmother's house, she cordially greeted him and informed him that he should have come to her front door. This made such an impression; he repeatedly related the story throughout his life."

Throughout the decades, in the face of countless changes, the central commandment to put others at their ease would remain constant. "Do unto others as you would have them do unto you," the agnostic etiquette expert maintained. One's clumsy guests, for instance, must be made comfortable over any mishap their carelessness might have caused: "If a guest knocks over a glass and breaks it, even though the glass be a piece of genuine Stiegel," the host's only concern must appear to be "that her guest has been made uncomfortable. 'I am so sorry' that your meal is spoiled, and I will replenish it at once: 'The broken glass is nothing.' " The "right and wrong" of the situation centered not on events themselves but on how those involved reacted. People and their feelings always came first.

To wittingly cause distress to others was, to Emily, the antithesis of good manners. Even as *Etiquette* gently instructed women innocently but unsuitably dressed for a solemn occasion, she upbraided those who dared to disdain the newcomers' naïveté: "How often has one heard said of a young woman [whose mother has died] who was perhaps merely ignorant of the effect of her inappropriate clothes or unconventional behavior that the girl didn't really respect her recently deceased mother, for instance, or she would now be dressed in proper mourning?" The cruelty of such "thoughtless" remarks ranked far higher than mere ignorance.

But the heart of *Etiquette* is a succinct five-page model of glacial prose, "Fundamentals of Good Behavior," delineating moral conduct from dishonorable actions. Most of all, for those who remembered her divorce, the brief chapter resurrects the pain that Edwin's ignoble debauchery had caused her personally. "Far more important than any mere dictum of etiquette is the fundamental code of honor, without strict observance of which no man, no matter how 'polished,' can be considered a gentleman. . . . The man who publicly besmirches his wife's name, besmirches still more his own, and proves that he is not, was not, and never will be, a gentleman."

In years to come, she would modify the assumptions that had governed her relationship with her ex-husband, back when a father's rights counted for little. But the ignominy her failed marriage had imposed ensured that she would remain ferocious in other respects until her death. It is difficult to read the author's cool, crisp dispatch of a spousal cad without wincing at her payback. "Fundamentals of Good Behavior" is built upon clean, tense sentences that bend but don't break, as Emily's unyielding decree on marriage and divorce resurrects her own past. She believed in being generous, but even now, she could not forget that Edwin Post had humiliated her.

Etiquette CANTERS ALONG genteelly, its charismatic cast put through their own paces and sometimes in their place. Certainly Emily had her pet peeves, superficial but telling denotations of class that she believed put the speaker at a disadvantage. "Illiterate" pronunciations prevented movement into a better order, because others, fairly or not, disdained the speakers for their ignorance: say "family," not "fambly," and "picture" instead of "pitcher," Emily crisply instructed. Higher on her list of don'ts was anything that suggested overrefinement: "Saccharine chirpings should be classed with crooked little fingers, high hand-shaking and other affectations. All affectations are bad form." She aimed a quiver of arrows at pronunciations such as "iss-you" instead of "ishue," and at the silliness of enunciating *Paris* "with trilled r's and hissing s's." "I used to cringe when I heard Johnny Carson being hyper-correct," her grandson recalls. "He would always say 'I' when a simple 'me' was called for, and that unnecessary attempt to sound correct, thereby getting it wrong, was the kind of tension that trying too hard created. That kind of thing used to make my grandmother wince."

In the first edition of *Etiquette,* Emily's list of "Never Say"s (NS) paired with "Correct Form" (CF) included the following:

NS: In our residence we retire early (or arise); CF: At our house
   we go to bed early (or get up).
NS: I desire to purchase; CF: I should like to buy.
NS: Lovely food; CF: Good food.
NS: Attended; CF: Went to.
NS: Converse; CF: Talk.
NS: Perform ablutions; CF: Wash.
NS: Phone, photo, auto; CF: Telephone, photograph, automobile.

"Bovine continuation" instead of "cow's tail" was typical of affected speech, she explained, incredulous herself at such locutions. "The very worst offenses" in language were overwrought diction such as "Pray, accept my thanks for the flattering ovation you have tendered me," with the speaker tripping over her own grandiloquent speech. In 1937, Emily would shorten her list of "Never Say"s, admitting slang to "appropriate contexts." But "I desire to purchase" rather than "I should like to buy" or "Will you accord me permission?" instead of "Will you let me?" remained the type of overspeak that made her shudder until she died.

Even more than overreaching through ignorance, Emily was deeply offended by the pretentious and the pompous, and she disparaged especially the supposed "omniscience of the very rich." Nonetheless, she had her inconsistencies. As one otherwise admiring critic lamented, while declaring "few rules of etiquette" to be "inelastic," she had nonetheless weighted *Etiquette* down with an ample use of "never" and "always." It seemed that at least in the writer's psyche, there were still absolutes.

THE GIRL WHO had pouted when denied the stage was a self-possessed woman come full circle: she had got her chance, after all, to be famous. This time, however, her narcissism would work to the good of others as she freely dispensed her knowledge and the fruits of her background. Emily Post's genuine if confused respect for all people registered on page after page of *Etiquette*. The subject hardly mattered: funerals or flower arrangements, broken hearts or broken glasses, Emily held her audience in esteem, and she meant to teach her readers, would-be "Best People," whatever their background, race, or creed, to do likewise:

> The endeavor of a hostess, when seating her table, is to put those together who are likely to be interesting to each other. Professor Bugge might bore you to tears, but Mrs. Entomoid would probably delight in him; just as Mr. Stocksan Bonds and Mrs. Rich would probably have interests in common. Making a dinner list is a little like making a Christmas list. You put down what they will (you hope) like, not what you like. Those who are placed between congenial neighbors remember your dinner as delightful—even though both food and service were mediocre; but ask people out of their own groups and seat them next to their pet aversions, and wild horses could not drag them to your house again.

Tellingly, as the book's "Best Society" became more elusive with each revision, it also became more egalitarian. Emily's "Society" eventually grew into "a corporate concept—not simply about individual display, but about a class and its cohesion and dominance," historian Eric Homberger maintains. But *Etiquette*'s principle of practicality remained the same: if you wanted to belong, if you wanted to get ahead and join the "Best People," you needed to know the rules. "Good manners open many doors that money will never move!" an advertisement for *Etiquette* claimed several years after its initial publication.

The 1922 publication of *Etiquette: In Society, in Business, in Politics and at Home* was an epochal moment. On an average of every five years, a revised edition of those original 250,000 words would track the changing conventions, revisiting and reenvisioning society. Most extraordinary, the name Emily Post, associated with elegance, would nevertheless signify the democratization of manners into the next century.

⁂

TEN YEARS BEFORE SHE DIED, EMILY POST WOULD RANK SECOND ONLY to Eleanor Roosevelt in a *Pageant* magazine list of the midcentury's "most powerful women in America," in which 272 women journalists judged the influence of the country's prominent females. In 1990, decades after her death, *Life*'s "The 100 Most Important Americans of the 20th Century" included Emily in its celebration as well. From the frequency with which she retold the story, however, Emily's keenest pleasure would still have come from the statistic citing *Etiquette* second only to the Bible as the book most often stolen from public libraries, an honor it would hold through the end of the twentieth century.

A month after *Etiquette*'s publication in July 1922, Anne Whitney Hay conducted an extensive interview with the author for the Sunday *Morning Telegraph,* a New York City newspaper. Accompanied by a flattering sketch drawn by the well-known illustrator James Montgomery Flagg, the article allowed Emily to stake a claim with her audience as a trustworthy arbiter of manners. She also began spinning her story of *Etiquette*'s difficult birth. Far more concise than the versions to follow, that early account cast Funk and Wagnalls as supplicants, imploring her in vain to write on the subject. Only when the publishers convinced her of the "ignorance and inaccuracy" filling the current etiquette books did she acquiesce. She felt compelled to help rescue, she implied, the "uninitiated." Her motivation was not purely altruistic, Emily hastened to add: "Few of us write entirely for the love of seeing our names in print. Frankly, the money appeals."

The reviews of *Etiquette* came fast. They were, for the most part, favorable, with the August issue of the highly respected *Literary Digest* even starting its review with Matthew Arnold's statement "Conduct is three-fourths of life." What Emily Post had achieved was impressive by any measure, its writer noted: "Not to teach us to display our sophistication, but to enable us to live without friction. Such is the real object of a book on etiquette, and the recent resurgence of such books is perhaps a sign of the times." Uneasy about endorsing a retrograde subject, however, the *New York Times* nearly apologized for supporting the book: "It is so easy to grow baldly clownish over the various dicta in the book that one is tempted to lose sight that many a person may receive needful instruction from it."

There were plenty of raves. The *New York Tribune* claimed that "not since Mrs. Sherwood" had there been such a thorough compendium; the *Chicago Sunday Tribune* called it "the most complete book on social usage that ever grew between two covers. . . . It is a readable, interesting book on a subject which becomes dull and 'precious' only when it is disassociated from life"; the *Philadelphia Inquirer* declared that it "should be in every library"; and the Cleveland *Plain Dealer* believed "the book is invaluable to the average thinking man or woman who wishes to live today's life in as polished and near-conventional a manner as possible." Particularly gratifying was the endorsement Emily received from the bestselling author Gertrude Atherton, who wrote that *Etiquette* "reads like a fine high-society novel, without a trace of snobbery, and is both convincing and entertaining."

Many smaller newspapers outside the large cities defensively adopted a superior air toward what they considered indulgence in a trivial topic: "The introduction on morals and manners by Richard Duffy (a scholar of classics) is of no use to us whatsoever, as our morals are exemplary and our manners are beyond criticism. One gets that way after 20 years in the newspaper business," the *Nevada State Journal* writer sneered.

THOUGH THE READER would never know it from her son's memoir or see even a single mention of it in any of the countless interviews Emily gave through the years, *Etiquette* had serious competition. Emily Holt's 1901 *Encyclopaedia of Etiquette: A Book of Manners for Everyday Use,* the out-of-date etiquette book reenvisioned by the recent high school graduate Lillian Eichler, alternated with Emily's for top sales position. Eichler is without a doubt the great forgotten figure in American manners. For those who aspired to the middle class after World War I—especially those who had only a basic knowledge of English—the young copywriter proved a great teacher,

her voice "friendly and accessible," as Edmund Wilson remarked. Literary histories may have anointed one history of twentieth-century etiquette books as orthodox, but until the late 1940s, the actual sales figures for the competing works shifted back and forth.

Decades after Lillian Eichler and Emily Post ran neck and neck, the younger writer would share her story with Arthur Schlesinger, who was researching *Learning How to Behave,* his historical study of etiquette books. Eichler (by then Mrs. Lillian Watson) was thrilled to get credit at last: "The true story of [my] 'Book of Etiquette'—how it came to be written and how it helped start the widespread vogue for etiquette books back in 1921—has never been told, and I think your readers might find it interesting."

To help Doubleday deplete its company's remaining stock of the outdated etiquette book by Emily Holt, the large and important advertising firm Ruthruff and Ryan put together what they believed to be a simple campaign. Figuring that one or two mail order coupons in magazines would do the trick, one of the partners assigned the job to his clever relative Lillian Eichler. The nineteen-year-old, in touch with the younger, less affluent readers of the period, promptly devised a cartoon ad that showed a guest spilling a cup of coffee on the hostess's fine table linen. " 'Has This Ever Happened To You? What would *you* say?' I asked. 'What would *you* do?' " Eichler explained to Schlesinger.

Her ads proved immensely popular, bringing in an unexpected "avalanche of coupons" that depleted the remaindered stock, her success forcing the company to reissue the book they had thought to bury. Again, Eichler prepared catchy drawings showing puzzled but well-meaning guests fumbling at every social juncture. But almost as soon as Doubleday shipped out the orders, they confronted a serious new problem: Holt's actual books were dated, unlike the of-the-moment ad campaign. Within days, disappointed customers returned the misrepresented books.

Doubleday immediately commissioned Eichler to draft an updated version of the original. Writing after business hours, she finished it in two months. "I made *myself* the thing that was wrong in the picture, and wrote the kind of book I felt would be helpful to people like me—just beginning to be successful and just beginning to go out socially. The book was an instant success, and has continued to be a big seller for 20 years," she proudly wrote Schlesinger in 1946.

Only one article had ever told the real story behind her book, Eichler lamented. Emily Post instead became "so well known" because "her name was used in all the advertising of her book—but my name was never so used. That was *my* mistake!" Her magazine cartoon ads, she proudly believed, "helped make America etiquette-conscious back in the 20's."

WHEN FUNK AND WAGNALLS had first mentioned Doubleday's competition to Emily, they had downplayed her potential rival, a mere girl, after all. Now every week Emily found herself staring at advertisements for the rejuvenated book in the newspapers and bookstores around town. As soon as Emily's *Etiquette* had begun selling well, Doubleday had redoubled its own ad campaign. To combat the challenge, notices for Emily's book stressed its authority, the author's ability to share precious knowledge with those not so fortunate. "A guide to Good Form in speech, to charm of manner, and to those refining influences that serve to smooth and sweeten modern social life," read a typical ad. "Information on personal manners . . . practically from the cradle to the grave," another one claimed.

Caricaturing a young couple's ignorance in the midst of society, Eichler's tableaux, in contrast to Emily's regal stage characters, depended upon embarrassment as their motivation. However whimsical, the cartoons were meant to shame readers into buying the guide that would save them from sure ignominy. Starring Ted and his wife, the pictures showed a young couple embarrassed repeatedly as they tried to impress their employers or neighbors or fellow diners at a fancy restaurant. The couple proved so inept that they even managed to offend the waiter escorting them to their table.

Emily found Doubleday's ads insulting. She believed that humiliation and intimidation had no place in a civilized society. She was even more dismayed when she realized that Lillian Eichler was a Jewish teenager barely out of school. In one sense, the quick young woman was obliquely acknowledging the special needs of the immigrant class to which she herself belonged, intelligently using pictures to explain the abstract. The cartoons that advertised her book were easy to understand, transparent shorthand about a subject that terrified many. If Lillian Eichler's age, occupation, and cultural standing were ordinarily beneath Emily's notice, she was now forced to pay attention. Doubleday's campaign was ideally suited for its era because young Lillian Eichler belonged to it. Her book sold for $3.50, versus Emily Post's $4.00.

Almost immediately, Eichler began building strategically on the audience she had tapped into with her cartoons. Brilliant if clumsy, her own *Etiquette Problems in Pictures*—her quick follow-up to the outdated Emily Holt publication—promised to teach the untutored how to behave in a cultured manner. Eichler's social misfits wore business suits instead of evening clothes to the opera, where they illustrated their "lack of good taste by studying the people in the audience." At home a well-meaning hostess making a "most uncompromising blunder" even served the male guest first, "instead of his wife!" At this point, any reader familiar with Emily Post's book must have wistfully recalled the thoughtful Mr. Kindhart, reassuring the distraught young wife at her first dinner party, "Cheer up, little girl, it doesn't really matter."

By the time of her death, Emily's *Etiquette* had sold close to 1.5 million copies and Eichler's revamped Emily Holt book only half that; Eichler's volume had faded from view by 1960. To some extent, the sales comparisons had been flawed from the beginning, Edmund Wilson among others noting the odd discrepancies in the figures from the early 1920s through the 1950s. Various reports showed Eichler wildly outselling Post; other charts suggested a sudden reversal of figures. The problem stemmed largely from Nelson Doubleday's innovative selling techniques, which, in Lillian Eichler's case, meant repackaging the author's original version into so many commercial variations that accurate sales were impossible to track.

Over those three decades, Doubleday experimented with countless variations, ranging from 59-cent volumes to elaborately boxed editions. In 1947, the firm licensed promotional rights for an adaptation packaged by Old Dutch Cleanser. The irony of Eichler, a daughter of immigrants, touting a product that played on its Knickerbocker past wasn't wasted on her biggest rival.

OVER THE YEARS Emily would increasingly emphasize the surprise of *Etiquette*'s success, though she generally failed to mention the threat posed by Lillian Eichler. In light of the glut of etiquette books in the early 1920s, the publishers, anticipating a small initial draw that summer, had printed only 5,000 copies. But after a week or two of sluggish sales, word of mouth sold so many books that Funk and Wagnalls was motivated to pump money into expensive advertising. Before long, newspapers were paying for syndication rights, with urban centers, such as Boston, running excerpts daily for several weeks, starting that September. As 1923 began, announcements for *Etiquette* implicitly acknowledged the competition with Eichler: "Friendly Example—Not Ridicule," a typical notice declared. Funk and Wagnalls launched another campaign, this one touting *Etiquette*'s "50,000 copies" sold in six months. The race was on.

⁂

EMILY WAS PLEASED AT THE ATTENTION SHE WAS GETTING, BUT two worries continued to nag at her. She wanted her twenty-eight-year-old son to find himself. After the war, Bruce—who, as his mother had predicted, hadn't returned to college—tackled several jobs with only minor success, probably because none of them interested the artistic young man. Suddenly coming upon a solution, Emily arranged for him to apprentice with architect Kenneth Murchison, a family friend with whom Emily's father had occasionally worked, and who was like a favorite uncle to Bruce Price's namesake.

Satisfied that her younger son finally seemed well situated, Emily turned to her other challenge. Determined to finish a novel started years earlier, she found her days at home distracting and concluded that she should make this year's trip to France longer than usual to escape the daily disruptions. As usual, she would stay with the widowed Minnie Coster, who was raising her granddaughter abroad, while the child's flighty mother, Matilda, sampled one royal liaison after another.

On April 25, Emily sailed to Europe on the *Paris,* a year before the ocean liner was sold for scrap. The travel notice in the *New York Times* included unusual detail about the passengers on board, possibly because its readers were weary of the Teapot Dome scandal and craved some relief. In any case, these travelers were more interesting than the average social crowd. Anne Morgan, for instance, was returning to Europe a hero because of her earlier unstinting war efforts on behalf of the French. Dr. Katharine Bement

Davis, former commissioner of the New York City Department of Correction, was also on board. The manifest read like a roll call of the new woman.

While Emily was traveling, she was honored in absentia: Will Rogers believed *Etiquette* important enough to use for an extended comedy routine. Everyone knew you had "arrived" when the popular humorist used your work as the butt of his jokes. Now he played with the differences between "out West" in California and eastern traditions. "Allow me to present" versus "May I introduce": How, Rogers implored, was he to know that the first was supercilious and the second correct? Emily Post's *Etiquette* would save him, he quipped.

Just now Emily felt in need of salvation herself, still unable to move her novel in the directions she'd wanted. Remaining abroad late that season, she chose to miss the annual autumn ball at Tuxedo, in spite of the advance notice that this was to be an especially grand year. On October 27, 1923, the party met with record attendance. "Every resident of the Park entertained guests over the week end at their villas," the *New York Times* announced—the shift in idiom from "cottage" to "villa" as striking as the cache of new hosts unknown to Emily.

Katharine Collier's married daughter, Katharine St. George, headed a dance committee this year, while others her age arranged for side rooms where they could play mah-jongg. This wildly popular game of Chinese origin, which had first appeared in the States around 1850, was suddenly new again in the 1920s. Ned and his wife, "Mr. and Mrs. Edwin Main Post Jr.," friends of the St. Georges', were in residence for the fall festivities as well. Barbara Loew Post, now a new mother, especially enjoyed the mix of the young and old at Tuxedo Park: "My mother was very interested in people of all ages, very social, but rather restrained nonetheless," her son, Bill Post, related, offering a description that could have fit his grandmother Emily at the same age. Regardless of the group's welcome, however, neither Emily nor Katharine Collier attended this year's gala, their absence signaling Tuxedo Park's changing of the guard.

By Thanksgiving, the fifty-one-year-old writer had returned to Manhattan. A week before Christmas, she gave a dinner for Ned and Barbara, where her little grandson was treated to Uncle Bruce playing Santa Claus. Determined to help her son (whose bachelor status increasingly worried his mother) find himself, Emily had begun inviting eligible young women to dinner, including the recently relocated daughter of a family friend.

The journalist Nanette Kutner told the story many years later about that Christmas "during a dark year of her life" when Emily sensed her loneliness and invited the depressed girl to a Christmas Eve celebration. Everyone drank southern eggnog and opened presents around an enormous tree. Eager to do good all around, Emily hoped that Bruce and Nanette might connect romantically. There was no spark, however, at least from Bruce's side. Emily's talented and clever son had not given serious thought to any girl, but his mother persevered in trying to jump-start his romantic life, regardless of how difficult a prospect it seemed.

THE NEW YEAR BEGAN with another salute to Emily in the *New York Times*. On January 6, 1924, Delight Evans, usually one of *Screenland* magazine's reporters, instead interviewed for the newspaper "Mrs. Price Post," whose society novel *Parade* would be published soon. Uncharacteristically late for her noontime meeting, Emily rushed into the drawing room for her interview. She apologized, explaining that she had been "dashing" about since six-thirty that morning, typical of her daily routine. "When I work I forget everything else in the world. I work ten hours a day as a rule. . . . I give up everything except reams and reams of paper and my typewriter." She went on to share more details about her writing, admitting that she jabbed at her typewriter with four fingers, entrusting the stenographer with the final draft only. Implying a tension about the demands of her job that would resurface throughout her life, Emily seemed to be answering an unspoken complaint uttered by her still uncomprehending family and friends: "I cannot be flying here and dashing there when I am writing."

Finally deep into the novel that had given her such difficulty, Emily would reveal only that it was about a contemporary "soulless butterfly" who breaks the hearts of those who woo her. The excited reporter, however, allowed her no pause, imploring her to work "even more than ten hours a day" so that she could finish and get the novel into her audience's eager hands. As if overcome in person by Emily's compelling authority, the journalist eagerly ranked her among Edith Wharton's literary company, elevating her diverse abilities above anyone of her own acquaintance, and causing Emily, actually delighted, to protest: "Super-woman has an unpleasant sound. . . . There is not a nice ring to it. It is smug. One visualizes a somewhat stodgy female of imposing proportions and the courage of her convictions. Super-woman!" Such modesty merely egged on the writer to try harder: "Books should be written about [Emily Post], if they haven't been. She is one of the most interesting women of her day."

As Emily was basking in public admiration, she continued to observe the disintegration of her personal retinue of Best People. She witnessed the humiliation of her good friend Juliet Morgan when a short, pithy article in the *Times* announced William Hamilton's trip to Nevada to remarry, mere weeks after his divorce from Juliet had become final. (Hamilton had recently retired from J. P. Morgan and Company, where everyone knew he had served as an executor of Morgan's will in 1913.) Nine months after the divorce, the *Times* would feature a much longer article with the headline "Mrs. Hamilton Gets Country Seat Back." Before leaving Juliet, Hamilton had sold her family's 760-acre "country seat" to Dwight Morrow, the sale forcing Juliet to vacate the grounds at the time of her divorce. Morrow, also professionally involved with J. P. Morgan and Company, was now selling the land back to Juliet.

The land was important to Emily's longtime friend for more than monetary reasons: it defined one of the fledgling attempts Juliet had made to break out of the mold she'd assumed unreflectively when she and her girlfriends had married. Like Emily, she, too, had found ways to grow. Inspired by her younger sister, Anne, sponsoring her similar wartime projects overseas on behalf of Frenchwomen, Juliet (vice president of the Women's Land Army of America) had underwritten even more extensive professional training for "farmerettes" in New York than she had originally planned at the start of the war. But the grounds abutting Tuxedo Park had eventually gone fallow once the women's work was deemed no longer necessary. Juliet Morgan Hamilton saw no reason that she should not reclaim the land.

THOUGH EMILY AND JULIET occasionally lunched together in the city that year, the novelist went into near hibernation following her interview with the gushing journalist who was certain that the talented writer could work harder. Determined to finish *Parade* by late autumn, she succeeded. Soon after, as if rewarding herself, she briefly spoke twice on the radio, enamored of this new art form. She was deeply disappointed that her voice came off sounding so tinny, but soon she had her proofs to correct, and she once again happily sequestered herself, this time to prepare her novel for its publication.

Perhaps the subject of *Parade*—a poor but clever girl finagling a marriage proposal from a Gilded Age socialite—caused Emily to forget the real world she inhabited nowadays. During the lull before publication, uncharacteristically finding herself with little to do, Emily became involved in a very public and unattractive conflagration concerning race and, inevitably, class. Leonard Kip Rhinelander had recently made headlines when the *New York Times* learned of his secret marriage to Alice Beatrice Jones, a laundress and the "daughter of a Pelham taxicab driver and odd-job man." More important, Alice's father was "colored."

Tuxedo Park (where Kip's mother, Anna Kip, had died in a fire in 1916) was agog. Over the subsequent drawn-out newspaper coverage, the Rhinelanders would repeatedly be labeled as "one of the wealthiest New York families" and "one of the oldest Dutch families in the country." For six weeks the press hounded the Jones family, exposing what did, in fact, look like a conventional hasty marriage between a lovesick young man and a crafty opportunist. Inevitably, Kip's love proved no match for the Rhinelanders' might. Filing for an annulment, the young man claimed that Alice had sworn that she had no touch of Negro blood when he proposed to her. Since he had been dating her for three years, regularly visiting the family home, his professed shock didn't convince anyone. But the truth was not the point.

In support of Kip's family, in March 1925 Emily wrote to the social register (at its peak that year, containing twenty-one individual city directories), requesting that the blue book of society omit the name of a new bride who, according to New York state law, was guilty of miscegenation.

Related to the Posts by marriage, the Rhinelanders had always awed Emily. Now she made it her cause to help save them; several fine women, including at least one countess, had been dropped for what many considered minor bad behavior. The alarmed officials quickly explained that they had included Mrs. Rhinelander only to denote the change in status for Mr. Rhinelander; the couple would be omitted from future issues.

Not everyone in society approved of the stuffy register. Though some members of the social registry, like Emily, found the list a practical way to locate their friends, many of the oldest names as well as the newly rich city residents found it an anachronism, embodying an absurd, misplaced notion of class. Such iconoclasts refused permission even to include their names. One of that group sent the *New York Times* a copy of what was meant to be Emily's private letter of protest to the register, to be read only by the secretary, not by the *Times*' audience. A subsequent newspaper article about the

Rhinelander affair shamelessly quoted it: "I happen to know that you announce all the misalliances [members' ill-advised engagements or marriages] of those on your list, ... a stand which I have greatly admired and one which in certain prominent cases has shown no little courage of principle on your part. . . . [F]or the sake of race, as well as for the decency of society, which you do uphold, please explain." Miscegenation was widely believed to weaken the gene pool of everyone involved.

Delighted, for reasons unclear, at the chance to flaunt her disregard for Emily Post, a previously outcast member of the register immediately wrote a letter to the editor, snidely skewering Emily for being pompous: "To an arbiter of social etiquette such as Mrs. Emily Post has proved herself to be in the outlying villages of the United States (I hear the sale of her book was very large), this exchange should indeed be final, and yet now that a touch of the tar brush has dimmed the luster of the Social Register, who knows?" The truth underlying the woman's sarcasm lay outside the scope of Emily's imagination, and that of other American citizens as well. By the end of the decade forty-two states still banned marriages between whites and citizens of color, whatever that meant.

In spite of the prevalent mythology that the Roaring Twenties was a time of unshackled freedom, the era's ethnic stew boiled over after the war's end. The middle years of the new decade would prove one of the most vicious periods in America's tortured history of black-white relations. Many intellectuals had assumed that the teamwork of men fighting side by side in the trenches of World War I would finally put an end to the Civil War. Instead, from Chicago to the Deep South to the nation's capital itself, lynching proliferated. Following the brief color-free brotherhood occasioned by the Great War, enmity toward people with dark skin triumphed once again.

CHAPTER 44

❧

IN THE MIDDLE OF THE DECADE, EMILY WAS WRITING THE RULES of proper behavior for a population whose first lady wore flapper clothes so effectively that the couturier Charles Worth awarded her a French locket on behalf of the garment industry. Unlike the increasingly plump author, Grace Coolidge, with her slender, athletic body and her interest in sports, captured the epoch perfectly. Rumor had it that female skiers were even training to compete in the next Olympic games.

Though Emily didn't measure up to the era's demanding physical standards, she had nonetheless anticipated perfectly the new model of the self-determined woman accepted on her own terms. Emboldened by the spirit of the age, taking herself seriously as an amateur architect, she finally decided to design a building herself. She had long had the project in mind, she happily confessed to a *New York Times* reporter, noting, "But the sites offered from time to time by various brokers were either inaccessible or unpromising of sunlight." For now, she moved into a luxury rental—in part to study its operations.

The Gladstone, centrally located at East Fifty-second Street and Park Avenue, was heavily advertised in 1925 as "a definite departure in apartment hotel arrangement," an "artistic and distinctive home plus superb hotel service"—upper-class accommodations perfect for Emily's needs at the time. Living at the Gladstone offered conveniences that enabled occupants to dispense with the tedious details of running a house. And, for Emily, observing up close how the building worked helped her plan the dream residence she planned to build. By pursuing such a course as if she were a professional, she was again traveling the path laid down by Edith Wharton, who had written *The Decoration of Houses* in 1897.

Emily was also capitalizing on a mid-1920s conviction that Manhattan was "just a village," as Harold Ross, whose *New Yorker* magazine had made its first appearance in February, insisted. As she analyzed life at the Gladstone, she realized that her ideal home would be a building whose inhabitants were all friends and acquaintances. They would invest monthly in the building—covering the expenses of its maintenance and staff—and they would buy their individual apartments just as they would a house. Yet again, Emily was following her father's lead. In the late 1880s, soon after he'd moved to Manhattan, Bruce Price had scandalized old-liners with the multiunit buildings he had designed and built. Within another few years, single-family dwellings, mansions and humble houses alike, had begun yielding to apartments, where people lived under shared roofs. Now, in 1925, his daughter felt she was taking up his cause, though in truth the starchy resistance of forty years earlier had almost entirely crumbled.

Emily scoured the city, deciding upon a good Upper East Side location at 39 East Seventy-ninth Street, at Madison Avenue. Next, she invited Minnie Coster and Alice Beadleston Post to lunch to help her work out the logistics. Then, following several mistrials, she obtained architectural blueprints to her exact specifications. Within a few weeks, over half of the still unplotted units were presold. Eventually, seventeen of Emily's friends invested in the fifteen-story building, which cost a total of $1.3 million, roughly the equivalent of $13 million today. In contrast to the 60 to 80 percent membership in the social register that most Park Avenue apartment buildings boasted, 100 percent of Emily's co-op members were listed.

Still standing, the co-op on the northeast corner of Madison Avenue and Seventy-ninth Street retains its appeal today, largely because of Emily's attention to detail. The layout of two apartments on each floor allowed residents to convert rooms into closets and add extra windows and dining rooms as they wished. An "average apartment" consisted of two to four bedrooms, two to three servants' rooms, and three to five baths. Emily's own apartment, 9B, was decorated with "chintzes and murals . . . and large oil portraits of her ancestors, odd carvings and a liberal spattering of good Chinese furniture." Most impressively, it boasted a rather grand nineteen-by-twenty-five-foot living room. Emily would eventually own two units, her office situated on the ground floor while her home remained on the ninth.

Years after the building's completion, she wrote that "the house which is to be your home—in short, your background—should unmistakably suggest you." As architecture critic Christopher Gray has mused about Emily's achievement: "Most people don't have the energy to do their own brain surgery, their own haircutting, whatever, and they also don't have the energy to build their own house, especially build their own apartment building." Especially impressive is Emily's emphasis on the less than glamorous details: developers usually design the "big splashy parlor, or library or dining room, to hell with the servants . . . [but Emily] knew that if the servants were unhappy, the household would be unhappy."

Besides the obvious reward to Emily and her friends of living among acquaintances, the project also allowed Bruce Post to further his reputation. Emily hired her son along with Kenneth Murchison as the building's architects, creators of the place she would call home for the rest of her life. What pleasure for Emily to partner her younger child with her father's old colleague. Bruce was turning out to be more like his namesake than she had dared imagine, even when she had observed his artistic inclinations in childhood. Now that he didn't have to compete with his older brother, her younger son was finding himself. And what he found proved more gratifying to his mother than even her own work. He was becoming the architect heir her father had always wanted.

PARADE, ONE OF FUNK AND WAGNALLS'S rare forays into fiction, was published on August 25, 1925. The early reviews were positive, but even the most favorable made the obvious connection between the novelist's expertise with manners and her new book. If she didn't realize it earlier, Emily must have sensed that from now on, her identity as the author of *Etiquette* would trump any critical consideration of her fiction.

In prepublication publicity, Funk and Wagnalls played heavily on the author's own social position. "A novel by Emily Post, author of *Etiquette*, . . . said to be a story of life in the inner circles of the '400.' Mrs. Post can be trusted to make her characters behave as society people should," one ad crowed. The novel was "written by a woman who, through life-long association and personal observation, knows the characters she introduces, and is herself of their social environment." Funk and Wagnalls promised that the plot would create a new guessing game, with readers arguing over which of the author's acquaintances had inspired the characters. Some re-

Emily Price, circa 1882, with Josephine Price, her mother, New York City.

Bruce Price, architect,
overseeing construction of
Tuxedo Park, 1885–86.

Bruce Price,
architect's apprentice,
Baltimore, 1872.

Emily in 1890, when she disappeared from society, probably due to illness.

Rocklawn, the Price family home in Tuxedo Park, 1891.

*Edwin Post and his fiancée,
Emily Price, early 1892.*

*Emily and Edwin Post,
newlyweds, 1892.*

Emily Post, society wife
and mother, circa 1894.

Emily and Edwin Post's
modest cottage on
Staten Island, circa 1893.

Bruce Jr. with his grandmother Caroline Post, Babylon, Long Island, 1897.

Bruce Jr. and Ned with their other grandmother, Josephine Price, on the stoop of one of their father's Tuxedo Park houses, 1897.

*Emily reading to
her sons, one of her
favorite maternal
activities, circa 1898.*

*Edwin Post, his son Ned,
and Bruce Price,
Tuxedo Park, circa 1898.*

Emily swimming with the boys in Babylon, circa 1899.

The Tuxedo Park train station, 1904. This was where Emily would wait for her husband to return from Wall Street every night.

THE FLIGHT
OF A MOTH
by EMILY POST

Emily's first novel, based on her letters to her father from abroad, 1904.

*Ned and Bruce,
Tuxedo Park,
circa 1904.*

Emily and Edwin in Gramercy Park, New York City,
setting out on their cross-country trip, spring 1915.

The spring rains of 1915 made the Lincoln Highway impassable at times. Emily experienced frequent delays on her trip out west.

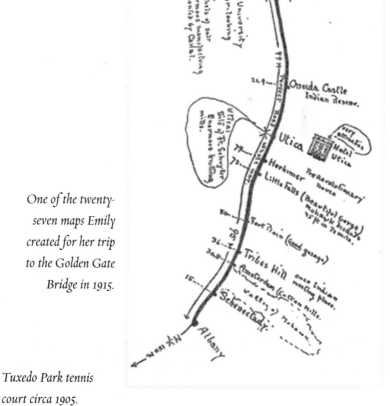

One of the twenty-seven maps Emily created for her trip to the Golden Gate Bridge in 1915.

Tuxedo Park tennis court circa 1905.

Selling benefit tickets for the Architects' Emergency Relief Fund. From left: Mrs. Goodhue Livingston, Emily, Alfred E. Smith, and Emily's favorite cousin, Sadie Price Turnure.

Emily (right) with Sadie Price Turnure, participating in a shoe drive for Belgian children displaced by World War I.

The successful author, circa 1923.

Emily in her New York co-op, the apartments of which were all occupied by personal acquaintances, Christmas 1935.

Emily tutoring a young woman during World War II in the best way to hitch a ride.

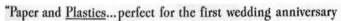

"Paper and Plastics...perfect for the first wedding anniversary

...and they offer such a broad new range of beautiful and practical gift possibilities," says

Emily Post

MONSANTO
CHEMICALS · PLASTICS

Emily promoting Monsanto plastics, mid-1950s.

Emily and her Edgartown gardener, John, admiring her latest blooms.

Emily with her great-grandson William Post, Jr., late 1940s.

Emily on CBS radio in 1932.

Emily and Ned in Edgartown, 1951.

Emily (left) with Mary Margaret McBride, the radio host, early 1950s.

Emily Post with "Suzy," her Dictaphone, in her favorite position, early 1950s.

viewers suggested smugly that the author wasn't very polite herself if she had used people she knew personally to make her case for courtesy.

Parade took as its theme the exchange of one's integrity for a place in society. Geraldine was a girl from a poor though honorable family, befriended by a cheerful, kind, but completely uneducated newly rich family called the Jimpsons, whom she accompanied to seaside resorts. Soon she met Oliver Townsend, a wealthy, cultured suitor. Using all her wiles, she convinced him to propose marriage, after which she deserted the naive Jimpsons.

Though the heroine tried hard to love her rich husband, she found his sexual ardor overwhelming. Facing her husband on her wedding night, she reflects, "Perhaps it was only her excited imagination that made her think he kissed . . . differently—with less restraint. And there swept into her mind the consciousness that there was no longer any barrier between them. She belonged to him, body and soul. In sudden panic she struggled against him. He released her at once."

In her depiction of a woman, like herself, disdainful of sexual pleasures, Emily describes Geraldine as remote throughout her marriage, her lack of physical passion finally helping to drive her kindhearted husband to suicide when she flirts heavily with another man. Turning to her old beau, whom she had really loved but had discarded for the far richer Ollie, she is shocked to discover that he had encountered his own good fortune and now, as a millionaire, is engaged to marry the Jimpsons' daughter.

Within ten years of Geraldine's marriage, the Jimpsons had been thoroughly absorbed by Best Society, with even Mr. Jimpson braided into its political structures—all without compromising the Jimpsons' native kindness. Mrs. Jimpson, whose gaudy ball gowns had originally earned her the nickname the "Circus Queen," commands the moral center of the novel. She is a woman who never forgets the highest claims of ethics: a woman can go as far as she desires if she possesses charm that comes from within and as long as she has integrity—without integrity, not even charm counts.

The writer Katherine Anne Porter appreciated the novel: "The helter-skelter of the times breaks down all the barricades. The newly rich climbers come stampeding in, and Geraldine faces the great crisis of her life when she discovers that in her early climbing days she had snubbed all the wrong people." Though she didn't grasp its significance, Porter isolated a major realization that Emily had developed over the decade: "There is nothing to do but cultivate [these vulgar new rich]," the novel emphasized. When the

Old Guard relented, they found "hearts of gold beating under these over decorated bosoms. Besides, they all learn quickly, and shortly they are scarcely distinguishable from the elect."

IN THE WAKE of the attention following *Parade*'s publication, Emily gave several interviews unrelated to her novel, aimed at the women's pages of newspapers and magazines. With the same voice of authority she used whatever the subject, she gamely discussed anything the journalist pursued, including who looked best in the new short hairstyles for women. The lengthy article she wrote for *McCall's*, "They Who Are Fat Must Suffer to Be Thin," proved disarmingly honest. No longer the wasp-waisted debutante, she acknowledged her own inability to look as up to date as she might wish. The current fashion of extreme thinness put people who liked to eat fatty foods—like Emily—at a distinct disadvantage, she lamented.

The "New Woman" of the mid-1920s was "elegant and lean, tall and linear, alluring yet remote." The olden days were easier for those who liked to eat: in 1892, a Smith College girl had written her parents that she was well on her way to meeting her goal to increase her 137 pounds to 150. Now, a different Smith student wrote her family that "I had the worst scare the other day." She had weighed in at a shocking 136½ pounds, having weighed a feminine 119 pounds only the semester before.

Emily believed that her young readers' plight was even worse than hers had been several decades earlier: "Never . . . has fat been held in such abhorrence. . . . Thinness to the point of emaciation, is the outline of fashion's decree." To women who expressed horror at the girdles used to achieve a wasp waist in the 1890s, she remarked that the strapping down of their chests to achieve the new boyish look was surely just as irritating.

The worst of Emily's own weight struggle was her discovery that, as an older woman, she could eat no more than eight hundred calories a day if she wanted to become slim again. For the past thirty years, ever since Ned's birth, she had tried intermittently to shed pounds. Anytime she had succeeded on a diet, she'd quickly gained the weight back. Clearly enjoying her subject, Emily couldn't resist sharing some of her "wild diets" throughout the years. Once, after losing twenty-six pounds in seven weeks on nothing but milk and potatoes, she'd wound up unable to even look at a glass of milk again. When she found herself overweight once more, she began a stewed-fruit-and-vegetable diet, which upset her stomach violently. Her favorite diet actually caused her to gain weight: its protocol dictated eating as much of one isolated food as desired at every meal. Emily merrily ate her way through stacks of pancakes or chocolate for breakfast, lunch, and dinner, not really surprised when this regimen proved too good to be true.

Aside from the nearly constant presence of hunger one had to accept in order to maintain a sleek profile, another major problem with staying thin was the toll the effort took on one's social life. No one liked being around dieters: not only were their menus restricted, but their usual expansive natures seemed temporarily corseted as well. "I can lose [weight] when I make up my mind that I must and I do lose periodically but I do NOT enjoy the process, nor have I ever found it possible to stay permanently under-weight and at the same time be contented, except morally and esthetically with my character and outline! . . . Dieting is NOT conducive to amiability, vitality or well being. It is entirely a triumph of vanity over mind!" She concluded by admitting that, at present, her only constant diet practice was substituting crystallose (saccharin) for sugar.

Emily's ease in talking confidently about the trends of the day suggests the self-assurance of an only child, evident throughout her life. She had always observed others closely, and now she noted the drastically different shapes women were currently adopting today—in every way. By one estimate, during the 1920s nearly one-half of all girls had sexual intercourse before marriage. Equally significant, young men tended to lose their virginity with women of their own class instead of paying prostitutes. Even more radically, people were demanding that marriage be funded by love. Emily Post was quite taken with this new Jazz Age, and she was determined to keep her finger on its pulse whatever birthday she was celebrating.

IN EARLY FEBRUARY 1926, Emily gave an interview to Katharine Brooke Daly, an Albany newspaper reporter. Still living at the Gladstone while workers applied the finishing touches to her co-op, she dazzled the writer, from the casually open door Daly discovered upon her arrival to Emily's "long, slender hands . . . [accompanied by] diamonds and rubies." In her "fifties, though she scarcely looks it," Mrs. Post is "distingué," Daly observed, though, for the sake of the "men who will read this," she noted, she is still "pretty in the tall patrician way."

After being further introduced as the "social arbiter from Baltimore, New York [and] Tuxedo," Emily commandeered the interview, expanding on her new (convoluted) personality theory, the emblem of which was the "enneagram," a nine-pointed diametric symbol based on an ancient secret

numbers system, to some extent connected to the Kabbalah. The enneagram's current popularity began when American soldiers learned the
quasi-spiritual system from their Russian counterparts during World
War I. Back home, it fit in perfectly with the success-based how-to books
of the age. More important to Emily, it spoke to a long-implied but mostly
buried need she felt to locate something spiritually meaningful about life
itself, whether exploring metaphysics with Mr. G. or table tapping with
Julie Olin Benkard, or ruminating abstractly with the reporter from the
Morning Star, investigating "things that mattered."

Users of the enneagram believed that everyone was dominated by one
of nine personality types, due to their inborn temperament and the child
rearing by their parents. People were also primarily "outgiving" (good) or
"intaking" (bad), Emily explained. Her recent novel *Parade* had used this dynamic to characterize two sisters, the selfish Geraldine and the generous
Dora, who was "beloved by everyone."

Warming up to her subject, she discussed how successful marriages
thrived on wives who were themselves contented: a woman who complained as soon as her husband reached the door would surely soon find
herself alone at night. Deliberately or not, her advice echoed that of birth
control pioneer Margaret Sanger, whose newly revised book *Happiness in
Marriage* claimed that it was up to women to "keep romance alive in spite
of the influence of the prosaic demands of everyday life." Growing expansive, Emily enthusiastically enjoined the young reporter, now utterly transfixed by the older woman, to reflect upon her own marriage from such
angles.

After leaving the apartment, the writer paused, lauding the generous
gaze Emily had allowed "into her ideas and feelings.... It is an outgiving
door." Emily was, of course, far too strategic for the exchange to have been
as "natural" and uncontrived as the young reporter assumed; it was her skill
as an "outgiver" that enabled her to seduce the woman so completely.

Discoursing on such an of-the-moment trend as enneagrams positioned Emily as someone who, no longer young, nonetheless stayed current.
Despite doing her best to ignore chronological years as a determinant of attitude, the fifty-three-year-old Emily Post was feeling the gulf between her
sons' age group and her own more than she had anticipated. In an era
fiercely focused on and celebrating the new, she had started thinking about
growing old, and how to best exploit where she was now. That spring,
McCall's published her essay "The Young Woman of Forty," a thoughtful but

confused commentary promoting the youthfulness of the middle-aged matron, *une femme d'un certain âge.*

A "very curious thing" had occurred in the last few years, regarding a woman's age, Emily opined. "Age values have changed—are changing. Today the sophisticates and the intolerants and the disillusioned are the young men and women in their early twenties, even in their teens. And the ingenuous, spontaneous qualities that once belonged to youth, are becoming the attributes of age. . . . The woman of forty, even of fifty," she daringly continued, "is, in the big cities at all events, much younger in her viewpoint, and her interests and her sympathies than she was at thirty. But her daughter is not only older in every way than her mother WAS, she is older than her mother IS, today."

The middle-aged crowd had rediscovered dancing, though Emily herself, she lamented, was not up to it. "At thirty-eight, I who danced was exceptional. Women of my age went to balls and sat as dowagers watching the season's debutantes. Today, I am almost exceptional because I don't dance. Being myself rather old-fashioned, I cannot yet contemplate with any sentiment resembling envy the actions of cavorting fifty year olds—perhaps in ten years I may join their ranks. Who knows?"

Around the same time that Emily's article about forty-year-old women appeared, the *New York Times* "Books and Authors" column took note of Lillian Eichler's forthcoming book, *Well-Bred English,* reminding readers that the author was broadcasting from WGBS every Monday afternoon from three-twenty to three-thirty, such a regular routine far more impressive than the brief appearances her competitor had made. To Emily's dismay, Eichler was working hard to establish her radio presence. Because she worked in a major advertising firm, the younger woman was well positioned for such an industry.

Wisely, Emily played to her own strengths. That September, based on the popularity of her distinctive articles, *McCall's* magazine began to run a column called "The Post Box," a series of questions and answers by Emily Post that would run through the first half of 1928. The "back page" of each month's magazine continued to belong to the advice column of the austere-looking Mrs. Winona Wilcox, though the following year, she and Emily would alternate that position. Writing regularly for *McCall's* was no small achievement—Dorothy Parker contributed as often as Emily, and Booth Tarkington, Carl Sandburg, Rudyard Kipling, and Scott and Zelda Fitzgerald wrote occasional pieces as well.

During the December holiday season, within a month of Emily's return from an early autumn trip overseas, a full-page ad in *Vanity Fair* showed the local linen guild proudly quoting an endorsement by Emily Post, who claimed, imperially, "We dine on linen damask." For just twenty-five cents, the viewer could receive a booklet on the subject of setting a fine table, "its foreword written by the author of *Etiquette*." In light of Emily's typical simple dinner for one these days, along with her equally strong preference for simple language, her friends must have smiled at the royal "we."

⌖

THOUGH BY THE MID-1920S IT WAS ALREADY A POPULAR VACATION spot for the well-heeled, Martha's Vineyard, cold in the winters, remained a natural paradise for foxes and pheasants, dunes and marshes. Emily's annual visits to Katharine Collier's summer rental finally convinced her to buy her own house on what she had begun to consider an almost magical island. She had been looking for a replacement for Tuxedo Park for a while, and not just because of the humidity: her time there had passed. It was right for her sons' generation to hold their own autumn balls these days.

At her leisure over the past few years, she had considered everything from the Morgan acreage in the Adirondacks to a seaside location on Long Island. Once she visited Katharine on Martha's Vineyard, however, she knew she was home. Later she explained that her ancestral link to John and Priscilla Alden of *Mayflower* fame called her to Massachusetts. What's more certain is that before making a final commitment, she ensured that her immediate family would cooperate: "She worked out a deal with my parents before making the purchase," Bill Post recalls fondly. "I would spend every summer shuffling back and forth between Grandmama's and my parents', two or three weeks in Edgartown then the next 'session' at Tuxedo and so forth."

The white-clapboard, green-shuttered cottage she finally settled on included a private beach about a quarter of a mile from her door on Fuller Street. Within view of the harbor, within walking distance of the village, the location was perfect for a woman unable to drive a car. Even the name of the real estate agent who sold her the property, Littleton C. Wimpenney, seemed scripted for the creator of *Etiquette*'s flamboyant characters.

The house had been remodeled several times already before she bought it. While tearing down the roof and the widow's walk, Emily uncovered a piece of tile bearing the words "This house was reshingled in 1828." Romantically, if inaccurately, Emily described the 1778 residence as an "old, gray fisher cottage, weather-beaten and squatty." She loved how her new home balanced a sense of the timeless with the temper of the modern day, the island's slightly stodgy reassurance anchored to the busyness of Boston, less than an hour and a half away by a pleasant ferry and car trip.

Most important, her son was going to help her renovate the entire house. She and Bruce spent the beginning of 1927 happily arguing over the best ways to update the friendly miniature farmhouse, so appealing that the young architect pushed her to travel to the island early, even before the season began. It was easy for Bruce to plead his case for an early departure as they celebrated his thirty-second birthday at the beginning of February: Manhattan was cold and bleak, the forecast predicting more of the same. Admittedly, it was cold near the water too, but at least they'd be able to get to work on the inside of their new property. He was pleased that he and his mother had one move behind them: he'd overseen Emily's installment at her new co-op, the unpacking finally complete, including a cache of his clothes and favorite bedroom pieces as well.

But Bruce's mother, excited to be updating *Etiquette,* was determined to finish the revisions due to her publisher first. She exulted in how perfect her life was just now: her public clamoring for more, her younger son at her side, about to help her rebuild her "new" home. This latest maternal excursion suited him well, she knew. He was impatient to get to "the other island," as they had taken to calling Martha's Vineyard, where he could begin work on his next project. Emily told Bruce he would simply have to wait a few weeks; he was acting, she said with a smile, much as he had as a little boy, begging to open his Christmas gifts early.

An abstemious, unmarried attractive man, Bruce was known for his friendships but not for any romance. If, as several elderly distant relatives have suggested, Bruce was gay, he would almost surely have remained closeted. He was no Oscar Wilde or Noël Coward, and he would have been horrified at the thought of humiliating his mother again, after what his fa-

ther had done to her. Emily's son loved her far too much to put his own desires first.

His sexuality would become a moot point. Just as Emily finally felt able
to leave Manhattan, her son got a bad stomachache that refused to go away.
Against his protests, she finally took him to the nearest hospital, where, on
February 25, 1927, Bruce Post, the joy of his mother's life, died from a ruptured appendix.

For the only time that anyone remembers, Emily Post faltered. Devastated by a grief she hadn't imagined possible, she shut down. Though her
surviving son alludes to this terrible sorrow in his memoir, he quickly passes
it by, as if too hard even at a distance to relive—both the loss of his brother
and his mother's pain. "For weeks she was unable to realize it or accept it as
a fact," he quietly observed. A prominent obituary in the *New York Times*
lauded "Bruce Price Post" as "high among the younger architects." Over the
last several years, Post had "given evidence of inheriting the talent of his
grandfather, Bruce Price, who planned Tuxedo Park and designed many of
the houses there." A rising young star, already a member of the Beaux-Arts
Institute of Design, he had designed the New Colonial Hotel in the Ba-
hamas and the Tuxedo Golf Club, closer to home. Bruce's father went unmentioned.

Emily was too shattered to consider the irony that must have struck
others: the best way for loved ones to tend to her now was to heed the
counsel she herself had offered in 1922. The advice would never waver, un-
revised from this first edition of *Etiquette* until her death:

At no time does solemnity so possess our souls as when we stand deserted at the brink of darkness into which our loved one has gone.
And the last place in the world where we would look for comfort at
such a time is in the seeming artificiality of etiquette; yet it is in the
moment of deepest sorrow that etiquette performs its most vital
and real service.

All set rules for social observance have for their object the
smoothing of personal contacts, and in nothing is smoothness so
necessary as in observing the solemn rites accorded our dead.

It is the time-worn servitor, Etiquette, who draws the shades,
who muffles the bell, who keeps the house quiet, who hushes voices
and footsteps and sudden noises; who stands between well-meaning

and importunate outsiders and the retirement of the bereaved; who decrees that the last rites shall be performed smoothly and with beauty and gravity, so that the poignancy of grief may in so far as possible be assuaged.

She had learned from her parents' deaths and from observing reactions of close friends to their own tragedies that grief skewed one's equilibrium:

Persons under the shock of genuine affliction are not only upset mentally but are all unbalanced physically. No matter how calm and controlled they seemingly may be, no one can under such circumstances be normal. Their disturbed circulation makes them cold, their distress makes them unstrung, sleepless. Persons they normally like, they often turn from. No one should ever be forced upon those in grief, and all over-emotional people, no matter how near or dear, should be barred absolutely. Although the knowledge that their friends love them and sorrow for them is a great solace, the nearest afflicted must be protected from any one or anything which is likely to overstrain nerves already at the threatening point, and none have the right to feel hurt if they are told they can neither be of use nor be received. At such a time, to some people companionship is a comfort, others shrink from dearest friends. One who is by choice or accident selected to come in contact with those in new affliction should, like a trained nurse, banish all consciousness of self; otherwise he or she will be of no service—and service is the only gift of value that can be offered.

JOAN DIDION, IN *The Year of Magical Thinking*, identifies explicitly with Emily's words about mourning. The unlikely pairing of Didion and Post was cited often in the impressive array of reviews showered on the bestseller, a winner of the National Book Award and a runner-up for the Pulitzer. Many journalists couldn't understand why someone as edgy and postmodern as Didion chose *Etiquette* to succor her. Didion explained: she had been taught from childhood to "go to the literature" in "time of trouble," and so she pursued everything she could find about death's anguish: memoirs, novels, how-to books, inspirational tomes, *The Merck Manual.* "Nothing I read about grief seemed to exactly express the craziness of it," Didion says. The one thing that spoke to her, finally, was the "Funerals" chapter in Emily Post's 1922 blue book on etiquette. Only Emily Post understood the power of routine to hold one's raw emotions at bay. Only Emily Post made suffering bearable.

"There was something arresting about the matter-of-fact wisdom here. [Post] wrote in a world in which mourning was still recognized, allowed, not hidden from view," Didion explained. Like Didion herself, who wanted to "bring death up close," Emily Post needed to acknowledge desolation as part of life. Her ability to confront sorrow in a straightforward manner seemed, to Didion, a success unmatched by other writing on the subject.

Didion remembered that her mother had given her a copy of *Etiquette* to sweeten a snowbound stay in Colorado during World War II. This time, in 2004, enduring another cold winter in a different era of her life, she could read it online in the solitude of her home.

WHEN HER SON DIED, Emily lost her bearings. Her suffering alternately numbed and roiled her for months, and then she fought to find her way back. From the few accounts of this period, Emily's ability to carry on depended upon her filling every moment of her day. From developing her garden skills, to working crossword puzzles, to writing, to creating intricate models for her friends' architects: she wanted no time to reflect. In addition to projects already under way, including reading the proofs for the first revision of *Etiquette,* she piled on new assignments, overextending herself in order to be saved. A decade later, she admitted that she had "worked with a furious concentration, taking on whatever jobs came along, until they often occupied sixteen hours out of twenty-four."

Shrewdly, she figured out a way to keep her loss at bay while staying connected to those she had loved: through writing a textbook on architecture, she would instruct others in the "Bruce" tradition. That spring, while everyone around her talked of nothing but Charles Lindbergh squiring his *Spirit of St. Louis* from New York to Paris, Emily immersed herself in the libraries of her father and her son, creating from their volumes complex building diagrams and explanations. Though it professed to be the work of an amateur decorator, the book that resulted was a systematic compendium of architecture, enthusiastically detailing everything from color wheels to histories of furniture. Even as she paid tribute to them, Emily was now free to become her own version of the wide-ranging architects her father and then her son had been.

—

CAUGHT UP IN her enthusiasm for this new book subject, Emily began rendering intricate replicas of houses she was helping remodel, using detailed cardboard constructions created from cigar boxes, decorating each room with diminutive papier-mâché furniture. If they suited the owners, she added tiger-skin rugs made of wax, with the stripes carefully etched. John Russell Pope, with his reassuring ties to her father, bought several of her models. Though Emily had meant from the start to produce the miniatures primarily as a hobby, her friends had insisted on compensating her, further confirming her status as a professional. She quickly discovered that prospective customers would "pay her plenty," especially when she had to travel. Soon her architectural and design consulting skills became valuable enough that she started charging strangers for long-distance phone advice. During the next ten years, she would create twenty-five models.

Clients and architects alike enjoyed working with her. Without seeming overbearing or condescending, she employed a foolproof method of getting her way with both of them. An admiring journalist explained: "She tells them what she thinks and what she wants, quickly, in a level voice; and then, before even the most embattled antagonist has time to argue with her, she says, 'you see, don't you?' leaning forward a little and speaking in a tone so suddenly warm and winning that there is no possible answer except 'Yes, Mrs. Post.' "

But if her attention to architecture kept the departed close, she sometimes needed ways to avoid thinking about them entirely. Within a few months of Bruce's death, Emily turned to a hobby she had occasionally indulged throughout her adulthood, gardening. This time, however, there would be nothing of the amateur about it. Fastidiously organized, her garden log reveals an obsessively detailed description of the grounds surrounding the house that she and her son meant to restore together; now the flowers she planted would be Bruce's eternal flame. "Gardens are a blending of nature and artifice; they are the product of horticulture and architecture," remarks the anthropologist Yi-Fun Tuan. Control over nature reassures uneasy souls, especially those, like Emily's, in turmoil. Her garden would be the perfect monument to her son.

Used to small plots rather than to her current expansive outdoor environment, she asked friends how to proceed, but they tried to discourage her from undertaking such a large project, for which she had little background.

Undaunted, she defended her plan: "Lots of people have grown flowers who have not graduated from a horticultural college." She "read literally every book on gardening" that she could "beg, borrow, or buy." Studying the elaborate grids, Emily created her own chart, "not only painted in color, [but] the plants grouped according to time of blooming, height, sun and shade requirements and type of soil." Color began to dominate her vision: her main requirement was to avoid "egg-yolk yellow or turkey red, neither of which I can endure." Red, her favorite choice for human-made items, seemed grotesquely unnatural and attention-seeking in nature.

Pausing during her workday, she often found herself eyeing a bold defector from her master plan:

I am drawn to a window—and there is a red flower standing out like a gash! Then out I go and pull it up. I go indoors, and from the window see the hole where it was taken out. Well, I'm not going to do anything about it! I sit at my desk and begin my day's real work, but instead of seeing the words I write, I see the hole where the red plant was. Within fifteen minutes I am out of the house walking around the garden looking for something to transplant. Then the hole made by the flower that is moved has to be filled—and so it goes.

House and Garden editor Dominique Browning has poignantly explained how her garden rescued her after her marriage failed: "I took care of the garden, then the garden took care of me." Gardening became her way "of digging into the new life—digging in for the long haul, connecting, committing to a patch of soil, rooting in and under and around and through it all." For the first few seasons following her loss, Browning, like Emily, lacked energy to lavish on her new garden. "But the garden went on. A few more springs passed in the same sorry state, and then one day I noticed a profusion of weeds and decided to do something about them. . . . Enough to get by, enough to get going again."

As if a stranger to her newly bountiful countryside, Emily emigrated to the outdoors. She was mimicking, unknowingly, the newcomers to the United States who had long used personal gardens, however small their piece of land, to re-create the feel of their old lives and to offset the deracination they inevitably experienced. Planting a square, however humble, but full of the same herbs and foods that fed them back home, kept the dispossessed in touch with the lives they had lost. For Emily, whose child had been an aesthete, the planting of architecturally perfect grids of flowers was surely, if unconsciously, a potent way to connect with the land of her dead son.

Though new to gardening on such a large scale, Emily had the instincts of a survivor who intuitively knows what to do. Researchers at New York University Medical Center have measured brain-wave changes in a group of women presented with flowers; they were shocked at the rate of genuine smiles, as measured by brain-wave changes. The investigators claimed "never [to] get 100 percent in any experiment"—until now: patients at NYU's Rusk Institute of Rehabilitation Medicine seemed "to forget about their pain" when spending time among the hospital's flower beds.

As she assuaged her own pain, Emily reached out to connect with others. She took pleasure in delighting passersby with lively flowers in riotous bloom outside her picket fence. One day, however, it dawned on her that they were invisible to any spectator inside the gate; she and her servants could not enjoy them. Her new driver (like his predecessor, though far younger, also named John) took her to the town hardware store, where, newly determined to sponge sword-shaped leaves all over her side of the fence, she quickly decided to buy three colors of green paint. Several hours later, her house windows looked out upon a forest of painted foliage, replacing the previous starkness of the white wooden planks. Like Bruce Price designing skyscrapers—finishing all sides of the building instead of only those that showed—his daughter believed in considering the total picture.

EMILY'S WELL-WORN GARDEN log bears in equal measure the marks of her pain and her resolve to be happy. To this day, her descendants marvel at her intricate notes on each bed of plants: their favorite fertilizers and elaborately detailed planting schemes colored with every shade of crayon she could find. She designed the garden on her own, with the help of a seed merchant in Philadelphia to whom she wrote detailed letters. Henry Dreer served, without knowing it, as a surrogate therapist to help the bereft mother avoid thinking too often of her son's empty room inside.

"Dear Madame," the fastidious merchant responded that first July after Bruce died. "There isn't any doubt but that the combination of one part of Muriate of Potash and four parts of Bone Meal [are] better for your dahlias than Stim-U-Plant." A long letter ensued, the patient Dreer explaining every facet of fertilizer Emily must have queried, from the proper bone meal mix to the proportions of nitrogen and ammonia. It was almost as if she became a midwife to her flowers.

John Enos, serving as both her gardener and her handyman, proved as loyal in his way as her old coachman in Manhattan and Tuxedo Park had been. John's now elderly successor, Tony Bettencourt, still remembers the daily routine: Emily walked into her garden right after lunch. After a thorough discussion of any horticultural activity during the preceding twenty-four hours, she'd go sit in the shade (usually pleased at the growing success of her latest enterprise) and watch Tony nurse the weakest plants back to health. She was always "thinking big," he recalls fondly.

Over the subsequent summers, she would record everything planted: "June 5, 1st iris (one) in bloom (about 30 spikes).... 2 Lupins (1 blue in longbed—1 white in picking and in first bloom). Nearly all lupins dead.... First Dalilias [sic] (house plants 4 to 10 millimeters high). Gladiolii planted in keg about May 1 well out of ground (1 to 3 inches)." The chronicle continues, her planting and watering and fertilizing detailed fastidiously, almost as carefully as she measured the growth of her flowers. Determined to repair any omissions in her garden that compromised its health, she could have been documenting Ned's height every month, as she had over thirty years before, implicating with each note the swift passage of time: "Too tall for path beds" she marveled now when her progeny exceeded her expectations.

Putting things together, piecing a whole out of its parts, making sense of things: this theme was a constant in Emily Post's adult life. Now, at quiet times when neither hired help nor friends were at hand, Emily enlisted new support: hand-cut plywood puzzles that Parker Brothers had recently begun selling. She chose traditional scenes of English history or American landscapes. "I don't remember much from that period—I was only five or six—but I do recall the summer when my grandmother became dedicated to the Pastime Picture Puzzles. She'd get so involved she wouldn't hear anything else," Bill Post reminisces. "They became a family hobby, with all of us joining in. She and I had an ongoing mock argument about the better way to arrange the pieces: I preferred to group by shape, but not Grandmama.... She'd lose herself in the pieces. She'd select by colors and organize the blues and the reds together."

Crafted in 1926 or 1927, each high-quality puzzle piece cost 1.5 cents. Typically a scene would require 100 pieces, twelve deliberately shaped like recognizable objects. A complex 750-piece puzzle would cost $7.50, with 1,000-piece puzzles commanding $10 ($100 today). Emily scoffed at the "exorbitant" price: she and her grandson would make their own puzzles, she said. But, Bill recalls clearly, she bought a secondhand saw, a "cheap model" that no one could make work. Before long, she was forced to cede the ground to Parker Brothers.

The boxes still stacked high in her grandson's closets suggest that Emily was rarely without a puzzle in progress after Bruce's death. On the top of each cardboard container she scribbled the date she finished it, noting as well any help she wangled along the way. Recording the visits her family and friends made, the carefully documented lids substitute for a more conventional diary of her life. One obvious favorite, its box tattered and held together with string, displays the first Thanksgiving dinner at Plymouth Rock. As if reminding herself of her family's perpetuity and renewal—her connection to the *Mayflower*'s John and Priscilla Alden—she framed a reality that helped reorder her shattered life. It is hard today to finger the tiny irregular pieces and not feel close to the woman who used them to heal herself.

But of her myriad diversions, the most reliable, the sturdiest, was the revision of *Etiquette* she had been working on for months. Although subsequent newspaper advertisements emphasized society's need for an updated version, her publisher had an added incentive: Emily's contract expired at the end of the year. They wanted to keep their star, and from now on, her royalty rate would be whatever she negotiated. Funk and Wagnalls placed a large ad in the *New York Times* on the last day of November, trumpeting, "The first edition of Mrs. Post's *Etiquette* has already gone through seventeen printings." The continued interest in the subject, and the "many changes that have occurred in the social amenities in recent years," had required modifications. Emily, desperately in need of more diversion than gardening and puzzles could provide, relied on *Etiquette* to save herself.

※

THE 1927 EDITION OF *ETIQUETTE*, APPEARING THE YEAR HER SON died, reflected Emily's growing awareness of life outside the circle she knew best. The booming postwar economy had contributed to a confused new social blend, the same people showing up at a speakeasy one night and a Southampton dinner party the next. How did—how should—Best Society (whatever that was) act these days?

Americans had witnessed radical changes over the past five years, since *Etiquette*'s original publication. Emily explained that "the increased pace of living," embodied by the "automobile, airplane, radio" and, as well, by "apartment-dwelling," had created a new sensibility, even allowing for a "young woman [to go] out alone with a man." The new car culture, especially, had changed the rules; in 1921, Warren Harding had governed a nation that boasted one automobile for every eleven residents. By the end of the decade, the number of cars had almost tripled, with one for every four and a half residents. Sanguine about the inevitable battle between parents and their children that such significant and rapid changes created, Emily agreed with correspondents who thought it unrealistic for a mother to expect her daughter not to do what all her friends were doing with the new freedoms they'd been handed, including going on late-night dates that ended with good-byes said in the car.

That December, *Time* magazine published a slightly smug review of the new edition of *Etiquette*. The writer summed up the genre, as he saw it: "The Idea: A dictionary of etiquette for 1928. The Motive: To tell those who do not set standards what is being done by those who do". The *Washington Post* was more flattering, believing the new edition important enough to be reviewed on Christmas Day. "The customs and manners of a people" decidedly "change with the times," the article observed, and Emily Post's revisions neatly illustrated radical changes in the conduct of men and women since the early twenties. Young girls, for instance, now did pretty much whatever they wanted, the review pointed out, a change that had caused Etiquette's 1922 chapter "The Chaperone and Other Conventions" to be replaced with "The Vanishing Chaperone and Other Lost Conventions." This revised edition included instructions for a woman to go "out alone with a man." Such a shift in emphasis exemplified "the wind of women's independence," the Post opined.

Even more important than the trials of the newly liberated flapper were the fears of housewives who had read the 1922 edition and become totally confounded about what to them was a major issue: how to give a formal dinner party without the staff Emily assumed readers had. Trying to host a dinner based on the descriptions in Etiquette, women readers had frequently failed. They lacked the butlers that seemed pivotal to formal entertaining, and so they wrote to the author, earnestly wondering, "What shall I do?" How could they entertain with the requisite style and grace though lacking six or eight servants?

Emily had been so impressed with the deluge of mail on this topic that by the end of 1922 she had already devised a solution, and now she included it in the newly revised Etiquette: Mrs. Three-in-One, the hostess, cook, and waitress. Pondering the anxious letters, she had invited six friends to dine with her and Bruce in their apartment. From this experience came her story of dinner with the "Toploftys, the Gildings and the Worldlys," all of them delighted by their hostess's ingenuity. Emily admitted that the efficient Mrs. Three-in-One she created did employ a kitchen helper; nonetheless, the menu didn't depend on such luxuries. Emily's main course was "chicken hash." For a surprise, there was ice cream cranked earlier in a dessert freezer, which she'd cheerfully concealed under her chair. At the end of the meal, reaching below and extracting the finale "caused a mild sensation," with her guests clapping delightedly. Essentially the ambassador of a highly organized method that enabled food to be served from the head of the table, Mrs. Three-in-One, following her formal debut in 1927, would become almost as much a part of Etiquette's iconography as its royal blue cover.

Mrs. Three-in-One represented a huge leap of Emily Post's imagination. In the five years since her book had made its debut, Emily had come to realize that the issues that resonated most deeply with her readers had to do with their insecurity over class. Now she was taking into consideration more fully the amorphous group striving always to belong to the chimerical all-knowing group they believed would validate them. This middle class, its economic and social status fluctuating along with its definition, feared above all else looking ignorant. Thus, with respect and aplomb, Emily gracefully explained what Josephine would have thought beneath her daughter: how service pieces were used, where they were set on the table, how to talk to servants if you were lucky enough to afford them. She had come to realize that the lack of savoir faire displayed by Bruce Price's newly rich customers, such as George Gould and his family, was not idiosyncratic after all. The very notion of the middle class was starting to refer to desire, to the effort to become upwardly mobile. Being rich, as the Prices had always known, was not in and of itself a virtue.

Though sensitive to her audience's anxieties, Emily urged her readers to exchange confidence for ill-placed alarm: "One of the fears expressed time and again in letters from readers is that of making a mistake in selecting the right table implements, or in knowing how to use one that is unfamiliar in shape. In the first place queerly shaped pieces of flat silver, contrived for purposes known only to their designers, have no place on a well appointed table. . . . [E]tiquette is founded on tradition, and has no rules concerning eccentricities. In the second place, the choice of an implement is entirely unimportant—a trifling detail which people of high social position care nothing about."

Realizing, nonetheless, that those in the middle class—not "people of high social position"—were the ones dog-earing the pages of her book, she continued in a practical vein, aware that before indulging in the luxury of breaking the rules, one had to know what they were: "In order that you may make no mistake, you need merely remember that you are to take the outside, that is the furthest from the plate, spoon or fork first. If the places are not set in this order, then the fault is that of the person who set the table, and not yours. If you are in doubt," wait until your host or hostess has picked up his or her utensils, "and do likewise."

The majority of the 1922 text didn't change. "Best Society" was still defined "not [as] a fellowship of the wealthy, nor does it seek to exclude those who are not of exalted birth; but it is an association of gentlefolk. . . . [G]ood form in speech, charm of manner, knowledge of the social amenities and instinctive consideration of the feelings of others are the credentials by which society the world over recognizes its chosen members." But to her chapter on the businessman, she added an equally long section on the ways for the "business woman" (whom she clearly admired) to get ahead: working long days, almost like an "efficient machine," was an order of the first importance.

Furthermore, one's entire career could be sidetracked by the seemingly trivial, making it no wiser to ignore the banal than the profound. Overlooking "careless" odors, for instance, whether from eating garlic "or neglecting frequent bathing or because of digestive or chemical defects," might well subvert one's best efforts, causing people to dwell on the superficial before there was any chance to get to the core.

Most of all, Emily quietly acknowledged the larger field she was playing on. Her book no longer even pretended to be about things less than vital: "Etiquette must, if it is to be of more than trifling use, include ethics as well as manners." "One's Position in the Community" (the Choice) became "Making One's Position in the Community," the egalitarian implications of the new heading no doubt horrifying the Old Guard. Tellingly, another chapter, "American Neighborhood Customs," contained advice meant for the first-generation Americans she now realized she was tutoring. "The history of New York City cannot be told without figuring in immigration," as Pete Hamill has said. Nor could the story of the rest of the country.

The letters that poured in after Etiquette's first edition had made her conscious that her real public was this vast national community, from lower middle class to rich or aspiring to be, all seeking to learn courtesies from A to Z. Such a response encouraged her to address Americans outside the East Coast that she knew so well, a task she now realized had begun during her cross-country car trip on the Lincoln Highway. Even the immigrant soccer league players common to New York City knew—or their wives did—that there were occasions when everyone needed to play by the same rules. Women moving to the city from rural communities and new citizens arriving from foreign countries: Emily wanted these transplants to know how to get ahead. To Emily Post, knowledge and the choice to use it wisely were all anyone needed for a good life.

Over the years, she would come to better understand the dynamics of social power that undergirded her life versus those of a struggling underclass, and her awareness allowed her to address more clearly the need of that world's inhabitants to fight their way up the ladder to success. In order to remain relevant, Emily was forced to open her eyes to the grim realities with which Jacob Riis, a photographer dedicated to social reform, had confronted the nation years earlier. At some level, she was beginning to understand that her turn-of-the-century New York "had reeked of racism, religious bigotry, class prejudice, and sexual exploitation." Emily had grown since those Gilded Age days, and her new edition, with its genuinely democratic ideals and sympathies, made that clear.

PART FOUR

. . .

Write the name and address on the envelope
as precisely and as legibly as you can.
The post office has enough to do in deciphering
the letters of the illiterate, without being asked
to do unnecessary work for you!

—ETIQUETTE, PAGE 460

CHAPTER 47

THE CONTEST TO BUILD THE TALLEST SKYSCRAPER WAS BACK ON. In the booming economy steadily heating up ever since the troops came home, the leading architects waged bets against one another, speculating about who they thought would go highest and how long it would take them to get there. Their rivalry reminded a wistful Emily Post of how her father had been a key player in the similar competitions at the turn of the century. His aging friends were amused and a little nostalgic to see what they had assumed to be their story now being told for a second time. These days, everyone was talking about the Chrysler Building, two years from its completion, and how it had just been blindsided by the Empire State Building, scheduled to enter the race as well, with its driven architect determined to bludgeon his competition if only by a measure of inches. Both skyscrapers would be more than three times the height of Bruce Price's American Surety Building on Broadway.

But Bruce's daughter was too busy these days writing about more modest dwellings to waste time speculating on the grandiose. That spring, she herself was engaged in a competition centering upon the leading contemporary aesthetic. Aware of the heated contest between old and new, representatives from the International Exposition of Art in Industry chaired an afternoon debate between Emily Post and eminent photographer Edward Steichen. During his talk entitled "The American Point of View in Modern Decoration," Steichen urged his audience to embrace the modernist position that valued function over ornamentation: "Consign . . . useless bric-a-brac" to the attic, he urged. Emily's impassioned defense of the individual's right to her own aesthetic won the greater applause, if only because the event was held at Macy's department store: "I hope modern decoration won't lead any of you to throw away your old pieces," she told her well-heeled audience, "for I am especially fond of eighteenth-century works. While I think the new movement is a serious one, combining beauty and utility, I feel each home should represent the taste of the individual living in it, and not be filled with things some one else said were the things to have."

Without a doubt, Emily was her own woman—or at least she meant to be. Before retreating to Martha's Vineyard that summer, she posed for Old Gold Cigarettes' ad campaign, a commission her mother would have found shocking: tobacco, messy and masculine, was clearly never meant for a woman. Josephine might have been somewhat mollified had she noticed the familiar names imbedded deep in her daughter's assignment. Pierre Lorillard's dynasty included the American Tobacco Company, with Edward L. Bernays (a nephew of Sigmund Freud's) the corporation's public relations genius. Shrewdly, Bernays encouraged women to take up smoking by linking it with the suffrage movement. During the Easter parade on Fifth Avenue the following year, ostensibly promoting "equality of the sexes," he would choreograph debutantes marching in public as they puffed away on "torches of freedom," in the name of the emancipated female.

Many professional models sought the Old Gold assignment, which would involve a blind taste test of various brands of cigarettes, but Emily was actually approached by the company's executives, who knew her advocacy would matter, especially among all those potential clients still unsure if they should smoke at all. Although the number of women smokers had tripled in the past ten years, the *Washington Post* commentary from a decade earlier still seemed prudent to a certain set of worried females: "A man may take out a woman who smokes for a good time, but he won't marry her, and if he does, he won't stay married."

Emily, who saw no reason these days to censure women's use of tobacco, agreed to accept the assignment only if she be allowed to tell the truth about her choice. After all, she had yet to take up smoking and didn't intend to start now, as she would make clear in a later interview: "Personally I have never acquired a taste for tobacco. For most cigarettes seem to burn my tongue and sting my throat. The only time I ever smoke, therefore, is in courtesy to someone coming to my house, who would lay her accustomed cigarette aside unless I at least lit one too. It seemed absurd, at first, that I should be chosen to attempt this blindfold test . . . except that never having become a smoker, my taste is extremely sensitive to the burning harshness of the average cigarette." Choking after each puff, she went through four cigarettes, gulping coffee because she kept getting dizzy.

Fortunately for the sponsors, Emily not only chose Old Gold but lauded it for being "perceptibly smooth, stingless and pleasant to taste. In fact," she added, "I now quite easily understand why the OLD GOLD compartment in my general cigarette box must be so constantly refilled." Later, describing the blindfold test, she explained that the advertising executives were extremely jumpy throughout it, their nervousness adding to her own tension. After she announced her decision, Old Gold's representatives practically bounded around the room in pleasure. But as soon as the ad appeared, Emily herself spent several restless nights, unable to sleep, worried what her friends would think.

Or so she said, fobbing off her current relentless insomnia upon such concerns. In fact, as ill-advised as it may have been, the cigarette assignment had helped distract Emily from her sadness. Now she just needed to get out of the city and clear her head. For several months, she had been arising before daybreak, after tossing restlessly for hours, and writing notes for her gardener about preparing her soil in Edgartown, then shooting off inquiries to the expert at her Philadelphia seed store after she chose the garden's colors. One typical order, placed unseasonably early while Emily was still in New York, requested eight varieties of gladiolus bulbs, all by their botanical names.

By late spring, finally in Edgartown, she was sending detailed records to the Philadelphia store and commending Dreer for his advice, which had helped her attain the exact shade of red she had doggedly pursued. "I HATE crimsons and the red of scarlet sage and the yellow of golden glow. These two [*sic*] colors are pulled up the instant they appear. Also all purples and Jacquemenot [*sic*] red. But I LOVE the pale yellows—especially lemons and pale lacquer vermillion, the brilliant orange and salmon like the Prince of Wales. Richard Deiner [one of the varieties she has ordered] is wonderful, but Mrs. Pendleton with large globs of blood I detest." The almost manic letter continued for several jarring, energetic paragraphs, surely taking aback the readers at Dreer's. They realized they were dealing with yet another high-minded lady, but this one, at least more personable than most, was also far more eccentric: pleasant as could be, she was particularly opinionated and strong-willed about her garden plot. Never, Dreer mused, had any customer talked about yanking out perfectly formed flowers just because they proved the wrong shade of pink.

On May 28 Emily's journal practically shimmered with excitement: her garden, she believed, was now in full bloom. Two days later, however, she noticed where improvements were needed. Out of all the cornflower blues she had planted, very few had survived the winter. Next year, she decided, she would have to do better.

WHILE EMILY POST weeded her garden to make peace with one son's death, she heard from her older child, Ned, about a calamity that had recently upset him. In 1928, twenty-two years after his divorce from Emily, Edwin Post was living with his spouse and their three children—two boys and an infant daughter (soon to die)—in an inn near Babylon. He was content with his life, the balance just about right at last: a loving family that embraced his passion for the sea, a theatrical wife like the woman he'd thought he was marrying the first time around.

One summer day, acting as the broker for a friend and client, Edwin volunteered to deliver a twenty-five-foot secondhand speedboat to the new owner's summer home near Stamford, Connecticut. The wealthy young medical student eagerly accepted Edwin's offer, then thought to go along as well, inviting two friends, one a noted art historian, to accompany them. Against the entreaties of his apprehensive twelve-year-old son, Henry, who thought the boat unseaworthy, Edwin, impetuous as always, insisted he could navigate around Long Island. Including Henry, three generations of Posts had sailed these waters. The foursome passed through the Great South Bay, then headed toward Fire Island Inlet, a rough spot that connected the bay to the Atlantic Ocean. They planned to continue west, toward New York City, then motor through the East River to reach Stamford, located on the north side of Long Island Sound.

As Edwin steered, the *Ethel Ray* ripped through the tricky currents of Fire Island Inlet; from descriptions of similar trips, the excursion was well known as a scary ride for even the most experienced navigators. Suddenly, unaccountably, just three miles offshore, the craft capsized. A few days later, two of the bodies were retrieved, the other two eventually surfacing as well. Edwin's body was the last to be recovered.

He was laid to rest in Woodlawn Cemetery, among the rich and famous he had always admired most, his family name ensuring his admission to this exclusive acreage. Jay Gould, R. H. Macy, and other notables faced each side of the imposing Post ancestral vault: Edwin was part of the big money at last. According to their grandson, Emily never said a word about Edwin's death. She may not have known that his widow, whom he had married in 1911, resumed her stage name upon his death. Nellie (Eleanor) Malcolm acted with a professional company, the Idle Hour Playhouse, located on the former Vanderbilt estate at Oakdale. Remembered by her great-grandchildren as "delightful, imperious, kind, and, of course, theatrical," Nellie sounded a lot like Emily Post.

THAT FALL, WHILE the nation went about electing its new president, Emily sought to take advantage of the lively speculation her whimsically themed pieces for *Vanity Fair* had created over the past year. Originally she had written "How to Behave—Though a Debutante" at editor Frank Crownin-shield's behest, as a series of magazine articles, illustrated handsomely by the well-respected graphic artist John Held Jr. The writing by "Anony-mous" appeared monthly, and some readers had even assumed the story to be a satire aimed at the writer of *Etiquette*. Few had identified the real au-thor, and Emily's successful subterfuge pleased her enormously—so much so that by April she had not only met with Doubleday editors about ex-panding the collection into a book but she had suggested to (or been con-vinced by) them, that she leave Funk and Wagnalls for good in the process.

Even in the 1920s considered something of a musty publisher, Funk and Wagnalls was associated largely with dictionaries and encyclopedias. Emily, a fifty-five-year-old woman in an era glorifying youth, worried that publish-ing with the specialized company ossified her name, handicapping her against ever-younger writers. To make matters worse, in 1927 Doubleday had merged with the George H. Doran Company, creating the largest pub-lishing business in the English-speaking world. Emily hadn't failed to notice, either, that sales of Lillian Eichler's books continued to increase. Accord-ingly, as she worked out her contract for the *Debutante* book, the shrewd busi-nesswoman, false pride never her weakness, concluded that she would do better to turn *Etiquette* over to Doubleday as well, regardless of the company's fondness for Eichler.

To her surprise, however, the Funk and Wagnalls executives removed their gentlemen's gloves and prepared to do battle—however genteelly. This time Emily Post lost, though at least it was edifying that the publisher wanted her so much. "Dear Madam," the letter of April 18, 1928, read (no "Mrs. Post" now). "We have seen yours of April 3rd, 1928"—presumably about Emily's intention to take *Etiquette* to Doubleday. "Notice is hereby given you that we have instructed our attorneys to take the necessary steps against you and against Doubleday, Doran & Co. and that all further proceedings by either of you will be taken at risk."

Emily didn't know that this brisk communication was far more genteel than Funk and Wagnalls's law firm, Griggs, Baldwin and Baldwin, had first urged be sent. Either more charitable by nature or worried about irreparably offending its author, Emily's publisher had replied to the lawyers' initial draft with polite alarm: "On reading [your suggested letter] over we thought the phraseology was a bit abrupt, and I have tried my hand at a letter which will probably have the same effect, at the same time not be such a direct blow. Will you kindly look this over and let me know what you think of it and make such changes as you may deem proper." Though no names are legible, the company's president apparently signed it. Emily did not defect to the competitor, and Funk and Wagnalls continued to publish *Etiquette* until after its author's death.

HOW TO BEHAVE—THOUGH A DEBUTANTE debuted in the fall of 1928. Whimsical and charming, the parody promoted the notion that youth was its own category, one that deserved respect—as did one's parents, though the burden fell largely on the older generation to accept gracefully the passage of time. The *Times* reviewed it positively a few days before Thanksgiving. Questioning whether the market could support yet another book on etiquette or on the new generation, the reviewer answered, "Exactly. Both." A "distinctly likable book" because of its author's charitable persona, *How to Behave* allowed Emily to revisit the debutante as the 1920s drew to a close. Whatever nostalgia the romp inspired in the author, her creation Muriel, neither "snobbish" nor "purse proud" nor "cynical," was a distinctly modern creature. With divorced parents, she was forced to cope with various second-marriage relationships. Through it all, whatever the trials, the girl remained compassionate and likable: "With her breezy honesty, she is very attractive; she is, really, lovable," the *New York Times* reviewer concluded.

Muriel is sad that she can talk only "emptiness to Mamma . . . because she doesn't really want anything else. . . . She cares nothing for all the problems of human nature. . . . Originality, independence, and breadth of experience are simply bad form!" Given how the girl continues, forthrightly pouring out her feelings about topics unthinkable, let alone mentionable, in Emily's age, it's easy to see why few guessed the author's identity: "We of today,"

Muriel explained, "believe in freely discussing everything we can think of—especially if it is a Problem. We talk quite a lot about sex, of course, ... and we quite often analyze its unexpected appeal—or failure to appeal. We believe that every serious problem of human nature is discussable." This casualness in mentioning what was still unmentionable to many readers even of *Vanity Fair* hardly seemed the natural terrain of an etiquette adviser.

A week before Christmas, with Emily's identity divulged, the *Washington Post* lauded her acceptance of the day's youth on its own terms. The modern debutante was "no doll baby," after all. "She is a high-powered individual who cannot be coaxed, coerced or driven." Most important, the reviewer concluded, no matter how "brazenly unconventional" Muriel's decisions seemed to her elders, they succeeded ethically because they were "for the most part predicated on kindliness and consideration for the other person."

ETIQUETTE, HOWEVER, DID NOT commend silence when speaking up was the ethical thing to do. Provoked by a writer whose disdainful comments about women were several decades out of date, Emily finished the year with a diatribe. Her aggrieved, aggressive rejoinder appeared in the December issue of the *American Magazine,* its take-no-prisoner intelligence causing it to be included in the *New York Times Magazine*'s list of must-read articles. Whether she now realized that she was tough—she had survived many women's worst fears—or whether her outburst was simply a signpost of the age's newly liberal society, she reproached Clarence Budington Kelland mercilessly for his anachronistic assumptions.

Money management within marriage was the subject. Kelland claimed that women tended toward two extremes, the "parsimonious" or the "predatory," and that only after a husband signed a release for his wife to purchase on credit should he be legally responsible for any purchases she made. Wives were destined to be either tightwads or spendthrifts; with women, there could be "no happy average."

To Kelland's picture of the industrious husband in "last year's pants" while his wife wore the latest extravagant fashions, Emily contrasted the reasons why she herself had sometimes reused her own fashionable outfits long ago: "Plenty of wives ... are wearing much farther back than last year's clothes, and worrying themselves to death about every expenditure, even necessities for the children's well-being, when up drives husband in his expensive new car, clothed according to fashion's best and latest." There existed, she quickly agreed (misusing a word she thought meant *spendthrift*), "penurious wives," but more often, in her experience, women were the prudent "little partners, trying their best to keep the firm solvent despite whatever form of expenditure happens to be the policy—or weakness—of their men!"

She cited from her own acquaintances and their friends twenty women suddenly thrown back upon their resources, widows who belatedly discovered that their husbands had rifled the family bank accounts and who thereupon squared their shoulders and made a living for themselves and their children. A wife's overspending of the budget, she charged, was due to the husband's failure to consider her an equal who should be included in all financial decisions. The real problem at the root of marriages was that a "certain kind of husband—the '100 per-cent he-man type' especially" treated his spouse "as though she were a moron" instead of valuing her as an intelligent and dependable companion.

Repeatedly, Emily returned to her thesis: women were capable of being valuable lifetime partners, but men—"about a hundred years backward—and then some"—arrogantly prevented them from contributing their expertise to the marriage or to the larger world outside, for that matter. Angrily rejecting Kelland's accusation that financial problems were usually due to the woman, she lashed out, motivated by her own past, and insisted that "the money difficulty in family life is chiefly the fault of the husband, who, for reasons known only to himself and the Almighty, tells his wife nothing whatever, or as little as possible, about what he is doing, or trying to do, or failing to do"—even when he is on edge of bankruptcy.

This was Emily Post at her finest, crusading out of personal conviction, not as part of a movement supporting the strong women who populated her nation. Instead, though singular, she nonetheless spoke from experiences that others shared. She strove to be fair, admitting that more than men's ill-placed contempt motivated marital failure: the social system was set up to overvalue one sex at the expense of the other. Even this observation, however, had been born out of the muddle of her own marriage. The rebuttal to Kelland was Emily's final rejoinder to her dead ex-husband, unwitting but therefore all the more passionate, unleashing her frustration at Edwin's carelessness and at the conjugal lack of trust that had ruined their marriage. Edwin might have died in an accident, but it was no accident that the ethical, hardworking Emily Post, not the man whose name she shared, was still alive and thriving.

CHAPTER 48

⊕

S HE REVELED IN THE DIVERSITY OF HER READERS, PROUD THAT
the people who wrote to her for advice by now included "every type imaginable: simple people, smart people, gay people, quiet people." A new equality had seized the day: even the changes in fashion supported egalitarianism.
A decade earlier, clothes had divulged one's place among the Best People,
but by 1929 such distinction was no longer possible. A businessman complained to reporters, "I used to be able to tell something about the background of a girl applying for a job as stenographer by her [dress] . . . but
today I often have to wait till she speaks, shows a gold tooth, or otherwise
gives me a second clue."

If, as Emily maintained, how one spoke would always indicate one's
class, gold, in a tooth or otherwise, would prove far less reliable. On
March 4, 1929, helped by the phenomenal economic boost of the 1920s,
Herbert Hoover became president, elected largely because of his association with the preceding two Republican administrations and their legacy of
monetary success. But in late March, just after Hoover's inauguration, a
worried Federal Reserve Board started meeting every day behind closed
doors. The first of numerous minor crashes and rebounds began on Monday, March 25, but a seemingly quick recovery reassured the jittery market.

In contrast to the excitement Josephine would have felt, Emily was relieved that she didn't have to think about high-stakes finances. Her family
inheritance, along with the money she believed she would earn from future
revisions of *Etiquette* and apparently endless magazine assignments, re-

assured her that she could support herself, no matter what happened to the economy.

Most important was her understanding that her success lay in writing about what she knew, a reality she no longer fought, whatever dreams she had once held about becoming a great novelist. That spring, she worked on several articles for *Collier's,* all of them centered on the family. The magazine's July issue featured "How to Be Happy Though a Parent," which Emily had aimed at mothers and fathers of up-and-coming flappers. Reminding her older readers that mores inevitably altered as times changed, she nonetheless agreed that the current generation's behavior could be exasperating. For the most part, however, she sided with the younger crowd. Far more upsetting than the silliness of a misguided youth was the "stupidity" of a parent "who complains and nags and asks questions and illustrates all arguments with bygone pictures." Earnestly, she continued: "As a grandmother, I ought to be far less in sympathy with the youngest generation than with that of their mothers who are usually much younger than I. Instead of which, I have an enormous sympathy and liking for what I should call the 'typical moderns' of the younger generation. I like their honesty of outlook, their complete frankness (if given a chance to be frank), I admire their courage, their self-confident pride in being able to cope with whatever may turn up."

She continued to promote accommodation to change, though obliquely, in her September article "What! No Chaperones?" America's economy had forced young women to work outside the home, mixing with men on a daily basis. This new reality made the very question of a chaperone irrelevant. "The things that she existed to prevent," Emily pointed out, "are no longer banned; girls are free to go about with boys as much as they please—even to go after them to a reasonable degree. The restraints of formality and superficial conventions have been exchanged for unselfconscious frankness." By and large, Emily Post thought this was all for the better.

BUT THIS EXHILARATING new world, negotiated by young and old alike, was stopped short in its tracks by the stock market crash. Tuxedo Park denizens, excitedly putting finishing touches on late-season events, frantically canceled their plans. On October 24, 1929, which would become infamous as "Black Thursday," 12,894,650 shares changed hands on the New York Stock Exchange—a record that made the previous high of 3,875,910 shares from a year and a half earlier seem modest. This time, however, everybody was selling, nobody was buying, and the market came tumbling down. The next week, on an even darker day, "Black Tuesday," October 29, many who were fabulously rich the day before suddenly became the infamous poor. By three P.M., when traders heard the gong (later replaced by a less Gothic-sounding bell), 12,880,900 shares had been traded. The ticker tape was so backed up that it took another two and a half hours after the doors closed just to print it.

Within a few weeks, $30 billion had evaporated. Thousands throughout the nation lost their massive fortunes as stock prices crumbled. Emily herself was barely affected; she had already been too badly burned by Edwin's gambling to invest much in stocks and bonds anymore. Her closest friends—Juliet Morgan Hamilton, Minnie Gray Coster, Katharine Delano Collier—were also free of husbands whom Wall Street had mesmerized, even as the women themselves were supported by hefty family inheritances. They rightly considered themselves among the lucky ones.

No fireworks exploded over Times Square when the New Year shrugged its grim way into the city. Over the next five years, one-third of the nation's banks would close. In 1930, Freud's *Civilization and Its Discontents* seemed to document culture's reluctant capitulation to repression, the severe price civilization exacted in order to sustain the social order. Individuals would be forced, inexorably, to sacrifice the personal, existential freedom the 1920s had encouraged. At times it felt as if Americans were paying for the decadent excess of the preceding decade. At Tuxedo Park, houses stayed closed for the season. Some of the cottages were torn down or fell prey to arson, the fires assumed to be the desperate acts of owners unable to pay their taxes.

During the worst periods of the Depression, about one-third of the male labor force was out of work. Over the next five years, the lack of jobs for the traditional family breadwinners motivated laws in twenty-six states that forbade the hiring of married women. When both sexes did work, the yearly salaries averaged $525 for women and $1,027 for men. Yet in spite of the lack of jobs, as the Depression deepened, new opportunities for women arose—just as in wartime. The American Woman's Association, determined not to see females devalued again as soon as the hard times receded, quickly created a series of talks centered upon safeguarding women's employment. Anne Morgan and Alva Vanderbilt sponsored seminars where attendees could meet motivational leaders, with Eleanor Roosevelt, the wife of the New York governor, occasionally chairing a panel. Such earnest mingling substituted for the dances that Emily's crowd had enjoyed when they were young.

Emily believed that the current emphasis on women taking whatever jobs they could find would serve them and their families well in the end. Ten years later, in 1940, she would write a newspaper article on how to get ahead in the modern-day workplace. Urging women to make their own way, she recalled her experiences of working hard without a clear sense of the forthcoming rewards. Whether she was thinking of her first novel or her manual of etiquette, she concluded, "I can write from first hand knowledge that there is a great joy to one who, expecting little, finds much. To undertake to do a job because it is offered and then to do the very best one can do with it because of one's obligation to what one has undertaken, and in the end to find that one has really made something of it, is a story with a very happy ending."

At the end of 1930, professional women were still learning about the extra roadblocks they faced on their quest to be taken seriously in their jobs. That December, for instance, speakers tackled the stigma that the marketplace attached to aging. Anticipating by over fifty years *AARP: The Magazine* and the plethora of articles on midlife careers, business executives confronted the problems women over forty faced in the professional world in 1930. An industrial relations expert theorized that although "gray" increased men's power, it inevitably diminished women's, whose maturity was thought detrimental to the workplace. Because of such discrimination, women should feel justified in lying about their birth dates when applying for jobs, he said. But at least age did give the advantage to the female in one field: longevity. The overall life expectancy for American women was 61, while men lived an average of 58.1 years. Emily was 58.

CHAPTER 49

✠

PUBLISHED IN APRIL 1930, *THE PERSONALITY OF A HOUSE,* IN SPITE of moderate sales figures, was among Emily's proudest achievements. Several professors around the country would adopt the architecture volume for classroom use, a fact proudly noted by the woman who never considered attending college herself. Its initial run proved too small for its audience, and between January 1933 and January 1937, *Personality,* newly revised, would be reprinted four times. That the dense volume was ready for spring publication confounds the imagination still: while she was constructing her literary edifice, Emily was also writing occasional pieces for *Collier's* as well as finishing her *Debutante* book.

Dedicated "in memory of the architects of my family," the book was a lanyard linking her accomplishments with those of her two Bruces. Edith Wharton's 1897 *The Decoration of Houses* had been written with an architect, and so had Emily's book, in a manner of speaking. Candidly, she wrote a sympathetic interviewer, "This book is different. I've written all my other books calmly enough, but this subject is so utterly bound up in the memories of those who were dearest to me—my father and my son—that I was on edge with nerves! Terrified lest critics make fun of me for daring to attempt such a subject, as the principles of beauty in architecture—yet how could I leave the foundation out? My other books—oh well, if kind things are said—then that is very pleasant; if rude things—then try to do better next time, but in writing this my heart was on my sleeve."

She explained that until recently she had taken her knowledge of building and decorating for granted, as though it was her birthright. One day,

however, the editor of *Ladies' Home Journal* and she found themselves talking
about houses "for three hours," she said, adding,

> and he asked me to write a series of articles on the principles of archi-
> tectural beauty, the theory of color, and the details which produce—
> charm!
>
> I answered—"oh, but I couldn't! The subject is more near to me
> than any other, but I don't know enough!"
>
> Mr Schuler [the editor] smiled. "You may not know as much as
> your father and the other architects of your family did, but you know
> far more than I do and I've always thought I knew a great deal! I'd
> like you to write out exactly what you have said—you've outlined a
> whole book on the personality of a house."
>
> "That's a perfect title," I exclaimed.
>
> "All right," he said, "call it that."

An in-depth, meticulously detailed five-hundred-page book, *The Personality of a House* ambitiously sought to address the novice and the professional
at the same time. Its twenty-two chapters began by urging that every house
must, most of all, express its owners' personalities. To help novices decide
upon structure and interior design, several chapters then set out a history
of architecture and, specifically, of houses in America. Suggesting that her
artist readers skip the chapter titled "Principles of Color Harmony," Emily
detailed a highly technical explanation of everything from color theory to
mixing paints: the "colorlessness . . . [of "neutral gray"] is made by mixing
equal portions of your original primary red, yellow, and blue. . . . To prove it,
take a small circle of paper painted yellow, red and blue in three equal divi-
sions, like a pie cut into three pieces, and fasten it on a child's top. When it
is spun, three colors thus fused but not mixed will turn to white."

The book contained an extraordinary 171 small pen-and-ink illustrations and sixty-three full-page cartoons and photographs. Whether of a
Palladian window or a wrought-iron New Orleans balcony or her own
Cape Cod–style house, photographs that she believed would be educational for her mostly novice audience filled the book.

Samuel Graybill, the Yale architecture student who, in the 1950s, wrote
his dissertation on Bruce Price, believes Emily's book "odd and offputting,"
though, he admits, his impression is skewed because he disagreed so radi-

cally with her aesthetic. "When I met her, she and her house were dressed the same—somewhat grotesquely, all flowers and prints. And cabbage roses," Graybill recalled, gently but disdainfully, fifty years later. But Emily's rose chintz, however dated, was true to her message. "The personality of a house is indefinable, but there never lived a lady of great cultivation and charm whose home, whether a palace, a farm-cottage or a tiny apartment, did not reflect the charm of its owner. Every visitor feels impelled to linger, and is loath to go. Houses without personality are a series of rooms with furniture in them."

Unobjectionable to architecture critic Christopher Gray, *The Personality of a House* is nonetheless, he believes, "uninspired." All the same, the book is stamped with Emily's own personality and concerns, especially her attention to the pragmatic. She even devoted five pages to financing, distinguishing for first-time buyers the difference between an "amortizing" and a "permanent" mortgage. True to form, the author lavished attention on the nuts and bolts of the business. "Above everything," she instructed, "you must notice whether every working part of the house is practical."

She meant her book to be used by people who would truly inhabit their homes, emotionally as well as physically, as she did hers. Regarding the formal aesthetics of the new residence, she advised; "When rules hamper—discard." The "qualifications" of an "enchanting" house are "suitability to situation and to purpose. . . . Its personality should express your personality, just as every gesture you make . . . express[es] . . . whichever characteristics are typically yours." The thesis was well suited to a Depression era forced to create its aesthetic out of the affordable, leftover materials at hand.

One of the book's first major reviews appeared in the magazine section of the *New York Herald Tribune,* entitled "The Etiquette of Home Decoration." Uneasy initially over the technical chapters that alternated with "intimate experiences and suggestions," the journalist concluded that the book perfectly merged advanced and beginner skills. *The Personality of a House* was "one of the best books on planning and decorating a home which has appeared in a decade," he opined. Everything was presented "in a delightful personal style, garnished here and there with humor." Instead of the stage settings of Mrs. Toplofty and Mr. Gilding that she used in *Etiquette,* Emily had created scenarios for real people, whatever their tastes or income. Most impressive was her ability to apply a "sweet reasonableness" to "period decoration, principles of line, mass, balance and color and the fundamentals," the reviewer noted. There was nothing theatrical about this book; instead, it at times hovered on the academic.

The *New York Times* also addressed the book promptly. "Mrs. Post puts as much personality into her book as she wants her readers to make evident in their homes," the journalist said, declaring her work "wholly unlike" the "scores" written by architects or designers of late and "in a class by itself. . . . The vigor and the individuality with which the author invests each theme and makes it warmly and appealingly expressive give the volume a distinction and an interest unusual in books of this sort." But the review that meant the most to her appeared in the *American Architect*. "Seldom has anything been written which so delightfully tells just how the person-about-to-build thinks as this book by Emily Post, the daughter of the late Bruce Price and quite evidently an inheritor of his architectural flair," that journal averred. The following year, in a rare confessional moment, she told a *Better Homes and Gardens* interviewer, "I wish my life were at its beginning, instead of being on the down slope, that I might be a really professional architect and not just a halfway one. . . . [I] finally wrote about the personality and comfort and charm of a house. . . . I don't know why I ever wrote about anything else."

THAT MAY, EMILY was the subject of a popular *Boston Globe* column, "Meeting the Big Names." However selectively, she was now using her clout with the public to campaign openly for causes she believed important to everyone. In Chicago, the labor reform advocate (and the first American woman to receive the Nobel Peace Prize) Jane Addams censured all proposals to end Prohibition, embracing complete abstinence instead, hardening Emily's attitude toward what her mother had considered radical women activists. As if assuming Bruce Price's crusade against restricting civil liberties, she volunteered to help rescind Prohibition. Particularly because Emily herself rarely used alcohol, her protest proved powerful. She wrote proudly to the *Jefferson County Union,* "I think the repeal cause is going splendidly, and the people of the United States are beginning to understand that prohibition is not encouraging temperance." At the Women's Organization for National Prohibition Reform, she joined "eight prominent women of New York" to reject a Main Line socialite's suggestion to officially ban alcohol from all social register gatherings.

In spite of being bothered by a noticeable lack of energy, Emily could afford to push herself hard in the city, as long as she knew that her island re-treat lay ahead. By July, the rituals and more leisurely pace of Martha's Vineyard had clearly revitalized her. She even joined other seasonal resi-dents to fête the yachts arriving at the island for the warm months. Invig-orated, she hosted a reception for Garden Club members following the summer opening. After visits to seven luxuriously manicured grounds, par-ticipants ended the afternoon by drinking tea among Emily's begonias and hydrangeas. Increasingly vivacious and buoyant, the invigorated amateur gardener proved in high spirits these days. She knew that the New Yorker was soon to publish an extensive interview with her.

That reporter, however, proved as gullible as others who had been se-duced by Emily's charm. Helen Huntington Smith swallowed whole Emily's favorite chestnut: Writing about etiquette "was an accident in [Emily's] life," Smith authoritatively proclaimed. Now, eight years after Etiquette's publication, the colleges at "Cambridge and New Haven," she said, were ordering copies of the preternaturally famous blue book on behavior—surely an exaggeration that referred more accurately to the university li-braries.

While Emily tried to keep Smith focused on her professional life, the journalist kept returning to the class difference between author and read-ers: most of Emily's audience, Smith pointed out, though they "belong to the flower of American womanhood . . . would not find their names" in the social register. "In a way," Smith concluded, Emily Post was "a link be-tween two worlds." While with the one hand she reached back "to the redoubtable Mrs. William Astor and Ward McAllister," with the other hand she touched modernity itself. "Her talents and energies have led her to the edge of that extraordinary modern world which is half-social, half-professional." When Smith urged her subject to talk about society matters, Emily dutifully rehashed the Canadian train trip Bruce Price took with the Duke of Connaught, Queen Victoria's son, forty years earlier. Probably boring herself with the overused anecdote, she embellished her previous accounts. Now, not at just one stop but at every train station, the crowds had mistaken the gallant, princely Bruce Price for royalty.

Deeply disappointed when she saw the New Yorker article, Emily scrib-bled furiously in the margins of the published interview. At the bottom of a page detailing tedious points of official State Department protocol that she had helped to construct, she scrawled, "I mind this more than any other mistake [the interviewer] made because it presented me as exalting the silliness which I most detest." She added, "All of this is offensive, very quaint," and "This is where M. C. Harrison [another journalist] got that stupid mistake." She snorted indignantly through a series of flamboyant exclamation marks, the pages practically crackling with her disdain.

Her mood couldn't have been improved by the magazine's strained compliment to her faded looks: at fifty-eight still "a good-looking woman," Mrs. Post had been a "perfect" beauty just a few years ago. Perhaps Smith, clearly irritated that Emily refused to discuss her "long ago" marriage to Edwin Post—"a member of one of New York's pre-Vanderbilt families"— was carefully retaliating. In any event, the writer was never invited back.

❈

HOWEVER PROUD EMILY WAS TO APPEAR PROMINENTLY IN THE *New Yorker,* becoming a regular over the airwaves was her real goal. After all, people speaking on the radio reached millions. A year before the stock market crashed, Walter Damrosch (the son of Leopold, the founder of the New York Symphony Society) had acted as a missionary to the American masses, delivering to them, over the airwaves, the New York Symphony Orchestra. Now he became the musical adviser at NBC, ensuring that by the early 1930s six million American schoolchildren were regularly listening to his *Music Appreciation Hour.* By offering to the multitudes what used to be accessible to the very few, the nation built on its democratic foundation. In 1920 most Americans had never been to an opera or a symphony, but by the decade's end, "millions had enjoyed music of all kinds through the medium of the radio, and a cultural miracle occurred: Classical music, which had never played a significant role in American life, became a widespread form of entertainment," notes the historian George H. Douglas. Radio was the innovation that would revolutionize the culture, providing a free education for Americans of all ranks, further diluting the sovereignty of high birth or money alone.

Sound resonating in their living rooms also encouraged listeners to visualize an idealized world, just when they needed dreams to refurbish their imaginations. Without a doubt, the 1930s edited over the airwaves sounded more cheerful than the reality camping outside most people's doors. Helping to lift listeners out of the Depression's bleak amphitheater, broadcasting during the 1930s was not just a business or a job: it was magic. Announcers and musicians wore tuxedos to work, and female performers dressed in evening attire—even when there was no studio audience. Such respect by the performers paid homage to the costly walnut behemoth as well as the cheap do-it-yourself radio kit, both of which staked a place in the nation's living rooms. Stentorian tones only added to the broadcast's allure, transforming homes across the nation into fantasy escapes from the world outside.

Emily would often recite the story of her audition for radio, and her surprise at getting on the air. She enjoyed describing how she had assumed that her voice, which she considered "thin and feminine," would disqualify her—though in fact she had already broadcast several times in the preceding years and had been greeted with an enthusiastic response from her listeners in spite of the poor-quality sound. Sometime in mid-1930, remembering those crude early 1920 transmissions and unaware of the dramatic studio innovations over the last decade, she shared her worry with potential sponsors, saying that her voice would probably come across as too squeaky on the radio.

She was, uncharacteristically, a bit behind; not only sound quality had changed but even the way the stations pinpointed their audiences had. Since 1927, NBC, a subdivision of RCA, had split its programming into the NBC Red Network, offering entertainment and music programming, and the NBC Blue Network, primarily carrying news and cultural shows. After the various changes were explained to her, Emily, reluctant but excited, allowed NBC's Red Network station WEAF to line up seven commercial representatives to hear her audition. According to her favorite account, they all "stampeded" to sign her to advertise their products.

Her grandson recalls a different spin: "She explained to me that her radio success, mostly the etiquette question-and-answer show she would present off and on for years, was partly due to her unobjectionable voice at a time when women weren't used that much on the radio. Her voice came out well, and in spite of her constant worries when sponsorship of her show changed that she would be dropped, the new sponsors always kept her on." The opportunity to be onstage again would prove irresistible to Emily: "She loved broadcasting," Bill Post remembers. "It was her passion." She was one of the lucky ones; radio was entering its golden age even as her late son's architect friends stood in breadlines.

Depending on the audience, Emily continued to change her story throughout her life. Most often, she would describe how the eager compet-ing sponsors had queried her about salary requirements, eliciting her bold response that she would be "willing to accept whatever 'Amos and Andy' get," causing the executives to "pale visibly." Those who knew the history of the hit show understood her reference: two weeks after its debut a year ear-lier, *Amos 'n' Andy*, Emily's favorite comedy, had proved such an immediate success that the network soon moved it from its late-night spot to a prime-time slot at seven P.M. The actors' salaries escalated accordingly.

Though today perceived as denigrating black Americans, the ostensibly good-natured comedy, starring white men using black vernacular speech, was destined to become the nation's longest-running broadcast in radio's history. It was also one of the country's first successful on-the-air serializa-tions, mesmerizing black and white audiences alike. Radio's crashing of racial barriers would prove pivotal to later developments far afield of com-edy. White performers such as Elvis Presley, growing up amid segregation, were tutored by radio, with its overspill of black gospel music and "sinful" black rhythm and blues.

Into the hodgepodge of the day's broadcasts marched a jubilant Emily Post. From the few extant records, her short-term deals followed the pe-riod's typical protocol, which included high pay for radio stars. In the heart of the Depression, she negotiated a contract for $500 per week (or about $6,000 today), nowhere near what the top celebrities received. Still, she was pleased, especially because her show would be broadcast nationally. Her exclusive six-month agreement with Procter & Gamble to speak on NBC was renewable after it expired on April 30, 1932, as long as both parties agreed. In November 1930, Emily began appearing regularly on New York City's WEAF, speaking on Friday mornings over the Columbia Broadcasting System.

SHE WAS AN immediate hit. Her listeners regularly wrote heartfelt compli-ments to the radio's office, and her sponsors, of course, were delighted: "I like your voice best of any on the radio. I look forward every Saturday to hearing it. And I bought Camay soap because if you stand for it, it must be good and I like it very much." The letters came from all over the country, reinvigorating their recipient. It appeared that there was a second act—or a third or fourth—to her already impressive career. She was part of the new age, not a dinosaur, as she had feared. And, much to her pleasure, Lillian Eichler's voice, which had seemed to intone the modern age so thoroughly that sponsors had aired her often in the late 1920s, had proven too "New York" after all.

By now, newspapers routinely listed information about radio programming, and the *Brooklyn Eagle* wasted no time in announcing Emily's new venture. "Mrs. Post" would be talking about "Etiquette," her program "intensely interesting and instructive," it noted. More than the mere problems of manners, the author planned to discuss how ethics and etiquette were connected subjects. With a good-willed petulance, Emily complained to a reporter about her more typical experience when speaking to the public: "Every time I have tried to get to the root of the matter and talk about these really important things," she said, a deluge of mail had arrived soon afterward, inquiring about which fork to use.

Procter & Gamble exercised its option to renew the original contract through the end of the following June, at the same rate of $500 per week. Camay soap also commissioned her to prepare twenty-seven talks on etiquette, its series to run on CBS's national radio network WABC throughout the same months. For eight years, until 1938, Emily would average one fifteen-minute radio program broadcast nationally three times a week. Among her sponsors were Procter & Gamble, Tangee lipstick, White Owl cigars, and Crane paper, several of them ahead of the times and already prerecording their studio ads; a few still broadcast live, the musicians set up behind Emily. Her new notoriety prompted various sidelines as well, neatly supplementing her income: endorsements for a gingerbread company earned her $3,000, and she got paid $5,000 for a generic pamphlet in which she lauded upscale linen, silver, and glass.

Endearingly, she opened her initial broadcast a bit self-consciously:

> Good morning! Having just been introduced to you, I ought to have said, "How do you do." No one knows this particular rule of etiquette better than I. But I think this introduction of me, to you, is different. We are not meeting as strangers, out in public—we are not even meeting in the house of one of our friends! I have actually come into the privacy of your home—of course I don't know where! I may be in your living room, but it is quite as likely that I am in your kitchen or at your breakfast table, or sitting beside your bed—or wherever you happen to be! And so—I can't quite picture myself as being shown into your drawing room as an afternoon visitor with my card case in my hand, and saying formally, "How do you do."

Turning to the day's topic, she cleverly incorporated the task of greeting her audience into the program's first subject, how to make introductions. "Informal introductions are made about nine hundred and ninety-nine times out of a thousand," she began. Summoning encounters between old and young, woman and woman, formal, half formal, warm, cool, and stilted, Emily lauded the effective approaches and fingered the weak ones: "Many of us actually suffer from name-blank news and suddenly find a name that we know perfectly well, has vanished from memory. So you say helplessly, to the nameless one, 'Oh, don't you know my husband?' or, 'You have met Mrs. Elder, haven't you?' I must confess that the subterfuge does not often work very well, and the nameless one is rather apt to announce herself—not fooled by your chicanery at all."

Even before the program was over, her audience inundated the station with questions for Emily Post. One anxious listener actually telegrammed her, frantic about the social situations that might ensue following an introduction. Because of such interest, Emily's second broadcast set out detailed scenarios that encompassed all possible punctilios regarding introductions. She suggested that upon walking into a room, the first thing one should do was quickly scan the faces to see if any were familiar. If not, one should stand near the hostess, who, if she was worth her salt, would then surely introduce another guest nearby. Upon being introduced, one could discuss what had appeared in the morning's paper or talk about the weather or the latest radio show. Contributing to a small group conversation created connection, which was the key objective: to show a genuine interest, no matter the subject.

She concluded with one of her pet topics. A person's speech, she told her listeners, however unfairly, was a ticket into society—or an excuse for exclusion. Thus, if the object was to fit into the social world, attention must be paid. "The words and phrases accepted or taboo are utterly without reason," she said. "And yet nothing in the entire subject of etiquette is so important and so devastating to those who happen not to have had wide worldly experience, and yet want to be recognized as persons of cultivation and social position." She ended her tutorial by announcing that the following week she would finally "turn away from these seemingly trifling but very nagging rules and choose one of the nicest subjects possible. I'm going to talk to you about the spirit of hospitality."

But she had miscalculated: apprehensive listeners guaranteed that she could not tackle her favorite subject yet. Letters flooded the radio office, sometimes begging for help: "How many inches should I sit from the edge of the table?" and "When taking my place at table, should I approach my chair from the right or the left side?" Later, her confused audience would ask why they should never sign a letter "Mrs." It was all about being pretentious, Emily explained. To sign a letter "Mrs." indicated that the writer considered herself of a "higher class socially than the one to whom she is writing . . . a shocking breach of good manners." The correct way to sign a letter was "Mary Brown" with "(Mrs. Arthur Brown)" to the left of the signature.

With as much aplomb as an experienced schoolteacher, Emily forged on, pointing out that pioneer women had been forced to preface their names with "Mrs." to ward off the overfamiliarity of rough men. "Kings and Queens sign their Christian names, Albert or Marie; Dukes and Earls and all those of highest title sign their last name alone—Broadlands or Everton—while the rest of us sign two or more—Mary Allerton Jones or John Henry Huntington Jones or whatever our full names may be," she explained. Thus, to sign one's own name with the honorific "Mrs." smacked of the gauche and the parvenu. Those easterners secure in their manners had "continued tranquilly the precepts of established precedent," she said, realizing that nowadays, in fact, names become more complicated as one's "importance decreases."

Though she didn't refer to them as such, Emily didn't flinch from addressing class issues. She herself continued to blur distinctions in her definition of Best Society (a term that, like most of her labels, she capitalized erratically). Best Society's Perfect Human Being mixed Old World genes with the classless Christian Golden Rule. Avoiding self-importance and treating others as you wished to be treated were key to becoming part of Best Society, whatever and wherever it was.

Etiquette, both in 1922 and throughout its subsequent revisions, supplied the meat of her radio broadcasts. In both, she warned against the worst impostor, the social climber, inevitably exposed: "A man whose social position is self-made is apt to be detected by his continual cataloguing of prominent names. Mr. Parvenu invariably spices his conversation with, 'When I was dining at the Bobo Gildings,' or even 'at Lucy Gilding's' and quite often accentuates, in his ignorance, those of rather second-rate though conspicuous position. 'I was spending last week-end with the Richan Vulgars,' or 'My great friends, the Gotta Crusts.' When a so-called gentleman insists on imparting information that is of interest only to the Social Register, shun him!... The born gentleman avoids the mention of names exactly as he avoids the mention of what things cost; both are an abomination to his soul."

But, however paradoxically, the notion of a "born gentleman" had little to do with genes or inheritance. It was relayed by one's behavior. To illustrate the danger of playing the social impostor, she told a story on the air about a party she had attended: a man boasting of his close friendship with Theodore Roosevelt asked his listener if he had "ever seen T.R.?" The man quietly replied, "Yes, I have seen Mr. Roosevelt." Everyone present except the social climber knew that the speaker was a member of Roosevelt's family.

BILL POST BELIEVES that broadcasting and, eventually, writing her syndicated advice column were his grandmother's greatest pleasures, even beyond the books she published. Radio and newspapers allowed her an immediate connection—however scripted—that her novels and even *Etiquette* deferred. Now she regularly hailed a taxi to the radio station at 485 Madison Avenue, where she had become an instant favorite of the studio staff because of her fastidious use of a stopwatch. Emily Post was no diva needing to be cajoled to yield the stage.

She took her listeners seriously. Among the few papers she preserved was a page of excerpts from fan letters written by aspiring middle-class Americans: "I am greatly interested in your talks every Saturday on the Procter and Gamble Hour. I am sure they are a wonderful help to thousands" and "Your talks are wonderful, I enjoy them a lot. I try not to miss any and I take notes."

In a period when actors and broadcasters routinely adopted stagy upper-class Philadelphia accents, Emily's voice, a blend of Baltimore, New York, and a bit of the ubiquitous Main Line, was repeatedly singled out for its "sweetness." So was her "sweet personality." Her listeners were correct: buoyant, alive, generous, outgoing, she was lovable. Her sometimes annoying obsessiveness was obscured in the short radio broadcasts. "Your talks are most instructive and entertaining," a listener in Cambridge, Massachusetts, wrote. "Your talks are ever so interesting and Mother and I enjoy them so much, and hope that they will continue indefinitely. We listen each week."

Emily reveled in the feedback from her radio show, gradually realizing that her word actually mattered to thousands of people around the country.

"I listen to your talks and enjoy them so much. I am trying hard to learn about what should be and what should not be done," said a fan from Providence; another noted, "Many persons in Massillon, Ohio, are enjoying your clever talks on etiquette. Your voice and charming accent are delightful, and we hope you continue advertising something or other for many months." "I take this opportunity to thank you for all your splendid, helpful talks which we farm women enjoy, too" came from Seaford, Delaware, and, from McLean, Virginia, next door to the nation's capital: "Never do I go to town on Fridays now, but I stay home to listen to your talks which are very enjoyable and instructive to me. How good it is that your voice doesn't sound affected as do those of so many women we hear on the air. I treasure your Blue Book highly and am always hoping for time to study it most thoroughly and to read all your other books, too." Page after page: Emily recorded sheaves of such comments, as if to remind her sponsors of her worth when renewal time came along. Or to remind herself.

The person behind the voice was a palpable intelligence. Today, it is impossible to read *Etiquette* without wishing the author were still pronouncing on the best ways to create a harmonious life. In the 1930s, it was hard to listen to Emily Post's radio broadcasts without wanting her to be around to share a cup of tea and an insight or two.

CHAPTER 51

⚜

THE NEW YEAR STARTED SADLY, WITH EMILY RECEIVING WORD THAT her favorite cousin, Baltimore's Sadie Price—Sarah Price Pell Turnure— was dead. Months earlier, after a series of illnesses had left her with pneumonia, Sadie's husband, the physician Percy Turnure, had interrupted the couple's vacation on the French Riviera, in the belief that complete rest in the City of Light would allow Sadie to recuperate. More recently, in desperation at his wife's weight loss and recurrent fevers, Percy had had her admitted to a private clinic in Paris. Now, her wasted body was returned to New York, where Emily attended the funeral services, held at Grace Episcopal Church.

The season's social distractions, geared to her favorite profession, proved a tonic for Emily, shocked by her cousin's death. On January 23, 1931, Ken Murchison, a family friend, Bruce Post's mentor, and his grandfather's beloved colleague, yet again joined the antics of the Society of Beaux Arts Architects, founded in 1894 with Bruce Price and his colleagues at the fore. Its balls highlighted Venice one year, a Renaissance reconstruction the next. A certain playfulness had always helped undercut the public's suspicion of a lurking elitism, such misgivings aroused by the frivolity and the high ticket prices ($15 in 1894). Money and architecture seemed interbred. Now, with large numbers of the profession standing in breadlines, even the well-heeled and best-known architects could no longer take their jobs for granted.

An advertisement in early January had described the ball as "modernistic, futuristic, cubistic, altruistic, mystic, architistic and feministic." "Fete Moderne—a Fantasy in Flame and Silver" prophesied a new architectural surge just around the corner. The organization staged a "tableau vivant" of Manhattan's skyline, a dramatic contrast to the pastoral tableaux Bruce and Josephine had created at the Academy of Music when Emily was a little girl. The runway was festooned with several dozen architects-as-models dressed to recall the buildings they had designed, including the Empire State Building, the Chrysler Building, the Fuller Building, and the Waldorf-Astoria Towers. Though this group was known for its disdain toward contemporary art, the artists still swayed with the times, at least tonight: Main Street was done up as a Cubist "midway" with "modernist trees dotting the village green."

PUBLICITY GENERATED BY the gala disguised for a few more weeks the toll the Depression was exacting from Bruce's profession. The *New York Times* reported in mid-January that more than 500 architects had registered at the Emergency Employment Committee in Manhattan, 180 of them in "desperate need" with two or more children to feed. Over the next months, the profession's employment rate dropped further; new buildings were not on anyone's list of priorities. Emily was a near-constant presence at fund-raisers led by the Women's Auxiliary of the American Architects Society, whose volunteers tried to help architects find work. Even Alva Vanderbilt Belmont, who typically supported feminist agendas these days, sponsored relief events for the men (and more than a few women).

But by March the situation had only worsened, and Emily's organization enlisted the *New York Times* to again publicize the architects' plight. Socialites with their wealth intact devised a strategy to employ architects on their abundant private lands, with these "owners of country real estate" funding the project. After all, roofs still needed mending, and the exteriors of many houses shouted for a new coat of paint. Porches, stairways, stone fences: the architects, when hired, found that they could build such necessary country improvements by themselves, their assistants no longer necessary.

While her father's revered profession stagnated—men her dead son's age suffering the most—Emily was interviewed by the Associated Press on the question of "to dunk or not to dunk corn pone in potlikker," the habit of soaking eggless cornbread in leftover green bean juice a well-publicized characteristic of Louisiana's notorious Governor Huey Long. "I can't set down rules that conflict with neighborhood customs," Emily politely responded. "The only thing I can offer is when in Rome, do as the Romans do. . . . The only thing I really care about is rudeness of the host or hostess. Their business is to see that the guests enjoy themselves. If it is going to make somebody unhappy to have to dunk, let him be allowed to crumble. We can't set rules here in New York for the rest of the world without knowing neighborhood custom." Emily Post had become a relativist, whether she knew it or not.

THOSE OWNERS OF country estates suddenly needing repairs were responding to President Hoover's plea: private citizens and charities had a duty to bail out the homeless and unemployed. Worried that federal charity programs would inure Americans to helping their own, Hoover urged states to succor their individual communities. Cities, bearing the greatest burden, were already strained beyond their resources, and this new mandate only made things worse. Chicago fired policemen, firemen, and teachers, many of whom had already gone eight months with no paycheck. Franklin Roosevelt, the governor of New York, worked with aides to develop a work relief program.

The Depression encouraged Americans to close ranks as the financial crisis reached global proportions, and Maryland politicians, determined to boost morale, decided that 1931 would be the year to make "The Star-Spangled Banner" the national anthem. In March, the words of Emily's relative Francis Scott Key, composed during the British attack on her beloved Baltimore, finally became official. Not everyone supported the choice: set to the tune of an old English drinking song, Key's piece hardly seemed a logical choice to celebrate the routing of the English enemy. But most Americans felt only kinship these days to their ancestors across the sea. Less easy to ignore was the argument that the song was too hard to sing. Two amateur sopranos, known locally and brought in to perform for the House Judiciary Committee, proved to the officials' satisfaction that the notes were well within most people's reach.

That same month, the second revision of *Etiquette* was published, the changes few but significant. Funk and Wagnalls's advertising exploited the country's current insecurity and need for reassuring national rituals. On the one hand, Emily's diplomatic protocols, based on recommendations she had written when queried by the country's Department of State, were still included in the book, striking a high tone. At the same time, *Etiquette* no longer even pretended to address primarily people of financial means or those underwritten by a predominantly Knickerbocker lineage. The ads emphasized that "special chapters [were] written in answer to countless requests from the smaller communities, and from young householders" lacking servants. New instructions explained "the simplest wedding," as well as discussing ceremonial differences to observe for diverse religions. Matter-of-factly, Emily even suggested the most tactful ways to deal with brides and grooms who had previously been divorced.

IN SEPTEMBER, *VANITY FAIR* published a series of readers' questions answered by a panoply of experts, Emily Post side by side with prominent ministers, educators, and columnists. Her success in the limelight emboldened her the following month to hire another agent, the first since she'd parted with Paul Reynolds ten years earlier. Holman Harvey would not handle her books or magazine articles—she settled those business deals herself nowadays—but would help her negotiate with newspaper syndicates. She hoped to land a contract for a weekly or perhaps even daily column. Harvey, with extensive experience at *Reader's Digest,* promptly approached executives at the Bell Syndicate, one of several newspaper consortia. Emily liked the idea of being responsible for her own success: writers were paid according to the number of newspapers that subscribed to each columnist.

Through Harvey she negotiated hard, requesting a minimum $500 monthly cash guarantee, but the Bell representative balked. The two sides finally came to an agreement: Bell offered Emily a three-month trial period, followed by a guarantee of $150 a week. At any time she could give thirty days' notice and cancel her contract. Her column, to be titled in all the newspapers some variant of "In Good Taste," would debut in the fall of 1932. It would eventually be featured in two hundred newspapers, the daily readership totaling 6.5 million people.

By the time she'd completed her negotiations with Bell, Emily was back on the air. That October, General Electric inaugurated the *GE Radio Hour,* a series of weekly programs carried by fifty-four NBC stations. The show featured nationally and internationally prominent women, including Emily Post. Throughout 1931 (and for the early part of 1932), Emily spoke for six minutes twice weekly on WEAF Red, appearing on the well-respected journalist Heywood Broun's *Newspaper* show for thirteen weeks. At the bottom of her tattered sheet of appearances, one of the few such memorabilia that she saved, she placed an asterisk after Broun's name: "Only woman on a man's program. Had top popularity rating. Terhune; Erskine; Van Loon;

Morley, on one night each; EP on 2 nights." Without a doubt, Emily Post was as competitive as anyone. Never, though, did she indulge such ambition over the obligation to act honorably. As she stressed to her public, she meant to talk with them "not so much [about] the mere problems of etiquette, but the more profound things in life, such as morals, ethics and good taste."

❊

ILL POST REMEMBERS FONDLY HOW, DURING THE EARLY PART of the 1930s, his grandmother reserved Sundays as their day, "just for Grandmama and me. The elevator man always greeted me, then took me to the ninth floor. Grandmama loved sitting on the floor even as an old woman, and with me, she never sat anyplace else, especially when we did projects together." Until he was eleven or twelve, Bill, Emily at his side, spent his Sundays casting soldiers from lead molding sets his grandmother combed stores and catalogs to buy for him.

She spoiled him, he admits today: "She devoted those afternoons to me. I couldn't do anything wrong, in her eyes: I was her only grandchild." Such singularity came at a cost. Emily had a "tendency to be demanding" when the two got together. It was all or nothing. "When she was ready to turn her full attention onto you, it could be suffocating," Bill recalls, reluctantly. "She was 'focused' on me, almost obsessive. Or maybe a better way to say it is that she cared very deeply about me. But sometimes it felt claustrophobic." Emily's loyal secretary, Yvonne Sylvia, who worked for her during the last decade of her life, says carefully, "Even when I was her seasonal worker on the Vineyard, she could be smothering, kind of overwhelming even if she didn't mean to be. I felt sorry for her sometimes, as if she was a little sad though she was happy."

But not even for her Billy would she shirk her work. If, as the historian Frederick Lewis Allen maintains, the five-day workweek was the decade's most significant innovation, Emily Post kept to her old pace, her only regular break Billy's Sunday afternoons. "Nothing, including me, could interrupt her morning writing," her grandson states emphatically. Another un-alterable routine was mealtime regularity—and brevity, as if Emily was making up for those endless hours at the table when she and Edwin enter-tained or, even worse, dined with their showier friends: "Grandmama ate at strict times, at one P.M. for lunch and seven P.M. for dinner, always leaving the table within ten or fifteen minutes. The longtime maid stood in the stairwell five minutes before the hour so she could walk in at the exact time. Or if my grandmother was out on the upstairs porch the maid would go halfway up the stairs and wait for the hall clock to strike seven before going the rest of the way up, to say 'Dinner is served.' I would run home from playing with neighbors to avoid being two minutes late, and if I was, she just ate without me, cheerfully requesting that I be served once I was com-fortably seated. If I came very late, she'd sit there while I ate to keep me company, even though she was already finished with dessert. She wasn't an-noyed, she just had a regimen and not wasting time was a big part of it."

AT LEAST FOOD and shelter would never be a problem for Emily, though the majority of Americans would find 1932 the hardest of the Depression years. Around 13 million people, a third of the nation's workforce, were now unemployed. Steel production dropped to 73 percent, with a further decline predicted. Comparisons of the Federal Reserve Board's Index of Industrial Production put numbers on the despair: U.S. Steel, for example, registering $261^3/_4$ early in October, then on November 13, 1929, falling to a shocking 150, now—three years later—was at $21^3/_4$. General Electric, a few years ago at $168^1/_2$, came in at 34.

However inconsequentially, even Emily was affected. "My grandmother was especially concerned about getting her contract renewed for 1932," Bill Post remembers. "To her credit, she understood that while for her this was a matter of pride more than anything, for most people out of work, it was a matter of feeding their families." Her anxiety proved ill-placed anyway: on January 4, she was back on New York City's WJZ, giving the first of fifteen talks on etiquette to be delivered daily at 4:00 P.M.

For those whose finances and families were stable—or who could rely upon long-guarded family income—there were still frivolities to attend. That spring, Minnie Coster's daughter remarried, this time to royalty whose family always staged its weddings in Monte Carlo. And there were chastening reminders of sorrows worse than poverty. The kidnapping of Charles and Anne Lindbergh's baby played out daily on the front pages of the city's newspapers from the first day of March until the middle of May. Soundly asleep in a bastion of love and protection, far from harm's way, the baby had nonetheless been stolen from his home, the kidnapping striking at the heart of American hero worship and seeming to imply some decrepitude in the state of the union. After all, publisher Henry Luce had made Lindbergh the first "Man of the Year," his image gracing *Time* magazine's cover in 1927. Now the crime riveted the nation's attention upon Lindbergh again as it conferred a measure of schadenfreude upon the suffering masses, reminding them that money alone didn't cure all ills. If Charles Lindbergh's family wasn't safe, whose was?

While most of America seemed transfixed by the kidnapping, Emily was pouring her energies into revoking Prohibition. Finally, here was an issue where she agreed with President Roosevelt: he should endorse the Twenty-first Amendment at once, stimulating the economy even as he rooted out the corruption bred in Prohibition's wake. As part of a coterie of prominent New York women convinced that for thirteen years the ill-conceived law had wreaked havoc on the nation, she urged that political candidates be judged primarily upon their position on repealing the Eighteenth Amendment. Emily's outspokenness was noticed, and a letter to the *New York Times* praised her for the spirit, courage, and frankness she showed in indicting the politics of "dry" citizens.

Before she left for Edgartown that spring, she again worked on relief projects for unemployed architects, their increasing numbers distressing her. The Women's Division of the Architects' Emergency Committee creatively conceived of every possible mission that could help feed a hungry family, including a survey of traffic conditions along Fifty-ninth Street; a campgrounds appraisal in Beacon, New York; an industrial study of steel, brick, and mineral resources for Columbia University; and an assessment of the city's food-storage systems required by the Welfare Councils of New York. After these projects were depleted, the committee scoured the outlying areas for any remotely related work. Ambitious young college graduates as well as their experienced elders vied to design and build a gas station. Over two thousand architects entered the contest, where the winner and thirty-five runners-up would split a "pot" of a mere $975.

That summer the market hit bottom, down 89 percent from its high in September 1929. Emily's new advice column for the Bell Syndicate might well prove disastrously ill-timed, she realized, with few newspapers in a financial position to take on new commitments. Instead, she proved such a hit with readers that papers soon appraised her domestically oriented column as one of their surest assets. On September 14, hometown papers from Appleton, Wisconsin, to Hoboken, New Jersey, ran her opening "Good Taste Today" column, subtitled "Tea Trays and Service Plates." "Dear Mrs. Post," the first letter asked—it was "from a man," Emily noted— "should one use a small hemstitched cloth or the bare table" when serving tea? Readers looked to her for a reality outside the financial crisis of their times. She wrote with authority and with a compassion that presupposed everyone was on her side—and she on theirs; she spoke to equals, even as she clearly assumed command.

The easily tired woman now seemed indefatigable. In December 1932, she broadcast from New York City's WJZ Blue several times a week, concluding her month's appearances on December 26 by appearing on WJZ at 10:45 A.M. and then on WEAF at 6:45 that evening. She shared the program with a baritone soloist, a sister team of organ players, and various other speakers. Judging from the grainy newspaper photographs that remain, she was finally showing her age. Her plump if pasty skin still retained some of its natural translucence, her face now settling into a consistent look of contentment. The hunger shadowing her wary posed photographs from the past had finally been appeased by her current satisfaction: sixty-year-old Emily Post was fulfilled. Emily Post was happy.

CHAPTER 53

✸

MID THE FRANTIC, HOPEFUL HILARITY OF STILL ILLEGAL MID-
night toasts as 1933 got under way, there lurked forebodings of evils far
greater than Prohibition or the Depression. That January, Germany's new
chancellor, Adolf Hitler, was sworn in; the next month, his Nazis, in order to
seize power, burned down the Reichstag building. The almost immediate
consequence to the United States was the migration from Germany of approximately sixty thousand artists—writers, painters, musicians, actors—
many of whom headed for the sanctuary of Ellis Island, where the Great
Lady of Emily's childhood stood atop Uncle Frank's stone base to welcome
them ashore.

In general, however, Americans were roiled by their own misfortunes,
able to pay little attention to newcomers. In 1933, at the nadir of the Great
Depression, one in four Americans who sought work was unable to find a
job. Harlem had an unemployment rate of over 50 percent, and within the
next three years property owned or managed by African Americans fell
from 30 to just 5 percent. New York City would vote in a new mayor, who
had represented in Congress a district that included several minorities.
Fiorello La Guardia, from the time of his inauguration in early 1934, carefully but joyously glued the fractured city back together again. Riding into
office on the "Fusion ticket," a party formed from an amalgam of political
perspectives, the chubby, five-foot-two man joked that he balanced the
ticket all by himself. The child of Italian and Jewish immigrants, La
Guardia was married to a Jewish Lutheran, with whom he had adopted two
Scandinavian children. Facile in six languages, he met with inhabitants of a

Yiddish neighborhood one day, a Puerto Rican one the next. Here was a man who represented everything good about America, shoring up the dreams of the poor, the worried middle class, and those who had been refugees themselves not so very long ago.

For the most part, Emily filtered her experience of such urban politics through the radio and, even then, primarily through her favorite commentator. Though she enjoyed several newscasters, her loyalty lay with Lowell Thomas. "Grandmama had a brightly painted radio in every room of her house," Bill Post recalls, "even a pink one and one with glitter she had pasted onto it. And Thomas on NBC was one constant, an absolute in her life at this time, no matter how busy she was." Until the mid-1930s politically left-leaning, by the end of the decade Lowell Thomas would claim that President Roosevelt's reliance upon government spending had turned the reporter into a conservative. Thomas was the kind of person Emily admired: true ladies and gentlemen, she believed, did not depend on the felicities or fortuities of wealth to define themselves. The homeschooled boy could recite by heart hundreds of "great" poems by the time he was ten. After a stint out West for Thomas's father to (unsuccessfully) mine for gold, his family moved back to Ohio, his birthplace. While still friendless in his new school, he was elected captain of the football team, in part because of his excellent speaking skills, and most of all because he was a hard worker.

Lowell Thomas also appealed to Emily's sense of wanderlust, something the writer too seldom felt able to indulge these days, except in memory—or through newscasts. She identified with him as a New Yorker as well: both Thomas and newsman Edward R. Murrow lived in Pawling, just over an hour from Manhattan. In a manner similar to Murrow's—and one that allowed Emily herself to happily fantasize—Thomas delivered reports "from airplanes, from balloons, from mountain tops, from ships at sea, from battlefields, from the depths of mines."

And yet, very much in the style of Emily herself, who treasured stability in the midst of change and excitement, Thomas achieved popularity for his calm, predictable nightly opening and closing words as much as his sense of adventure. "Good evening, everybody," he greeted his listeners; "So long until tomorrow," he concluded, warmly bidding them good night in a voice that conveyed his certainty about the future.

EMILY CONTINUED WITH her project of helping the bludgeoned architects, the previously privileged profession as devastated as any other except for the most radically destitute, such as farmers, particularly in the Midwest. The Women's Division of the Architects' Emergency Committee funded a new relief "pot" of $100,000, not only sponsoring house-repair jobs but also selling objets d'art for those still able to afford them. Emily was one of six committee women who commissioned a Lenox china limited-edition tea set. The Architects' Tea Set, decorated with colonial scenes, was displayed at a shop on Park Avenue and Fifty-seventh Street. Unlike the days when her links to society might have secured the project, now it was her business connections that eased the women's way; Lenox had recently hired her to write a promotional brochure.

The tea set's theme was keyed to the upcoming inauguration. Franklin Roosevelt's old Dutch family had preceded the British. He had grown up in privilege, moving among the Best People represented by such nostalgic china, with its colonial scenes of quiet affluence. Americans now turned to him in hope and desperation. As if signaling a new day, this March 4 inauguration would be the last controlled by the threat of bad weather. Times had changed, and Roosevelt's leadership would not allow a blizzard to forestall the government. Hereafter, there'd be no waiting for a month with a milder forecast; American presidents would assume office in January.

If only because of her personal connections, Emily was more interested in this administration than usual. Franklin Roosevelt was the beloved nephew of her dear friend Katharine Collier; Katharine was the sister of Sara Roosevelt, the new president's mother. "I remember," Bill Post comments, "when FDR won his first term as president, it delighted my grandmother, who disliked Roosevelt's policies, that Katharine Collier, FDR's aunt, sent him a lighthearted telegram saying 'Personally I congratulate you, politically I abhor you.' "

As part of his efforts to get Americans to believe in themselves again, in the heart of the Depression Roosevelt would initiate a series of "fireside chats," laying the groundwork for his New Deal. Enormously popular, the thirty talks, which the president used to gain support for his agendas against a conservative Republican legislature, were broadcast on an irregular schedule from March 12, 1933, until June 12, 1944. Although Emily never missed a chance to convey her dislike of Roosevelt's politics, she would proudly relate, any chance she got, FDR's comment to his aunt Katharine that the greatest compliment he received when he began his fireside chats was "You're as Good as Emily Post."

WHATEVER THEIR POLITICS, most people sympathized with the new president's challenge. When Roosevelt took office, unemployment had risen from 8 to 15 million (roughly one-third of the nation's nonfarmer workforce) and the gross national product had decreased from $103.8 to $55.7 billion. That March, 40 percent of the farms in Mississippi were on the auction block. Roosevelt's near-immediate action upon becoming president was to close the banks for a full week, a decision not designed to reassure the class Emily (as well as the president himself) hailed from. His radical action was aimed at rescuing a banking system that had failed to function.

It seemed as if nothing would stay fixed. Whenever the country felt itself on the mend, able to imagine standing tall again, something would knock it off course. Less than a week after Roosevelt took office, over 130 Californians died in a deadly earthquake that ripped through Long Beach. For those who were superstitious, the passing of an era, when all things in California seemed golden, was formalized in April once the United States decided to go off the gold standard. The optimism of San Francisco's world's fair eighteen years earlier, when Emily had made her cross-country car trip, suddenly seemed from another age.

Almost everyone felt the trickle-down effects of the Depression. Doctors were not paid because their patients had no money. Construction slowed to a dribble. Manhattan was rife with the savaged remnants of the upper class, its citizens so accustomed to keeping up appearances that even now they sometimes chose to hide their reduced circumstances. When one man Emily knew slightly lost his Wall Street job, he and his wife, hungry and unable to make their mortgage payments, lived in their mansion while they awaited the bank's foreclosure. His friends assumed he was still a millionaire until the couple was turned onto the street.

Difficult for the middle class to sympathize with, Emily's social community, brimming with bank executives and stockbrokers, was especially hard hit. In some cases, the owners themselves destroyed their houses in hopes of collecting insurance money. Colonel Frank B. Keech, a proud descendant of John Jay, arranged for a spectacular fire to burn down his house near Tuxedo Park. Insured for $232,000, the building netted him $177,000 in the settlement. Five years later, the Orange County Grand Jury would indict the seventy-seven-year-old colonel, a member of General Pershing's staff in World War I, for paying his former chauffeur to commit arson. Keech was spared the ignominy of a public trial when he jumped under the Lexington Avenue subway train on March 9, 1937.

LIKE THE PRIVILEGED president whose politics she disdained, Emily Post remembered and represented an earlier age, even as she eagerly greeted the future. She registered history's minutiae, capturing the moment with every step she took and every page she wrote. On April 16, still self-conscious over her lack of formal schooling, she nonetheless moderated a debate between Smith and Lafayette colleges on New York City's WJZ; the topic was "Resolved: That Modern Manners Should Be Deplored." Two women defended the "social conduct of the modern girl," while their male counterparts upheld the "degradation" of today's etiquette. Those listening to the four-thirty broadcast could act as judges, mailing in their votes. The timing for such an event was perfect: this April, for the first time since Prohibition began, beer (3.2 percent) could be sold legally. The moment was ripe for college-aged drinkers to discuss proper behavior.

Emily's confidence, always abundant, had grown steadily through the years since *Etiquette* had proved a success; now she was willing to tackle just about anything. After all, having concluded that Paul Reynolds was no longer useful, she had been without an agent since the beginning of the 1920s, and she had done just fine. To negotiate her newspaper deals, two years earlier, she had shrewdly hired Holman Harvey to represent her. That spring, when she renewed her contract with the Bell Syndicate, she realized that she was ready to take charge of those negotiations as well. Nervous as a rookie columnist, she had subsequently become, in business parlance, a newspaper veteran—as long as she was willing to write about etiquette.

The contract Harvey had brokered was typical for its time: the Bell Syndicate received 40 percent of the net profits, Emily 50 percent, and the agent 10 percent. Now, applying her mother's business savvy, Emily informed Bell's representative H. Sniveley (named, improbably, like a guest at one of *Etiquette*'s fictional dinner parties) that she expected to receive 60 percent of the profits. She was forcing Bell to either cut out Harvey as middleman or reduce its own profit. Shocked, Sniveley wrote a frantic note to Harvey (whom Emily had not fired, since, she reasoned, she had never rehired him). Do you understand, he implored, that Bell can't possibly afford to receive only 30 percent of the total profits? That you are out of a

job? Sniveley had explained all this to Mrs. Post, he lamented, but she'd refused to budge. He had stressed to Emily that Bell couldn't possibly give up
more than the 60 percent it was already spending for her interests. Nonetheless, Emily had held firm, he said. Sniveley clearly was worried that Harvey would come after the Bell Syndicate if Bell didn't convince Emily to
retain him.

Harvey, pontificating, finally wrote to her: Emily must stay with Bell or
risk losing her readership, he lectured. The letter, suggesting how little
Harvey understood his client, only stiffened her resolve to do things her
own way. On November 3, 1933, Emily signed a contract with Bell that she
alone had negotiated: 60 percent of the profits would now go directly to
her, in addition to Bell's generous provision of secretarial support. Harvey
was told that his services were no longer required.

ON MAY 27, while Emily was reviewing her strategy with Bell, the 1933
Chicago world's fair opened, its theme "A Century of Progress." In the
flush of Roosevelt's first months in office, in spite of the country's nonstop
dramas, the president had convinced the nation that there was room for
optimism. As usual, the exhibits at the fair were aimed at the cantilevered
middle class. Fan dancer Sally Rand drew large crowds, but so did the Lin-
colns, Cadillacs, Pierce-Arrows, and, anointed best of show, the Packard,
the stuff of dreams. Among the largest moneymakers were a "midget village" peopled with "Lilliputians," an exhibition of baby incubators lined
with live infants, and exotic displays of dancing African Americans, their
lavish headgear alone causing spectators to gasp.

In its two years, the fair attracted nearly 50 million visitors, making this
the first time in American history a truly international fair had paid for itself. In defiant contrast to the 1893 "White City" that George Post had
helped a troupe of architects build for Chicago's beige-and-white world's
fair, this spectacle was splattered in an Art Deco array of rainbow colors.
Scheduled to close in November, the Century of Progress Exposition
proved so popular that after a winter break, it reopened the following May,
finally shutting its doors in October 1934.

During the summer of 1933, Emily bypassed the fair she heard about
constantly, a pageant she wouldn't have missed a decade earlier. By now,
however, her Edgartown routines had taken on their own rhythms, and she
found the hoopla surrounding overwrought exhibits too taxing. A week or
so after the other servants had aired out the seaside house and stocked it

with groceries, she and Hilda Ogren traveled to the Vineyard. The house staff had grown to love the seasonal rituals. Loyal and trustworthy, her longtime employees were close-lipped, feeding gossip to no one; they were invested in their employer's well-being and genuinely fond of her as well. On the other hand, even Hilda always acted "as a maid, doing Emily's hair and helping her dress every morning. And Hilda only ate in the servants' dining room—never at the table," Bill Post remembers. Yet in many ways, Hilda was more of a companion than a maid, a paid friend who, conveniently, never forgot her place. If Ned and Bill could make a polite getaway whenever Emily threatened to smother them, Hilda was fixed fast: she couldn't afford to offend. Nor did she want to. At least once a week the two women attended the local movie theater, where Emily could see her beloved Shirley Temple movies, the spunky child star surely reminding Emily of herself as a girl. (She was not alone in her adulation but part of a Depression-era worship that, from 1933 to 1935, would triple the number of newborns named "Shirley.") Vineyard residents knew Emily as an "inveterate movie-goer" always accompanied by "her companion . . . Miss Hilda Ogren." The two were "seen so often at the movies, or going to and fro, that this was one of the most familiar of seasonal patterns." Hilda, inevitably grumbling that she didn't even like the movies, was nonetheless always at Emily's side, linking arms with her employer afterward to walk to the local ice-cream parlor. She and Emily often commiserated over trying— and failing—to lose weight.

Back in Manhattan that fall, Emily toured NBC's new eleven-story building, just west of the seventy-story RCA Building. NBC had outgrown its former headquarters on Fifth Avenue in just six years; this current structure housed two national networks and two local stations. Barely open by Armistice Day, the facility would be tested during November, when the stations themselves seemed besieged by endless accounts of unremitting dust storms battering the Great Plains. The storms that had been sweeping the prairies throughout the decade failed to abate, until, on November 11, 1933, they seemed to climax in a final defeat when "the farms blew away." The swirling dust would blanket the land for the next three years. On the holiday, tales of the storms' horrors competed for airtime with celebrations, grit and glory paying a belabored tribute to the battered farmland.

In spite of—or because of—the seemingly nonstop chronicles of sand everywhere and warnings of financial ruin almost as common, the end-of-year *Vanity Fair* eschewed the sensationalist reports of desperate citizens all over the country "fighting for scraps of food like animals" as they picked over restaurant garbage, and emphasized the paying customers instead. In its feature "Private Lives of the Great," the magazine published caricatures by Mexican society painter Miguel Covarrubias. "Emily Post, social arbitress, in a moment of quiet abandon chez elle" was shown relaxing at home, her bare feet propped up on a table, next to a framed portrait of Queen Victoria. Pictured reading about scandals in the *Police Gazette,* she drank from a cup with her pinkie raised disdainfully (a gesture she had in fact repeatedly disavowed as supercilious). Her filmy coral-toned dress with its long pearls looked graceful and sophisticated, more redolent of the late 1920s than the somber 1930s.

In annual reports on the year's major trends, jigsaw puzzles headed most lists. An odd accompaniment to the finally relaxed alcohol laws, the fad apparently fed the citizens' need to reunite broken parts into a whole, a desire to exert control and a sense of mastery amid the seemingly endless chaos. This was one of the few times when Emily Post was in the vanguard; she'd ordered her Parker Brothers sets years earlier, when jigsaw puzzles were new and she needed help putting herself back together again. From the time that her father helped her build her first dollhouse, she had always liked making the pieces fit.

CHAPTER 54

✠

THE 1934 RIOTS IN PARIS STARTED AMERICANS WORRYING THAT
France was on the brink of civil war and that their ally's internal conflicts
might spread. American tabloids were riveted by killings, from the Nazis'
assassination of the Austrian chancellor to Bonnie and Clyde's dramatic
final shootout. The very symbols of youth gone wild, the twenty-three- and
twenty-five-year-old renegades, sitting in their car, listening to "Blue
Moon" on the radio, required a posse of police and sharpshooters and 167
bullets to bring them down. No fingers remaining on her right hand, Bonnie was photographed still clutching a bloody pack of cigarettes in her left,
as if a sign that the Roaring Twenties had expired for good.

But there were broadcasts of public events that felt less foreboding as
well, those that proved a tonic even to the underfed, such as the birth of
quintuplets to Canada's Oliva Dionne, all of whom, miraculously, survived.
Such signs of better times to come were instantly transmitted nowadays.
With 60 percent of the nation's households owning a radio, the airwaves
spread a shared culture among a wildly disparate audience. If you had a job
and one of the country's 1.5 million automobiles with radios, you could
even listen to the news on your way to work.

From January through April 1934, several times a week Emily appeared
on WOR's ten A.M. half-hour variety show for a fifteen-minute segment,
sharing the venue with musicians and guests such as cosmetics queen Elizabeth Arden. She also stayed busy revising *Etiquette,* grateful that Funk and
Wagnalls saw the need for another update. Lillian Eichler was rewriting her
own *Book of Etiquette* as *The New Book of Etiquette,* to include passages on serv-

ing wine, divorce, and plane travel. At least Eichler's books didn't appear on
the bestseller list, if only because their purchase was not calculated in a traditional way: Doubleday routinely included pamphlets and excerpts sold
separately in sales tabulations for her book. But now the publisher advertised *Book of Etiquette* as having sold a million copies, a distortion of the truth
that irritated Emily profoundly.

The numbers game was particularly vexing in the case of *Etiquette,* because Funk and Wagnalls's incomplete reporting had created an illogically
static number—around one million—which writers had begun using to
convey its popularity as early as the mid-1920s. Even after subsequent revisions had sold well, the national press and Funk and Wagnalls continued
to use the same fixed figure—regardless of the intervening years.

HOWEVER CROWDED HER WORKDAYS had become, Emily always made
room for promoting her books. That spring, partly as her effort to prop up
sales of a second edition of *The Personality of a House,* she talked to the *American Home* about her gardening experiences. In a move that anticipated
today's product placement, Emily's article contained a cordoned-off ad for
the new General Electric refrigerators, capitalizing on GE's prominent
sponsorship of Emily's current radio appearances. "My Gay Little Garden"
is an informal reminiscence of the novice gardener's experiences over the
previous five or six years, her loyal assistant John at her side, a faithful
"young man" who really wasn't "anything of a gardener." Though she probably didn't even acknowledge the truth to herself, the faithful young man
had filled in for her dead son, allowing Emily to heal as she incorporated
nature's reassuring rhythms into her own. For her present audience, she
emphasized the learning curve both she and John had confronted as they
studied how to "to plant and pluck and fertilize."

Rehearsing aloud the pleasures awaiting her, Emily decided to leave
early for Martha's Vineyard. But just before she departed, her old friend
Phoenix Ingraham died of a heart attack, at his side the woman he had finally married after Emily refused to take his courtship seriously. A year
after *Etiquette* was published, Phoenix had been elected to the New York
Supreme Court, following the path that his father and grandfather, both
judges, had established before him. Corpulent and pleasure-loving to the
end, Emily's longtime ally was eulogized at society's Madison Avenue Presbyterian Church, home of the crusading minister and Bruce Price's bête
noire, Reverend Parkhurst, many years before. Accompanied by a store of

bittersweet memories, Emily walked to the service from her apartment on East Seventy-ninth Street.

She arrived in Edgartown eager to escape from the overload of bad news that seemed her lot these days. She certainly had no desire to read more about the dust storms pummeling the plains, especially since, much to her surprise, she had now confronted their horrors firsthand. On May 11, a dust cloud had dumped dirt over Manhattan for five hours straight, obscuring even the Statue of Liberty. On the Vineyard, she determined to seek out city papers only once or twice a week, her commitment to tuning out an overload of news making it likely that she missed the snide early summer reference to her in the *Washington Post*.

Ominous in its tinge of condescension, the tone anticipated the amused tolerance younger reporters would soon begin to exhibit. "Devoted as we are to Emily Post, it becomes necessary once in a while to reprimand her severely," the journalist smugly intoned. Emily had erred a few weeks earlier when she'd answered a fan with rules from a bygone era. When asked if a woman could use the word "swell" and not be stamped "ordinary," she had gone all "high-hats" instead of sticking to her typical "simple, kindly answer." Admitting that "swell" was perfectly acceptable as slang, Emily had "incorrectly" deemed it inappropriate in "My dear, I have had a swell time." The *Post* admonished her, however playfully, for being twenty years behind with this answer. "We do wish that Emily, swell girl that she is, would keep abreast of the current," it concluded.

In fact, swimming in the same stream as the modern crowd, Emily, as she prepared to join Lillian Gilbreth and Eleanor Roosevelt as a panelist at the fourth annual Conference on Current Problems, found herself in the middle of a domestic crisis that smacked all too painfully of the current. Social critic Kenneth Burke, writing in 1935 of the success of *Etiquette*, would speculate that in times of social heterogeneity, such guides were necessary: social labels could no longer be taken for granted. Its author, herself divorced, certainly understood that; now her son was getting divorced. "When I got back home from a trip to Montana, early that September," Bill Post remembers, "my parents said they had to talk to me." He was given little time to adjust before he left for his first year of boarding school. "They asked me to sit down," he recalls, "and they told me of their plans to separate, and that they had enrolled me at St. Paul's, in Concord, New Hampshire. I left the very next day."

The scenario was eerily like the one Emily had presented her sons with when she'd sent them to Pomfret almost thirty years before. She was distressed anew, still convinced that divorce harmed children no matter how hard the parents tried to protect them. Though the publicity during the breakup of Ned's marriage was nothing like what Emily had endured, the announcement nonetheless proved irresistible fodder for the gossip columnists. Unlike in her case, where her husband was at fault, the speed with which Barbara Post remarried suggested that she'd decided on a new spouse before getting rid of Emily's son. Ned's ex-wife planned to wed playboy millionaire Nicholas Holmsen—once he disposed of his current spouse, Mildred Tilton Holmsen, in Reno. Unfortunately, Mildred delayed the path to freedom with her "scandalous" attire at the Nevada court hearing, whereupon the judge demanded that she "dress properly" before appearing in court to end her marriage. Back home, the New York social register very publicly dropped Mrs. Holmsen because of equally "scandalous" though undisclosed behavior its members had uncovered. Barbara Post, finally Barbara Holmsen, would live with her new husband at the conjugal home she and Ned Post (and Bill) had shared. Within a few years of the Posts' divorce, Barbara inherited her share of the $4 million estate left by her recently deceased mother.

During the summer of Ned and Barbara's separation, Hilda proved a particularly reassuring presence to her distressed employer, a sign of constancy while Emily worked on her upcoming panel presentation on contemporary social problems. At least the current forum allowed Emily to ponder families outside her own. On September 26, 1934, Eleanor Roosevelt opened the Conference on Current Problems, its theme "Changing Standards." Ranging from crime prevention to vocational opportunities for youth, the event was the equivalent of today's invitation-only retreat for high-powered female achievers. Emily's panel featured the redoubtable Amelia Earhart, but it was Lillian Gilbreth, only six years younger than she, with her determination and near worship of "common sense," who was perfectly positioned to become her ally and friend.

Both Emily and Lillian, from similarly privileged backgrounds, put efficiency at the center of their lives. Lillian's marriage and children had been immortalized by the bestselling book *Cheaper by the Dozen,* written by her now deceased husband, Frank, an engineer who studied motion and how to help people do their jobs faster. Lillian, with her master's degree from the University of California at Berkeley and her Ph.D. from Brown University, was, according to some worshipful commentators, a potential candidate for sainthood. While a widow tending her eleven children (one of the dozen died young), she maintained a high-level appointment in the Hoover administration, heading various building projects. Emily appreciated Gilbreth's intelligent grasp of the rudiments of construction. Yet in spite of their shared enthusiasms and similar age, Emily and Lillian Gilbreth remained mere acquaintances. Probably Lillian's elevation of "efficiency over graciousness" discouraged any overtures Emily might have made, since Gilbreth wouldn't have thought an expert on etiquette worth much of her time.

Shortly after their panel participation, Emily worked with Gilbreth on yet another project. At the beginning of the Depression, to sponsor affordable housing for the middle class, Herbert Hoover had helped found the organization Better Homes in America. (Bill Post's great-grandfather George F. Baker had funded its beginnings.) The group had recently commissioned a model Georgian cottage, the temporary display built on top of the CBS recording studio; the station cooperated fully, even broadcasting news on the construction's progress. America's Little House, as it was called, opened on the morning of November 7, 1934. The line outside its doors extended several city blocks until four-thirty P.M., when the exhibit closed, disappointing hundreds who never got inside. More than sixteen hundred men and women had walked through the domestic display.

Emily's admiration of Lillian Gilbreth's practical "efficiency model" for the kitchen and nursery was shared by the public, who oohed and aahed over Gilbreth's feat. Designed "with a view to lightening the household duties of a wife and mother," Gilbreth's mock-up addressed housewives' real needs. On her next day's CBS broadcast, Emily would review the most popular parts of the exhibit, highlighting "labor-saving devices in the kitchen" along with a home library and basement playroom, all representing "the type of dwelling which the family of moderate means might acquire." Awed visitors had also been impressed by the "large amount of closet space, the efficient use of racks and shelves behind kitchen doors and other inconspicuous places, and the convenient layout of rooms."

Alongside her genuine interest in innovative building, Emily remained keenly aware of the hit her father's profession had taken. Family friend Kenneth Murchison, who had hired young Bruce Post a decade earlier, was urging that the arts be privately as well as publicly funded. In January, he spearheaded yet another Beaux Arts Ball, held earlier than usual in order to assist the unemployed architects. Heavily publicized throughout the month, the affair at the Waldorf was well attended, its three thousand patrons including Ned Post, who even played a part in one of the skits. He appeared on behalf of his mother, who wanted familial respect paid to Bruce Price and his grandson Bruce Post.

Even while Emily continued pushing architects' appeals and fund drives, she was busily endorsing products in order to increase her own income, as long as such support didn't compromise her beliefs. Her grandson believes that, however irrationally, she always worried about having enough money, probably because of the quagmire Edwin had made of their marital finances. But he also agrees that it was her ambition for her career, not for income, that continued to motivate her work. She was shrewd, and she knew, better than anyone, that the cultural winds could shift along with the weather. Keeping one's name in front of the buying public was crucial. In February, Macy's advertised stationery under her name. A few months later, the Hamilton Watch Company (today owned by Swatch) contracted Emily to write a booklet about time, an assignment that couldn't have been more suitable.

She herself was driven by punctuality. The studio's engineers revered her because she carried a stopwatch to each broadcast, timing herself to the minute, never failing to finish exactly "on the nose," showing an "Old World punctiliousness." She had no trouble approving the general subject of this new brochure sponsored by Hamilton Watch. Even the company's location in the coal county of Pennsylvania bespoke Washington and Emily Lee and their daughter Josephine.

The brochure, *Time Etiquette,* is a long essay Emily pieced together the summer of 1935 from her earlier writings. Clever illustrations of well-heeled women driving Pierce-Arrows, even now, in the heart of the Depression, made the subject suddenly attractive. Emily exploited the power of appearances to make her argument for being on time: "We all know people who are good-looking, amusing—attractive as they can be. And yet when we think of asking them to lunch or dine—to play bridge or go to a play—we hesitate. Simply because we know that half an hour after every other guest has arrived," the attractive, well-known young socialite, inevitably and baldly, appears. It was pure "nonsense" for any host to accept "the belief among the unknowing" that "it is smart to be late." Although the latecomer might possess great talent or charm, she should be allowed a free pass only once.

After Emily made her salient points about behavior, finally, as if reluctantly, she inserted the name of her sponsor, Hamilton Watch. Citing

Hamilton watches a total of five times in the sixteen-page article, she seemed to be winking to a knowing audience, her nods to her sponsor almost gratuitous. "Lunching in a great city like New York it is difficult to get through traffic and arrive with the exactness of a Hamilton watch," she noted. Without a doubt, she sanctioned the larger truth: time is money and power, and until recently, women had neither. They had had no need for a real watch. "My idea of a watch was of an ornament rather than of an accurate time-piece," she confessed. "In the present day when time is of such vital importance to most of us, a watch may very well be an ornament, but it is first of all an essential equipment.... Almost every phase of effectiveness in modern life is a matter of perfect timing."

※

*O*N NOVEMBER 24, 1935, A NOTICE IN THE *TIMES* ANNOUNCED THAT *Let's Talk It Over* would debut nationally the next day on WJZ at four-thirty. Sounding remarkably like shows aimed at women in the early twenty-first century—from *Oprah* to *The View*—the program was "designed to reflect feminine opinions on current topics." The informal half-hour spot would "follow the conversational attitude of the tea table in an earnest attempt to mirror national interest." A well-known soprano, Alma Kitchell, would be the mistress of ceremonies, with two authors and one editor the guests. Emily was the only participant needing no introduction.

Her radio appearances gave her an excuse to forgo traveling to Washington that December to hand out photography awards, the prizes totaling an impressive $10,000. Sixty-four national newspapers had selected 250 amateur photographs to hang on the walls of the National Geographic Society's Hall of Explorers exhibition. Though she'd been happy to lend her name to the panel of five judges, among them Sara Roosevelt and, more exciting to her than the president's mother, Lowell Thomas himself, Emily had few Baltimore relatives now to motivate her to make the trip south, and Roosevelt and Thomas were not certain to attend anyway. Nonetheless, she was gratified with the reports: the winner of first place, a $1,000 stipend, was a young southern high school teacher, described as "all warm and pink with excitement" when she heard the news. Emily had been especially pleased when informed of the industrious young winner's routine: she had compulsively taken seventeen photographs before she stopped, sure at last that she had gotten just the right pose of a little girl holding a balloon.

Emily felt her absence justified by her need to prepare for her radio appearances. She had continued speaking on *Let's Talk It Over,* along with ever more substantial women, motivating her to research their causes and achievements. By the spring of 1936, the radio panels would include presidents of two powerful women's groups, the New York State Federation of Women's Clubs and the National Federation of Business and Professional Women's Clubs; the head of the Russell Sage Foundation; Josephine Roche, assistant secretary of the treasury; and Mrs. Herbert Hoover. Not all weeks highlighted heavyweight topics: Carmel Snow, the editor of *Harper's Bazaar,* chatted quite happily about the "philistines of fashion," a topic that surely prompted Emily to warn, gently, against automatic dismissal of others' tastes. Given her interest in the younger generations, she probably enjoyed most the president of the Kappa Kappa Gamma sorority, who discussed "the new seriousness of college women."

Such a varied, fast-paced schedule had helped her deny a problem that was threatening to demand her attention, whether she wanted to give it or not. Sometime during the preceding year, Emily, who, at sixty-two years old, had long been proud of her faultless vision, had started noticing an occasional blurriness as she wrote. Assuming she finally needed glasses, she'd kept postponing going to the doctor's. Then, on the Fourth of July, 1935, when she and Bill watched the fireworks together at Martha's Vineyard, she was startled: the blasts were much nearer this year than usual, so close they seemed threatening. Dreading the loss of control that imperfect vision would imply, she was finally forced to admit that there were too many vivid, scary explosions bursting within her line of vision to be real. Bill urged her to see a doctor, but again, she waited. By late autumn, after her vision had become undeniably blurry, Emily capitulated. The doctor diagnosed an advanced case of double cataracts; she would need two operations per eye. She should be prepared for total blindness if the surgeries were not successful, he said.

Ned wondered how his commanding mother would handle this possibility, because she "loathed dependence in any form; freedom of movement was as necessary to her as freedom of thought. The possibility of losing this cherished independence was distressing beyond words." But Emily spent no time brooding. Instead, she asked her son to take her to a nearby farm where Seeing Eye dogs were trained, so she'd be comfortable around the animals before she needed to rely on one as her constant companion. Then she wrote away for information on Braille and investigated recordings for the blind.

She scheduled the first set of her cataract surgeries for April and May 1936, when her radio programs were off the air. Typical of the procedure that was used until midcentury, her post-op recoveries required she spend several weeks in bed in a darkened room, with sandbags braced against each ear to prevent her from lifting her head while her eye healed. The already avid radio listener now commanded everything to cease while Lowell Thomas was on the air: only through the airwaves could she "read" the news as she healed, and she trusted Thomas to give it to his audience straight.

At least she missed the fluffy press about the current Broadway production of *A Private Affair*, heralded in the *New York Times* that spring, the cast prominently listed. If Emily had not followed her star onto the stage, Edwin's second, more suitable wife had: among the eight actors the *Times* was fêting was Nellie Malcolm. Just as Emily had sought to justify her writing career through financial need, Nellie now insisted she had returned to the stage only because of her husband's drowning and the need to support herself—in spite of her sons' private educations and her entreaty to the social register to be readmitted. From the positive reviews that followed her successful stage career as a character actor, it seems that Nellie Malcolm, like Emily Post, had a superb sense of comic timing. She would go on to get larger parts, until it would become impossible, a decade later, for Emily, impaired vision or not, to miss the theater reviews of Miss Malcolm's impressive performances.

Stretching her own dramatic limits whenever she had the chance, the writer crafted an account of her tedious confinement that she would trot out for reporters every year or so. The story referred not to her courage or to her condition but to an amusing if self-congratulatory anecdote about Walter Winchell, that "New Yorkiest" of all writers. When the popular Winchell, wishing her well, broadcast news of her operation one Sunday night, she received hundreds of telegrams, homemade jelly, and a roomful of flowers—the belle of the ball once again.

Luckily, the eye surgery proved moderately successful, and Emily was eventually able to manage her permanently weakened vision by using three pairs of glasses, each with a different prescription. So that she could easily tell them apart, she painted the frames various bright colors, notching them according to their ocular strength. Even so, her trouble seeing caused Emily to turn over more of the detail work of her columns to Anne Kent, the secretary she had, at Ned's urging, recently hired. She knew that she'd have to train someone to help her answer her mail from now on.

THAT FALL, RADIO PROVED more powerful than ever. Father Coughlin, the latest incarnation of Reverend Parkhurst's self-righteousness, formed the Union Party and used radio to attempt to jettison the president. In the November election Roosevelt, running for his second term, and his relatively moderate Republican opponent, Alfred Landon, each spent $2 million on radio appearances. Though she was still recovering from her surgeries, Emily, who felt strongly that Katharine's nephew was steering the wrong course, acted atypically and took her politics public. On October 5, 1936, she appeared on the *Landon Radio Club Program,* where she emphasized her support of Landon, whose triumph over a hardscrabble past—he had grown up even poorer than Abraham Lincoln—she particularly admired, believing it an advantage in the prevailing economic climate. Unlike Lincoln, however, Landon would carry only two states, Maine and Vermont, making Roosevelt's election the largest landslide since 1820.

For the most part, the convalescent was still confined to listening to, not broadcasting on, the airwaves. And at times they seemed to be wafting by just fine without her. Benny Goodman had successfully introduced his big band (the first popular multiracial group to play at Carnegie Hall) to radio that year, the medium and music a perfect match for the jitterbug. Tuning in, Emily realized she'd now have to deal with parents lamenting about how their daughters used "dabs of nail polish" on their ankles "to hold [their] bobby socks up." Still a different audience worshipped Artie Shaw and Glenn Miller: lately music, not the news, seemed to hold the nation in its thrall, as if the voiceless songs of the airwaves succeeded in drowning out sounds of the Depression.

Regardless of her limited sight that winter, Emily couldn't escape the news of the king of Great Britain's romantically doomed reign. In addition to the radio's feverish daily updates, Hilda kept her abreast of the ongoing drama. After 327 days, Edward VIII had decided to give up his crown for the commoner he loved, and on December 10, 1936, he turned over the throne to his brother George VI. Some people believed that such a scene— a king renouncing his throne for a woman—would have been inconceivable thirty-five years earlier, when Queen Victoria died. But now the truly unimaginable had occurred. On December 11, Edward VIII announced on the radio, "I have found it impossible to carry the heavy burden of responsibility and to discharge my duties as king as I would wish to do without the help and support of the woman I love"—a Baltimore girl, about whom Emily surely knew the suspicious scuttlebutt whether she wanted to or not. Edward was a hero to many, though the ever-practical Emily Post considered such a match foolish, not romantic.

"When I listened to the abdicating King's address," she later recalled, "I saw those rows and rows of crosses in France, the graves of Englishmen who gave their lives 'For King and Country.' I felt they had been betrayed. Who cares whether the king is happy or not? Happiness is less important than many other things." Emily had not changed her mind at all: marital happiness ranked far below duties to others.

When the newly common ex–royal husband and his wife visited the United States the following year, Emily was sent a question she would answer briskly. How do we address the new "queen"? she was asked. "If you happen to meet the duke and duchess of Windsor while they are in America, call the duke 'Your Royal Highness' but his wife just plain 'you.' " The answer was picked up and reprinted by hundreds of the country's newspapers.

To capitalize on the fairy-tale Windsor marriage, CBS began broadcasting a fifteen-minute show, *Our Gal Sunday*, about a Colorado orphan who marries a British aristocrat. Originally a Broadway play starring Ethel Barrymore, this radio version, complete with the theme song "Red River Valley," would air until 1959. Every episode of the soap opera began with a kind of rehashed thesis from Emily's own days as a novelist: "Can this girl from a little mining town in the West find happiness as the wife of a wealthy and titled Englishman?"

CHAPTER 56

◆

B Y THE END OF 1936, *ETIQUETTE* WAS SELLING BETTER THAN
it had in a decade, and Emily was contemplating her next major revision.
Funk and Wagnalls, planning a strong campaign for the following autumn,
urged their author to take time to reassess the culture: What advice should
she modify? Could she preserve the gist of her 1922 volume and still sound
modern now, fifteen years later?

If only because of the span of topics her book encompassed, Emily felt
she had no choice but to stay up to date. How else could she justify herself
as an authority of the age? And certainly radios, now sprouting pushbut-
tons, made it impossible for anyone to ignore completely the nation's political, economic, and cultural changes. President Roosevelt signed the U.S.
Neutrality Act, while the British would try to appease Hitler with the Mu-
nich Agreement. No one could escape political realities, nor was the United
States singular in its financial woes. Britain had hit bottom toward the end
of 1932, with France following a few years later. As if reflecting the uncer-
tainties of the age, the nostalgic novel *Gone with the Wind,* an almost instant
classic in 1936, would vie with Dale Carnegie's of-the-moment *How to Win
Friends and Influence People* for bestseller of 1937. Readers might immerse
themselves in the past, but most didn't blink at the present either.

Yet another sign of the changing times occurred on January 2, 1937,
when Emily and Ned attended the wedding of Katharine Collier's granddaughter, Priscilla St. George, to Angier Biddle Duke. The union presaged
an American dynasty. Held at Tuxedo's St. Mary's, where Bruce and Ned

had been baptized four decades earlier, the wedding was a homecoming for Emily. Her retinue of friends from the past were all in attendance, the bride's mother, Katharine Collier St. George, having grown up under Emily's watch. Bouquets of blossoms alternated with hothouse flowers in full bloom, all tied in baskets at the rails of each pew. The St. Georges held the wedding reception at their Tuxedo Lake home, built by Bruce Price. It seemed a bower of bliss, but this radiant couple too would be divorced.

The illustrious list of invitees included President and Mrs. Roosevelt. Though Priscilla's great-aunt Mrs. James Roosevelt was present, Franklin and Eleanor did not attend. The Tuxedo Park crowd tended toward the conservative in their politics. An interviewer would report that while Emily Post counted Sara Roosevelt, "mother of the president, as an old and valued friend, . . . she has no more sympathy for the New Deal than have her other friends of the Tuxedo Park tradition. Her views on labor were conservative. 'I wish,' she says of the demands of factory strikers, 'that I had to work only thirty hours a week.' "

THE WEDDING'S OLDER GUESTS hardly had time to reminisce about days gone by when the media reminded them of the newfangled age they inhabited. On January 19, Howard Hughes broke the transcontinental speed record, flying nonstop from Burbank, California, to Newark, New Jersey, in a record seven hours and thirty-one minutes. It was as if, after the ground had been conquered with the automobile, which ambitious men had created, the sky became the new limit. And in the fight of man against nature, women too were gaining ground: the previous year had closed with the spellbinding news of Amelia Earhart's plan to fly around the world the following summer.

In yet another reminder that people were no longer limited by their environment, the inauguration for President Roosevelt's second term was held on January 20, just as planned, weather forecasts and naysayers aside. Whether or not she wanted anything to do with Franklin's administration, Emily was increasingly often consulted by his State Department on matters of etiquette. Not everyone, however, believed protocol important. Major General Johnson Hagood, who had recently retired from the army after clashing with President Roosevelt's administration, weighed in once more, this time haranguing the *Chicago Daily Tribune:* "Shooting should come before saluting," he declared. Too much emphasis was placed on military etiquette these days, he practically spat, with the result that saluting was "the Emily Post of military training," and expenditures for smart uniforms were overriding practicality: "Let 'em wear overalls," the general huffed.

Though not as eager to indict her, another writer dubious of Emily's currency interviewed her in February for the *New York Woman* magazine. Speaking energetically, Emily obliquely referred to Lillian Eichler's book (still selling strong) as the motivation behind *Etiquette* in 1922. A recent bestselling etiquette book had wrongly implied, she explained, that "the American woman, to whom it was addressed, had neither common sense nor kindliness. It patronized the reader." But the journalist was completely uninterested in the author's tales of her competition, instead positioning Emily's *Etiquette* as a relic, "like the Bible . . . a perfect picture of a sort of society that is fast disappearing from the world, if it has not already vanished."

By early spring, Emily was engaged with the lawsuit her former newspaper agent, Holman Harvey, had been pursuing since she'd cut him from her professional life in 1933. Now, in April 1937, his case finally came to trial in New York County Supreme Court. Court records revealed that 10 percent of the net profits from Emily's newspaper columns, spanning November 16, 1931, to February 27, 1937, totaled $8,616.14. Emily's net came to around $45,000 ($950,000 today)—if, that is, she were paid only 50 percent of the profit, the deal Harvey was insisting still held, and not 60 percent, the new deal she had brokered herself with the Bell Syndicate.

In his suit Harvey maintained that his contract had guaranteed a permanent percentage of any new agreements Emily signed with the Bell Syndicate for the life of their connection. Both Emily and Bell refused to budge: the agent's original contract was a one-time arrangement, and the writer hadn't needed him since. They were, in fact, no longer connected. After losing his case, Harvey would appeal the decision again in Albany, on June 3, 1938, at the State of New York Court of Appeals, where he would lose one last, definitive time.

PRESCIENT CITIZENS COULD HARDLY be blamed, during the cold spring of 1937, for equating the late blossoms that year with the worldwide chill that threatened them. Those who read omens in misfortune grew pale at the explosion on May 6 of the two-year-old German zeppelin named for the country's previous president, Paul von Hindenburg, and one of the two largest aircraft ever built. Just as it started to land in Lakehurst, New Jersey, near the George Gould estate Bruce Price had created, the bullet-shaped "ship"—its nationality already making it suspect to many Americans—blew up, killing thirty-six of the ninety-seven aboard. The stunned reaction of Herb Morrison, a visiting broadcaster from Chicago's WLS, would itself be recorded in history, transforming news coverage more than the actual event did.

Forcing herself to turn off her radio, Emily ceded some of her precious listening time to the heavy schedule of print interviews Funk and Wagnalls had arranged to promote *Etiquette*'s forthcoming revision. In May, before she set out for Edgartown, she welcomed to her co-op apartment a *Saturday Evening Post* reporter, Margaret Case Harriman.

Harriman was the kind of woman—from a hardworking family—that Emily admired. Her father was Frank Case, the éminence grise of the Algonquin Hotel's bar, the now famous hangout for writers. Case had started there as a clerk in 1907, buying the Algonquin by the time he was twenty-seven. He had carefully cultivated the bar as a watering hole for the best and brightest of the 1920s, especially the loosely connected *New Yorker* writers. Among a crowd at the Round Table that included Robert Benchley and Dorothy Parker sat Robert Sherwood. Destined to win the Pulitzer, among other prizes, he was the son of Rosina Emmet Sherwood, who had urged Emily, while painting her portrait in the 1890s, to make something of herself. Because Rosina Sherwood was the first woman Emily had encountered who had both a successful home and a professional life, she'd always remembered her and her family fondly.

Now, in the spring of 1937, from Harriman's perspective, Emily Post looked "considerably younger than her age, which is sixty-four . . . her face still has that fine transparency of line and texture that never quite leaves a woman who has been beautiful." The interviewer noted that Emily's "compelling manner" and unusual height might intimidate some people. Fortunately, such daunting authority was tempered by her "fluttery way of talking and a nervous habit of moving her hands continuously in small gestures—pleating a fold of her dress, fussing with a cushion or a letter or anything that happens to be within reach. She doesn't smoke or drink, but her hands are as unrelaxed as those of any habitual cigarette smoker or cocktail nurser. She is endlessly careful about her own choice of words in formal conversations." But her "contacts with the world of industry" had clearly colored" Mrs. Post's language, even allowing her to emit the occasional "damn" or "godawful" during the jovial interview.

Emily opened up to Margaret Harriman more than usual. She admitted that she sometimes wished she were "celebrated as an architect and designer of houses rather than as an etiquette expert," though "she had no quarrel with the kind of fame the years have brought her." She struck the reporter as an almost dauntingly friendly woman, still listing her phone number in the Manhattan directory and, in spite of her rigid schedule, spontaneously meeting almost anyone who stopped by to see her, especially university students. Sometimes she'd even invite sightseers in for a cup of tea. But the journalist missed the underlying message: Emily was lonely. With her career stabilized, one son dead, Ned and Hilda were her only constants. Ned came to dinner only once a week during the city months; in the summer, she barely saw him at all. He didn't like Martha's Vineyard, and nowadays Emily was staying in Edgartown almost six months of the year.

Harriman's impression of Hilda didn't do the servant justice. Though Emily's personal housekeeper was not, even her employer admitted, the perfect maid, she was far more than the "dour and devoted" employee Harriman observed. The reporter noted, with some mystification, the sororal relationship, uneasy that Hilda and Emily dryly referred to servants who had been in the house for several decades as "the new" girls. Yet Emily was clearly the boss: she admitted to dragging Hilda along to the movies because she was her first choice of companions, not because of interest on her maid's part. An odd turn of phrase suggested Harriman's preoccupation with the class issues that domestic hired help raised, even when employers like Emily meant to avoid them: "Like most people who are resigned to what life has brought them, Hilda is a fine restful companion."

Servants were a mainstay of Emily's adult life. Years after Harriman's interview, one of Emily's summer secretaries would recall "how jealous the servants always were of Mrs. Post's attention." Surely Emily was pleased at such a show of "love," reminiscent, on some level, of being courted in her debutante days. What needs the gruff servant with a heart of gold Hilda Ogren fulfilled through her relationship with her employer are unclear. No records of Hilda's life remain, and no family members or friends have yielded clues to interested queries. What seems evident is that neither Hilda nor any other woman or man, after her divorce, entered into an intimate relationship with Emily Post. Apparently, she was celibate after Edwin betrayed her. But what Emily obviously received from this long-term relationship with her servant was a seminal friendship, secured by an excellent salary and personal concern for Hilda's well-being.

In effect, Emily bought the human contact she needed. Her relationship with Hilda didn't require complicated human interactions: the line of command was clear, and Emily could afford to be unfailingly gracious and generous, because she was in charge. It was a striking instance of the way one woman married the conflicting legacies of her upbringing to the desires and possibilities bred by the current age. She finally was able to get what she wanted, as long as she didn't expect others to give her such close attention free of charge. But the cost was high, the combination of loneliness and sadness, as she aged, a harsh price to pay for having things her way.

During Emily's interview with Margaret Harriman, she reassured her audience that she was well taken care of and that her health was now in good order following her eye operations. Walter Winchell's earlier public conveyance of good wishes was flattering, but it had also alerted her entire audience to her possible blindness. Emily emphasized how she had completely recovered from her cataract surgery, and Harriman dutifully reported her progress: "In spite of the restrictions put upon it in the past year, Mrs. Post's daily routine continues to be a considerable whirl. She wakes up regularly at half past five in the morning and has her breakfast—coffee in a percolator which she plugs into an electric-light socket in the early dawn, and a slice of zwieback—from a tray arranged beside her bed the night before. After breakfast she works, lying in bed in a flurry of pencils, paper and galley proofs, until half past seven, when her servants get up. She writes fluently." In light of the reality—the astonishing amount of rewriting and self-editing sprinkled throughout her transcripts and rough drafts—Emily had cleverly managed to tell the story her way once more. She made things look easy—part of her code as a lady—but the truth was otherwise. For a long time, Emily Post had worked harder than anybody she knew.

⋇

CHAPTER 57

*I*N AUGUST 1937, WHILE AWAITING THE OFFICIAL SEPTEMBER RE-
lease of *Etiquette's* fourth edition, Emily was saddened to hear that John Russell Pope, Bruce Price's apprentice and good friend, had died. Because of
her father's clear regard for Pope, Emily had grown even closer to him and
to his sister Minga after she lost Bruce, and she'd seen the two frequently.
After her father's death, she had given Pope the portfolios of photographs
and drawings he had collected, an assortment he was observed "poring
over" in the final months of his illness. Not only had Jack Pope kept vigil at
Bruce's bedside with her and Josephine; he had subsequently steered
Emily's way countless people seeking an interior decorator with a knowledge of architecture to help them design their houses.

Now Jack was gone too, but, thankfully, other traces of her father bespoke a fruitful regeneration. That year, Frank Lloyd Wright would create
Fallingwater, a country house in Pennsylvania that many experts, including
Vincent Scully, have maintained had its roots in Bruce Price's Tuxedo Park.
Chris Sonne, Tuxedo Park's historian, also feels certain that Wright worked
briefly in the atelier of Bruce Price. Amid Lorillard's planned community,
as a result of the wood and stone and landscaping he used, Emily's father
had made it seem as if nature itself encouraged the rusticated development
to flourish. Similarly, Wright's outwardly organic structure, growing out of
trees and a waterfall, was in fact a highly calculated building that managed
to convey the absence of design instead.

Visiting with Minga at the end of the summer, Emily confided that even
though the fourth edition had not officially been released, Funk and Wag-

nalls staff claimed that sales figures had risen more than 117 percent over those for the same period the preceding year. *Publishers Weekly* was sure that "the appeal of the new edition" lay "in the fact that Mrs. Post's dicta as to correct behavior have undergone great amendment, and have been adjusted to the changing usages in present-day society." The historical reality driving the sales—the country was pulling out of the Depression, happy to reconsider and reenter the world of etiquette—went unremarked.

In September, Funk and Wagnalls unleashed a massive fusillade to launch the book. The publishers claimed that the company's advertising campaign for this fall list, "headed by the modernized *Etiquette,* by Emily Post," was the "most ambitious in [its] fifty-year history." Ads would appear in the *New York Times Book Review, This Week,* the *New Yorker,* and *Bride's Magazine,* and booksellers pledged to display *Etiquette* in windows and on counters. The *Times'* "Book Notes" announced that "Emily Post has completely rewritten her book, 'Etiquette,' according to her publishers. . . . The book is now aimed at a wider audience than previously." Emily's own favorite work, *The Personality of a House,* which she had revised slightly in 1933, was reissued simultaneously. Still, though Funk and Wagnalls sporadically marketed the books together, as a package, it was clear that their commitment was to their moneymaker.

A NEW FLUIDITY among the American social classes replaced the strict demarcations of her own past, and Emily welcomed the change. In *Etiquette*'s 1937 revision, she modified her first chapter's title, implying her increased discomfort with absolutes. "What Is Best Society?" now became "The Growth of Good Taste in America." In many instances, she sought to show that a more casual tone had eclipsed the earlier age's formality. Even when she disliked certain modifications, she emphasized that manners evolve with the times and the citizenry would do best to adapt to change. Something as basic as the matter of introductions had transmuted into a far more reasonable, casual routine, leaving behind the intricate calling cards from her day. Using first names for people outside one's own circle was still not good form, but "Hello, everybody, this is Sally" was now an acceptable, casual introduction at the local country club or the neighborhood prayer meeting.

These detailed amendments were due in part to Emily's boredom while confined to bed after her eye surgeries. Even without seeing, she had been able to dictate to her machine, "Suzy," and she certainly wasn't about to stay idle. The result was impressively inclusive, taking account of subtle social changes. Women should pay for themselves when on a date, decreed one forthright new prescription—followed immediately with a list of exceptions. Much of the advice had already been incorporated into the second or third edition, such as the sections on "American Neighborhood Customs" ("*do exactly as your neighbors do, is the only sensible rule*") and "The Vanished Chaperone and Other Lost Conventions." Admiring reviewers who compared the fourth edition with the original gave Emily credit for having added these updates all at once.

Some of the changes startled readers more than others. *Time* magazine noted the ones its reporter found most remarkable:

- Emily Post had been forced to deal with divorce. As she herself noted, "The epidemic of divorce which has been raging in this country for the past 10 or 15 years must be rated with floods, dust-storms, tornadoes and other catastrophes."
- A man no longer had to pay the check for a woman on every occasion.
- An adult woman could take care of herself. An unmarried girl over eighteen could go unchaperoned to the theater with a man, even to dinner in his apartment—if, the always sensible adviser added, such a move would not agitate her own social circle. The young woman could also take the initiative and invite the man to a game or to the theater. Nor, in the city, did she need to lean fetchingly upon a man's arm, as if relying on his protection.
- Corn on the cob, one of Emily's own favorite foods, could now be eaten (neatly) at a formal dinner, using both hands for every ear. Whatever the host preferred, cigarettes at the dinner table were de rigueur, according to the day's mores. Emily herself admitted that the practice was "an innovation she herself cannot approve," but when in Rome . . .
- Slang had become progressively more permissible in good society, and nothing was gained from resisting. "O.K.," "swell," "divine," "and how!," "so what?," and "you betcha" were expressions Emily had often heard. But mispronunciations were another thing entirely: "colyum," "ottawobile," "eggsit," "tomayto," and "cult-your" kept people out of good society: there was a titanic difference between deliberate slang and ignorant speech.

Emily had long hammered home the importance of correct speech. As far back as 1931, she had urged her radio audience to reflect upon the "old saying that in spite of a dowdy or otherwise undistinguished appearance, purity of speech proclaims [a lady's] background or her education to have been one of culture." After all, learning to speak well did not depend upon wealth or status. But, she continued, "people of imitation elegance who mince their words and strangle their throats and enunciate too precisely, almost invariably break the worst tabu of all, which is that of pretentiousness." She added, "By the way, do not confuse illiteracy with accent"—of which the country contains countless varieties, "north, east, south and west. Some of them have distinction, some are charming, some are distorted, and some are just ugly—but none (not even these last) are illiterate." In 1937, her pet peeve remained pretentious circumlocutions; the use of "permit me to assist you" instead of "let me help you" made the otherwise forgiving author shudder.

THE REVIEWS WERE RESPECTFUL if at times more grudging than in years past, as though some of the journalists were annoyed that a writer could devote serious energy to a subject they believed to be trivial. Impatient reporters scoured the book for missteps, statements they could genially ridicule as daffy or outdated. A longtime supporter from the *Washington Post* was perplexed that Emily insisted on four table settings, regardless of the number of people expected for dinner. Presumably, Emily's advice was motivated by her belief in being prepared. Often she and Katharine Collier dined together in their adjacent New York apartments, and having places already set waylaid any sense of discomfort on the part of a sudden guest and allayed inconvenience for the servants, their well-being always a consideration for Emily.

In yet another friendly though condescending notice, the *Post* published a small essay, "Why We Behave," which led with a loaded sentence: "Thomas Wolfe and Margaret Mitchell might as well give up. For when it comes to turning out reams of copy, Emily Post makes them look like pikers." The writer explained that Emily had beat her own record, with this latest etiquette tome boasting 860 pages, compared to its immediate predecessor of "a mere 723."

Time magazine had begun its review of the revised edition by claiming that etiquette was in fact a game in which everyone was trying to one-up the neighbors. Emily Post, in reality "a prosperous businesswoman," was, in the end, just like Samuel Johnson—he the "first great English lexicographer," she the "first great lexicographer of U.S. manners, . . . imposing many of her personal prejudices as rules for contemporary and future generations to follow." Gratuitously trotting out the details of Emily's divorce, which turned her into a "comely divorcee somewhat in need of cash," the *Time* writer downgraded her significance into the "autocrat of U.S. etiquette." She had assumed this role, he surmised, by virtue of the "6,000 questions a week which pour in upon her from millions who have never seen Newport or Park Avenue." Irrationally, the reviewer disdained the idea of commoners outside of society or beyond the rungs of higher education turning to an insider to find out how they might get in too.

In fact, what sometimes seemed her natural inclusiveness, enveloping dissimilar readers and wide-ranging subjects, was proving among Emily's most remarkable strengths. Relentlessly, according to her grandson, she sought the opinions of everyone around her, "cabdrivers, house servants, socialite friends she lunched with, personnel she met through her radio or newspaper business." On society's behalf, as her personal mandate, she had, over the years, honed her powers of observation until they were almost preternaturally alert to nuances of change.

That September she wrote in her newspaper column of being surprised at the reemergence of the afternoon tea party among the young cognoscenti. She believed that such a seemingly trivial event reflected a significant cultural shift. As she described it:

> Not everywhere—but certainly in the majority of American communities—the invitation "Will you come in for a cocktail?" outnumbers every other. And yet there is no question at all that the trend of the moment—I am perfectly serious—is back to tea! I am not writing about people of yesterday; as far as I can see, they are not changing. I am writing of the youngest and the most fashionable of this modern day. By this I do not mean that cocktail parties are not given by the smartest and youngest, but I do mean that there is a decided return to popularity of the old-fashioned five o'clock tea table—muffins, crumpets, strawberry jam, and all.

By the time Prohibition ended, Emily explained, it had become quaint to ask anyone over for "a cup of tea." Paradoxically, when alcohol was forbidden, hard liquor was all that was served at chic parties; if a guest didn't want to drink, she or he had to go without. Rarely were substitutes offered. Once liquor was legal again, orange and pineapple juice, as well as tomato juice seasoned with lime, celery salt, and pepper, became newly chic—as did tea. Now the recently alcohol-saturated "horse's neck," which back in the 1910s had been just a tumbler of ginger ale with long lemon twists, could fashionably return to its nonalcoholic roots. People no longer felt compelled to drink—not even the ubiquitous import Dubonnet, newly popular among the social set—because, once again, they had a choice.

Answering the confused queries filling her in-box, Emily instructed women in how to serve tea. Assuming that young children probably accompanied the hostess and her women guests during their afternoon visits, she suggested ways such a group could take turns caring for the youngsters, teaching children in the process a gentle etiquette for visiting among themselves. She urged the mothers to encourage the oldest child to take over the "host" role and to supervise the cookies and milk, allowing the children to feel worthy and important and providing their mothers a well-deserved break; meanwhile their offspring painlessly learned good manners.

INCREASINGLY IN DEMAND as a radio spokesperson for major marketing campaigns, Emily Post began telling Americans how to get more out of life while they grew healthier in the process. By 1937 she had received enough offers for sponsorship that she could pick and choose. She opted to talk about ways to become stronger, physically and mentally, through one's diet and one's attitude, a combination she had long wanted to discuss on the air. In September, Emily began commanding a twice-weekly fifteen-minute spot, a six-month radio show sponsored by the Florida Citrus Commission on New York City's WABC, heard nationally. Her talks not only helped Florida oranges outsell those from California, at least according to her typed notes, but were greeted by an amazing number of letters that shared a common theme—a family's modest budget and queries about how, with such limited resources, to "get the most out of life."

Emily was impressed by the earnestness of her fans. "Every letter strengthens my faith in the basic goodness of human nature. In every question I read a sincere desire for those intrinsic qualities which mark the person of taste and cultivation," she wrote. Her listeners frequently asked her about social change and its impact on the mores of the young, a subject always dear to her heart. "There is nothing new in the fact that youth is the backbone of our nation—it always has been; it always must be," she said.

"Don't worry when you hear laments against modern youth. Youth is far better prepared to face the new problems of a changing world than are those who would be its teachers. Do all you can to encourage—never discourage—and never try to force any one into a pattern chosen by you."

She herself had found endorsing Florida citrus an easy fit because it was an obviously beneficial, nourishing product—and, she explained, because she could honestly vouch for the grapefruit-centered diet, which she had tried more than once herself. Smaller, more frequent portions, fresh vegetables and fruit (no dressing), and grapefruit juice or grapefruit as often as you want: those were her recommendations for losing weight. She also urged her readers to exercise, not mentioning that she herself rarely managed to do so. "Unused muscles often become flabby, and it is important to prevent this if you want to look trim, slim, youthful and attractive," she advised.

Still, in spite of the commission's emphasis on nature's bounty, Emily, almost defiantly, promoted even more strongly the importance of financial stability over any produce on the market: "The happiness of every family is dependent on financial solvency. It does not matter what your income is, if you can live within it you are rich—if you go beyond it, you are bankrupt."

OCTOBER ENDED WITH a large display ad for the new edition in the *New York Times*: "Today, As Always EMILY POST is the supreme authority on MANNERS—good taste, not only in the things we do and say—but in the things we think and are," it boasted. The following month, among dozens of prominent speakers at Rockefeller Center's *New York Times* National Book Fair, Emily's appearance merited a headline in the *New York Post*: "Etiquette Author Tells of Her Woes." The article reported on her attempts to adapt conventions to modern behavior, noting that she had written five million words on the subject in the last fifteen years. Emphasizing how much she disliked the word *etiquette* because of its unfairly high-toned attitude, Emily pulled out her old saw. Telling people what fork to use held no interest for her, she said. After all, she was as likely to pick up the wrong utensil as her neighbor, for two reasons: she was absentminded and nearsighted. As for propping your elbows on the table at dinner? "It really makes no difference," she answered airily.

The interviewer, hoping for less sanguine copy, was clearly taken aback at Mrs. Post's unwillingness to indict the day's behavior. This maven of etiquette, rather than deploring recent changes, considered herself "the living record of the change in manners and customs." She even chuckled over intriguing new questions that had arisen. More surprising to the reporter, Emily eagerly took credit for expanding society's boundaries. "Mrs. Post says she feels she has done more to 'knock down the social walls which used to enclose fashionable society than even Mr. Roosevelt has done,' " the reporter noted. Fifteen years ago, Emily claimed, "fashionable society consisted of a small group of people living within the walls of their own selection here in New York, in Boston, Baltimore, London and Paris. They fixed the rules of etiquette and used them as part of their social walls. It became my mission to tell people who did not know the rules what they were."

As a result of the shift in demographics since 1922, Emily herself had adjusted to a slightly altered role: rather than dictating from above, she said, "I find I have to adapt the conventions to my younger readers." Acknowledging the power of the postwar adult generation, she declared that they had "taken the bit in their teeth [and] I have been running after them ever since. I can tell that I am still keeping up with them, however, by the letters I receive." Such attention to generations far younger than her own proved rejuvenating, as the genial woman quizzed the children and grandchildren of her associates and friends, sometimes questioning them openly and occasionally observing them quietly, as if they were invaluable laboratory specimens.

At the end of 1937, a lengthy essay in the *New York Times* rewarded her fastidious attention to the world around her. Deferential, it was nonetheless tinged with the condescension common to so many of the reviews of the current edition. In part such a response reflected the times: facing global conflict and trying to recover from the long national financial debacle, the populace and its pundits were in no mood to honor the work of a mistress of manners, set on ensuring that etiquette stayed up to date. Teasingly, the reviewer noted that "it still isn't proper for Mary to take John's arm except when approaching a puddle." But Emily's 1937 text didn't endorse this kind of rule at all, and only an already prejudiced reader could have made such a misinterpretation; instead, she asserted women's new rights to walk the streets without any ironclad rules at all, except for respect for others. Too many strictures about how men and women should interact landed people back in the Victorian age, and Emily saw nothing laudatory in that. As she had asserted on her radio show six years earlier, "If a rule seems to be like sand in the gear box instead of the lubricating oil it is intended to be, get rid of it and use home made oil instead."

Unremarked by the mainstream press, a major shift had occurred in *Etiquette*'s original purebred assumptions. Emily's book was now a crossbreed, absorbing new codes and passing them on, observing the country's mutations as they traversed young and old, immigrants and citizens, women and men. *Etiquette* was a maelstrom of the culture that had spawned it, a palimpsest replacing the prior version of its behavior and beliefs with a new one every five to seven years.

※

*I*F EMILY THOUGHT ATTENTION TO HER EYE PROBLEMS WAS A THING of the past, she was in for a rude surprise at a most unlikely venue: as the evening's speaker at New York's Gourmet Society banquet. Held for the first time "across the East River," the *Times* noted, in unfashionable Brooklyn, the dinner proved a culinary extravagance that would have done even Sam Ward proud: "Breast of England Pheasant en casserole with champagne sauerkraut Continentale, to serve seventy-five," the paper reported in loving detail. "Russian hors d'oeuvre first, followed by clear green turtle soup, Japanese toasted rice crackers, Chinese celery, assorted national breads and a lavish French dish: ragout fin en coquille, Madame Pompadour fleurons"—followed by a dessert of lingonberries.

But the event proved most remarkable for Emily Post's blunders: she spilled her lingonberries and spent most of the three-hour dinner with her elbows on the table. The scarlet fruit thoroughly soaked the tablecloth, the mishap causing the president of the society to jump in quickly to explain that Mrs. Post's "elbow had been jiggled," no doubt "by a careless waiter." Emily would have none of it and insisted on taking full responsibility for the gaffe: "People . . . generally think I'm made of tin, a sort of mechanical robot, but it is not so," she explained as the mess was cleaned up. She smiled, then propped her elbows back on the table again. The woman who, in the privacy of her home, preferred corn on the cob, meat loaf, and chocolate ice cream, graciously exclaimed, "Never have I eaten such beautiful foods. Or observed such wonderful table manners."

The Associated Press quickly circulated a wire, provoking newspapers everywhere to reprint their own version of the dinner, always starring the shocking etiquette blunder of Emily Post, turning her slipup into fodder for their public's amusement. "Mrs. Post Unbends at Gourmet Dinner" and "Here's Real News! Emily Post Spills a Cranberry Dish" typified the genial if condescending titles. "Emily Post . . . has spilled something on the tablecloth," the *Times* gossiped. "And of all places. It had to happen at a dinner of the Gourmet Society, which includes some of New York's fanciest feeders."

The topic proved fascinating enough that a week later, on January 30, the *New York Times* reprised it. At least Emily's writing received attention in the process. The sixty-five-year-old author was famous not only for the five million words she had reportedly printed on etiquette but also for texts on architecture and interior decoration, as well as several novels. "Even official Washington is said to have accepted her authority," the article avowed, referring to the State Department protocol. The overwrought, disproportionate coverage of the inconsequential event highlighted the nation's insecurity about manners. Forcing Emily Post to stand in for the one thing she had always emphasized should be forgotten and forgiven—an innocent mistake—journalists were gleefully casting the doyenne of etiquette as part of a system they feared, not one that she endorsed. They thought they were getting some of their own back, but Emily Post, more than willing to confess her faults, had never sanctioned these journalists' notion of income or prestige-driven "Best Behavior." She may have thought of her compeer Edith Wharton, who had famously lamented, "After all, one knows one's weak points so well, that it's bewildering to have the critics overlook them and invent others."

In spite of the catty coverage, Emily chose not to reveal the true reason for the accident. The operations, while successful in saving her sight, had left her vision impaired. She had no intention of trading on pity, however, so she briskly and cheerfully dispatched the gossipmongers, determined not to skip a beat. From February through April, she accepted advertising appearances on shows such as CBS's popular soap opera *Aunt Jenny's Real Life Stories* as well as continuing her own weekly etiquette program. Eager to stay current, she tackled ever more modern social issues, including "Problems of the Second Wife"—a subject that, thirty-two years ago, during those grueling weeks she'd spent testifying against her husband in court, she'd never dreamed she'd discuss with anyone.

———

EXCITED WITH THE LOOK of what she had achieved with a few fledgling attempts the previous season, in late spring Emily instructed John to help her coat just about everything else in the house with oil-based paint, resulting in compliments from the neighbors, sincere or merely polite. Color, always a pleasure to her, now became a vital part of her life, compensating for the dull glaze her damaged eyes spread over everything. What seemed to others in Edgartown yet another whimsical project was as much Emily's response to her continuing vision problems as it was her latest aesthetic. "Red, red, red," recalls her grandson. "The house also had lots of red-and-blue combinations. And when Grandmama wanted something done, she wanted it done yesterday. So she'd try to do lots of things herself, often succeeding. Now she decided to paint her mahogany dining room table blue, and after deciding it looked very nice, she painted many other items in bold color. Every few years she would repaint—often all on her own—to keep the colors fresh." No doubt she also repainted to lift her spirits when she was feeling low, as well as to remind herself that an intelligently conducted life could always accommodate change.

She spent the rest of the summer catching up on her personal correspondence. Not only her social or professional acquaintances but her employees would vouch for her genuine concern over their lives, and the complete trust she inspired in them. More than Manhattan, Martha's Vineyard, with its seasonal, less formal attitude, allowed Emily to blur the boundaries between workers she employed and island friends. One such helper, young Betty Osborne, had written Emily about the exciting changes she'd undergone. Betty's family lived on Martha's Vineyard, and through her mother, the town librarian, Emily had discovered the recent high school graduate to be an excellent secretary during the summers.

Betty had recently moved to Virginia, to live with her grown sister, and Emily took the time to write her a loving, detailed letter to catch her up on local news: "Partly busy and completely happy re-doing a house that some very old friends of mine have just bought—the Furlauds from Tuxedo," Emily related. Eleanor Furlaud was the daughter of Richard Mortimer, an early resident of Tuxedo Park. Eleanor's sister and her brother both owned houses in the park, and when it turned out Eleanor would be living at Martha's Vineyard, the women had excitedly realized that Emily could re-design the Furlaud residence in Edgartown.

Betty's ancestors had once lived in the Furlaud house, Emily reminded the young woman. "It had a big piazza across it until yesterday, when I had the pleasure of seeing it taken off. As soon as I finish this letter I have to go over to design the top of the door which will need some sort of entablature where the roof of the porch has been torn away. I have also designed new doors for the old school house–Boys' Club. It is a lovely old building and it is too good not to repair correctly." She closed by reassuring the young woman of "how much and how often I miss you." Generously praising Betty's replacement, she elevated the earlier employee at the same time: "Natalie is a darling child, she *couldn't* be sweeter, but she is not you."

Emily talked easily to young people, engaging especially in conversations with the daughters and granddaughters of friends and acquaintances. Such encounters had shaped her opinions when, in August, she wrote candidly about the characteristic girl of sixteen. "Emily Post says the typical 16-year-old American girl has boy friends, uses lipstick, talks about sex and has radical political opinions," announced the *Dallas Morning News*. A Hollywood studio, developing the screen character of Nancy Drew, had sent education and social leaders a questionnaire, seeking to define the female youth. Emily's responses captured the headlines. "Mrs. Post was short and to the point in her answers," the paper related. "She said the typical American girl of this age does not smoke, uses lipstick but no rouge, has a spending allowance of 50 cents a week, has no steady beau, is athletic but has a sketchy musical education, belongs to one club, expects to marry, is a tomboy by day and thoroughly feminine by night, talks about sex matters with other girls but doesn't know as much about the subject as she pretends she does, can cook a little, is more obedient to her father than her mother." But, the article went on, "Mrs. Post protested the narrow choice of answers, saying that to expound on the 'typical' sixteen-year-old was useless." There was no such thing as "typical."

That September, her concerns were refocused dramatically on the home front, when she was affected by a historical event that touched her personally, a natural disaster that gave her little choice but to get involved. A storm that had percolated off the coast of Africa paused, on its way to New England, long enough to ravage Long Island. The hurricane obliterated the Dune Road area at Westhampton Beach, smashing her son's house into oblivion. Ned, who spent his weekends on the beach until it turned uncomfortably cold, was lucky to escape injury; twenty-nine people in his area died, and an additional twenty-one deaths occurred over the eastern end of Long Island. The storm flooded the South Fork, obliterating the tracks of the Long Island Rail Road, so important long ago to the fortunes of Emily's father and grandfather and their good family friend Hop Smith. Montauk, where the Tile Club members had finished their hike, was turned into a temporary island.

Nowadays referred to as the Great New England Hurricane or the Great Hurricane of 1938, the storm killed between five and seven hundred people on Long Island and in New England while causing what would be today $6 billion in damage. Finally Emily had an indisputable edge in the gentle running argument between mother and son over which beachfront was superior.

As usual, in the aftermath of upheaval, she converted her anxiety into action, helping Ned draw up plans to rebuild. Just as she herself felt emotionally settled, in December she received a desperate letter from Betty, her summer secretary. Could Mrs. Post send her some money and perhaps even allow her to come stay with her temporarily in Manhattan? "Betty dear, what can have happened?" Emily began her alarmed response. "Your great distress is hard to understand. If I only knew more about it I might be better able to help. One thing of course I can do—tide you over temporarily, but not for very long. Nor can I advise you to come to New York to get a job. Jobs are scarce, pay low and living high. But if that is the only thing you can *bear* to do, I can stake you to room and board—expenses at the 'Y.' For a few weeks in which to find a job—or at least find yourself."

Still, Emily beseeched her to explain: "Only please tell me what it is. Is he married or has he a baby or *what* has he done?" The unsaid question was, Has he gotten you pregnant?

Apparently Betty had implied that she had serious romance problems. Emily's advice sounded like what she would have told her own children, parental dicta she believed led to healthy independence: "I know it must be something serious—yet I hate to have you who are blameless of whatever it is run away from it—because the things we don't face leave us weaker. The things we face leave us, after the encounter, stronger."

Worried that the girl would feel deserted, Emily added, "Anyway, my thoughts *are* with you—if necessary you can come to N.Y.—but then? I don't know—but my love to you. And I am sorry." She signed the letter with a few indecipherable letters, an *E* and a scribble, followed by a *P* and quick lowercase *t*—not so much a sign of her hurry as a signature that bridged the way she signed professional or business letters and those she wrote to friends and family. She added a P.S., saying that she had just made out a check, which she had already put in the mail.

Years later, Emily's baby gifts to Betty and her husband suggested that the girl's dilemma—whatever it had turned out to be—had had a happy ending.

⚜

CHAPTER 59

*A*TTENTION TO ITS OWN DIDN'T MEAN THAT THE COUNTRY
was tuning out the rest of the world entirely. The bombing of the Spanish
town of Guernica on April 26, 1937, by the German Luftwaffe and their
Italian subordinates had inspired Norman Corwin to write, for his *Words
Without Music* radio series, "They Fly Through the Air with the Greatest of
Ease," a song Emily loved to hum. Directed at the horrors of fascism, the
song premiered on February 19, 1939, prompting one thousand favorable
letters to be sent to CBS.

However much she hummed the theme, Emily spent the winter far
from its concerns, busily compiling a commercial brochure of popular etiquette queries for Bab-O cleanser. By the spring, Bab-O had announced
that it would be conducting an extensive campaign through newspapers,
national magazines, and radio to publicize its exclusive offer of *101 Common
Mistakes in Etiquette—and How to Avoid Them,* by Emily Post. A slender book of
popular questions, their subjects ranging from table settings to bridal invitations, the brochure was not about "mistakes" at all. How Bab-O convinced Emily to use a title that was so contrary to her whole philosophy
about manners—perhaps by not telling her before publication—is unclear.
Obviously the company was building on the enormous success of the earlier Lillian Eichler book that had contained both corrections and cartoons
on every page.

SIGNS OF A SOCIETY still in need of simple instructions—two steps forward, one back—abounded, nowhere more than in the inconsistent racism

that usually went unnoted by the press, its attention focused on covering the war. Louis Armstrong was at the Met one day, and the next day he'd be recording "Jeepers Creepers" for Decca Records. Even when the nation relapsed into the racism of its past, it seemed intent on making amends, on creating a country for everyone. After they realized she was black, for instance, the Daughters of the American Revolution refused to allow opera singer Marian Anderson to perform at Constitution Hall, but citizens protested. Black soldiers could die abroad under the American flag, but black musicians couldn't perform on sanctified American soil. That Easter Sunday, April 9, 1939, before a live audience of seventy-five thousand and a radio audience of millions, NBC broadcast a free concert by the rich-sounding contralto. From the steps of the Lincoln Memorial, she began by singing "My Country 'Tis of Thee."

THAT SAME APRIL, television would make its national debut at one of the largest imaginable venues, the New York world's fair. Emily watched at home as Franklin Roosevelt, officially opening the fair, delivered the first presidential address over the new medium. For four years, a committee had worked on this exhibition organized around "The World of Tomorrow," making it the largest international event in twenty years. Now, the grand opening registered 200,000 people, all eager to glory in America's newest technological achievement. Americans, feeling themselves recovering from the decade's financial chaos, were willing to spend the reasonable prices the fair commanded. Over the next two spring seasons, the 45 million visitors would generate approximately $48 million.

Even so, the spectators' pleasure was offset by organizational bad planning: the expensive fair proved a complete financial failure. There were just too many serious exhibitions for a nation in need of fun. Neither the Jewish Palestine Pavilion, promoting the concept of a modern Jewish state, nor the grandly reassuring medical arts building, displaying methods to administer safer anesthesia, interested journalists or the public. At least the IBM and the Ex-Lax exhibits drew crowds. Then, of course, there was always the car, a winner every time it roared into life. This year General Motors exhibited a seven-lane cross-country highway system meant to give it room to roam.

Another innovation with more immediate gains for residents as well as the tourists who would continue to flood the city was the special subway line (the 7) built to transport traffic to and from the fairgrounds. The fair was held at what is now Queens's Shea Stadium, a site that would become the home of the New York Mets and remain in use until the season's opening day in April 2009, when a newer, bigger stadium next door, Citi Field, was scheduled to take its place.

THE SUMMER OF 1939 was Emily's idea of perfection. Though not the princess of the park that Tuxedo had anointed her, she was now a revered fixture in Edgartown. A local journalist invited to her house marveled that Mrs. Post was "absolutely modern not only in ideas" but in her appearance and conversation: "Gowned in a simple frock of red and white crepe, her costume was completed by a wide-brimmed red straw hat and large pearl earrings. The red color scheme was becoming to her dark hair and seemed to reflect the vigor and brightness of her personality." A grumpy writer from the New York Times instead fussed on her behalf that summer about the busload of tourists "walking on her grass" and "peering about," in general "making a nuisance of themselves. Thus is rewarded labor in behalf of etiquette," he sniffed grandly. Clearly, he'd failed to understand how much Emily herself genuinely enjoyed the tourists and the respect their interest implied.

Between the strangers who gawked at the exterior and the local residents who gained access to the inside, Yvonne Sylvia sometimes felt responsible for protecting her boss from potential embarrassment. She laughs when she recalls how humiliating it was when her employer held garden club meetings at the house: "The kitchen desperately needed new appliances to be seen by the public, I finally told her. She never went into the kitchen herself, and her food tastes were so simple that it just hadn't occurred to her how antiquated everything was. Mrs. Post quietly listened to me and ordered all the equipment I suggested."

Emily relished the equilibrium she achieved by balancing the island against the city. In June, Bill had graduated from St. Paul's, his elite boarding school in Concord, New Hampshire, and he would be leaving soon to attend MIT. More than ever, as her family pursued new places and relationships, Emily found herself appreciating the familiar. Back in New York, the co-op that she had so carefully designed and filled with people she loved continued to be a major stalwart in her life. Foremost remained her friendship with Katharine Collier. Katharine's great-grandson remembers what steadfast companions the two women remained through the years. "When I was a little boy, I used to go over to 39 East Seventy-ninth all the time," A. St. George B. Duke, or "Pony," recalls fondly. "And they'd always be together—whenever Emily wasn't working, that is." Katharine "was a very dear person," he says, and "it's no wonder that Emily was over at the apartment" so often. For their lunches, at least several times a week, they alternated homes, "both feeling lucky to be living right next to the other."

Almost as important, there was Hilda, who continued to occupy a seminal role in Emily's life. She supervised the other servants: Ebba, the cook, Girda, the housekeeper, and Ailfi, an all-around helper. That year, the movie everyone had to see was the blockbuster made from the novel *Gone with the Wind*. When asked if their great-grandmother saw the film, Cindy Post Senning replies, "She must have, and Hilda would have gone with her. That film had to resonate with a Baltimore woman from Emily's generation and background, the way Scarlett knew in the end it was all up to her." Given the auguries of war threatening the Western world by the end of the year, you didn't have to be southern to vibrate to the epic scenes of death and decay on the larger-than-life screen.

To counter isolationists who demanded that the United States remain neutral, Roosevelt and his cabinet tried to enlist Hollywood's help to mobilize American opinion against Hitler. President Roosevelt even roped a cowboy, matinee idol Gene Autry, into helping fight the enemy abroad. Dining at the White House with the president, Autry was asked to travel to Great Britain and assure the British of American support. The sandy-haired, pink-cheeked, blue-eyed, baby-faced fellow with the slow smile and easy drawl was thought a perfect representative of the iconic American ethos. "Right thinking, clean living, and a devotion to duty are the ingredients necessary to success," the singing cowboy affirmed. That offscreen he would soon play loose with his marriage vows and go heavy on the alcohol were both beside the point.

THROUGHOUT MOST OF THE FALL OF 1939 NED DINED WITH HIS mother every Monday night in Manhattan. She treasured their routine and kept urging her son to come to the Vineyard the next spring for a visit, but he wasn't interested, even after his property on Long Island had proved no sanctuary. Since the end of the war, Ned had been working as an executive advertising manager for Mack Trucks. For now, his frequent presence in New York City helped compensate Emily for her loss: her grandson was rarely around anymore. Because his studies at MIT had been compressed into an accelerated three-year program, Billy was working nonstop these days. His grandmother was amazed; the eighteen-year-old Billy already planned to join the navy upon graduation and move to Washington, D.C., to design training simulators. Clearly he was cast in her mold, someone who acted methodically and with foresight.

By the beginning of the new year, Emily was hard at work on the next revision of *Etiquette,* following, after only three years, on the heels of the fourth edition. Sales had climbed, in part because of a lessening of the nation's financial crisis, but also because of Emily's radio appearances. Now she meant to incorporate feedback provided by her listeners, some of them a new audience to her book. Mrs. Three-in-One, the servantless wonder woman Emily had devised with her younger son just before his death, now (at the end of the Depression) occupied not two or three but nine pages of text. "The Vanishing Chaperone" of 1936 (already reduced from "The Chaperone" in the first *Etiquette*) was unceremoniously laid to rest, dispensed of in a few sentences headed by "The Vanished Chaperone."

In "New Aspects of Hospitality," Emily took on the changing norms of kitchen etiquette. She pointed out that nowadays many men cooked routine meals, unlike the "terrapin or canvas-back duck" specialties that husbands of old undertook. Addressing readers both with and without servants, she acknowledged, through her easy juxtaposition of different classes, the fluid nature of her audience. Suggesting that some couples might enjoy eating in the kitchen, where it was informal—even having friends join them there—she also comfortably discussed how to train and treat a servant if one was suddenly able to afford such assistance, stressing that a loss of privacy was the price of hiring help: "All-time occupancy of the kitchen by the family is possible only in the house of Mrs. Three-in-One, whose kitchen is her own. In the house of Mrs. One-Maid, the kitchen should be considered available only when the maid is out. And in the house of one who has many servants, the kitchen, of course, belongs to them as entirely as the front of the house belongs to the family."

With the nation in better financial shape than during the past ten years, Emily felt justified expanding the subject of hired help into a more detailed discussion, in essence tutoring readers in the art of treating underlings with respect. In the section "An Obligation of Courtesy to the Servants," she wrote: "The kitchen should be returned to its rightful tenant, the cook, in just as good order as it was turned over to the family when she went out. The same is true of the pantry and even the dining room. A few pots and pans left filled with water in an otherwise clean sink in an otherwise tidy kitchen, is reasonable. But it would not be fair to the cook, any more than it would be to the maid alone, to leave her a kitchen that requires hours of scrubbing and polishing to put it back in order."

A stronger economy demanded advice on etiquette for passengers on airplanes. This newest form of travel required decisions about choosing the best seats, considering others in new ways (wipe out the restroom sink when you are finished), and understanding the rules that governed group conversation in the air (where talking was expected to cover nervousness) versus those applicable to less communal train travel. In turbulent weather, "laughter and conversation by the other plane passengers is always reassuring as well as diverting," Emily noted.

She also covered bumpy territory back on the ground, appending a section ostensibly about drinking but couched vaguely enough to cover sexual freedom as well. In addition to "Saying No to Cocktails," Emily's advice for "Young People Afraid to Say No" at various moments seems to be aimed at men, at others, women. "A real leader," Emily explained, was one who said " 'No' lightly, and yet this 'No' has an immutable finality. Such a person says very little about what he will or won't do. In fact, he rarely forces his opinion upon anyone, but if asked, he gives his answer as truthfully, as uncritically and as briefly as possible—especially if he thinks his opinion may be in serious disagreement with that of the other persons. Such people never lose the confidence of their friends." She emphasized the point that tone told as much as the words themselves:

> It is quite amazing how frank we can be when our manner is sympathetic, eager, or appreciative. We can say "No" and make it sound almost as nice as "Yes." On the other hand, we can say "No" and make it sound cold, critical, and almost as affronting as a blow. We can say "I'm sorry, no," and make it sound a poignant regret; or make it sound as casual and lighthearted as the flitting of a butterfly. Or it can come down upon the sensibilities of others with the weight of a sledge hammer. The secret of how this is done is first of all an innate attitude by which, while we refuse, we hold no criticism of those who do not refuse. At the very moment we set ourselves up with an "I am better than thou" attitude, we become as intolerable to others as we ourselves are intolerant.

In some of her new pronouncements, Emily's unchecked earnestness opened her to a mild degree of ridicule, and journalists, predictably, emphasized her more provocative comments. Women, Emily had warned, should avoid gaining weight, if only because it was hard for an overweight woman to look dignified. "The tendency of fat is to take away one's gentility; therefore, anyone inclined to be fat must be ultra conservative—in order to counteract the effect." If all else failed, a fat woman (she minced no words) should wear black. There were more than a few who snickered at the notion that dignity had anything to do with appearance.

SOON AFTER SHE ARRIVED at Edgartown in late spring, Emily holed up to write *Children Are People,* spending the entire summer of 1940 working on the manuscript and delivering it to Funk and Wagnalls in time for December publication. According to Yvonne Sylvia, this, not *The Personality of a House,* was her favorite book. "One of the least sentimental of women," according to her son, she related to the young as if she and they were a natural fit, as if being an only child had taught her the importance of adults to children. At a birthday party she had given for a young Billy, for instance, she had noticed that "one little boy, younger and less assertive than the others, was left behind in all the games." Her grandson observed Emily "calling Hilda to bring her bag of wools of which she had quantities in all colors and shades. She snipped several small pieces from all of these, tossed them out in a heap on a table and offered a prize to the child who could match the most colors in a given time." Bill's father marveled, years later: "How she knew that the shy little boy who hung back from the active games could and would be the winner at this she herself could not have told you."

Children Are People exhibited an intuitive grasp of child psychology. Almost seventy years later, the book still rewards a close reading. Though it discusses basic questions about child care and training, even more, it assumes that parenting should be a positive experience, producing offspring who become self-confident adults. Aware of its audience of young parents, Funk and Wagnalls set the price at $2.75, lower than that of any of Emily's other nonfiction.

Early in the book, Emily described the challenges of the new decade. Parents of the day faced "restlessness, . . . craving for novelty and excitement, the lack of resources within ourselves. The radio turned on—just to make noise; hordes of people encouraged to come in at all hours of the day and night, or else each separate member of the family going out somewhere. The homes of many might just as well be railroad stations. . . . I am afraid [this is] a not unusual picture . . . not alone in the great cities, but in countless small ones as well." She hoped to offer parents ways to sustain "the spirit of home" and the "beauty of living."

Surely it was no accident that Emily chose gardening as her metaphor for effective parenting—tending the pliant stalks, protecting them from chaos, ensuring that no harm comes to them until they have a chance to blossom; all these impulses she had exercised on her soil at Edgartown after she lost her son. Such careful tutelage, she conceded, wasn't always necessary: there existed "flower seeds blown by the wind and falling upon the bare earth, and babies without cradles or any . . . tender care," who mysteriously have grown to "perfect maturity." More often, though, a successful adult evolved from careful parenting: "As a usual thing, the flowers watched over by a skilled gardener, and the children watched over by skilled parents, have far greater perfection. . . . [J]ust as flowers bloom for those who wisely understand and patiently supply their needs, so too does wise understanding, known by the name of comradeship, bring to full flower the heart and mind of a child."

Far more explicitly than in the past, she addressed issues of class and money. "It is not necessary for parents to have had the advantages of more than humble education to set an example to their children while they are little, and also to inspire them with a lifelong ambition to live up to the standards their parents set," she wrote. Refusing to flinch in the face of social realities, Emily acknowledged that "this does not mean that the advantages of cultivation and sufficient wherewithal to insure beauty of home surroundings are not valuable, or that anyone of us would choose illiteracy ever!" Still, it was "the greater value of fundamental character" that directed the growth of a child: "Self-control, integrity, trustworthiness, patience, kindness, tolerance, and common sense are qualities that can be possessed by those in humble circumstances quite as fully as those who from a material standpoint are far more fortunately placed."

As if awakened to the reality confronting many American families, she rode her theme hard: "The belief sometimes expressed that ideal parents are necessarily rich, could not be farther from the truth. Poverty is a handicap certainly, and illiteracy is a greater one. Yet the history of our country gives proof after proof of parents who have triumphed over both. In the world of today—in spite of its disintegrating tendencies—many a mother and father whose backgrounds were of the simplest, have succeeded in creating a home that has never ceased to satisfy, to hold, and to influence their children."

Equally important were the manners parents showed their offspring. To expect children to contribute to the household was essential. To interrupt Johnnie or Jane and ask them to perform tasks for lazy parents, however, was just rude. "The child who is at the moment doing nothing but loll in a chair, trying to make up his mind *what* he wants to do or where he wants to go, can certainly be sent to fetch anything for anyone. . . . But if a child is really engrossed in doing something, whether it be work or play, interrupting should be avoided almost as much as it should be for a grown person." Clearly speaking from her own frustrations as a writer whose schedule was not always respected, she added: "As a matter of fact, few people, except composers or writers, have any idea of the meaning of interruption! Every writer knows the impulse of people to whisper an interruption, as if it made any difference whether the announcement, 'Mrs. Jones is on the telephone,' is whispered or shouted—if it is necessary to go to the telephone."

Her chapter "The Stepchild and the Adopted Child" boldly instructed "mixed families" how to make their new lives run smoothly, even as Emily rehashed her arguments against divorce, all centered on the children's welfare. Only cruelty or abuse, not venial unhappiness or lack of compatibility, justified wrenching a family apart. Just as she'd believed so long ago, she still maintained that one should keep up pretenses, however unhappy the marriage was, for the sake of the children. Refusing to blink at the price children paid for divorce, she completely sidestepped the physical or emotional well-being of the unhappily married couple.

She also plunged into the turbulence of remarriage and stepparenting, an issue she had given little thought when she was a young wife. Unconsciously implying her own low expectation of men's domesticity and her assumption of the husband as breadwinner, she explained that a stepfather naturally had a "comparatively easy" task, since earning a living required most of his time. The man, the "family member least often at home" had only to be "kind and decent," and he would win everyone's affections. In contrast, fairy-tale lore had forever tainted the word *stepmother,* an image Emily suggested upending by showing steady, patient love. "A stepmother has a dozen quicksands to build bridges across, before she can reach firm ground on which to meet the temperament and gain the confidence of each child in turn," she said. The stepmother who "inherits" the children when they are babies faces the problems typical of new mothers everywhere. Then, when she gives birth to her biological children, "tactless people say to the older child" things like "The boy is her *own* baby—you're only her stepchild!" Such people, Emily practically spat out, "ought to be boiled in oil."

Months after the book's publication, while speaking in Edgartown, Emily advised her audience to tell children "early" of their parentage. "One tactful parent" she knew well had told her adopted child that "out of all the babies in the world we had to choose from, we chose you because we felt that you were the very nicest."

Children Are People was dedicated "To Billy." "I knew the book was for me, in essence," Bill Post says. "In many ways, especially compared to relationships today, my grandmother and I had a rather formal one. Yet we loved each other deeply, and I never doubted how important I was to her. Grandmama enjoyed providing for me many of the things she recommended in her book for children," he recalls fondly. "Most of all, I know where those pages that urge parents to read to their children came from—she read aloud to me all the time. Books such as *Alice in Wonderland,* Kipling's *Jungle Book*—that kind of thing." One of the few early photographs of Emily with her young sons shows Ned sitting at her knees and Bruce on her lap, listening as she concentrates hard on the text, her senses clearly engaged. She continued the tradition with her grandson and later, in spite of her eyesight, tried her best to read aloud to her great-grandchildren as well.

The young war widow Libby Cookman didn't read this book upon its publication, four years before she married Bill Post. But her fiancé had been brought up in large part on its precepts, his grandmother influencing him as much as anyone, he believes. Libby's baby son Allen was a Post from the first day Emily held him in her arms, the child not of her blood but of her heart, and she made sure everyone knew it. Yvonne Sylvia remembers that "Bill Post was especially kind and generous to Allen's biological grandparents, whose son had been killed in the war." There would be no legal ambiguities after her death, either: her will specified that equal estate portions be granted to her great-grandchildren, including Allen Post, "adopted son of William."

CHAPTER 61

❖

$\mathcal{U}$NTIL MAY 1940, WHEN GERMANY DEFEATED FRANCE, AMERICANS couldn't be blamed for conspicuously ignoring the escalating terror in Europe. During September, however, London became the target of sustained bombing, which continued for the next eight months. Emily's friends living in the city left for the English countryside within weeks of the first attack. An average of two hundred bombers battered London nightly, with the Blitz claiming forty-three thousand lives and a million residences. On October 15 alone, a six-hour attack by four hundred bombers was resisted by a meager forty-one RAF fighters. Along with most middle-class Americans, Emily listened to the voice of Edward R. Murrow; using shortwave, he described the scene on *London After Dark*. The radio refused to let the war stay overseas, as citizens around the nation sensed the conflict creeping closer to their hitherto invulnerable homes.

That autumn, however, Emily addressed office, rather than national, politics. On September 22, her syndicated newspaper column (a copy of which she uncharacteristically saved) tackled the workplace. Detailing ways that smart office protocol made employees appear indispensable, she wrote with the enthusiastic, sure tone that guaranteed her an audience. Now she constructed a scenario about a highly successful worker quietly commanding the office. To the reader's presumed surprise, this superworker turned out to be a woman. Today, Emily emphasized, this composite was characteristic of many fifty-year-old women spearheading America's workplaces. Minimally trained upon their hiring, they had quickly become exemplars for their fellow citizens. Such an employee represented "the typical competent American woman whose heart is in her job, and who is blessed with plain common sense!"

Focusing on office life afforded Emily a subject many less intrepid columnists would avoid even today. Refusing to flinch from the awkward, even back in 1922, when she addressed the matter briefly in *Etiquette,* she now used *Good Housekeeping* magazine to promote awareness of possible "personal" offenders, from onions to "bodily defects," which, presumably, included everything from bad breath to flatulence to hygiene: "If [a woman] should ever notice that people seem to draw away from her, she should ask a friend the reason. If she tells her that it is a personal unpleasantness she shouldn't resent her friend's truthfulness. The chances are that her druggist can give her an immediate cure, but if he can't then she can go to her doctor." Otherwise, she reasoned, an embarrassed employer, too shy to tell her the truth, might fire the unsuspecting worker with a trumped-up reason. "The strangest angle of this not uncommon situation," Emily pointed out, "is that the sufferer is herself completely immunized and therefore unaware of this unpleasantness."

Having stayed on the Vineyard later than usual that year, in early October, before returning to New York, she spoke about her forthcoming book on children to a group of sixty women from the Edgartown Women's Club. During her appearance, she was interviewed by a local reporter, who was surprised when Emily used his forum to campaign for Republican presidential contender Wendell Willkie. Though she seldom talked about politics, "Mrs. Post wanted to speak about the third term that President Roosevelt was seeking: 'Washington and Jefferson . . . refused third terms because they knew the love of power would overcome the good they'd achieved,'" she explained. Though Willkie had initially sounded suspiciously idealistic to scared voters, with his "one world" concept of global cooperation, now, as the election drew closer, the candidate took a hard line, accusing the government of being soft on defense preparations. To Emily, who had also campaigned for Al Smith, Wendell Willkie just sounded practical.

GRADUALLY, REVIEWS OF ANYTHING Emily Post wrote began to exhibit a subtle smugness, inspired by a faint shift in journalists' attitude toward what she stood for as well as to her advanced years. Occasionally, the implication that an aged Emily Post was necessarily out of date underlay the prose. Gentle prodding, making fun of an authority no longer in command, suddenly went with the territory that Emily had comfortably overseen for the past two decades.

By the end of 1940, she was reading polite but lackluster reviews of her *Children Are People: And Ideal Parents Are Comrades.* The unenthusiastic responses almost apologized for endorsing a near dinosaur of an author. "At first glance the idea of 'etiquette for children' may seem artificial or stereo-typed," wrote the *New York Times,* "but readers should be assured forthwith that the principles and precepts here underscored are neither of those things." In her "essentially human pages," Emily "wisely" harnessed her high "ideals . . . to specific conditions and problems." The author "believes that the happiest homes are those in which courtesy, consideration and self-control are joined with comradeship between parents and children; she be-lieves in gentleness and resourcefulness and poise." *Time* magazine seemed to review her book out of a bored courtesy: "Today, at 67 [she had turned sixty-eight that fall], Mrs. Post is still undisputed autocrat of U.S. etiquette. Mrs. Post has long had another ambition: to write a Blue Book for raising children. . . . Mrs. Post likes old-fashioned ways best." Emily had argued against the "unrestrained self-expression" currently in fashion, believing children needed to be kindly kept in check instead, a position she did not believe old-fashioned at all.

At least the public school principal Angelo Patri, a writer of a syndi-cated newspaper column himself, "Our Children," sent a more than polite thank-you letter to Emily in early December, which the usually unsenti-mental woman kept. Like Emily's *Etiquette,* Patri's book *Child Training* had been published in 1922, the year New York City's boxing enthusiasm peaked; the innovative educator and immigrant subsequently used the ac-tivity to channel the anger of troubled boys in his Bronx school. Emily ad-mired him and had mailed him an advance copy of her own child-rearing book, an act he promptly acknowledged: "I have been enjoying your book, every word of it is so true and so helpful—before writing to thank you for your kindness in sending it to me. Your thoughts of me touched and de-lighted me beyond words. I shall treasure the book doubly: as a fine piece of work, and as a cherished gift from a great lady of America. Sincerely, An-gelo Patri." Emily was so gratified that her book passed muster with Patri that she would later share the letter, "proud and pleased," with Yvonne Sylvia, on Martha's Vineyard.

Patri's widely publicized work in support of educating the nation's chil-dren and directing their frustrations outward must have been much on her mind these days, or she would never have sent him a gift copy of *Children Are People*. On December 13, an audience crowded the grand ballroom of the Waldorf-Astoria Hotel for an afternoon panel sponsored by the National Association of Manufacturers, "Women's Responsibility in Preparing America's Future," with national defense obviously the real subject under discussion. Emily, part of a panel of four, turned the topic into improving educational systems instead of pouring the government's money into general relief causes, as she believed was now the case. She was deeply dismayed at the expense of Roosevelt's New Deal, especially in its diversion of money to artists, who, she thought she had helped prove, could be privately subsidized. She urged women to learn the record of candidates "even for local offices" and, most of all, to be sure to cast their ballots. If she was chastened at the memory of her lack of enthusiasm when asked to campaign for the vote years ago, she gave no sign.

IN SPITE OF THE distressing condescension directed toward her the past few years, Emily had reason to feel content. The 1941 edition of *Current Biography* began her entry by noting her cultural importance: "It seems incredible that as late as 1921 [Emily Post] was not part of our national vocabulary." The essay noted that "Mrs. Post's own views on etiquette have changed considerably" since her earlier writings, her advice in 1940's *Children Are People* minimizing the importance of proper "form" even further. For Emily, the titles following her name said it all: "author, radio commentator, arbiter of etiquette." A well-respected encyclopedia had finally granted precedence to her life as a writer—not first and foremost an authority on etiquette. Almost defiantly, she had submitted to the editors an older photograph that highlighted her short hair, softly waved above her ears. Her skin was still translucent, and in the picture her small mouth didn't yet turn down at the corners. Two strands of pearls, one long, the other lying against her neck, adorned a flowered blouse, which, she vaguely suggested in a subsequent interview, she had designed and even sewn herself.

Between sponsoring lunches for business contacts and sharing meals with her son or Katharine Collier, Emily had developed a satisfying daily routine. Katharine, with her frequent chitchat about the Roosevelts' contentious affairs, state and otherwise, provided a perfect forum through which the writer could keep in touch with the political world, motivating Emily to register change on grounds other than the domestic, cultural level of etiquette and ethics. Both women leaned toward a libertarian position, wherein the "defense of every conceivable freedom" resulted, paradoxically, in a free market that pitted poor and rich, native and immigrant, man and woman—all in theory—against each other as equals. The friends believed in freedom and dignity for all the world's people, but they also thought that human beings saw the world refracted through their "national community"—in Emily's case, as "an American"—where they had to work hard in order to achieve equality for all of its citizens.

Katharine's daughter, Katharine Collier St. George, would serve as New York state representative from 1946 until 1964. Her complicated politics shed light on the beliefs of her mother and her mother's best friend, fleshing out ideas about women's abilities that the older women considered sacred. An "ardent Republican," the younger Katharine was also known as an outspoken advocate of equal rights for women (supporting an early equal rights amendment). Like Emily and Katharine, whom many believed to be elitists, Katharine Collier St. George was strongly opposed to "protective legislature" for women, claiming women neither "need nor want" such paternalism. Instead, they sought "to be free to work as equals, asking for no special privileges, but insisting on equality of opportunity and pay." Yet in spite of their political differences, Katharine St. George maintained a cordial relationship with the president, who would die just before she first took office.

Because of her close association with Katharine Collier, Emily occasionally socialized with President and Mrs. Roosevelt. From vague comments she made to her grandson, however, it was not only the president who failed to win Emily's vote; she didn't admire the first lady either. Echoing the lessons of Josephine Price, Emily deemed Eleanor far too pushy about getting things done. Though the first lady was twelve years younger, she still came from the Gilded Age that had produced Emily Post, and she exhibited some of the same personality traits. Possessed by a deep-rooted horror of wasting time, Eleanor was impatient with the slowness of ocean liners, choosing the new option of the airplane every time, while Franklin solicited "her companionship on languid trips by boat and train" to no avail. Just like Emily Post, when she had a mission, she wanted to execute it at once, without delay. Lillian Gilbreth, Emily Post, Eleanor Roosevelt, even Alva Vanderbilt: it's as if the new professional woman, sure of her right to be where she was, didn't have time to waste anymore, nor the emotional reserves to spend on the maintenance of a husband.

Perhaps Emily also mistrusted the aura of do-gooder some believed clung to Eleanor Roosevelt. But the deeper reason surely included the envy the first lady bred. After all, she conducted her marriage as a throwback to Emily's parents' generation, primarily for the sake of the children, redefining ways to live together in lieu of a divorce. Though her husband's mistresses were more than suspected in government and social circles, Eleanor—and the president—maintained appearances, however minimal. The family came first, at least in its public persona.

Like Emily, Eleanor Roosevelt did not depend on men for her emotional life after her de facto separation from her husband. Unlike Emily, she was still married, creating her private space within the context of a very public marriage. It was what Emily would have liked to salvage with Edwin. Somehow Eleanor Roosevelt had managed to keep her marriage without compromising her individuality—and certainly without shortchanging her work. Seeing such a success story, in its own way, must have galled Emily, who had tried hard but had failed to dictate her own marital terms.

IN FEBRUARY 1941, Hitler, seeking sovereignty over the Atlantic, began attacking British port cities. The Germans aimed the bombs at civilian rather than industrial targets, but with Britain's increased radar-controlled defenses, the Luftwaffe's losses mounted dramatically, increasing from 28 planes in January to 124 five months later. Finally, if only to prepare for the invasion of Russia, the German command ended the Blitz in May, just after the British Museum and Houses of Parliament were severely damaged in one of Germany's strategic demoralization attacks.

As if to stay distracted—she had friends and relatives overseas, including in England—Emily granted more interviews than usual. She had no intention of ceding control over her schedule just because she had hired efficient secretaries. Juggling her radio broadcasting and her column, she fit in a lengthy interview for *Reader's Digest* with Hildegarde Dolson, a young woman determined to be a second Dorothy Parker.

From the beginning of their encounter, a friendly tug-of-war seemed the order of the day. Dolson would seek personal information, either about Emily's divorce or her income, and Emily would parry cleverly. Dolson then feinted, and Emily dodged. This back-and-forth went on for several hours, intricate enough that years later Dolson, by then a *New Yorker* writer, would include a humorous piece about the interview in her collection of essays, concluding that Emily was a "very nice woman" in spite of it all.

In June, another friendly dialogue was published. Probably because Margaret Case Harriman had produced such a strong interview several years earlier in the *Saturday Evening Post,* Emily had consented to a second meeting with her, this time for *Reader's Digest,* the audience enthusiastic for more about Emily Post after the interview with Dolson that spring. While the women talked, Emily sat comfortably on the couch with her legs drawn up and her feet tucked under. Her hands nonetheless fluttered compulsively, "busy with one of the gadgets—eyeshades, file boxes, and so on—she likes to make out of colored pictures clipped from magazines and stuck together with gummed tape," Harriman reported. The sign of a person on the go, Emily's edgy hands were often remarked upon as she grew older, as if age was not going to slow her down. Clearly startling Harriman, Emily, after she'd finished eating, plopped "her elbows on the table."

AT THE END of the year, questions about good taste lost their fascination as the nation shifted from debate to commitment in a matter of minutes. On Sunday, December 7, the Japanese killed or wounded over three thousand American military personnel at Pearl Harbor, sinking or crippling eight battleships and thirteen other vessels and destroying nearly two hundred aircraft. On the day after the debacle, the roll call on the floors of the House and Senate met with a near-unanimous accord: the Senate voted 82 to 0 and the House 388 to 1 to grant President Roosevelt's request to declare war on Japan.

"We interrupt this program to bring you a special news bulletin. The Japanese have attacked Pearl Harbor, Hawaii, by air" framed America's collective memory of December 7, 1941. Contrary to those recollections, no bulletin actually interrupted network programming that day. Instead, exploiting new technologies seven years later, engineers spliced together two separate recordings to "re-create" FDR's famous radio message. In a testimony to the power of the radio, even now, the catastrophe seared into their minds, people still swear they heard the announcement themselves, just hours after the attack.

⊱⊰

PEARL HARBOR CHANGED EVERYTHING—FOR THE COUNTRY, AND for Emily's radio career. The war quickly rendered niche shows expendable, even as the Armed Forces Radio Service, or AFRS, boasted 306 stations for military personnel worldwide. Nonetheless, as Emily focused her daily newspaper column on questions created by the war, ranging from private Department of State inquiries about protocol to suggestions on carpooling, she secured a fresh currency. She reveled in having her advice sought, and to matter during wartime was a great acknowledgment indeed.

Though not signed to a show of her own that season, she began the year by appearing on Alma Kitchell's radio program on WJZ. But soon she found even such guest slots becoming scarce, as being nice to one another hardly seemed relevant to the order of the day. The columnist Henry McLemore, complaining irately that military training was too soft, wrote, "Uncle Sam, let's take the likes of Emily Post off the General Staff. Please, let's forget the military counterparts of how to hold your fork, which spoon to use and when to use it, and who leads whom into the smoking room. . . . Hasn't Hitler been in operation long enough for us to have learned that when he dropped his first calling card in the form of a bomb, Adolf ended all national courtesy?"

After the United States officially entered the war at the end of the year, Funk and Wagnalls, deciding that their bestseller needed to be revamped to fit the times, suggested that Emily plan an amended version of *Etiquette,* to be published in 1942. Relieved to have the assignment distracting her from worrying constantly about Bill and his friends, Emily revised the 1940 edition by adding a thirteen-page "War-Time Supplement" to the book's conclusion. Ernie Pyle, the popular journalist who was in London describing the unimaginable for Americans back home, suggested in one of his newspaper columns that British officers in training be required to read *Etiquette*—thus they would become officers and gentlemen at the same time. The plucky trainees subsequently adopted as their nickname the "Emily Posters," with Betty Grable and Emily Post the military's new favorite pinup girls. When the *Chicago Daily News* picked up the story and embellished it, orders flooded Funk and Wagnalls's office within hours. After Pyle's remark, requests to USO clubs for *Etiquette* ran second only to orders for the *Rand McNally Atlas.* Ninety military chaplains, endorsing Emily Post's marriage of etiquette with ethics, would use the book "to advise men under their guidance."

The new supplement was, above all else, pragmatic, explaining that it was not only acceptable but necessary at times to ignore certain conventions on the nation's behalf. "Etiquette," Emily stressed, "is not a fixed subject." Unexpected drama called for improvisation. From permitting women to write to anonymous soldiers, to girls dancing with strangers, to weddings performed on furlough and marriage reunions held "at [military] camp," etiquette, she explained,

> like our living language is seemingly rigid but actually fluid. The times in which we live are constantly producing new and, therefore, puzzling situations. We gladly accept forms that are helpful but we have little patience with those whose purpose is the preservation of form for form's sake. It has long been my particular occupation not only to urge keeping those precepts and customs of practical use and to discard those which no longer serve, but also to meet the new problems constantly arising. It is this increasing fusing together of the new with the old, that has kept this book from becoming a collection of dry-dust maxims, to which "Finis" might otherwise have been written twenty years ago.

Of all the revisions of *Etiquette* since its initial publication in 1922, the 1942 version bore the most specific marks of its moment in American history. Where else would she discuss the returning veteran? If the soldier was an old friend, "tell him how glad you are to see him back; and show that you are, not only by looking glad but by paying enough thoughtful attention to adjust your mood to his." He might seem "absent-minded, untalkative or tense: try to realize what he has been through and be patient." Don't badger him about a job: let him find his own way back. "Try to follow his lead with friendly but uninquisitive interest in anything he has to tell you. But whatever you do don't ask him questions about what the war was like, or what he thinks or feels about getting home—unless he himself brings up these subjects."

Emily also warned—carefully—against subversive activity that endangered the country. Acknowledging the inherent dangers a nation at war faced, she nonetheless cautioned against suspecting aliens unfairly. Stressing consideration for recent immigrants, Emily tried—with her usual tact and a bit more circumlocution than normal—to urge citizens to be fair and patriotic both. Her opening is worth quoting:

> Because in us Americans flows the blood of every race and creed, there is no country in the world where there is so great a need of wise appraisal, of sensitive understanding of our countrymen.
>
> The Janus-faced difficulty of this most important aspect of [wartime] etiquette is, on the one side, the need for alertness lest subversive elements take us unawares, and on the other the equally great need to avoid mistrusting those who are completely loyal to the principles of our Founding Fathers.
>
> When we encounter one whose behavior causes doubt of his loyalty, censorship of our impulses is only fair play, both now and in the years after the war. There is, however, this warning which must be given: IF someone does or says something definitely threatening to our government, write a letter to the F.B.I. or to the governor of your State, or the mayor, or to the sheriff of your township. Or, if you prefer, you can telephone. In any case make your evidence definite and brief.

As she was finishing her revisions, which inevitably engaged profoundly important national issues, Emily fussed privately about what she knew to be trivial by comparison: finding appropriate help for her upcoming summer on the Vineyard. She was apprehensive; the greater she felt the infirmities of age, the more she realized she depended upon others. Worst of all, her beloved Hilda Ogren had died that year, the elderly servant's cause of death and place of burial unremarked in Ned Post's memoir of his mother, almost as if he was fighting his own jealousy of this loyal longtime companion. With her passing, Emily's last full-time, consistent connection with a professional servant ended.

Even her local help had changed: Natalie (Betty's cousin) had proved unable to return that spring. Luckily, Edgartown's librarian heard that Emily Post needed a secretary, and she urged her daughter, about to graduate from high school, to apply for the job. Yvonne Sylvia was hired on the spot, assisting Emily each summer for the next fifteen years. Still a teenager, Yvonne was especially eager to help her employer stay up to date. Soon Emily was quizzing her, just as she did anyone who would indulge her, on everything from current wedding details to the best ways of dealing with wartime privations. "It was kind of exciting to see things I knew were modeled on my wedding appear in Mrs. Post's writing," Yvonne remembers to this day.

"Even though we were several generations apart, you could say we were two women aging together," she suggests. "Emily Post was always so easy to work for. She was warm, really human, especially with her grandson, Bill. She loved children. After my first child was born, I took my infant with me to work each day, and Mrs. Post bought clothes and furniture for him." Nor did Emily forget that mothers needed a break. Emily paid for a babysitter on the premises, and sent Yvonne's children to camp when they were older. "If it was a particularly miserable day, Mrs. Post would give me a check and say, 'Go buy yourself a hat in a bright color to cheer up your family and yourself while it's dismal outside.'"

Yvonne found her employer's lack of ceremony remarkable, both in the 1940s and thereafter. "She was never really formal with me; often she'd dictate into her Dictaphone, that vivid red 'Suzy,' while she was still in bed, and I'd go into her bedroom and she would sit there, completely at ease. Half the days, she worked in her bed jacket, but other times she was dressed. Sometimes she used the library-office she kept downstairs. Almost always, though, she had her feet up, on the bed or on a sofa.

"She really spread out on that sofa—it was wide and comfortable—with Suzy set up beside her, like her best friend," Yvonne recalls. "She spoke to it in a low voice, but every once in a while she'd burst out laughing, hard, almost a guffaw. She had a great sense of humor and was always smiling." Asked what, in light of such vivid memories, she considered Emily Post's most dominant characteristic, Yvonne Sylvia barely paused: "Her sweetness . . . she was truly a sweet person. And I could tell she missed Hilda, and that made her even more human."

BESIEGED WITH QUESTIONS about state and military protocol, Emily continued focusing on the ever-changing rules and rituals of the American armed forces. That winter, she sent advice about hitchhiking to the Regional News Bureau of the Office of War Information. With gasoline at a premium in 1942, the war effort demanded that everyone, including those working for the Defense Department, wherever they were stationed, endorse conservation measures. In her typically detailed fashion, Emily explained the safest ways for women to "hitch" rides to and from work with men they had never before met. It was crucial, she explained, to follow the Defense Department rules: one must exhibit one's identification badge prominently, just as police officers did, so that it would be clear why a girl was thumbing a ride, as well as what direction she needed to take. The badges' designations, B or C, saved the driver from going out of the way to deliver a hitchhiker in the opposite direction.

Moreover, as unfeeling as it seemed, hitchhikers should remember that these charitable shared rides were professional, not social occasions. Talk should be confined to a minimum, for everyone's sake—in part to avoid unintentionally disclosing "dangerous information." The *New York Times* reprinted most of the lengthy disquisition.

But though Emily Post endorsed the logic of the age in urging women to hitchhike, she failed to accept that "anything goes." In December, a gossipy *New York Times* column, "Heard in New York," reported the kind of anecdote about her that at least amused the younger press corps, not convinced of etiquette's value. A soldier, a marine, and two women, waiting for a United Press photographer to shoot scenes of Emily showing them how to conduct themselves at USO canteen dances, did or said something offensive to their earnest instructor. "Mrs. Post suddenly left without being part of the pictures," the *Times* announced. The tag line of the newspaper article hinted at the jocular disrespect Emily was continuing to experience as she grew old. "Miss Post," the photographer shouted after her, "you didn't even say 'Pardon me.' "

The year ended with a more solemn reminder of the country's new reality. Blackout restrictions throughout the East Coast cities meant that no glittering ball would welcome in 1943. Instead, there was one minute of si-

398 | LAURA CLARIDGE

lence, followed by a recording of church bells. As far as America was concerned, radio remained the major revolution of the day, in spite of the handicaps hobbling its progress. Only 700,000 radio sets were sold in 1943, due to the wartime ban on nonessential electronic manufacturing, down from the 13 million sets bought in 1941. The scarcity of shellac, a strategic war material, caused the number of phonograph records to decline, the lack causing the Armed Forces Radio Service to distribute vinyl records to its military radio stations. In spite of the temporary restrictions, radio remained a racehorse just waiting for the gate to lift, television right on its heels.

⨳

*S*HOWN ACCEPTING A HEAVY BAG FROM A GROCER, THE SEVENTY-year-old Emily Post explained to the readers of the *Washington Post,* "I carry my own parcels home. . . . A bulky parcel is a woman's badge of wartime service." Exhibiting the same self-assurance she had used to describe Mrs. Three-in-One a decade and a half earlier, now, on behalf of the war effort, she was photographed for the newspaper's February 2 edition to illustrate "Emily Post's Wartime Rules." One picture showed her repairing a worn outlet plug on an electric beater, confidently teaching a young woman to restore the damaged product herself, rather than discard her appliance. Had her sight not been impaired, Emily undoubtedly would have actually carried her own packages and made her own repairs. Instead, she used her celebrity clout, urging readers to do so, as well as to donate books for the "boys at the front"; she herself was photographed giving the Office of Civilian Defense "as many books" as she could.

She fed several well-rehearsed anecdotes to those older reporters who knew they could depend upon Emily Post for intelligent domestic news. Of recent note, she recounted, she had felt terribly irritated when an officer had suggested that military women, the Waves and the Waacs, address all superiors—male and female—as "Sir." "There's nothing that denotes masculinity so much as 'sir,' " Emily insisted. "Holding out for 'ma'am,' " the reporter wrote, "she scoffs at women officers who think the word isn't stylish."

Newsweek noted that the Bell Syndicate was now distributing Emily's daily column to ninety-eight newspapers, with 5.5 million readers, "said to be at its highest popularity in its twelve-year history." The Office of War Information and army and navy officials practically badgered her for information about manners. *Etiquette*'s recently enlarged wartime edition had been selling a steady one thousand copies weekly throughout the war, its greatest popularity in army camps, "where soldiers want to know how to act on blind dates" the *Newsweek* journalist opined, amused, in spite of her indisputable popularity, at Emily's status.

It may have been Emily's undiminished success that caused envious or resentful editors to feature her as such an amusing anachronism. In May, adjacent to the *New York Times*' Letters to the Editor page, headlining "Punishment for War Guilt" as the day's weighty subject, and under the title "Topics of the *Times*," appeared "Etiquette and the War," a reprint of a recent article Emily had published. "To knit or not to knit when one is part of a large audience listening to an important speech" was its topic. Recently Emily had been besieged by women who worried that they appeared rude while knitting socks for the troops: "Even in these days when one should not waste a minute, does it not seem disrespectful for a number of the women in an audience, listening to a speaker, to continue their knitting?" her readers questioned. Emily waffled: she herself wouldn't mind listeners knitting while she spoke, but ideally, one would simply ask speakers their preference before the lecture began. Whatever the answer, the newspaper's trivialization of her topic, by printing it side by side with a discussion of war guilt, seemed newly mean-spirited.

JUST AS EMILY POST was feeling the insults of what would be called "ageism" in the twenty-first century, American women were forging ahead in her own. Visibly needed, they proved irreplaceable cogs in a successful national endeavor to safeguard the nation. And with their centrality to the war effort came respect. There was nothing frivolous about being female these days. In 1942, Westinghouse for War Production had published a poster, *We Can Do It,* by J. Howard Miller, in which a physically strong and relentlessly cheerful young female assumed a mythic persona. As part of the government's ambivalent campaign to encourage paid work for women, the character Rosie the Riveter began to appear everywhere after a song in early 1943 saluted the working woman of the age as "loyal, efficient, patriotic, and pretty." On May 29, 1943, the *Saturday Evening Post* published on its cover what would become the most widely circulated visual image of Rosie, by Norman Rockwell. After Rockwell's illustration appeared, Rosie images became ubiquitous, and soon ads were created showing women competing to drive the most rivets into bombers.

Rosie the Riveter was in many ways the kind of woman Emily had been promoting all her adult life. It was as if the model Emily had endorsed since 1922 suddenly, finally, commanded center stage. If she was too old to take the leading role, by rights Emily should have received credit for the script. Independent, cheerful, hardworking, socially responsible to one's community: Rosie was even attractive, beauty a quality that Emily had never denied made life easier. It was as if Emily Post's intuitive version of the capable, modern woman had come to life. She had believed in her even before Rosie had a name. Now, as the number of women working outside the home increased over 50 percent from 1940, numbering 20 million by 1944, she was pleased, even if it had taken a war to prove that women were capable beings.

Emily and an ever more infirm Katharine Collier each pitched in for the war effort as best they could, contributing money to charitable causes and lending their names whenever someone they deemed worthy asked. According to Yvonne Sylvia, Emily seemed slightly dejected during this period. From the spring to the fall, Edgartown's distance from the city made Ned reluctant to visit his mother, and she rarely saw Bill these days, Washington demanding most of his attention. Many of her friends were living with their own offspring, and even Katharine was spending more time at Tuxedo Park, with the St. Georges. "Maybe that's one reason Mrs. Post was so naturally kind to the servants," Yvonne suggests. "They were like her surrogate children."

That summer, the *Saturday Evening Post* paid Emily what turned out to be a double-edged compliment by selecting her to be part of a series of cartoons. In "People You Know," Emily's caricature showed a woman caught dunking a doughnut in her coffee. Accompanied by whimsical, good-natured doggerel, the last four lines implied a stuffiness that had never conveyed what Emily Post stood for.

Gravy-soppers, table hoppers,
Swear off while you're able!
He who dunks may dine in heaven,
But not at Emily's table.

As usual, the truth about etiquette was otherwise: Emily considered it fine for knowing adults to "dunk," if the circumstances were informal. Dinner parties, of course, were something else entirely. So were the rules for children who were still learning basic good manners.

In September, widely syndicated maverick journalist Henry McLemore, the gadfly who had already written off Emily Post as an artifact two years earlier, now penned a column sarcastically but half-seriously proclaiming that her rules for gracious living had damaged the war effort. The parodic article, entitled "Doughboy Etiquette for Occupation of Italy," began: "I am beginning to believe that courtesy is the secret weapon of the Allied invading forces. Our boys kill the enemy with kindness. If you doubt me, then you haven't read that guidebook to social behavior issued to the members of the British Eighth Army just before they took off from Sicily for a landing on the Italian mainland. It lays down the rules for almost everything except how to eat spaghetti and the proper use of the finger bowl. Let me quote a few of the paragraphs of instructions, and then you try to figure out whether Eisenhower, Montgomery, Alexander or Emily Post is in charge of the occupation." He then cited what he considered extraneous rules aimed at adapting to local customs: "don't consider that you have the right to be served before any civilian" and "don't drive furiously down narrow village streets, scaring pedestrians and livestock in all directions." The wisdom of honoring the conventions of the defeated escaped him entirely.

As the year came to its wobbly conclusion, *This Week* magazine published Emily's article "How to Treat Them," which *Reader's Digest* reprinted the following February. The essay was updated from the advice she'd given in the wartime edition of *Etiquette*: disabled veterans required special tact; a "wife or mother or sweetheart" must prepare herself ahead of time for whatever she would discover. Emily's description reads like an incident from William Wyler's *The Best Years of Our Lives,* the lessons of which were served up in *Etiquette* first. Her insistence that physical injuries obvious to the eye somehow be acknowledged—even as love reduced them to insignificance—would be a theme of Wyler's 1946 movie.

"From now on," Emily noted in *This Week,* "more and more of our seriously wounded will appear in public. What are we going to do and say when they leave the hospitals and take their places in the world for which they have given so much? We will do well to follow the first rules of good manners, which are: don't stare, don't point, don't make personal remarks."

Some soldiers, Emily conceded, might want to talk about their injuries, a desire to be respected and responded to. "But most of them will resent such callous impertinence—bitterly." What they and people close to them inevitably sought in potentially awkward situations was to be treated without fuss. "The greatest kindness we can show our injured is not to let our own thoughts dwell on their handicaps," she wrote. To that end, when their impairments created special needs, one must proceed as if "matter-of-fact," whether leaning over to cut a man's steak or helping him into his coat when he stood up.

Most challenging would be the need for courage in the case of great disfigurement: "The supreme requirement of tact will be exacted of the one whom a badly hurt man most longs and yet most fears to see—that first meeting when a man searches his wife's or mother's face to measure the degree of his handicap. Both wife and mother must school themselves to keep tears under control. They must remember that the one thing that helps is to make him realize he is not any different from the man he was—and to assure him that he is NOT to be set apart."

CHAPTER 64

❖

AS THE WAR INCREASINGLY OCCUPIED THE SCHEDULES NOT only of middle-class workers but of America's young socialites as well, who volunteered to wrap bandages, visit the sick, or provide transportation, their mothers gathered at a series of forums chaired by Eleanor Roosevelt. At one such seminar, Emily met Doris Stevens, a well-known leader of the suffrage movement and Alva Vanderbilt Belmont's assistant years earlier. There is no trail for their friendship, no clues suggesting how it deepened, but their epistolary exchange casts important light on Emily's awareness of her own limitations and her lifelong resolve to rise above them.

After the colloquium, Stevens wrote Emily a letter, offering her a copy of her autobiography. Upon receiving the book, even before opening it, Emily immediately sent off a chipper thank-you note, accompanied by a newspaper clipping from the pen of *Christian Science Monitor* reporter Mary Hornaday, a watchdog over the first lady. Hornaday's article apparently criticized Eleanor Roosevelt, including her support of suffragettes, quoting disparagingly some of Roosevelt's opinions, which Emily assumed Doris too would disdain. "I can't bear to have you miss [Roosevelt's] 'garblings' enclosed. Of all the glamourous sobbings this is the sobbingist! It was so nice seeing you—do make it soon again and *here*." It was signed, "Affection- ately, Emily Post" with a scribble on the bottom: "*Many* thanks for lovely card."

Her deep respect for Doris Stevens and her desire to be liked by her peer resonate in their correspondence. But Emily had miscalculated her new friend's own highly political history. Snuggled down in her bed to read

Stevens's *Jailed for Freedom,* seventy-one-year-old Emily stayed up through the early morning to finish the activist's memoir. Horrified, she soon realized that she had not only inadvertently insulted its author with her flippant note but had dishonored herself as well. She tried to phone Stevens several times, getting no answer.

A note from Stevens soon arrived, remonstrating with Emily for her disrespect toward those early feminists who had marched for voting rights. Chastened, Emily immediately replied. After typing "Dear Mrs. Stevens," then nervously crossing out the "Mrs." and writing "Dr." instead, she began in earnest: "Please forgive what I said about being against Suffrage—what a dreadful thing to say to you! Moreover, it is not true. (I have never been an obstructionist, but I find I was appallingly ignorant of what you went through.) Having had no interference with my own liberties, the right to earn a living, to keep what I earned, to have entire guardianship over my children and to get *extraordinary* credit for efforts that would have been nothing for a man (or a *trained* woman worker), left me sitting in the situation of having everything pleasant brought to me on a silver platter." As if afraid she had not been frank enough, Emily scribbled next to the typed paragraph, "I was very unaware of other points of view."

Whatever response Stevens sent to the apology, the ease of Emily's subsequent note wishing her correspondent a good trip implied she had been forgiven. As further appeasement, she offered to lend Stevens "Suzy," her Dictaphone, for the activist's summer project. She explained eagerly that she herself could carry a duplicate machine from Manhattan to the Vineyard. She signed her brief reply "Affectionately," in a communication that sounded wistful, as if Emily Post wished, after all, that she'd gotten a real education too.

In its own way, Emily's belated acknowledgment of her privileged position echoed the confession Virginia Woolf had made to working women the previous decade: "to show you how little I deserve to be called a professional woman, how little I know of the struggles and difficulties of such lives, I have to admit that instead of spending [my earnings] upon bread and butter, rent, shoes and stockings, or butcher's bills, I went out and bought a cat."

Privilege, however, saved a person from only so much. Though basically healthy, Emily herself didn't travel much anymore, finding that her infirmities drained her energies if she wasn't careful. On August 5, 1944, Billy got married in a wartime ceremony without his grandmother present. William

Goadby Post and Mrs. Elizabeth Lindley Cookman wed in the nation's capital, where they would live throughout his tour of duty. "Libby," whose first husband had been killed in the Pacific theater the year before, brought to the marriage her infant, Allen, immediately adopted by her new husband. As soon as they had a chance to slip away, the couple visited Emily in Edgartown, where she was already planning an addition to the cottage for baby Allen and the other children she was sure would follow.

"Upon our first meeting," Libby Post recalls, "she greeted me in the doorway of her house in Edgartown, with a broad smile and warm greeting. I particularly remember her bright red dress and red shoes—her favorites. Later I found out she had a closet full of red shoes. She made me feel very comfortable and immediately welcome." Bill and Libby saw Emily frequently for the next several years. The relationship between granddaughter-in-law and Emily was "extremely cordial if never intimate." But then, looking back, Bill remembers, "Grandmama and I always maintained a certain distance ourselves." Fond of the elderly woman so dear to her husband, Libby was nonetheless aware "of a certain narcissism, of her needing to be the center of attention. And of being very much into control."

Emily returned to Manhattan that fall to gratifying press: *Time* magazine cited her as one of the Bell Syndicate's stable of prize writers, used to woo Washington columnist Drew Pearson away from United Feature Syndicate. And she had the pleasure of hearing her name invoked by one of her favorite comedians, the ventriloquist Edgar Bergen, on his prime-time NBC radio show, with its nationwide audience of millions. Using his puppet Charlie McCarthy, Bergen routinely poked gentle fun at national figures, and teasing Emily Post, who later appeared on one of his broadcasts as "a vulture for culture," elicited one of the incongruous horsey guffaws her grandson remembers so vividly.

For the next few months, Emily worked on what Funk and Wagnalls correctly assumed would be her postwar version of *Etiquette*—essentially the same edition published three years earlier, except for minor changes. The "War-Time Supplement" was retitled "Military and Post-War Etiquette." Material added in 1942 would be reprinted in the 1945 version, including the espionage chapter, which would be dropped in 1950.

For the first time since 1922, there was a price hike, from $4 to $5. More significant to Emily, however, was her new dedication page, years after she had stopped dedicating *Etiquette* to anyone: "To Anne Kent, My invaluable assistant in affectionate recognition of her liberalizing influence throughout our long association." Kent had been clever from the start, carefully but quickly consolidating her power over Emily's "empire," becoming, she believed, indispensable. Emily, who in her younger days would not have tolerated the implicit disrespect, now looked the other way. The daily columns were beginning to wear on her, and she knew efficient help was hard to find. She wasn't about to play the prima donna with an impressive woman her son had, with great diligence, finally located for her. Still, it is hard to imagine Emily Post comfortable around someone who pretended not to hear her employer when she called upstairs for assistance.

Determined to keep current, Emily had hired the much younger woman in part to keep herself in touch with changing trends. Often, Emily used the daily column to address issues new to her and, she assumed, to others as well. In January 1945, the *Journal of the National Education Association* reprinted an article by a teacher complaining about high expectations and low pay. Most of all, the young woman felt imprisoned by the expectations governing her conduct and appearance. In the same issue, Emily responded:

> There are a number of things that I have long wanted an opportunity to say. One of these is to protest against those who seem to have kept a mid-Victorian hold on the conduct of teachers—and on them alone.
>
> The point I should like to make, to parents and school boards both, is that teachers are exactly like the rest of us. They must possess normal intelligence and sufficient education. They must be citizens. Surely then, they should not be denied the normal pleasure of social contacts, and the right to free expression of their views. To keep watch on how they spend their free time, what they say in the company of their friends, and to dictate the cut of their clothes, makes us look like Gestapo agents. On the other hand, a teacher— either young or old—has to realize that like the perfect parents, she is an unceasing example to the children in her class. If she is a really qualified teacher, her influence is immeasurable, and can easily be permanent.

Emily's unfortunate use of "Gestapo" in the context of teachers' wardrobes was motivated by her immersion in all things war, as she prepared her new edition of *Etiquette*. But however inappropriate her choice of words, she didn't deserve the comparison she would draw to the German führer just after the war ended. Speaking to 150 welfare workers at the Gary, Indiana, YMCA, a psychiatrist from Buffalo, Dr. Nathaniel Canton, told his audience that "Hitler and Emily Post are the two most detrimental personalities to present society." After all, he explained, grievously misreading one of his exemplars, both popular leaders bullied people to fit only one pattern, exerting "insidious control" over society as they did so.

DURING THE WAR, more copies of *Etiquette* were requested by GIs than any other book. As they prepared to return to civilian society, soldiers ordered an average of 16,000 copies a week. Impressive sales figures even today, in part because *Etiquette* was published only as a hardback and never sold through a club, they were by no means singular. By 1946, Dr. Benjamin Spock's *Common Sense Book of Baby and Child Care* would hit the marketplace, soon to leave numbers such as Emily's far behind. The war produced a flurry of popular paperbacks, with book clubs driving hardcover figures back up soon after it ended.

Emily was sick for longer periods those days. In a letter she wrote in March 1945 to Betty ("Mrs. Kyle Ward"), her young secretary on the Vineyard years before, she explained why she was late congratulating the Wards on their new baby: she had been "contagious up to now" and unable to get to the post office. Working hard to make up for lost time, she had suffered a relapse. Then, trying to send a telegram of congratulations to the Wards, she had learned that during wartime, "telegraph and telegrams of congratulation are *out.*" Only now was she strong enough to walk to the bank, buy the baby a bond, and put it in the mail.

Her illness delayed slightly her preparations for the Vineyard. She was in New York to read the perfervid headlines of a world still in the clutch of anxiety. On April 12, 1945, before she left for Edgartown, sixty-three-year-old President Roosevelt died suddenly of a cerebral hemorrhage, just three weeks before the Allies accepted Germany's surrender on May 8. Six days after the president's death, forty-four-year-old Ernie Pyle was killed by a sniper as he stepped ashore on a small island west of Okinawa. It was unsettling to lose two national icons so close together; the president had been in office for twelve years, and the reporter had followed the war from its beginnings. Sandwiched between their deaths, on April 15, Edward R. Murrow reported the liberation of the Buchenwald concentration camp. The fateful month came to a grisly end with the indelible image of Benito

Mussolini hanging upside down by his ankles in the center of Milan. At least the war would be over any day now.

As if promoting business as usual, in early July, New York's Mayor Fiorello La Guardia read the Sunday comics over the radio during a newspaper strike, emphasizing that the world did not depend on the print media, even for the frivolous. *Meet the Press* began on NBC, and it, not a music show or soap opera, would become the longest-running radio program in history.

In August, there would be Hiroshima and Nagasaki.

FOLLOWING THE WAR'S END, marriages seemed to dissolve at an accelerated pace. Except for the Depression era of the 1930s, the decade ahead would witness divorce rates rising to the highest in American history, with almost one in three marriages ending during the 1950s. But there were immediate positive social changes as well, with Americans widely embracing the concept of "the weekend," the employees' right to enjoy two entire, adjacent days of leisure in lieu of their jobs. Just as in Edwin's age, when the stock market and the fast car proved epochal markers, those two days off guaranteed that workers would become, according to some scholars, "the chief temporal institution of the modern age," a force to be reckoned with because now their presence couldn't be taken for granted. Suddenly bosses had to plan around their workers' schedules, with the weekend the new regulator of twentieth-century life.

Emily's problem was the opposite of seeking time off: she disliked days when she wasn't occupied with her job. Nonetheless, she was forced to take more breaks, if only to protect her eyes. Enforced recreation had its own rewards once Libby and Bill, who had accepted a job with Pan American airlines, moved to Rye, New York, just as Ned moved overseas. A reasonable thirty-minute drive to Manhattan, Rye wasn't a particularly strenuous distance from Martha's Vineyard either. "Emily was delighted to have great-grandchildren and was very fond of them, as they were of her, even as babies," Libby remembers. Yet in a bemused afterthought, she adds: "But I could never forget that she was definitely a character, very different from other women of the time. From all the women I knew, at least."

It was around this period that Bill first met his half uncles, the children born to Emily's ex-husband after the couple's divorce. At a Palm Beach hotel, a man in the lobby greeted Bill with "Hi, I'm your uncle Henry, your father's half brother." Neither Ned nor Emily had ever mentioned to Bill the existence of a second family, though Ned had enjoyed many summers at Babylon with the boys when he and Bruce were young men. "If I had pursued all this, and asked Grandmama about them, she would have answered. But she never would have talked about my grandfather," Bill asserts. In spite of Ned's closeness to Edwin, Ned too would fail to discuss him with Bill. Implicitly, Emily demanded a kind of allegiance from those she loved that proved their loyalty.

A few years later, in Boston, Bill would encounter his grandfather's widow, Eleanor ("Nellie") herself, in the dining room of the Ritz Carlton: he had heard nothing of her either. Asked what he thought of the "dauntingly dramatic English actress" that her granddaughter Nora Post recalled, Bill answered simply, "She seemed nice . . . perhaps a bit flamboyant."

A LOUD EXCLAMATION mark punctuated the end of 1945 for Emily, who, twenty years earlier, had written for *McCall's* magazine that she herself was "rather old-fashioned and, reluctantly, didn't feel confident enough" of her appearance "to dance in public these days." Now, at seventy-three years old, America's first lady of manners lost her panties in the middle of Manhattan. After watching them fall unceremoniously "to the pavement," she bent down and, "stuffing them" in her purse, proceeded. A rare reference to this bizarre episode was her offhand remark to an interviewer who, at length, had won the aging woman's trust. To Jeanne Perkins, Emily Post joked that she had finally "dropped her drawers on Broadway," the shocked reporter failing to connect the elderly woman's lifelong love of center stage to her cheerful pun.

Several years later Emily recast the incident into a more polite anecdote for an interview with *Suburbia Today*, reprinted in *Reader's Digest*. In this telling, an embarrassed lady, waiting in a White House receiving line, "realized with horror that a piece of her underwear was slipping. Before she could think what to do, her feet were entangled in a web of lace-trimmed silk. Instantly the aide was at her side. With grave dignity, he bent, picked up the offending panties and disappeared. Only the couple directly behind saw what had happened. Later, as she left, a footman offered her, on a silver tray, a discreetly wrapped package."

The actual, less elegant event on the sidewalk was oddly out of character not only with Emily's sense of decorum but with her meticulous grooming as well. One factor might be that her eyes had not fully recovered their earlier vision after the cataract surgery; even at their best, they would never allow her completely clear sight again. Or possibly Emily was losing physical control as she aged, ignoring mundane everyday maintenance such as replacing worn underwear (she had gained enough weight by now to stretch them severely). Perhaps she wanted to deny the change in her size, even if her servants had tactfully suggested buying new garments.

However embarrassing the dropped drawers must have been, the accident that followed at the end of the month brought the year to a more precipitous close than humiliation alone. On December 25, Emily broke her ankle, falling down the stairs as she was leaving her Upper East Side apartment for Christmas dinner. The only public comment about the matter was her own, when, the following spring, she told a reporter that she was grateful for two things at the time of the accident: "Thank heavens, I did not throw up," she recalled, and, as if mocking herself, added, "What's more, my hat was on straight the entire time!"

*L*ETTERS EMILY WROTE OVER THE FIRST FEW MONTHS OF 1946 TO her summer assistant suggest that her injuries were more serious than she admitted publicly. Thanking Yvonne Sylvia for the "delicious" holiday "chocolates—which I opened!!!"—Emily explained her silence of late: "Yvonne dear, I thought a floor was level and I fell down 3 marble steps! Am laid up in bed with two broken bones in my ankle and torn tendons and most of me black and blue."

While recuperating, Emily reread her 1922 edition of *Etiquette,* leading her to compare women in the business world of 1946 to the almost nonexistent scene a quarter of a century earlier. Inspired, she began writing newspaper columns about the transformations. "Ever-Changing Rules of Etiquette Must Conform to Modern Business" appeared on January 20. How should today's woman employee courting a man's business account deal with the social niceties? The seventy-three-year-old's advice was as practical as ever: treat a man just as you would any business associate whose business you sought. It was a good idea, for instance, to settle a luncheon bill out of sight or to establish a running account at one restaurant that would allow the woman to sign as she leaves. "To insist that a man pay a taxicab fare, lunch check, or even dinner check on an occasion that is strictly business and by rights her obligation is not only uncomplimentary to the woman, but belittling to her job," Emily noted. If, however, a man hoping to land an account were to ask the woman manager to lunch, he would pay. Emily paused to remind businesswomen that in general, male executives were accustomed to concise lunches: "This is not the place to practice leisurely conversation"—which, she implied, was a finely honed art among well-brought-up women.

Emily couldn't afford to grow complacent. Just as in the aftermath of World War I, when the market for etiquette books had exploded, a sudden show of interest requisitioned the subject of manners again. Even *Vogue* magazine had published a book of etiquette. Though she would prove a minor threat, the young Elinor Ames, a prominent Hunter College graduate, surely made Emily nervous. Ames produced a daily "behavior photograph" distributed by the Chicago Tribune–New York News Syndicate. With the unblushing confidence of youth, the twenty-something writer would soon publish *Etiquette for Moderns: A Guide for the Executive's Wife.*

As if in retaliation for the threat of defection to a competitor, Emily, albeit gently, began to criticize her beloved New York City. On February 22, 1946, she wrote to Yvonne of her pleasure that her husband had found a good job near Edgartown, saying, "I think it is wonderful!" The young wife had apparently been considering a move to Manhattan, and Emily thought the Vineyard a far better choice: "I should have hated to see you one little atom in a great city like this—or any other! To live where you are among people *who know you* (and *love* you—as they do you) is the real beauty of life." She continued, complaining about the city she used to be in love with, and, an even more startling change, was careless with her punctuation:

At the present time N.Y is almost impossible!!—except to sit at home in (or unless one is able to walk miles!) It has never been like it before. People who have cars are not allowed to park outside of parking lots—far away and jammed! Buses are packed people stand as long as an hour on the corner. Taxis so scarce I had to wait the one time I've been out 1 hr 10 minutes before the doorman at a 5th Ave apartment house got me a taxi.

In other words I don't dare go out because I can't walk home!!! As for theatres—unless you have a car and a chauffeur who drives round and round the block—or can walk 2 miles, only those who live in a theatre district can make it. (Most people go to nearby churches)

I don't know what all this is about except I've only been able to walk (limp) around the house for about 2 weeks. The bones mended nicely in a month but all the ligaments were torn are taking their own time. So no places in busses or empty taxis. I go around saying

"I think I'll go out and then stay home and complain about being 'so tired!!'"

After citing her plans to go see her two great-grandchildren, Emily launched into a poignant discussion of the portrait that Funk and Wagnalls had recently commissioned:

F and W Co have had my portrait painted by the Miss Havill whose pictures I was so crazy about. I said I thought she did old people so well!! Now I wonder *how* old those old ones were? I saw my picture the day before yesterday and have been in a state of collapse ever since. White-haired, stoop-shouldered dowdy and slouching old crooked-faced woman aged 88!!! (Possibly 96!!!) It wasn't finished. And maybe my shock impressed her. I am feeling very much that she is one of those artists who do not believe in painting pretty people. Perhaps I won't care if age makes a lop-sided jaw and a peanut shaped nose interesting meanwhile an old friend who paints handkerchief-box prettiness has come home from London. But I really *can't* sit again.

Her next paragraph, however, switched determinedly to a subject that made her happy: "*Etiquette* is selling more than ever! 3800 last week! Perhaps the portrait will end it—or who knows, it may sell more than ever because a freaky frump wrote it. Or maybe the 'FF' will be lovely when finished—(the picture I mean)."

Over the next few months, Emily and Yvonne exchanged several letters, mostly to discuss Yvonne's pregnancy. Yvonne would continue to work for Emily over the coming summer, though with shorter hours since she would be tiring easily, and with "a little higher than 'fair' pay," according to Emily's offer of "$35 a week for 5 hr days." Emily emphasized that she would be counting on Yvonne's competent secretarial skills to "keep her on track" when her own great-grandchildren stayed at the Edgartown cottage from the middle of June to August 1.

As Emily and her assistants made their annual transfer to the Vineyard that spring, the last truly revelatory interview she would give was published in *Life* magazine. The article began with the prototypical Emily Post anecdote: sharing a taxi with a pleasant stranger, Emily had ended up bailing out the embarassed passenger when the woman realized she'd left her wallet at home. But the description tendered by the well-meaning, enthusiastic Jeanne Perkins must have disconcerted readers who thought of Emily as ageless, as well as jolting Emily herself: in her favorite winter outfit, including a formidable black velvet hat and exotic Persian lamb coat, she impressed the journalist as an "attractive, elderly dowager."

Perkins led off her story with a heartfelt royal coronation: "Emily Post has ceased to be a person and has become a noun, a synonym for etiquette and manners, more widely used perhaps than even the words themselves." Since *Etiquette*'s appearance in 1922, it had been "reprinted 65 times, [and] has never sold less than 30,000 copies in one year. During the past few months demand for it has unexpectedly risen and recently it reached a new high of 5,602 copies per week." The accelerated sales, speculated the journalist, reflected the large number of postwar weddings and divorces, the quantities of money "changing hands," and the subsequent need to learn behavior that would serve in the postwar boardroom, a fancy restaurant, or at a neighborhood barbecue.

Perkins remarked carefully on Emily's bright red nail polish, "blended especially for her." As had others, she noted her "rather fluttery hands." Seemingly at odds with the sure demeanor she otherwise presented, the quick, lissome movements no doubt marked instead a woman who did not, metaphorically, enjoy sitting still and wasting time. Cataloging Emily's "iron-gray hair" and her careful rouge and lipstick, along with her decision to wear "a lot of jewelry," the reporter noted that the author's usual summer dress color was red; in the city, Emily also often wore black softened with touches of pink. Because of eye operations, the author now carried three pairs of glasses. Emily's ten radios impressed Perkins, whom Emily told, "I would rather broadcast than eat."

Emily perked up when she started talking about her newspaper column, which now elicited an average of five thousand pieces of mail a week, including letters written on "a perforated sheet of loose leaf notebook paper." From a woman wondering what to wear to visit her boyfriend in prison to a man writing to complain about his wife's crude habit of putting salt and pepper shakers on their dinner table instead of keeping the condiments in the kitchen, Emily was speaking to all classes and every sort of problem these days. Predictably, she advised both writers to pursue the practical: dress brightly and smile a lot, she told the worried girlfriend; do what feels best to you in your own home, she enjoined the irritated husband.

For years, Emily's more intrepid fans had occasionally phoned her in

Manhattan, where they usually ended up talking to Hilda. Still not wanting to discourage this sort of random contact, even after Hilda's death, the author had continued listing her number (under Mrs. Price Post) in the New York City telephone directory. When frantic callers from Detroit or Washington reached her, begging for emergency information, such supplicants were graciously accommodated. Yet what impressed Jeanne Perkins most was not Emily's accessibility but her claim to rarely notice "errors in the mechanics of etiquette."

The reporter waxed nostalgic, wondering aloud why, in her seventies, Mrs. Post remained "the unchallenged authority on manners." Ever the architect at heart, Emily offered two earthbound reasons: one, her book was truly encyclopedic and authoritative; and two, even "more important," her philosophy was expansive, not restrictive. "Manners are like primary colors," Emily explained. "There are certain rules and once you have those you merely mix, i.e., adapt, them to meet changing situations."

Regardless of such flexibility, Emily knew she could no longer do everything herself. From paying secretaries in Manhattan to transcribe her recordings, to handing over more of the business matters to her son, back in New York City after his stint abroad, she was suddenly a fan of outsourcing before the concept even existed. Recently retired from his job with Mack Trucks, Ned Post developed a way for his mother to keep more of her earnings by enfolding her work into a true mini-corporation. That summer, the organization Ned had helped put in place finally came together. Funk and Wagnalls's treasurer agreed that future royalties and statements would be made out and sent to the "Emily Post Institute, Inc."

THE MANUFACTURING OF RADIOS resumed as soon as government controls were lifted. In 1947, Bell Laboratories would launch the portable transistor. The AM stations increased in number, from 961 in 1946 to 2,006 three years later. But if this period was important to radio, it also ushered in the next medium to explode: television. As soon as TVs were widely advertised, Emily had arranged to purchase one in New York City. Now she decided she had to have one in Edgartown as well. Someone at the Vineyard sold her a set with "a rotating antenna, so you could point the antenna to get the station you wanted," Bill Post recalls. " 'Okay, I want WBZ in Boston,' she said, and the salesman told her, 'I'll fix it.' " But instead he stabilized the television reception to receive only the Boston station. "That was enough for Grandmama; she still loved it. But clearly the salesman had flimflammed her!" Bill still chuckles.

She stayed active in local Edgartown projects, and the townspeople enjoyed spotting her riding in the front seat of the repair shop's pickup truck, insisting on taking her radios into town herself. "Compared to the past, though, she went out infrequently by then," Yvonne recalls. "When Hilda was alive, she would walk down to an early movie with her. After she died, Mrs. Post seemed to stop going much of anywhere. But now that I think about it, she'd never really been one for going out a lot anyway. What I remember most is how she loved to throw a ball for the little boys [Bill and Libby's two young sons] to catch." Smiling, Yvonne recollects: "Work and grandchildren were her life, and by the time that her grandson and his wife had produced four great-grandbabies for her, she was in heaven." When they weren't there, she was lonely.

That November, Emily made a radio appearance on WOR's popular quiz show. Along with five or six other guests, Emily, who received star billing in the list of the week's radio programs, was asked to answer twenty questions. There is no record of how she did. Fred Van Deventer and Florence Rinard, the show's sponsors, took the popular show to television a few years later, but Emily Post would not be included among their guests that time.

EVEN FOR SOMEONE determined to stay current, the years immediately after the war were throwing more fastballs than anyone could catch. Race and class barriers seemed to be crumbling in the euphoria following V-J Day. Jackie Robinson, a brand-new Brooklyn Dodger, became the first "Negro" to play on a modern major league baseball team; and GIs fresh from the battlefield could rent an entire house for their young families, due to the gritty hands-on efforts of Abraham Levitt and his sons, self-taught builders, their innovations shaping the country's new landscape. On May 7, 1947, Levitt and Sons publicly announced its plan to build two thousand mass-produced rental homes for veterans, and within two days, one thousand had already been leased in advance. Levittown, as the new development would be named, was made possible by the ways architecture had moved forward over the decades, but it was also enabled by the ever-expanding population who relied upon Emily Post the most.

This was the same year that Metropolitan Life built the nation's largest housing project seen to this day, Stuyvesant Town and Peter Cooper Village. Manhattan's returning veterans and their young families were finding affordable housing even harder to come by than soldiers plumbing the suburbs, and the blocklike red-brick structures, 11,232 apartments in 110 buildings between Fourteenth and Twenty-third streets, provided them a built-in community as well as a new home. Met Life would more than double those numbers in New York City with more affordable residences throughout the decade, housing the very class and age and multifariousness of people who yearned for a firm but compassionate, flexible but knowing advice giver like Emily Post.

Certainly her world was expanding everywhere she looked. She reveled in changes that seemed to call out for her interpretation, eager to understand their rationale. She chatted eagerly with her friends' grandchildren about their favorite books one afternoon, then spent the next flipping through a fashion standard, *Vogue* magazine, begun at the turn of the last century by Arthur Turnure, the uncle by marriage to Emily's dear cousin Sadie Price Pell Turnure. To Emily's amusement, up-to-date women were now wearing Christian Dior's New Look, inspired by the end of the very belle époque that had witnessed Emily's and her friends' debuts as well as the magazine's. But many of those friends were gone now, she sometimes realized with a start. She found herself thinking about her own death, and taking steps now to ensure that her work would continue after she was gone. Under Ned's tutelage, she expanded her legal corporation into the Emily Post Institute for the Study of Gracious Living.

"She didn't do this for the family's future income," Emily's grandson maintains today. "She was concerned instead about the legacy of what she stood for and believed in. She really wanted her work to survive, and the kind of work she supported to survive." It was, in part, such healthy narcissism that motivated Emily to stay on radio. Before she went to Edgartown that year, she appeared at least once on the air, the guest for WJZ's half-hour show *Betty Crocker Talk*. Bill remembers the taping being set up in Emily's Seventy-ninth Street apartment, because she had trouble getting to the studio.

But there was a far less self-interested side to Emily Post that her own family knew nothing about. In early June, as part of her spring trip abroad, she spent several weeks in Germany, working to bring orphaned Jewish children to America, an activity she kept secret even from her son. Now, informed of her charity, her family doesn't understand her silence. The reasons run a gamut of possibilities: she might have been asked by American authorities not to talk; she might have been helping the children avoid undue interest from tedious officials; she might have disliked the thought of being congratulated for simply doing good; she might have been worried that her fame would make her the target of overwhelming numbers of requests for help.

Whatever the grounds for her silence, she worked tirelessly and anonymously during her time in Frankfurt, searching out young victims to help. One documented assistance centers on Isaac Hass, a Holocaust survivor later interviewed for the Steven Spielberg Holocaust archives project. Transported to Auschwitz, where his parents and six sisters had been gassed immediately, Isaac was then transferred to Buchenwald. After incarceration in five concentration camps, he had been shot by the SS and left for dead. In May 1945, he was rescued near Schwandorf, Germany, by American soldiers from Patton's Third Army.

At that point, the teenager weighed seventy pounds; he barely survived typhus while he was cared for by nuns in a German hospital. After he regained his strength, he began working in an American officers' club. "One day a very nice lady visiting the Frankfurt club on behalf of the Red Cross talked to me," Isaac recalled. According to Isaac's daughter, Bonnie Hass, Emily had volunteered with UNRRA (United Nations Relief and Rehabilitation Administration) to help orphans abroad. UNRRA, founded in 1943 as an organization of fifty-two countries, helped around eight million refugees from at least seven European countries, excluding Germany. Even there, if a German child sought to be united with a family member already in America, efforts would be made to find the relative.

"Emily Post somehow ended up at the officers' club, where she inquired about young Holocaust survivors," Bonnie Hass explains. "The officers told her about my father, and she met and spoke with him. He told her that he had been going all over Germany, by bicycle, poring over lists of survivors, hoping some of his family was still alive. He had found none," she recalls. "But he did remember an uncle in Brooklyn, his father's older brother, who had emigrated to the United States after World War I." At this news, in her straight-ahead manner, Emily set her sights on getting the boy to New York. But he was twenty years old by then, and the children's immigration bill had a mandatory cutoff of eighteen. To ensure his entry into the United States as a juvenile, Emily briskly instructed Isaac: "From now on, you are seventeen."

On the Spielberg Holocaust survivors' series, an aged Hass cried as he explained, "Emily Post helped me get documentation saying I was under age; she wanted to make sure I was even a year younger than the cut-off date. All of this was her idea, not mine."

Isaac Hass left Germany on June 12, 1947, after being given instructions by Emily to be at the dock in Bremerhaven, where he would board the USS *Ernie Pyle*. On July 22, he entered New York Harbor, greeted by the statue that had served as his benefactor's dollhouse a half century earlier. Realizing Emily Post's celebrity only years later, he told his daughter his story, adding that "Mrs. Post was such a great, fantastic lady, and I want you to be a great lady too." Bonnie Hass was sent to finishing school, where she learned etiquette. She also learned, from her father, to give people the benefit of the doubt. "He never let me forget that good people went out of their way in order to help others," she says quietly. "Emily Post saved my father's life."

After a few years in his new country, Isaac Hass was drafted into the U.S. Army. Upon completing his tour of duty, he became an executive vice president of the American Machine and Foundry Company of New York. But he always owned his own small business on the side to make sure he could feed his family, no matter what happened. He was exactly the kind of man Emily Price admired.

Though she could not work a similar magic for the elderly Bertha Leach, her faithful New York City seamstress, Emily returned home, tired but determined to ameliorate the woman's poor health. She knew that her longtime acquaintance was seriously ill, so in mid-July, in spite of her own fatigue, Emily took Bertha on a car trip upstate, centered upon a visit to the curative waters at Saratoga Springs. In the Adirondacks, however, Bertha became so sick that she required immediate surgery. The ensuing operation revealed that she had advanced stomach cancer—the disease that had killed Emily's father. Told she had at best weeks to live, Bertha was reassured by her friend and client that she, Emily Post, would take care of everything. Upon dying at the end of July, the woman was buried at Emily's expense. Bertha's family had little money, and Emily sent them $1,300 to cover the fuel bill for the upcoming winter, as well as a present on her old friend's behalf. She asked that they buy a bassinet for Bertha's newborn grandniece.

EMILY CONTINUED TO be deeply interested in the generations that would follow hers. On Martha's Vineyard, residents welcomed her into local activities, even appointing her president of the Edgartown Boys' Club for a short period. Once, in an apparent social misstep that gave rise to gossip that she was "losing it," when it was her time to serve refreshments for the Garden Club, Emily sponsored a barbecue instead of setting out the regular tea sandwiches. Rather than the gaffe others assumed, this was entirely intentional: grilled meats seemed a more festive offering than old-fashioned ladies' food, in her practiced opinion.

She still reveled in the attention drawn by her well-tended gardens, with their shoulder-high dahlias. Tourists routinely paused to observe, saying, "Oh, this is Emily's Post's home." Occasionally, she would ask someone admiring her flowers to come inside and join her for tea. She was proud that each summer her house was included on the tour of Edgartown benefiting the local hospital. Every year, Emily trotted the paying guests to her closet, with its munificence of red shoes, which ranged in number from twenty-five to one hundred, depending upon the imagination of the visitor. Eileen Robinson, a longtime resident, recalls observing Emily on her daily walk each midday to the post office, always "very very erect in those red shoes, and beautifully dressed."

Eileen remembers vividly the time that she had a "close-up with Mrs. Post, after I told my mother that I wanted to get married. I was about to graduate from high school and had met my future husband already. Mom secretly asked Emily to counsel me, and one day I was asked to her house for 'tea.' I thought this was for several people, but I arrived to find only Mrs. Post and me, which alerted me to something from the start. She started right in, telling me how important an education was, and that I was too young to get married. She did not mention that she had married at the same age I planned to, at nineteen! What I actually remember most vividly is the glass walkway over Mrs. Post's garage leading to the upstairs living room, where we had tea."

Toward the end of July, in the co-op at 39 East Seventy-ninth Street she had helped Emily and her son design, the seventy-nine-year-old Minnie Gray Coster succumbed to an illness of several years' standing. In Minnie's obituary, the New York Times again concentrated on her late husband's feat, highlighted in newspaper accounts of their wedding in 1900 as well: William Coster, who had died in 1919 from aftereffects of the Spanish flu epidemic, held the record for walking fastest to the stock exchange from the New York Athletic Club. As if only yesterday, her daughters' marriages to foreign titles were rehashed, as well as the Times' moniker for Minnie, the "leader of the American colony in Paris" until World War II. In recent times, she had become a "supporter for the benefit of various activities for the blind," including the Lighthouse on East Fifty-ninth Street, the donation in homage to the sight problems of her dear friend. Ned urged his progressively frail mother not to return to Manhattan to attend the funeral; he would go in her place. Reluctantly, she agreed.

That autumn, while Americans rationed themselves one slice of bread daily and endorsed meatless Tuesdays to help feed the needy abroad, Anne Kent, without fanfare, took her employer's place on the Emily Post segment of a radio quiz show. No explanation was offered to family members or to the media. Kent also commandeered the daily newspaper column, although Emily insisted on responding herself to questions that required more than a routine answer. Several years into the next decade, readers would still be writing Emily Post about war-related anxieties. Occasionally she would use a "composite of a half dozen [letters] sent . . . within the week" to illustrate a recurring theme: "I married a war widow. Her ex-mother-in-law is having the son's body brought to this country for burial here. (1) Should my wife go the funeral? (2) If so, alone or possibly with his family? Should I be with her in either case? (3) Also, what about our sending flowers? From my wife or both of us? (4) Would the fact that I had not known her first husband alter your answers?" Emily responded, "(1) yes. (2) This depends upon your, as well as her, relationship with his family. (3) Yes, but from her alone. (4) No, but the relationship between you and his family does matter."

As 1947 came to a quiet end, wrapped in almost twenty-six inches of snow blanketing New York, Emily mourned again. On December 29, she attended the funeral of Frank Crowninshield, against the protests of her protective son. Weather be damned, as Crownie would have expected. Three hundred close friends showed up. The service was held at St. James Protestant Episcopal Church on Madison and Seventy-first Street, no walk at all for Emily in the old days. This time she took a cab.

✠

ON JANUARY 18, 1948, THE *BOSTON GLOBE* PUBLISHED AN EDITORIAL lauding Emily so celebratory that Funk and Wagnalls reprinted the article as a full-page ad. "Emily Post will be remembered, says a friend, as the great revolutionist of this age," the essay began. The postwar class revolution had created her largest playing field yet, the *Globe* explained, one including not only the children of immigrants but others wanting to join the Best People. "*Etiquette* is carrying the nation a long way in the direction of equality," the article celebrated in italics. "In a country where education is spreading, and the people possess Code Emily Post, all those who seek to maintain an aristocracy of any sort will find the going exceedingly hard."

In spite of such perceptive analysis, the press more often sounded as if it were humoring a nice, slightly eccentric old lady. In April, the *New Yorker* wrote up the high-profile "tea party" Funk and Wagnalls sponsored at Emily's apartment in honor of her forthcoming fourth edition of *The Personality of a House,* the publisher even providing a "willowy young lady" to host the event. When the efficient helper guided a new arrival toward Emily's chair, saying, "Mrs. Post, I'd like to present Mrs. Chase, of *Vogue,*" Emily's face lit up. "Why, Edna! . . . My very old friend! How nice of you to come!" Edna Chase, *Vogue*'s editor, had insisted on attending Emily's tea, in spite of her own terrible cold.

Emily had honored another friend, the popular radio host Mary Margaret McBride, by asking her to "pour." The two women had met in the studio years before, when their paths crossed while they were recording their shows. "My grandmother really liked Mary Margaret, her honesty and spontaneity and good nature," Bill Post recalls. "Once, when Emily was on her way to appear on the Edgar Bergen show with Charlie McCarthy, we rode to the studio with Mary Margaret, and they chatted like old friends the whole way." Initially the cheerful country woman had demurred at Emily's request, protesting that she had never "presided at a tea table" in her life, but her friend had insisted.

In spite of McBride's celebrity, many critics regarded the radio star with near contempt. Nor was such disdain unusual: as one commentator has noted, "In a lot of cases . . . the [media] historians were men and didn't regard 'women's shows' or what women broadcast as particularly important. Historically, the voice of 'authority' was a male voice." Where there were famous pairs, like Gracie Allen and George Burns, or Lucille Ball and Desi Arnaz, the men were ceded control even if the ditzy wife wielded the power behind the scenes—or the apron. American culture since the Civil War had depended on ensuring that women and black men were kept in their place: "It was men who could vote, men who made decisions, men who were out in the public sphere. . . . When radio came along, it was gendered the same way society was. . . . [Women] were supposed to be good at conversation but not terribly knowledgeable the way men were expected to be. Jokes about how dumb women were permeated popular culture," notes social historian Donna Halper. For better or worse, Emily was in a "female" arena: women were the bearers of a society's manners, where at least they could hope to influence its mores as well.

A year after serving at her friend's tea, Mary Margaret McBride would make public the inner strength that supported her cordiality, a characteristic that had clinched Emily's affection and respect. Like Emily, Mary Margaret wed ethics to etiquette. At the Yankee Stadium fête of her radio show's fifteenth year on the air, she enthusiastically, to the shock of the crowd, bear-hugged the celebrated head of the NAACP, Walter White.

THAT SUMMER, A NEW sign adorned the tour buses that for years had regularly made a stop at Emily's Edgartown house. Instead of the usual ads, this banner read "Grand Old Lady of Etiquette." Indeed, Emily now seemed to represent the island. Neighbors on Fuller Street routinely returned home from running errands to find that strangers had walked into their unlocked houses and were resting for a minute while they reloaded their cameras to shoot the house where Emily Post lived. The Lamborns, Emily's neighbors across the street, found themselves entertaining sightseers more than once, motivating their teenagers to paint their own sign, which read "The Lamborns live here," and prop it up on their lawn.

One day, Mrs. Lamborn (whose daughter would marry Emily's great-grandson Peter) apologized for the noise her children had made the night before while walking home from the yacht club, their singing and chattering easily heard on a summer evening when everyone's windows were wide open. "I hope you could sleep, Mrs. Post," the worried neighbor said. "My dear," Emily answered, "it is I who should apologize to you for my snoring." Mrs. Lamborn admits today, "She snored so loud it was almost a village legend. If you walked out of the club on one end of the street, you could hear Emily Post snoring at the entire other end. All the way down Fuller Street."

If Emily could have done something about the snoring, she would have. As she grew older, considering others' feelings only became more important to her philosophy of life. People reacted to tone and implication, she was convinced, even more than to the actual message. That November, unlike much of the nation, she was not shocked when Governor Dewey lost to Harry Truman. She thought the outcome was predictable if one contrasted Dewey's hauteur with Truman's unfailing ability to put others at their ease, the mark of the true gentleman or lady. Even when an impudent reporter from the *Washington Post* beseeched Emily to confess her age, she teased him gently as she impugned his insensitivity: at seventy-five, she considered it "downright cruel" of him to ask. (She was, in truth, seventy-six.) When the journalist explained more carefully that he needed to record Emily's correct age to update his publication's file for 1948 (or its morgue, in newspaper lingo), Emily perked up: "Oh, an obituary. Well, if they're not going to print it until I'm dead, I don't care."

The logic of a dramatically younger audience being tutored by a woman whose photographs and interviews seemed increasingly of another era began to sit uneasily with everyone, from Emily to her publishers to her fans. As the publication of Simone de Beauvoir's *The Second Sex* became a defining moment the following year, Emily Post's tenor bespoke a woman come of age in the gay nineties. Gently reporting that "the years are catching up" with Emily Post, a reporter from the *American Weekly* would quickly add, as if a gentleman always cushioned the truth, "But she will never grow old." Instead, the very idea of Emily Post was starting to seem tarnished.

EVEN AS WORLD WAR II began to recede mercifully into the past, Emily's columns continued to be loaded with war-related questions, the aftereffects of battle clearly not yet exhausted. Her columns that autumn reflected the odd dissonance of real life as it was being experienced. A typical day's questions would include unrelated themes. Should dinner-table candles be lit on a daylight summer evening? It's up to you, she answered. Should a newly engaged war widow finally remove her dead husband's wedding ring from her right hand, or could she continue to wear it until she and her fiancé actually married? Emily dispatched her wisdom as briskly as ever, urging the woman to take off her wedding ring when her engagement was announced.

But such lucidity was unreliable. Yvonne Sylvia remembers a new suspicion of others cropping up in her employer around this time, partly the result of Emily's growing old and feeling defenseless, especially without the loyal Hilda at her side. There were also signs of incipient senility. "Mrs. Post sometimes decided someone in the house, one of her trusted servants, had taken something," Yvonne recalls regretfully. "Later she always found it." At least once, Emily used the local paper to locate a "prized gewgaw" she thought had mysteriously disappeared from her breakfast tray. She placed a discreet item in the local newspaper, appealing for the object's return by "the person, perhaps young and certainly thoughtless, who yielded to impulse." Inevitably, the anecdote was repeated in a national publication, *Time* magazine. No one remembers the fate of the missing object.

IN THE MIDST of such domestic dramas, sometime in 1949, in the middle of a bridge game, fifty-six-year-old Ned had a serious stroke, and Emily suddenly found herself needed again.

Bill and Libby and their children had moved that year to Bogotá, Colombia. Visiting their families back home for long periods each summer, they would return to New York permanently five years later, in 1954, four children in tow. Now, on the day of his father's stroke, when Emily phoned her grandson early in the morning, Bill at first assumed the call to be routine: the woman so centered on the most efficient use of time kept forgetting the one-hour time difference between Bogotá and Manhattan. "Grandmama often phoned; she absolutely refused to write," he recalls. "Once in a while she even rang us at bizarrely early hours, while she lay in bed eating her zwieback toast. So I wasn't alarmed when I heard her voice." But then Emily explained the reason for this early morning call: Ned's stroke was severe, though Bill was to sit tight for the time being, not uproot everything to return home precipitously. Within days, it was clear that Ned would recover, though he was left with a permanent limp and other minor deficits.

Travel, however, Ned's passion, would be limited hereafter. As if to compensate for his inability to tour again, Emily, though exhausted from tending her son, accepted an assignment to write a pamphlet to be called *Motor Manners,* under her own name but certainly informed by Ned, the longtime automobile buff of the family. The woman who had never driven a car in her life now very publicly contributed to the fourth national highway safety campaign. Free to readers of *Look* magazine and Bell Syndicate newspapers, Emily's pamphlet, published by the National Highway Users Conference, seemed to reprove her audience, her slightly irritable tone out of character. Barely engaged press coverage quoted the same material in papers throughout the country: "A gentleman will no more cheat a red light or stop sign than he would cheat in a game of cards. . . . A courteous lady will not 'scold' raucously with her automobile horn any more than she would act like a 'fish wife' at a party. Primitive, irresponsible, discourteous and impatient behavior behind the wheel of an automobile has no place in society."

Always one to rework her material, she proceeded (with Ned's help) to write several promotional columns about safety on the highway. That spring her newspaper column headed "Etiquette for Truck Drivers" must have startled some of her readers. Finally, as if her career had been revitalized by this foray far afield, in June, the *New York Times* announced that Emily Post would be heading for television, "where she would be co-featured in a five-minute film series with animated puppets dramatizing etiquette subjects. Mrs. Post had signed a television contract with Telescoops, and the production firm already was at work on the initial series for fall broadcast."

There is no sign that the program went forward, and her family doesn't believe she completed the project. "I was there the first few times people tried to film her," Bill recalls. "I remember the acute embarrassment on everyone's part as they realized my grandmother simply wasn't capable of this. It was a disaster." Intrepid as ever, Emily was stepping up to participate in the latest medium, but even she wasn't agile enough this time to make the leap.

CHAPTER 67

H OWEVER SHE FAILED AT TELEVISION, EMILY WAS STILL AT
the helm of her Blue Book. To help Funk and Wagnalls promote the upcoming 1950 edition of *Etiquette,* Emily invited several executives from
Franklin Spier, the advertising agency her publisher had hired, to her apartment for lunch. Peggy Brooks, an enthusiastic young account executive, accompanied her boss to talk over publication strategies for the new edition.
Because of Funk and Wagnalls's identity as a "sort of fuddy duddy publisher," with "only the dictionaries and Emily Post," Brooks assumed Emily
herself would be dry as dust. "I was a bit intimidated," she recalls, "until the
moment when Mrs. Post invited us all to inspect her new walk-in closet.
She was just folks after that."

It was an awareness of the firm's stuffy image that motivated Funk and
Wagnalls to update the language of *Etiquette,* or at least edit a few of the
mise-en-scènes. Peggy Brooks was not sympathetic to such changes: those
characters that had amused Edmund Wilson and Scott Fitzgerald delighted
her as well, and she believed the publisher's choice to minimize their appearances wrong-headed. "They were old-fashioned but vivid just the
same," she says. In spite of the strategy session, very little of *Etiquette* was altered. But the occasional compressed sentence, as if Emily's Gilded Age lo-
quaciousness needed cutting down to size, subtly echoed the waning of the
real presence behind those words, someone who must be ancient by now,
many book buyers believed. Squeezed out as well were some of the quintes-
sential Emily Post–isms of a paradoxically ageless quality. The 1950 revi-

sion "didn't sell as well as later etiquette books did, written by more contemporary authors than Emily Post," Brooks remembers.

Only the rare reviewer noticed minor but meaningful shifts from *Etiquette*'s edition of five years earlier—or, for that matter, the changes made periodically from its beginning. Instead, writers, without acknowledging the decades of incremental revisions, typically compared the original 1922 edition to the current adaptation, pronouncing "startling evidence" of the social changes—both "manners and morals"—that had occurred over a "short span of thirty years." Those critics who had followed *Etiquette* throughout its lengthy career observed Emily's increasing if reluctant accommodation to divorce, one of the most telling demarcations of the book's social history. Emily Post, in book or newspaper, now routinely tackled realities ranging from shared custody to couples living with in-laws to multiple families occupying one house. It appeared that she flinched from nothing.

Now she had new irritants. She devoted two pages of the 1950 *Etiquette* to a problem she hadn't needed to address in 1922: the etiquette of the radio. Being such an avid listener herself, she professed shock at the "gross inconsistencies of [otherwise polite people] interrupting friends who have perhaps forgone other pleasures to stay home in order to hear a broadcast." Perhaps, she suggested, one could simply list the title and duration of the program under way on a slate marked "Please Enter Silently" and hang the notice "where visitors can see it."

As always, Emily had worked hard to stay up to date, the now stout seventy-seven-year-old seeming to instinctively register cultural shifts as if adapting to such changes were second nature. In an observation later borrowed by Cleveland Amory as the linchpin for his bestselling book *Who Killed Society?*, she explained the evolution of the social world: "In the general picture of this modern day, the smart and the near-smart, the distinguished and the merely conspicuous, the real and the sham, and the unknown general public, are all mixed up together. The walls that used to enclose the world that was fashionable are all down. Even the car tracks that divided cities into smart and not-smart sections are torn up. . . . There is nowhere to go to see Best Society on Parade," she professed boldly in her introduction to the 1950 *Etiquette*.

If Emily needed proof that she—and her writing—still mattered, early that year she got it. The staff of the women's magazine *Pageant* (its cheesecake cover shots the sexy progenitors of today's *Cosmopolitan* magazine, its contents more like *Redbook's*) queried 272 American newswomen to select the five women who had most influenced "modern life" in the twentieth century. An executive editor called Emily to announce that she had placed second—just behind Eleanor Roosevelt. Though the official list was said to be secret, her publisher steadily leaked the list to major news outlets for several weeks. In March several of the top five winners, Emily and Eleanor Roosevelt among them, appeared more than once on Mary Margaret McBride's radio program.

Finally, in April, the magazine officially released the results of the poll, the lead shared with the cover story, "Giving the Lie to 25 Sex Beliefs." "If it really takes a woman to judge a woman, this is The Word. Here's how 272 women journalists ranked for *Pageant* the influence of America's most famous women," the feature announced. "The Most Powerful Women in America: Who Are They?" it asked, answering: "Number 1 was Eleanor Roosevelt; Number 2 was Emily Post."

Eighteen names followed, most of whose company Emily was proud to keep: Sister Elizabeth Kenny; Clare Boothe Luce; Dorothy Thompson; Senator Margaret Chase Smith; Dorothy Dix (Elizabeth Meriwether Gilmer); Princess Elizabeth; Hattie Carnegie; Anne O'Hare McCormick; Mary Margaret McBride; Representative Helen Gahagan Douglas; Grandma Moses; Vijaya Lakshmi Pandit; Mary McLeod Bethune tied with Helen Keller; Lillian Gilbreth tied with the Duchess of Windsor; Kate Smith; and, tied for No. 20, Eve Curie and Irene Dunne.

Emily's citation stressed her unswerving authority and her paradoxical timeless timeliness: "She still influences the manners and perhaps the morals of the nation," *Pageant* noted.

BUT WHEN 1951 OPENED, the curtain was slowly closing on the drama of Emily Post, as America's cast rehearsed a new play. Korea and Joe McCarthy were peeking around the corner. Already the new decade vibrated to the sounds of Nat King Cole, Hank Williams, and Louis Jordan, even as it sponsored innovative faces that would become icons of their age, Audrey Hepburn and Hubert de Givenchy. Emily's nation, composed of thirty-seven states at her birth, now encompassed forty-eight. An equally seismic expansion, much too late for her generation, was the discovery—or acknowledgment—that healthy women liked sex. In 1953, Alfred Kinsey's *Sexual Behavior in the Human Female* would recount the stories of six thousand women willing to detail their most intimate sexual practices, an exposé unimaginable since the year after Emily's birth, when the anti-pornography and—at least as significant—the contraceptive-banning Comstock law had erected barriers to pleasure in Americans' bedrooms.

That January, Anne Kent gave an interview to the omnibus magazine *Cosmopolitan* in her employer's name. Identified as "personal assistant to Emily Post for more than 15 years," Kent was tasked with listing the most important social changes Emily's recent revision of *Etiquette* had recorded. Quickly, however, the emphasis shifted from Anne Kent as Emily Post's amanuensis to Kent the authority, heir presumptive: "Miss Kent finds no fault with this practice [of calling people by their first names] in circles where it's taken for granted. She says that position and age should be respected, and children shouldn't call adults by their first names." Kent cataloged Emily's latest changes: women could now wear slacks, though they remained "improper for city wear." Typewriters could be used even for personal notes, though formal correspondence was still better written by hand, and sympathy letters seemed "warmer and more sincere if handwritten." And Anne Kent delivered the definitive answer to the question of the day: a woman could now smoke in public whenever or wherever she had the whim.

Partly to stake a claim in territory unmarked by her aggressive assistant and, even more, as a gift to Ned, a gourmet from the earliest days of his father's training, Emily agreed to do a cookbook with her son, who, she would later admit, had "written every word of it." She added, "Calling this book *The Emily Post Cookbook* is evidence of the degree to which untruth can go! I have never cooked a single dish in my life." After his early retirement, Ned had renewed his amateur's interest in culinary arts. *The Emily Post Cookbook*, published in 1951 by the Emily Post Institute, gave the gourmet something to focus on following his stroke. "My son Ned," Emily would later write to her longtime friend journalist William Hunt, "is a cook of really wide reputation—particularly in France."

Emily's mark was nonetheless present, as if she refused, for ethical reasons, to contribute nothing but her name to a book she had supposedly written. Just as she had provided advice booklets for almost any commercial product she had endorsed, now she supplied the foreword, skirting the subject of Emily Post in the kitchen. She concentrated on the economic changes of the day that made "good professional cooks" far too costly for most homes, with "expensive restaurants" off-limits as well. She explained to Hunt privately that "I think there is a real need for this book on the part of the many who can no longer keep pace with soaring prices and wages— and must now learn to cook! Hoping this doesn't mean you!!"

The Emily Post Cookbook book still reads as an exemplar of an easy-to-follow guide to basic popular foods. Its preface contains a thorough, well-translated list of cooking terms, many foreign; measurements and equivalents; and menus accompanied by recipes. Family and friends remember that Ned expected the book to be highly successful, in spite of Irma Rombauer's The Joy of Cooking having cornered this particular market in the early 1930s. To launch "her" cookbook, Emily (or probably Ned) convinced Funk and Wagnalls to fly thirty-two food editors and writers on a DC-3 from New York (plus a few from Boston as well) to Edgartown, where an entire meal was constructed of recipes from the cookbook. Clam bisque, oxtail stew, and apple pandowdy were all on the menu, but Emily later gave the game away when she told an interviewer from the Vineyard Gazette that other than the "Baltimore caramels," she had made nothing. "If I were forced to cook for myself, my diet would be bread and water," she cheerfully admitted.

The introduction to the cookbook concluded with her supposed "favorite dessert, Pennsylvania Apple Pandowdy." Her friends must have laughed: the simple, sweet country mixture of sliced apples, brown sugar, molasses, and cinnamon, with a thick latticed top, was famously southern. Trying to credit the menu with more national appeal—or just out of ignorance—Ned had misrepresented its regionality. The woman with chocolate ice cream on her mind day and night may well have yearned for an occasional home-cooked pandowdy instead, but not one that came from Pennsylvania, where, Josephine had often lamented, coal came quicker than cuisine.

That October, Emily revised her earlier will (no copy of which survives), perhaps to remove formally a beneficiary she had planned to reward. Anne Kent, the one-time dedicatee of Etiquette, "mysteriously disappeared" from Emily's life around this time, Bill Post remembers. "Because my family and I were living in Bogotá, I didn't get much firsthand information about Anne Kent's disappearance," he says. He assumes there was a falling-out: "It had been a great personal relationship at first," he recalls. "Grand-mother was very fond of her. But I did hear suggestions that Anne Kent assumed she was Emily Post's heir. My grandmother wanted family, not outsiders, handling the institute after she died, mostly for the continuity of her personal vision, not for financial reasons, in spite of the money being good. Perhaps the Anne Kent schism was due to this situation. Libby and I decided to return from Colombia primarily because of Grandmama's needs for the institute. She was reaching the point where someone had to take over, and my father just wasn't able. All I know is that when Libby and I moved back to New York, Anne Kent was gone, and she was never mentioned again."

Emily rarely left her apartment those days. "Pet," as Emily fondly called her new assistant and secretary, Isabel Paulantonio, had a small lobby office in the co-op building Emily had created, and her employer phoned her to come upstairs whenever she was needed. "I was with her every day, I think, throughout the fifties. Mrs. Post was very kind, very generous, very, very nice; we had lunch together often," Isabel remembers. "But she sometimes didn't remember who I was or what I was doing there."

By 1952, many of Emily's friends had died, and at times, it almost seemed as if there were no real Emily Post either, just a symbol instead, to be used by the public as it best served them. On May 23 newspapers around the country reported on a Los Angeles lawyer's wife who had sued the Pacific Telephone and Telegraph Company. The phone company had ignored the woman's demands to list only herself, not her husband's ex-wife too, as "Mrs. Carl Warner." The divorced wife should go by "Mrs. Jeanne Warner," with the man's first name reserved for the current wife alone, decreed the supreme authorities of the land, quoting from "English common law," "social usage," "American custom"—and, they claimed, "Emily Post." Once again, Emily's words were twisted to suit the governing assumptions: *Etiquette*'s dictum, both in 1922 and now, stated the contrary to such a ruling. "A woman who has divorced her husband retains the legal as well as the social right to use her husband's full name, in New York State at least"—thus spake Emily Post for real.

CHAPTER 68

⁜

OVER THE NEXT FEW YEARS, THE DICTION OF EMILY'S DAILY COL-
umn changed, enough to alert an especially observant reader to an outside
presence. Lacking Emily's genteel though quick rhythm, the answers,
though largely written by Emily, became artfully efficient, crisply edited by
Ned and Isabel. Enough moments that were "pure Emily" assured the careful reader that she was nonetheless still in command: "The test of a lady is
nowhere greater than in situations where the advantage is her own. It isn't
possible to advertise lack of quality more blatantly than the overbearing,
inconsiderate shopper, who rudely criticizes everything a saleswoman
shows her, who treats her as though she were someone of a completely inferior class."

In her June 15, 1952, column, Emily addressed a question from a mother
who thought it more polite for her child to leave food on her plate at every
meal. During World War II, the writer acknowledged, "when food was
scarce, it was considered proper to eat all the food on one's plate, but does
that same rule apply today?" For Emily, there was no ambiguity: "Leaving
food on your plate is not good manners—and never was because it not only
shows lack of appreciation of your hostess' food, but also 'wanton' priorities. Wasting a precious commodity could never be an ethical choice." Immediately following this quick dispatch, the second query concerned an
"innocent offender" in the office who had the habit "of spraying everyone
in the face whenever he talks to them." Because much of the colleagues'
work demanded that the two sit side by side, the writer said, he was "fre-

quently sprayed," "a most unpleasant experience." Emily cut to the quick: "Unhappily, I know of nothing except trying to keep out of his range."

Most important, in 1952, Emily Post would confront a real contender for her position as front-runner in all things etiquette, the first serious threat since Lillian Eichler. Amy Vanderbilt's *Complete Book of Etiquette* would sell 900,000 copies by the end of its first six months on the market. Vanderbilt's book sales quickly overtook Emily's oddly stagnant—and undoubtedly inaccurate—figure, "1 million copies," cited repeatedly over the years. Asked if she was bothered that other books were copying her own— politely, no names were cited—Emily amicably responded that the more good books on the subject of good manners, the better. For most of the decade, Amy Vanderbilt's book ran neck and neck with *Etiquette*. Doubleday was the publisher, and this time, in contrast to the anonymity Lillian Eichler had been dealt decades before, the book cover included the author's name.

Later that summer, as if proving that she was still current, Emily Post tackled beach manners—her way. She wrote a lengthy column comparing European with American beach habits; she noted that on "European beaches . . . sex is always dominant, whereas in America, it does not count!" Perhaps her awareness that swimming in Edgartown was easy and relaxing— no shame involved when neighbors walked by—caused her to prefer her own country's habits to beach protocols in Europe. There, she pointed out, the beaches were meant for spectacle rather than exercise. At "Trouville-Deauville or the Lido," she estimated, "not more than 25 per cent" of those in swimsuits go in the water, unlike the nearly "100 per cent" of American beachgoers so attired. As usual, she saw nothing inherently wrong with either choice: they were simply different, demanding sensitivity to one's environment. Emily, who for years had lauded the habits and manners of sophisticates overseas, now found herself more comfortable in her own American skin.

She held no truck with those wistful for the past. Women today, unlike in her youth, were not weighed down by "yards and pounds of water-soaked flannel," almost drowning as they tried to learn the breaststroke, she said. One of Emily's readers protested against the skimpy swimming suits showing up on the beach. "One might as well go bathing with nothing on at all," she complained, adding, "I trust you don't approve of young women in those postage-stamp suits." Emily responded that, as always, it depended on the context. But does Mrs. Post condone such immodest clothing? Emily knew her fan would wonder. Bluntly, she answered the imaginary query: "Young women, I do! Old women, decidedly not! . . . 'Modesty,' says the cynic, 'is consciousness of one's own imperfection.'"

That September, in response to Amy Vanderbilt's competition, the Bell Syndicate issued a press release commemorating the thirtieth anniversary of "what has become the definitive handbook of social usage, Emily Post's *Etiquette.*" The feature, "Emily Post's Etiquette Book Has Changed Startlingly in 30 Years," compared the first edition to the most recent one. Readers who had not bought the revised editions through the years wouldn't have realized from the ads how little the essentials of the current volume differed from the one in 1945.

ON OCTOBER 1, in the house at Tuxedo Park that Bruce Price had built and given to Emily, Katharine Collier, age ninety-four, suffered a heart attack in her sleep. She was dead within minutes. At least there were other things to balance Emily's loss: not only did Emily's great-grandchildren bring her a sense of revitalization, but finally, her son and his longtime companion, loved by Bill and Libby as well as by Emily, were free to wed. On April 9, 1953, after obtaining a divorce in Mexico City, Marietta Szveteney Persico married Edwin Main Post in Rockleigh, New Jersey. The daughter of the late Baron and Baroness George Szveteney of Budapest, Marietta had moved to the United States in 1936 and become an American citizen in 1944. Legally separated in 1930 from her husband, the Italian ambassador Giovanni Persico, consul general for Italy in Berlin, Marietta had a long-standing agreement that as soon as the ambassador had retired and was no longer vulnerable to public scrutiny, he would support their divorce.

Ned and Marietta had been patient, their family, including Emily, entirely sympathetic all these years. "We adored Marietta," Bill remembers, "Grandmama as much as anyone. There was no question of disapproval. There were no children whose parents were damaging their lives."

In 1954, with their four toddlers, Bill and Libby resettled in Rye, New York, ensuring that Emily would always have her family nearby. Living again in the United States, the timing of his move due mostly to his grandmother's frailty, Bill started his own company. Libby tended their four young children—and painted, whenever she got the chance.

After Ned worked out a system to continue the newspaper column abroad, he and Marietta, secure that Bill was on hand for Emily, moved to

Italy, where they already owned a house. For a short while the plan worked: Isabel helped Emily choose a few of the new letters, sometimes pulling from the files an old one not previously used. Then the secretary wrote down Emily's responses, sending the selections and answers to Ned, who, after "editing"—in truth, often writing—the column, mailed everything back for Isabel to transcribe. "The system proved unwieldy and didn't last for very long," Bill Post remembers. After a few years, as his mother became less capable, this complicated scheme became too great a strain on everyone, and Ned resumed living in Manhattan for a few months each year to oversee Emily and the institute.

There were other signs that Emily was gradually ceding control of her life. That summer she reluctantly parted with the ebony jewel box her father had made for Josie, donating it to the Museum of the City of New York. The *New York Times,* detailing the twenty-five sets of fine gemmed jewelry inside the velvet-lined drawers, described Emily's father as "one of the foremost architects in this country," who, while "struggling" and "young" at the early stages of his career, had married Josephine Lee. Around the same time, though she generously lent her name to the *Reader's Digest* twenty-fifth anniversary of the magazine's Braille edition, her solicitation letters for charity subscriptions were clearly written (Emily's signature imitated) by an assistant.

Emily herself still traversed the ages. That August, for instance, when a salesman complained about the "TV Boors," she sought to clarify the new rules governing a subject she cared about deeply: the use of media within the home. If an appointment had been previously arranged, she ruled, the household television must be turned off when the salesman arrived—if he was on time. If the salesperson came earlier or later, or did not have an appointment, no such rules applied, and the viewer's wishes received priority.

At the very least, television reminded Emily that women inhabited a modern world she hadn't even dreamed of. That same year, in 1954, a poor southern girl, Brownie Wise, began selling a bowl that unceremoniously burped its way right into the American kitchen, Tupperware making Wise and many other savvy women rich. *Business Week* would anoint Brownie the first woman ever to appear on its cover. It was the kind of success story Emily Post would have been thrilled to read about—she never forgot that she herself had felt compelled to talk down her success when she first began to work.

Even now, years after seeking entry into such a world, Emily enjoyed the chance to appear as a professional businesswoman whenever she could. Though her increasing forgetfulness surely gave pause to her sponsors, if not to herself, she accepted a television spot on behalf of rayon, a no-iron fabric marketed in the early 1950s as a labor saver for housewives. No copies of Emily's appearance have been located, and her grandson doesn't recall such a project, but Emily clearly followed through. A news release for the American Rayon Institute confirms that "Mrs. Post recently made a television appearance, her debut, in a film released by the institute, which was formed by the producers to step up promotion in line with expanding production." When the institute opened new offices at 350 Park Avenue that October, the president of the New York City Federation of Women's Clubs gave her an award, recognizing her "contribution to gracious American living."

The following May, Emily had the chance to put into practice her lessons from the past, presiding over a meal that was, at least in theory, under her control. Funk and Wagnalls invited forty guests, mostly journalists, to a buffet lunch at the St. Regis Hotel in Manhattan, to celebrate the forthcoming 1955 tenth edition of *Etiquette*. Even the venue implied a connection between the modern and the past. The Waldorf-Astoria, with its restaurant and hotel, had long since overtaken Delmonico's as "the place" to dine; now the St. Regis trumped the Waldorf. The publishers had clearly been unsettled by Amy Vanderbilt's book for Doubleday, which, though no more modern in its advice, was written with a more casual diction, suggesting a younger writer assumed to be suitably current. Doubleday's publicity emphasized that its author (meant to supersede the now dated Lillian Eichler) was a working woman supporting children in school—and that, in addition, she was a Vanderbilt. Just as Emily's *Etiquette* had, early on, depended upon her presence in Best Society, so Amy Vanderbilt's familiarity with the café set that had overtaken old money vouched for her credibility.

Ned returned for the launch of the new edition, helping to host the party at the regal St. Regis. Bill received guests alongside his grandmother, both he and Emily seated on a "settee," the *New Yorker*'s dated locution meant to imply the era the party seemed to evoke. "William Goadby Post," in "his thirties," was "wearing a Countess Mara tie crawling with monkeys," while Emily wore a straw hat with red trim and a black crepe dress with red and white silk pleats. For the most part, the press simply ignored the author. Ned smoothly chatted to the reporters, explaining the current shape of his mother's empire: Emily's column appeared in 160 newspapers seven days a week, inspiring around three thousand letters weekly. About 5 percent of the letters were nonroutine and were forwarded to Emily herself to address. Otherwise, her full-time, year-round secretaries stationed in Edgartown and New York worked with Ned to answer nearly all of the letters on his mother's behalf.

Interested in scoring some juicy quotes, the reporter asked Ned what Emily most disliked about the current era. The loyal son parried, responding with a stale canard: "She regrets most the loss of the art of conversation. . . . Discussing a book doesn't exist today. No one's read a book." Anxiously listening in on the interview, the Funk and Wagnalls's representative rushed forward "to clarify their own case: The advance sale [of this edition of *Etiquette*] is three times that of any previous revision." Perhaps frustrated by the lack of frisson in the air, the petulant *New Yorker* reporter noted sourly the absence of water glasses. Even worse was the bland menu—chicken consommé, chicken Tetrazzini, and ice-cream cake. Ned explained apologetically that desserts were the only part of a meal that really interested his mother, "especially ones with chocolate and whipped cream. . . . She doesn't like the rest of the meal at all," he said. As if to dispel the myth of the preternaturally perfect Emily Post, *Time* magazine noted that "as reporters dawdled over cocktails, the arbiter of proper behavior cried: 'I'm hungry. Where's the food?' "

⚜

CHAPTER 69

A FEW YEARS AFTER EMILY DIED, THE NEW YORK STATE DEPART-
ment of Education would conduct a survey it called "The Ten Reference
Books Indispensable in Any Public Library." *Etiquette* came in fourth. But in
1955, the last edition of *Etiquette* officially revised by Emily Post met with a
noticeable lack of enthusiasm. Nonetheless, it was enough of a literary
touchstone of its time that one sharp critic, at least, considered its appearance noteworthy. Comparing the original version of 1922 with its present
incarnation, Geoffrey Hellman, who had written thoughtfully about Frank
Crowninshield just before his death, now detailed "The Waning Oomph of
Mrs. Toplofty" in the *New Yorker*. Some of the changes Hellman enumerated
had occurred as Emily herself matured, such as her renunciation of wit used
at another's expense. Showing greater sensitivity to the damage language
can cause, she had also toned down some of her theatrical descriptions
from the early version of *Etiquette:* "How can you go about with that moth-
eaten, squint-eyed bag of a girl!" asked a charmer in 1922 who "admired her
own facile adjectives" and wanted to impress a young man. His answer had
been a one-two knockout: "Because the lady of your flattering epithets
happens to be my sister." The updated version, over thirty years later, now
read, "How can you go about with that squint-eyed girl!" "Because she is my
sister," this aggrieved brother responded.

On a larger social scale, Emily's famously creative names had, by 1955,
and at the insistence of her publisher, yielded their implicit Knickerbocker
heritage to a mixed crowd from Boston or Philadelphia: Mrs. Katharine de

Puyster Eminent, for instance, was now Mrs. Katharine Sedgwick Penny-backer. The seemingly minor changes throughout the book suggested to Hellman that a "regional expansion," marked by "flights from provincialism," had taken place on Emily's part. Certainly she had bowed to majority opinions. She, who treated the punctuality of her own meals as sacrosanct, now omitted completely the Toploftys' earlier stern solution for latecomers.

These days, Emily had decided, the polite response was to welcome the tardy guests to the table and help them catch up on the meal. In 1922, the Toploftys had simply bid the servants serve the latecomer whatever course everyone else was then eating. In spite of her relaxed vigilance, however, Emily held tight to a few nostrums. Mrs. Toplofty's initial response to an obnoxious guest, for instance, remained intact. Both in 1922 and 1955, "Mrs. Toplofty, finding herself [at a dinner party] next to a man she quite openly despised, said to him with apparent placidity, 'I shall not talk to you—because I don't care to. But for the sake of my hostess I shall say my multiplication tables. Twice one are two, twice two are four'—and she continued on through the tables, making him alternate them with her. As soon as she politely could, she turned again to her other companion."

Funk and Wagnalls's nearly frantic promotion of the 1955 edition as "new" obscured how Emily's book had regularly adjusted to its moment throughout the years, at least twice each decade. What were now touted as radical changes—the disappearance of fingerbowls, the appearance of divorced parents, maids allowed to entertain male friends—had been made gradually throughout the preceding years. The presumption that etiquette was somehow timeless tricked journalists and even, arguably, Funk and Wagnalls into defining the subject at its most trivial level, shortchanging the constancy of Emily's record of social changes through the decades. The publisher had deliberately dated its author by claiming that until four years ago she'd taken for granted that everyone had maids—a bizarrely inaccurate assertion. This error was further compounded in publicity for *The Emily Post Cookbook,* which portrayed Emily as having assumed until recently that everyone had a cook. Suddenly, Funk and Wagnalls proclaimed, she was coming "to [the] help" of people without a "calling card."

While the *New Yorker* engaged in a comprehensive comparison of Emily's early and late texts, *Newsweek* simply avowed that "Mrs. Post had made heroic efforts to keep her advice current," citing as one example her recent advice on women helping their dates pay for restaurant meals. To such modern positions, the journalist contrasted her edict from 1922, when Emily had written that a lady was always seated in the back of a car, to the right of the gentleman, noting that "a lady 'on the left' is NOT a 'lady.' "

Long ago, Arthur Schlesinger and Edmund Wilson, followed by contemporary writers such as Michael Korda and James Cate, had drawn attention to the contradictions that plagued Emily's early discussions of the mythical "Best People." By 1955, however, she had staked her claim clearly: Best People weren't born, they were made. In 1922, she had trotted out a nominee's pedigree, rather than her true practice of etiquette: "Mrs. Titherington Smith . . . is the daughter of the late Rev. Samuel Eminent and is therefore a member in her own right, as well as by marriage, of representative New York families," she wrote as an example of a letter of recommendation. By 1955, birth no longer determined desirability; distinction according to one's merits was what mattered. "Mrs. Titherington Smith," this passage now read, "is a person of much charm and distinction and when you meet her I am sure you will agree with me in thinking that she will be a valuable addition to the club."

Hellman also observed how Emily's treatment of class had changed from that of 1922. Her tone was "less snobbish, for Mrs. Post has replaced social inferiority with ignorance as a whipping boy." Emily, however, had always maintained that social inferiority came from lack of knowledge, however poorly she had expressed that conviction. Ignorance had consistently been her primary target. Emily's current locution, "people who know better," revised from her 1920s "persons of position," reflected a pivotal change in American culture between the Gilded Age and the post–World War II era, when the doors to a rarefied class had been shown breachable after all. Emily had understood this from the beginning.

DEMENTIA GAINED GROUND toward the end. As other cultural icons located their bearings, Emily lost hers. Civil rights, the cold war, and rock and roll: they would proceed without Emily Post. From the creator of the Eames chair, to a young and earnest Abigail Van Buren, to an even younger and more tenacious Martin Luther King: Emily Post would offer no comment on society's incipient revolutions, her confused private world finally fixated on the past. By the time that Soviet and American rockets were vying for supremacy, the woman who had never driven a car had nonetheless weathered enough cultural change to cede the stage to others.

Sometimes Emily's confusion was merciful. It is unclear whether she

understood fully at this point that eighty-one-year-old Alice Lee Beadleston Post, her longtime travel companion and "double" relative from both
her mother's and ex-husband's sides, died after a long, difficult illness. A
few years earlier, President Eisenhower had begun the great interstate
highway project, enabling car trips that Emily and Alice would have taken
in a heartbeat, back in the old days.

At the end of 1957, Bill arranged for round-the-clock nursing for his
grandmother, shortly before an article appeared in *Newsweek* lauding both
Etiquette and Amy Vanderbilt's book on manners, currently in its fourth edition. *Newsweek* described the latter as more modern in tone. While Emily
Post "is more inclined to act as a gracious Delphian oracle proclaiming
How to Behave," Amy Vanderbilt instead reported "How the Best People
Are Currently Behaving," the journalist opined. In a sentence Emily herself
would never have used, Vanderbilt explained that she was trying "to find
out what the most genteel people regularly do" and then report on those
practices. What gentility is, how it is defined, who the "most genteel" are:
Vanderbilt's implied roster suggests the metaphysically vague notion of
"Best People" Emily herself had acknowledged to be a cultural, not a natural, construction. *Newsweek* fêted Vanderbilt's forthcoming publication,
adding that Amy Vanderbilt had been writing a column syndicated by 150
newspapers for the past four years. At this point, it is unlikely that Emily
knew or cared about the competition.

Ned, staying for ever longer periods in New York City as his mother
grew more disoriented, finalized an agreement with freelance writer
Dorothy Giles of Cold Spring, New York, to ghostwrite what would become *Truly Emily Post*, published by Funk and Wagnalls within months of his
mother's death. On March 13, 1958, Giles—who would die the same year as
Emily—signed the contract for a biography "by Edwin Post," with herself
"nowhere to be credited as author or collaborator." She would be paid
$5,000 in three installments: $1,250 on signing the letter of agreement;
$1,250 upon delivery of half the manuscript; and $2,500 when the complete
text, in final typed form, was delivered to the publisher on January 1, 1959.
If Emily had been sentient, she would have been more interested in the financial arrangements than in revisiting the ledgers Ned turned over to
Giles.

IN 1960, THE GRANDSON of a poor Irish immigrant like those Emily's
book had tutored was elected as the United States' first Roman Catholic

president. Less than two months earlier, on September 25, 1960, at 39 East Seventy-ninth Street in the co-op that her younger son had helped her design, Emily Post died in her bed. Officially, her cause of death was pneumonia, but in the fashion of those who watch a loved one deteriorate month after month, her companions insisted it was just "old age."

The obituaries followed fast and furious, the news appearing on the front page of the *New York Times* and the Los Angeles papers. The *Chicago Tribune* claimed that her age, treated with such reticence that it was not mentioned in her sketch in *Who's Who in America,* had "finally" been disclosed. Then its reporter too got it wrong by a year: "She was born in Baltimore on October 27, 1873." The year of her birth (usually a toss-up between 1872 and 1873) and her age when she left Baltimore (ranging from five to twelve years) depended upon the newspaper. *Life* magazine remembered her fondly and respectfully: "In a favorite position on her wide sofa, Mrs. Post dictated answers to her daily mail in a low voice with a good deal of laughter."

What impressed commentators most was Emily's willingness to confront reality. "Emily Post took the world of people as she found it," the *New York Times* reported. "Probably you were never going to meet the Grand Duke and so it didn't matter much whether you knew exactly how you should address him. But when the daughter was married it was useful to know such things as what the father of the bride should do at the wedding reception. The advice she gave was often little more than simple common sense, but her reputation as an authority made this advice easy to follow. Having easy good manners herself, she succeeded in taking a lot of the la-di-da out of cultivated living. She was the enemy of the little finger that extended elegantly from the teacup. She decried the supercilious gape through the lorgnette." A few days later, the *Times* commended Emily Post as a "pioneer" who simplified etiquette "in a time when many believed that good manners were necessarily elaborate." Her local *Vineyard Gazette* recounted her "primary rules": "use your common sense" and "don't be self-conscious," and then "you'll be all right. . . . I'm firmly against doing things by rote."

The accolades at least hinted at the historical distance Emily and *Etiquette* had spanned. Emily Price Post was a product of the defeated and desiccated South, born when her parents and their families had barely recovered their balance after the Civil War. She grew up in the dual shadow of the Gilded Age and the skyscraper, a blend of nostalgic looking back at what never was and an aggressive interaction with the future. Railroads and agriculture, dependent on each other, had boomed. Electricity, the telephone, the automobile, the radio, the television: each fed the others. By the time Emily Post died, her country was launching rockets into outer space. *Etiquette*, a "ticket" to society, was also a cultural history of her nation. She didn't know when she played in the base of the Statue of Liberty that Miss Liberty would one day welcome an audience who would read her book to learn how to be proper Americans.

Other women who had tried to buck the system on their own weren't so fortunate as Emily Post. On the same page where the *Washington Post* announced Emily's death, a much smaller column announced that of fifty-nine-year-old Ruth Rowland Nichols, "world famous flier . . . society girl . . . regarded with Amelia Earhart as one of the pioneering women in American aviation." A few years earlier Nichols had flown an air force jet faster than one thousand miles an hour at 51,000 feet, setting another record for women. Now, it appeared, the lonely woman had taken her own life. The roster of firsts for the twentieth-century woman could have contained thousands of names. Emily Post was one of the lucky ones.

JUST OVER TWO WEEKS after Emily's death, during a General Assembly meeting at the United Nations, Comrade Nikita Khrushchev removed his shoe and banged it on the table. Connecting two radically disparate moments, *Life* magazine immediately responded to the comic spectacle with the article "What Would Emily Post Have Said?" Khrushchev's boorish behavior, which would have worldwide repercussions, had taken place "not far," a mere two miles, from Emily's deathbed. "It may seem frivolous to discuss [the Assembly's] breaches of etiquette, as though the menace of Castro, for example, were his careless choice of forks," *Life* noted. But in the end, there was "a connection worth tracing between manners and politics. *Etiquette*, as Mrs. Post always insisted, is 'the code of instinctive decency, ethical integrity, self-respect.' Politics is a branch of morals, too."

The funeral was private, though carefully, lovingly redolent of her past. The church at Madison and Seventy-first, within walking distance of her apartment, had witnessed many such ceremonies for Emily's crowd these past few years. Practical to the end, and following her parents' example, Emily Post was cremated. Her ashes were buried in the cemetery at Tuxedo Park, the date of her birth, 1872, chiseled in stone at last. Not even a lady's prerogative could bend the truth now.

ACKNOWLEDGMENTS

TWO GENEROUS GRANTS, A NATIONAL ENDOWMENT FOR THE HUMANI-
ties yearlong fellowship and the J. Anthony Lukas Work-in-Progress Award,
jointly sponsored by the Columbia University Graduate School of Journalism and the Nieman Foundation at Harvard, sustained me in multiple ways
while I wrote this book. Financially, they were godsends. Even more important, they reassured me that I had something worth saying and the wherewithal to say it. I am especially grateful to Marion Lynton for endowing the
Lukas award, and to Linda Healey, Susan Braudy, Kevin Coyne, Richard
Pollak, and Nicholas Lemann for their votes of confidence.

Joseph Wittreich at CUNY Graduate Center and Arthur Danto at
Columbia University have remained stalwart supporters for many years,
professors who showed me the way and then graciously stamped their im-
primatur on my studies a long time ago, loyally staying my course however
tortuous its direction. Their gracious sustenance has, over the decades, emboldened my critical enterprise. They are exemplars of public intellectuals,
those individuals whom Richard Altick, mentoring me even earlier, called
scholar-adventurers.

Far less directly, but proving again the power of the text, a scholar from
afar, chronologically and otherwise, also lit the path of my inquiry. Years
ago, while living in Stuttgart, I spent months studying Norbert Elias's astounding *The Civilizing Process,* originally published in Germany in 1937,
within two years of his parents' deaths at Buchenwald and Auschwitz. I
stumbled upon the book long after Elias had achieved renown and re-
spectability in the 1960s, and I was not prepared for its breadth and erudi-

tion. I strongly suspect that its trenchant chapters on manners and the organizations of society and state played a part, decades later, in leading me backward to Emily Post. I hope so. I believe, though they'd initially be astonished at their pairing, that Emily Post and Norbert Elias would have appreciated each other.

The family of Emily Post has been unfailingly gracious and supportive. William (Bill) Goadby Post, Emily's grandson, and his wife, Elizabeth (Libby), have brooked, with charm, my near-constant interference these past seven years. Cindy Post Senning, Peggy Post, and Peter and Tricia Post have gone out of their ways to accommodate my needs, often at great inconvenience to themselves. Allen Post and William Post Jr. have also been willing and ready whenever I asked for their input. Matt Bushlow and Katherine Meyers and, especially, Elizabeth Howell, at the Emily Post Institute in Vermont, never demurred those times I needed extra help, even meeting me in their New England office on early Saturday mornings, always at the ready, cheerfully filling my endless requests.

On the other side of the genealogy charts, Nora Post, the granddaughter of Emily's ex-husband, has steadily made herself available to me, by e-mail and, more delightfully, once we realized we lived within miles of each other, in person. Though she is not of Emily Post's blood, Nora's unflagging energy and unflappable good spirits make it seem as if she came from a similar mold—one that makes sense of her grandfather's attraction to my subject so many years ago.

INVALUABLE AFFILIATIONS THAT PROVED seminal to this book include a disproportionate number of librarians and private archivists. Anyone who has tapped the unflappable David Smith at the New York Public Library for his vast knowledge and his unfailing willingness to find whatever is needed knows him as a giant to writers lucky enough to cross his path. The Hudson Valley's Fran Shapiro, at the Kingston Regional Library, along with Christian R. Sonne, the historian of Tuxedo Park, have gone far beyond the norm, insisting kindly that all their work was in the line of duty. Roberta Fiore, of Long Beach Historical Society, mailed me her private copies of books impossible to obtain otherwise. Donna Halper answered my confused questions about the beginnings of radio with humor and grace and, most of all, with alacrity. Eric Homberger read the early sections of my text when the Astors and Vanderbilts had really pulled me down: How would I ever keep them all straight? That he lives in England mattered not a whit: within hours, I received his detailed emendations. Pony Duke was tireless in his generosity, whether from the mountains of Montana or up close, in Manhattan. Correction upon correction: he cheerfully undertook vetting my genealogy and anecdotes until—I think—I finally got it right. His sister, Katharine Selznick, even went so far as meeting me for pizza in Pacific Palisades. From obtaining obscure, hard-to-find copies of hundred-year-old texts to tracking down quotations I couldn't identify, these sources, these friends—anonymous when we started—were indefatigable. This book would have been several more years in the making without their knowledge.

Research assistants were loyal no matter what challenge I frantically issued, including my willing soldier at Bard, Rebecca Jones, who inherited all the tedious details at the very end. But most of all, my dear Tracey Middlekauff was my ally in arms, the stalwart who tended me and mine in Baltimore and Brooklyn in ways that elicit awe among my fellow writers. She also mentored two hardworking young writer interns, Jessica Ruggieri and David Hillstrom.

Closer to home, my Hudson Valley writers' group offered advice that was inevitably useful: Sue Erikson Bloland, Richard Hoffman, Holly George-Warren, and John Milward. Sue and Andrea Grunblatt, both psychoanalysts, were also tireless in answering questions dealing with Emily Post's psychological makeup. On a personal level, Sue and Marilyn Manning sacrificed their own work when I needed transportation after I fell ill. Lorraine Johnson, Jennifer Naidich, Jen Dragon, Leslie Siegel, and Robert Warren seemed always at the ready, whatever my needs, however inconvenient for them. Richard and Alice Hoffman, who moved out of their house in Woodstock to give me a place to recuperate when I was sick, were extraordinary in their kindness.

At Random House, publicists, designers, and copy and production editors who have ensured this book shows to its greatest advantage include Bonnie Thompson, Judy Eda, Robbin Schiff, Sally Marvin, Karen Fink, and especially Steve Messina.

My editor, Susanna Porter, once again made the always fearful and fearsome task of revising a manuscript if not exactly a piece of cake, at least a medicine that went down easy. Of all her "suggestions," I suspect I rejected only one, and even that was so I'd have some self-respect left. In addition to her editorial legerdemain, Susanna showed a benevolence of spirit in urging me to take all the time I needed to write this book. There was no hurry, she emphasized. It is to Random House's credit, and particularly to Susanna's faith, that I was allowed to finish at my own pace.

Flip Brophy was equally steadfast, never pushing me but emphasizing that whenever I was ready, she was there, to guide, to encourage, to support. Probably neither Susanna nor Flip has any idea what their confidence meant to me.

I have discovered that each book is empowered by a gift of good fortune that at first seems pleasantly incidental but proves providential instead. Miriam Medina, the creator of thehistorybox.com, was the angel sent my way for this one. She read my author's inquiry in the *New York Times* and, from that point on, freely and magnanimously gave me the benefit of her wide-ranging genealogical knowledge and research skills. Over the past seven years, we have e-mailed weekly, sometimes frantically several times within an hour—and we've still never met face-to-face. If it were not for the extraordinary personal circumstances of my writing this book, I would dedicate it to Miriam—she was that important.

Individuals who assisted on this project include but are not limited to Wint Aldrich, Gabriele Almond, Mary Alstrup, Bob Armstrong, Samantha Barbas, Neil Bascombe, Allen Bell, Tony Bettencourt, Michelle Boxley, Tsofit Butler, Mark Caldwell, Joan Didion, Stephen Dubner, A. St. George B. Duke, Michael Fredman, Ross Freier, Rev. Edwin A. Garrett III, Courtney Goines, Christopher Gray, Samuel Graybill, Bonnie Haas, Nancy Hadley, Paige Horn, Laura Jacobs, Susan Jacoby, Jeffrey W. Jarrett, Michael Kammen, Beverly Rae Kimes, Chuck Klosterman, Catherine Lynn, Karal Ann Marling, Margie Menard, Nancy Milford, Gary Nigh, Cesar Pescolini, Lori Plutchik, Julia Reed, Wayne Reilly, Mark Renovitch, Kate Rounds, Shelby Scates, Vincent and Catherine Scully, Katharine Selznick, Dori and David Sless, John Siemon, Jane Smith, Patrick J. Stevens, Jean Strouse, Yvonne Sylvia, Anita Whitehead, Barbara Dafoe Whitehead, Linda Zeller, and Kristy Zornig.

Institutions and their representatives also contributed generously: Allegany College of Maryland; Allegany County Public Library, Cumberland, Maryland; Bob Flesher, American Banjo Fraternity; American Institute of Architects, Washington, D.C.; Valerie Hawkins, American Library Association, Chicago; Susan Robbins Watson, Hazel Braugh Records Center and Archives, American Red Cross; Terri Chiao, Architectural League of New York; Babylon (New York) Public Library; Adam Gross, James T. Wollon Jr., and Carlos Avery at the Baltimore Architecture Foundation;

the online 1864 Baltimore City Directory Project; Elizabeth Rafferty, Baltimore County Public Library; Bar Harbor (Maine) Historical Society; Braille Institute of Los Angeles; Bucks County (Pennsylvania) Historical Society; Gillian Thorpe, Julia L. Butterfield Memorial Library; Charnley-Persky House Museum Foundation, Chicago; Colony Club, New York City; Jennifer B. Lee, Rare Book and Manuscript Library, Columbia University; Patrick J. Stevens, Rare Book and Manuscript Collection, Cornell University Library; John G. Langley, Cunard Steamship Society; Sallie Bingham Center for Women's History and Culture, Duke University Library; Edgartown (Massachusetts) Library; Diana Carey and Mary Jo Price, Lewis J. Ort Library Special Collections, Frostburg State University; Surrogate Courthouse and County Clerk's Office, Orange County Courthouse, Goshen, New York; Town and City of Goshen, New York; Larry Ashmead and Helen Moore, HarperCollins Publishers; Harvard Alumni Association; Giordana Mecagni, Doris Stevens Collection and Jessie Tarbox Beals Papers, Arthur and Elizabeth Schlesinger Library, Radcliffe Institute for Advanced Study, Harvard University; Deb Whitehorse, Iceboat.org, Four Lakes Ice Yacht Club; Indiana University Archives (Dodd, Mead); Kingston (New York) Public Library; Lynn Rankin, Ladies' Tea Guild of Southeastern Massachusetts; Lagrange Historical Inn; Travis Westly, Newspaper and Current Periodical Room, and Patrick Kerwin and Jeffrey M. Flannery, Manuscript Division, Library of Congress, Washington, D.C.; Leslie Gottlieb, Lighthouse International; Lincoln Highway Association; Long Beach (New York) Historical Society; Long Island Museum of American Art; Eulalie Regan, *Vineyard Gazette* and Martha's Vineyard Historical Society; Carol Fleeger, Martha's Vineyard Inn; Linda Wilson, Martha's Vineyard Museum; Maryland Diocesan Archives; Melissa Ray, Maryland Historical Society; Carl Spadoni, McMaster University Library Division of Archives and Research Collections; Mercer Museum/Bucks County Historical Society; Abigail Grotke and Miss Abigail's Time Warp Advice; Christine Nelson, Morgan Library, Archives Committee; Museum of the City of New York; Ken Beck and Shu Lin Lee, Museum of Television and Radio (New York and Los Angeles); Renee Braden, National Geographic Archives and Special Collections, Washington, D.C.; Rajal Lele, NBC Archives; Miriam Touba, New-York Historical Society; Eric Robinson, New-York Historical Society Library; Arnold W. Roepken, Archives, New York Stock Exchange; New York University Archives; New York Yacht Club; Enoch Pratt Free Library of Baltimore City; Margaret Sherry Rich, Rare Books and Special Collections, Princeton University Library; Sallie Sypher, Putnam County (New York) Historical Society; Nancy Kelly, Rhinebeck (New York) town historian; Marjorie Strong and Alycia J. Vivona, Franklin D. Roosevelt Presidential Library, Hyde Park; Rosina Sherwood Collection, Emmet Family Papers, Archives of American Art, Smithsonian Institution; Society of Architectural Historians, Chicago; Kathy DiPhilippo, South Portland (Maine) Historical Society; St. Clement and St. Peter's Episcopal Church, Wilkes-Barre (Pennsylvania); St. Mary's Episcopal Church, Tuxedo Park; Staten Island Historical Society Library; 3quarksdaily.com; Kate Nielsen, Tuxedo Park Public Library; Carrie T. Hayter, Union League Club; Lynn E. Eaton and Rachel Sailor, Rare Book, Manuscript, and Special Collections Library, University of Iowa Libraries; Ann Hudak, Maryland and Rare Books Department, University of Maryland Libraries; Vermont Historical Society; Carl Spencer, Wagnalls Memorial Library; Jennifer Dintaman, Washington County Historical Society, Hagerstown, Maryland; and Edmund Wilson Papers, Beinecke Rare Book and Manuscript Library, Yale University Collection of American Literature.

IN THE FALL OF 2003, I was diagnosed with primary CNS lymphoma, a particularly aggressive brain cancer. Six months later, when I came to know myself again, I could barely remember Emily Post at all. Memorial Sloan-Kettering, where the latest research helped save my life, provided first-rate care. Doctors Lisa DeAngelis and Lauren Abrey, Joachim Yahalom and his kind, intelligent assistants (as well as the adjunct care of Dr. Jackson Coleman, next door at New York Presbyterian–Cornell), and, especially, the dedicated, intellectually capacious, brave, and kind Dr. Craig Nolan healed me. Craig's medicine even went one better: he asked me to autograph a copy of my last book, as strong an incentive to get well as any chemical agent the devil could devise, a reminder of who I was and who he believed I would be again. If Craig kept me from dying, Dr. Stephen Foster, clinical professor at Harvard Medical School and president of the Massachusetts Eye Research and Surgery Institute, saved my sight, and I am deeply grateful for his courage in expanding conventional treatments in order to help me see again.

My longtime friends Azra Raza, Sughra Raza, and Abbas Raza kept insisting I would eventually be well, and I figured they must know. The first two, doctors at august medical institutions themselves, were always at the ready, time and again consulting with my retinue in New York. Abbas was the don of my brain, writing so lucidly on his brilliant 3quarksdaily.com Web site that I could almost understand the science his sisters were trying to teach me.

From my own sister, Marybeth Powell, boarding a plane on the West Coast within hours of getting a phone call, to in-laws spanning Atlanta to Ireland and phoning daily, my family has been unstintingly loyal and fluent with their love. And then there are my four progeny, my tight little mixed clan of genes and glory. Two of them, though they were not, at the time, living in Manhattan, nonetheless made themselves present in every possible way, Colin, the youngest, interrupting his first semester at college to be by my side, Geof, by age the ringleader of our combined family, reassuringly next in command after his father. Even so, for this book, the dedication is a natural, Geof and Colin agree.

My resolute New York triumvirate of daughter, son, and husband, holding faithful watch at my hospital bedside that interminable night of the soul when even the doctors had given up hope, singing to me, whispering in my ear, insisting (so nurses, friends, and visitors report with awe), against all evidence, that I would be fine: "Just come back," they urged fiercely, a force I couldn't resist. "Come back to us." I am here because of them as much as anything or anyone else.

N O T E S

Works listed in the Bibliography are referred to in these notes by only the author's name and short title. All citations of *Etiquette* are from the 1922 edition unless otherwise noted.

PART ONE

CHAPTER 1

4 *for the same "project":* The travails of Edwin Main Post and of Colonel William D'Alton Mann's cohorts come from the following newspaper accounts: *New York Tribune,* July 12, 1905, p. 1; *New York Tribune,* July 15, 1905, p. 1; *New York Times,* July 12, 1905, p. 1; *New York Times,* July 22, 1905, p. 7; *New York Times,* July 15, 1905, p. 1; *Evening Post,* July 14, 1905, p. 1; *Evening Post,* July 13, 1905, p. 1; *New York Times,* July 16, 1905, p. 6; *Evening Post,* July 12, 1905, p. 2; for a more complete account of Mann's continued problems, relevant to much more than Post's own ordeal, see Andy Logan's *The Man Who Robbed the Robber Barons.* Information about Emily's reactions to her husband's misalliance comes from family recollections, twice-told tales, and reminiscences of Edwin Post's daughter-in-law about family gossip. Also relevant was a letter from Stephen G. Post to Barbara Dafoe Whitehead, February 17, 1998.

5 *"Stockbroker's Way of Dealing":* New York Tribune, July 12, 1905, p. 1.

5 *any chance it got:* Baltimore Sun, July 13, 1905, p. 1.

CHAPTER 2

6 *bravos all around:* Lately Thomas, *Delmonico's,* 147.

7 *"Everyone" revered him:* Samuel Graybill, "Bruce Price, American Architect," quoting Countess Pesciolini, 25.

8 *out of expedience:* Bruce Price came from an old Scottish family, one that, by his birth on December 14, 1845, had its roots deep in the Maryland countryside. The most useful sources for information on Price's genealogy are as follows: the Maryland State Archives; J. Thomas Scharf's *History of Baltimore City and County,* 1881; Clayton Colman Hall, ed., *Baltimore: Its History and its People,* vol. 1, *History;* Henry Whittemore's *The Heroes of the American Revolution and Their Descendants: Battle of Long Island,* 1897; and J. Thomas Scharf's *History of Western Maryland.* Also see the Federal Census

of 1860, p. 90, Eleventh Ward, Baltimore City in the County of Baltimore of Maryland, June 13, 1860. The historical societies of Luzerne County, Pennsylvania, and Cumberland, Maryland, were useful in helping me understand the family lore.

For the most meticulous account of dates for events in Price's relatively short life, see Samuel Graybill's 1957 Yale dissertation, "Bruce Price, American Architect"; microfilm copies are available through most major academic libraries. Graybill was a student of architect critic and historian Vincent Scully. Graybill interviewed Emily Post, who consulted family histories no longer extant; and she provided the Ph.D. student with a list of friends and family (all since deceased) to contact as well. The *New York Times,* the *New York Herald,* the *New York Post,* and *Town Topics* all provide exhaustive coverage of the buildings Price created and the social events he attended.

10 **throughout the war:** Many of the exchanges between Price and Lincoln can be found in Lincoln's correspondence at the National Archives, Washington, D.C., and in the well-indexed, eight-volume *Collected Works of Abraham Lincoln,* edited by Roy P. Basler (New Brunswick, N.J.: Rutgers University Press, 1953). For the type of trusting relationship Price and Lincoln enjoyed, see e.g., "This letter being written by the U.S. District Attorney I have concluded to grant the pardon requested," from the middle of the war (letter dated December 11, 1862, vol. 6, p. 2, of Basler).

Price had served as the Baltimore delegate to the House of Delegates Special Session in December 1861, when the urgency of Baltimore's loyalty was nearly palpable. President Lincoln appointed Price to two terms as U.S. district attorney, beginning the following year.

CHAPTER 3

11 **It was a new day:** For Washington Lee's family, I have relied heavily on census data and Luzerne County histories, land deeds, church records, and old newspaper accounts. The Luzerne County Historical Society is a first-rate resource for both specific research on the Lee family and on the coal area itself, as are the archives of the *Wilkes-Barre Record* newspaper. Again, excellent resources also now exist on the Web: lowerluzernecounty.com/nanticokeborohistory.htm is one of them. Other pertinent documents include George W. Howard's *The Monumental City: Its Past History and Present Resources* (Baltimore: J. D. Ehlers, 1873–76); Henry Blackman Plumb's *History of Hanover Township and Wyoming Valley* (Wilkes-Barre: Robert Baur, 1885); Oscar Jewell Harvey's *The Harvey Book: Giving the Genealogies of Certain Branches of the American Families of Harvey, Nesbitt, Dixon and Jameson* (Wilkes-Barre, 1899); George B. Kulp's *Families of the Wyoming Valley: Biographical, Genealogical, and Historical; Sketches of the Bench and Bar of Luzerne County, Pennsylvania* (Wilkes-Barre, 1890); *History of Luzerne, Lackawanna, and Wyoming Counties, Pa., with Illustrations and Biographical Sketches of Some of Their Prominent Men and Pioneers* (New York: W. W. Munsell, 1880); and *Memorial of the Mayor and City Council of Baltimore* (Baltimore: Wm. M. Innes, 1861).

Local newspaper articles from the nineteenth century, death certificates, obituaries, probated wills, and notices of inheritances helped me re-create a past that—oddly, in light of her compulsive tendencies—Emily Post didn't preserve. Regional libraries and historical societies repeatedly filled in gaps.

Priscilla and John Alden did join Plymouth Colony for the country's first Thanksgiving. Arguably more important are the histories of Luzerne and Washington counties' early ore deposits and the carving of millionaires out of the countryside. The history of Emily Post's ancestors, trailing opulent black coal, is rich for those concerned with early commercial enterprise. In 1823 Colonel Lee (Emily Post's great-uncle) and George Chahoon leased a mine in Newport and contracted for the mining and delivery of one thousand tons of coal in arks at Lee's Ferry, Pennsylvania, at $1.10 per ton—the coal selling at Columbia at a loss of $1,500. But by 1829, the coal in the area had gained a reputation as the finest in the country, causing Baltimore capitalists to invest heavily. Pennsylvania, in essence, subsidized the coal industry's future in the state by allowing for the incorporation of the Baltimore and Pittsburg Coal Company, publicizing the anthracite veins as the best in the nation. The legatees of the Lee family estate sold it to the Susquehanna Coal Company, which rented it out as a tenant house. Josephine Lee didn't come by her business smarts by accident.

Washington Lee, Josephine's father, went to Dickinson College, in Carlisle, Pennsylvania, and graduated in 1843. He studied law, subsequently practicing his profession for several years in Wilkes-Barre, where he was elected county district attorney. After a few years of comparing incomes from the law with those of the furnace, Lee left the bar and engaged in business enterprises with his uncle Colonel Washington Lee, operating coal mines at Nanticoke and becoming very rich.

On June 29, 1846, he married Emily Laura Thomas (for whom Emily Post would be named), the daughter of Abraham Thomas. The Lees had five children; their daughter Josephine would be the mother of Emily Price Post. A common cause of confusion for those few interested in researching the beginnings is the following: one of Washington Lee's daughters, Emily Thomas Lee, married Benjamin C. Barroll Jr. on September 8, 1874. Emily Thomas Lee is the sister of Mary Josephine Lee and aunt of Emily Post. Of their children, a daughter, Emily's first cousin, was named Josephine Lee Barroll. The Washington Lee family lived part-time in Baltimore—where Josephine and Bruce Price met—and afterward moved to New York, where the patriarch died on March 26, 1883.

12 *picked quality ore by hand:* Tall, dignified, studious, and well liked, Colonel Washington Lee was one of the native sons (named by an Alden woman in honor of the new country's founding father) destined to become a legend himself in certain parts of Pennsylvania. He became the prime mover in Luzerne County. In 1825, he bought the on-site store and began operating a distillery, probably aimed at the immigrant workers he hired. (Lee's uncle had ceded him the title to the property just after the War of 1812.) By now hard work came naturally to his family, built into the tradition they passed down. Luckily, hard work paid well, the Lees discovered: by 1828 Colonel Lee was selling bar iron at $120 per ton. It was dirty work, he used to say, but it cleaned up real nice.

The colonel left an impression on his grandniece Josephine Lee. His gentleness and intelligence struck people as his salient characteristics, and in many ways, including his height, Bruce Price must have reminded Josephine of her favorite uncle. Bruce visited Wilkes-Barre before his marriage, where he was entertained either at the "comfortable mansion" (as county histories described it) erected on the east bank of the Susquehanna River or at the nephew's estate down the road, the home of Bruce's betrothed. Colonel Lee's nephew—this Washington Lee so named in honor of a local empire—had inherited the bulk of his relative's fields and fortune. The childless old colonel had been quite the businessman, buying a farm of one thousand acres in the early part of the century that he sold several decades later for $1.2 million, a neat inheritance for Josephine Lee's father.

13 *created a rebound:* Lately Thomas, *Delmonico's,* 101.

15 *nothing if not romantic:* See Kenneth D. Ackerman, *The Gold Ring.*

16 *very large baby:* According to her tombstone, Emily was born on October 27, 1872. In addition, the 1900 Federal Census asserts that she was born in Baltimore that year. But records from the period are not always reliable; she may have been born five days later, or even during another year: October 27, 1873, is the date of birth on her passport from 1923.

16 *every bulb she planted:* Baltimore vital records don't exist for the 1870s. Throughout her life, Emily would evince a psychologically complicated reaction to substituting for the baby brother so close in age, his gender of such obvious importance to her father.

CHAPTER 4

17 *from her stock investments:* Edwin Post, *Truly Emily Post* 3, 8, 31. In otherwise rare praise, Emily consistently emphasized Josephine's practical nature and frequently remarked how her mother used her idiosyncratic shrewdness to good effect playing the stock market.

Truly Emily Post, Edwin (Ned) Post's ghostwritten biography-memoir of his mother, was compiled during the last few years of Emily's life, when the ghost-writer, Dorothy Giles, had access to whatever logs Emily had kept over the years. From the time she was a debutante, Emily filled ledgers with the minutiae of her days. Unfortunately, except for a garden book, such accounts have disappeared. The surviving family assumes that when Emily's son moved abroad, the materials got lost in the transition. "We have no idea what happened to those records," says Cindy Post Senning, Emily's great-granddaughter. "We have searched everywhere in hopes of them turning up, but they're gone with the wind or, probably, lost in the various shuttles my father and his wife made between Italy and the United States those last years" (interview, August 3, 2002).

The only way to confirm the often misdated and exaggerated accounts in *Truly Emily Post,* whose author died only months after Emily herself, is to cross-reference any anecdote or to present it as conjectural.

18 *fueled their concerns:* Jean Strouse, *Morgan,* 152. More than anything, as Strouse emphasizes, it was this six-year depression that purged the country's near-fairyland obsession with the past. Now an expanding economy would be forced to confront urgent monetary issues of the current day, instead of rehashing times past.

18 *he inevitably answered:* Quoted in Harold Evans, "Follow the Money."

19 *the Four Hundred:* Jerry Patterson, *The First Four Hundred,* 87.

19 *really only 273 names:* Ward McAllister, "The Only Four Hundred: Ward McAllister Gives Out the Official List," *New York Times,* February 16, 1892, p. 5. The list had varied, depending on who was in and out of society at the time.

20 *like Uncle Charlie:* Truly Emily Post, 68.

20 *until the beans were gone:* Emily Post, "Kelland Doesn't Know What He Is Talking About, Answers Emily Post," *American Magazine,* December 1928, p. 13.

20 *and proper pencils:* Eleanor Garst papers, courtesy of the Iowa Women's Archives, University of Iowa Libraries.

21 *90 percent rate:* Samuel Graybill, "Bruce Price: American Architect," conclusion.

22 *"into towering cubes":* Etiquette, 2.

22 *into the urban fold:* By Motor to the Golden Gate, 240.

CHAPTER 5

23 *Baltimore houses he had loved:* Truly Emily Post, 38.

23 *"Clearly custom hammered":* Transcript of interview with Christopher Gray, May 22, 2001, courtesy of Laura Jacobs.

24 *when they weren't in residence:* Truly Emily Post, 68.

24 *age of commerce and creativity:* The birth of the skyscraper, the competition between Chicago and New York, and the major players of the times are the subjects of an ever-increasing library. Two sources particularly user-friendly for the nonprofessional are Sarah Bradford Landau and Carl W. Condit, *Rise of the New York Skyscraper,* and Erik Larson's *The Devil in the White City.* The latter is the dual story of the Chicago world's fair and a mass murderer, its subtext the fight between New York and Chicago architects to take the lead in the skyscraper race.

25 *French women around her husband:* Truly Emily Post, 23.

26 *the buyer's prestige:* "A Glimpse of Fairy Land: 'The Sleeping Beauty' at the Academy, Remarkable Success of Benefit Performance for the Mount Vernon Endowment Fund—Brilliant Audience," *New York Times,* April 26, 1878.

27 *paid off when he was able:* "Newsboys in High Feather," *New York Times,* July 23, 1878. Catharine was related to the Bruces of Scotland, for whom Emily's father was named. David Wolfe Bruce, one of the executors of Catharine Lorillard Wolfe's estate, was a cousin of the Lorillards and Bruces, making Emily a true blueblood.

28 *sputter to a wan conclusion:* Classified ad, *New York Times,* May 6, 1879.

CHAPTER 6

30 *anyone else in her life:* For a detailed account of the trip up the Hudson, see Ronald G. Pisano, *The Tile Club and the Aesthetic Movement in America* (New York: Abrams, 1999), 30–33.

31 *everything from painting to textiles:* In the 1880s a worldwide movement occurred in almost all areas of art and design, from jewelry to architecture. Western art was newly inspired by the simple beauty of Japanese, Celtic, Viking, and Islamic art and by plant and animal life (including the human female). An aesthetic rebellion aimed at decades of classical repetition in art and Victorian excess in architecture swept across Europe. The movement was called Art Nouveau in Belgium and France, Secession in Austria, Jugendstil in Germany, Modernismo in Spain, and Stile Liberty in Italy (the nomenclature stemming from Arthur Liberty, whose firm crafted jewelry and homeware in the new style). The Tile Club, inspired by such energies, was part of the American reaction.

31 *even consider moving to New York:* Lloyd Morris, *Incredible New York,* 168.

31 *travel, painting, and antics:* In his *The Tile Club and the Aesthetic Movement in America,* Pisano emphasizes Frank Hopkinson Smith's status as talented and genial gadfly. Additional information on the club can be found in William H. Shelton, *The Salmagundi Club: A History* (Boston: Houghton Mifflin, 1918), and Constance Koppelman, "Nature in Art and Culture: The Tile Club" (Ph.D. diss., State University of New York, Stony Brook, 1985).

32 *an ill mix:* *Harper's Weekly,* August 14, 1880, p. 516. The hotel had officially opened on July 13, 1880, with the *New York Times* hailing the "new watering place" in its coverage the following day.

32 *oversee company operations:* The Long Beach Hotel was leased by the Long Beach Improvement Company. A requirement of the rental agreement between Lee's company and the hotel owner was that $25,000 had to be spent on property improvement the first year of occupancy.

33 *long-promised railroad stop:* The increasingly worried investors were granted an artificial reprieve when President Garfield was shot in the back as he boarded a train—confounding the already confused markets further but in the process deflecting creditors from Long Beach. The country was distracted from its longtime financial fears by the drama being played out publicly, with unsettling medical bulletins issued daily for the next two months. Peculiarly blunt, as if clarity would ward off disaster, they went further than we do today in our supposedly more open age: it was announced, for instance, that Garfield's heavy discharge of pus appeared healthy. Even after the president's death, every detail of the surgery to remove his spine for the jurors to examine was covered, including a description of the spine itself.

33 *progressed nicely:* Lately Thomas, *Delmonico's,* 192–93.

34 *structures over the past year:* His workload was staggering. Samuel Graybill's biography provides drawings of more than eleven projects, all believed to have been built, not just designed, during 1880 alone. Graybill, "Bruce Price, American Architect," 273–74.

34 *half of that number:* In 1860, New York City's population stood at 1,174,000; just twenty years later, it topped 2,000,000.

34 *"of much moment":* "Thayer and Barroll," *New York Times,* February 2, 1881.

35 *side that his daughter adored:* "Events in the Metropolis: Seventy-Three Giants; The Grand Classical Banquet of the Titans in Delmonico's," *New York Times,* May 22, 1882, p. 2.

35 *obtain better sight lines:* "James Barton's New Theatre," *New York Times,* August 30, 1883, p. 5.

35 *with gusto decades later:* Eleanor Garst papers, courtesy of the Iowa Women's Archives, University of Iowa Libraries.

35 *couldn't make a go of it:* For the history of the Long Beach investment and construction during this period, Roberta Fiore, historian and founder of Long Beach Historical Society, proved irreplaceable. She turned over every stone and found some truly unexpected gems.

36 *New York State:* Washington Lee's will left an estate of about half a million dollars in today's currency. What that valuation consisted of—did it include the property in Wilkes-Barre? the house for the poor female relatives?—is unclear. Certainly he did not leave his five adult children or his wife conventionally wealthy in the terms of the Gilded Age in which he lived.

CHAPTER 7

38 *owned a large part of it:* The story of Alva Vanderbilt's entry into society has been told countless times. Several of the best and most readily accessible descriptions appear in Eric Homberger's *Mrs. Astor's New York,* Jerry Patterson's *The Vanderbilts,* and Lloyd Morris's *Incredible New York.*

38 *anything even she had sponsored:* Alfred Allan Lewis, *Ladies and Not-So-Gentle Women,* 112.

38 *the Astors' daughter:* Lately Thomas, *Delmonico's,* 238.

39 *back home in Alabama:* Ibid., 88.

40 *in the age to come:* Ibid., 89.

40 *bungalows by the sea:* *New York Times,* May 9, 1883.

41 *she would claim:* Truly Emily Post, 8, 31.

42 *at the top:* "The Base for Liberty's Statue," *New York Times,* August 15, 1883, p. 2.

42 *"almost twelve":* For an excellent discussion of this legislative issue and the period in general, see Susan Jacoby, *Freethinkers,* 180.

43 *memories rarely exhibited:* Truly Emily Post, 39.

43 *partner and eventual successor:* Ibid., 5.

CHAPTER 8

45 *facedown, on silver trays:* Cleveland Amory, *Who Killed Society?,* 206.

46 *disrespect toward the South:* In her talks with Samuel Graybill, Bruce Price's biographer, Emily Post emphasized that her father belonged to all clubs except the Union League (Graybill, "Bruce Price, American Architect," 6).

47 *sat among them:* An extensive account of the evening at Delmonico's appeared in the *New York Times,* November 23, 1884.

48 *captured the popular imagination:* Land-based expeditions reached the pole first in 1909.

49 *Sunday night alone:* "Crowds at the Seashore," *New York Times,* July 20, 1885.

CHAPTER 9

51 *his—or Cora's—vision:* Alfred Allan Lewis, *Ladies and Not-So-Gentle Women,* 81–82.

51 *be put in his name:* For a thorough account of Tuxedo Park's founding myth, see

Emily Post, "Tuxedo Park: An American Rural Community," *Century Magazine* (October 1911). The prestige of being a member of the club's fifteen-man board of governors caused such excitement that the governors cheerfully paid the annual dues deficit themselves, a debt that ran to $50,000 a year. Until the Depression, no statement was ever sent to the other members.

51 *played in its genesis:* Cora Brown Potter, "The Age of Innocence and I," *Hearst's International Cosmopolitan* (March 1933).

52 *brown and rust red:* Samuel Graybill, "Bruce Price, American Architect," 28.

52 *"to the kitchen-maid":* Cleveland Amory, *Who Killed Society?,* 284; *Etiquette,* 438.

52 *"bore anyone had ever met":* Papers of Geoffrey Hellman, untitled notes from an interview with Frank Crowninshield in preparation for a *New Yorker* profile.

53 *decorous personal behavior:* "Lorillard and his son were big philanderers," Tuxedo Park historian Christian Sonne claims, as do virtually all the gossip columns of the period as well.

54 *it was not fashionable:* "Society Topics of the Week," *New York Times,* January 31, 1886, p. 3.

54 *"all had been lost":* Julia Reed, *Queen of the Turtle Derby,* 120.

54 *"lineage mattered most of all":* Ibid., 121.

CHAPTER 10

57 *many of the Price family friends:* There would be gloomier assessments of Tuxedo Park's conversion from resort to residence. Cleveland Amory claimed that old-timers deserted it because it was too hot in the summer and too cold in the winter, so it became an ordinary year-round residence for the wealthy instead. "No other community in this country ever started off on a grander social scale, and therefore no other may be said to have fallen so hard," he noted in *The Last Resorts,* 79.

57 *"American domestic building":* Scully is quoted in Samuel Graybill, "Bruce Price, American Architect." See Vincent Joseph Scully's *The Shingle Style Today* and various volumes of *American Architect and Building News* for a useful catalog of Bruce's contributions. Also see Graybill, 83.

58 *"nothing extra to them":* Christopher Gray, interview with Laura Jacobs, May 22, 2001. For other appreciations of Price's work, see Russell Sturgis, "The Works of Bruce Price," *Architectural Record,* Great American Architects Series, 5 (June 1899), and, in the same publication, Barr Ferree's "A Talk with Bruce Price." Also see "The Suburban House," *Scribner's,* July 1890, pp. 3–19, reprinted in Russell Sturgis, et al., *Homes in City and Country* (New York: Scribner's, 1893).

58 *most by her gender:* "The Statue Unveiled," *New York Times,* October 29, 1886.

59 *"to a closed circle":* Elsie de Wolfe, *After All,* 19.

59 *"in his own right":* Ibid.

60 **Town Topics** *herself:* See Eric Homberger, *Mrs. Astor's New York,* 20, for a particularly compact account of Elsie's relationship with Lorillard and Tuxedo Park. Also see Alfred Allan Lewis, *Ladies and Not-So-Gentle Women,* 82.

60 *when an audience responded: Truly Emily Post,* 24.

CHAPTER 11

62 *forever at Tuxedo Park:* Cleveland Amory, *The Last Resorts,* 100–101.

65 *"in American history":* Jean Strouse, *Morgan,* 215.

66 *complete equality with men:* Lloyd Morris, *Incredible New York,* 15.

66 *movement for women's clubs:* For an excellent overview of Sorosis, an important women's club, see Lately Thomas, *Delmonico's,* 138–43.

66 *older sister, Juliet:* Jerry Patterson, *The First Four Hundred,* 129.

66 *mocked their appearance:* Thomas, *Delmonico's,* 201.

CHAPTER 12

69   *suddenly busy with purpose:* Dozens of newspaper articles, long features on Gilded Age debutante balls, and so on inform this account of Emily's debut. Among the most pertinent documents are "The Patriarchs' Guests: A Notable Social Event at Delmonico's," *New York Times,* December 17, 1889; Elsie de Wolfe, *After All;* Karal Ann Marling, *Debutante;* Eric Homberger, *Mrs. Astor's New York;* and "Society Topics of the Week," *New York Times,* April 12, 1891. Also of particular relevance are Joseph Epstein's *Snobbery* and Jerry Patterson's *The First Four Hundred.*

69   *Philadelphia or Washington:* Marling, *Debutante,* 11 and 19.

69   *court of St. James's:* Ibid., 28.

69   *their quest for a title:* In *The Custom of the Country,* Wharton seemed to take especial delight in showing parvenus longing to become part of old society, and she detailed their coarseness. Henry James, in *Daisy Miller,* allows the rich American ingénue abroad to be at times truly innocent, if alarmingly simple.

70   *ball held outside the home:* The restaurant was not afraid to take risks: though it was an extremely controversial decision, Lorenzo Delmonico allowed the country's first all-female club, Sorosis, one that furthered the cause of universal suffrage, to meet at the restaurant, unescorted by men. Lloyd Morris, *Incredible New York,* 147.

70   *The fanciest dances:* One of the best manuals on the dances of the period is Elizabeth Aldrich's *From the Ballroom to Hell,* which exhaustively details everything from the language of the fan to the various moves of dances throughout the nineteenth century.

70   *sometimes, a quadrille:* For a concise portrait of Ward McAllister, see Marling, *Debutante,* 31, 62–66, 67, 69, 74, 78.

71   *menu reverted to type:* Ibid., 69.

72   *men they were riding:* For an informative essay on such a school, see Henry Collins Brown, *Valentine's Manual of the City of New York, 1917–1918* (New York: Old Colony Press, 1917).

72   *Thursday, and so on:* Patterson, *The First Four Hundred,* 76.

72   *would ever complete:* See Marling, *Debutante,* 67; and see Patricia Beard, *After the Ball,* 163.

73   *"gloves of different lengths":* de Wolfe, *After All,* 14.

73   *debutantes to their own:* "The Patriarchs' Guests," *New York Times,* December 17, 1889.

74   *how to cross a ballroom:* Emily slipped this observation into as many interviews as possible throughout the years. Sometimes she was one of two debutantes, other times one of ten ladies in all New York who could cross a ballroom correctly. See Cleveland Amory, *Who Killed Society?,* 20, and *The Last Resorts,* 99. See also Jeanne Perkins, "Emily Post," *Life,* May 6, 1946, p. 60.

74   *to be plucked:* Robert Tomes, *The Bazar Book of Decorum* (New York: Harper & Brothers, 1870), 229, quoted in Aldrich, *From the Ballroom to Hell,* 113.

74   *until supper was announced:* The *New York Times*' coverage of the evening on December 17, 1889, was unusually long, running to three columns.

75   *her haul to the table: Truly Emily Post,* 34. Emily retold the story often, with minor variations, including during a long *Saturday Evening Post* interview with Margaret Case Harriman, "Dear Mrs. Post," p. 56. She always sought to emphasize her popularity among the men at her debut.

75   *compensate for much: Etiquette,* 261 and 268.

CHAPTER 13

76   *into his life's plan:* "Society Topics of the Week," *New York Times,* December 29, 1889.

77   *Emily as a guest:* "Society in Baltimore," *New York Times,* May 4, 1890, p. 11.

77 *noted in the society pages:* "Bar Harbor: Every Available Inch Filling Rapidly," *New York Times,* July 6, 1890.

78 *liked the water or not:* Jerry Patterson, *The First Four Hundred,* 62.

78 *family visitor, Edwin Post:* The photos from Emily's personal picture album are annotated with "Papa" and "Amherst, Winter of 90–91, Jack and Edwin."

78 *a syndicated society notice:* Fort Wayne Sentinel, January 31, 1891.

78 *the newspaper recounted:* Ibid.

79 *distressed the old-timers:* So many white men wanted to play in blackface that competition was limited to them alone. The style of banjo playing in the minstrel shows was different from society picking as well: the strummer knocked down on the string with the back of his fingernail, "African" style, unlike the European picking style society ladies used (thanks to Bob Flesher, the American Banjo Fraternity, for this information).

79 *was the perfect hook:* Fort Wayne Sentinel, January 31, 1891.

79 *prospective bride's "illness":* New York Times, October 11, 1891. The concise announcement mangled the names, combining that of Emily's good friend Juliet Morgan's fiancé, William Hamilton, with Edwin's: "It is understood that the marriage of Hamilton Post and Miss Bruce Price has been postponed, owing to the ill-health of Miss Price."

80 *"He rumbled me so!":* Macy log (unpublished handwritten manuscript owned by Colonel Post's great-granddaughter Nora Post, of Kingston, New York), courtesy of Nora Post, November 6, 1890, p. 189, and August 6, 1909, p. 85. Commissioned in 1886, the boat stayed in the Post family until the death of Edwin's father, Colonel Henry Albertson Van Zo Post, in 1914. Edwin Main Post wrote most of the entries. Colonel Post, his crew members, and the guests on board made additional entries. Edwin would write the last entry when his father, whom he loved deeply, died: "Colonel HAV Post, owner of the 'Macy' died at 11:15 PM. Thus passed away one of the truest gentlemen and one of the best sportsmen the world ever knew. Signed by his son Edwin Main Post February 7, 1914." Edwin had voiced the praise earlier in his "Brant Shooting on Great South Bay," pp. 197 and 204.

80 *making a good match:* "The Desecration of a Graveyard in Southampton," *Brooklyn Eagle Daily,* July 23, 1887.

81 *with the requisite eagle:* "Dancing in Washington: Mrs. McLean's Cotillion in Honor of Miss Bonaparte," *New York Times,* February 6, 1892, p. 3.

81 *"it cost was $11.79":* Truly Emily Post, 41.

81 *has her heroine say:* The Flight of a Moth, p. 3.

82 *"stranger to the other":* Etiquette, 299.

82 *total killed that season:* Macy log, November 6, 1890, pp. 22 and 189, and August 6, 1909, p. 85. Also "Brant Shooting on Great South Bay," pp. 197 and 204.

83 *"And yourself":* Truly Emily Post, 19–20.

84 *manageable for all that:* Ibid., 21–22.

84 *planted in Emily Post as well:* Margaret Case Harriman, *The Vicious Circle,* 133.

85 *"faithfully yours, Bruce Price":* Emmet Family Papers, Archives of American Art, Smithsonian Institution, 4755: 774–75.

86 *"occupation of a woman writer":* Virginia Woolf, "Professions for Women" in *The Death of the Moth* (London: Hogarth Press, 1943).

87 *"always have a breeze":* Macy log 1889, p. 19.

87 *descendant of Oliver Cromwell:* Thanks to Nora Post and Miriam Medina for information on Caroline McLean's ancestry.

87 *the letter "Affectionately":* Emily Post Institute archives, letter, dated from internal evidence to between 1890 and 1895

88 *had both clearly dissolved:* "Calls Post Home to Answer Charges," *New York Times,* November 15, 1907.

88 *holes in the country:* New York Times, December 31, 1884.

89 *mid-seventeenth-century migration:* All Post family genealogy comes from *The Post Family,* by Marie Caroline De Trobriand Post (Mrs. Charles Algred Post). That sometimes convoluted tome was made clearer by Nora Post, Edwin and Eleanor's granddaughter, who graciously tracked the lines with me far more than once.

90 *of snagging a title:* "The Newport Season: Late Arrivals at the Hotels and Cottages," *New York Times,* June 11, 1888, p. 5.

CHAPTER 14

91 *"reminds her of me":* The rest of this account of the engagement dinner and the invitation list is taken from *Truly Emily Post,* 38–45.

92 *reforming the city government:* Jerry Patterson, *The First Four Hundred,* 153.

92 *"kick him downstairs":* *Truly Emily Post,* 40.

93 *"free-and-easy town":* The description is from Lloyd Morris, *Incredible New York,* 227.

93 *assumed benefited everyone:* "Saloons All Closed: The Police Aroused by Dr. Parkhurst and the Grand Jury," *New York Times,* April 3, 1892, p. 3.

94 *in this family circle:* *Truly Emily Post,* 43 and 41.

94 *"chagrined at their choice":* *Etiquette,* chapter 21.

95 *"both are commonplace matters":* *Etiquette,* chapter 20.

95 **point d'Alençon:** Syndicated columns in regional newspapers, such as the *Daily Northwestern,* in Oshkosh, Wisconsin, ensured that their readers were tuned in to the wedding's importance; see, e.g., "Society Wedding Near New York: Elaborate Costumes," *Daily Northwestern,* June 1, 1892. Locally, not only the wedding party but its weather captured headlines: "A Very Muggy Day: Only One June 1 on Record That Beat Yesterday for Heat," *New York Times,* June 2, 1892.

96 *quick and pointed substitutions:* "Society Topics of the Week," *New York Times,* December 29, 1889.

96 *"too stupid to discuss":* *Etiquette,* 1927, chapters 21, 31.

96 **Times** *boldly pronounced:* "All Sorts of Pretty Things," *New York Times,* June 5, 1892, p. 12.

96 *and her physical beauty:* *Truly Emily Post,* 23 and 46–47.

PART TWO

CHAPTER 15

101 *twenty-minute face-to-face:* A particularly detailed account of society women's days is contained in M.E.C., "Daily Life of an Ambitious Society Woman," *New York Times,* February 9, 1902, p. SM4.

101 *"to squander it":* *The Flight of a Moth,* 53–55.

101 *($55 in today's terms):* Her friend Frank Crowninshield would recall the protocol for producing first-rate terrapin dinners: "We were at the Ritz . . . and we had terrapin and it wasn't so awfully good. . . . When I was a young man and a rich fashionable man was giving a dinner, we'd telephone the Baltimore Club, tell steward to prepare and cook terrapin for twelve. No males used. No female could be used if over seven inches from tip to tip of shell. Put on one o'clock train, $5 bill to conductor, and my valet will meet the train, take it home, heat it, chafing dish, serve at K [Knicker-bocker] club at eight o'clock" (notes from Geoffrey Hellman's interview with Frank Crowninshield, courtesy of the Hellman collection, Bobst Library, New York University).

Forty years later, *Vogue* magazine, in a retrospective of the Gilded Age, would claim that "hostesses . . . were thought niggardly if they failed to serve both terrapin and canvasback duck" ("Men About Town," *Vogue,* October 1, 1937, pp. 155–57).

101 *his infamous terrapin suppers:* Upton Sinclair, *Candid Reminiscences,* 10.

102 *"necessary to every gentleman":* *Etiquette,* 229

102 *"removing the bouquet":* Alessandro Filippini, *The Table.*
103 *"lore about wine":* James Lea Cate, "Keeping Posted," p. 24.

CHAPTER 16

104 *picked up their tab:* Jerry Patterson, *The First Four Hundred,* 151.
104 *a million oysters each day:* Mark Kurlansky, *The Big Oyster,* 234.
104 *Washington and New York:* Ibid.
106 *"never in formal Society":* Quoted in Cleveland Amory, "Tuxedo: All Club and 5,000 Yards Wide," *Washington Post,* July 19, 1953, p. S4.
106 *Edwin lived on the island:* "Staten Islanders' Fete: Given Jointly by the Cricket and Ladies' Clubs. Dancing, Refreshments, and Many Booths Presided Over by Young Women, All Out of Doors—Large Attendance of Society Fold," *New York Times,* June 23, 1892.
107 *to reach the mother-to-be:* Truly Emily Post, 10.
107 *his mother-in-law's approval:* Ibid., 4–6.
108 *better commute as well:* Ibid., 13.

CHAPTER 17

110 *a bad mother:* Truly Emily Post, 22.
112 *"only its freaks—himself":* The Flight of a Moth, 14.
113 *winter of 1893–94:* Thanks to the New York City Social Register for sharing its records with me.
113 *two leading men:* "Yachtsmen Enjoyed the Race," *New York Times,* October 14, 1893, p. 2.
114 *best by being predictable:* Children Are People, 7.
114 *hurting others' feelings:* The Flight of a Moth, 50–51.
114 *"image of a duke":* See Margaret Case Harriman, "Dear Mrs. Post"; Cleveland Amory, *The Last Resorts;* and William Engle, "The Emily Post Story," *American Weekly,* February 6, 1949, p. 19.
115 *"all during prayer":* Truly Emily Post, 66.
115 *"come too close":* Ibid., 72.
116 *content with her solitude:* "The Social World," *New York Times,* December 8, 1893, and *New York Times,* December 19, 1893.
116 *"height of the structure":* Warren Briggs, quoted in Samuel Graybill, "Bruce Price, American Architect," 190.
116 *fifteen stories high:* Sarah Bradford Landau and Carl W. Condit, *Rise of the New York Skyscraper,* 231.
117 *Briggs remembered happily:* Quoted in Graybill, "Bruce Price, American Architect," 190.
117 *to rest on bedrock:* Landau and Condit, *Rise of the New York Skyscraper,* 231–35, and *Truly Emily Post,* 26.
117 *tallest building in the world:* Landau and Condit, *Rise of the New York Skyscraper,* 235. In 1895 the Astors brought suit against the owners for blocking the light and air of their own Schermerhorn edifice next door, but the matter was resolved by American Surety leasing the family's building for the next ninety-nine years.
117 *"careful refinement":* Many years later, in the early twenty-first century, *New York Times* critic Christopher Gray would say this about Bruce's achievement: "It's built in the round, so it didn't have these awful blank walls. That was a point of very hot contention; I mean a tall building is criticized for many things but none more pointedly and more brutally [than] for the awful blank walls that we still see today. Now, at the beginning of the century this was really [considered] . . . offensive, especially at a time when there was a City Beautiful movement. . . . And so the American Surety Building . . . was designed to be seen from all sides and . . . didn't just

present a rude face to the rest of the city." Courtesy of Laura Jacobs, interview with Christopher Gray, May 22, 2001.

118 *gifted father decades later: Children Are People,* 23.

CHAPTER 18

119 *"Ancient Mariner":* Macy log, courtesy of Nora Post. Apparently the time of year didn't affect the boating: on December 1, 1893, Edwin filled the log with Coleridge's "Ancient Mariner," and throughout the winter months he continued taking the boat out.

119 *"really big money":* Jerry Patterson, *The First Four Hundred,* 140.

120 *one of the will's executors:* "Hamilton's Remarriage Reveals Divorce from the Late J. P. Morgan's Daughter," *New York Times,* January 4, 1924; *New York Times,* April 22, 1894, p. 11; and Jean Strouse, *Morgan,* 332.

120 *"homes at reasonable rents":* "The Social World," *New York Times,* May 26, 1894, p. 8; and see "Opened Its New Clubhouse: Staten Island Ladies Club Holds Reception and Open-Air Ball," *New York Times,* June 2, 1894, p. 8.

122 *"never spank him again":* Truly Emily Post, 75–76.

123 *bequeath his daughter:* "Drank Eggnog as Was Eggnog: People from Dixie Land Observe an Old Southern Custom," *New York Times,* December 23, 1894.

CHAPTER 19

124 *"And that's coming":* Stephanie Coontz, *Marriage,* 194.

124 *"everlasting bow-wows":* "Mrs. Sherwood's Mistake: She Told Only of the Wrong Side New-York Society, Scheduled Bow-Wows Far Away," *New York Times,* May 26, 1895.

125 *documented by excited reporters:* Lately Thomas, *Delmonico's,* 255 and 256.

125 *could be collected:* Shadi Rahimi, "Next to 1936, '05 Is No Sweat," *New York Times,* August 3, 2005.

126 *nomenclature of the sea:* Macy log.

126 *invalids' friends and family:* Truly Emily Post, 84.

126 *a friend of Emily's:* Town Topics 36, no. 15 (April 15, 1897).

126 *formerly august club:* Lloyd Morris, *Incredible New York,* 239–42; Jerry Patterson, *The First Four Hundred,* 187–97; and Truly Emily Post, 11.

127 *"blazoning it, either":* Purple and Fine Linen, 178.

127 *Emily almost apoplectic:* Truly Emily Post, 116.

128 *and left the room:* Ibid.

129 *Emily remembered it:* Ibid., 54.

129 *Dr. Charles Parkhurst:* "Resorts on Long Island," *New York Times,* May 30, 1897, p. 20.

129 *increasingly silly:* Truly Emily Post, 11.

130 *build for her and her husband:* Ibid., 71.

CHAPTER 20

131 *and Niagara Falls:* "Canadian Hotel Syndicate," *New York Times,* January 6, 1898.

132 *the animals didn't:* "E. R. Thomas Injured in an Auto Smash," *New York Times,* August 15, 1908, p. 1.

132 *help him heal faster:* "E. R. Thomas Taken South: Sent to Atlanta for a Change of Scene—Stands the Trip Well," *New York Times,* November 3, 1908, p. 1; "Mrs. E. R. Thomas Sues for Divorce," *New York Times,* March 20, 1912, p. 1.

133 *"happy tho unmarried!":* Macy log, p. 63.

134 *often absent husband:* "Status of Married Women: American Wives Not to Be Envied, Says an Englishwoman; Marriage Crushes Her Life; Friendships with Men,

Participation in Sports, Even True Companionship of Her Husband, Denied Her," *New York Times*, August 14, 1898.

134 *"a bit gray now"*: "Brant Shooting on Great South Bay," p. 197.

135 *"best in class"*: "Racing with Tiny Yachts," *New York Times*, July 4, 1899, p. 5.

135 *assets of $2.6 million*: "Business Troubles," *New York Times*, June 23, 1899, p. 8, and July 8, 1899, p. 9.

135 *Tuxedo horse season would open*: Jerry Patterson, *The First Four Hundred*, 118–20, and "Orange County Horse Fair: Numerous Entries at the Fifth Annual Exhibition at Goshen," *New York Times*, October 8, 1899, p. 10.

136 *Times solemnly reported*: "Society at the Opera: The Wealth and Fashion of the Metropolis on View Last Night," *New York Times*, December 19, 1899, p. 3.

136 *she hadn't been forgotten*: "The First Assembly Ball: Society Out in Force Last Night at the Astoria," *New York Times*, December 15, 1899, p. 7.

136 *($5 million in today's dollars)*: "The Gould House Party: New York and Philadelphia Guests Lavishly Entertained," *New York Times*, December 22, 1899, p. 1.

137 *designing their house*: Cleveland Amory, *The Last Resorts*, 58.

137 *"find your way around"*: "Georgian Court," *New York Times*, July 23, 1899, p. SM6.

CHAPTER 21

139 *she said, would disapprove*: Truly Emily Post, 125.

139 *"a little turtle"*: Ibid., 124–34.

140 *"every vestige of formality"*: "A Day's Wedding," *New York Times*, October 2, 1900.

140 *theatricality and flair*: "Broker Roughly Handled," *New York Times*, November 3, 1900, p. 14. Edwin M. Post was a member of the NYSE from August 22, 1900, to December 13, 1906. (Thanks to Steve Wheeler, the archivist for NYSE Luncheon Club, for this information.)

140 *would join him*: Truly Emily Post, 131.

140 *exulted in it*: The purely masculine profession was a chimera, it is true: in January 1870, Victoria Woodhull and Tennessee Claflin had been backed in opening the first female brokerage house, at Twenty-fourth Street and Broadway.

140 *"even try to sleep"*: Julie Chanler, *From Gaslight to Dawn*, 49.

141 *enormous, dated cupola*: Samuel Graybill, "Bruce Price, American Architect," 210.

141 *farm in New Jersey*: Reported earlier in "Tuxedo's Society Event," *New York Times*, September 29, 1900.

CHAPTER 22

142 *New York Yacht Club*: Thanks to M. Watson at the New York Yacht Club for researching the club's records.

142 *than the Macy*: Edwin Main Post, "Brant Shooting on Great South Bay," p. 204.

142 *"for the rich"*: "Scenes of Disorder in Stock Exchange," *New York Times*, May 10, 1901.

143 *often spent their autumns*: Truly Emily Post, 170.

143 *toward the dark side*: Ibid.

143 *or the local hostilities*: More importantly, on July 7 Katharine asked her half brother for a loan: "My dear Warren, I find that, for certain reasons I shall require some money and although I have it in my bank account I cannot very well get it [without being obvious]." In light of the lavish house the Colliers were building, the reason for the loan remains a secret; money was not the issue. Delano Family Papers, Box 35, FDR Library, Hyde Park, New York.

144 *"very slim one"*: "Pierre Lorillard Sinking: Members of His Family Remain Constantly at His Bedside," *New York Times*, July 7, 1901, p. 5; "Pierre Lorillard's Will," *Baltimore Sun*, July 13, 1901; "Report on Lorillard Will: Estate's Value When He Died $1,797,925.53, and the Executors Now Hold $1,589,725," *New York Times*, August 15,

1902, p. 5; "How Mr. Lorillard Divided His Estate: Bequest of Rancocas to a Woman Arouses His Family," *New York Times*, July 14, 1901, p. 10.

145   *"wore no mourning whatever":* "Mrs. T. Suffern Tailer Obtains Her Divorce," *New York Times*, August 15, 1902.

145   *gagged its citizens:* C. F. Talman, "Long Heat Waves Are Often Costly," *New York Times*, August 6, 1933.

147   *her husband's attention: Truly Emily Post*, 98–100.

147   *she would later remember: The Flight of a Moth*, 7.

147   *end of the race:* Emily's anger and her failure ever to appreciate Edwin's passion are described, in *Truly Emily Post*, 105–15.

148   *"and at Newport":* Ibid., 108. See also "Yachting Notes," *Brooklyn Eagle*, September 21, 1901, p. 8, and "News of the Yachting World," *Brooklyn Eagle*, February 7, 1902, p. 17.

148   *reflect years later: Truly Emily Post*, 115.

148   *happiness shocked her:* In contrast to the Victorian ideal of near-perfect happiness, it was becoming hard to believe that there were any satisfying marriages among the rich. The exceptions—at least those who made their affection public—were so notable as to become inscribed in the history books of the Gilded Age. Mamie and Stuyvesant Fish had one of the few high-society marriages widely believed to be based on mutual love, even devotion, in spite of the rumors about their own sometime irregular behavior. Perhaps Mamie Fish's defiant refusal through the years to play the proper society wife made her a real, multidimensional person to her spouse. Just before the irrepressible, flamboyant Mrs. Fish died in 1915, her husband celebrated her: "In looking back over the many bitter and sweet but ever pleasurable memories of long years of married life, I can recall no moment when I failed to be thankful for my action and above all my choice" (quoted in Jerry Patterson, *The First Four Hundred*, 203).

148   *Mrs. Lorillard's revenge:* "Tuxedo Park's Gayeties," *New York Times*, August 4, 1901, p. SM17.

149   *by the younger set:* "Gayety at Tuxedo," *New York Times*, October 13, 1901, p. 24, and "Autumn at Tuxedo," *New York Times*, September 8, 1901, p. 7.

149   *Colliers and St. Georges:* The Colliers and at least one of their four children would spend part of each year in Tuxedo Park, in the house Bruce Price built them, through the 1950s.

149   *a plan of reorganization:* "Financial Announcements," *New York Times*, November 24, 1901, p. 18.

149   *working extra hours:* "At the Hotels," *New York Times*, September 13, 1901, p. 3.

CHAPTER 23

150   *the New Year:* "Baltimore's Social Season," *New York Times*, January 19, 1902.

151   *"Bruce Price, the architect":* "Clubmen," *New York Times*, August 10, 1902.

151   *"gossip about the matter":* "Mrs. T. Suffern Tailer Obtains Her Divorce," *New York Times*, August 15, 1902.

151   *lose its luster:* "Dull Week at Tuxedo," *New York Times*, September 21, 1902.

151   *hosted by the Posts:* "Society at Tuxedo," *New York Times*, September 14, 1902.

152   *"Huguenot family":* *New York Times*, May 2, 1899, p. 2.

152   *Vogue magazine:* "Arthur Turnure Dead," *New York Times*, April 14, 1906, p. 11.

152   *when Edwin was away: Truly Emily Post*, 133.

152   *New York Supreme Court: New York Times*, October 9, 1902, p. 7.

153   *"when we are working": Truly Emily Post*, 118.

154   *to the opening:* "Dinner and Musicale at George J. Gould's: Remodeled Town Residence the Scene of a Brilliant Function," *New York Times*, January 23, 1903, p. 9.

155   *"sympathy and condolence":* "Death List of the Week," *New York Times*, May 31, 1903, p. 18; "Decisions and Calendars," *New York Times*, June 13, 1903. *La Savoie*, the ship returning Bruce Price's body to the United States, was later used in World War I to

land troops in the Dardanelles and eastern Mediterranean operations. For comprehensive studies of Bruce Price's work, see Russell Sturgis, "The Works of Bruce Price," *Architectural Record,* Great American Architects Series, 5 (June 1899), and issues of the *American Architect and Building News* throughout his life.

A list of Price's major achievements, all but the first three still standing, includes: East End Station, Montreal; West End Hotel, Bar Harbor, Maine; Long Beach Hotel; Cathedral, Savannah, Georgia; Lee Memorial Church, Lexington, Virginia; cottages and clubhouse, Tuxedo Park; American Surety Building and St. James Building, New York; Hotchkiss School, Lakeville, Connecticut; Georgian Court, Lakewood, New Jersey; Château Frontenac, Quebec; Windsor Station, Montreal; Royal Victoria Academy, Montreal; Osborn Memorial, Yale College; Welch Dormitory, Yale College; and Colonial Historical Society Building, New Haven, Connecticut. Price also invented, patented, and built parlor bay-window cars for the Pennsylvania and Boston and Albany railroads. (Information courtesy of the Enoch Pratt Free Library, Baltimore, Maryland.)

155 *Emily mourned alone: Truly Emily Post,* 162–63.

CHAPTER 24

157 *actually giving it up:* "Receivers for Post & Co.: Special Partner Objects to Assignee of Firm of Brokers, Says General Partners Hypothecated His Personal Deposit and Tried to Sell Firm Seat on 'Change," *New York Times,* November 7, 1903, p. 13.

157 *turn-of-the-century dollars:* "Two Trust Companies Fail in Baltimore: Liabilities of Concerns Estimated at $10,000,000," *New York Times,* October 20, 1903, p. 3.

157 *"International Silver securities":* "Two Firms Dissolved," *New York Times,* October 9, 1903.

158 *through the bad times: Truly Emily Post,* 200.

158 *and the Robert Goelets:* "Tuxedo Park Social Events," *New York Times,* October 4, 1903, and "What Is Doing in Society," *New York Times,* November 14, 1903, p. 9.

159 *thirty-eight drafts:* Gretta Palmer, "Mrs. Post Regrets," *New York Woman,* February 3, 1937, p. 11.

159 *"talk of the town":* Advertisement, *New York Times,* October 1, 1904, p. RB653.

159 *"as I do, would I?": The Flight of a Moth,* 32–33.

160 *knowledge of society:* "Recent Fiction: Emily Post's Study of the Restless American Woman," *New York Times,* October 1904.

160 *Hamilton gently counseled: Truly Emily Post,* 140.

160 *Duer, and Emily Post: New York Times,* November 26, 1904.

160 *Paris and Brussels in 1903: Truly Emily Post,* 158.

161 *to keep her attention:* Ibid.

161 *in Purple and Fine Linen: Purple and Fine Linen,* 172.

161 *was in the works:* "Society at Tuxedo," *New York Times,* September 18, 1904, p. 7.

162 *Emily left early:* "Tuxedo Society Gossip," *New York Times,* December 4, 1904.

CHAPTER 25

163 *at Times Square:* William B. Scott and Peter M. Rutkoff, *New York Modern,* 14.

163 *earth in this city:* Ibid., 14–17, 20–21.

164 *to society women:* Jerry Patterson, *The Vanderbilts,* 153.

164 *"off to Europe":* William Engle, "The Emily Post Story," *American Weekly,* February 6, 1949, p. 19.

165 *attending as well:* "Miss Mable Mcafee Wed," *New York Times,* May 17, 1905, p. 9.

166 *"get away from": The Flight of a Moth,* 30.

166 *hero in the process:* "May Confront Ahle with Society Leaders: Prosecutor Says They Were His Victims, Perhaps," *New York Times,* July 13, 1905, p. 3.

166 *confessed to his wife:* For a strong sense of the immediate excitement, see: "Got $500

from Post, Then Was Arrested: Blackmail Charge Against 'Society Editors' Solicitor'; A Promise to Hide Scandal; Ahle Also Took to Broker at Stock Exchange a Note from a Town Topics Editor," *New York Times*, July 12, 1905, p. 1; "May Confront Ahle with Society Leaders," *New York Times*, July 13, 1905.

166 *caught his man:* Andy Logan, in *The Man Who Robbed the Robber Barons*, gives a detailed account of the affair and the trial. See also *New York Times*, July 15, 1905, p. 1; *New York Times*, July 16, 1905, p. 3; *New York Times*, July 23, 1905, p. 12; *New York Times*, December 3, 1905, p. 1; *New York Times*, January 20, 1906, p. 1; *New York Times*, January 23, 1906, p. 1; *New York Times*, January 27, 1906, p. 1; *New York Times*, January 28, 1906, p. 1; *New York Times*, February 6, 1906, p. 5; *New York Times*, December 18, 1906, p. 3; and *New York Times*, December 29, 1906, p. 1.

167 *city's newspapers:* "Stockbroker's Way of Dealing with Bribe Offer," *New York Tribune*, July 13, 1905.

CHAPTER 26

168 *"the strangest":* "Authors in Vacation Time: Where Some Are Recreating and Others Are Working—the New Books Some Are Writing," *New York Times*, July 1, 1905; Michael Decourcy Hinds, "Adirondack Survivors: Rustic 'Grand Camps,' " *New York Times*, August 27, 1981.

169 *to her fingernail polish:* Marie Weldon, "Society at Home and Abroad," *New York Times*, July 23, 1905, p. SM8.

170 *"bearable or unbearable":* "Love Triumphant," *New York Times*, October 28, 1905.

172 *"let you go!":* *Purple and Fine Linen*, 9, 5, 10, 6, 11, 2, 125, 196–97, 195, 238, 22, 240, 21, 216.

173 *"gray in their hair":* "Celebrate Mark Twain's Seventieth Birthday," *New York Times*, December 6, 1905. On December 5, 1905, the newspaper had trumpeted the "notable gathering of authors"—150—invited to the dinner to be given at Delmonico's, using, as if influenced by the tenor of the event, "woman" instead of "lady" throughout the long essay. See also Justin Kaplan, "A Rose for Emily," p. 108, in "Books," *Harper's*, March 1969, pp. 106–9.

173 *May Sinclair:* Thanks to Robert Hirst, who has served as the general editor of the Mark Twain Project and Papers at the University of California, Berkeley, for over a quarter of a century, for helping me identify pictures of the dinner's attendees. Thanks also to Professor Fred Kaplan at the Graduate Center, CUNY, whose biography of Twain has long been a touchstone for research on the writer.

173 *"another man's road":* "Celebrate Mark Twain's Seventieth Birthday," *New York Times*, December 6, 1905.

174 *as in years past:* "Good Skating at Tuxedo," *New York Times*, December 26, 1905.

CHAPTER 27

175 *father and grandfather:* "Justice Ingraham Dead in 60th Year," *New York Times*, May 1, 1934, p. 24.

176 *keep their secrets:* "Federal Divorce Hunt Makes Much Uneasiness; Papers Long Kept Secret Will Be Opened by Labor Clerks," *New York Times*, August 14, 1906, p. 12; "Sealed Divorce Papers Cause Census Wrangle; Court Clerks Won't Allow Them to Be Examined," *New York Times*, August 19, 1906.

176 *mad for divorce:* At least one sociologist believes that the rising divorce rate in post-Victorian America was directly related to the increased expectations now aimed at the institution (see, e.g., David Shumway, "Something Old, Something New," in Peter N. Stearns and Jan Lewis, eds., *Battleground of Desire*, 306). Men and women had learned enough about sexuality that they no longer viewed themselves as aberrant for expecting emotional and physical satisfaction in their marriages. Emily and

Edwin inherited a Victorian model for their marriage, and unlike other such couples, they proved unable to escape it without divorce.

176 *"herself to fiction"*: "Women of Wealth," *Washington Post*, March 25, 1906.
177 *"far more treacherous"*: *Town Topics*, June 7 and 14, 1906, and June 21, 1906.
177 *wife wasn't present*: "Happenings at Tuxedo," *New York Times*, June 17, 1906, p. 12.
178 *November 6*: The stenographer's minutes from the New York Supreme Court records, Orange County, October 25, 1906, to November 6, 1906. Emily's signature on the court testimony was her only statement, the dramatic flourish beneath her name the equivalent of a lady's act of defiance.
178 *final workday*: According to New York Stock Exchange records, Edwin Post's last day as a member of the NYSE was December 13, 1906.
178 *afloat financially*: "Divorce for Mrs. E. M. Post," *New York Times*, January 23, 1907, p. 1.
178 *asked for alimony*: Upon Edwin's remarriage four years later in New Jersey, where punishment for the guilty adulterous party was not lifelong bachelorhood, as it was in New York, newspapers would report facts at variance with Emily's version, even getting the date of the decree wrong: "Mr. Post said that he had been married before, but that his wife had obtained a divorce [in Orange County, New York] on March 4, 1907" (*Washington Post*, December 30, 1911). Furthermore, the Supreme Court Justice had supposedly ordered Edwin to pay $200 a month in alimony to Emily Price ("College Socialists Meet: Victor Berger and Other Leaders at Mrs. Finch's Reception," *New York Times*, December 29, 1911). The families don't know which account is true—was there alimony or child support or not? New York State archivists are unable to resolve the ambiguity.
178 *upon his divorce*: "Banker Post Gets Divorce," *Washington Post*, January 24, 1907.
178 *assessed or not*: Divorce papers, State Archives, Albany, New York, December 1906. For details, see "Divorce for Mrs. E. M. Post," *New York Times*, January 23, 1907, p. 1, and *Washington Post*, December 30, 1911.
178 *British stepmother, Eleanor*: Nora Post, Edwin Post's granddaughter, has been an invaluable source of information on Edwin and on his second wife, Eleanor Malcolm.
178 *"become public, ever"*: William G. Post, phone interview with the author, September 26, 2005.

CHAPTER 28

180 **en plein air:** *Truly Emily Post*, 157.
181 *"society, literature, and art"*: "Keats-Shelley Meeting Pleases: Much Money Obtained for the Purchase of the Memorial in Rome," *New York Times*, February 15, 1907.
181 *anything she'd ever done*: *Truly Emily Post*, 199.
181 *"the boys call you?"*: Ibid., 157.
182 *"did not happen"*: Ibid., 155.
182 *"push her away"*: William G. Post, interview with the author, February 15, 2003.
183 *"was your own"*: Lately Thomas, *The Astor Orphans*, and Julie Chanler, *From Gaslight to Dawn*.
183 *was not his wife*: Chanler, *From Gaslight to Dawn*, 62 and 70.
184 *both great satisfaction*: Evelyn Perrault, phone interview with the author, July 23, 2006.
184 *"great friends"*: Chanler, *From Gaslight to Dawn*, 60, and Jerry Patterson, *The First Four Hundred*, 147.
184 *her hostage again*: William G. Post, interview with the author, April 3, 2004.
184 *pursuit of the trivial*: Claudia Roth Pierpont, *New Yorker*, April 2, 2001, pp. 68–69.
185 *"a one-time suitor"*: *Truly Emily Post*, 152.
185 *noted one newspaper*: *Town Topics*, February 14, 1914.
185 *had a woman chef*: Jane Smith, *Elsie de Wolfe*, 111.

186 *"conspicuous luxury"*: "Women's New Club, the Colony, Opened," *New York Times,* March 12, 1907.

187 *"system never failed"*: *Truly Emily Post,* 161.

188 *"must needs pursue"*: *Woven in the Tapestry,* 69.

188 *"height it reflects"*: Review, *New York Times,* June 27, 1908.

188 *concept of "healing"*: *Mark Twain's Letters to Mary,* printed by Columbia University Press in 1961 and edited by Lewis Leary, explains the magnet that drew Twain to Tuxedo: "Mary" was young Mrs. Henry Huddleston Rogers Jr. Her father-in-law, the senior Henry Rogers, a founder of Standard Oil, came to Twain's rescue frequently. Around the time the publishing house venture with Twain as chief partner failed and went into bankruptcy, Mary and her husband bought a house on the north shore of Tuxedo Lake. See also Tuxedo Park historian Doris Crofut, Tuxedo Park internal library records, "Mark Twain and Tuxedo Park," and Ron Powers, *Mark Twain: A Life,* p. 614.

188 *"mortal mind"*: *Truly Emily Post,* 155.

CHAPTER 29

189 *into her stories:* *Truly Emily Post,* 83.

189 *short-story contest:* Jeanne Perkins, "Emily Post," *Life,* May 6, 1946, p. 65, and Gretta Palmer, "Mrs. Post Regrets," *New York Woman,* February 3, 1937, p. 11.

189 *up her back:* Patricia Beard, *After the Ball,* 71.

190 *she had experience now:* "Charles Coster Lost $1,000,000 in Stocks," *New York Times,* April 30, 1908, p. 1.

190 *with her ensemble:* "Dark and Subdued Hints Find Favor with the Best Dressed Woman Rather Than the Bright Ones," *New York Times,* November 15, 1908.

190 *through September 1909:* *Everybody's Magazine,* chapters from *The Title Market,* February through September 1, 1909. Details about publication in letter from Emily Post, July 8, 1909, and "Memorandum of Agreement, 5 April 1909, Dodd, Mead and Co. and Emily Post," Dodd Mead Manuscripts, Lilly Library, Indiana University, Bloomington, Indiana.

191 *in familiar surroundings?:* *New York Times,* August 21, 1909.

191 *"very serious item":* *The Title Market,* 55.

191 *the* **Tribune** *pronounced:* *Tribune,* January 23, 1910.

191 *even her closest friends:* Emily Post, "On the Care of Husbands," *Life,* April 22, 1909, p. 552.

192 *a married woman's success:* " 'Outrageous to Wed Titles': Mrs. Post Blames Mothers," *New York Journal,* August 1909.

CHAPTER 30

194 *a few years later:* Patricia Beard, *After the Ball,* 347.

195 *as she read it:* For an extended comment on the explicitness of the *Times'* coverage of disasters for the fifty-year period following Adolph Ochs's stewardship, see Michael Barton, "Journalistic Gore: Disaster Reporting and Emotional Discourse," in Peter N. Stearns and Jan Lewis, eds. *Battleground of Desire,* 164–69.

195 *would recover:* "Auto Smash Kills Mrs. Bruce Price: Wealthy Tuxedo Woman, Widow of Architect, Flung Against Tree Near Arden," *New York Times,* October 18, 1909. At least one obituary, in the *Wilkes-Barre Record,* mentioned that the car was traveling at a "high rate of speed" (October 19, 1991, p. 9).

196 *she went to work:* *Truly Emily Post,* 160.

196 *New York City as well:* Orange County Surrogate's Court, Liber 81, W80, 234.

196 *"pointing backward":* Jerry Patterson, *The First Four Hundred,* 127.

197 *"bad investments":* Margaret Case Harriman, "Dear Mrs. Post," p. 56.

197 *instead of her books:* *Publishers Weekly,* November 26, 1909.

197   *wherever the wives lived: Manfield News,* December 28, 1909.
198   *about politics anyway?:* "Girl Strikers Tell the Rich Their Woes," *New York Times,* December 16, 1909, p. 3, and "Women Socialists Rebuff Suffragists," *New York Times,* December 20, 1909, p. 5.

CHAPTER 31

199   *the* **Smart Set:** Edwin Main Post, "The Blue Handkerchief."
199   *and Louis Untermeyer:* "Among the Magazines: Many Articles of Importance and Much Entertaining Fiction," *New York Times Book Review,* January 15, 1910.
200   *understand her writing:* Paul R. Reynolds, *The Middle Man,* 13–16.
202   *"houses come high":* Paul Revere Reynolds, Paul Revere Reynolds Papers 1899–1980, internal memorandum, January 26, 1910, Rare Book and Manuscript Library, Columbia University Libraries. Reynolds's intraoffice memo records his author's payment arrangements, his notations useful though difficult to translate into today's jargon. Emily received $3,000 for the novel's serial rights in magazine form, with an additional $1,000 for each 15,000 copies of the published novel sold.
202   *"the* **Atlantic's** *covers":* April 8, 1910, to April 19, 1910, Paul Revere Reynolds Papers.
203   *"who seem happy":* Emily Post, "What Makes a Young Girl Popular in Society?," *Delineator,* November 1910, p. 254.
203   *"a line from you?":* December 10, 1910, Paul Revere Reynolds Papers.
203   *redefining herself publicly: Washington Post,* December 15, 1910.
204   *awed by her concentration:* Albert Foster Winslow, *Tuxedo Park: A Journal of Recollections,* p. 102.
204   *Winslow said: Washington Post,* December 15, 1910.

CHAPTER 32

205   *the heroine's death: The Eagle's Feather,* 242.
206   *"been the neck":* "141 Men and Girls Die in Waist Factory Fire," *New York Times,* March 26, 1911, p. 1.
206   *near their home: Delineator,* July 1911, pp. 8, 68.
207   *the summer before:* Letters from Emily Post to Ray U. Johnson. The letters to the editor of the *Century Magazine* are undated until the final note on May 31, 1911.
207   *her work for her:* Ibid., May 31.
208   *"won't have it":* F. Hopkinson Smith, *Kennedy Square* (New York: Scribner's, 1911), 9, 10, 26, 35, 39.
208   *leavened her reprimands:* "The Traveling Expenses of the Stork," *Delineator,* July 1911, p. 8.
208   *prodded her agent:* Letters from Emily Post to Paul Reynolds, April 15, 1911, Paul Revere Reynolds Papers.
209   *"this?" he pleaded:* Letters from Paul Reynolds to Emily Post, April 20, 1911, and June 2, 1911, Paul Revere Reynolds Papers.
209   *hard at work:* Letters from Paul Reynolds to Emily Post, June 27, 1911, Paul Revere Reynolds Papers.
210   *manners in the country:* Arthur M. Schlesinger, *Learning How to Behave,* 7.
210   *"or other later on":* Paul Reynolds to Emily Post, July 7, 1911, and Emily Post to Paul Reynolds, July 25, 1911, Paul Revere Reynolds Papers.

PART THREE

CHAPTER 33

213   *"intense spiritual energy":* Dominique Browning, *Around the House and in the Garden,* p. 13.
214   *to do something similar:* Samuel Graybill, "Bruce Price, American Architect," 6.

214 *of her social contacts:* Neal Bascomb, "For the Architect, a Height Never Again to Be Scaled," *New York Times,* May 26, 1905, p. F10. Bruce's former associate would one day convince his friend's namesake to follow in his grandfather's footsteps.

214 *to overextend herself:* Jean Strouse, *Morgan,* 643.

214 *laughter all the way:* Elsie de Wolfe, *After All,* 132–33.

215 *to their limits:* William G. Post, letter to the author, February 28, 2006.

215 *self-help genre:* Michael Korda, *Making the List,* 24–25.

215 *yards of fabric:* Frederick Lewis Allen, *Only Yesterday and Since Yesterday,* 105.

216 *branch of the bank:* "Woman Wins Place as Bank Executive," *New York Times,* February 13, 1925, p. 1.

216 *"economic factor":* Ibid.

216 *on the bestseller list:* Nelson W. Aldrich Jr., *Old Money,* 58.

217 *Lincoln Highway:* Pete Davies, *American Road,* 28 and 30.

CHAPTER 34

218 *admitted into society:* "Brilliant Dance Assemblies and Weddings Attract Society," *New York Times,* January 11, 1914.

219 *unformed child?:* Morgan's articles were collected and reprinted as *The American Girl;* see pp. 5 and 9.

219 *wrote her encouragingly:* Paul Reynolds to Emily Post, May 25, 1914, Paul Revere Reynolds Papers.

220 *"enough with* **The Title Market***":* Emily Post to Paul Reynolds, June 4, 1914; Paul Reynolds to Emily Post, June 6, 1914, Paul Revere Reynolds Papers.

220 *"scarlet upholstery":* Beverly Rae Kimes, "Emily's Great Adventure," *Star* (Mercedes-Benz Club of America), September–October 2001, p. 27. On the occasion of the club's one hundredth anniversary, in 2002, Kimes did extensive research on the Mercedes Ned customized in London.

221 *paid $5 a day:* Jean Strouse, *Morgan,* 636.

221 *the supposed upgrading:* Kimes, "Emily's Great Adventure," 27.

221 *reached the port:* Edwin M. Post Jr., "Henri, War Dog, to the Rescue," *New York Times,* April 18, 1915.

222 *in northwestern Burgundy:* "Mrs. Percy Turnure Dies of Pneumonia," *New York Times,* January 5, 1931, p. 14.

222 *graceful prose:* Edwin M. Post Jr., "Henri, War Dog to the Rescue." A sequel appeared the following year in the *New York Times,* on June 4, 1916. A reprint of the original story about "Henri the War Dog" was sold as a booklet for the benefit of the wounded at an Allied bazaar.

222 *to Ober directly:* Emily Post to Paul Reynolds, June 9, 1914, Paul Revere Reynolds Papers.

223 *at the president's side:* At *The Birth of a Nation's* February 8 premiere in California, the twelve-reel-long silent was accompanied by the Los Angeles Philharmonic playing in the cinema pit, while the movie's actors (including John Ford) appeared dressed in Klan robes. The movie debuted only after Griffith obtained an injunction from the court overruling the city council members who had ordered the movie suppressed due to its inflammatory racism. The publicity would more than compensate for the delay. What is often forgotten in modern retellings of the film's release is the less than monolithic support its appearance engendered. Repeatedly, local groups supporting the rights of African Americans to fair representation protested the hate message that spilled across the big screen.

223 *"scrap of a pickaninny" son:* Francis Hopkinson Smith, *Colonel Carter's Christmas,* 47.

223 *not to use it:* William G. Post, phone interview with the author from Naples, Florida, April 3, 2004.

224 *"timekeepers of progress":* J. C. Furnas, *Great Times,* 181.

224 *"he was one":* Letter to the editor, *New York Times,* April 13, 1915.

CHAPTER 35

227 *"the punishment severe":* By Motor, 21–24, 26, 57–58. In 2004, the book, edited by Jane Lancaster, would be reissued by McFarland and Company in North Carolina.
228 *"same of the city":* "Mrs. Post Was Not Well Posted," Iowa City Daily Press, September 23, 1915.
228 *"Southwest existed":* By Motor, 88.
228 *"treasured memories":* Ibid., 60.
228 *countries in one:* J. C. Furnas, Great Times, 181.
228 *"upstart crass":* Ibid., 182.
229 *"values startlingly":* San Diego Historical Society, www.sandiegohistory.org.
230 *for the Golden State:* Walter Lippmann suggested that the Panama Canal was "perhaps the greatest victory an army ever won" (quoted in Furnas, Great Times, 182–83).
231 *"to unimportance":* By Motor, 189, 193, 233, 226, 238–40.
231 *"O.K., Emily Post":* Emily Post to Paul Reynolds, November 4, 1915, Paul Revere Reynolds Papers.

CHAPTER 36

232 *times had changed:* "Buy Tickets for Allies' Bazaar," New York Times, June 2, 1916; "Honeymoon Trips Are Sold at One Dollar at Bazaar," New York City Herald, June 9, 1916.
233 *muddy battlefields:* By Motor, 86.
233 *due for pilot training:* "Mrs. Post and Her Son at Lenox," Washington Post, July 10, 1916.
234 *"a tarantula":* "Society Is Moving to Mexican Border: Fiancées, Wives, and Parents of Guardsmen are Braving the Torrid Heat of Texas," New York Times, July 12, 1916.
235 *she asked proudly:* "What Sons Can Do for a Mother," Morning Telegraph, October 15, 1916.
235 *"Hurray!":* Emily Post to Paul Reynolds, December 17, 1916, and Paul Reynolds to Emily Post, December 19, 1916, Paul Revere Reynolds Papers.

CHAPTER 37

236 *war against Germany:* John M. Barry, The Great Influenza, 120.
236 *disparaged the American government:* World War I was an aristocrats' war. See Nelson W. Aldrich Jr., Old Money, 178.
236 *true or false:* Barry, The Great Influenza, 124.
236 *for the arts:* "Fund for Authors' Relief," New York Times, March 18, 1917.
237 *reported for military duty:* New York Times, April 9, 1918; "Town of Tuxedo Centennial Commemorative Program," Tuxedo Park Recreation Commission, 1990; and Tuxedo Park local history, courtesy of Chris Sonne, town historian.
237 *"night of terror":* Doris Stevens, Jailed for Freedom, p. 203.
238 *"glad to congratulate him":* "Two American Soldiers Cited by French Army," New York Times, December 28, 1917.
238 *"besides, The Title Market":* Flying, February 1918, p. 50.
238 *the following world war:* Barry, The Great Influenza, 130.
239 *in twenty-four years:* Ibid., 92. Many scientists believe that the "bug" scientists discovered in fall of 2005 was the genealogical precursor to the avian flu many epidemiologists predict will be the next international bug to sweep society; see: "Avian Virus Caused the 1918 Pandemic, New Studies Show," by Betsy McKay, Wall Street Journal, October 6, 2005, p. B1.
239 *400 of whom died:* "War Records of the Town of Tuxedo, NY," compiled by Susan Tuckerman, Tuxedo Park historian, 1923; Gina Kolata, "Experts Unlock Clues to Spread of 1918 Flu Virus," New York Times, October 6, 2005. At least the epidemic led to one of the most important scientific discoveries of the twentieth century, one

that resonates powerfully to this day: in seeking to stop future devastations, Alexander Fleming discovered penicillin.

240 *reign at Tuxedo Park:* Property maps and records courtesy of Chris Sonne, Tuxedo Park Realty.

CHAPTER 38

241 *one of their daughters:* United States Census, 1920.

241 *charming six-footer:* Pony Duke, phone conversation with the author, July 18, 2005; throughout the years of interviews Emily gave, whenever she recounted her childhood, she'd often invoke the nasty-tempered German nanny who didn't like the French.

242 *man in New York City:* The New York Times included him, along with John D. Rockefeller, Henry Ford, and Andrew Carnegie, among the six richest men in the country, based on income tax recorded a decade before. The Times reminisced about how it was customary to speak of George Baker, J. Pierpoint Morgan, and John D. Rockefeller as the "The Big Three." His funeral at Tuxedo Park included lengthy readings from condolences from presidents Hoover and Coolidge and every business titan alive. "Funeral of Baker at Tuxedo Today," New York Times, May 5, 1931, p. 20; and "Simplicity Marks G. F. Baker Funeral," New York Times, May 6, 1931, p. 23.

242 *late Bruce Price:* "In the Social World, California Tech," New York Times, February 22, 1920, p. 23. Edwin Sr. was making a successful if muted life for himself; he had served as a lieutenant commander of reserve troops during the war. According to his daughter-in-law Marguerite Post, he never had enough money to live the way he wanted to.

Following the war, in order to gain additional income, Edwin's wife, Eleanor, resumed her stage name, Nellie Malcolm, and started acting again. "Edwin had a small brokerage, and he was happy with a much simpler life than he had known as a wealthy socialite," according to Post (Marguerite Post to Barbara Dafoe Whitehead, early 1998).

242 *"extant in whites":* William B. Scott and Peter M. Rutkoff, New York Modern, 136.

243 *sex education:* Peter N. Stearns and Jan Lewis, eds., Battleground of Desire, 92.

243 *"midwife of 1885":* Stephanie Coontz, Marriage, 199 and 197.

243 *just as men did:* Ibid., 201.

243 *for five hundred:* "Society Throng Sees Miss Loew Married," New York Times, May 7, 1920, p. 11, and "Easter Monday Nuptials," New York Times, April 12, 1898, p. 5. George Baker's status had been emphasized years before, at his daughter's wedding. The guests included President and Mrs. Benjamin Harrison among a list of equally illustrious officials. Florence Baker had married a Loew, a family that spent the majority of their "in-between season" time on Jekyll Island and in Tuxedo Park. The couple had become good friends of Emily's, and their children spent summers together—even though Ned's parents were divorced. Florence's sister wed B. St. George; Katharine Collier's daughter married into the St. George family as well. Florence Loew, Barbara's mother and Emily's friend, left over $4 million to her children and husband when she died in 1937—worth over $50 million today.

CHAPTER 39

246 *"couldn't see straight":* "She Was Leading Lady in American Life to Millions," Vineyard Gazette, September 30, 1960.

246 *"made me do it":* Sue Erikson Bloland, interview with the author, January 20, 2005.

246 *"hundred years hence":* Etiquette, 303.

247 *being "in society":* Stephen Birmingham, "Our Crowd," 75–76; and James Lea Cate, "Keeping Posted," p. 26. Arthur Schlesinger, in Learning How to Behave, asserts that the "lack of a hereditary aristocracy, the constant frontier, the repeated waves of im-

migrants, and the scarcity of women in new settlements" worked against a codifed behavior for the vibrant middle class. The challenge created the spectacle of etiquette books being published ever more frequently, as publishers tried to keep pace with the settlers' need for instruction (viii).

247 *"of democracy" itself:* Schlesinger, *Learning How to Behave,* vii.

247 *" 'Emily Post' was sufficient":* Quoted in Deborah Felder, *A Century of Women,* 126.

CHAPTER 40

248 *hairstyles was abbreviated:* Stephanie Coontz, *Marriage,* 197.

249 *to their core:* Edmund Wilson, *To the Finland Station,* 65.

250 *Ned remembered: Truly Emily Post,* 208.

250 *or fashion consultant:* Mark Caldwell, *A Short History of Rudeness,* 7 (see, too, pp. 60 and 21), makes the point that "civility and rudeness" are subjects that must be submitted to the resources of multiple disciplines: "history, sociology, anthropology, psychology, communications theory, language, and linguistics" as well as "the hard sciences." To this catalog could be added philosophy and women's studies, the latter because of the preponderance of women working in the field of etiquette, at least throughout the twentieth century.

250 *genteel Tuxedo Park: New York Times,* September 30, 1921, p. 11.

251 *January 27, 1922:* Courtesy of HarperCollins, from Funk and Wagnalls archives. Drawn up on behalf of Mrs. Emily Price Post, State of New York, and Funk and Wagnalls Company of the City of New York, the original contract, dated January 27, 1922, states that Mrs. Post "has a certain book . . . the subject or title of which is Etiquette" (courtesy of e-mail from Helen Moore, HarperCollins, October 4, 2005). The publishers agreed to pay the author 10 percent of the retail price of every copy sold. In five years, Funk and Wagnalls would be allowed to drop the contract or buy it out, if the writer would purchase the remainder of any leftover stock. Instead, when that five-year deadline arrived, Funk and Wagnalls would publish a second edition, after Emily Post had negotiated an entirely new contract first. And "Emily Post Is Dead Here at 86," *New York Times,* September 27, 1960.

251 *"Society is incidental": Etiquette,* xvii.

252 *"changes in the mores":* James Lea Cate, "Keeping Posted," p. 34.

CHAPTER 41

253 *more than money:* The bestseller list was firmly established by 1902 (Michael Korda, *Making the List,* xvii).

254 *"its chosen members": Etiquette,* 3.

254 *Emily's vivid characters:* Quoted in Edmund Wilson, "Books," *New Yorker,* July 19, 1947; the essay also appears in Wilson's *A Literary Chronicle, 1920–1950* (New York: Anchor, 1952), 380–89.

254 *"the right thing":* Pankaj Mishra, "The Unquiet American," review of *Edmund Wilson: A Life in Literature,* by Lewis M. Dabney, *New York Times Book Review,* January 12, 2006, p. 31. Wilson, eventually to be termed a "national cultural institution" just like Emily Post, sought hard to reconcile "the aggressively commercial culture of post–Civil War America" with the "genteel idealism" he believed had ruled until then.

255 *"California, and Nevada":* "Men About Town," *Vogue,* October 1, 1937, p. 155.

255 *"to the heart": Etiquette,* 373.

256 *were close friends: Truly Emily Post,* 97–99.

256 *to her servants: Etiquette,* 510.

256 *"throughout his life":* Letter to the Post Institute from Elizabeth Tocher Peck, Sandia Park, New Mexico, 2006.

257 *"glass is nothing": Etiquette,* 218.

257 *"in proper mourning?"*: Ibid., 405.

258 *"are bad form"*: Ibid., 58–64.

258 *"my grandmother wince"*: William G. Post interview with the author, Naples, Florida, April 22, 2002.

258 *until she died*: Etiquette (1937), 8.

259 *were still absolutes*: James Lea Cate, "Keeping Posted."

259 *"your house again"*: "Formal Dinners," *Etiquette*, chapter 24. For comparisons of their treatment of the same issue, see Mrs. John Sherwood, *Manners and Social Usages*, chapter 30, "The Modern Dinner Table," and Lillian Eichler, *The Book of Etiquette*, "Planning the Formal Dinner," vol. 2, chapter 2.

259 *Homberger maintains*: Eric Homberger, e-mail to the author, November 1, 2005.

259 *its initial publication*: Display ad, *New York Times*, October 1, 1925.

CHAPTER 42

261 *celebration as well*: *Life*, fall 1990 Special Issue, "The 100 Most Important Americans of the 20th Century," and April 1950 *Pageant* magazine, "The Most Powerful Women in America: Who Are They?"

261 *"the money appeals"*: Anne Whitney Hay, "Mrs. Price Post, Her Book on Etiquette," *Morning Telegraph*, August 1922.

262 *"sign of the times"*: "How to Watch Your Behavior," *Literary Digest*, August 19, 1922, p. 33; "How to Be Happy Though Decent," *Literary Digest*, September 1922.

262 *"instruction from it"*: *New York Times Book Review*, December 17, 1922.

262 *"convincing and entertaining"*: *Literary Digest International Book Review*, March 1923, and Alice Payne Hackett, *Sixty Years of Best Sellers*, 96.

262 *"the newspaper business"*: *Nevada State Journal*, September 29, 1922.

262 *American manners*: The Library of Congress bibliography of Lillian Eichler Watson lists nineteen books.

263 *Edmund Wilson remarked*: Edmund Wilson, "Books of Etiquette and Emily Post," *Classics and Commercials*, 375–76.

264 *"back in the 20's"*: Letter from Lillian Eichler Watson, May 2, 1946, Schlesinger papers, Radcliffe Institute for Advanced Study.

264 *another one claimed*: Display ad, *New York Times*, August 27, 1922; *Philadelphia Inquirer*, n.d.

264 *explain the abstract*: "Advertising News and Notes," *New York Times*, August 20, 1941, and May 30, 1962. To some extent, Emily Post's lifelong silence on things Jewish issued from her confusion over class.

264 *cultured manner*: Recounted in several dozen interviews, this version is most thoroughly aired by Edmund Wilson in the Post essay in *Classics and Commercials*. That the literary Wilson would take on a mere etiquette book as one of his subjects was considered so singular that mention of his essay on *Etiquette* was included in his *New York Times* obituary.

265 *"doesn't really matter"*: *Etiquette*, 183.

265 *biggest rival*: Internal Notes and Contracts, Doubleday/Garden City Publishers, August 18, 1923, to November 19, 1957, courtesy of Doubleday.

265 *that September*: See, for instance, "Etiquette by Emily Post," *Boston Globe*, September 18, 1922, p. 12.

265 *sold in six months*: Display ad, *New York Times*, February 21, 1923.

CHAPTER 43

267 *the new woman*: "Many Tourists Sail for Europe Today," *New York Times*, April 25, 1923, p. 26.

267 *he quipped*: *Boston Globe*, September 9, 1923, p. 41. Thanks to Donna Halper for pointing out that "of course you knew you had 'made it' when humorist Will Rogers joked about your work in his stage routine"; e-mail to the author, April 8, 2006.

267 *festivities as well:* "Debutantes Out at Tuxedo Ball," *New York Times,* October 28, 1923, p. 22, and "Mr. and Mrs. Edwin Main Post Jr.," *New York Times,* December 14, 1923.

267 *at the same age:* William G. Post, e-mail to the author, June 5, 2004.

268 *from Bruce's side:* Nanette Kutner, "Emily Post Is Only Human, Too," *Family Circle,* November 1955, p. 14.

269 *"of her day":* Delight Evans, "Mrs. Price Post," *New York Times,* January 6, 1924.

269 *back to Juliet:* "Hamilton's Remarriage Reveals Divorce From the Late J. P. Morgan's Daughter," *New York Times,* January 4, 1924, p. 1.

271 *"please explain":* "Society Youth Weds Cabman's Daughter," *New York Times,* November 14, 1924; "Rhinelanders Flee Glare of Publicity," *New York Times,* November 15, 1924; "Rhinelander Sues to Annul Marriage: Alleges Race Deceit," *New York Times,* November 27, 1924; "To Drop Mrs. Rhinelander: Social Register Will Omit Her Name," *New York Times,* March 16, 1925, p. 19.

271 *"who knows?":* The landmark case *Perez v. Sharp* made California the first state to overturn a miscegenation statute when a "white" woman and a "Negro" man successfully sued to marry in 1948.

271 *whatever that meant:* "Mrs. L. Kip Rhinelander in Social Register, Despite Race Assertions in Husband's Suit," *New York Times,* March 11, 1925, and "To Drop Mrs. Rhinelander," *New York Times,* March 16, 1925. See also Earl Lewis and Heidi Ardizzone, *Love on Trial.* The Jones family had emigrated to the United States from England, where the parents were born; their ancestors were from the West Indies. In the language of the period, their daughters were at best mulattos, which meant that marriage to white men was illegal. Until 1948, laws prohibiting marriage between races preempted interracial romance throughout the country. New York State, notoriously conservative in its marriage laws, at least proved consistent by disallowing race alone as grounds for divorce. Injured parties had to prove fraud, and even the all-white male jury agreed that Kip Rhinelander had known he was marrying a "mixed blood" woman. No annulment could be granted. Kip would file for divorce later in Nevada, and neither he nor Alice would marry again.

CHAPTER 44

272 *Olympic games:* Frederick Lewis Allen, *Only Yesterday,* 104 and 105.

273 *members were listed:* Christopher Gray, *New York Times,* November 14, 1999, p. 197, and "Women Will Erect Apartment Deluxe," *New York Times,* May 14, 1925, p. 10. According to *Dau's New York Social Blue Book 1930,* the tenants included, in addition to Emily, Mrs. Price Collier, Mr. and Mrs. J. O'Hara Cosgrave, Mr. and Mrs. Curtis Bean, Miss Katharine Gandy, Mr. and Mrs. C. Godwin Goddard, Mr. and Mrs. Charles Hopkins, Mrs. John Torrey Linzee, Mrs. Horace H. Martin, Mr. and Mrs. Victor Morawetz, Mr. and Mrs. Louis Carbery Ritchie, Mr. Alexander M. Stewart, Mr. and Mrs. Albert Tilt, Mrs. Stanford White, and Mrs. Frederick W. Whitridge.

273 *living room:* See also Jeanne Perkins, "Emily Post," *Life,* May 6, 1946, p. 59.

274 *"suggest you":* *The Personality of a House,* p. 2.

274 *"would be unhappy":* Courtesy of Laura Jacobs, interview with Christopher Gray, May 22, 2001.

275 *case for courtesy:* see "Books & Authors," *New York Times,* August 16, 1925, p. BR15, and also *New York Tribune,* July 26, 1925; "A Professional Beauty," *New York Times,* August 1925, p. 2; review of *Parade, New York Times;* "Funk and Wagnalls' Latest Volume," *Yorkshire Herald;* "Book Reviews in Tabloid," *Atlanta Constitution,* September 27, 1925, p. D3.

275 *"her at once":* *Parade,* 92. The sexual attitude of Geraldine is oddly akin to that of the heroine in Ian McEwan's 2007 novel *On Chesil Beach.*

276 *"from the elect":* Katherine Anne Porter, "Etiquette in Action," *New York Tribune,* December 26, 1925.

276 *hairstyles for women:* "Is the Bob Here to Stay?" *Washington Post,* September 27, 1926, p. SM7.
276 *semester before:* C. J. Furness, ed., *The Genteel Female,* 39.
276 *just as irritating:* "They Who Are Fat Must Suffer to Be Thin," *McCall's,* March 1926.
277 *funded by love:* Stephanie Coontz, *Marriage,* 200–201.
278 *"of everyday life":* Margaret Sanger, *Happiness in Marriage* (New York: Brentano's, 1926; Maxwell Reprint, 1969), 177.
278 *so completely:* Katharine Brooke Daly, "Emily Post Points Out Success Factor," *Morning Star,* February 7, 1926. The enneagram was sometimes referred to as the "Enneagon."
279 *"Who knows?":* "The Young Woman of Forty," *McCall's,* April 1926, pp. 54–55.
279 *competitor had made:* "Books and Authors," *New York Times,* May 16, 1926.
280 *"linen damask":* *Vanity Fair,* December 1926.

CHAPTER 45

281 *magical island:* Pony Duke, phone interview with the author, July 18, 2005.
281 *"so forth":* William G. Post, e-mail to the author, September 6, 2004.
282 *she bought it:* "Edgartown House Exemplifies Real Hobby of Emily Post," *Vineyard Gazette,* May 1939, and T.N.J. Dexter, "What Mrs Post Has Done with an Old Place," p. 8, in Historic Notes on Vineyard Houses, Envelope MS, Box 24B, Archives of Martha's Vineyard Historical Society, internally dated.
282 *"in 1828":* "She Was Leading Lady in American Life to Millions," *Vineyard Gazette,* September 30, 1960.
282 *"weather-beaten and squatty":* "Edgartown House Exemplifies Real Hobby of Emily Post" and T.N.J. Dexter, "What Mrs Post Has Done with an Old Place," p. 8.
283 *ruptured appendix:* Bruce Price Post, death certificate 5121, Department of Health, City of New York.
283 *he quietly observed:* *Truly Emily Post,* 231.
283 *went unmentioned:* "Bruce Price Post, Architect, Dies: Son of Novelist a Victim of Acute Appendicitis," *New York Times,* February 26, 1927.
284 *can be offered:* *Etiquette,* chapter 24. During the last minutes spent by persons in the World Trade Center on September 11, when they knew death was imminent, they quickly passed around the only cell phone operating, so that everyone would have a chance to say good-bye. As authors Jim Dwyer and Kevin Flynn somberly note, "Even in a time of confusion and coursing fear, small courtesies survived" (*102 Minutes* [New York: Henry Holt, 2005], 126).
285 *World War II:* Joan Didion, *The Year of Magical Thinking,* 57–59.
285 *"out of twenty-four":* Margaret Case Harriman, "Dear Mrs. Post," *Saturday Evening Post,* May 15, 1937, p. 18. Emily's determination to function alongside of her tragedy recalls Rose Kennedy's diary entry soon after President Kennedy's assassination: "My reaction to grief is a certain kind of nervous action.... I just keep moving, walking, pulling away at things, praying to myself while I move, and making up my mind that it is not going to get me. I am not going to be licked by tragedy, as life is a challenge and we must carry on and work for the living as well as mourn for the dead" (Rose Fitzgerald Kennedy papers, John F. Kennedy Presidential Library and Museum, Boston).
286 *" 'Yes, Mrs. Post' ":* Margaret Case Harriman, "Dear Mrs. Post," p. 52.
286 *in turmoil:* Yi-Fu Tuan, *Dominance and Affection,* 18–21.
287 *"and so it goes":* Emily Post, "My Gay Little Garden," *American Home,* April 1934, pp. 245–46, 307–8.
287 *"get going again":* Dominique Browning, *Around the House and in the Garden,* 51 and 48.
288 *they had lost:* Patricia Klindienst, *The Earth Knows My Name.*
288 *hospital's flower beds:* Michele Owens, "The Healing Power of Flowers," *O Magazine,* November 2006, p. 314.

289 *midwife to her flowers:* Letter from Henry A. Dreer to Emily Post, July 20, 1927, courtesy of the Emily Post Institute.

289 *her expectations:* Emily Post's Garden Log, courtesy of the Emily Post Institute.

289 *recently begun selling:* Thanks to Bob Armstrong and to Anne Williams for sharing their research on jigsaw puzzles.

289 *"reds together":* William G. Post, phone interview with the author, from Naples, Florida, April 3, 2004.

290 **Etiquette** *to save herself:* Display ad, *New York Times,* November 30, 1927.

CHAPTER 46

291 *four and a half residents:* Ron Chernow, "How It Sparkled in the Skyline," *New York Times,* May 26, 2005, p. F8.

291 *"those who do":* *Time* magazine, December 12, 1927.

292 *the* **Post** *opined:* "Social Laws Are Changed in Blue Book," *Washington Post,* December 25, 1927, p. S9.

293 *"and do likewise":* *Etiquette* (1927), 631–32.

294 *"its chosen members":* Ibid., 3.

294 *"as well as manners":* Ibid.

294 *Pete Hamill has said:* Pete Hamill, *Downtown,* 20.

295 *"sexual exploitation":* William B. Scott and Peter M. Rutkoff, *New York Modern,* 22.

PART FOUR

CHAPTER 47

299 *measure of inches:* Ron Chernow, "How It Sparkled in the Skyline," *New York Times,* May 26, 2005, pp. F8–F9. Admiration for the Art Deco icons would ebb when critics such as Lewis Mumford and Alfred Barr promoted European modernism instead of what they believed to be products of mere "real estate speculators."

300 *"were the things to have":* "Value of Antiques Debated at Macy's," *New York Times,* May 18, 1928.

300 *"he won't stay married":* Cynthia Crossen, "When Worse Than a Woman Who Voted Was One Who Smoked," *Wall Street Journal,* January 7, 2008, p. B1.

301 *friends would think:* Margaret Case Harriman, "Dear Mrs. Post," *Saturday Evening Post,* May 15, 1937, and Display ad, *Morning News Review,* Florence, South Carolina, May 3, 1928.

301 *readers at Dreer's:* Letter to Henry Dreer, Philadelphia, n.d., part of Emily's private Garden Log, courtesy of the Emily Post Institute.

302 *have to do better:* Garden Log, n.p.

302 *surfacing as well:* "Post's Capsized Boat, 4 Missing, Washed Ashore," *Herald Tribune,* July 4, 1928; and "Edwin M. Post's Body Recovered on Beach," *New York Times,* July 11, 1928.

302 *last to be recovered:* "Launch Floating on Side Points to Tragedy," *New York Times,* July 3, 1928, p. 3, and "Columbia Students Missing from Boat," *New York Times,* July 4, 1928, p. 9.

303 *big money at last:* "Edwin M. Post's Body Recovered on Beach."

303 *a lot like Emily Post:* "Mrs. Post Back on Stage," *New York Times,* August 8, 1929, and Nora Post, interview with the author, Kingston, New York, June 5, 2005.

304 *its author's death:* Letter to Mr. Edwin N. Moore, n.d. (around April 18, 1928), courtesy of Funk and Wagnalls; letter to Emily Post (with a copy sent to Doubleday, Doran and Co.), April 18, 1928, Funk and Wagnalls; courtesy of Helen Moore at HarperCollins.

304 **Times** *reviewer concluded:* "A Debutante's Code," *New York Times Book Review,* November 25, 1928.

305 **"human nature is discussable":** *How to Behave—Though a Debutante*, 56, 62, 227.

305 **"for the other person":** R.R.W., *Washington Post*, December 16, 1928, p. S12.

306 **"of their men!":** "Kelland Doesn't Know What He Is Talking About, Answers Emily Post," Emily Post, *American Magazine*, December 1928, pp. 13, 111–13, and "Notes on Current Magazines," *New York Times*, December 2, 1928, p. 93.

CHAPTER 48

307 **"a second clue":** Quoted by Liesl Schillinger in "The Beautiful and Damned," *New York Times Book Review*, April 16, 2006, p. 18. See also Lillian G. Genn, "Society Is Changing—and How: Life of New York's Aristocracy 'Not What It Used to Be,' " *Washington Post*, March 10, 1929, p. SM5.

308 **"may turn up":** Emily Post, "How to Be Happy Though a Parent," *Collier's*, July 20, 1929, pp. 17–18.

308 **"unselfconscious frankness":** *Collier's*, September 7, 1929.

309 **family inheritances:** Frederick Lewis Allen, *Only Yesterday*. Some scholars date the beginning of the Depression to October 24, 1929, Black Thursday, the day the stock market crashed. Undoubtedly a traumatic day for those who owned stock as sales volume broke all records, Black Thursday nonetheless registered a deterioration in overall stock prices of about 2.5 percent, from 261.97 to 255.39, as measured by the *New York Times* index of fifty stocks. The worst still lay in the future; the market hit bottom on July 7, 1932, when the *Times* index was only 33.98, a decline of over 89 percent from its high of 311.90 on September 19, 1929.

309 **pay their taxes:** Courtesy of Chris Sonne, Tuxedo Park historian.

309 **$1,027 for men:** Deborah Felder, *A Century of Women*, 144.

310 **"happy ending":** Bell Syndicate, "Good Taste Today," *Roanoke Times*, September 22, 1940.

310 **to the workplace:** Alfred Allan Lewis, *Ladies and Not-So-Gentle Women*, 419–20.

CHAPTER 49

311 **her two Bruces:** In February 1993, Mitchell Owens, a columnist for the magazine *Decorating Remodeling*, would list *The Personality of a House* as one of three "must reads" on the art of decorating. The other two imperatives were *Mark Hampton on Decorating* and Stephen Calloway's *Twentieth-Century Decoration*, both written more than fifty years later.

311 **"on my sleeve":** Letter from Emily Post, Eleanor Hubbard Garst letters, courtesy of Special Collections and University Archives, University of Iowa Libraries, circa May 1931.

312 **"call it that":** Ibid.

313 **fifty years later:** Samuel Graybill, phone interview with the author, July 13, 2005. Now the proprietor of an inn in Provincetown, Massachusetts, Graybill interviewed Emily in the 1950s. She told him that she believed her father's Quebec hotel, the Château Frontenac, to be his greatest achievement. Graybill held out for Tuxedo Park and the American Surety skyscraper.

313 **"furniture in them":** *The Personality of a House*, 3, 66, 74.

313 **"house is practical":** Interview with Christopher Gray, May 22, 2001, courtesy of Laura Jacobs.

313 **"typically yours":** *The Personality of a House*, 206.

314 **"and the fundamentals":** "The Etiquette of Home Decoration," *New York Herald Tribune*, magazine section, 1930.

314 **"of this sort":** "Home Decoration," *New York Times*, April 27, 1930, p. 68.

314 **"anything else":** Eleanor Hubbard Garst, "Book-Helps for the Busy Homemaker," *Better Homes and Gardens*, September 1931, p. 27.

314 **"Big Names":** Edwin Alger, "Meeting the Big Names," *Boston Globe*, May 22, 1951.

314 **women activists:** "Social Leaders Here Reject Cocktail Ban," *New York Times,* June 10, 1930.

314 **"not encouraging temperance":** "Famous Woman Says WCTU Should Be Changed to WCPU," *Jefferson County Union,* July 4, 1930.

315 **and hydrangeas:** "Vineyard Haven Fetes Yachts," *New York Times,* July 27, 1930.

316 **was carefully retaliating:** Helen Huntington Smith, "Profiles: Lady Chesterfield," *New Yorker,* August 9, 1930, and Smith, "Ask Mrs. Post," *New Yorker,* August 16, 1930.

CHAPTER 50

317 **Music Appreciation Hour:** George H. Douglas, *The Early Days of Radio Broadcasting,* 161.

317 **"form of entertainment":** Ibid., 153.

317 **most people's doors:** The growth and prosperity of national radio networks was linked tightly to the number of potential affiliates. RCA was the first to recognize that independent organizations could manage broadcast services more efficiently than one giant umbrella corporation. With this realization, RCA created NBC in 1926 and purchased the WEAF and WCAP radio stations and network from ATT, merging them with RCA's own major network, the WJA New York/WRC Washington chain. NBC was divided into two networks, called the Red and the Blue. Similarly, CBS debuted during this period, its parent, United Independent Broadcasters, barely solvent until 1929, the year after William Paley, investing his own money, bailed it out and spearheaded its new operation. See also Nicholas Lemann, "Amateur Hour: Journalism Without Journalists," *New Yorker,* August 7, 2006.

318 **"her passion":** William G. Post, phone interview with the author from Naples, Florida, April 3, 2004.

319 **"pale visibly":** *Truly Emily Post,* 235. Even theaters dared not open their doors until *Amos 'n' Andy* was over. At one point the nightly show was listened to by one-third of those owning radios. Some historians credit its popularity for increasing radio sales during the Depression.

319 **rhythm and blues:** Frederick Lewis Allen, *Only Yesterday,* 352.

319 **broadcast nationally:** Contracts between the Blackman Company Advertising and Emily Post, October 22, 1930, and November 28, 1930, courtesy of the Emily Post Institute; and William G. Post, e-mail to the author, June 7, 2006.

Emily was paid well by her sponsors, though she never commanded the salary of the major stars. According to the reliable radio (and later television) critic of the *Chicago Tribune,* Larry Wolters, Major Bowes's sponsors, including Chase and Sanborn coffee, paid him $18,000 a week for his beloved amateur hour (which would stay on the air until 1970), the first year of its radio network broadcasts auditioning more than thirty thousand acts in the talent contest program, among them Frank Sinatra. Singer-comedian Eddie Cantor was paid $14,000 a week (though he paid much of that to his bandleader and other sidekicks), Jack Benny made $7,000 a week, and Burns and Allen received up to $8,500. The higher their ratings, the more their sponsors paid them. (*Chicago Tribune,* November 15, 1936, p. SW4; thanks to Donna Halper for this information.)

319 **their recipient:** *Mrs. Post's Radio Talk,* November 1, 1930, Procter & Gamble radio script, courtesy of the Library of Congress, Manuscript Division.

320 **fork to use:** Jo Ransom, "Radio Dial-Log," *Brooklyn Eagle,* November 16, 1931.

321 **"chicanery at all":** Procter & Gamble radio talk, November 8, 1930.

321 **"spirit of hospitality":** Procter & Gamble radio talk, November 15, 1930.

322 **left of the signature:** Excerpts from *Emily Post Inquiries,* typed list from Emily's file, courtesy of the Emily Post Institute, Burlington, Vermont.

322 **the parvenu:** Procter & Gamble radio talk, March 14, 1931.

323 **"abomination to his soul":** *Etiquette* (1922) 508, and *Etiquette* (1937), 617–18.

323 **of Roosevelt's family:** "Mussolini: Mispronounced," *New York Times,* May 14, 1939.

323 **"I take notes":** Comments courtesy of the Emily Post Institute, Burlington, Vermont.

324 **remind herself:** Ibid.

CHAPTER 51

325 **Grace Episcopal Church:** "Mrs. Percy Turnure Dies of Pneumonia," *New York Times,* January 5, 1931, p. 21.

326 **"the village green":** C. Gray, "A New Age of Architecture Ushered in Financial Gloom," *New York Times,* January 1, 2006, Section II, p. 2.

326 **children to feed:** "$10,000,000 Asked for Jobless Here: Republican Aldermen Request Fund for New City Work—Plea Sent to Committee. Breadline Control Urged: Relief Agencies to Plan Revision of 82 Mass Feeding Stations—Architects Seek Aid to Mobilize Relief Agencies. Architects Appeal to Hoover," *New York Times,* January 21, 1931, p. 14. See also "Asks Aid for Draftsmen: Architects' Committee Says Many Idle Men Are Destitute," *New York Times,* March 23, 1931, p. 40.

326 **no longer necessary:** "Jobless in Distress Put at 160,000 Here: Gibson Estimates Half Are Family Heads and About Third Are in 'White-Collar' Class. Women to Organize Today; Mrs. Belmont Hopes to Enroll 500—Walker Seeks to Have Harvard Play the Army Here. Job Bureau to Be Used. 1,200 Architects Seek Jobs. Charity Games Yield $107,777," *New York Times,* September 30, 1931, p. 6.

327 **knew it or not:** "Emily Post Rules on Potlikker Etiquette About Dunking," *New York Times,* February 19, 1931.

327 **most people's reach:** "Enactment Meeting Held in Baltimore," *Frederick Post,* April 7, 1931.

328 **been divorced:** Her heart lay with her radio audience, which was even taking priority over her magazine readership. She hurried off an apology to an interviewer from *Better Homes and Gardens,* explaining that she was answering her query belatedly today, on Sunday, her day off, because it had been "lost under the avalanche of radio letters." Letter to Emily Post from Eleanor Hubbard Garst, late May 1931, courtesy of Special Collections and University Archives, University of Iowa Libraries; and Garst, "Book-Helps for the Busy Homemaker," *Better Homes and Gardens,* September 1931, p. 27.

329 **"EP on 2 nights":** Contracts between the Blackman Company Advertising and Emily Post, October 22, 1931, courtesy of the Emily Post Institute.

329 **"and good taste":** Procter & Gamble radio talk, November 1, 1931.

CHAPTER 52

330 **"her only grandchild":** William G. Post, phone interview with the author, October 24, 2002.

330 **"it felt claustrophobic":** Ibid.

330 **"she was happy":** Yvonne Sylvia, interview with the author, Martha's Vineyard, October 20, 2002, and by telephone October 23, 2002.

331 **"part of it":** Letter to the author, February 28, 2006.

331 **"feeding their families":** E-mail to the author, July 22, 2004. Emily's tension every time she needed a contract renewal was motivated partly by the financial concerns evident even in the magical world of modern entertainment. *Time* magazine announced that radio moguls would begin charging their sponsors, such as General Electric, more, even as they paid the radio entertainers less. Emily was able to relax once everything settled down. Her own contracts were unaffected, and she was beginning to realize additional profit from an informal relationship between the Bell Syndicate newspapers and the radio stations. The earlier antagonism between newspapers and radio had yielded to an alliance wherein Emily's mutual promotion

was the current gold standard. Columbia's radio systems had already affiliated thirty-five newspapers with its ninety radio stations. Walter Winchell, Little Orphan Annie, and Emily Post were held up as celebrity examples of mutually beneficial crossover. (*Time,* May 9, 1932.)

332 *"dry" citizens:* "Ask Women to Make Repeal Sole Issue: Mrs. Post and Mrs. Sheppard Want Candidates Judged by Their Attitude on Prohibition," Letter to the Editor, *New York Times* March 30, 1932, p. 21.

332 *Welfare Councils of New York:* "A Garden Party: Events to Raise Funds for Unemployed Architects," *New York Times,* May 29, 1932, p. X8, and Anne Lee, "Real Aid for Architects: Emergency Committee Has Created Useful Jobs for Many," *New York Times,* June 13, 1932, p. 14.

332 *a mere $975:* "Contest for Beauty in Filling Stations: Awards of $975 Offered for Designs by Unemployed Architects," *New York Times,* April 3, 1932, p. RE20.

333 *when serving tea?:* Emily Post, "Good Taste Today," *Appleton Post Crescent,* September 14, 1932.

CHAPTER 53

335 *"busy she was":* William G. Post, telephone interview with the author from Naples, Florida, April 3, 2004.

335 *"depths of mines":* George H. Douglas, *The Early Days of Radio Broadcasting,* 109–12. Lowell Thomas was a man after Emily's own heart: he indulged in so many different activities that when the Library of Congress librarians cataloged his memoirs, they had to place them in "CT," the section for people whose lifework doesn't fit any one category.

335 *about the future:* Ibid.

336 *and Fifty-seventh Street:* "Sale Will Aid Architects," *New York Times,* January 18, 1933, p. 6.

336 *"I abhor you":* William G. Post, phone interview, April 3, 2004. Pony Duke says he "seriously doubts" that Katharine would have said such a thing. Given Emily's propensity to take the kernel of a true story and exaggerate it into a better one, she probably doctored Katharine's statement.

336 *"Good as Emily Post":* Truly Emily Post, 236.

337 *hailed from:* Alfred Allan Lewis, *Ladies and Not-So-Gentlewomen,* 102.

337 *from another age:* Ibid.

338 *March 9, 1937:* Thanks to Chris Sonne, Tuxedo Park historian, for his April 22, 2006, e-mail to the author and two interviews at Tuxedo Park, in 2002 and 2005. The insurance detectives had been watching the chauffeur for years as he had been blackmailing Keech—another instance of Colonel Mann's premise that servants were the best spies into the households of the wealthy.

338 *could be sold legally:* "Citizens of 19 States Get Legal Beer Today," *Charleston Gazette,* April 7, 1933, p. 10.

339 *held firm, he said:* From the New York Supreme Court records. Records from an unsuccessful lawsuit Holman would file at the end of the decade reveal Emily as making an average of $10,000 a year ($137,000 in 2006 dollars) for the daily column from November 16, 1931, until February 27, 1937.

340 *Bill Post remembers:* William G. Post, phone interview with the author, November 17, 2004.

340 *"of seasonal patterns":* "She Was Leading Lady in American Life to Millions," *Vineyard Gazette,* September 30, 1960.

340 *battered farmland:* Frederick Lewis Allen, *Only Yesterday,* 196.

341 *paying customers instead:* Quoted in ibid.

341 *as supercilious:* "Private Lives of the Great," *Vanity Fair,* December 1933. Miguel Covarrubias's linear drawing style influenced other caricaturists, including Al Hirschfeld.

CHAPTER 54

343 *irritated Emily profoundly:* "Book Notes," *New York Times,* May 9, 1934, p. 17.
343 *"pluck and fertilize":* Emily Post, "My Gay Little Garden," *American Home,* April 1934, pp. 245–46, 307–8.
344 *Seventy-ninth Street:* Obituary, *New York Times,* May 1, 1934, p. 23.
344 *Statue of Liberty:* Timothy Egan, *The Worst Hard Time* (Boston: Houghton Mifflin, 2005), 152.
344 *"of the current":* "Slapping Emily's Wrist," *Washington Post,* July 13, 1934, p. 8. Over seventy years later, another *Washington Post* critic, Tim Page, would recall how, "in a moment of early-teen hippie scorn," he had begun to read *Etiquette* in order to mock it, certain he would find an " 'uncool' justification of bourgeois rules and regulations." Instead, to his amazement, the book offered "clearly stated reasons for courtesy, gentility and scrupulousness." It became, says Page, who suffered with Asperger's syndrome, "the book that helped pull me into the human race" ("Parallel Play," *New Yorker,* August 20, 2007, pp. 38–41).
344 *"very next day":* William G. Post, phone interview with the author, May 19, 2006.
345 *members had uncovered:* "N.Y. Social Register Dropped Mrs. Mildred Tilta Holmsen Because of Her Scandalous Behavior and Attire," *New York Times,* November 24, 1934.
346 *much of her time:* The two women would serve jointly on several committees during the Depression years, working alongside other illustrious figures eager to see women succeed at home and in the workplace. Lillian Gilbreth's biographer has pondered the reason that no further connection between the two women occurred: "Odd, but not unexpected. LMG was probably too busy to make many friends, especially in the 30s. Also she lived in NJ, not Manhattan, and spent a lot of time at Purdue where I imagine EP would not have been very much at home. Also, she favored efficiency over graciousness" (Jane Lancaster, e-mail to the author, May 18, 2006).
346 *"layout of rooms":* "Model Home Opens: Throng Inspects It," *New York Times,* November 7, 1934. "America's Little House" was the Depression's version of New York City's 2006 Kips Bay house, designed professionally and benefiting charities into the early twenty-first century.
347 *grandson Bruce Post:* "Society and Fine Arts Join in Gay Pageantry of the Beaux Arts Ball: Event Epitomizes Beauty and Style," *New York Times,* February 2, 1935, p. 8.
347 *"Old World punctiliousness":* *Time Etiquette* (Lancaster, Pa.: Hamilton Watch Company, 1935 [probably September]).
347 *"smart to be late":* Ibid.
348 *"perfect timing":* Ibid.

CHAPTER 55

349 *needing no introduction:* New York Times, November 24, 1935.
350 *holding a balloon:* Time, November 18, 1935.
350 *"of college women":* "Today on the Radio," *New York Times,* January 6, 1936, p. 35, and April 13, 1936, p. 33.
350 *"distressing beyond words":* Truly Emily Post, p. 240.
351 *to be readmitted:* "News of the Stage," *New York Times,* May 14, 1936; see also "Volpone Opens Play Series," *New York Times,* September 8, 1948.
351 *"New Yorkiest":* Ann Douglas, *Terrible Honesty,* 111.
351 *ball once again:* Herman Klurfeld, *Winchell,* 34.
352 *"bobby socks up":* Richard Yates, *Revolutionary Road* (London: Methuen, 2001), 256.
353 *"many other things":* Gretta Palmer, "Mrs. Post Regrets," *New York Woman,* February 3, 1937, p. 13.

353 *country's newspapers:* Larry Wolters, "News of Radio," *Chicago Daily Tribune,* November 3, 1937, p. 21.

CHAPTER 56

355 *would be divorced:* "Priscilla St. George Is Married to Angier B. Duke in Tuxedo Park," *New York Times,* January 3, 1937, p. 85; "In Washington Tomorrow," *Syracuse Herald,* January 19, 1937; and "Roosevelt Pledges to 'Blot Out Injustice,'" *Fitchburg Sentinel,* January 20, 1937.

355 *"hours a week":* Gretta Palmer, "Mrs. Post Regrets," *New York Woman,* February 3, 1937, p. 11.

356 *general huffed:* "Hagood Scorns 'Emily Post' in Army Training," *Chicago Daily Tribune,* February 9, 1937, p. 13, referring to Dudley Harmon, "Top Hats and Tiaras," *Washington Post,* February 7, 1937, p. S1.6.

356 *"already vanished":* Palmer, "Mrs. Post Regrets," p. 11.

356 *last, definitive time:* Court case, Court of Appeals, State of New York: *Holman Harvey v. Bell Syndicate,* 541–42.

358 *"restful companion":* Margaret Case Harriman, "Dear Mrs. Post," *Saturday Evening Post,* May 15, 1937, p. 51.

359 *things her way:* Ibid.

359 *"writes fluently":* Ibid.

CHAPTER 57

360 *two frequently: Truly Emily Post,* 162–63.

360 *fruitful regeneration:* John Russell Pope, *New York Times,* August 28, 1937, p. 15.

360 *of Bruce Price:* Chris Sonne, phone interview with the author, August 7, 2002.

361 *"present-day society":* "Etiquette up to Date," *Publishers Weekly,* September 18, 1937.

361 *"fifty-year history": New York Times,* September 8, 1937.

361 *on counters:* Display ad, *New York Times,* September 19, 1937, p. 112.

362 *ignorant speech: Time,* September 20, 1931.

363 *"are illiterate":* Procter & Gamble radio broadcast, March 21, 1931, rough draft, courtesy of Cindy Post Senning.

363 *consideration for Emily: Washington Post,* February 7, 1937.

363 *"a mere 723":* "Why We Behave," *Washington Post,* September 3, 1937, p. 8.

364 *"or Park Avenue": Time,* September 20, 1937.

364 *"newspaper business":* William G. Post, phone interview with the author, May 2, 2003.

365 *had a choice:* Eric Felten, "How's Your Drink?," *Wall Street Journal,* July 15–16, 2006, p. 14.

365 *good manners:* Emily Post, "Good Taste Today," *Los Angeles Times,* September 12, 1937, p. K16.

365 *"out of life":* A typical column of Emily's from this period can be seen in ibid. The promotion was announced in the *New York Times:* "Florida Campaign Detailed," October 23, 1937, p. 33. Given her penchant for details, Emily must have known that the prestigious advertising agency handling the fruit commission's massive new campaign that fall was none other than Ruthruff and Ryan, the launchpad fifteen years earlier for Lillian Eichler, copywriter, and the sure beneficiary of the cartoon advertising campaign Eichler had spearheaded for Doubleday. Now the vice president of Ruthruff and Ryan announced "an elaborate advertising program for the citrus products of Florida" to be unveiled at the Waldorf-Astoria, with the Florida governor as the guest of honor (Emily Post radio programs courtesy of the Emily Post Institute).

365 *"taste and cultivation":* From a brochure she wrote for the commission, *How to Get the Most Out of Life* (Lakeland, Fla.: Florida Citrus Commission, 1937).

366 *"are bankrupt"*: Ibid.; pages quoted are 3–5, 12–13, 15, 21, 28.

366 *"we think and are"*: Display ad, *New York Times,* October 31, 1937.

367 *"younger readers"*: "Etiquette Author Tells of Her Woes," *New York Post,* November 19, 1937.

367 *laudatory in that:* New York Times, December 11, 1937, p. 11.

368 *"oil instead"*: Emily Post, radio broadcast, January 10, 1931.

CHAPTER 58

369 *"table manners"*: "Mrs. Post Unbends at Gourmet Dinner," *New York Times,* January 24, 1938.

370 *State Department protocol: New York Times,* January 30, 1938, p. 2.

371 *"colors fresh"*: William G. Post, phone interview with the author, from Naples, Florida, April 3, 2004.

371 *residence in Edgartown:* Thanks to Tuxedo Park town historian Chris Sonne for an e-mail to the author, May 5, 2006.

372 *thing as "typical"*: "Typical Girl of 16 Outlined by Emily Post," *Dallas Morning News,* August 21, 1938, p. 11.

374 *a happy ending:* Courtesy of Betty Osborne, letters from Emily Post, n.d., and October 31, 1949.

CHAPTER 59

376 *for Decca Records:* In 1939, music still dominated radio programming. It was good to laugh along with Jack Benny and with George Burns and Gracie Allen, but even more people preferred to escape with Glenn Miller's band. Between 1928 and 1939, major symphony orchestras in American towns and cities had grown from ten to seventeen, while the number of small orchestras had increased from 60 to 286. Pianos, even during the height of the Depression, sold faster than ever before. When the 1920s began, music instruction was nonexistent in most public schools; by the late 1930s, nearly all schools had music courses, along with 30,000 school orchestras and 20,000 school bands. It wasn't as if the radio had corrupted musical taste: the legendary Walter Damrosch, Leopold Stokowski, and Arturo Toscanini, among others, were "early advocates of radio music." See R. LeRoy Bannerman, *Norman Corwin and Radio,* 43, and George Douglas, *The Early Days of Radio Broadcasting,* 154.

376 *room to roam:* "Advertising News and Notes," *New York Times,* April 18, 1939, p. 30. Two of the most vivid fictional re-creations of the fair are E. L. Doctorow's *World's Fair* and *The Amazing Adventures of Kavalier & Clay,* by Michael Chabon. "Fifty Years After the Fair" is a song written and recorded by Aimee Mann. See also "World's Fair Opens!," *Hammond Times,* April 3, 1939.

377 *"of her personality"*: "Edgartown House Exemplifies Real Hobby of Emily Post," *Vineyard Gazette,* May 1939.

377 *interest implied:* Charles Hanson Towne, "Jogging Around New England," *New York Times,* June 6, 1939, p. 27.

377 *"equipment I suggested"*: Yvonne Sylvia, interview with the author, Martha's Vineyard, 2002.

378 *"next to the other"*: Pony Duke, phone interview with the author, July 18, 2005.

378 *"all up to her"*: Cindy Post Senning, interview with the author, April 5, 2004.

378 *beside the point:* Holly George-Warren, *Public Cowboy No. 1: The Life and Times of Gene Autry* (New York: Oxford University Press, 2007).

CHAPTER 60

379 *fourth edition: Truly Emily Post,* 245.

380 *"to the family"*: Etiquette (1940), 871.

380 **"back in order"**: Ibid.
380 **"as well as diverting"**: Ibid., 828.
381 **"of their friends"**: Ibid., 876.
381 **"are intolerant"**: Ibid.
381 **"counteract the effect"**: Ibid., 714.
381 **her favorite book**: Yvonne Sylvia, interview with the author, Martha's Vineyard, 2002. See also William Engle, "The Emily Post Story," *American Weekly*, February 6, 1949.
382 **"not have told you"**: *Truly Emily Post*, 233.
383 **"mind of a child"**: *Children Are People*, x–xii.
383 **"fortunately placed"**: Ibid., 4.
383 **"influence their children"**: Ibid., 3.
383 **"grown person"**: Ibid., 92.
383 **"to the telephone"**: Ibid.
384 **everyone's affections**: Ibid., 189.
384 **"boiled in oil"**: Ibid., 188.
384 **"the very nicest"**: *Vineyard Gazette*, October 4, 1940.
385 **anyone, he believes**: William G. Post, phone interview with the author, September 5, 2002.

CHAPTER 61

387 **"this unpleasantness"**: "Good Taste Today: Full Knowledge of Job Makes Worker Valuable," *Good Housekeeping*, September 22, 1940.
387 **defense preparations**: *Vineyard Gazette*, October 4, 1940.
388 **"and poise"**: "Brief Reviews," *New York Times Book Review*, December 8, 1940.
388 **old-fashioned at all**: *Time*, December 9, 1940.
388 **"Angelo Patri"**: Letter from A. Patri to Emily Post, December 18, 1940, archives, Emily Post Institute.
388 **on Martha's Vineyard**: Yvonne Sylvia, interview with the author, Martha's Vineyard, 2002.
389 **their ballots**: "Tasks for Women in Defense Urged," *New York Times*, December 13, 1940.
389 **"form" even further**: *Current Biography: Who's News and Why*, ed. Maxine Block (New York: H. W. Wilson, 1941), 681–83.
390 **other as equals**: Francis Fukuyama, *America at the Crossroads*, 28.
390 **its citizens**: Kai Bird and Martin J. Sherwood, *American Prometheus: The Triumph and Tragedy of J. Robert Oppenheimer* (New York: Vintage, 2006), 5.
390 **first took office**: "Katharine Collier St. George, Former GOP Representative, Dies," *Washington Post*, May 6, 1983.
390 **and Mrs. Roosevelt**: Phone interview July 18, 2005, with Pony Duke. The Delano-Collier-Roosevelt crowd fueled social events to the north and west of Tuxedo Park. Pony Duke remembers how often "family" and friends flocked to the Hudson Valley Staatsburg estate, called "Evergreen Lands," where his distant cousin Laura Delano lived. "Laura even hosted several unpublicized cocktail hours on the porch with the president, her cousin, when he wanted to see Churchill privately," he recalls. "I remember playing around the chairs while the two men talked in August [1943], and I climbed all over them. I watched the president being carried by his Secret Service men to sit in a chair in the pool."
390 **without delay**: Doris Kearns Goodwin, *No Ordinary Time: Franklin and Eleanor Roosevelt: The Home Front in World War II* (New York: Simon & Schuster, 1995), 409.
391 **a second Dorothy Parker**: Hildegarde Dolson, "Spilling Tea," *Sorry to Be So Cheerful*, 43; Dolson, "Ask Mrs. Post," *Reader's Digest*, April 1941; "Doomed but Happy," *New York Times Book Review*, August 21, 1955.
391 **in spite of it all**: Dolson, *Sorry*, 41.

392 *"on the table":* Margaret Case Harriman, "Don't Call Me Lady Chesterfield," *Reader's Digest,* June 1941.

392 *after the attack:* The attack on Pearl Harbor occurred on a Sunday, so there was no immediate confirmation. Sunday was the day off for major radio news reporters and executives. As the story broke over the shortwaves and telegraphs, everyone rushed to cover it and discover what had really happened. Thanks to Donna Halper for her detailed e-mail to me, July 3, 2006.

CHAPTER 62

393 *"national courtesy?":* Henry McLemore, "It's a Tough War," *Dallas Morning News,* December 29, 1941.

394 *"under their guidance":* Etiquette (1942), 896.

394 *"twenty years ago":* Truly Emily Post, 246.

395 *"definite and brief":* Etiquette (1942), 896.

397 *"even more human":* Yvonne Sylvia to the author, Martha's Vineyard, 2002.

397 *" 'Pardon me' ":* New York Times, December 23, 1942, p. 16.

398 *military radio stations:* Big-business machinations continued, and a federal antitrust ruling transformed NBC Blue Network into the American Broadcasting Company (ABC).

CHAPTER 63

399 *as she could: Washington Post,* February 2, 1943, p. B4.

400 *at Emily's status:* "Thumbing à la Emily Post," *Newsweek,* February 22, 1943, pp. 71–72.

400 *newly mean-spirited:* "Topics of the Times," *New York Times,* May 17, 1943.

401 *rivets into bombers:* J. Howard Miller's poster was published by the Westinghouse for War Production Co-ordinating Committee in February 1942. Special thanks to Linda Pero, curator of collections at the Norman Rockwell Museum, Stockbridge, Massachusetts, for her correspondence of July 10, 2006.

401 *"surrogate children":* Yvonne Sylvia, interview with the author, Martha's Vineyard, 2002.

401 *"not at Emily's table":* Poem by Ethel Jacobson, "People You Know," *Saturday Evening Post,* July 10, 1943.

402 *"in all directions":* "Doughboy Etiquette for Occupation of Italy," *Dallas Morning News,* September 11, 1943.

402 *Wyler's 1946 movie: Etiquette* (1942), 878.

403 *"to be set apart": This Week Magazine,* December 12, 1943, pp. 72–73.

CHAPTER 64

405 *real education too:* Letters in the Doris Stevens archives, Schlesinger papers, Radcliffe Institute for Advanced Study, December 28, 1943: "[indecipherable] of piece 'Eleanor Roosevelt' by Mary Hornaday." Also letters to Doris Stevens, Schlesinger Library, from Emily Post to Doris Stevens, December 1943; July 22, 1944; and August 22, 1944.

405 *"bought a cat":* "Professions for Women" in *The Death of the Moth* (reprint, London: Harvest, 1974), 236.

406 *would follow:* William G. Post, letter to the author, February 28, 2006. Emily would have loved one result of her accommodations: Bill's son Peter, Emily's youngest great-grandchild, would marry one of his summer childhood friends from the Vineyard. Tricia Post recalls: "When we were thirteen–fifteen, Peter and I were part of a rat pack of about fifteen–twenty kids that used to hang out [on the Island]—mostly playing Hearts! We 'remet' in college. I transferred to the University

of Pennsylvania as a junior. Second semester, Peter was sitting behind me in an art history class. I recognized his voice! The rest, as they say, is history!" (From an e-mail to the author, July 11, 2006.)

406 *"into control":* Elizabeth Post, e-mail interview with the author, September 26, 2005.

406 *so vividly: Time,* November 20, 1944, and November 27, 1944.

407 *upstairs for assistance:* Nanette Kutner, "Emily Post Is Only Human, Too," *Family Circle,* November 1955, p. 14.

407 *"be permanent": Journal of the National Education Association,* January 1945, p. 22.

408 *as they did so:* "Emily Post Put on Pan," *Hammond Times,* November 12, 1945.

408 *after it ended:* Alice Payne Hackett, *Sixty Years of Best Sellers,* 12.

408 *to the post office:* Letter from Emily Post to Betty Ward, March 1945.

409 *any day now:* "Nations Gather to Make World of Peace," *Oakland Tribune,* April 30, 1945, and *Berkshire County Eagle,* April 25, 1945.

409 *the frivolous:* Universal 18-414 newsreel, July 9, 1945.

409 *during the 1950s:* Stephanie Coontz, "A Pop Quiz on Marriage," *New York Times,* February 19, 2006, p. 12.

409 *twentieth-century life:* Witold Rybczynski, *Waiting for the Weekend,* quoted in the *New York Times* by William Grimes, "Time Off for Good Behavior," April 28, 2006.

409 *"knew, at least":* Libby Post, interview with the author, December 15, 2005.

410 *discuss him with Bill:* Nora Post, interview with the author, May 5, 2005.

410 *"bit flamboyant":* William G. Post, interview with the author from Naples, Florida, November 10, 2002, and phone interview, April 3, 2004.

410 *cheerful pun:* Jeanne Perkins, "Emily Post," *Life,* May 6, 1946, p. 65.

410 *"wrapped package":* "Social Blunders, My Own and Others," *Reader's Digest,* July 1960.

411 *"the entire time!":* Perkins, "Emily Post," p. 62.

CHAPTER 65

412 *"black and blue":* Letter from Emily Post to Yvonne Sylvia, undated, circa early January 1946.

413 *well-brought-up women:* "Ever-Changing Rules of Etiquette Must Conform to Modern Business," *Zanesville News,* January 20, 1946.

414 *to August 1:* Letters between Yvonne Sylvia and Emily Post, circa February to April 1946.

416 *"changing situations":* Jeanne Perkins, "Emily Post," *Life,* May 6, 1946.

416 *"Emily Post Institute, Inc.":* Letter from Funk and Wagnalls to Emily Post, August 21, 1946. Courtesy of Helen Moore at HarperCollins.

417 *Bill still chuckles:* William G. Post, interview with the author in Naples, Florida, November 10, 2002.

417 *"in heaven":* Interview with Yvonne Sylvia in Edgartown, October 20, 2002.

417 *twenty questions:* "Twenty Questions Quiz: Emily Post, Fred Van Deventer, Florence Rinard and Others," WOR, November 23, 1946, 8:00–8:30 P.M.

418 *like Emily Post:* "Stuyvesant Town Sale Closes Despite Effort to Halt Deal," Charles V. Bagli, *New York Times,* November 18, 2006, p. B3.

418 *"supported to survive":* William G. Post, interview with the author from Naples, Florida, November 10, 2002.

418 *to the studio:* "Betty Crocker, Talk; Emily Post, Guest," WJZ, March 28, 1947, 10:25–10:45 A.M.

420 *Price admired:* Phone conversations and e-mails with Bonnie Hass, December 1 to December 7, 2006; interview with Irving Hass, March 24, 1992, Wyomissing, Pennsylvania (on behalf of the Holocaust Memorial Museum, Washington, D.C.); and interview with Irving Hass, October 10, 1995, by Rose Sher Weiss, Delray Beach, Florida, on behalf of Steven Spielberg's Visual History Foundation.

420 *newborn grandniece:* Evelyn Perrault, phone interview with the author, July 22, 2006.

421 *of the visitor:* Pat Lamborn Kolbe, phone interview with the author, July 15, 2006.
421 *"beautifully dressed":* Eileen Sibley Robinson, phone interview with the author from Edgartown, April 22, 2006.
421 *"where we had tea":* Ibid.
422 *her dear friend:* "Mrs. William B. Coster," *New York Times,* July 24, 1947, p. 21.
422 *Reluctantly, she agreed: Truly Emily Post,* 245.
422 *"family does matter":* Dallas Morning News, July 27, 1952.
422 *friends showed up:* "F. Crowninshield Is Dead Here at 75: Advisor to Conde Nast Firm Introduced French Modernist Painters to the Country," *New York Times,* December 29, 1947, p. 17.

CHAPTER 66

423 *"exceedingly hard":* "Emily at the Barricades," *Boston Globe,* January 18, 1948.
424 *"the whole way":* William G. Post, e-mail to the author, July 18, 2006. For a fully fleshed biography that makes it clear why Emily and Mary Margaret McBride would be natural companions, see Susan Ware's *It's One o'Clock and Here Is Mary Margaret McBride.*
424 *friend insisted:* "Tea Party," *New Yorker,* April 3, 1948, p. 22.
424 *"popular culture":* Donna Halper, e-mails to the author, June 22, 2006, and August 6, 2006. See also Halper, *Invisible Stars.*
425 *"down Fuller Street":* Pat Lamborn, phone interview with the author, July 14, 2006.
425 *"I don't care":* "Emily Post Gives Age, but Protests 'Cruel' Question," *Washington Post,* November 30, 1948, p. 4.
425 *"never grow old":* William Engle, "The Emily Post Story," *American Weekly,* February 6, 1949, p. 18.
426 **Time** *magazine: Time,* August 29, 1949.
426 *"heard her voice":* William G. Post, e-mail to the author, June 22, 2006.
427 *"in society":* "Emily Post Tells Drivers How to Act," *Washington Post,* May 10, 1949.
427 *some of her readers: Worcester Gazette,* May 10, 1949.
427 *"for fall broadcast":* "Radio and Television: Video Broadcasters Unit Asks FCC to Ease 'Freeze' on New Station Applications," *New York Times,* June 20, 1949, p. 34.
427 *"a disaster":* William G. Post, interview with the author in Burlington, Vermont, July 29, 2006.

CHAPTER 67

429 *Brooks remembers:* Peggy Brooks, e-mail to the author, June 9, 2002.
429 *"can see it":* Sonia Stein, "It's Tough Enough on TV Without 'Life' Horning In," *Washington Post,* February 18, 1951, p. L1.
429 *the 1950* **Etiquette:** Quoted in Cleveland Amory, *Who Killed Society?,* 19.
430 *Irene Dunne:* "Tri-City Herald Social Events: U.S. Newspaper Women Pick America's Influential Women," *Tri-City Herald,* March 23, 1950, p. 6. Newspapers such as the *Tri-City Herald* also touted the upcoming feature in *Pageant* in April 1950.
431 *Americans' bedrooms:* Ann Fessler, *The Girls Who Went Away* (New York: Penguin, 2007), 43. In 1961, however, Anthony Comstock's Gilded Age proscriptions still held sway in his home state of Connecticut, where the law prohibited contraception counseling for married couples.
431 *had the whim:* "Ten Important Etiquette Changes Listed by Emily Post's Assistant," *Denton Journal,* January 12, 1951 (reprint of *Cosmopolitan* interview).
431 *"particularly in France":* William Hunt, "Across the Desk," *Allegany City Newspaper,* October 2, 1960.
432 *"doesn't mean you!!":* Ibid.
432 *from the cookbook:* "Mrs. Post's Party," *New Yorker,* May 14, 1955.
432 *cheerfully admitted:* "She Was Leading Lady," *Vineyard Gazette,* September 30, 1960.

433 *"never mentioned again":* William G. Post, interview with the author, from Naples, Florida, April 2004.

433 *"was doing there":* Isabel Paulantonio, phone interview with the author, February 12, 2002.

433 *claimed, "Emily Post":* "Not Right, She Says," *Dallas Morning News,* June 23, 1952.

433 *Post for real: Etiquette,* chapter 10.

CHAPTER 68

434 *by Ned and Isabel:* Cindy Post Senning, e-mail to the author, July 19, 2006.

434 *"inferior class":* "Is the Customer Always Right?," *Dallas Morning News,* June 29, 1952, p. 2.

435 *"out of his range":* "Emily Post," *Dallas Morning News,* June 15, 1952.

435 *over the years:* "Literary News: Minding Our Manners," *Newsweek,* August 11, 1958.

436 *" 'one's own imperfection' ":* *Dallas Morning News,* July 27, 1952.

436 *one in 1945:* The Bell Syndicate, Inc., September 4, 1952.

436 *within minutes:* Obituary, *New York Times,* October 2, 1953, p. 21.

436 *"damaging their lives":* William G. Post, phone interview with the author, July 18, 2004.

437 *Emily and the institute:* Ibid.

437 *by an assistant:* "Emily Post Gems Shown," *New York Times,* July 1, 1954, p. 29, and letter to Mr. and Mrs. Donald Moore, courtesy of Michael Fredman, private collection. Also see "Book Notes," *New York Times,* January 7, 1938, about the 877-page edition of *Etiquette* the Braille Institute signed to publish with Funk and Wagnalls. The *Times* claimed it would fill eleven volumes. The expense proved prohibitive, and whether Funk and Wagnalls or the Braille Institute or Emily herself funded the project remains unclear; her family "never heard anything about such a volume," according to Cindy Post. The Library of Congress, where the trail stops, cannot locate the publication. Thanks to Julie Uyeno, Information Resources Librarian, Braille Institute Library Services, Los Angeles.

437 *received priority: Newport Daily News,* August 25, 1954.

438 *"American living":* "News and Activities in the Advertising and Marketing Fields Here and Elsewhere," *New York Times,* October 20, 1954, p. 48. During the fall and early winter of 1954, Emily again revisited the past, in what must have been a glorious occasion for the adoring daddy's girl. Samuel Graybill, a doctoral student of Vincent Scully's at Yale's School of Architecture, interviewed Emily repeatedly about her father, discussing his architecture and his life. (Samuel Graybill, phone conversation with the author, November 8, 2004.)

438 *trumped the Waldorf:* Justin Kaplan, "A Rose for Emily," *Harper's Magazine,* March 1969, pp. 106–9.

439 *"meal at all":* "Mrs. Post's Party," *New Yorker,* May 14, 1955, p. 15.

439 *" 'Where's the food?' ":* *Time,* May 2, 1955.

CHAPTER 69

440 *brother responded:* Geoffrey T. Hellman, "Onward and Upward with the Arts: The Waning Oomph of Mrs. Toplofty," *New Yorker,* June 18, 1955.

441 *"calling card":* Display ad, *New York Times,* June 24, 1951, p. 76.

442 *"NOT a 'lady' ":* *Newsweek,* April 25, 1955.

442 *"to the club":* Hellman, "Onward," p. 13.

442 *"a whipping boy":* Ibid.

443 *past four years:* "Literary News: Minding Our Manners," *Newsweek,* August 11, 1958.

443 *January 1, 1959:* Contracts courtesy of Helen Moore at HarperCollins.

444 *just "old age":* Isabel Paulantonio, phone interview with the author, November 21, 2002.

444 *"October 27, 1873":* Los Angeles Times, September 27, 1960, p. 1; also "Emily Post Is Dead Here at 86," Chicago Tribune, September 27, 1960, p. 1.

444 *"deal of laughter":* "Sensible Shaper of U.S. Manners," Life, October 10, 1960, p. 73.

444 *"through the lorgnette":* "Emily Post Is Dead Here at 86: Writer Was Arbiter of Etiquette," New York Times, September 27, 1960, p. 1. Over forty years later, the country would again pay homage to the importance of etiquette to a nation's welfare when, in 2006, Judith Martin ("Miss Manners") was crowned with the Presidential Medal of Freedom.

444 *"necessarily elaborate":* "Emily Post," New York Times, September 28, 1960, p. 38.

444 *"things by rote":* "She Was Leading Lady in American Life to Millions," Vineyard Gazette, September 30, 1960.

445 *"of morals, too":* "Sensible Shaper of U.S. Manners."

445 *redolent of her past:* "Emily Post" and "Rites for Emily Post," New York Times, October 2, 1960. Services in her honor were held at Manhattan's St. James Protestant Episcopal Church.

SELECTED BIBLIOGRAPHY

Abernethy, Rev. Arthur T. *The Jew a Negro: Being a Study of the Jewish Ancestry from an Impartial Standpoint.* Moravian Falls, N.C.: Dixie Publishing Company, 1910.

Ackerman, Kenneth D. *Boss Tweed: The Rise and Fall of the Corrupt Pol Who Conceived the Soul of Modern New York.* New York: Carroll & Graf, 2005.

———. *The Gold Ring: Jim Fink, Jay Gould and Black Friday, 1869.* New York: Carroll & Graf, 1988.

Adams, Sean Patrick. *Old Dominion, Industrial Commonwealth: Coal, Politics, and Economy in Antebellum America.* Baltimore: Johns Hopkins University Press, 2004.

Aldrich, Elizabeth. *From the Ballroom to Hell: Grace and Folly in Nineteenth-Century Dance.* 1991. Reprint, Evanston, Ill.: Northwestern University Press, 2000.

Aldrich, Nelson W., Jr. *Old Money: The Mythology of America's Upper Class.* New York: Knopf, 1988.

Allen, Frederick Lewis. *Only Yesterday and Since Yesterday: A Popular History of the '20s and '30s.* New York: Harper & Row, 1986.

Almond, Gabriel A. *Plutocracy and Politics in New York City.* Boulder, Colo.: Westview Press, 1998. Ph.D. diss., University of Chicago, 1938.

Alvarez, A. *The Writer's Voice.* New York: Norton, 2005.

Amory, Cleveland. *The Last Resorts.* New York: Harper & Brothers, 1952.

———. *Who Killed Society?* New York: Harper & Brothers, 1960.

Arditi, Jorge. "Etiquette Books, Discourse, and the Deployment of an Order of Things." *Theory, Culture & Society* 16, no. 4 (1999): 25–48.

Aresty, Esther B. *The Best Behavior: The Course of Good Manners.* New York: Simon & Schuster, 1970.

Arthur, Anthony. *Radical Innocent.* New York: Random House, 2006.

Auchincloss, Louis. *The Vanderbilt Era: Profiles of a Gilded Age.* New York: Charles Scribner's Sons, 1989.

Balsan, Consuelo Vanderbilt. *The Glitter and the Gold.* London: William Heinmann, 1953.

Banet-Weiser, Sarah. *The Most Beautiful Girl in the World: Beauty Pageants and National Identity.* Berkeley: University of California Press, 1999.

Bannerman, R. LeRoy. *Norman Corwin and Radio: The Golden Years.* Tuscaloosa: University of Alabama Press, 1986.

Barbas, Samantha. *The First Lady of Hollywood: A Biography of Louella Parsons.* Berkeley: University of California Press, 2005.

Barry, John M. *The Great Influenza: The Epic Story of the Deadliest Plague in History.* New York: Viking, 2004.

————. *Rising Tide: The Great Mississippi Flood of 1927 and How It Changed America.* New York: Simon & Schuster, 1997.

Bascomb, Neal. *Higher: A Historic Race to the Sky and the Making of a City.* New York: Doubleday, 2003.

Bear, John. *The #1 New York Times Best Seller.* Berkeley, Calif.: Ten Speed Press, 1992.

Beard, Patricia. *After the Ball: Gilded Age Secrets, Boardroom Betrayals, and the Party That Ignited the Great Wall Street Scandal of 1905.* New York: HarperCollins, 2003.

Beckert, Sven. *The Monied Metropolis: New York City and the Consolidation of the American Bourgeoisie, 1850–1896.* Cambridge, U.K.: Cambridge University Press, 2001.

Bedford, Steven McLeod. *John Russell Pope: Architect of Empire.* New York: Rizzoli, 1998.

Bellamy, Edward. *Looking Backward: From 2000 to 1887.* Boston: Houghton Mifflin, 1915.

Belmont, Eleanor. *The Fabric of Memory.* New York: Farrar, Straus & Cudahy, 1957.

Benedict, Ruth. *Patterns of Culture.* Boston: Houghton Mifflin, 1934.

Berlin, Ira, and Leslie M. Harris, eds. *Slavery in New York.* New York: New-York Historical Society/The New Press, 2006.

Birmingham, Stephen. *America's Secret Aristocracy.* Boston: Little, Brown, 1987.

————. *"Our Crowd": The Great Jewish Families of New York.* New York: Harper & Row, 1967.

Bourdieu, Pierre. *Distinction.* Cambridge, Mass.: Harvard University Press, 1984.

Boyer, Christine M. *Manhattan Manners: Architecture and Style, 1850–1900.* New York: Rizzoli, 1985.

Boyer, Paul S. *The Oxford Companion to United States History.* Oxford: Oxford University Press, 2001.

Boyle, Kevin. *Arc of Justice: A Saga of Race, Civil Rights, and Murder in the Jazz Age.* New York: Holt, 2004.

Bragdon, Claude. *More Lives Than One.* New York: Knopf, 1938.

Braudy, Leo. *The Frenzy of Renown: Fame and Its History.* Oxford: Oxford University Press, 1986.

Bridges, Amy Beth. "Another Look at Plutocracy and Politics in Antebellum New York City." *Political Science Quarterly* 97 (Spring 1982): 57–71.

Brooks, Van Wyck. *The Confident Years: 1885–1915.* New York: E. P. Dutton, 1952.

Brough, James. *Consuelo: Portrait of an American Heiress.* New York: Coward, McCann & Geoghegan, 1979.

Brown, Henry Collins. *In the Golden Nineties.* North Stratford, N.H.: Ayer, 1927.

Browning, Dominique. *Around the House and in the Garden: A Memoir of Heartbreak, Healing and Home Improvement.* New York: Scribner, 2002.

Bryce, Lloyd, ed. *The North American Review.* Vol. 161. (3 East Fourteenth Street, New York, 1895.)

Buckley, Peter G. "Culture, Class and Place in Antebellum New York." In *Power, Culture and Place: Essays on New York City,* edited by John Hull Mollenkopf, 25–52. New York: Russell Sage Foundation, 1988.

Burt, Nathaniel. *First Families: The Making of an American Aristocracy.* Boston: Little, Brown, 1970.

Bushman, Richard L. *The Refinement of America: Persons, Houses, Cities.* New York: Knopf, 1992.

Cady, Edwin Harrison. *The Gentlemen in America.* Syracuse, N.Y.: Syracuse University Press, 1949.

Caldwell, Mark. *New York Night: The Mystique and Its History.* New York: Scribner, 2005.

————. *A Short History of Rudeness: Manners, Morals and Misbehavior in Modern America.* New York: St. Martin's Press, 1999.

Cantor, Jay E. "A Monument of Trade: A. T. Stewart and the Rise of the Millionaire's Mansion in New York." *Winterthur Portfolio* 10 (1975): 165–97.

Caro, Robert. *The Power Broker: Robert Moses and the Fall of New York.* New York: Knopf, 1974.

Carson, Gerald. *The Polite Americans: 300 Years of More or Less Good Behavior.* London: Macmillan, 1967.

Castronovo, David. *The American Gentlemen: Social Prestige and the Modern Literary Mind.* New York: Continuum, 1991.

Cate, James Lea. "Keeping Posted." *University of Chicago Magazine* 64 (May–June 1972): 24–34.

Century Association. *The Century, 1847–1947.* New York: Century Association, 1944.

Chanler, Julie. *From Gaslight to Dawn.* New York: New History Foundation, 1956.

Chappell, George S. *The Restaurants of New York.* New York: Greenberg, 1925.

Churchill, Allen. *The Splendor Seekers: An Informal Glimpse of America's Multimillionaire Spender-Members of the $50,000,000 Club.* New York: Grosset & Dunlap, 1974.

———. *The Upper Crust: An Informal History of New York's Highest Society.* Englewood Cliffs, N.J.: Prentice Hall, 1970.

Clark, Champ. *Shuffling to Ignominy: The Tragedy of Stepin Fetchit.* Bloomington, Ind.: iUniverse, 2005.

Clews, Henry. *Fifty Years in Wall Street.* New York: Irving, 1908.

———. *Twenty-eight Years in Wall Street.* New York: J. S. Ogilvie, 1887.

Coontz, Stephanie. *Marriage: A History.* New York: Viking, 2005.

Copleston, Frederick. *History of Philosophy: Wolff to Kant.* Mahwah, N.J.: Paulist Press, 1960.

Cox, Anne F. *The History of the Colony Club, 1903–1984.* New York: Colony Club, 1984.

Crowninshield, Francis W. *Manners for the Metropolis: An Entrance Key to the Fantastic Life of the 400.* New York: Appleton, 1910.

D'Antonio, Michael. *Hershey: Milton S. Hershey's Extraordinary Life of Wealth, Empire, and Utopian Dreams.* New York: Simon & Schuster, 2006.

Davies, Pete. *American Road: The Story of an Epic Transcontinental Journey at the Dawn of the Motor Age.* New York: Holt, 2002.

Davis, John H. *The Guggenheims: An American Epic.* New York: William Morrow, 1978.

Deford, Frank. *There She Is: The Life and Times of Miss America.* New York: Viking, 1971.

Depew, Chauncey M. *My Memories of Eighty Years.* New York: Charles Scribner's Sons, 1922.

Desmond, Harry W., and Herbert Croly. *Stately Homes in America.* New York: Random House, 1903.

de Wolfe, Elsie. *After All.* New York: Harper & Brothers, 1935. Reprint, New York: Arno, 1974.

———. *The House in Good Taste.* New York: Century, 1915.

Didion, Joan. *The Year of Magical Thinking.* New York: Knopf, 2005.

Dodd, Edward H. *The First Hundred Years: A History of the House of Dodd, Mead, 1839–1939.* New York: Dodd, Mead, 1939.

Dolson, Hildegarde. *Sorry to Be So Cheerful.* New York: Random House, 1955.

Dorsey, John, and James D. Dilts. *A Guide to Baltimore Architecture.* Centerville, Md.: Tidewater Publishers, 1997.

Douglas, Ann. *The Feminization of American Culture.* New York: Random House, 1977.

———. *Terrible Honesty: Mongrel Manhattan in the 1920s.* New York: Farrar, Straus and Giroux, 1995.

Douglas, George H. *The Early Days of Radio Broadcasting.* Jefferson, N.C.: McFarland, 1987.

Dunlop, M. H. *Gilded City: Scandal and Sensation in Turn-of-the-Century New York.* New York: HarperCollins, 2000.

Eichler, Lillian. *Etiquette Problems in Pictures.* Oyster Bay, N.Y.: Nelson Doubleday, 1922.

———. *The Book of Etiquette.* Vols. 1 and 2. Garden City, N.Y.: Doubleday, 1923.

———. *Etiquette in Public.* Hoboken, N.J.: R. B. Davis, 1924.

———. *The Customs of Mankind.* Garden City, N.Y.: Garden City Publishing Co., 1924.

———. *The New Book of Etiquette.* Garden City, N.Y.: Garden City Publishing Co., 1924.

———. *Well-Bred English.* Garden City, N.Y.: Doubleday, 1926.

———. *The New Book of Etiquette.* Garden City, N.Y.: Garden City Publishing Co., 1941.

Elias, Norbert. *The Civilizing Process.* Translated by Edmon Jephcott. New York: Urizen Books, 1978. Originally published as *Über den Prozess der Zivilisation* (Basel: Haus Zum Falken, 1939).

Epstein, Joseph. *Friendship: An Exposé.* Boston: Houghton Mifflin, 2006.

———. *Snobbery: The American Version.* Boston: Houghton Mifflin, 2002.

Erenberg, Lewis A. *Steppin' Out: New York Nightlife and the Transformation of American Culture, 1890–1930.* Chicago: University of Chicago Press, 1981.

Erikson, Erik. *Life History and the Historical Moment.* New York: Norton, 1975.

Evans, Harold. "Follow the Money." Review of *Every Man a Speculator,* by Steve Fraser. *New York Times Book Review,* March 13, 2005, pp. 14–15.

Felder, Deborah. *A Century of Women: The Most Influential Events in Twentieth-Century Women's History.* Secaucus, N.J.: Birch Lane Press, 1999.

Fellowes, Julian. *Snobs.* New York: St. Martin's Press, 2004.

Filippini, Alessandro. *The Table: How to Buy Food, How to Cook It, and How to Serve It.* Rev. ed. New York: Charles L. Webster, 1891.

Fiske, Stephen. *Off Hand Portraits of Prominent New Yorkers.* New York: Geo. R. Lockwood & Son, 1884.

Fraser, Steve. *Every Man a Speculator.* New York: HarperCollins, 2005.

Fukuyama, Francis. *America at the Crossroads: Democracy, Power and the Neoconservative Legacy.* New Haven, Conn.: Yale University Press, 2006.

Furbank, P. N. *Unholy Pleasure: The Idea of Social Class.* Oxford: Oxford University Press, 1985.

Furnas, J. C. *Goodbye to Uncle Tom.* New York: Sloan, 1956.

———. *Great Times: An Informal Social History of the United States, 1914–1929.* New York: Putnam, 1974.

———. *Stormy Weather: Crosslights on the Nineteen Thirties.* New York: Putnam, 1977.

Furness, C. J., ed. *The Genteel Female.* New York: Knopf, 1931.

Garland, Hamlin. *Crumbling Idols.* Chicago: Stone & Kimball, 1894.

Geidel, Peter. "Alva E. Belmont: A Forgotten Feminist." Ph.D. diss., Columbia University, 1993.

Geist, Charles R. *Wall Street: A History.* New York: Oxford University Press, 1997.

Gladwell, Malcolm. *The Tipping Point: How Little Things Can Make a Difference.* Boston: Little, Brown, 2000.

Gordon, John Steele. *An Empire of Wealth.* New York: HarperCollins, 2004.

Graham, Lawrence Otis. *Our Kind of People: Inside America's Black Upper Class.* New York: HarperCollins, 1999.

Granger, Alfred Hoyt. *Charles Follen McKim.* Boston: Houghton Mifflin, 1913.

Graybill, Samuel Huiet, Jr. "Bruce Price, American Architect, 1845–1903." Vols. 1 and 2. Ph.D. diss., Yale University, 1957.

Hackett, Alice Payne. *Sixty Years of Best Sellers: 1895–1955.* New York: Bowker, 1956.

Hackett, Alice Payne, and James Henry Burke. *80 Years of Best Sellers, 1895–1975.* New York: Bowker, 1977.

Halberstam, David. *The Fifties.* New York: Villard Books, 1993.

Halper, Donna. *Invisible Stars: A Social History of Women in American Broadcasting.* Armonk, N.Y.: M. E. Sharpe, 2001.

Hamill, Pete. *Downtown: My Manhattan.* New York: Little, Brown, 2004.

Hansen, Marcus Lee. *The Immigrant in American History.* New York: Harper & Row, 1940.

Harriman, Margaret Case. "Dear Mrs. Post," *Saturday Evening Post* (May 15, 1937), pp. 18ff.

———. *The Vicious Circle.* New York: Rinehart, 1951.

Harris, Leon. *Merchant Princes: An Intimate History of Jewish Families Who Built Great Department Stores.* New York: Harper & Row, 1979.

Hillenbrand, Laura. *Seabiscuit: An American Legend.* New York: Random House, 2001.

Hokansen, Drake. *The Lincoln Highway: Main Street Across America.* Iowa City: University of Iowa Press, 1988.

Homberger, Eric. *Historical Atlas of New York City.* New York: Holt, 1994.

———. *Mrs. Astor's New York: Money and Social Power in a Gilded Age.* New Haven, Conn.: Yale University Press, 2002.

———. *Scenes from the Life of a City: Corruption and Conscience in Old New York.* New Haven, Conn.: Yale University Press, 1994.

Howe, Julia Ward. *Is Polite Society Polite? And Other Essays.* Boston: Samson, Wolfe, 1895.

Howell, Clark. "The World's Event for 1895: The Cotton States and International Exposition." *American Review of Reviews* 11 (February 1895).

Howells, William Dean. "Equality as the Basis of Good Society." *Century* 51, n.s. 29 (November 1895): 63–67.

Hughes, Kristine. *The Writer's Guide to Everyday Life in Regency and Victorian England from 1811–1901.* Cincinnati: Writer's Digest Books, 1998.

Jacobs, Laura. "Emily Post's Social Revolution." *Vanity Fair,* December 2001: 292–97, 316–19.

Jacoby, Susan. *Freethinkers.* New York: Metropolitan, 2004.

James, Henry. *The American Scene.* 1925. Reprint, New York: Penguin Classics, 1994.

Josephson, Matthew. *The Robber Barons.* New York: Harcourt, 1962.

Kammen, Michael. *American Culture, American Tastes.* New York: Knopf, 1999.

———. *In the Past Lane: Historical Perspectives on American Culture.* New York: Oxford University Press, 1997.

Kaplan, Fred. *The Singular Mark Twain: A Biography.* New York: Doubleday, 2003.

Kaplan, Justin. *When the Astors Owned New York: Blue Bloods and Grand Hotels in a Gilded Age.* New York: Viking, 2006.

Kasson, John. *Rudeness and Civility: Manners in Nineteenth-Century Urban America.* New York: Hill & Wang, 1990.

Kazin, Alfred. *On Native Ground.* 1942. Reprint. New York: Harcourt, 1995.

Kelly, Thomas. *Empire Rising.* New York: Farrar, Straus and Giroux, 2005.

Kimes, Beverly Rae. "Emily's Great Adventure." *Star,* September–October, 2001.

Klindienst, Patricia. *The Earth Knows My Name: Food, Culture, and Sustainability in the Gardens of Ethnic America.* Boston: Beacon Press, 2006.

Klurfeld, Herman. *Winchell: His Life and Times.* New York: Praeger, 1976.

Korda, Michael. *Making the List: A Cultural History of the American Bestseller, 1900–1999.* New York: Barnes & Noble, 2002.

Kurlansky, Mark. *The Big Oyster: History on the Half Shell.* New York: Ballantine Books, 2006.

Kyriakoudes, Louis M. "The Grand Ole Opry and Big Tobacco: Radio Scripts from the Files of the R. J. Reynolds Tobacco Company, 1948 to 1959." *Southern Cultures* 12, no. 2 (Summer 2006): 77–78.

Lamb, Mrs. Martha J., and Mrs. Burton Harrison. *History of the City of New York: Its Origin, Rise, and Progress.* 3 vols. New York: A. S. Barnes Company, 1877–96.

Lancaster, Jane. *Making Time: Lillian Moller Gilbreth—a Life Beyond "Cheaper by the Dozen."* Boston: Northeastern University Press, 2004.

Landau, Sarah Bradford. *George B. Post, Architect: Picturesque Designer and Determined Realist.* New York: Monticelli, 1998.

Landau, Sarah Bradford, and Carl W. Condit. *Rise of the New York Skyscraper.* New Haven, Conn.: Yale University Press, 1996.

Lapham, Lewis. *Money and Class in America: Notes and Observations on Our Civil Religion.* New York: Weidenfeld & Nicolson, 1988.

Larson, Erik. *The Devil in the White City.* New York: Vintage, 2003.

Laughlin, Clara E. *The Work-a-day Girl.* New York: Revell, 1913.

Leach, William. "Transformations in a Culture of Consumption: Women and Department Stores, 1890–1925." *Journal of American History* 71 (September 1984): 319–42.

Lears, T. Jackson. *No Place of Grace: Antimodernism and the Transformation of American Culture, 1880–1920.* New York: Pantheon, 1981.

Lee, Hermione. *Edith Wharton.* New York: Knopf, 2007.

Lemann, Nicholas. *The Promised Land.* New York: Vintage, 1992.

Levine, Lawrence W. *Highbrow/Lowbrow: The Emergence of Cultural Hierarchy in America.* Cambridge, Mass.: Harvard University Press, 1988.

Levitas, Susan, ed. *Railroad Ties.* Crownsville, Md.: Maryland Historical Trust Press, 1994.

Levitt, Sarah. *From Catherine Beecher to Martha Stewart: A Cultural History of Domestic Advice.* Chapel Hill: University of North Carolina Press, 2002.

Lewis, Alfred Allan. *Ladies and Not-So-Gentle Women.* New York: Viking, 2000.

Lewis, Earl, and Heidi Ardizzone. *Love on Trial: An American Scandal in Black and White.* New York: Norton, 2001.

Lhamon, W. T., Jr. *Raising Cain: Blackface Performance from Jim Crow to Hip Hop.* Cambridge, Mass.: Harvard University Press, 2000.

Lincoln Highway Association. *The Lincoln Highway: The Story of a Crusade That Made Transportation History.* New York: Dodd, Mead, 1935.

Logan, Andy. *The Man Who Robbed the Robber Barons.* Reprint, Pleasantville, N.Y.: Akadine Press, 2001.

Longstreet, Abby Buchanan. *Social Etiquette of New York.* New York: Appleton, 1879.

Longworth, Alice Roosevelt. *Crowded Hours.* New York: Charles Scribner's Sons, 1933.

Lott, Eric. *Love and Theft: Blackface Minstrelsy and the American Working Class.* New York: Oxford University Press, 1993.

Louis, S. L. *Decorum: A Practical Treatise on Etiquette and Dress of the Best American Society.* New York: Union, 1881.

Lundberg, Ferdinand. *America's 60 Families.* New York: Vanguard Press, 1937.

Lynes, Russell. *The Tastemakers.* New York: Harper, 1954.

Macdonald, Laura. *Curse of the Narrows.* New York: HarperCollins, 2005.

Maines, Rachel. *The Technology of Orgasm.* Baltimore: Johns Hopkins University Press, 1999.

Marling, Karal Ann. *As Seen on TV: The Visual Culture of Everyday Life in the 1950s.* Cambridge, Mass.: Harvard University Press, 1994.

———. *The Colossus of Roads: Myth and Symbol Along the American Highway.* Minneapolis: University of Minnesota Press, 1984.

———. *Debutante: Rites and Regalia of American Debdom.* Lawrence: University Press of Kansas, 2004.

Martin, Fredrick Townsend. *The Passing of the Idle Rich.* New York: Arno, 1973. First published 1911 by Hodder & Stoughton in London.

Martin, Judith. *Miss Manners' Guide for the Turn of the Millennium.* New York: Fireside, 1990.

Maxwell, Mrs. Sara B. *Manners and Customs of To-Day.* Des Moines, Iowa: Cline, 1890.

Mayer, Martin. *The Met: One Hundred Years of Grand Opera.* New York: Simon & Schuster, 1983.

McAllister, Ward. *Society as I Have Found It.* New York: Cassell, 1890.

McCabe, James Dabney. *Lights and Shadows of New York Life, or The Sights and Sensations of New York City.* Philadelphia: National Publishing Company, 1872.

McColl, Gail, and Carol McD. Wallace. *To Marry an English Lord, or How Anglomania Really Got Started.* New York: Workman, 1989.

McLuhan, Marshall. *The Mechanical Bride: Folklore of Industrial Man.* New York: Vanguard Press, [1951].

Milford, Nancy. *Savage Beauty: The Life of Edna St. Vincent Millay.* New York: Random House, 2003.

Mills, Kay. *A Place in the News: From the Women's Pages to the Front Page.* New York: Columbia University Press, 1990.

Montgomery, Maureen E. *Gilded Prostitution: Status, Money and Transatlantic Marriages, 1870–1914.* London: Routledge, 1989.

Moore, Charles. *The Promise of American Architecture.* Detroit: American Institute of Architects, 1905.

Morgan, Anne. *The American Girl: Her Education, Her Responsibility, Her Recreation, Her Future.* New York: Harper & Brothers, 1914.

Morris, Lloyd. *Incredible New York (1850–1950).* New York: Random House, 1951.

Morrison, Hugh. *Early American Architecture.* New York: Dover, 1952.

———. *Louis Sullivan, Prophet of Modern Architecture,* rev. ed. New York: Norton, 2001.

Myrdal, Gunnar. *An American Dilemma.* 1944. Reprint, New York: Harper & Row, 1962.

O'Neill, William L. *Divorce in the Progressive Age.* New York: Franklin Watts/New Viewpoints, 1973.

O'Rourke, P. J. *Age and Guile.* New York: Atlantic Monthly Press, 1995.

Ostrander, Susan A. *Women of the Upper Class.* Philadelphia: Temple University Press, 1984.

Patterson, Jerry. *The First Four Hundred.* New York: Rizzoli, 2000.

——. *The Vanderbilts.* New York: Abrams, 1989.

Pessen, Edward. "The Egalitarian Myth and the American Social Reality: Wealth, Mobility and Equality in the 'Era of the Common Man.' " *American Historical Review* 76 (October 1971): 989–1034.

——. "Philip Hone's Set: The Social World of the New York City Elite in the 'Age of Egalitarianism.' " *New-York Historical Society Quarterly* 56 (October 1972): 285–308.

——. *Riches, Class and Power Before the Civil War.* Lexington, Mass.: D. C. Heath, 1973.

Pool, Daniel. *What Jane Austen Ate and Charles Dickens Knew.* New York: Simon & Schuster, 1993.

Post, Edwin Main. "The Blue Handkerchief." *Smart Set: A Magazine of Cleverness* 30, no. 2 (February 1910): 69–72.

——. "Brant Shooting on Great South Bay." *Field and Stream* (January 1899). Reprinted in *Classic Hunting Stories,* edited by Lamar Underwood, 197–205. Guilford, Conn.: Lyons Press, 2003.

Post, Edwin Main, Jr. *Truly Emily Post.* New York: Funk and Wagnalls, 1961.

Post, Emily Price. *The Flight of a Moth.* New York: Dodd, Mead, 1904.

——. *Purple and Fine Linen.* New York: D. Appleton, 1905.

——. *Woven in the Tapestry.* New York: Moffat, Yard, 1908.

——. *The Title Market.* New York: Dodd, Mead, 1909.

——. *The Eagle's Feather.* New York: Dodd, Mead, 1910.

——. *By Motor to the Golden Gate.* New York: Appleton, 1916.

——. *Etiquette: In Society, in Business, in Politics and at Home.* New York: Funk and Wagnalls, 1922.

——. *Parade.* New York: Funk and Wagnalls, 1925.

——. *Etiquette: The Blue Book of Social Usage.* New York: Funk and Wagnalls, 1927, 1931, 1934, 1937, 1940, 1942, 1945, 1950, 1955, 1960.

——. *How to Behave—Though a Debutante.* Garden City, N.Y.: Doubleday, Doran & Company, 1928.

——. *The Personality of a House.* New York: Funk and Wagnalls, 1930.

——. *101 Common Mistakes in Etiquette.* New Haven, Conn.: Steinbach and Sons, 1939.

——. *Children Are People: And Ideal Parents Are Comrades.* New York: Funk and Wagnalls, 1940.

——. *The Emily Post Cookbook.* New York: Funk & Wagnalls, 1951.

Post, Marie Caroline De Trobriand. *The Post Family.* New York: Sterling Potter, 1905.

Powers, Ron. *Mark Twain: A Life.* New York: Free Press, 2005.

Pulitzer, Ralph. *New York Society on Parade.* New York: Harper & Brothers, 1910.

Ramsey, Alice Huyler. *Alice's Drive.* Utah: Patrice Press, 2005.

Randall, Monica. *The Mansions of Long Island's Gold Coast.* New York: Hastings House, 1979.

Randall, Rona. *The Model Wife Nineteenth-Century Style.* London: Herbert Press, 1989.

Ratner, Sidney, ed. *New Light on the History of Great American Fortunes: American Millionaires of 1892 and 1902.* New York: Augustus M. Kelly, 1953.

Rector, Margaret Hayden. *Alva, That Vanderbilt-Belmont Woman: Her Story as She Might Have Told It.* Wickford, R.I.: Dutch Island Press, 1992.

Reed, Julia. *Queen of the Turtle Derby.* New York: Random House, 2004.

Reynolds, Paul R. *The Middle Man: The Adventures of a Literary Agent.* New York: Morrow, 1971.

Richardson, Mark. *The Ordeal of Robert Frost: The Poet and His Poetics.* Urbana: University of Illinois Press, 1997.

Riis, Jacob. *How the Other Half Lives.* New York: Charles Scribner's Sons, 1890.

Roehrenbeck, William J. *The Regiment That Saved the Capital.* New York: Thomas Yoseloff, 1961.

Rogoff, Leonard. "Is the Jew White? The Racial Place of the Southern Jew." *American Jewish History* 85, no. 3 (September 1997): 195–230.

Rushmore, George M. *The World with a Fence Around It: Tuxedo Park, the Early Days.* New York: Pageant Press, 1957.

Russell, Charles Edward. "The Growth of Caste in America." *Cosmopolitan* 42 (March 1907): 524–34.

Schlereth, Thomas J. *Victorian America: Transformations in Everyday Life, 1876–1915*. New York: HarperCollins, 1991.

Schlesinger, Arthur M. *Learning How to Behave: A Historical Study of Etiquette Books*. New York: Macmillan, 1946.

Scott, Joan. *Gender and the Politics of History*. New York: Columbia University Press, 1988.

Scott, William B., and Peter M. Rutkoff. *New York Modern: The Arts and the City*, 1999. Reprint, Baltimore: Johns Hopkins University Press, 2001.

Scully, Vincent Joseph. *The Shingle Style Today: Or the Historian's Revenge*. New York: Norton, 1974.

Sennett, Richard, and Jonathan Cobb. *Hidden Injuries of Class*. New York: Random House, 1973.

Sheads, Scott Sumpter, and Daniel Carroll Toomey. *Baltimore During the Civil War*. Linthicum, Md.: Toomey Press, 1997.

Sheldon, George. *Artistic Country Seats*. Vol. 2. New York: D. Appleton, 1886.

Sherwood, Mrs. John [Mary]. *Manners and Social Usages*. New York: Harper & Brothers, 1884.

Shouter, D. C. "A Classification of American Wealth: History and Genealogy of the Wealthy Families of America." Available at http://www.raken.com/american_wealth/encyclopedia/1918.asp.

Sinclair, Upton. *The Autobiography of Upton Sinclair*. New York: Harcourt, Brace & World, 1962.

———. *Candid Reminiscences: My First Thirty Years*. London: Werner Laurie, 1932.

———. *The Coal War*. Boulder: Colorado Associated University Press, 1976.

Sloat, Warren. *A Battle for the Soul of New York: Tammany Hall, Police Corruption, Vice, and Reverend Charles Parkhurst's Crusade Against Them*. New York: Cooper Square Press, 2002.

Smith, F. Hopkinson. *Colonel Carter's Christmas*. New York: Charles Scribner's Sons, 1903.

Smith, Jane. *Elsie de Wolfe*. New York: Atheneum, 1982.

Smith, Matthew Hale. *Sunshine and Shadow in New York*. Hartford, Conn.: J. B. Burr and Co., 1869.

Smith-Rosenberg, Carroll. *Disorderly Conduct: Visions of Gender in Victorian America*. New York: Knopf, 1985.

Stearns, Peter N., and Jan Lewis, eds. *Battleground of Desire: An Emotional History of the United States*. New York: New York University Press, 1999.

Stevens, Doris. *Jailed for Freedom*. New York: Boni and Liveright, 1920.

———. *Tribute to Alva Belmont: Late President of the National Woman's Party*. Washington, D.C.: Inter-American Commission of Women, Pan American Union, 1933.

Stowe, Steven M. *Intimacy and Power in the Old South: Ritual in the Lives of the Planters*. Baltimore: Johns Hopkins University Press, 1987.

Strachey, Lytton. *Eminent Victorians*. London: Chatto & Windus, 1918.

Strausbaugh, John. *Black Like You: Blackface, Whiteface, Insult and Imitation in American Popular Culture*. New York: Penguin, 2006.

Strouse, Jean. *Morgan: A Biography*. New York: Random House, 1999.

Stuart, Amanda MacKenzie. *Consuelo and Alva Vanderbilt: The Story of a Daughter and a Mother in the Gilded Age*. New York: HarperCollins, 2006.

Sturgis, Russell. *The Appreciation of Architecture*. New York: Baker & Taylor, 1903.

Sullivan, Robert. *Cross Country: Fifteen Years and Ninety Thousand Miles on the Roads and Interstates of America with Lewis and Clark, a Lot of Bad Motels, a Moving Van, Emily Post, Jack Kerouac, My Wife, My Mother-in-Law, Two Kids, and Enough Coffee to Kill an Elephant*. London: Bloomsbury, 2006.

Susman, Warren I. *Culture as History: The Transformation of American Society in the Twentieth Century*. New York: Pantheon Books, 1984.

Sutherland, John. *Mrs. Humphrey Ward: Eminent Victorian, Pre-eminent Edwardian*. Oxford: Oxford University Press, 2002.

Tebbel, John. *Compact History of the American Newspaper*. New York: Hawthorne Books, 1963.

———. *A History of Book Publishing in the United States*. Vol. 1. New York: Bowker, 1975.

Tebbel, John, and Mary Ellen Zuckerman. *The Magazine in America, 1741–1990*. New York: Oxford University Press, 1991.

Thomas, Lately. *The Astor Orphans: A Pride of Lions*. Albany, N.Y.: Washington Park Press, 1999.

———. *Delmonico's: A Century of Splendor*. Boston: Houghton Mifflin, 1967.

Traub, James. *The Devil's Playground: A Century of Pleasure and Profit in Times Square*. New York: Random House, 2004.

Tuan, Yi-Fu. *Dominance and Affection: The Making of Pets*. New Haven, Conn.: Yale University Press, 1984.

Twain, Mark, and Charles Dudley Warner. *The Gilded Age: A Tale of Today*. 1873. Reprint, New York: Penguin, 2001.

U.S. Bureau of the Census. "Instructions to Court Clerks: Statistics of Divorce." Washington, D.C. [Government Printing Office, 1907].

Vanderbilt, Amy. *Complete Book of Etiquette: A Guide to Gracious Living*. Garden City, N.Y.: Doubleday, 1952.

Vanderbilt, Cornelius, Jr. *Farewell to Fifth Avenue*. New York: Simon & Schuster, 1935.

———. *Queen of the Golden Age: The Fabulous Story of Grace Wilson Vanderbilt*. New York: McGraw-Hill, 1956.

Van Rensselaer, Mrs. John King. "The Basis of Society in New York City," *Cosmopolitan* 27 (August 1899): 350–68.

Veblen, Thorstein. *Theory of the Leisure Class: An Economic Study of Institutions*. New York: Macmillan, 1899. Reprinted with a Foreword by Stewart Chase. New York: Modern Library, 1934.

Von Drehle, David. *Triangle: The Fire That Changed America*. New York: Grove Press, 2004.

Walker, Stanley. *The Night Club Era*. New York: Frederick A. Stokes, 1933.

Ward, Mrs. Humphrey. *Lady Rose's Daughter*. New York: Grosset & Dunlap, 1903.

Ware, Susan. *Holding Their Own: American Women in the 1930s*. Boston: Twayne, 1982.

———. *It's One o'Clock and Here Is Mary Margaret McBride: A Radio Biography*. New York: New York University Press, 2005.

Warren, Dorothy. *The World of Ruth Draper: A Portrait of an Actress*. Carbondale: Southern Illinois University Press, 1999.

Watkins, Mel. *Stepin Fetchit: The Life and Times of Lincoln Perry*. New York: Pantheon, 2005.

Watts, Steven. *The People's Tycoon: Henry Ford and the American Century*. New York: Knopf, 2005.

Wecter, Dixon. *The Saga of American Society: A Record of Social Aspiration, 1607–1937*. New York: Charles Scribner's Sons, 1937.

Weitzman, Lenore. *The Divorce Revolution*. New York: Free Press, 1987.

Wells, Richard A. *Manners, Culture and Dress of the Best American Society*. Springfield, Mass.: King, Richardson & Co., 1891.

Wertheimer, Barbara M. *We Were There: The Story of Working Women in America*. New York: Pantheon Books, 1977.

Wharton, Edith. *A Backward Glance*. New York: D. Appleton–Century Company, 1934.

Wharton, Edith, and Ogden Codman Jr. *The Decoration of Houses*. Reprint of 1902 edition. Introductory notes by John Barrington Bayley and William A. Coles. New York: Charles Scribner's Sons, 1978.

Wiener, Lynn Y. *From Working Girl to Working Mother: The Female Labor Force in the United States, 1820–1980*. Chapel Hill: University of North Carolina Press, 1985.

Wilson, Edmund. *Classics and Commercials: A Literary Chronicle of the Forties*. New York: Farrar, Straus [1950].

———. *To the Finland Station*. 1940. Reprint, New York: NYRB Classics, 2003.

Winchester, Simon. *A Crack in the Edge of the World*. New York: HarperCollins, 2005.

Winslow, Albert Foster. *Tuxedo Park: A Journal of Recollections*. Tuxedo Park, N.Y.: Tuxedo Historical Society, 1992.

Wish, Harvey. *Society and Thought in Modern America*. New York: Longmans, Green and Co., 1952.

Witwer, David. "Westbrook Pegler and the Anti-Union Movement." *Journal of American History* 92, no. 2 (September 2005).

Woloch, Nancy. *Women and the American Experience*. New York: Knopf, 1984.

INDEX

LAURA CLARIDGE is the author of several books, including *Norman Rockwell: A Life* and *Tamara de Lempicka: A Life of Deco and Decadence*. *Emily Post: Daughter of the Gilded Age, Mistress of American Manners* received a National Endowment for the Humanities grant and won the J. Anthony Lukas Work-in-Progress Award. Claridge has written features and reviews for *The Boston Globe, Los Angeles Times,* and *The Christian Science Monitor* and has appeared frequently in the national media, including *Today,* CNN, NPR, and the BBC. She lives in New York's Hudson Valley.

A B O U T   T H E   T Y P E

This book was set in Requiem, a typeface designed by the Hoefler Type Foundry. It is a modern typeface inspired by inscriptional capitals in Ludovico Vicentino degli Arrighi's 1523 writing manual, *Il modo de temperare le penne*. An original lowercase, a set of figures, and an italic in the "chancery" style that Arrighi helped popularize were created to make this adaptation of a classical design into a complete font family.